teach yourself...

Windows 3

AL STEVENS

ADVANCED COMPUTER BOOKS

MIS: PRESS

P.O Box 5277
Portland, Oregon 97208-5277

First Printing
ISBN 1-55828-065-0

Printed in the United States of America

TRADEMARKS

BIX is a trademark of McGraw-Hill, Inc.
CompuServe is a trademark of CompuServe, Inc.
Epson is a trademark of Epson America, Inc.
Genie is a trademark of General Electric Information Services
IBM AT is a trademark of International Business Machines Corporation
IBM PC is a trademark of International Business Machines Corporation
IBM Personal Pageprinter is a trademark of International Business Machines Corporation
Kermit is a trademark of Henson Associates, Inc.
MCI Mail is a trademark of MCI Telecommunications, Inc.
MS-DOS is a trademark of Microsoft Corporation
NetWare is a trademark of Novell, Inc.
Norton Advanced Utilities is a trademark of Symantec Corporation
PageMaker is a trademark of Aldus Corporation
PC-DOS is a trademark of International Business Machines Corporation
Procomm is a trademark of PIL Software Systems
Prodigy is a trademark of Prodigy Service
Radio Shack is a trademark of Tandy Corporation
Sidekick is a trademark of Borland International
Superkey is a trademark of Borland International
Telenet is a trademark of GTE Telenet
Teletype is a trademark of AT & T Teletype Corporation
Tymnet is a trademark of TYMNET, Inc.
Windows is a trademark of Microsoft Corporation
Word for Windows is a trademark of Microsoft Corporation
WordPerfect is a trademark of Wordperfect Corporation
WordStar is a trademark of MicroPro International Corporation
XYWrite is a trademark of XYQUEST, Inc.

Dedication

To Judy Stevens, wife and best friend

Acknowledgements

"I'd like to thank my parents for making this evening possible—and my children for making it necessary."

Victor Borge

Turning that quote around, I thank my children, now grown, for making these works possible by allowing me the freedom from convention that would otherwise keep one employed and not writing, and I thank my parents, now gone, for making these works necessary through the example of their boundless creative energies.

Thanks also to:

Microsoft for providing me with copies of Windows 3.0. All the Sysops and participants on the CompuServe MSWIN forum. Jim Conger for sending me the SNAP3 program. Bill Allred for providing the diversion that keeps me sane.

Contents

Preface

This book is a tutorial that enables you to teach yourself to operate Windows 3 on your personal computer. Windows 3 is an operating environment that adds three features to the IBM PC architecture: a graphical user interface; a user interface that can be consistent across applications; and the ability to multitask—to run more than one application concurrently. These features are important because they advance the personal computer into the family of operating platforms upon which the world is converging.

Windows 3 is the third version of Windows—with many improvements over earlier versions. Among those improvements is the ability to run DOS programs from within the Windows graphical operating environment. You can gain the benefits of Windows, gradually upgrade your software to applications that operate with the conventions of that environment, and never have to abandon the older DOS applications that you like or need.

This book ignores the earlier versions of Windows and usually refers to Windows 3 simply as "Windows."

HOW TO USE THIS BOOK

Teach Yourself Windows 3 is a tutorial book. Its purpose is to enable you to learn to operate in the Windows environment with a minimum of fuss. The book assumes that you have a basic understanding of DOS—not necessarily that of a power user, but sufficient knowledge to know how DOS organizes files into directories and subdirectories, what file names and directory names look like, and the differences between data files and program files. If you need to learn the fundamentals of DOS, read my book, *Teach Yourself DOS* (1989, MIS Press).

Proceed through the chapters of *Teach Yourself Windows 3* sequentially. This book is not a reference book in which you can look up a subject and find everything you need to know about it. It is a set of tutorial exercises designed to expose you to the features of Windows by using subjects already learned to introduce new ones.

As you leaf through the book, you will see many illustrations of screens and windows. The exercises in this book do not ask you to imagine what you will see when you try them out. Every exercise is fully illustrated to allow you to read and learn during those times when a computer is not handy and to reinforce your experience when you run the exercises. When what the book shows is what you see on the screen, you know you are doing it right.

Do not expect to learn Windows simply by reading this book. Use the book along with your computer to learn whenever possible. You will need an installed Windows configuration, preferably one that has not been heavily modified and enhanced. Ideally, you should start by installing Windows onto a computer that does not already have it. That way the examples and figures in this book will match the ones you see on your screen as closely as possible.

You have heard that Windows is a complex, difficult operating environment. It can be, but it doesn't have to start out that way. By learning its basic operations, you can rapidly become a productive Windows user. As you become more proficient, you can move on to the more advanced operations that Windows provides. This book follows that logic by presenting the easy topics first and saving the hard parts until later.

THE WINDOWS GRAPHICAL USER INTERFACE

The Windows graphical user interface (GUI) breaks the barriers of the traditional text-only screen. It presents the software operating environment in pictures—metaphors and icons—as opposed to the typically terse command-line syntax of DOS. DOS users must necessarily retain mental images of the files, subdirectories, programs, and other DOS resources. The GUI provide these images as pictures on the graphics screen, so you do not have to remember them. Many of the cryptic commands and command-line parameters that DOS and its applications use are replaced by point-and-shoot mouse or keyboard operations under a GUI. Such an interface is said, by its supporters, to be "more intuitive" than a DOS-like command line interface.

THE WINDOWS CONSISTENT USER INTERFACE

One of the problems with many computer systems and with DOS in particular, is that the user interfaces of the applications differ. A DOS user who runs spreadsheet, word processor, data base, electronic mail, and desktop publishing programs must learn the command and data entry languages for each of these programs, none of which might resemble the others. Even the DOS utility programs such as BACKUP, ATTRIB, and COPY use command-line syntax conventions that differ enough to cause confusion.

Windows users can, however, choose to operate programs that themselves use the Windows graphical user interface. Such programs employ input/output techniques that emulate those of Windows, including using standard menu and dialogue formats and layouts and using the mouse to select items from menus, scroll documents on the screen, and move the cursor. Users of these programs do not need to learn a new command language for every new program.

WINDOWS MULTITASKING

DOS does not exploit the power of most of the computers that run it. If you are running a program, you must terminate that program and return to DOS in order to run another program. Some users, however, have programs that they run frequently, and they do not want to save all their other work to disk and endure the overhead of startup time in order to run them. Other users run processes that consume time but do not require the user's attention—those users would also like to run other programs at the same time. Both groups of users need an operating environment that supports multitasking—an environment in which the computer runs more than one program at the same time.

DOS by itself does not support multitasking. Because of this, software developers have developed techniques for memory-resident utility programs that allow you to load more than one program into memory. When you want to execute one of these programs, you press a hot key, and the program "pops up." The task of switching from one task to another is the responsibility of the memory-resident programs themselves; DOS has nothing to do with it. As a result, each such program must record the state of the program it interrupts, establish its own state, coerce DOS into believing that the new program is the only one running, and restore the state of the interrupted program when it is done.

A drawback of the memory-resident program is that there are numerous differences between the conditions under which programs operate, not the least of which is the video mode. Unless every program is aware of every permutation, is able to switch to and from all possible permutations, and does it in a way that is compatible with all other programs, chaos reigns. Another disadvantage to the memory-resident program is that it occupies memory even when it is not executing. As you add resident applications, the residual memory available for other tasks decreases. Nonetheless, for years the memory-resident program was the only choice for DOS users who needed multitasking.

Windows is an application and file management shell program that runs on top of DOS. It can support true multitasking if you have an AT-class machine. True multitasking involves running several applications concurrently. While you write a letter with your word processor, the communications program collects your electronic mail, the spreadsheet application computes a large sheet, the data base program searches its files to answer a query you entered, and the printer prints the output from the other programs.

Windows can manage the execution of multiple tasks for non-AT users, too. The difference is that even though several programs are loaded and available, only one program is executing at a time. All the applications have access to the entire memory of the computer, however, and you can switch from application to application by letting Windows swap the running tasks in and out. Windows manages the multitasking and swapping of concurrently loaded programs in a way that allows each of them to have the full range of memory normally available to a single program in the DOS environment.

The multitasking environment is not restricted to applications that were developed to run exclusively in the Windows graphical operating environment. Windows can also switch between Windows applications and non-Windows DOS applications.

Windows allows applications to exchange data in ways not available under a single-tasking operating environment. You can move data from one application to another without the two applications knowing about one another—in fact the applications don't even need to know that data movement took place. Any Windows application that has a Paste command can receive text from any other Windows application that has a Cut or Copy command and that is running or has run in the recent past. A Windows application that can accept graphics data and has the Paste command can likewise receive graphics data from any other Windows application that displays graphics data and has a Cut or Copy command. Non-Windows DOS applications can similarly exchange textual data. You manage these data exchanges by using the Windows Clipboard as the intermediate repository for data that is to be exchanged.

Some Windows applications have a dynamic data exchange (DDE) facility built into them. These applications can exchange data among themselves without user intervention.

WHENCE WINDOWS 3?

Windows 3 is a product from Microsoft that culminates several generations of products that bore the Windows moniker. Its predecessors enjoyed less than moderate success for several reasons:

1) The hardware platforms required to run them were expensive;

2) The programs performed poorly;

3) You needed different versions of Windows, depending on your processor type;

4) The only applications you could run in the Windows environment were Windows-specific applications; and

5) Windows had no facility for true multitasking.

Windows 3 solves most of the earlier versions' problems; the computer industry solved the first one. Fast AT class machines with mice, high resolution color displays, and significant amounts of memory are now commonplace. Windows 3 senses what kind of hardware is running and adjusts itself accordingly—you no longer need different Windows versions for different hardware configurations. Windows also allows you to install and run non-Windows DOS applications, and, if you are using a 286 or 386 machine with sufficient memory, it allows several programs to execute at the same time.

HOW THIS BOOK IS ORGANIZED

Chapter 1 is an introduction to Windows. This is an important chapter. In it you discover what hardware and software you need to run Windows. You also learn how to install, start, and exit Windows, and you learn the basics of using the Windows graphical user interface. Subsequent chapters assume that you understand this interface. After Chapter 1 teaches you how to select an item from a menu with either the mouse or the keyboard, for example, other chapters simply tell you to select the item, assuming that you know how to do this. In Chapter 1 you will also learn how the Windows on-line Help system works.

Chapter 2 describes the Windows Program Manager. You learn how the Program Manager organizes programs into groups and how you can create, organize, and maintain your own groups of programs. You also learn how to operate DOS programs from within Windows and how to operate several programs at one time—multitasking.

Chapter 3 describes the Windows File Manager. You learn how to create and delete directories on your hard disk; move, copy, and delete files; format and copy diskettes; and run programs from within the File Manager.

Chapter 4 describes the Clipboard. You learn how to use the Clipboard to exchange text and graphics data among Windows and non-Windows DOS applications.

Chapter 5 describes the Windows Control Panel. You learn how to use the Control Panel to alter the appearance of the desktop; modify the performance of devices such as the mouse, keyboard, and communications ports; install, select and configure a printer; use the display and input conventions of other countries; set the date and time; and control the Windows beeper.

Chapter 6 describes the Windows Print Manager. You learn how to print from Windows applications with and without the queuing features of the Print Manager; print from DOS applications; delete and reorder entries in the print queues; and modify the Print Manager's processing priority.

Chapter 7 describes Windows Write, the word processor that comes with Windows. You learn how to use Write to create and modify documents.

Chapter 8 describes Windows Paintbrush, the graphics design program that comes with Windows. You learn how to use Paintbrush to create pictures, use graphics elements from other sources, and integrate your designs into your other applications.

Chapter 9 describes Windows Terminal, the communications program that comes with Windows. You learn how to use Terminal to connect to on-line services and bulletin board systems, send messages, and upload and download files.

Chapter 10 describes the Windows accessories programs. You learn how to use the Clock, Calculator, Notepad, Calendar, Cardfile, and Recorder.

Chapter 11 discusses the techniques that you will use when you become a Windows power user. You learn about the Windows operating modes and when and how to use them. You also learn how to use the Windows PIF Editor to integrate DOS applications into Windows and how to run applications that were developed for previous versions of Windows. Finally, you learn how to use Windows in a local area network work station.

Information sidebars, such as the one at the top of the next page, appear in each chapter to enhance your learning experience. These interesting detours are set apart from the rest of the text by asterisks. As you travel through the chapters, you will acquire added knowledge and skills by reading these sidebars.

***

WINDOWS: A QUANDARY OF ENGLISH USAGE

HOW TO USE THE WORD "WINDOWS?" IT IS A PROPER NOUN—THE NAME OF A PRODUCT—TAKEN FROM A PLURAL NOUN—THE NAME OF AN OPENING IN A WALL. FROM THAT USAGE, ONE COULD SAY, "I HAVE INSTALLED WINDOWS AND IT WORKS WELL," THE "IT" IN QUESTION BEING THE SINGULAR SOFTWARE PRODUCT NAMED "WINDOWS." WHILE A CARPENTER MIGHT BE CONFUSED BY THIS SENTENCE, COMPUTER USERS WILL NOT BE, AND SO THIS BOOK ADOPTS THAT USAGE.

BUT WHAT ABOUT THE PLURAL FORM OF WINDOWS? INASMUCH AS WE USE THE USUALLY PLURAL NOUN FORM "WINDOWS" AS A SINGULAR NOUN, WE NOW HAVE A PROBLEM WITH THE PLURAL. IF WE HAVE SEVERAL COPIES OF WINDOWS, HOW DO WE REFER TO THEM COLLECTIVELY. IT WOULD BE EASY TO SAY, "FETCH THOSE WORDPERFECTS, PLEASE," BUT "THOSE WINDOWSES" ROLLS INDELICATELY OFF THE TONGUE.

IN LIGHT OF THESE PROBLEMS WITH THE LANGUAGE, THIS BOOK USES THIS STYLE: "WINDOWS" IS A SINGULAR NOUN. IF A PLURAL USAGE IS NECESSARY IT TAKES THE EASY WAY OUT AND USES FORMS SIMILAR TO "COPIES OF WINDOWS"" AND "WINDOWS INSTALLATIONS."

THIS EXPLANATION ACKNOWLEDGES THE PROBLEMS THAT OFTEN PLAGUE THE WRITER WHO USES COMPUTER JARGON, AND IT ALSO ANTICIPATES AND—ONE WOULD HOPE—STAYS THE SELF-APPOINTED LANGUAGE COMMANDOS WHO LIE IN WAIT TO POUNCE UPON EVERY SMALL TRANSGRESSION OF THE UNSUSPECTING USAGE OFFENDER.

***

Chapter 1

Introduction to Windows 3

Following the section on "Installation" in this chapter, this book assumes that you have Windows installed in its default configuration. It is best that your Windows configuration not be heavily modified or enhanced when you begin so that the examples and figures in the book will come close to matching those on your screen.

GETTING STARTED

If you are a potential power user—perhaps you were a DOS power user—you will eventually want to customize, modify, and tweak your Windows operating environment to wrest the last ounce of performance from your computer and to personalize its appearance and behavior. There are many ways to do this and numerous third-party add-on products to enhance or otherwise change the way Windows works. This chapter could not possibly cover all the ways you can customize Windows, nor could the book. Chapter 11 will address some of the ways that you can modify the Windows operating environment. For now, however, the lessons assume that you will install Windows in its simplest configuration, out of the box, up, and running.

Required Hardware

You need a certain minimum hardware configuration to run Windows. You might hear that you can run Windows on almost any PC, and to a limited extent that is true. But Windows is a high-end software product that works well given the hardware horsepower it needs. Give it much less, and it will run so poorly that it is cumbersome to use and ineffective for the work it was designed to do. The hardware minimums given here are the recommended configurations for any reasonable operation of Windows.

Processor

You need a 286, at a minimum, to run Windows effectively. Even though Windows will run on the 8088 class of machine, most of the advantages offered by Windows are unavailable to that processor family, and the typical 8088's processor speed is too slow for reasonable use by Windows. For multitasking DOS and Windows applications, you will need a 386. Processor speed is important—even with 286s and 386s. Do not expect to be happy with Windows if you are running a 6 Mhz 286. You should have at least a 10 Mhz processor—the faster the better.

Memory

Windows needs 640K of conventional and 384K of extended memory for a total minimum of 1 Mbyte. You need 2 Mbytes of extended memory for multitasking or to run in 386 enhanced mode. (You will learn about Windows operating modes in Chapter 11, The Windows Power User.) The more extended memory you have, the more efficiently Windows will manage multiple tasks.

Disk

A Windows installation uses 6 Mbytes of hard disk storage. Do not consider installing Windows with less disk memory. Beyond this minimum, you will need room for applications programs, data files, DOS files, and the working files that Windows builds and uses. The 6 Mbytes that Windows uses must be on one hard disk drive. Applications and DOS can be on other drives if you have them. A good rule of thumb is to install Windows on a system with at least 8 Mbytes of disk storage available—the more the better. You also need a 1.2 Mbyte 5.25-inch floppy drive or a 1.44 Mbyte 3.5-inch floppy drive.

Video

You need a graphics adaptor to run Windows. All PCs have some kind of video adaptor, but Windows does not run on a machine that has the Monochrome Display Adaptor. You need an adaptor with graphics capabilities.

Although Windows works with the Color Graphics Adaptor (CGA), the displays are far less than appealing, and you will be unimpressed. At a minimum you should have the Enhanced Graphics Adaptor (EGA). The Virtual Graphics Array (VGA) is the recommended configuration. With that adaptor and a compatible color display monitor, Windows comes alive.

There are several other display adaptors and monitors that you might have and that Windows can use. The Setup procedure, described later, addresses the adaptors and monitors that come with Windows. Other hardware vendors include the necessary software drivers and installation instructions for adding their products to a Windows configuration. Be aware, however, that many such products include drivers for earlier versions of Windows. These drivers usually do not work with Windows 3.0 or, if they do work, it's only in a degraded mode. Make sure that you get the driver version for Windows 3.0.

Mouse

Although it is possible to run Windows without a mouse device, you should have one. Some Windows operations are easier with a mouse. Others lend themselves more readily to keyboard input. Windows is designed to support either mode and a mix of both.

Modem

Because Windows excels at multitasking, you might wonder how you would use that facility. The most productive use of a multitasking environment is to let the computer run some program that requires no attention while you use the computer for something interactive.

A frequent use for computers—and one that executes for long periods of time without operator intervention—is communication with other systems over telephone lines. By allowing Windows to run such communications applications in the background while you run an interactive application, such as word processing, in the foreground, you acquire a larger measure of productivity from your computer. Communications programs need a modem. You do not need a modem if you never telecommunicate, but if you do, Windows offers a good way to get it done.

Printer

Windows is a graphical operating environment. Because the environment offers a powerful and portable graphical engine, many graphics-based applications are available to run with Windows, and new applications surface monthly. Desktop publishers, CAD/CAM applications, and graphics design programs are examples of such applications.

The modern generation of laser printers is capable of printing the output from these applications with a high degree of resolution. A laser printer, while not required by Windows, is almost a necessity if you want to derive the maximum benefit from the Windows graphical operating environment.

Required Software

In order to run Windows, you must already have MS-DOS or PC-DOS version 3.1 or higher. Version 3.3 is the recommended version.

Installation

Windows installs itself. It comes with a package of numbered diskettes. You put the number 1 diskette in the A drive, log onto A:, and type SETUP. Then you follow the instructions. You must know the hardware configuration of the computer. The Setup program displays a list of hardware configurations based on its analysis of your system. You can modify that list by following the instructions. After you have specified a hardware configuration, the Setup program builds Windows onto your hard disk by copying the necessary files and stopping from time to time to ask you to insert a different diskette.

While Setup runs, it gives you a preview of what the graphical operating environment looks like. As it builds the application groups' icons into the Program Manager, it uses Windows-like displays. Soon you will learn what these things mean.

Setup offers to modify some DOS files named CONFIG.SYS and AUTOEXEC.BAT in the root directory of your boot drive. It even notices when you have certain incompatible hardware or software drivers installed and offers to disable those drivers. In most cases you can allow Setup to modify these files. Setup leaves copies named AUTOEXEC.OLD and CONFIG.OLD in the root directory of your boot disk for your review.

When installing your printer, Setup asks you several questions and gives you a list of printers from which to select. Follow the instructions at the bottom of the screen carefully during this procedure. You will need to know the port to which your printer connects. The choices are the usual LPT and COM ports, as well as the EPT port for the IBM Personal Pageprinter. In addition you can select to print to a disk file, but you will not normally make this last selection during initial Setup. Printing to a file is something you might need to do from time to time, and run-time Printer Setup options support that procedure and allow you to return to your usual printer after printing to the file.

Depending on which printer you select, Setup asks you some additional questions. Many printers have options—such as extra memory, font cartridges, landscape or portrait mode, and so on—that Windows can use to advantage.

One of the services performed by Setup is a search of your hard drives to find DOS applications that can run under Windows. You can choose not to do this search, but it might be worth the small amount of extra time that Setup uses to do it. Setup installs such applications into the Windows Program Manager so that they are ready to be run as soon as you have finished the Windows installation. Setup makes a list of the applications it finds and allows you to select from that list, installing the applications you select into the Program Manager.

When Setup is done it displays a text file with the new features and documentation corrections that have occurred since the User's Guide went to press. Setup uses the Notepad, a small text-editing Desktop Accessory program, to display the files. You can browse the files using the Notepad commands, which the text file itself describes well enough to allow you to use. You can rerun Setup whenever you want after Windows is installed.

When Setup is done it also advises you to reboot your computer. You must do this so that the changes to AUTOEXEC.BAT and CONFIG.SYS take effect. Reboot and proceed to the next section for your first step toward teaching yourself Windows.

Running Windows

If Windows will always be your primary operating environment, you might want it to execute automatically every time you boot the computer. Use EDLIN or another text editor to add this command to the end of the AUTOEXEC.BAT file in the root directory:

WIN

If you prefer to execute Windows yourself, do not modify AUTOEXEC.BAT, but rather type the WIN command from the command line when you want Windows to run. In either case, when Windows runs you will see a display very much like the one shown in Figure 1-1.

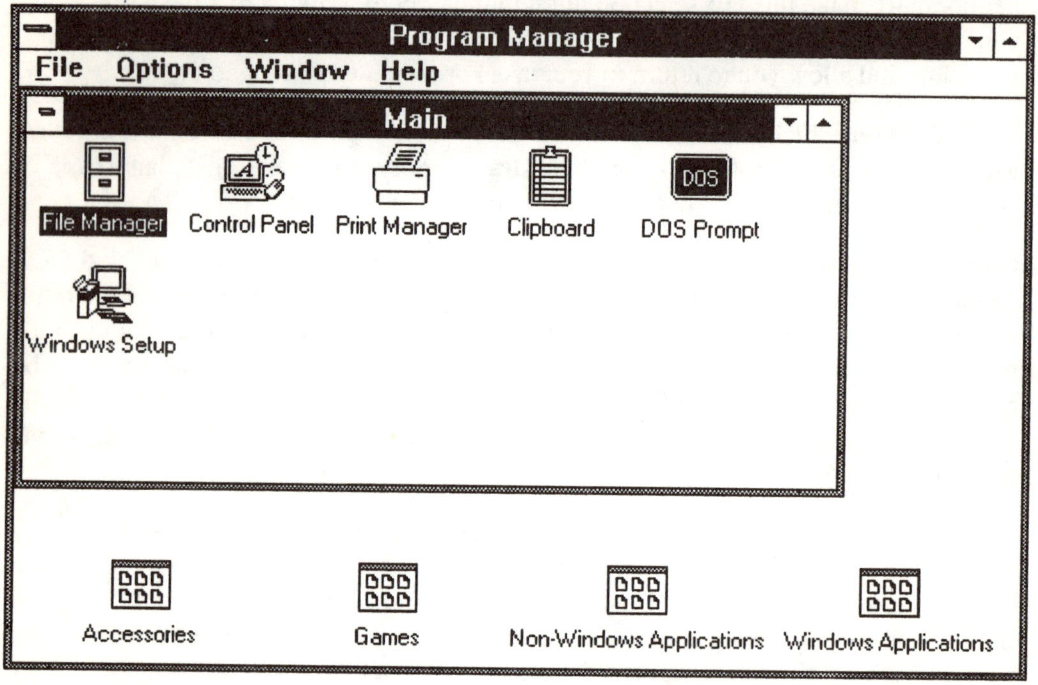

Figure 1-1. The Initial Windows Display.

This display is the Program Manager with the Main application group window opened. The Program Manager is the executive program with which you run all the other applications, utilities, and accessories. It is your introduction to the Windows way of doing things.

***

THE LITTLE SQUARE PICTURES WITH TITLES AT THE BOTTOM OF THE PROGRAM MANAGER WINDOW ARE ICONS THAT REPRESENT THE PROGRAM GROUPS. YOU WILL LEARN ABOUT THEM LATER. FIGURE 1-1 HAS THEM SPACED APART SO THAT THEIR TITLES ARE LEGIBLE, BUT WINDOWS IS NOT ALWAYS THIS NEAT. WINDOWS ARBITRARILY POSITIONS ICONS IN WAYS THAT SOMETIMES OBSCURE THE TITLES. THE SECTION "MOVING ICONS" WILL TEACH YOU HOW TO REPOSITION THE ICONS SO THAT YOU CAN READ THE TITLES. LATER YOU WILL ALSO LEARN HOW TO PERMANENTLY SPECIFY THE DISTANCE BETWEEN ICONS.

***

Exiting From Windows

You can exit from Windows back to DOS in one of three ways: by using the mouse or keyboard to select the Program Manager's Control Menu and then selecting the Close command; by double clicking (pressing and releasing the left button rapidly two times) the Control Menu selector box in the upper left corner of the Program Manager window; or by pressing Alt+F4 when the Program Manager is the current active window. The next sections of this chapter discuss each of these techniques.

You should always exit from Windows back to DOS before turning the power off or resetting the computer. This practice insures that Windows performs an orderly shutdown of everything it is maintaining. It also insures that all running applications get an opportunity to execute their shutdown procedures as well. Regardless of how you tell Windows you want to exit, you will see the window displayed in Figure 1-2.

Figure 1-2 is a dialogue box. Note the Save Changes box with an X in it. When you exit from Windows, it can remember the condition of the desktop so that when you restart Windows, everything is as you left it. The X tells Windows to save the desktop.

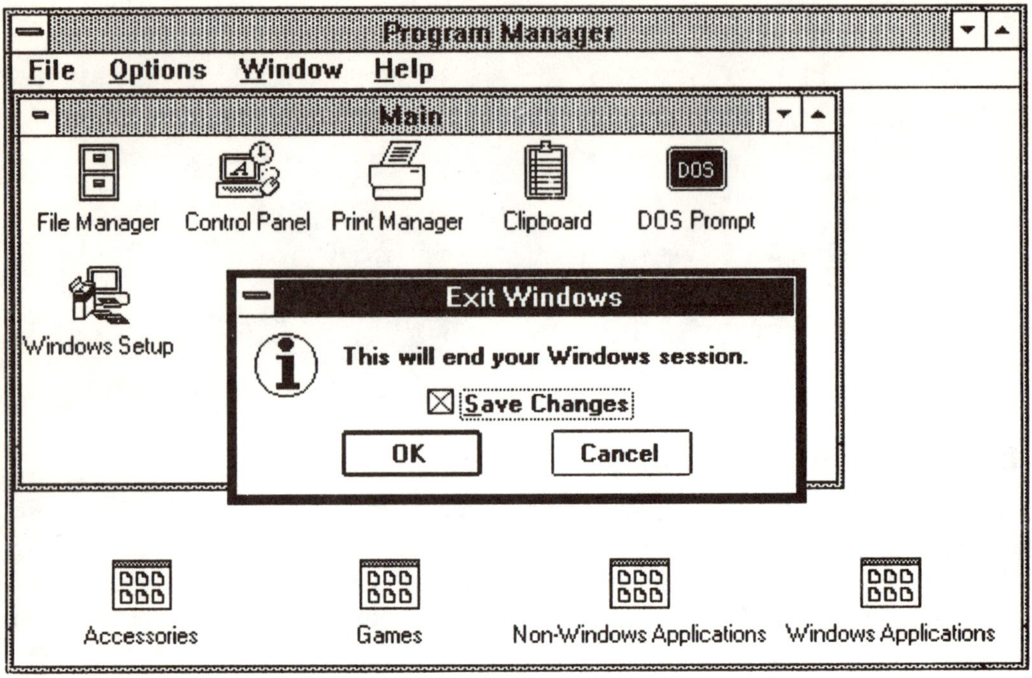

Figure 1-2. Exiting Windows.

While you are using the examples in this book, it is best to tell Windows to preserve the original, rather than the current, condition of the desktop. To make this specification, you must remove the X from the Save Changes box. You can do this either by moving the mouse cursor to the box and clicking the left button or by pressing the S key.

If you exit from Windows in the middle of an exercise or a series of related exercises, you can tell Windows to save the desktop so that when you return, you can start where you left off.

When the Save Changes selection is correct, you can exit by pressing the Enter key or by clicking the OK button. To ignore the request and return to Windows, click the Cancel button or press the Esc key.

Discussions of the mouse and dialogue boxes appear later in this chapter.

***

EVEN THOUGH YOU METICULOUSLY MOVE THE ICONS SO THAT THEIR TITLES ARE READABLE AND TELL WINDOWS TO SAVE THE CHANGES, WINDOWS FORGETS THIS WORK AND ARBITRARILY POSITIONS THE ICONS WHERE IT WANTS THEM WHEN YOU RESTART. AFTER A WHILE YOU WILL SIMPLY GIVE UP. YOU WILL LEARN HOW TO EXERCISE A MEASURE OF CONTROL OVER THIS BEHAVIOR IN THE "SETTING ICON SPACING" SECTION IN CHAPTER 5.

***

WORKING FROM THE DESKTOP

Windows operates with the Desktop metaphor. Programs and files display themselves on your screen in windows, which are rectangular subsections of the screen. Figure 1-1 shows two windows: one titled Program Manager and another titled Main. The windows appear as items on your desktop. The metaphor is of documents that lay flat on a desk. You can move documents around on a desk, and you can move the windows around on the Windows desktop. You can shuffle them, putting current ones on top of others. You can slide them around and make them smaller or make them occupy the entire screen. You can relegate a window to the bottom of the screen as an icon—a little picture with a title to remind you that the window is still active but set aside for the moment.

To teach the basics of operating Windows programs, this chapter will use many of the features of the Windows Program Manager. Chapter 2 describes the Program Manager and how it works, but you will get an early look at some of its operations in this chapter. Do not be concerned if you do not completely understand what you see in these examples. The discussions in this chapter are about the Windows common user interface, and their purpose is to teach you how to get around in any Windows program. The Program Manager is the first program you encounter, and it uses all the components of the Windows user interface. It is, therefore, a good place to begin learning.

Windows

A window can represent a program or a document. A program can be an application, one of the Windows utility programs, or a Windows accessory. Document windows display the data and files on which programs operate. Document windows are subordinate to program windows—you cannot move a document outside of the program window that owns it.

The Main window in Figure 1-1 is a document window that belongs to the Program Manager program window. The Program Manager is itself a Windows utility program. Its Main document window displays some of the data on which it operates, in this case one of the application groups from which you can execute programs. Sometimes, as in the case with a word processor, the program window uses itself to display the document.

Windows and its applications use other window-like display techniques for menus, dialogue boxes, and information displays. You cannot move all of these displays around like you can with program and document windows; it depends on how the application implements the display. You will learn about each of these display types as the lessons proceed.

The Format of a Window

Figure 1-3 shows the window that the Notepad Accessory program uses, with the standard window components indicated by labels. Chapter 10 discusses Accessory programs and describes the Notepad in more detail. You will use the Notepad's window here to learn the format of all windows.

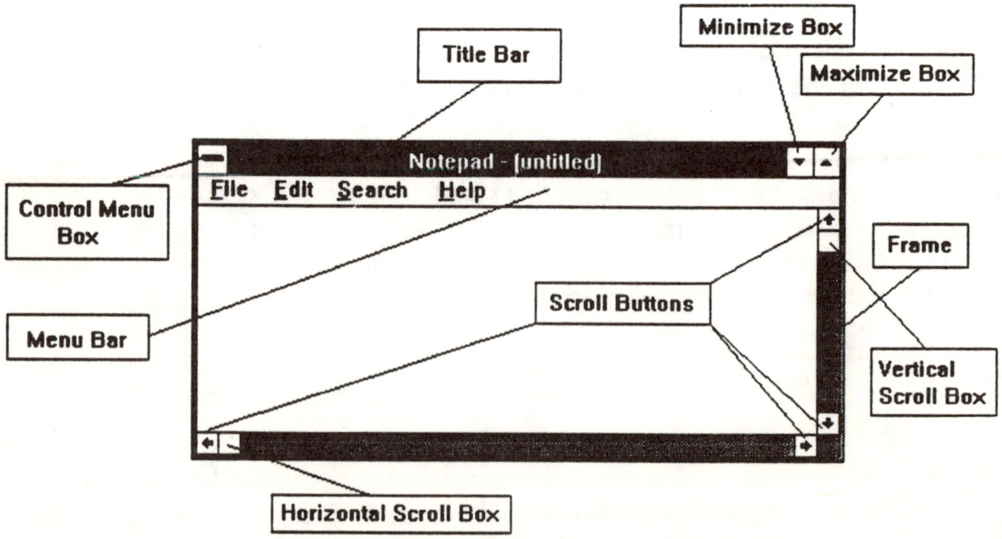

Figure 1-3. The Components of a Window.

Title Bar

The title bar serves three purposes: it displays the title associated with the window; it indicates when the window is active and when it is inactive; and it enables you to move the window when you point the mouse cursor to the title bar and drag the mouse. When a window cannot be moved, it has no title bar. You will learn several ways to move a window in a later exercise.

Frame

The frame surrounds the window. When you point the mouse to one of the sides and drag the cursor, you can shrink and expand the window size horizontally. The top and bottom of the frame allow you to shrink and expand the window vertically. When a window cannot be resized, the frame appears as a single solid line. You will learn several ways to resize a window in a later exercise.

Control Menu Box

The small box with the horizontal bar in the upper left corner of the window is the Control Menu box. It allows you to pop down a Control Menu. The Control Menu is the same for all windows, although sometimes some of its menu commands are disabled. You select the Control Menu by clicking the box with the mouse or by pressing the Alt+Spacebar key (for program windows) or the Alt+Hyphen key (for document windows). Figure 1-4 shows the Control Menu for the Notepad window.

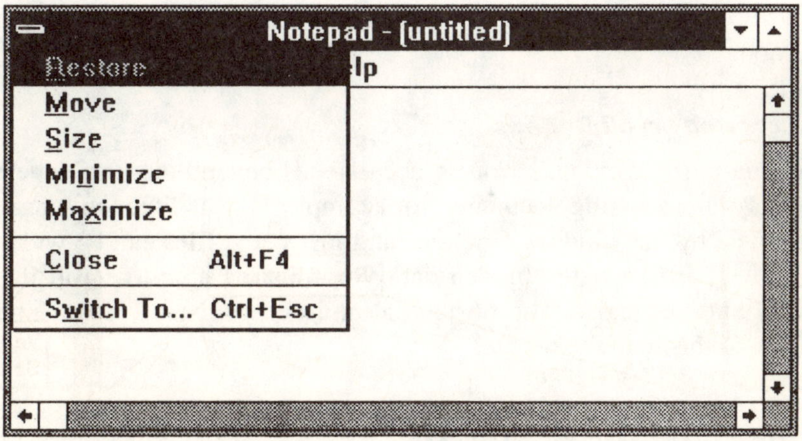

Figure 1-4. The Control Menu.

Menu Bar

The menu bar is the place on a window where the titles of pull-down menus appear. These titles vary from application to application, but certain standards have emerged. You will see File, Edit, and Help menu titles on the menu bars of many applications. A discussion of menu selections appears later in this chapter. Not all windows have menu bars because not all windows have operating menu selections for you to execute.

Work Space

The work space of a window is the portion that is inside the frame and under the title bar. This space is also called the "client area." The window displays its data in the work space.

Minimize and Maximize Boxes

A window can be in one of three conditions of display with respect to its size and placement: it can occupy a section of the desktop or parent window's work space; it can fill the desktop or parent window's work space completely; or it can appear as an icon at the bottom of the desktop or parent window's work space.

You control the window's placement with the Minimize and Maximize boxes in the upper right corner of the window. Return to the display shown in Figure 1-1—the Program Manager program window and its subordinate Main document window both have Minimize and Maximize boxes. You will learn how these buttons work in a later section.

Scroll Boxes and Scroll Buttons

Often the data in the window's work space extends beyond the area covered by the window. A word processing document, for example, is usually much longer than the space displayed by the window. Graphics and many text files can be wider than the window as well. To view the hidden data you must be able to scroll the window horizontally and vertically. The horizontal and vertical scroll boxes and buttons allow you to do this with the mouse.

The Mouse and the Keyboard

Windows seems to work best when you have a mouse. A mouse is not an absolute requirement because everything you can do with the mouse you can also do with the keyboard. But using the mouse relieves you from having to remember the different keystrokes that issue the commands. The mouse, being a pointing device, allows you to point at a visual symbol on the screen and click the appropriate action. The meanings of the symbols remind you of their purposes. Even the mouse cursor changes its shape to indicate the different effects it can cause.

With the screen still showing the display in Figure 1-1, observe the small arrow. That arrow is the mouse cursor. When you move the mouse around on your desk, the mouse cursor moves with it. To get something started, you move the mouse to someplace on the screen where the mouse has an effect and you press the left button. Sometimes you press the button once and release it. Sometimes you press it once, hold it down and move the mouse. This action usually moves something on the screen and is called "dragging" the mouse. Other times you double click the mouse to get the desired effect. Sometimes you press and hold the button down, observe its effect, and release it when you are done observing.

You use the keyboard in ways that emulate the mouse. Later you will see that many of the Windows displays tell you which keystroke can emulate what the mouse does. These keystrokes are called "shortcut keys." Menus are examples of displays that inform you of the shortcut keys.

In order to use either the keyboard or the mouse, you must first know how to select something. Among the many things from which you can select are icons on the screen.

Icons

The display in Figure 1-1 shows an active program window named Program Manager and an active document window named Main. You know these windows are active because their top borders are made up of a dark bar with the window title in white letters.

The Main window has some little pictures with descriptive titles. As mentioned above, these pictures are called icons. The Program Manager window has icons, too, at the bottom of the window. The Main window's icons are all different, while the Program Manager's icons are all the same. The Program Manager's icons represent groups of programs; all the icons are the same because each one represents a program group. The Main window's icons are all different because they represent individual programs.

Selecting Icons

When an icon's title is in white letters on a dark background, the icon is selected for the next action. The File Manager icon is selected within the Main window in Figure 1-1.

You can use the mouse or keyboard to select icons. By selecting icons, you specify programs that are to be run. You will use the operation of selecting icons as the first example in learning how to use the mouse and the keyboard.

Selecting Icons with the Mouse

Move the mouse cursor to an icon in the Main window and click (press and release) the left button. The title of that icon shows that the icon is selected. Try several other icons.

Now move the mouse cursor to one of the group icons at the bottom of the Program Manager window. Click the left button. If you chose the Accessories icon, for example, you will see the display shown in Figure 1-5.

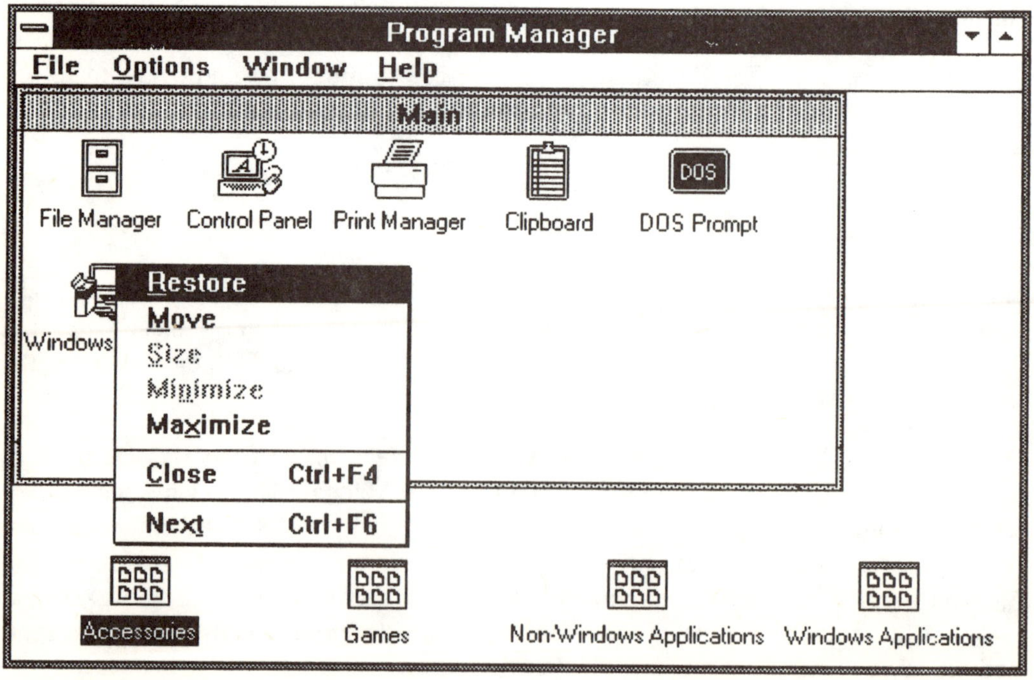

Figure 1-5. Selecting an Icon in the Program Manager Window.

Figure 1-5 shows you several things. First, the icon that you selected in the Main window is now de-selected, and the Accessories icon in the Program Manager window is selected. Second, the title bar of the Main window has a light background, indicating that you de-selected that entire window as well. (You will learn more about that later.) Third, there is a new display on the screen, a Control Menu window that controls the icon's position and status. (You will learn how that menu works later.) It contains the same selections as the Notepad's Control Menu in Figure 1-4. The menu in Figure 1-5 is for managing the placement and status of an icon; the menu in Figure 1-4 is for managing the placement and status of a window. The two menus are the same because those icons represent windows that are not currently being displayed.

To remove the icon's Control Menu for now, click the left mouse button a second time. Move the mouse cursor to the inside of the Main window, but not on one of the icons. Click the left button and observe that the Main window is active again, and the Main icon you selected last is also active. Click another icon at the bottom of the Program Manager window. Now click a specific icon in the Main window to select that icon instead of the icon you had previously selected in the Main window.

So far all you have done is select the icons that will be the object of the next action, if any. Now you will actually tell an icon to start running. Move the mouse cursor to the Control Panel icon and double click the mouse. You will see the display shown in Figure 1-6.

The display in Figure 1-6 shows the Control Panel as a running program, with its program window as the active window. To terminate the Control Panel, move the mouse cursor to the little box with the vertical bar in the upper left corner of the Control Panel window and double click the mouse.

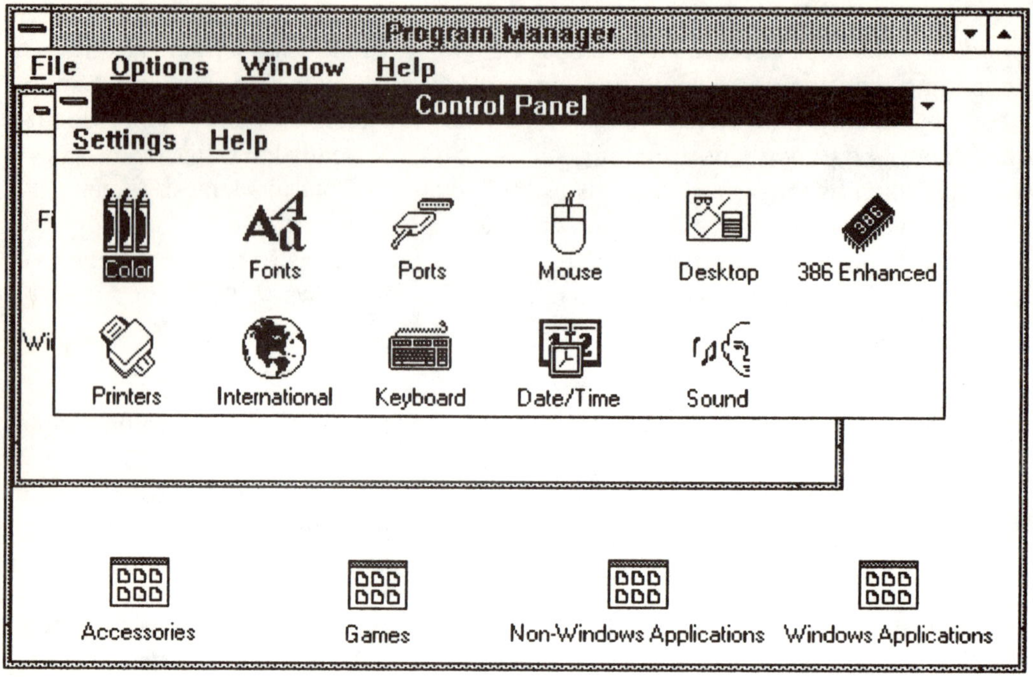

Figure 1-6. Activating an Icon.

Selecting Icons with the Keyboard

If you do not have a mouse, or if you prefer not to use one, you can use the following procedures to select icons with the keyboard. Start from the display shown in Figure 1-1 and use the arrow keys on your keyboard to change the selected icon in the Main window.

Press the Ctrl key and the Tab key at the same time. One of the icons in the Program Manager window becomes the active icon, and the Main window becomes inactive. When you press the Ctrl+Tab keys repetitively, program group icons in the Program Manager window alternately become active until eventually the program icon that you selected earlier in the Main window is the active one.

Using the technique just described, select the Control Panel icon in the Main window and press the Enter key. You will see the display shown in Figure 1-6. This display shows the Control Panel as a running program with its program window as the active window. To terminate the Control Panel, press Alt+F4. The display returns to the configuration shown in Figure 1-1.

Moving Icons

You can move some icons around on the screen with the mouse. If the icon represents a minimized window, you can move it with the keyboard as well. You will learn about minimizing and maximizing windows later. For now you have both kinds displayed. The group icons at the bottom of the Program Manager window are minimized icons. The program icons in the Main group document window are not minimized because they do not represent minimized windows.

Moving Icons with the Mouse

Move the mouse cursor to one of the icons in the Main window. Hold down the left button and drag the icon around the window. The icon changes to a black-and-white copy of itself, without its title, for as long as you drag it. If you try to drag the icon outside of its window, its shape will change to the slashed circle cursor shape to indicate that you are in forbidden territory. If another group window was displayed, you could drag the icon there to move the application into that group.

Moving Icons with the Keyboard

Press Ctrl+Tab to cycle through the groups until you reach the group icon you want to move. Press Alt+Hyphen to open the icon's Control Menu. If you chose the Accessories icon you would see the same display that you saw in Figure 1-5 earlier. Press the M key to select the Move option on the menu. A four-headed arrow cursor covers the icon. Use the arrow keys to move the icon around on the screen. Press the Enter key when the icon is positioned where you want it.

Note that if you move the Accessories group icon into the Main window, it goes there with no problem. You might think that you are transferring the icon to the Main group. You are not, however. You cannot move a group into another group. If you were to press Enter while the icon was in the Main window, the icon would appear to be properly positioned there. But if you were then to select one of the other icons in the main window, the Accessories icon would disappear when the Main window became active. Where would it go? It would be under the main window. You would have to minimize or move the Main window in order to see it. You will learn how to do those things later.

***

IF YOU ACTUALLY LOSE THE ACCESSORIES ICON AND DO NOT KNOW HOW TO GET IT BACK, HERE'S A HINT. WHENEVER YOU GET THE DISPLAY SO HOPELESSLY MODIFIED THAT YOU CANNOT FIND SOMETHING OR CANNOT FOLLOW ALONG WITH THE EXERCISES IN THE BOOK, EXIT FROM WINDOWS AND TELL IT NOT TO SAVE THE DESKTOP. WHEN YOU RUN WINDOWS AGAIN, THINGS SHOULD BE BACK TO NORMAL. IN EXTREME CASES, WHEN EXITING AND RERUNNING DO NOT HELP, SIMPLY REINSTALL WINDOWS. IT WILL TAKE SOME TIME, BUT IT WILL SAVE A LOT OF FRUSTRATION. LATER, AS YOU BECOME MORE FAMILIAR WITH MANAGING THE COMPONENTS OF THE DESKTOP, YOU WILL BE ABLE TO RESTORE THINGS THE WAY YOU LIKE THEM WITHOUT NEEDING SUCH MEASURES.

***

Selecting Windows

The display in Figure 1-1 has two windows: a program window, named Program Manager, and its document window, named Main. The Main window represents one of the program groups that the Program Manager manages. The group icons at the bottom of the Program Manager window represent the other program groups. The example used here has Accessories, Games, Windows Applications, and Non-Windows Applications. The Setup program installs the first two groups as a default. You might have either, both, or none of the other two groups, depending on whether you told Setup to scan for applications and, if so, what it found.

You can have several windows active at one time. From the screen shown in Figure 1-1, select the Accessories icon. Review "Selecting Icons with the Mouse" or "Selecting Icons with the Keyboard" if you cannot remember how to do this. You will see the display shown in Figure 1-7. This display shows the Accessories window as the active window on top of the Main window.

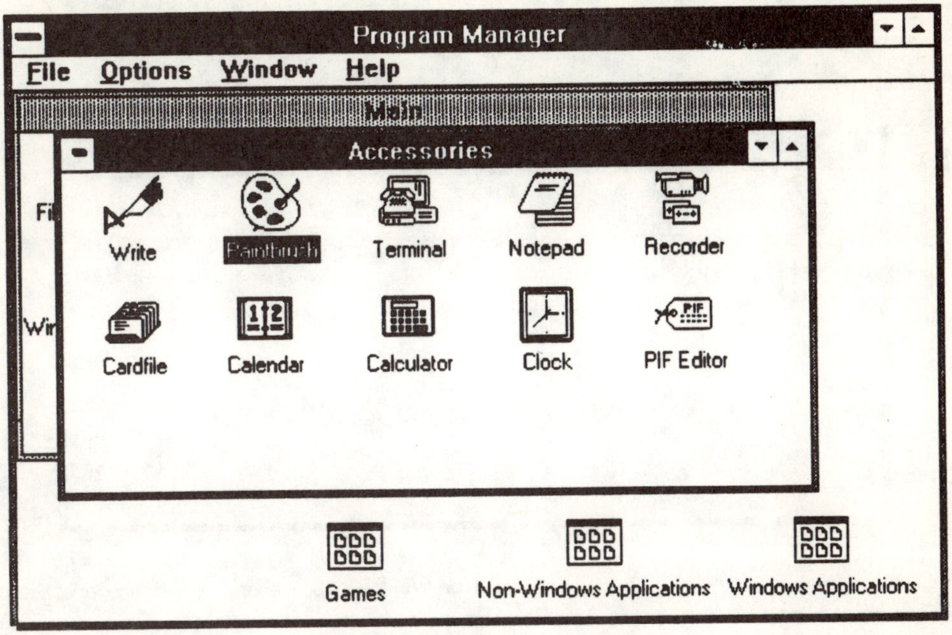

Figure 1-7. Two Document Windows.

Now select the Games icon. You will see the display shown in Figure 1-8. This display shows the addition of the Games document window. There are four windows displayed on this screen: the Program Manager program window and the Main, Accessories, and Games document windows.

***

Do not be confused by the phrases "program window" and "document window." At the moment there seems to be little difference between the two. Most of the windows you have seen so far have been nothing but boxes full of icons. The Program Manager program window does not seem to be an application, and the document windows do not seem to contain documents. In fact, both **are** what they seem not to be. The Program Manager is the executive program of Windows. Its document windows contain its data items, which consist of the groups of programs that it manages. The Windows lexicon uses "document" as a general reference to all things processed. To further confuse you, some program windows manage their own data from within the work space of the program window, not using document windows at all.

***

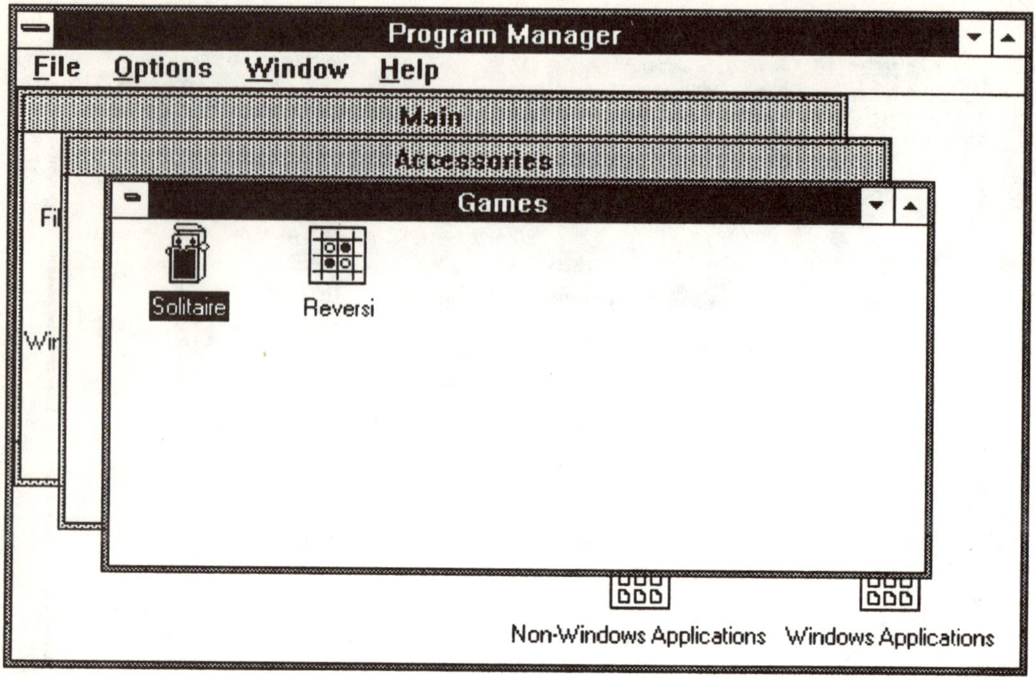

Figure 1-8. Three Document Windows.

Suppose that you want to see what is in the Accessories window. It is behind the Games window, and its work space is almost completely obscured. To bring it completely into view, you must select it.

Selecting Document Windows with the Mouse

Move the mouse to any visible part of the Accessories window and click. You will see the display shown in Figure 1-9.

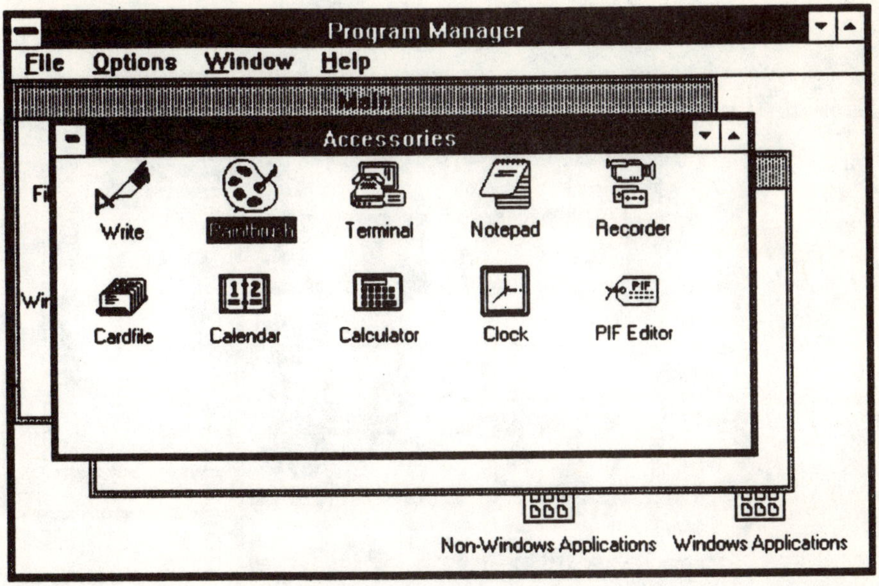

Figure 1-9. Pulling a Window Forward.

Selecting Document Windows with the Keyboard

Press Ctrl+Tab repetitively until the Accessories window is on top. You will see the display shown in Figure 1-9.

The Accessories window is now at the forefront and is the active document window. Each of its icons is an accessory program that you can use any time that Windows is running. You will learn all of them in time. For now, select the Calculator icon by double clicking it or making it active with the keyboard. You will see the display shown in Figure 1-10.

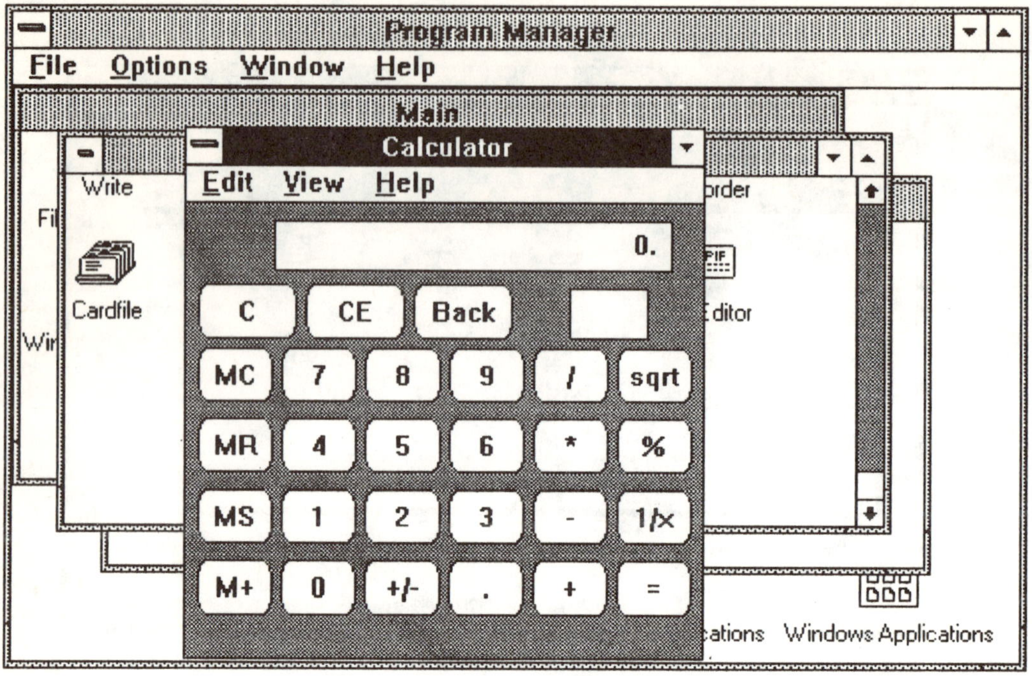

Figure 1-10. A Screen Full of Windows.

When you select the Calculator icon, you execute the Calculator application. The window at the front is the program window for the Calculator program. You now have two program windows on the screen: the Program Manager window and the Calculator window. The Calculator window is active. When more than one program window is displayed, more than one program is running—although only one of the program windows is active. You can select one of the inactive program windows to be the active one. To select a different program window, you select the window itself or one of its document windows, if it has them.

Selecting Program Windows with the Mouse

Move the mouse cursor to any visible part of the Program Manager window and click. The display now looks like Figure 1-9 again except that the Calculator icon's title is highlighted. But there is another difference: even though the display is the same as it was before, the calculator is still running. You cannot see it because its window is completely obscured by the Program Manager. Until you learn how to move windows out of the way with the mouse, you must use the keyboard to get the calculator back. Proceed to the next lesson to learn how to select a program window with the keyboard.

Selecting Program Windows with the Keyboard

Press the Alt+Esc key. This key cycles through the running programs, making the program window of each, in turn, the active one. Continue cycling through the program windows until the Calculator is active.

***

THE CALCULATOR WINDOW WORKS LIKE A DIALOGUE BOX. YOU CAN PLAY WITH IT BY TYPING NUMBERS AT THE NUMERIC KEYPAD OR USING THE MOUSE TO PUSH THE NUMBER AND OPERATOR BUTTONS IN THE CALCULATOR WINDOW. YOU WILL LEARN MORE ABOUT DIALOGUE BOXES IN A LATER LESSON.

***

Keep the display shown in Figure 1-10 on your screen—you will need it for the next section.

Moving Windows

Sometimes a window gets in the way. Sometimes you cannot see what you need to see on a window that is underneath the active one. You could make the hidden window active, but that might not be what you need. Earlier you used the mouse to make the Program Manager active, and the Calculator got hidden. You needed to go to the keyboard to get it back.

Sometimes you need to keep the current active window active while you look at the contents of another window. One way to do this is to move the active window out of the way. Suppose, for example, that you want to look at some of the icons in the Accessory window. The Calculator is in the way. You need to move it.

Moving Windows with the Mouse

Move the mouse cursor to the title bar of the Calculator window, press and hold down the left button, and move the cursor in the direction you wish to move the window. An outline of the Calculator window moves along with the cursor. When the outline appears where you want the window to be, release the mouse button. The Calculator window now appears in its new location.

Moving Windows with the Keyboard

Press Alt+Space to open the Calculator's Control Menu. The Control Menu pops down, as shown in Figure 1-11. Press the M key, and a four-pronged arrow cursor appears. Use the arrow keys to move the window horizontally and vertically. As you press the keys, an outline of the window indicates where the window movement will be. When the outline appears where you want the window to be, press the Enter key. The Calculator window now appears in its new location. If you decide to leave the window where it was, press the Esc key.

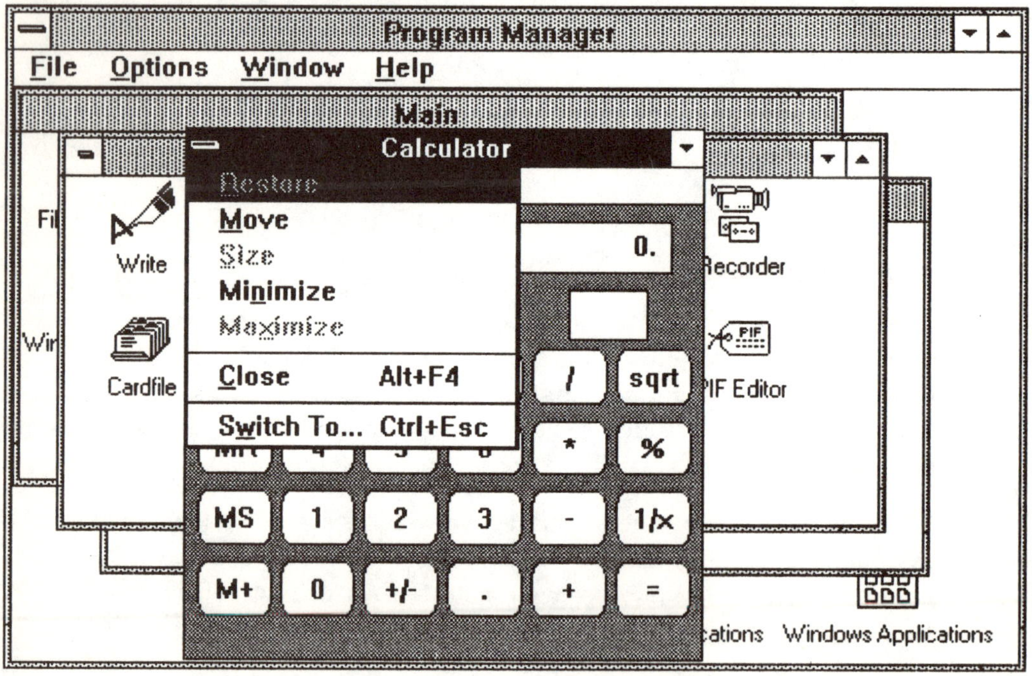

Figure 1-11. The Calculator's Control Menu.

Figure 1-12 shows the Calculator window moved to the upper right corner of the screen.

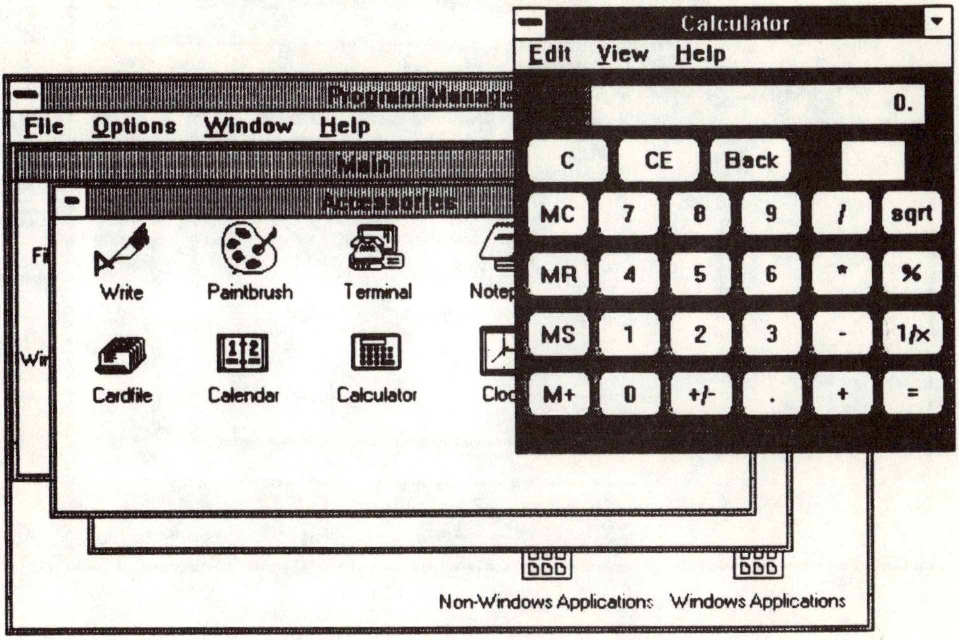

Figure 1-12. A Window That Has Been Moved.

Moving Document Windows

You can move a document window around inside the program window that owns it, but you cannot move it outside the program window. Select the Accessories Window by clicking somewhere inside its frame or by pressing Alt+Esc. The screen will look like Figure 1-13, with the Calculator in the background behind the Program Manager window. By selecting the Accessories window, which is a document window for the Program Manager, you made the Program Manager window the active program window; it now takes precedence over the Calculator, which is also a program window.

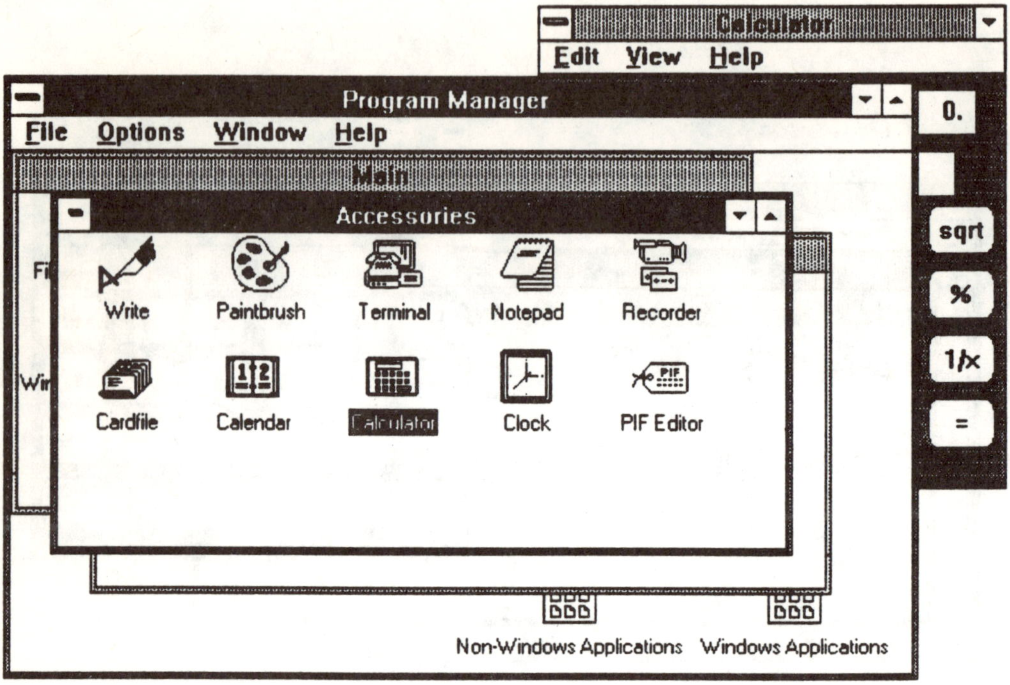

Figure 1-13. Moving a Document Window.

Use the mouse or the keyboard to move the Accessories window. Observe that when you move the Accessories window beyond the borders of the Program Manager window, the Accessories window seems to slide under the border and go out of sight. Observe, too, that when this happens, the Program Manager window gains scroll boxes and buttons. Figure 1-14 illustrates this behavior.

The Program Manager grew scroll boxes and buttons because the contents of its work space, in this case the Accessories document window, exceeded the limits of what the work space could display.

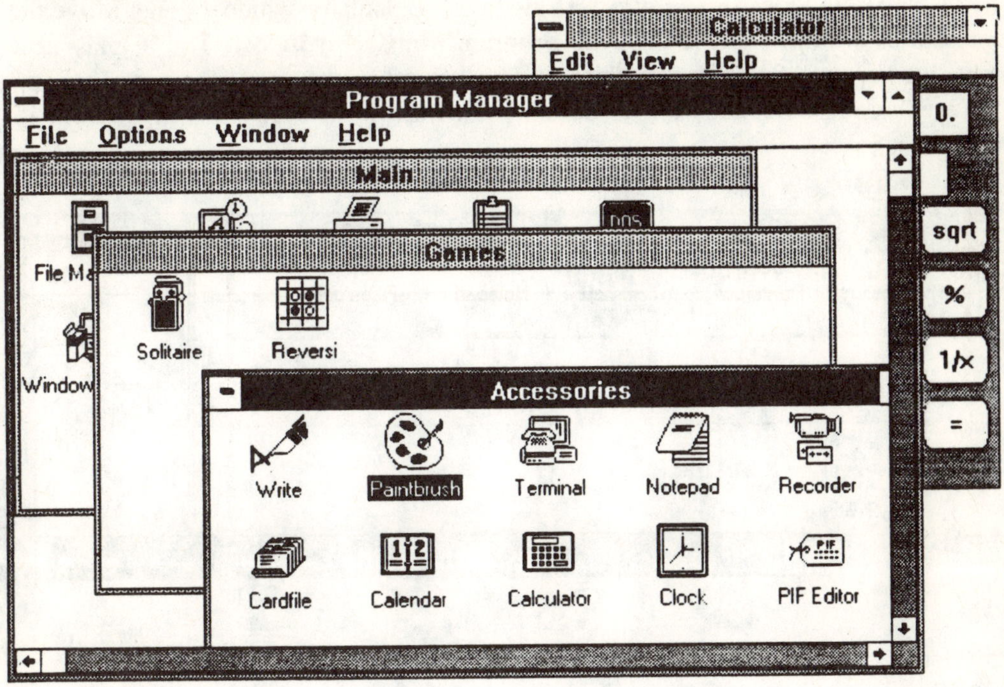

Figure 1-14. A Document Window That Has Been Moved.

Resizing Windows

You can change the size of windows that have frames. The Calculator does not have a frame and so its size is fixed. This is usually the case with dialogue boxes, too. The other windows in Figure 1-14 have frames, so any one of them can be resized. To resize a window, you must first make it active. When in doubt, look to see if the window has a frame. You cannot resize a window unless it has a frame. Another way to determine whether or not you can move a window is to look at the Control Menu. If you refer back to Figure 1-11, you will see that the Size selection on the Control Menu is displayed with a dim intensity. This means that the selection is not available.

Inasmuch as you cannot resize the Calculator, you do not need it for the next exercise. To get rid of it, select it with the mouse or press Alt+Esc. Now terminate it by pressing Alt+F4 or by double clicking the Control Menu selector box in the upper left corner of the Calculator window.

The display now looks like Figure 1-15, with the Calculator window gone. Move the Accessories window back inside the Program Manager window. The display now looks like Figure 1-9 again, with the scroll boxes and buttons gone from the Program Manager window because all its document windows now reside fully within its borders.

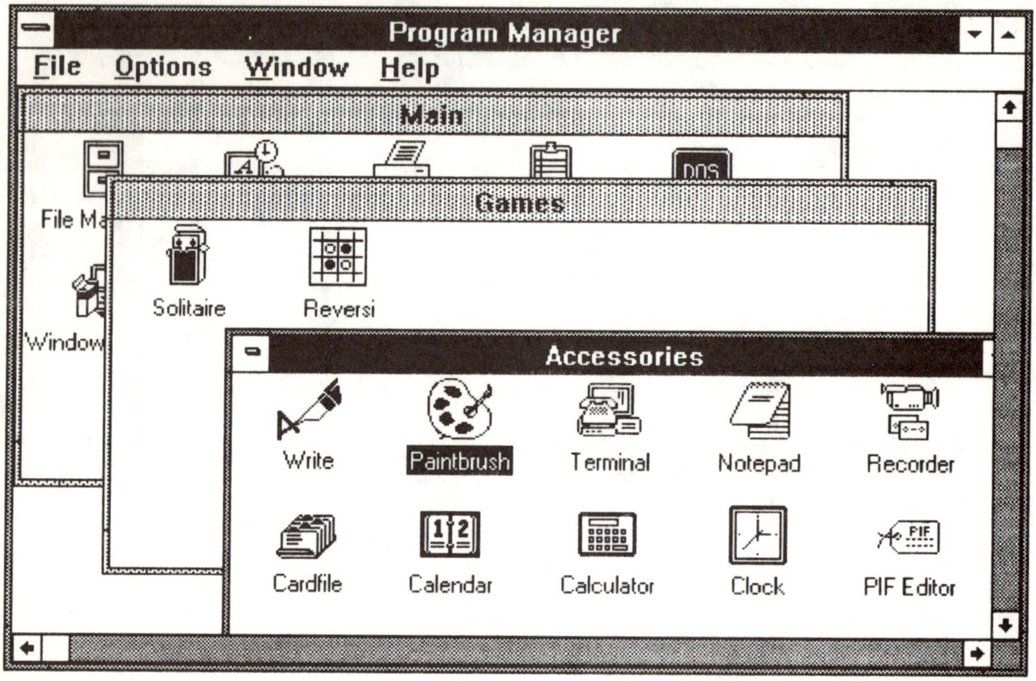

Figure 1-15. The Accessories Window with the Calculator Removed.

Resizing Windows with the Mouse

Move the mouse cursor to the right side of the Accessories window's frame. The cursor changes to a right-left pointing arrow. Hold the mouse button down and drag the cursor to the right and left. A rectangle describes the new window width dimensions. When the width is the way you want it, release the button, and the window appears with its new size.

You can do the same thing with the left, top, and bottom of the window frame, compressing and expanding the window on all sides. The size cursor for the top and bottom of the frame is an up-down pointing arrow.

When you point the cursor to one of the corners of the window, the cursor changes to a 45 degree two-headed arrow, and you can stretch or compress the window on two axes at the same time.

Resizing Windows with the Keyboard

Press the Alt+Hyphen key to display the Control Menu for the Accessories window. Press the S key to select the Size command. The four-headed arrow cursor appears in the middle of the window. Press one of the four arrow keys to select whether you are going to move the top, bottom, or one of the sides. The right-left or top-down pointing cursor appears on the part of the frame you selected. You can use an arrow key to change the position of the selected part of the frame, or you can use an arrow key to point to a corner where the slanted cursor takes over.

Figure 1-16 shows the Accessories window reduced in size on both axes. It has gained scroll boxes and buttons because the act of resizing it reduced it to the point that its work space could not display all its icons. Use the techniques you just learned to make your screen resemble the one in Figure 1-16 for the next exercises.

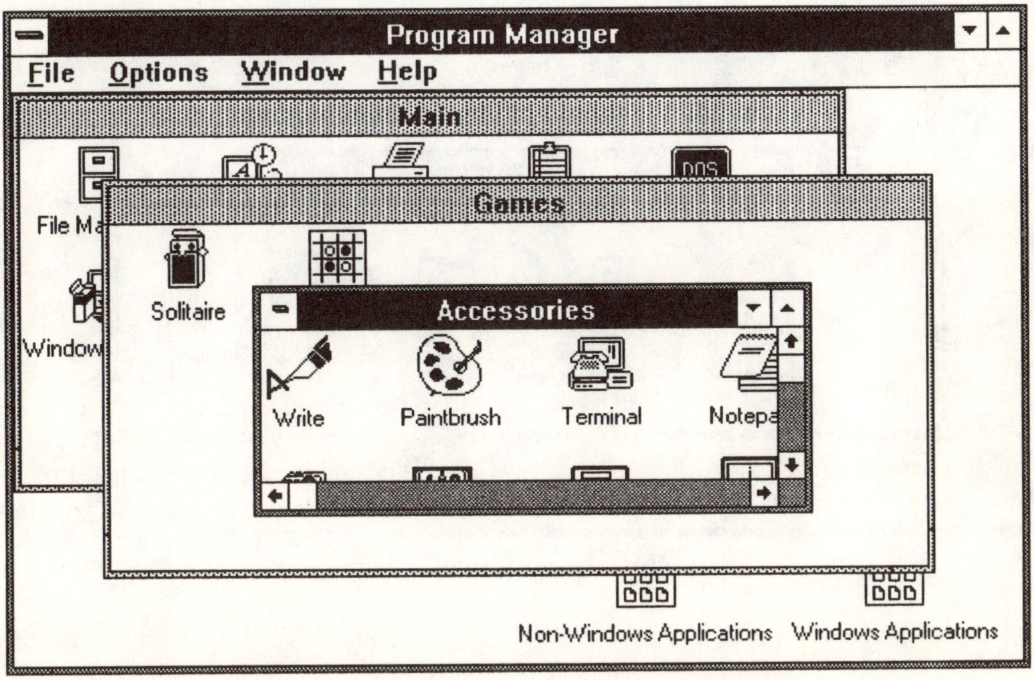

Figure 1-16. The Accessories Window Reduced in Size.

Scrolling the Work Space

You can now scroll the Accessories window both horizontally and vertically because it has both sets of scroll boxes and buttons.

Scrolling with the Mouse

To scroll the window's work space up, move the mouse cursor to the scroll button that points down. The scroll button is in the lower right corner of the window and has an arrow pointing down. Press the left mouse button and hold it down. You will see the window's work space scroll upward and the scroll box move downward. When the scroll box cannot move any further downward, the window appears as you see it in Figure 1-17. Use the same procedure with the upward-pointing scroll button to scroll downward.

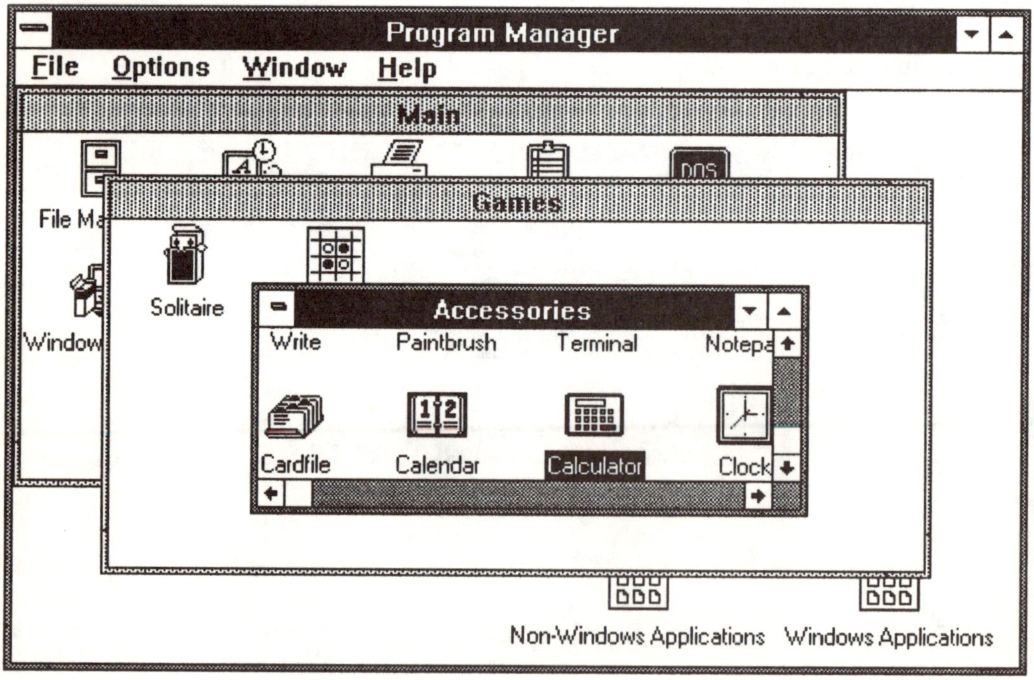

Figure 1-17. The Accessories Window Scrolled Up.

To scroll the window's work space to the left, move the mouse cursor to the scroll button that points right. The scroll button is in the lower right corner of the window and has an arrow pointing right. Press and hold down the left mouse button. Use the same procedure with the left-pointing scroll button to scroll to the right.

You can also use the cursor to drag the scroll box. The scroll boxes move in increments that are proportional to the length or width of the work space. For larger work spaces you can point the mouse cursor just ahead or after the scroll box in the scroll bar and click to move forward or backward one page.

Scrolling with the Keyboard

Use the arrow keys to scroll a window in any of its four directions. Use the PgUp and PgDn keys to page through the work space vertically and the Ctrl+PgUp and Ctrl+PgDn keys to page horizontally. Note that these keys are not as effective in small windows, such as the resized Accessories window, and they do not always work when an application is using the keyboard for its own use.

Minimizing and Maximizing Windows

As mentioned earlier in this chapter, a window can be in one of three conditions of display with respect to its size and placement: it can occupy a section of the desktop or parent window's work space; it can fill the desktop or parent window's work space completely; or it can appear as an icon at the bottom of the desktop or parent window's work space.

In Figure 1-17 the resized Accessories window, the Main window, and the Games window occupy a portion of the Program Manager's work space. Because these windows are child windows to the Program Manager window, they can each occupy some or all of the Program Manager's work space. The Non-Windows Applications window and the Windows Applications window are there too, but they appear as icons within the Program Manager's work space rather than as windows. You can use the mouse or keyboard to minimize and maximize the active window, which in this case happens to be the Accessories window.

If you do not have a mouse, you can skip the next two sections and proceed to "Maximizing Windows with the Keyboard." The keyboard sections will, however, refer to illustrations shown in the figures that accompany the mouse sections.

Maximizing Windows with the Mouse

Click the mouse in the Maximize box in the upper right corner of the Accessories window. The Maximize box contains an up arrow symbol. When you click the box, the window expands to occupy the entire work space of the Program Manager window, as shown in Figure 1-18.

The title bar in Figure 1-18 now appends the [Accessories] label to its title to indicate that it has dedicated its work space to the Accessories window. This title bar combines the titles of the two windows.

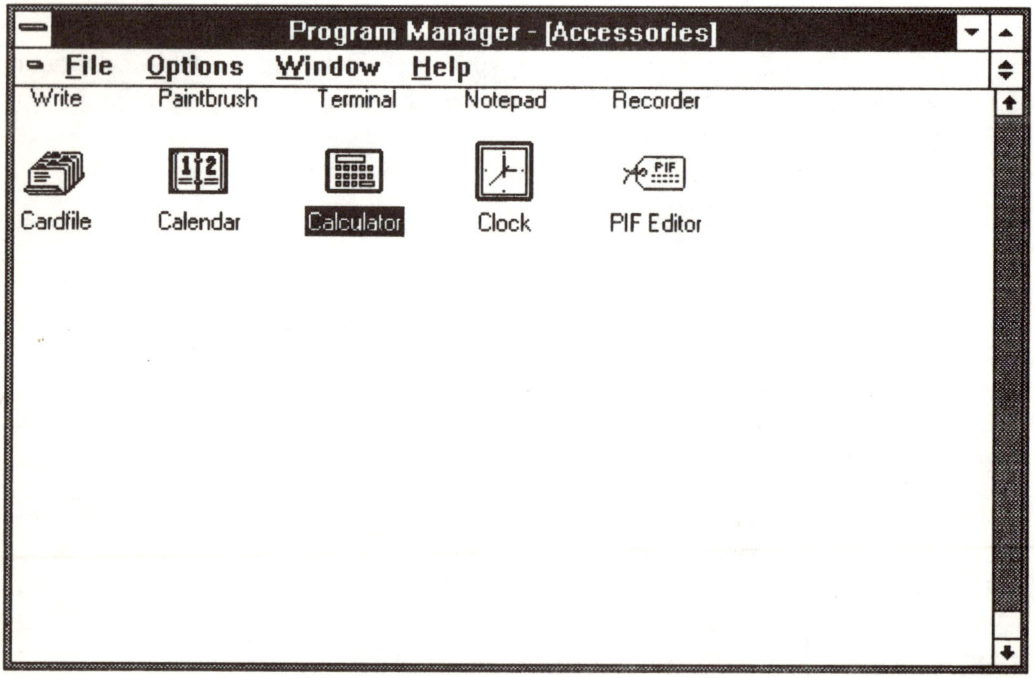

Figure 1-18. The Accessories Window Maximized.

The Minimize and Maximize boxes to the right of the title bar are for the Program Manager window. The box just under the Program Manager's Maximize box is the combined Minimize/Maximize box for the Accessories window. This box contains both the up and down arrow symbols. When you see such a box, it means that the window can only be normalized—returned to its original size. Because the window has been maximized, you can only normalize it.

Click the Maximize box in the Program Manager's window. This box is the one to the right of the title bar; it has an up arrow symbol. The Program Manager window now occupies the entire screen, as shown in Figure 1-19.

Observe that the Program Manager's Maximize box now has an up and a down arrow symbol while its Minimize box has only a down arrow symbol. This combination illustrates the difference between the two boxes. You use the Maximize box to toggle a window between its maximum display configuration or its normal one. You use the Minimize box to reduce a window to an icon.

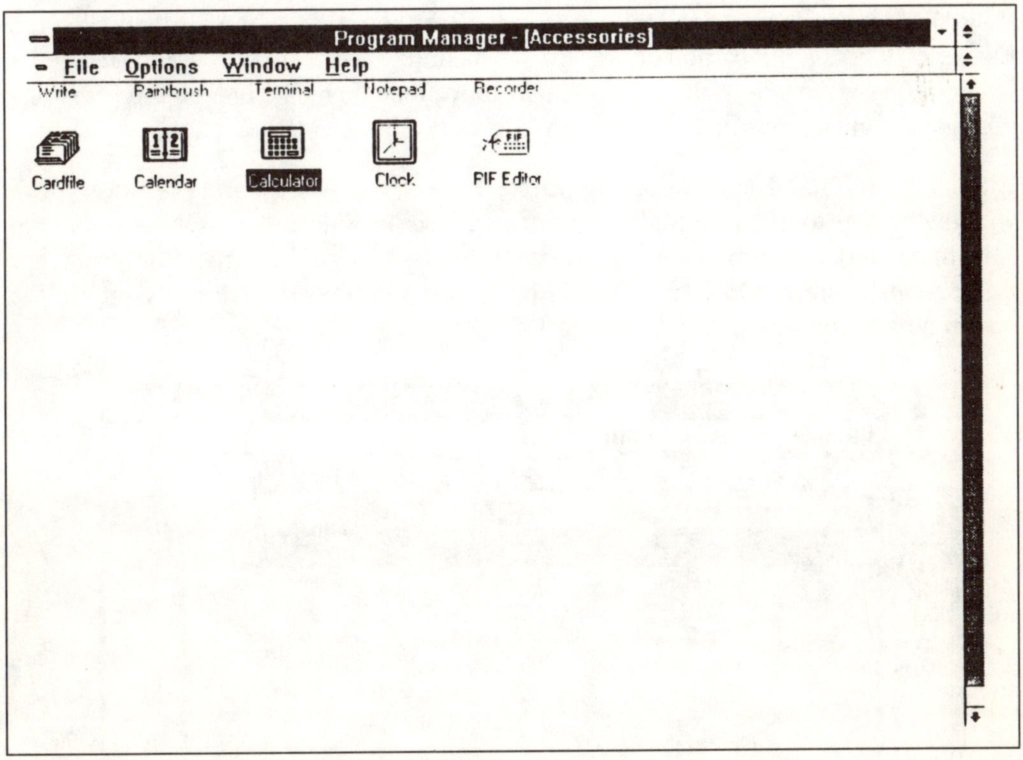

Figure 1-19. The Program Manager Window Maximized.

Minimizing Windows with the Mouse

Click the Minimize box in the Program Manager window. This box is the one with the single down arrow. The Program Manager window becomes an icon. Because no other programs are running, the icon is the only item on the screen, as shown in Figure 1-20.

Figure 1-20. The Program Manager Window Minimized.

Note that the title of the icon in Figure 1-20 is the same as the one that was in the Program Manager's title bar. Double click the icon to return to the display shown in Figure 1-19. Click the combined Minimize/Maximize box in the Program Manager's window. There are two of these boxes, one above the other. The one on top is the one you want to click to return to the display shown in Figure 1-18.

Click the combined Minimize/Maximize box in the Accessories window. The window returns to its prior configuration, as shown in Figure 1-17. Observe that the Minimize and Maximize boxes are in their own boxes again. Now click the Accessories window's Minimize box; it is the one with the down arrow symbol. The screen now appears as shown in Figure 1-21.

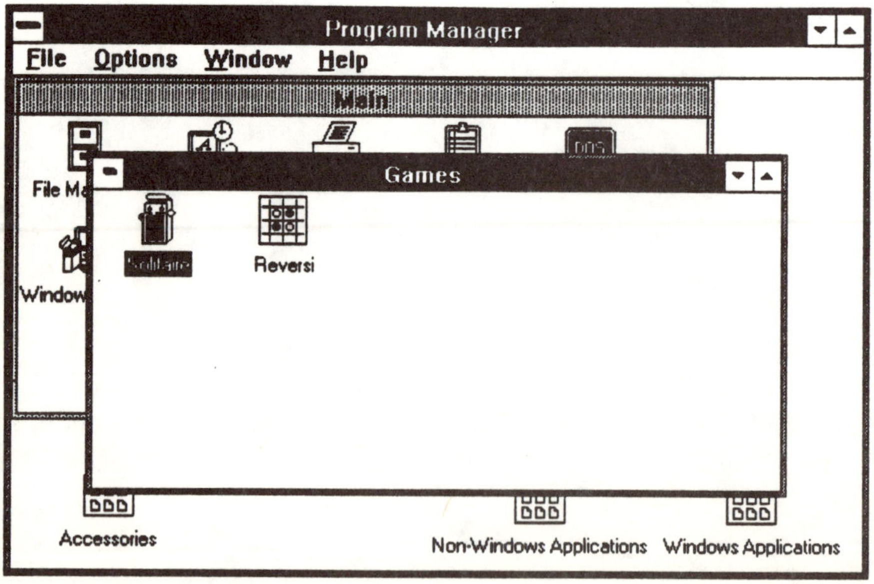

Figure 1-21. The Accessories Window Minimized.

The Accessories window is now an icon in the lower left corner of the Program Manager's work space and is partially obscured by the Games window, which is now active. Double click the Accessories icon to return to the display shown in Figure 1-17.

Maximizing Windows with the Keyboard

Note: These keyboard exercises use the figures from the preceding discussion on using the mouse to maximize windows, and they also introduce some figures of their own.

From the display shown in Figure 1-17, press the Alt+Hyphen keys. This command displays the Control Menu for the Accessories window, as shown in Figure 1-22.

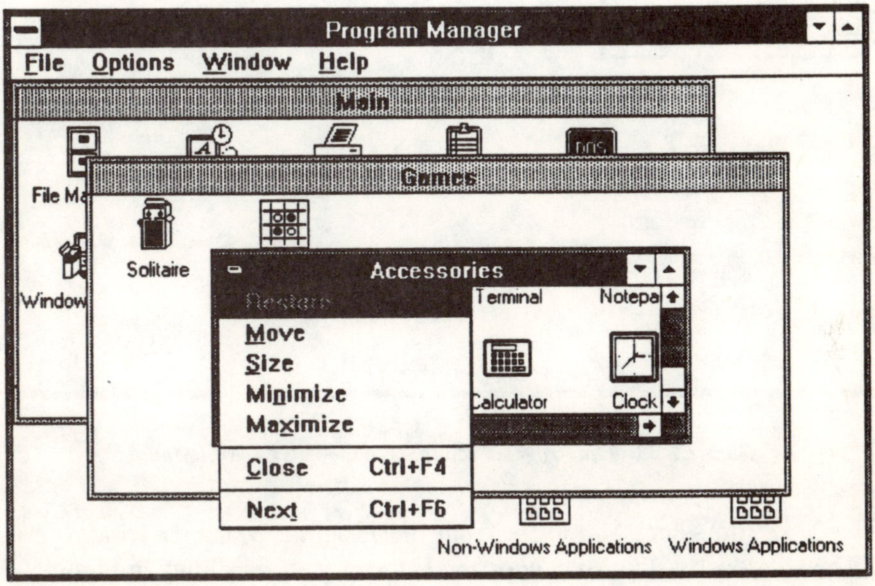

Figure 1-22. The Accessories Window's Control Menu.

Press the X key to select Maximize from the Accessories window's Control Menu. The window expands to occupy the entire work space of the Program Manager window, as shown in Figure 1-18.

The title bar in Figure 1-18 appends the [Accessories] label to its title to indicate that it has dedicated its work space to the Accessories window. This title bar combines the titles of the two windows.

Press the Alt+Spacebar keys. This command displays the Control Menu for the Program Manager window, as shown in Figure 1-23.

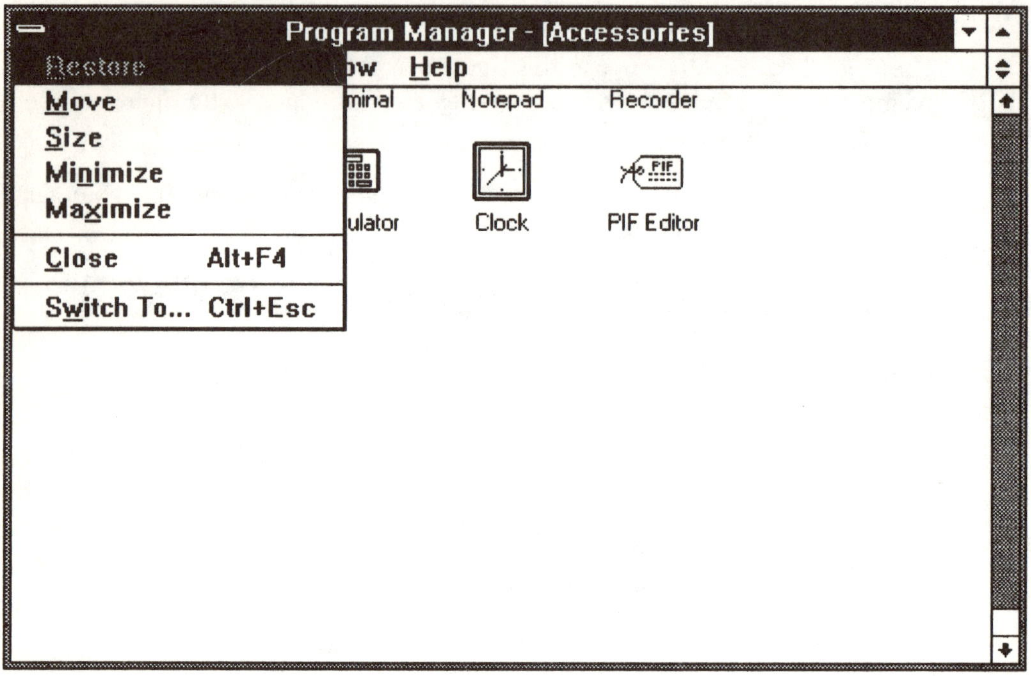

Figure 1-23. The Program Manager Window's Control Menu.

Press the X key to select Maximize from the Program Manager window's Control Menu. The window expands to occupy the entire screen, as shown in Figure 1-19.

Minimizing Windows with the Keyboard

Note: These keyboard exercises use the figures from the preceding discussion on using the mouse to minimize windows, and they also introduce some figures of their own.

Press the Alt+Spacebar keys to display the Program Manager window's Control Menu, as shown in Figure 1-24. Press the N key to select Minimize. The Program Manager window becomes an icon. Because no other programs are running, the icon is the only item on the screen, as shown in Figure 1-20.

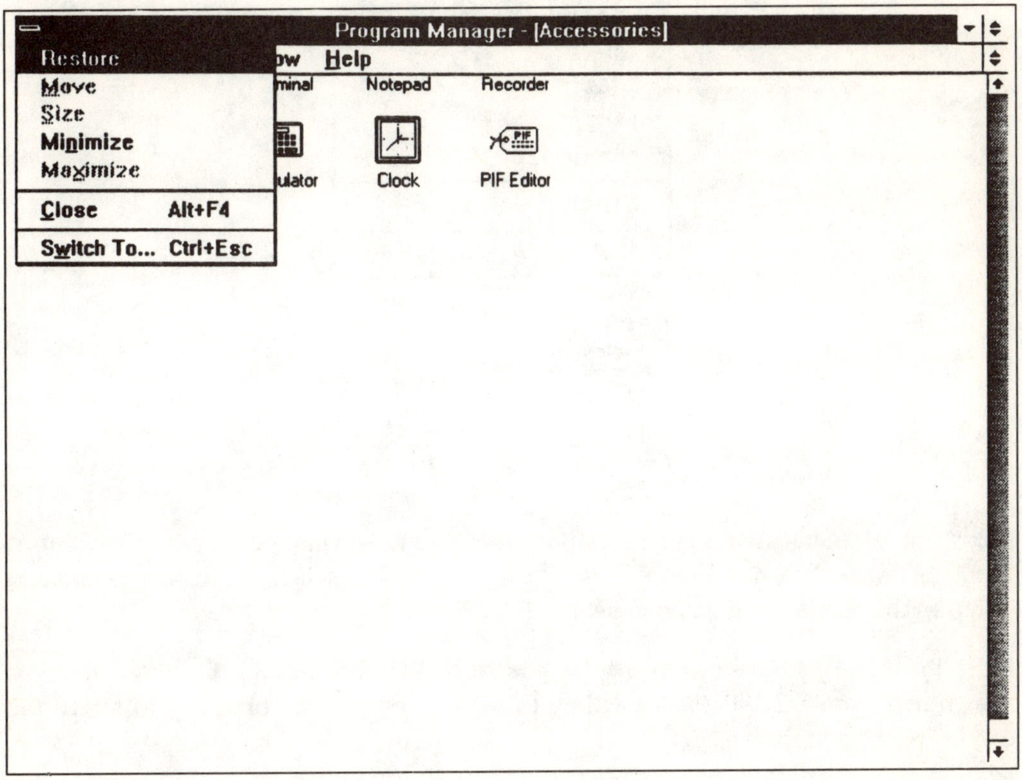

Figure 1-24. The Maximized Program Manager Window's Control Menu.

Notice that the title of the icon in Figure 1-20 is the same as the one that was in the Program Manager's title bar. To return to the display in Figure 1-19, you must reactivate the Program Manager window. Press the Alt+Space keys. You will see the display shown in Figure 1-25.

The window that appears in Figure 1-25 is the Control Menu for the Program Manager's icon. Press the R key to restore the Program Manager and return to the display shown in Figure 1-19.

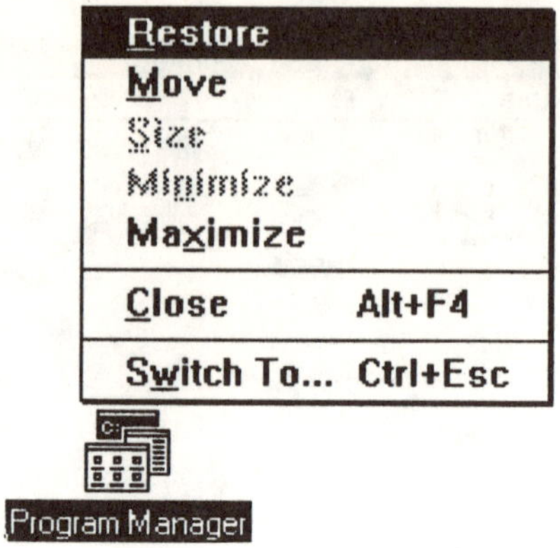

Figure 1-25. The Program Manager Icon's Control Menu.

Press the Alt+Spacebar keys to display the Program Manager window's Control Menu again, as shown in Figure 1-24. Press the R key to select the Restore command to return the display to the one shown in Figure 1-18.

Press the Alt+Hyphen keys to display the Accessories window's Control Menu, as shown in Figure 1-26. Press the R key to select the Restore command to return the display to the one shown Figure 1-17.

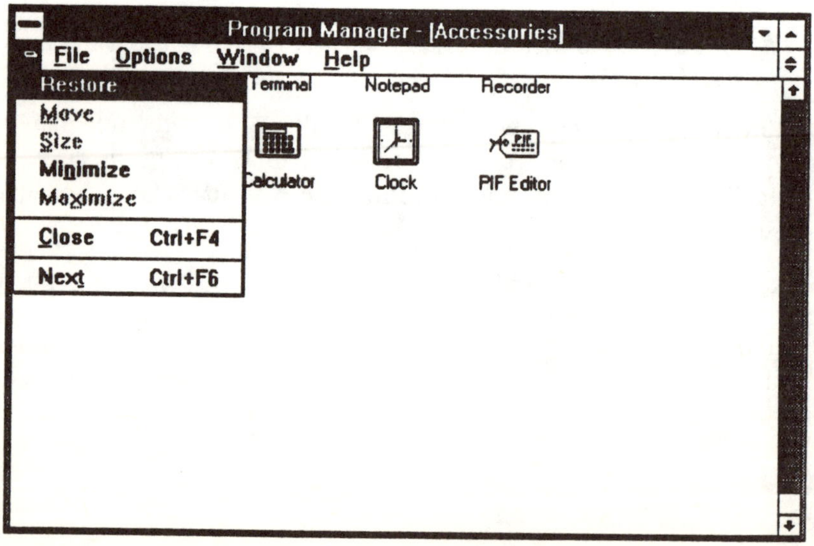

Figure 1-26. The Accessories Window's Control Menu.

Some Practice

Before proceeding, you must get the display back into its original configuration, as it appeared at the beginning of this chapter. One way to do this is to exit from Windows without saving the changes. Another way is to apply what you have learned so far to put things back the way they were.

Your display now looks like the one shown in Figure 1-17. Resize, rescroll, and move the Accessories window so that the display looks like the one shown in Figure 1-13. Bring the Games window to the foreground so that the display looks like Figure 1-8, then minimize the Accessories and Games windows to their icons in the Program Manager Window so that the display looks like Figure 1-1.

Do not worry if your display is not exactly like each figure. For one thing, Windows is contrary about placing icons. It does not always align them the way you want. For purposes of legibility, the figures in this book use consistent icon alignment, which took some effort to achieve. Furthermore, Windows will not always open a new window in the same place. For example, the Control Panel window does not always pop up in the precise location shown in Figure 1-6.

Most new subjects in this book begin with the display shown in Figure 1-1, so it is a good idea to use what you have learned so far to get your display to that point, save the configuration, and exit from Windows. The next time you reload Windows and exit from it, do not save the configuration. From then on you will always exit without saving and will always reload to the original starting place.

Menus

A program that runs in the Windows environment makes extensive use of menus. The Windows menu architecture is consistent across applications and within the Windows programs themselves. This consistency is part of the Windows common user interface.

You have already used one Windows menu: the Control Menu shown in Figures 1-5, 1-11, 1-22, 1-23, 1-24, and 1-26. This is a typical Windows menu. Applications and other Windows programs have menus as well, and they all work in much the same way. To illustrate this point, begin with the display shown in Figure 1-1 and de-select the Main window by double clicking the Control Menu box or by using the Minimize selection on its Control Menu. You will see a display similar to Figure 1-27, with the Main window minimized to an icon.

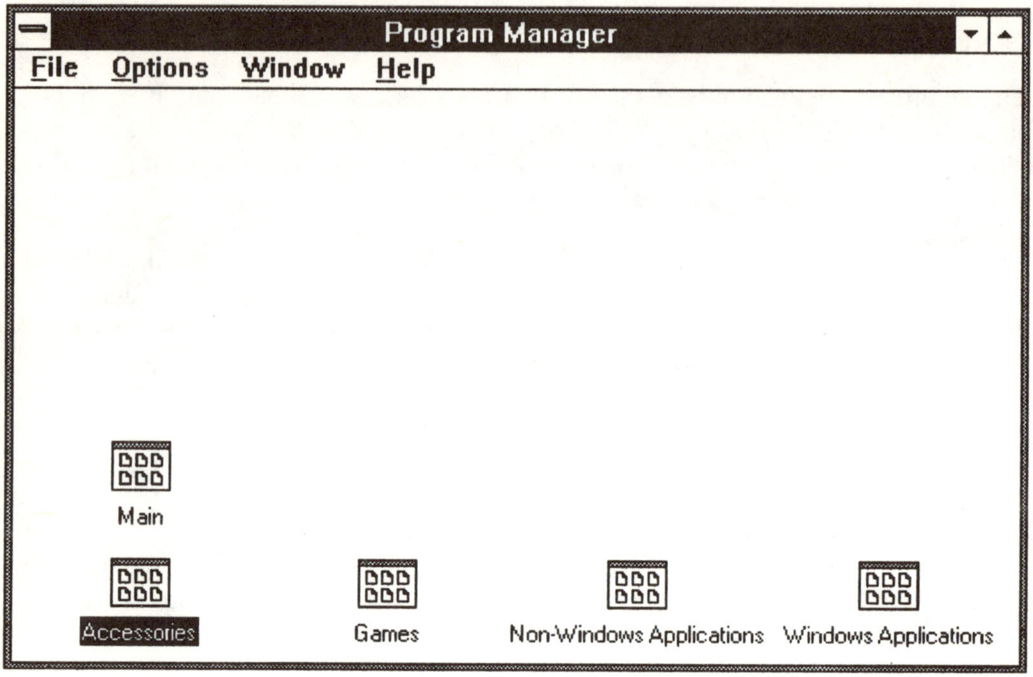

Figure 1-27. The Main Window Minimized.

The menu bar in the Program Manager window in Figure 1-27 is typical of menu bars for most Windows programs. Remember that the Program Manager is a Windows program itself. It is the executive program that manages the execution of other programs and, because it is a program, it uses the Windows conventions for a common user interface. Its menu bar contains four selections: File, Options, Window, and Help.

Most Windows applications have the File menu. It contains the selections to manage document files for the application, print documents, and exit the application. Many applications also have the Help menu. It is the entry to the conventional Windows context-sensitive help system that Windows itself and most applications use.

Other menus on a menu bar depend upon the nature of the application. Virtually every text editor and word processor that operates in the Windows environment includes an Edit menu. The Windows Notepad, Windows Write, and the Clipboard are examples of such programs, all of which you will learn in later chapters. Graphics programs—such as Windows Paintbrush and desktop publishing applications—include View, Font, Style, and other such menus.

Regardless of the nature and content of Windows menus, they all work the same way and have a given set of mouse and keyboard commands that enable you to navigate and select from them. There are three menu operations to learn: selecting a menu itself; moving from menu to menu; and selecting a command from a menu. You can use the menus of the Program Manager to learn these operations.

Selecting a Menu with the Mouse

Move the mouse cursor to the File label in the menu bar and click. You will see the display shown in Figure 1-28. This is a menu. It contains a list of selections and a menu selection cursor, which is a dark bar that extends the length of the selection's name on the menu. Observe the Move and Copy selections. They appear with characters of lesser intensity. These dim displays mean that, in the current context, the selections are not available to you.

You can select any menu by moving the mouse cursor to its title and clicking. To deselect the menu, move the mouse cursor outside the menu itself and click. The menu goes away and the screen looks like Figure 1-27 again. Do that now and proceed.

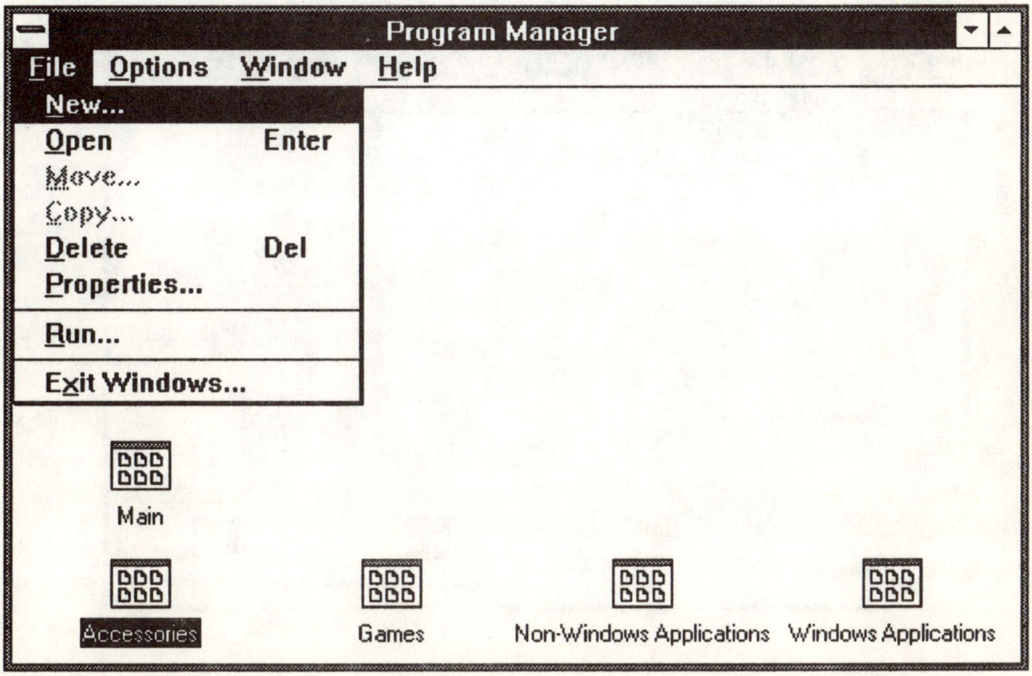

Figure 1-28. The Program Manager's File Menu.

Selecting a Menu with the Keyboard

Observe that each of the menu labels includes an underlined letter, in this case the first letter of the label name. These are the shortcut keys assigned to the menu names. Press Alt+F, and you will select the File menu, which appears as shown in Figure 1-28. Observe the Move and Copy selections. They appear with characters of lesser intensity. These dim displays mean that, in the current context, the selections are not available to you. To select another menu press the Alt+letter combination given for it. Observe that as soon as you press the Alt key, the earlier menu goes away. You can use the Alt key by itself to exit from the menu bar and go back to the application.

Moving from Menu to Menu

You move from menu to menu with the mouse simply by selecting the menus individually, but the keyboard offers several other ways to navigate the menu system. Select the File menu again by pressing Alt+F. The display is the same as it was in Figure 1-28 above. Now press the right arrow key on the cursor keypad. The File menu goes away, and the Options menu appears as shown in Figure 1-29.

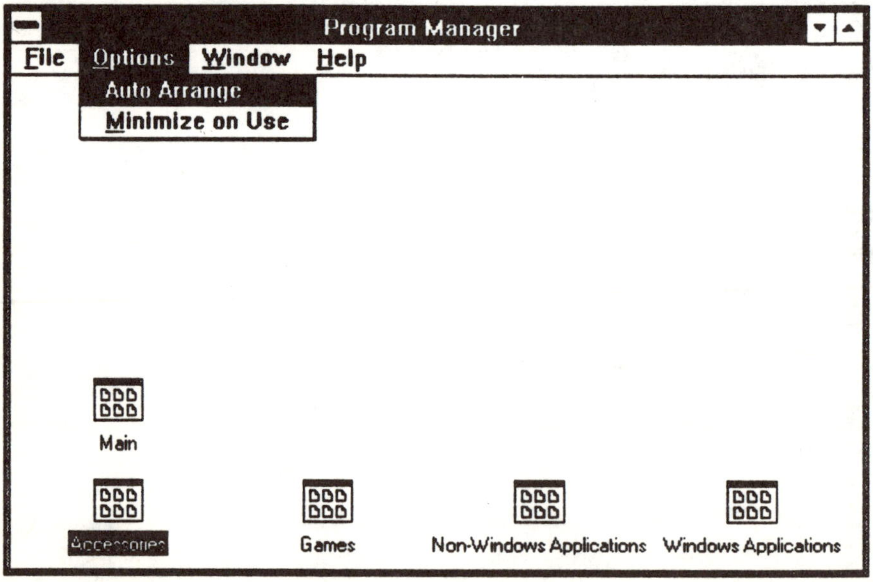

Figure 1-29. The Options Menu.

Use the right and left arrow keys to move from menu to menu. In addition to moving among the menus in the Menu bar, these keys move to the Control Menu for the Program Manager window and the Control Menu for whichever group icon is current as well. In this case, the Accessories icon is current. For applications that do not have child windows, there is no corollary to the icon's Control Menu, but the Control Menu for the application's window is included in the menu scan.

Press the Alt key (not the Esc key) to return to the display shown in Figure 1-27. Now press the Alt key by itself again and observe that the label for the File menu is highlighted, but the menu itself does not appear. Figure 1-30 shows this behavior.

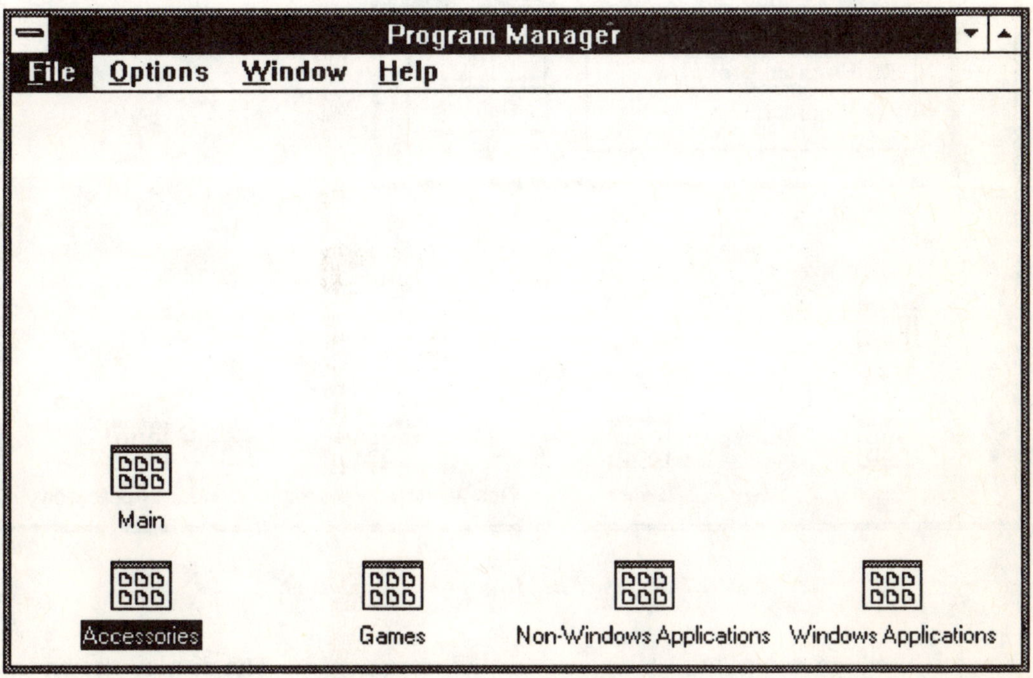

Figure 1-30. Selecting a Menu Label.

Use the arrow keys to move the label cursor from menu label to menu label. When the cursor is at the label of your choice, press the Enter key to select the menu.

Selecting a Menu Item with the Mouse

Move the mouse cursor to the File menu's label in the menu bar and click so that the display appears as it did in Figure 1-28. The File menu has six possible selections and two that are not available. The unavailable commands are indicated by their dimmed displays. Move the mouse cursor to the New... selection on the menu and click. You will see the display shown in Figure 1-31.

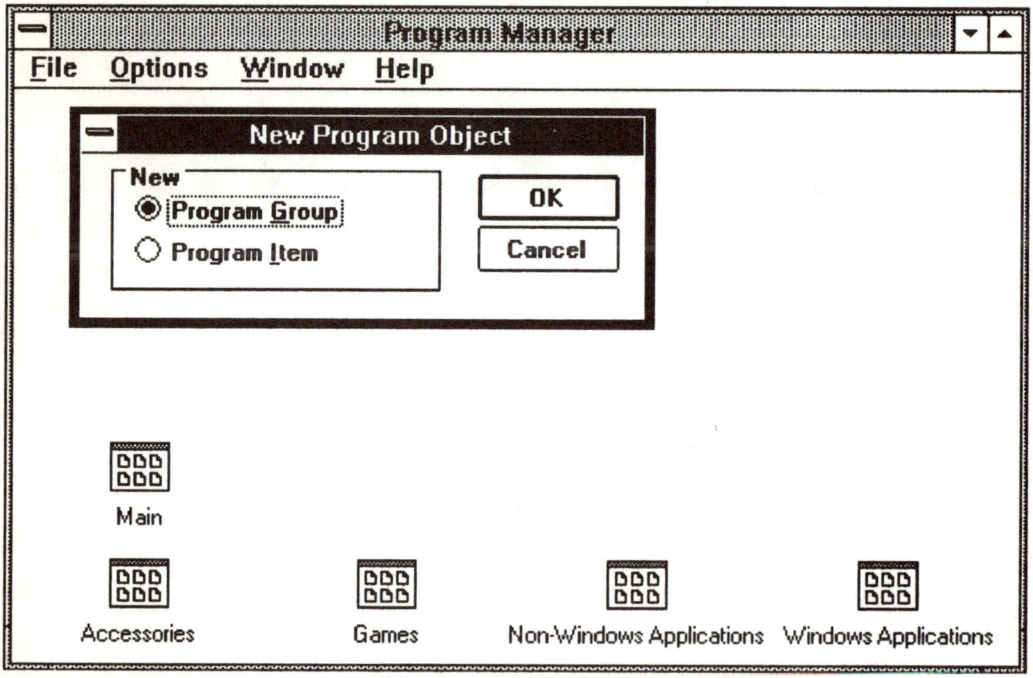

Figure 1-31. The File Menu's New... Command.

You just used the mouse to execute a command from a menu. The display shown in Figure 1-31 is the result of that command; it is a Program Manager dialogue box that lets you add new program groups and items to those managed by the Program Manager. You will learn about dialogue boxes later in this chapter and about the Program Manager in Chapter 2. For now click the Cancel button to exit from this process and return to the Program Manager's display, as shown in Figure 1-27.

Selecting a Menu Item with the Keyboard

From the display in Figure 1-27, press Alt+F to select the File menu, as shown in Figure 1-28. The File menu has six possible commands and two that are not available. The unavailable commands are indicated by their dimmed displays. There are several ways to select a command. One method is to move the menu cursor to the Run... selection on the menu with the down arrow key, and press Enter. You will see the display shown in Figure 1-32.

You just used the keyboard to execute a command from a menu. The display shown in Figure 1-32 is the result of that command; it is a Program Manager dialogue box that lets you run programs by typing their DOS command lines. You will learn about dialogue boxes later in this chapter and about the Program Manager in Chapter 2. For now press the Esc key to exit from this process and return to the Program Manager's display, as shown in Figure 1-27.

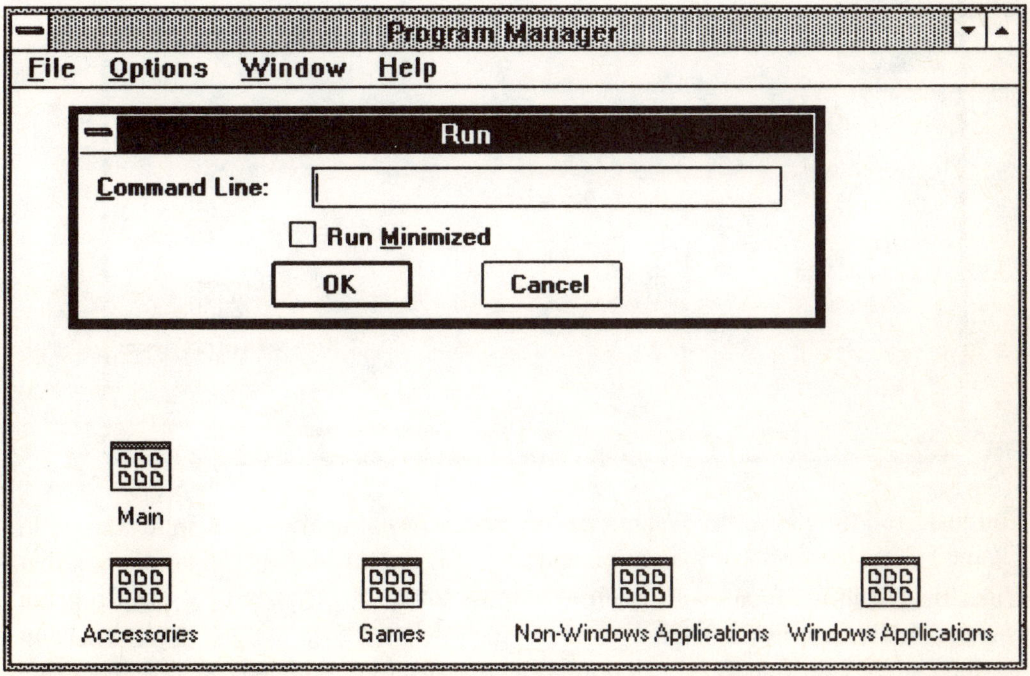

Figure 1-32. The File Menu's Run... Command.

Different Menu Selection Types

A selection on a menu can be one of three types: simple, context-sensitive, or toggle. The two selections you used in the mouse and keyboard exercises above were simple commands. When you use a simple command, you make a selection that executes the command immediately. The command is always the same, regardless of the surrounding circumstances.

Here is an example of another simple command. Use the mouse or the keyboard to move all the group icons into random locations within the Program Manager window's work space. Figure 1-33 shows how the screen could appear after you do this.

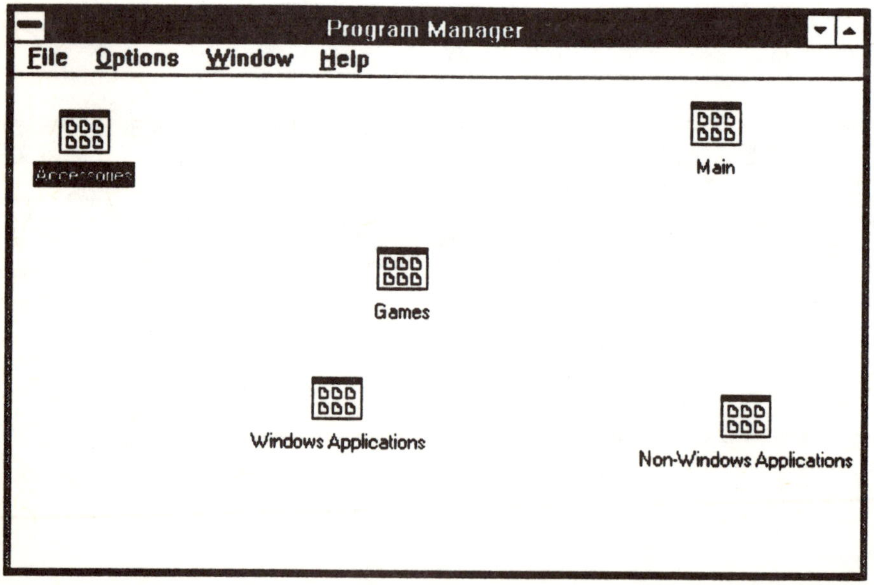

Figure 1-33. Rearranged Icons.

Open the Window menu, as shown in Figure 1-34, and select the Arrange Icons command. The command rearranges the icons into their original positions. You will see the display return to the configuration it had before you moved the icons around.

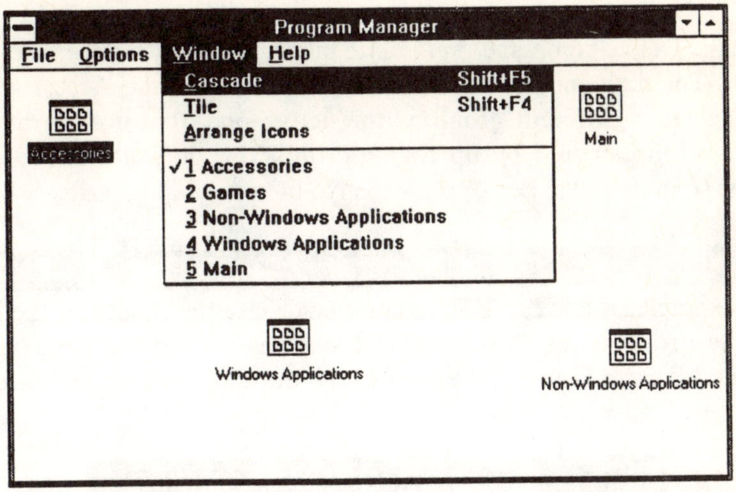

Figure 1-34. The Program Manager's Window Menu.

Other commands are context-sensitive. Their effects depend on external variable circumstances. For example, the Open, Delete, and Properties... commands on the Program Manager's File menu operate on the currently selected group icon or window. Select the Accessories icon as the current group and select the File menu so that the display appears as shown in Figure 1-35.

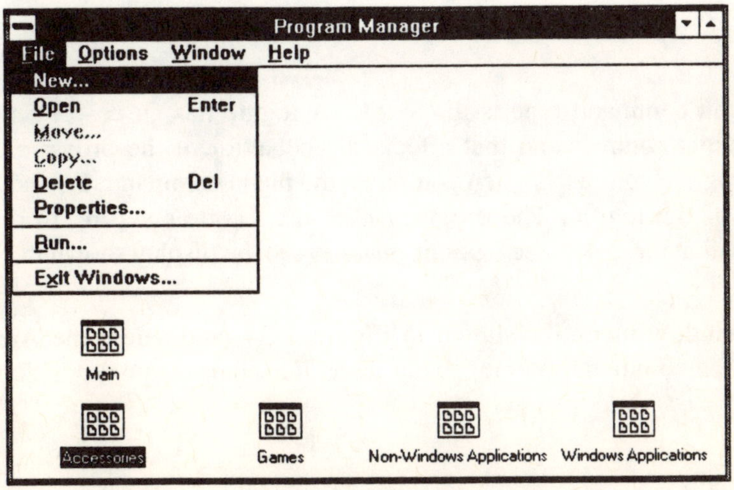

Figure 1-35. The Program Manager's File Menu.

Now select the Delete command on the File menu. You will see the display shown in Figure 1-36. The dialogue box asks if you want to delete the Accessories group. If you had selected a different group as the active one, that group, rather than the Accessories group, would be up for deleting. You do not want to delete your Accessories, so press the N key or click the No button.

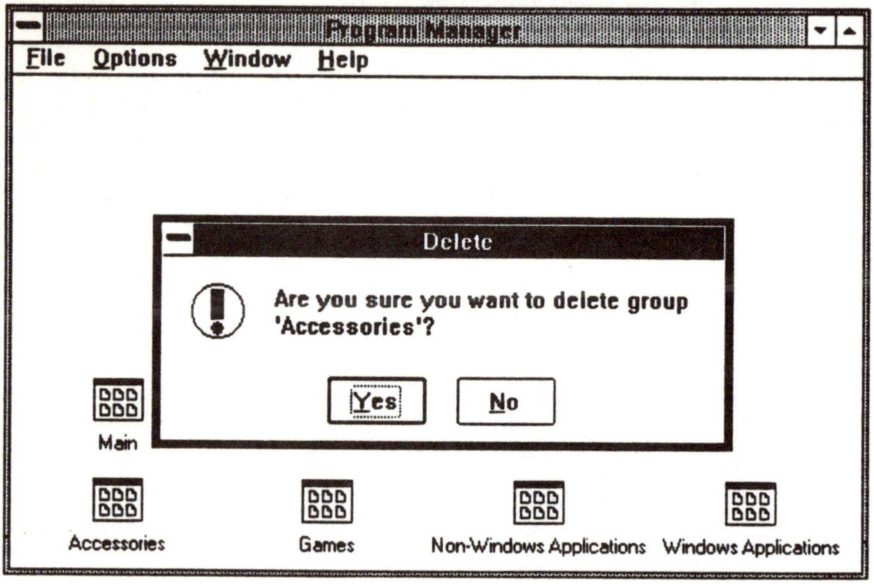

Figure 1-36. The Delete Group Dialogue Box.

Another menu command type is the toggle. A toggle has an on-off setting that the menu command controls and that affects the behavior of the program. You do not execute a program command when you select the menu command. Instead, you reverse the setting of the toggle. The program uses the toggle's setting to determine its subsequent behavior. Select the Options menu to see the display shown in Figure 1-37.

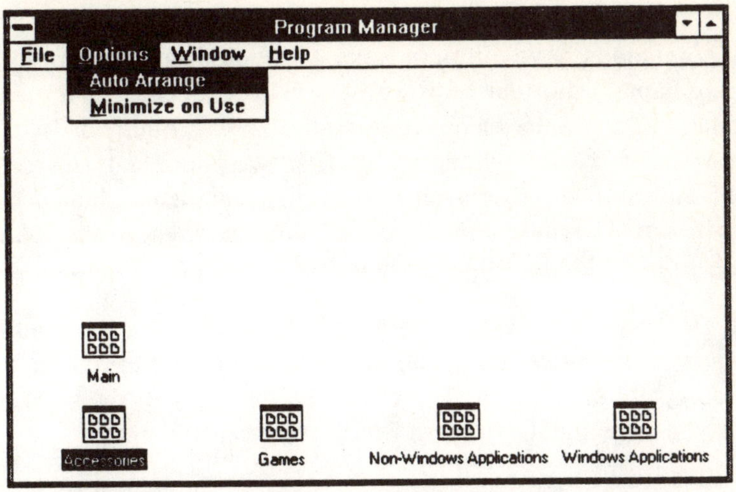

Figure 1-37. The Program Manager's Options Menu.

Select the Auto Arrange command on the menu. The Options menu disappears, and it seems that nothing has happened. If you select the Options menu again, however, you will see the changes shown in Figure 1-38. You can see that the Auto Arrange command now has a check mark to its left. That mark indicates that the toggle is on. Select the Auto Arrange command again—the toggle goes off and the check mark disappears.

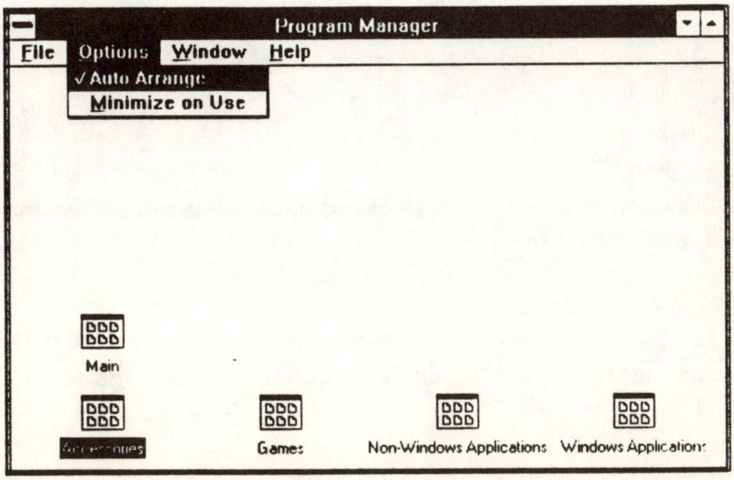

Figure 1-38. Auto Arrange Selected.

Menu Item Shortcut Keys

Some menu commands have shortcut keys associated with them. As mentioned earlier in this chapter, shortcut keys allow you to execute a command from the keyboard without opening the menu itself. Refer back to Figure 1-34, which shows the Program Manager's Window menu. The first two commands, Cascade and Tile, have Shift+F5 and Shift+F4 displayed next to their command names. These are the shortcut keys assigned to these commands. By pressing these keys, you can execute the commands from within the application without opening the menu.

Open all the group windows by selecting their icons one at a time until the screen looks like Figure 1-39. Since the default configuration is cascaded windows, this is how the windows initially appear. The order and visibility of the windows depends on the groups you have and the order in which you opened them.

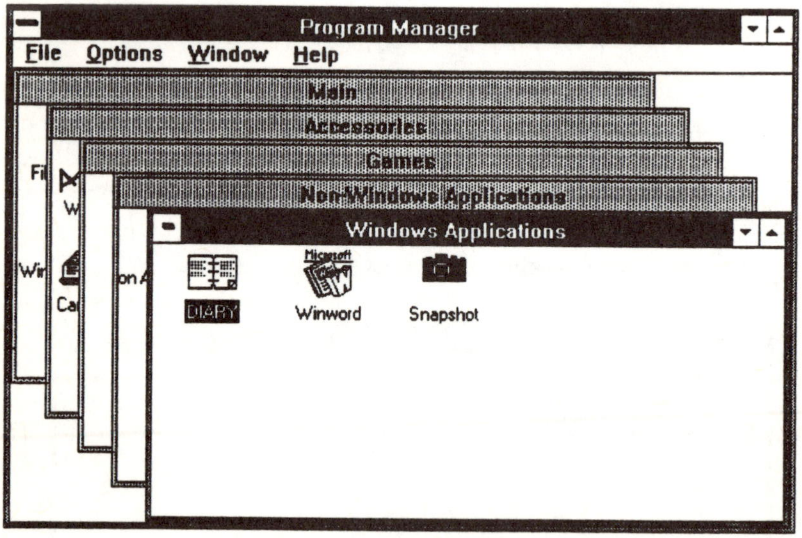

Figure 1-39. Cascaded Group Windows.

The shortcut key for the Tile command on the Windows menu is Shift+F4. Press that key combination and watch the windows appear in tiled configuration, as shown in Figure 1-40.

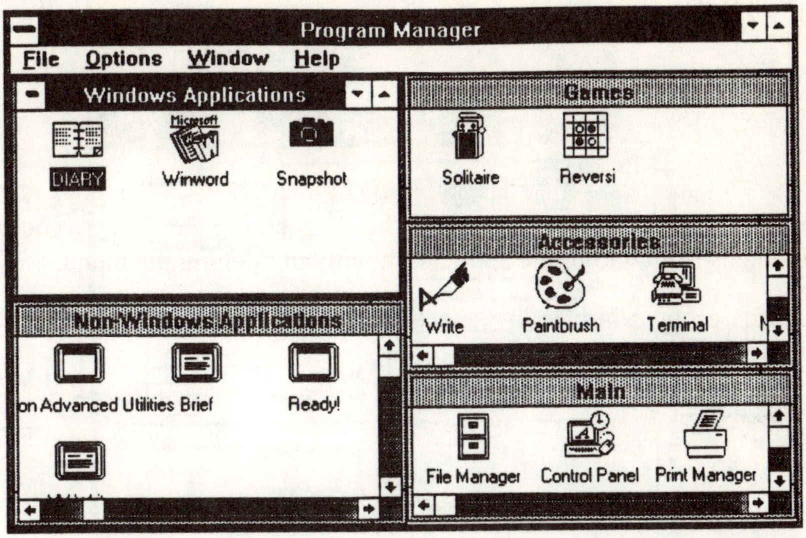

Figure 1-40. Tiled Group Windows.

The shortcut key for the Cascade command on the Window menu is Shift+F5. Press that combination and watch the windows return to their earlier cascaded configuration. Minimize all the group windows—except the Main group—to their icons to return to the original Program Manager window configuration.

Dialogue Boxes

Windows programs use the dialogue box to allow you to enter the data that the program requires. Data entry follows certain conventions that the dialogue box supports.

You have already seen dialogue boxes in earlier exercises, although none as complex as the one in Figure 1-41. Figure 1-2 showed a dialogue box that allows you to exit Windows specifying whether or not you want to save the changes. Figures 1-31, 1-32, and 1-36 showed dialogue boxes that the Program Manager's Run..., New..., and Delete... commands use.

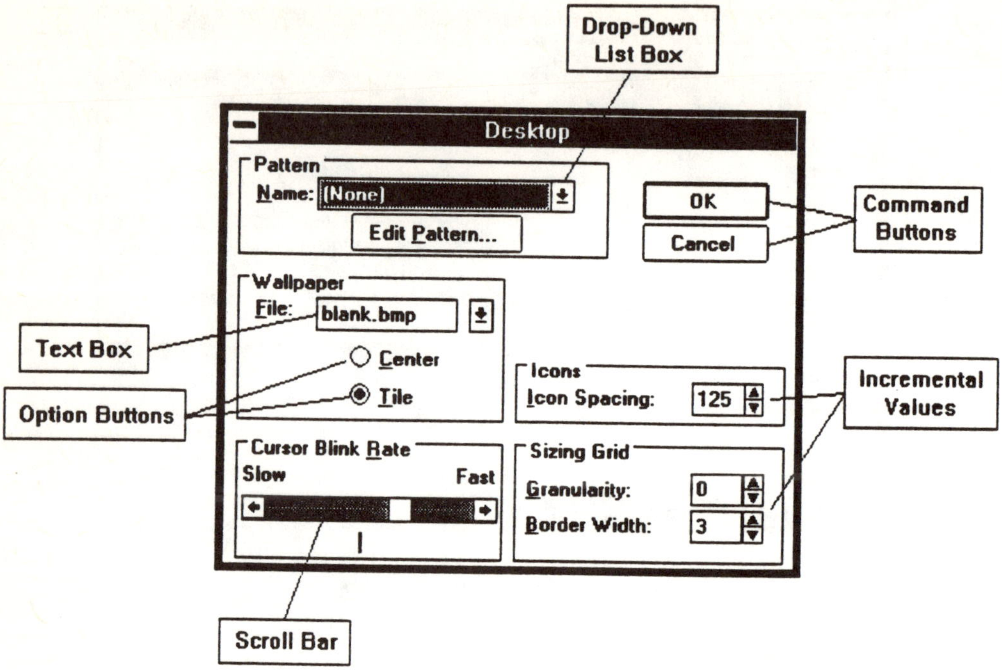

Figure 1-41. Some Dialogue Box Components.

Figure 1-41 shows a dialogue box taken from the Control Panel's Desktop command. This particular dialogue box allows you to modify the appearance of the Desktop by changing certain parameters, and it uses many of the features of the Windows dialogue box convention. To display the Desktop dialogue box, select the Control Panel icon from the Main group window and select the Desktop icon from the Control Panel window.

You will use the Desktop dialogue box to learn about dialogue boxes themselves. During the lessons that follow, do not press the Enter key or click the OK command button. If you do, the changes you make to the dialogue box will take effect whether you want them to or not. You will then have to work with a desktop that looks like whatever changes you made until you learn how to reset it in Chapter 5.

Moving Around the Dialogue Box

A dialogue box can contain several different data entry fields. At a given time you may enter data into one of them. To change to another field you must move to it. If you are using a mouse, you usually click to the field, although this action sometimes changes its value. The Tab key moves from field to field in a forward direction, and the Shift+Tab key moves to the previous field.

The dialogue box indicates the current field by surrounding it with a dotted line. The Pattern Name field in Figure 1-41, for example, has the dotted line indicating that it is the current field.

Some fields have names that include an underlined letter. You can press the underlined letter to move to the field or to select its value. For example, you can press the G key to select the Granularity field in Figure 1-41. There is a catch, though. The first field in the dialogue box is the Name field; it uses the keyboard for text entry. You must either use the Alt key in combination with the desired letter or Tab out of a text field such as the name field before you can use the underlined letters of the other fields by themselves.

Command Buttons

Most dialogue boxes have command buttons. The dialogue box in Figure 1-41 has two: one labeled OK and another labeled Cancel. These buttons are typical; most dialogue boxes have them. The OK button means that the values in the dialogue box are correct and may take effect. When you select the OK button, the dialogue box goes away, and its data values are posted to the application that uses them. When you select the Cancel button, the box goes away, and the application ignores any values that you changed.

You select a command button by clicking it with the mouse or by pressing the Enter key when the command button has a dark frame. Observe that the OK button in Figure 1-41 has a darker frame than the Cancel button. If you want to select Cancel with the keyboard, you can use the Tab key to step through the entry fields until the Cancel button has the dark frame and then press the Enter key. You can also select Cancel by pressing the Esc key.

When the dialogue box needs the Enter key for something other than selecting the command button with a dark frame, the frames of all the buttons have a light frame. If you step through the fields with the Tab key until you arrive at the Edit Pattern field, you will see that neither command button has a dark frame. In this case the Enter key selects another dialogue box for the Edit pattern process.

Text Boxes

A text box allows you to enter short strings of text data. The dialogue box in Figure 1-41 includes a text box named File to name the file that describes the Desktop's wallpaper. Once you have selected this field, you can place the cursor at its beginning and type a file name.

Lists

A dialogue box can display a list of items from which you can choose. The list appears within a small window. It has a vertical scroll box and buttons when its length exceeds the window's height. You use the scroll boxes and buttons the same way as you use these features with other windows. To select from a list, click the entry or use the up arrow, down arrow, Home, End, PgUp, or PgDn keys to move the cursor through the list. Then select the entry by pressing the Enter key. You will see an example of a list in the "File Selections" section later on and in the "Drop-Down Lists" section next.

Drop-Down Lists

The Wallpaper File file field and the Pattern Name field in Figure 1-41 both have drop-down list boxes. The fields themselves display the current values assigned to the data items. You can type into the Wallpaper File field because it is a text box as well as a drop-down list. The Pattern Name field is not a text box, so you must use its drop-down list box. To select the drop-down list, click the box with the mouse or Tab to the field and press Alt+Down Arrow. Figure 1-42 shows the Pattern Name field drop-down list after it has been selected.

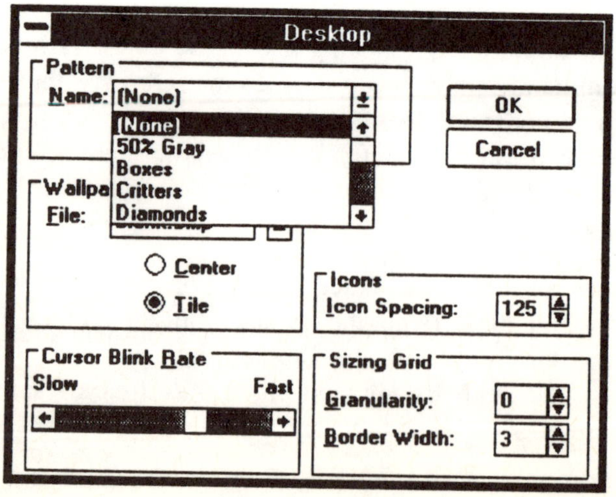

Figure 1-42. A Drop-Down List.

After the drop-down list has dropped down, it works just like a list, except that it goes away after you have made your selection.

Scroll Bars

Figure 1-41 shows the cursor rate as a scroll bar. This is one way that programs use the dialogue box to allow you to enter a sliding value where the precise value is not required. In this case you move the scroll box to change the cursor's blink rate. You are concerned with the abstract values Slow and Fast and the sliding values between them.

Incremental Values

In cases where a range of numbers is required and you must select a specific value, the dialogue box uses Incremental Value entries. The Granularity and Border Width fields in Figure 1-41 are examples of this technique. You can enter the specific value by using the left part of the field as a text box, or you step the value up and down by using the mouse to click the appropriate up and down arrow.

Option Buttons

Option buttons appear in groups where only one of a list of options can be selected. They are small circles where all but the selected one has a blank center, and the selected one has a dark circle in the center. Figure 1-41 shows option buttons that allow you to select between the Center and Tile options. These buttons are sometimes called "radio buttons" because they resemble the station selector buttons on older automobile radios; press a button, and the one that is currently pressed pops out.

You can click a specific button to select it. You can also Tab to the button group and use the arrow keys to change the selected button. When the button labels have underlined letters, you can use those keys with the Alt key to select the option button you want.

Check Boxes

The Desktop dialogue box does not use check boxes, but you already used one when you elected whether or not to save your changes when you exited from Windows at the beginning of this chapter. Figure 1-43 shows two copies of that particular dialogue box with the check box selected and de-selected.

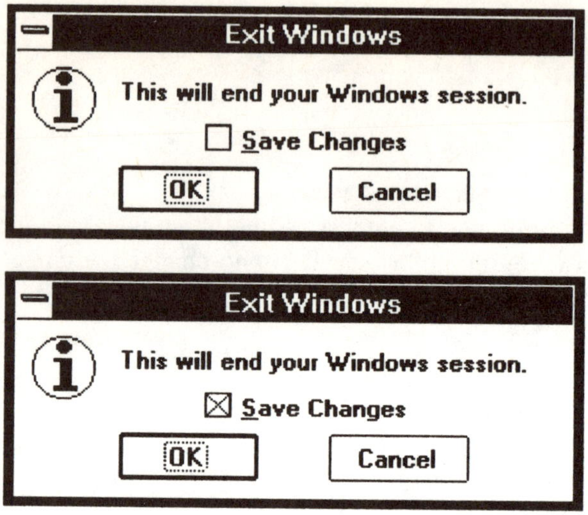

Figure 1-43. The Exit Windows Dialogue Box.

To select or de-select a check box you can click it with the mouse, press its underlined letter key along with the Alt key, or Tab to the field and press the Spacebar key.

File Selections

Dialogues often require that you specify the name and location of a disk file that you want the application to process. Windows uses a convention for file specifications that allows a dialogue box to display a miniature version of the more powerful File Manager from which you can select or enter a drive, directory, and file name. Figure 1-44 shows a typical File Open dialogue box. The Filename field in Figure 1-44 is a text box where you can enter an ambiguous DOS path and filename. You can specify the * and ? wild cards in this entry.

The Directory field shows the current drive and subdirectory. You do not change this field directly. It changes to reflect the changes you make to the other fields.

The Files box lists the files in the selected subdirectory that match the filename specification. The Files box is a dialogue box list, so you can click it to highlight a selection; Tab to the list to use the arrow keys to move through the list; or double click it to select the file name. Moving through the list changes the Filename field value. The list itself changes as you change the drive or directory.

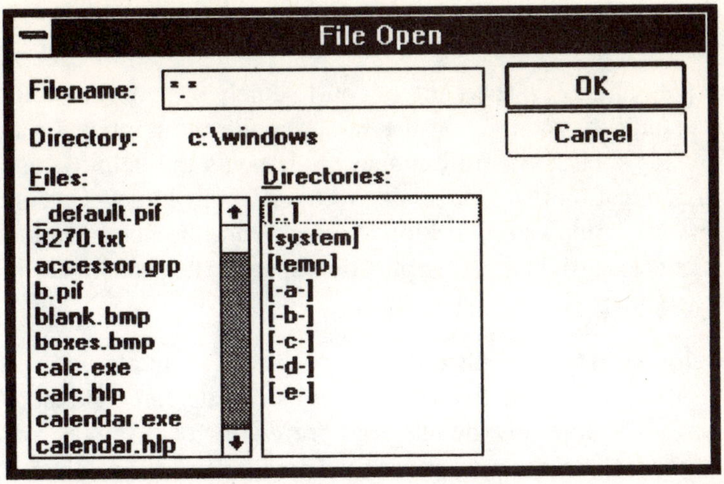

Figure 1-44. File Selection.

The Directories field is a list from which you select the drive and subdirectory. In Figure 1-44 the bracketed entries show the paths you can take from the \windows subdirectory of the C: drive. The [..] entry represents the directory that is the parent of the windows subdirectory, in this case the root directory of the C: drive. The [system] and [temp] entries indicate subdirectories that are subordinate to the \windows subdirectory. The [-a-] through [-e-] entries indicate other drives that are available. If the Directories list entries exceed the window's height, the list gains a scroll box. You select an entry by using the list selection procedures. If you are using a mouse, you click to point to an entry or double click to select it. If you are using the keyboard, you Tab to the field, use the arrow keys to move to an entry, and press Enter to select it.

If the application can work with more than one file at a time, you can select a group by holding down the Ctrl key and clicking each of the files or by using the arrow keys to select each of the files in the group.

If the dialogue box allows you to name a new file to be created, you must use the Filename text box to type in the new name; the Files box will not show it because it does not exist yet. When the Directory and Filename contain the file you want or the group is marked, click OK or press Enter to select it.

THE WINDOWS HELP SYSTEM

Contemporary computer systems employ on-line help systems that allow you to view operating hints and instructions on the screen while the application runs. Windows not only provides such a system but also implements the help system as a general-purpose help application that is available to other applications. This approach allows the developers of Windows applications to install on-line help information into their software systems by providing an application-specific help data base in a format that the Windows Help application recognizes.

A fully-developed help data base can make user's manuals and reference books unnecessary. A help data base that is tutorial in structure can make books such as this one obsolete. Most software developers prefer not to do away with bound and printed documentation for two reasons. First, the corporate buyers feel more comfortable selecting applications that have a preponderance of expensive-looking documentation. Second, the user's reliance on documentation makes the product less susceptible to piracy. Nevertheless, the time is coming when software will be self-teaching and self-explaining. The Windows Help system is a step in that direction.

Hypertext

Hypertext is a technique for browsing a textual data base. While looking at a body of text you can point to a word or phrase and execute a command that tells the software to display other text related to the subject to which you pointed. You can browse the text through several such retrieval layers, retracing your steps from time to time.

The Windows Help system incorporates a form of Hypertext. Many of the words and phrases in the help displays are described in a glossary that you can pop up. Others are topics that you can select and view in their entirety.

Context-Sensitive Help

A context-sensitive help system is one in which the content of the help information depends upon the program's current context. Some of the Windows help displays are context-sensitive. Others are constant—you must proceed through the text from a starting point to find what you want. The help files provided with applications may or may not be context-sensitive.

The Help Menu

Most menu bars in Windows applications include a Help selection, usually the right-most command on the bar. The Program Manager's menu bar is an example. When you select the Help command on this menu, the Help menu pops down, as shown in Figure 1-45.

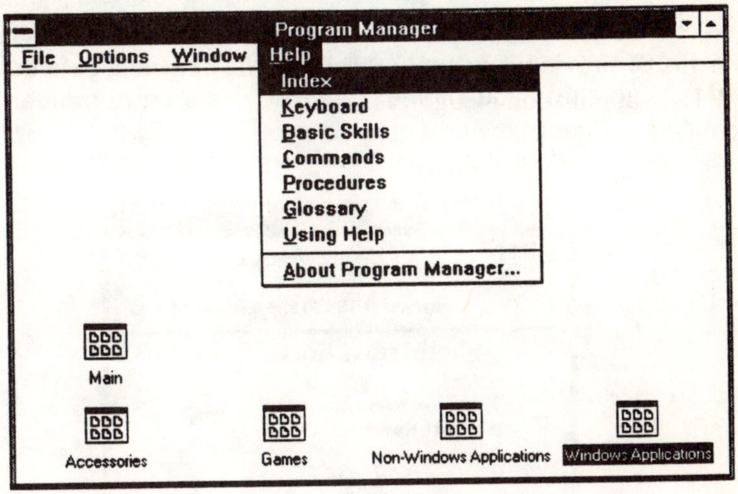

Figure 1-45. The Program Manager's Help Menu.

The Program Manager's Help menu commands are typical of those found in most Windows applications. The About... selection is worthy of mention because it provides more information than the About.. selections in most other applications. Figure 1-46 shows the Program Manager's About... display.

Usually an application's About... selection gives you a static display that tells you the name of the program, something you already knew; its version, which could be of some use; the copyright date, which you don't care about; and the names of the programmers, which are of interest only to them. The Program Manager's About... display goes farther. It tells you the current Windows operating mode, the amount of free memory, and the percent of system resources that are currently available. These values can be useful when you are having problems running programs. If a program will not run, for example, there might not be enough memory for it. The About... display might suggest that you should terminate some other programs to free up some of the memory for the new program.

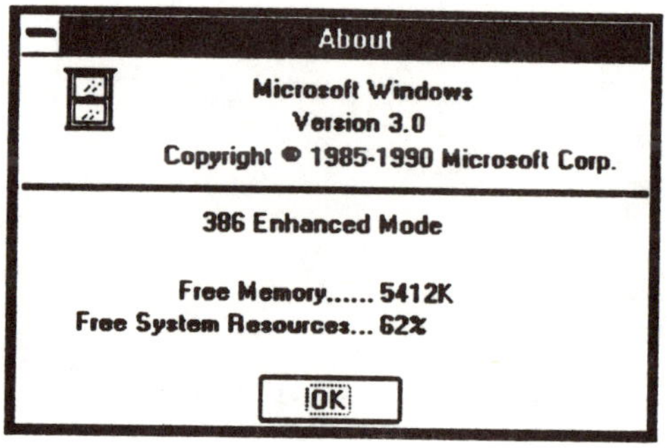

Figure 1-46. The Program Manager's About... Display.

The Using Help selection on the Help menu instructs you in the use of the Help system itself. This is an example of software that explains itself. When you select Using Help, you see the window displayed in Figure 1-47.

The display in Figure 1-47 is typical of the textual help windows that the Windows Help system provides. Remember that the Help system is an application itself, one that runs independently of the application it explains.

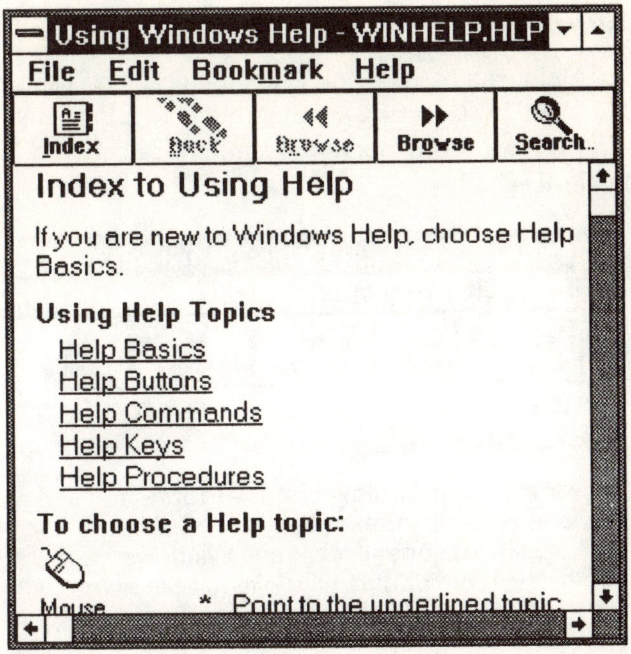

Figure 1-47. The "Using Help" Display.

If you were to minimize the window shown in Figure 1-47, you would see that the application becomes an icon, as shown in Figure 1-48. Exit from the Help application and select the Help menu command from the Program Manager's menu bar, as shown above in Figure 1-45.

Figure 1-48. The "Using Windows Help" Icon.

The Help Index

A well-organized Help data base begins with an index. You can start with the one in the Program Manager by selecting Index from its Help menu. You will see the display shown in Figure 1-49. Observe the similarities between this display and the one shown in Figure 1-47.

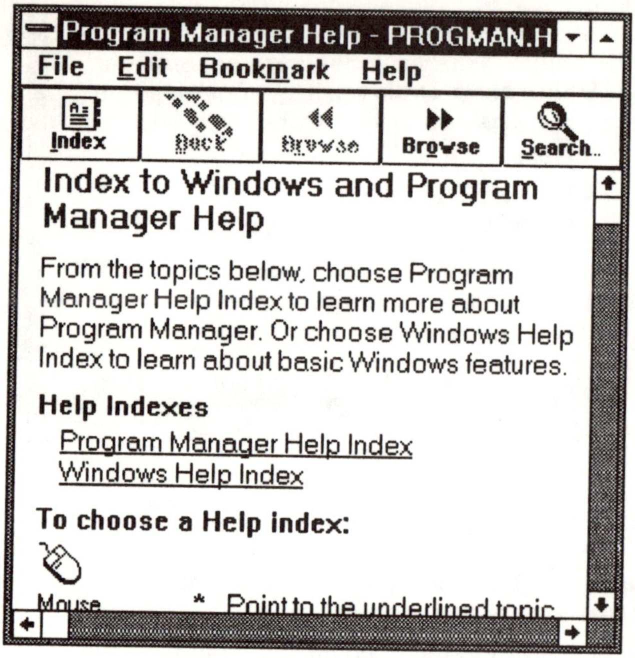

Figure 1-49. The Help Index.

Cross-References

Two of the lines in Figure 1-49 are underlined. These underlined titles are cross-references. You can select one of them by pointing the mouse cursor to it. The cursor changes from an arrow to a hand with a pointing finger. Click the topic you want when the finger is pointing to it. You can use the keyboard to select a cross-reference by pressing the Tab key until the desired topic is highlighted and then pressing the Enter key. Select the Program Manager Help Index topic now. You will see the display shown in Figure 1-50.

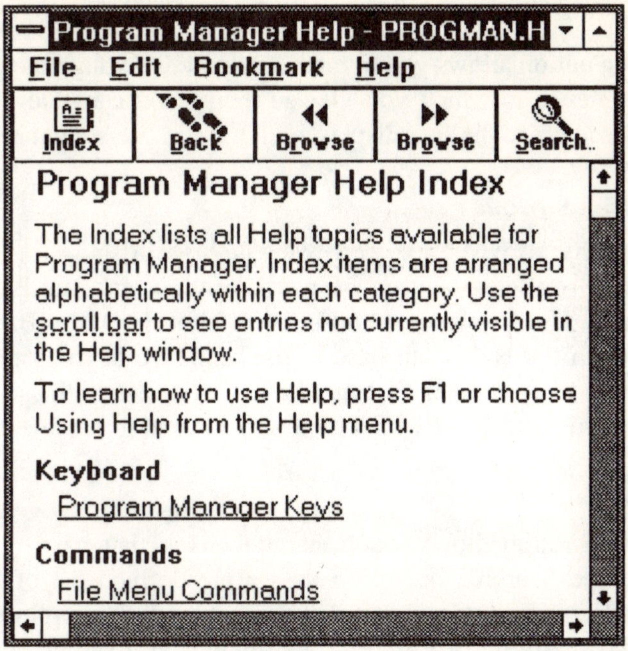

Figure 1-50. The Program Manager's Help Index.

Function Buttons

There are five rectangular buttons displayed across the top of the windows in Figures 1-47, 1-49, and 1-50. These are function buttons that allow you to move around in the Help data base. When a function button's display is dark, the button is available. When it is light, as are the Back and Browse << buttons in Figure 1-49, the button is unavailable. You select a function button by clicking it or by pressing the letter key that corresponds to the underlined letter in the button's name.

Index Button

The Index button returns you to the Index part of the Help data base. From the Program Manager Help Index in Figure 1-50, select the Index function button. You are returned to the Index to Windows and Program Manager Help, as shown in Figure 1-49, except that the Back function button is now available.

Back Button

The Back function button allows you to move backwards through the previous displays in the reverse sequence in which you viewed them. You can select the Back button repetitively until you get to the first display, which is the one shown in Figure 1-49.

Browse << and >> Buttons

The Browse buttons allow you to retrieve displays in their logical sequence of information. The Browse >> button browses forward, and the Browse << button browses in reverse. The Browse << button is different from the Back button in that you Browse through the Help data base in the sequence of the topics, whereas you use the Back button to cycle back through the topics in the reverse sequence in which you viewed them—regardless of which method you used to retrieve them.

Search... Button

The Search function button allows you to search the Help data base by specifying a key word or phrase. The Search... operation uses a pre-defined list of key values from which you can select. The entries in the list depend upon the application. Figure 1-51 shows the Search dialogue box that appears when you select Search... from the Program Manager's Help menu.

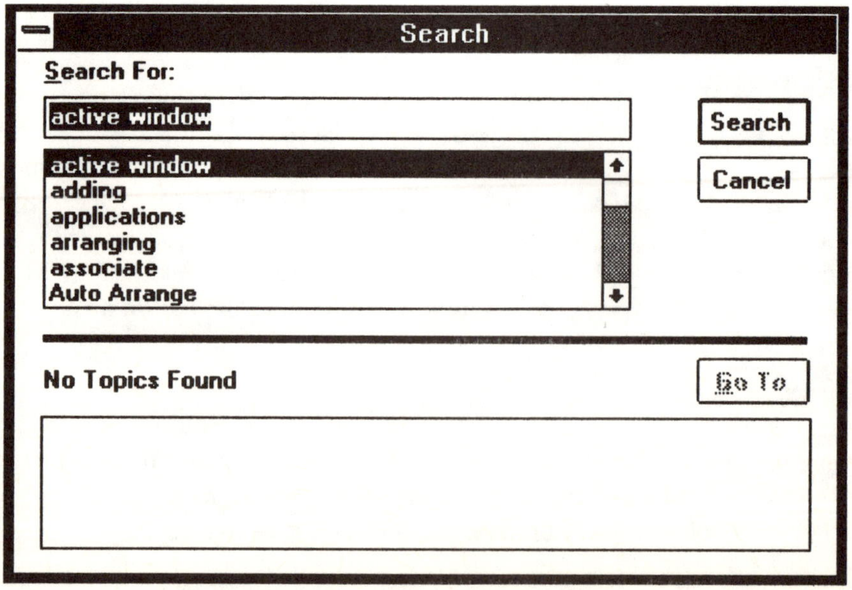

Figure 1-51. The Search Dialogue Box.

You can click or Tab to the key list in the Search dialogue box or you can type a key word of your own into the Search For field. As you type letters into the field, the list pointer moves to the entry that most closely matches the field you are typing. The Search process can search only for matches to entries that are in its list. Select the "opening" key word and then select the Search command button. You will see the display shown in Figure 1-52.

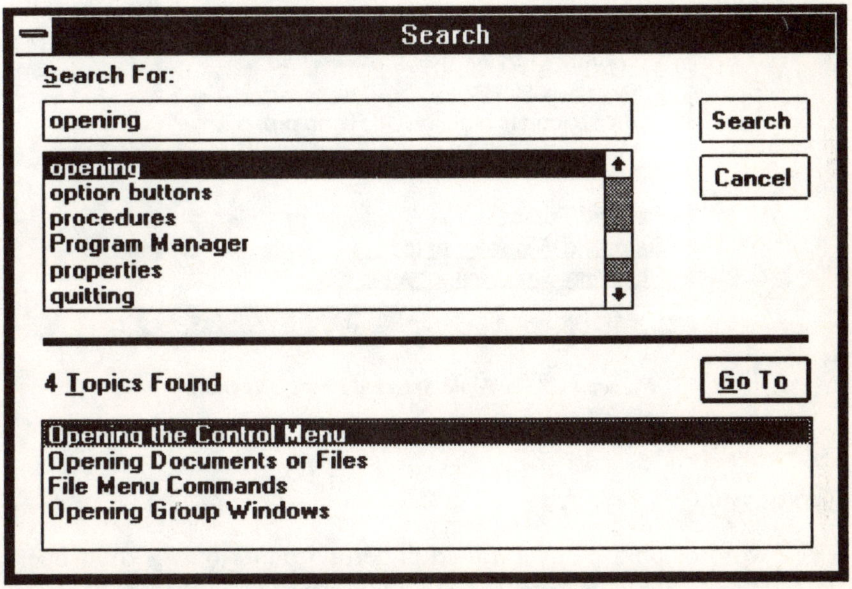

Figure 1-52. The Search Dialogue Box After a Search.

Figure 1-52 shows the Search dialogue box after the search has been completed. In this case there are four entries that match the "opening" key word. The list below the Topics Found field displays the topics that contain the matches. To retrieve the topic for one of the entries in the list, select that entry by double clicking it or moving to it and selecting Go To. Select the Opening Group Windows to see the display shown in Figure 1-53.

Figure 1-53. A Topic Selected From a Search.

The Glossary

When a key word or phrase has a dotted underline rather than a solid one, you can read a description of the item from the Help Glossary. The phrases "group window," "open," "application," and "document" in Figure 1-53 are glossary items. To view a glossary description with the mouse, move the mouse cursor to the phrase. When the cursor changes to the pointing finger symbol, press and hold the left mouse button. To view a glossary description with the keyboard, press the Tab key until the desired item is highlighted, then press and hold the Enter key. Figure 1-54 shows the Glossary display for the "group window" item. When you are done viewing the description, release either the mouse button or the Enter key.

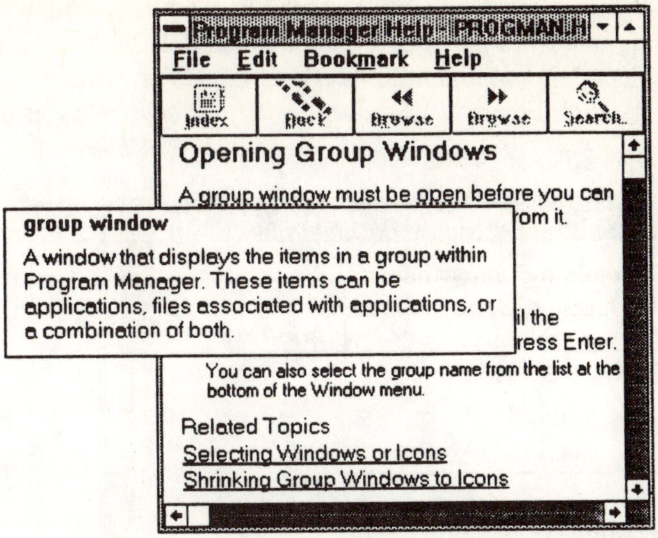

Figure 1-54. A Glossary Item Displayed.

You can view the list of items in the Glossary by selecting the Glossary item on the Help menu shown in Figure 1-45. Figure 1- 55 shows the display that the Glossary menu command produces.

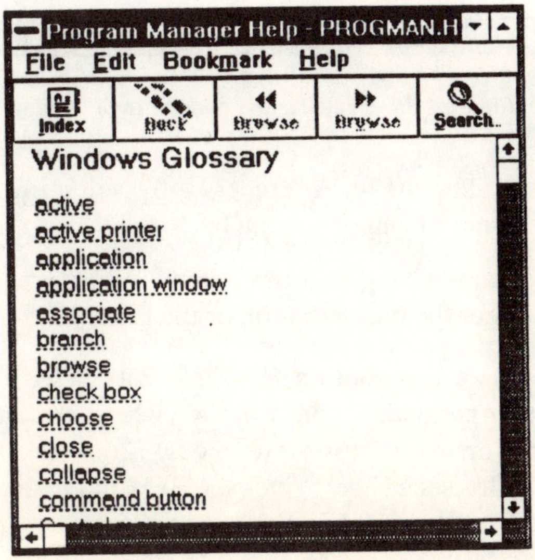

Figure 1-55. The Windows Glossary.

The procedures for viewing a glossary item from the list shown in Figure 1-45 are the same as for selecting one from the body of some other Help text. Click and hold the mouse button or select the item and hold the Enter key down while you read the description from the Glossary. Figure 1-56 shows the "check box" entry as displayed by the Glossary.

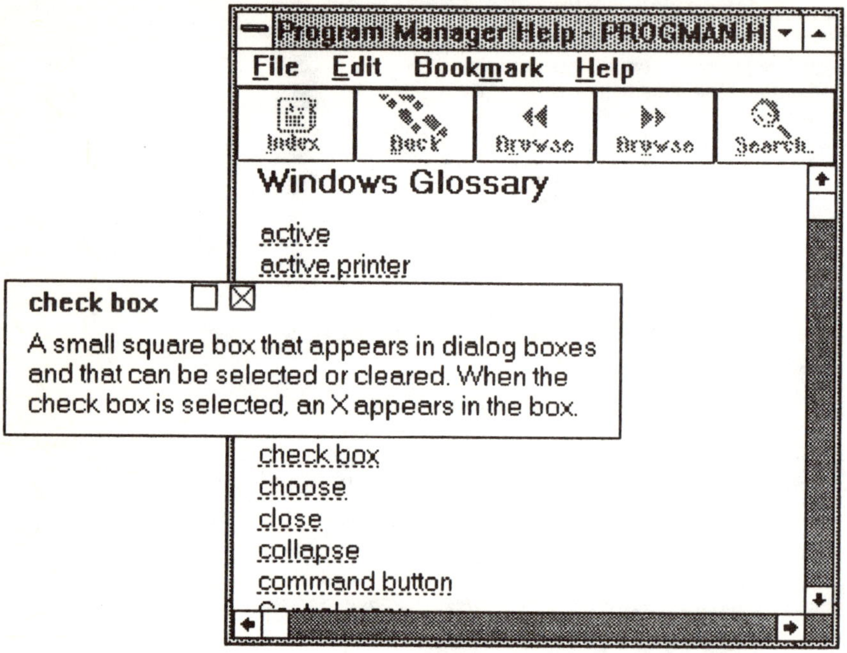

Figure 1-56. The Glossary with an Item Displayed.

Return to the display shown in Figure 1-47 by selecting Index from the Help command on the Program Manager's menu bar.

Bookmarks

You can insert bookmark icons into a Help text data base. These bookmarks allow you to go directly to a particular topic from anywhere else in the data base without searching, browsing, or using cross-references. From the Index to Windows and Program Manager Help, select the Windows Help Index cross-reference. You will see the display shown in Figure 1-57.

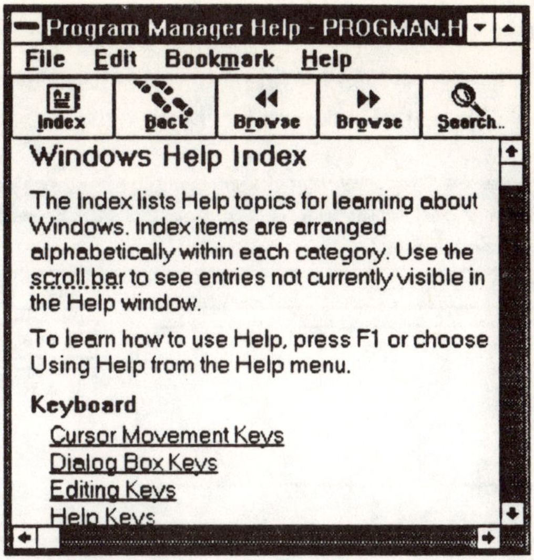

Figure 1-57. The Index to Windows and Program Manager Help.

Now select the Bookmark command on the menu bar. You will see the display shown in Figure 1-58, which shows the Bookmark menu.

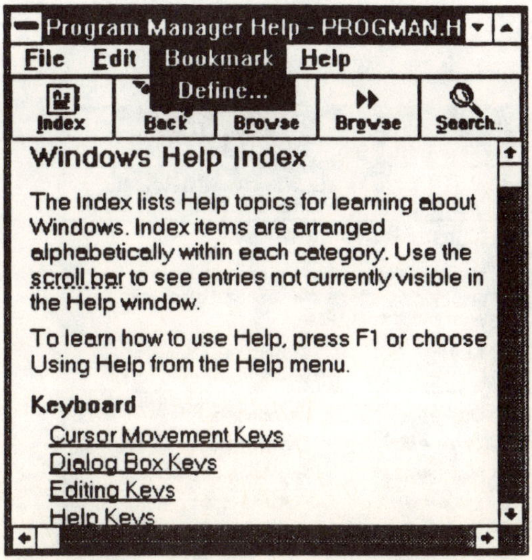

Figure 1-58. The Bookmark Menu.

Setting a Bookmark

The Bookmark menu in Figure 1-58 has only one command: the Define... command. When you select this command, you will see the Bookmark Define dialogue box shown in Figure 1-59.

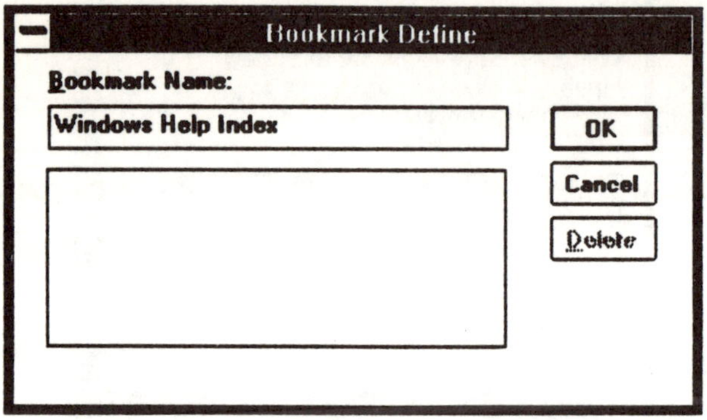

Figure 1-59. The Bookmark Define Dialogue Box.

You can accept the Bookmark Name as it is or you can change it by entering a different value into its text box on the Bookmark Define dialogue box. The name defaults to the title of the Help topic in which you are placing the bookmark. Select OK to insert the bookmark. Now select the Cursor Movement Keys cross-reference from the Windows Help Index in Figure 1-58 and select the Bookmark menu command again. You will see the display shown in Figure 1-60.

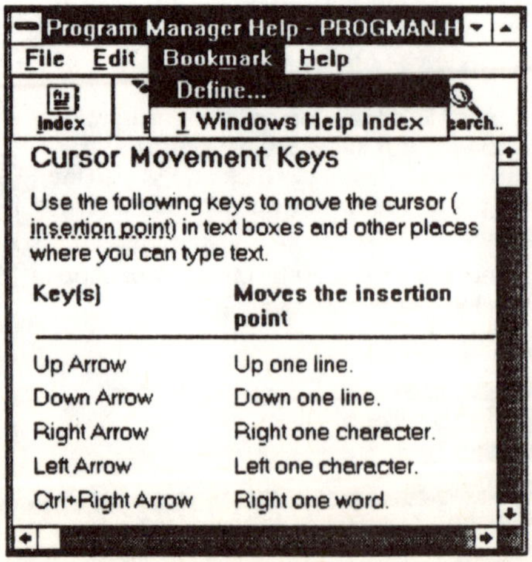

Figure 1-60. The Bookmark Menu with One Bookmark.

Observe that the Bookmark menu now has a second entry: the bookmark that you placed earlier. Select Define and you will see the Bookmark Define dialogue box shown in Figure 1-61.

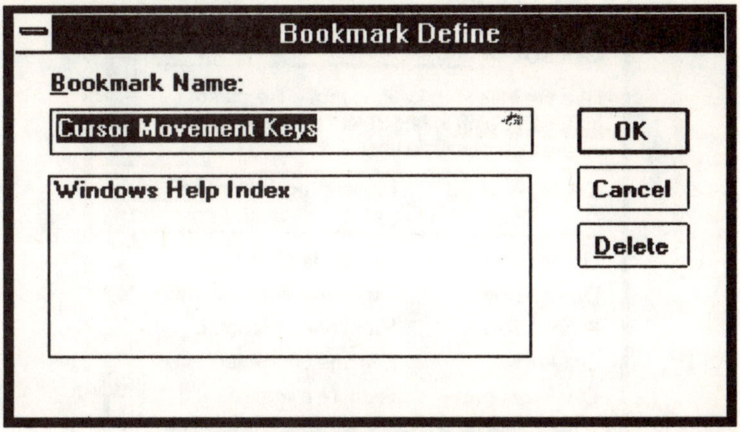

Figure 1-61. The Bookmark Define Dialogue Box with a Bookmark.

The Bookmark Define dialogue box is the same as the earlier one, except that its default Bookmark Name is that of the Cursor Movement Keys topic. The earlier bookmark title appears in a list in the lower box. You can select a name from the lower list box if you wish. For now, select OK to add the default bookmark. Now when you select the Bookmark command from the menu bar, you see that there are two bookmarks, as shown in Figure 1-62.

Whenever you select the Bookmark menu command from now on, the two bookmarks will be on the menu. You can select one of them and proceed directly to the topic that is marked. Observe that the bookmarks are numbered on the menu with underlines. You can also press the associated number key to select a bookmark.

Use the Index function button to return to the Index to Windows and then to the Program Manager topic, as shown in Figure 1-49.

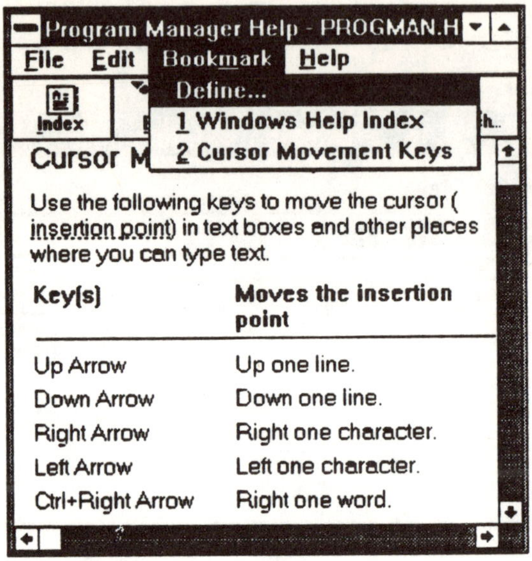

Figure 1-62. The Bookmark Menu with Two Bookmarks.

Deleting a Bookmark

To delete a bookmark, select the Bookmark menu and select Define. You will see the Bookmark Define dialogue box shown in Figure 1-63. Select the Windows Help Index entry in the lower list box. Then select the Delete command button. The entry disappears from the list box, and the bookmark no longer exists in the Help data base.

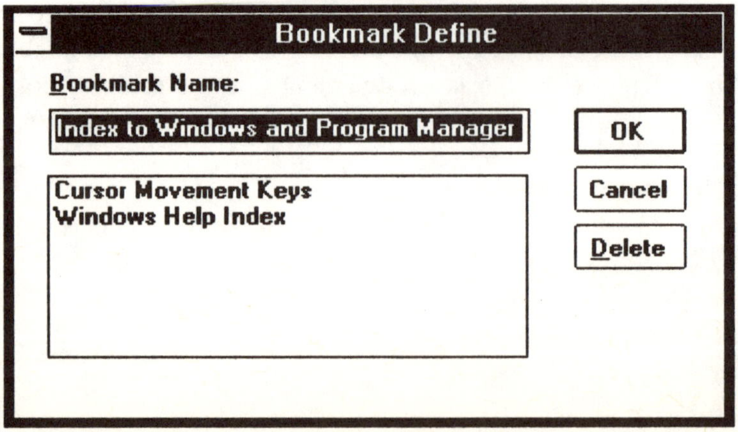

Figure 1-63. The Bookmark Define Dialogue Box with Two Bookmarks.

Annotate...

You can add your own notes to a Help Topic with the Annotate... command. Use the remaining bookmark to return to the Cursor Movement Keys topic and select the Edit menu command. You will see the display shown in Figure 1-64.

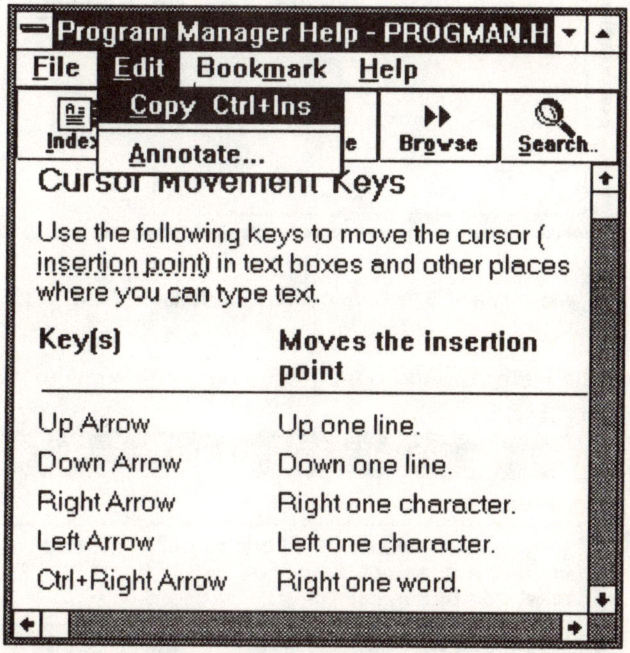

Figure 1-64. The Help Edit Menu.

Adding an Annotation

Select the Annotate... menu command and observe the Help Annotation dialogue box shown in Figure 1-65.

The small vertical bar in the text box is a text cursor. You can type the contents of your annotation into this box. As you type, you can use the cursor keys to move the cursor around in the text. The Backspace key deletes characters to the left of the cursor and the Del key deletes characters to the right of the cursor. You can mark blocks of text by pointing the mouse cursor to a point, holding down the left button, dragging the mouse, and releasing the button when the block is marked. The Del key deletes a marked block. The words wrap themselves to the next line. Do not use the Enter key to end a line.

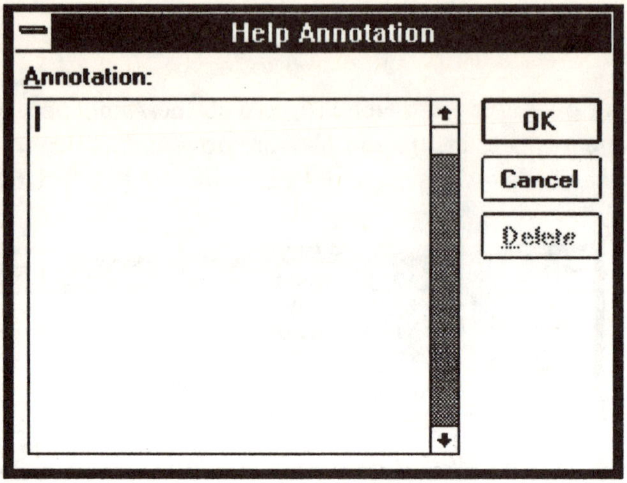

Figure 1-65. The Help Annotation Dialogue Box.

Figure 1-66 shows the Help Annotation dialogue box with some text entered.

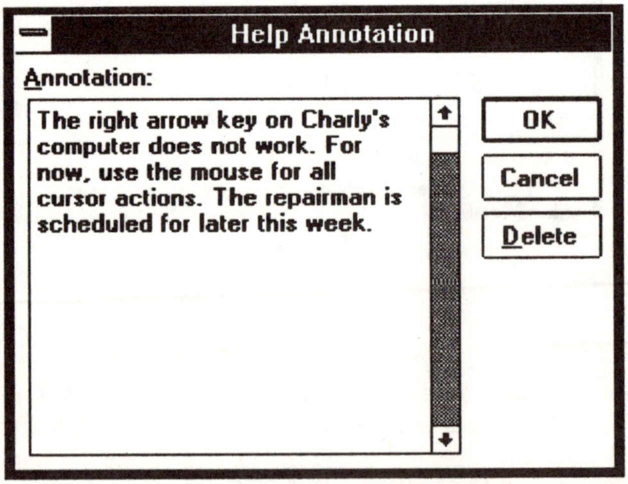

Figure 1-66. The Help Annotation Dialogue Box with Text Added.

When you select OK from the Help Annotation dialogue box, the annotation is added to the topic, and the Cursor Movement Keys topic appears, as shown in Figure 1-67.

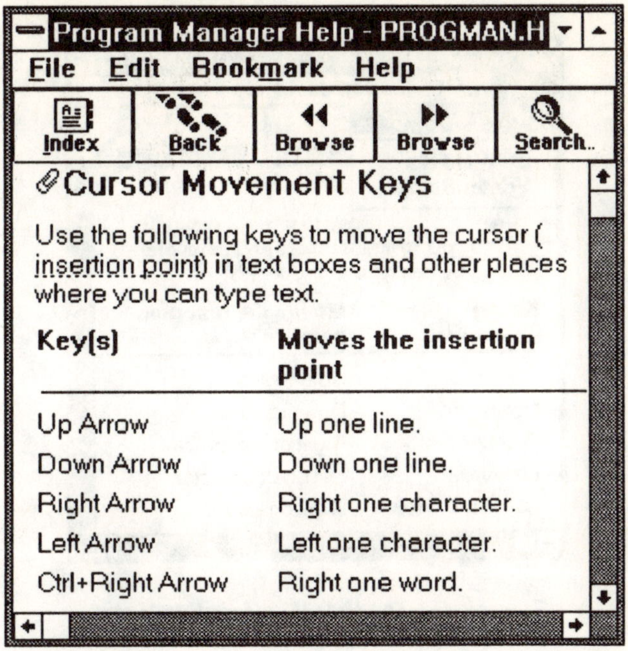

Figure 1-67. The Cursor Movement Topic with an Annotation.

Reading and Changing an Annotation

Observe the paper clip icon to the left of the topic's title in Figure 1-67. This icon means that the topic has an annotation. To read the annotation, click the icon or Tab to it and press Enter. You will see the Help Annotation dialogue box that you saw in Figure 1-66. You can modify the text and save it by selecting OK.

Deleting an Annotation

To delete an annotation, read it using the procedure you just learned. When the Help Annotation dialogue box appears, select the Delete command button. The annotation goes away, and the topic appears without the paper clip icon.

Printing a Topic

You can print the text of the current topic by selecting the Print Topic command from the Help window's File menu, as shown in Figure 1-68.

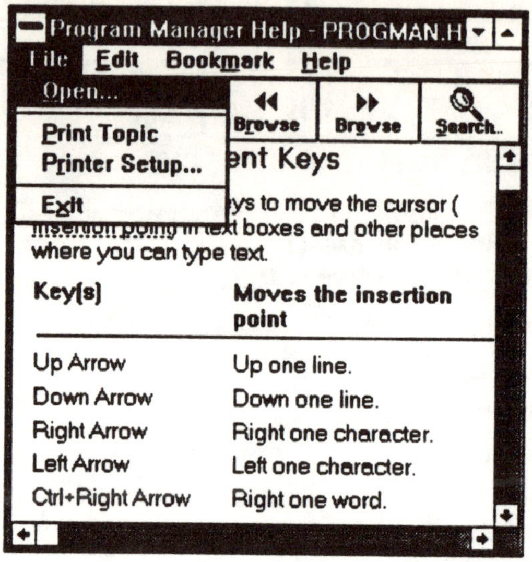

Figure 1-68. The Help Window's File Menu.

Figure 1-69 shows the printout of the Cursor Menu Keys topic.

Cursor Movement Keys

Use the following keys to move the cursor (insertion point) in text boxes and other places where you can type text.

Key(s)	Moves the insertion point
Up Arrow	Up one line.
Down Arrow	Down one line.
Right Arrow	Right one character.
Left Arrow	Left one character.
Ctrl+Right Arrow	Right one word.
Ctrl+Left Arrow	Left one word.
Home	To the beginning of the line.
End	To the end of the line.
PgUp	Up one window.
PgDn	Down one window.
Ctrl+Home	To the beginning of the document.
Ctrl+End	To the end of the document.

Figure 1-69. A Printout for the Cursor Menu Keys Help Topic.

Copying a Topic

You can copy the contents of a topic into another application with the Copy command on the Help window's Edit menu, as shown in Figure 1-64. When you select the Copy command, the textual contents of the current topic are copied into the Windows Clipboard.

You can also use the Paste command of the target application to copy the Clipboard's contents into the application's document. You will learn about the Clipboard in Chapter 4.

Loading Other Help Files

Windows and its applications have many different files in the Help data base. You can load a different Help file if you need help with another application. Select the Open... command from the File menu of the Help window. You will see the File Open dialogue box, as shown in Figure 1-70. Select any of the .HLP files from the dialogue box to change the active Help file.

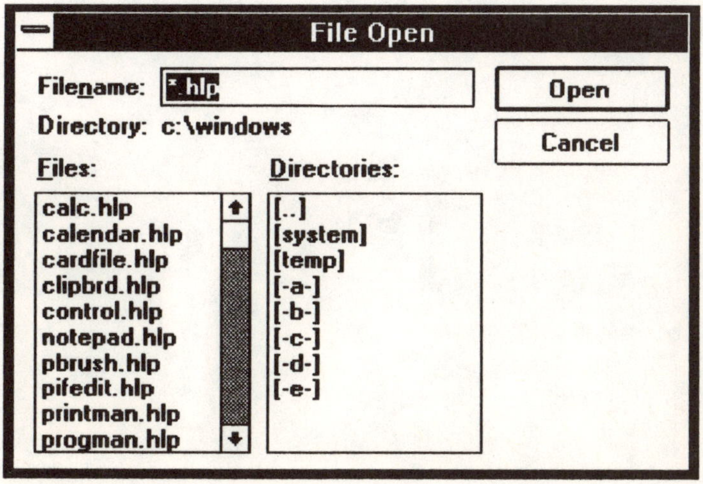

Figure 1-70. The Help Data Base File Open Dialogue Box.

SUMMARY

In this chapter you learned to use the Windows graphical operating environment. You now know how to use the mouse and keyboard to move around the Windows Desktop. You can execute commands from menus and enter data into dialogue boxes. You can rearrange the appearance of the Desktop, and you understand icons. These lessons are among the most important ones in learning Windows. Beyond this chapter, you will see little that will be unfamiliar to you because the applications that follow are functional entities that use the concepts you learned in this chapter in the expression of their user interface.

You used the Windows Program Manager extensively in this chapter to observe the behavior of the graphical operating environment. Chapter 2 teaches you the details of the Program Manager, including how you can use it to organize and manage your own system of programs.

Chapter 2

The Program Manager

In Chapter 1 you learned about the Windows graphical operating environment. The exercises in Chapter 1 used the functions of the Windows Program Manager to a large degree because the Program Manager is the first application you see when you run Windows. Unless you take steps to change it, the Program Manager runs automatically whenever you start Windows.

The Program Manager is a "shell" program. With it you manage your applications programs by organizing them into manageable groups. Windows begins with an installed set of groups. You can use the Program Manager to modify and expand these groups to create a personalized software environment.

GROUPS, APPLICATIONS, AND DOCUMENTS

The title of this section represents the view of a computer's work as seen by Windows through the Program Manager. Groups are collections of applications. Applications, in turn, are programs that work on collections of documents.

Suppose your work involves report preparation, bookkeeping for your business, and business correspondence. Besides those functions, you use a personal scheduler application, have utility applications to maintain your computer system, and sometimes knock off for a while and play some computer games. These categories could represent the groups into which you would organize your applications.

You could have a Reports group where you keep your word processor, style checker, paint program, chart program, and desktop publisher applications. Those applications each work on individual documents—the text and graphics that go into the reports you prepare.

You might then have an Accounting group for the general ledger, payroll, tax preparation, and spreadsheet applications. Those applications, too, work on other documents—the data bases and spreadsheet data files.

The Letters group could contain the same word processor application that you use in the Reports group, but with a different set of documents and perhaps different style sheets and default printer settings.

Your Utilities group could contain the hard disk management utility applications.

The Games group, of course, would have the computer games you like to play.

The Windows Program Manager allows you to control the software environment you use in ways similar to the model just described. Before you attempt to build your own customized Program Management environment, however, take the time to look at the configuration with which Windows starts.

GROUPS

Figure 2-1 is our usual starting point for most of the exercises in this chapter and in Chapter 1. It shows the Program Manager as it appears when you start a Windows session where little or no customization has taken place.

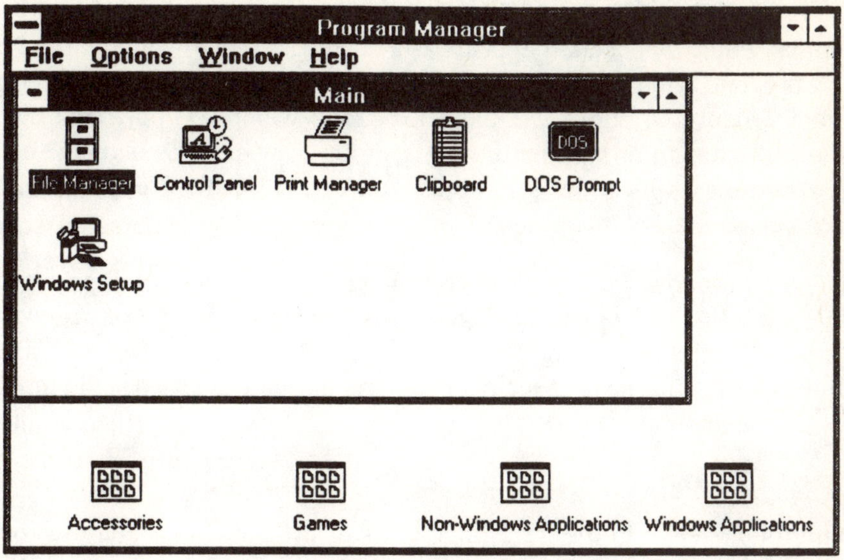

Figure 2-1. The Initial Windows Display.

The initial Windows display in Figure 2-1 shows that five groups exist: Main, Accessories, Games, Non-Windows Applications, and Windows Applications. Each of these groups contains applications that you will learn about in later chapters. Nothing requires you to preserve the default organization of applications within groups, and no doubt you will modify and expand it, particularly with respect to the last two groups. Nonetheless, the next several paragraphs discuss the contents of each of the groups to give you an idea of how applications might be logically arranged.

***

THE DISPLAY IN FIGURE 2-1 MIGHT NOT BE EXACTLY THE SAME AS YOURS. THE INSTALLATION PROCEDURE THAT BUILT THE SYSTEM USED IN THE PREPARATION OF THIS BOOK INCLUDED THE OPTIONS TO INSTALL SELECTED WINDOWS AND NON-WINDOWS APPLICATIONS. YOU MIGHT NOT HAVE ANY SUCH APPLICATIONS IN YOUR COMPUTER BECAUSE THEY DO NOT COME WITH WINDOWS. ANOTHER DIFFERENCE MIGHT BE IN THE SPACING OF THE ICONS AT THE BOTTOM OF THE PROGRAM MANAGER WINDOW. THE SPACING IN FIGURE 2-1 IS WIDER THAN USUAL BECAUSE IF YOU USE THE DEFAULT SPACING, THE TITLES OF THE ICONS TEND TO OBSCURE ONE ANOTHER. TO PRESERVE LEGIBILITY IN THE FIGURES, THIS BOOK USED A FEATURE OF THE WINDOWS CONTROL PANEL TO WIDEN THAT SPACE. YOU WILL LEARN HOW TO MAKE THAT MODIFICATION FOR YOURSELF IN CHAPTER 5.

***

Opening and Closing a Group Window

When a group window is open, it appears as a document window within the Program Manager's program window. When it is closed, it appears as an icon at the bottom of the program window. In Figure 2-1 the Main group window is open and the others are closed. To execute an application in a group you must first open the group window. When the application is running, you can close the group window from which it came.

To open a group window, you double click its icon, Tab to the icon, and press the Enter key, or select it from the Program Manager's Window menu. To close a group window you click its Minimize box, double click its Control Menu box, or select Close from the Control Menu itself. The next section considers the various groups in Figure 2-1.

The Main Group

The Main group, shown in Figure 2-2, consists of programs that you use routinely. File Manager, Control Panel, Print Manger, Clipboard, DOS Prompt, and Windows Setup are all utility applications that help you use and manage the Windows operating environment.

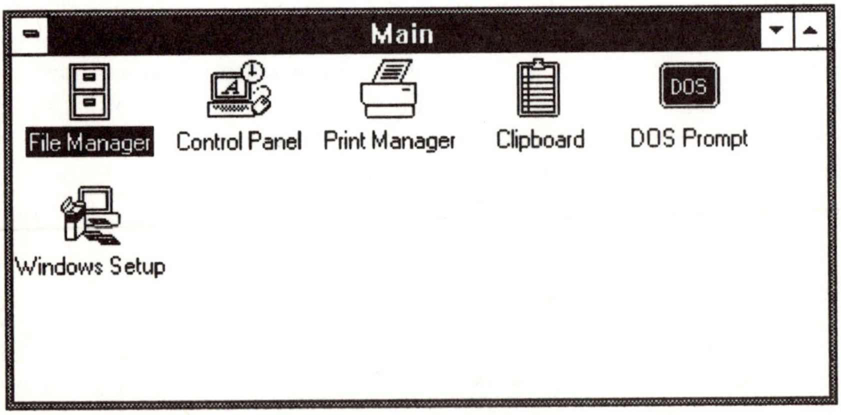

Figure 2-2. The Main Group.

The Accessories Group

The Accessories group, shown in Figure 2-3, is a set of small applications that by themselves could satisfy the computing needs of many users. Write is a word processor. Paintbrush is a graphical design tool. Terminal is a communications program. Notepad is a small text editor for the occasional memo. Recorder allows you to build keyboard and mouse macros to assign routine data entry functions to a single keystroke. Cardfile is a miniature text data base that emulates a 3x5 card file. Calendar is a personal scheduler and alarm clock. Calculator is a desktop calculator utility program. Clock is a time-of-day clock display. Only the FIF editor seems out of place. It is a utility program that you use when you integrate non-Windows DOS applications into the Windows environment.

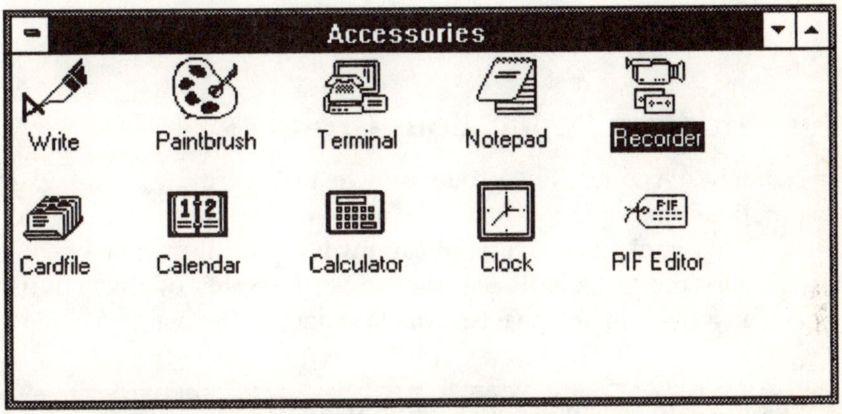

Figure 2-3. The Accessories Group.

The Games Group

The Games group, shown in Figure 2-4, contains two computer games that are included with Windows. This book will not dwell on them. They are there for your entertainment, and you might use them for a leisurely practice session to become comfortable with the system.

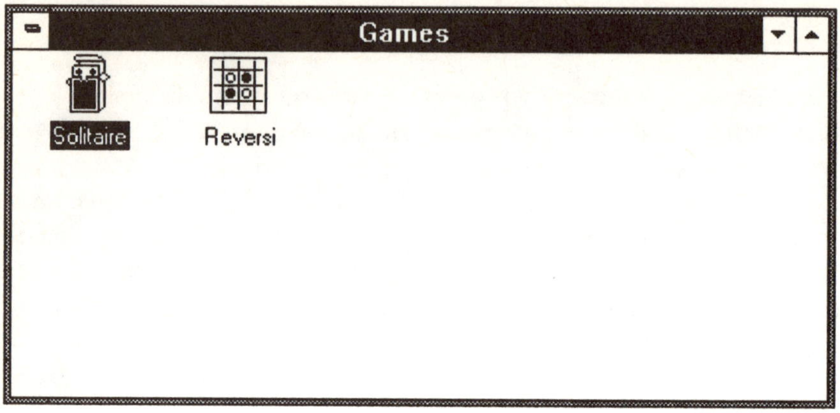

Figure 2-4. The Games Group.

The Non-Windows Applications Group

The Non-Windows Applications group, shown in Figure 2-5, displays the non-Windows applications included in the Windows installation that I used for the preparation of this book. The five applications are typical of non-Windows DOS applications, and the book will use them for examples of that environment, recognizing that you might not have equivalent programs in your own computer.

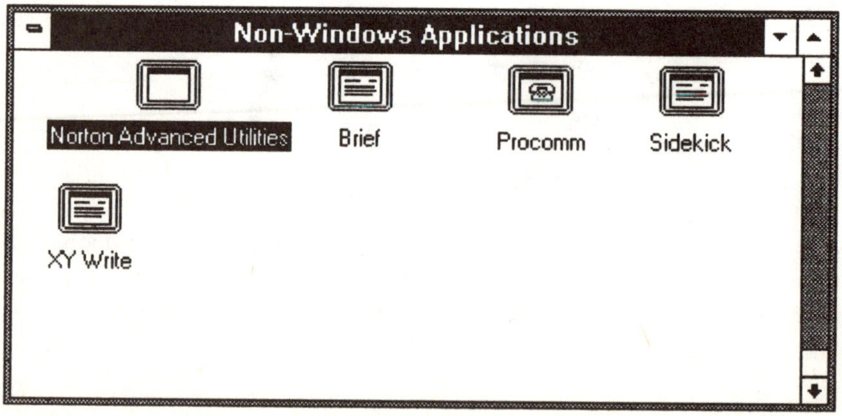

Figure 2-5. The Non-Windows Applications Group.

The Windows Applications Group

The three applications in the Windows Applications group, shown in Figure 2-6, represent programs from three different kinds of sources. The Diary application is a shareware personal manager that you can download from bulletin boards and on-line services. There are many such programs available that run under Windows. The second application is Microsoft Word for Windows, a high-end word processor that many users prefer. The third application is a screen snapshot program that was published in a magazine article and that I keyed in and installed for preparing some of the figures in this book.

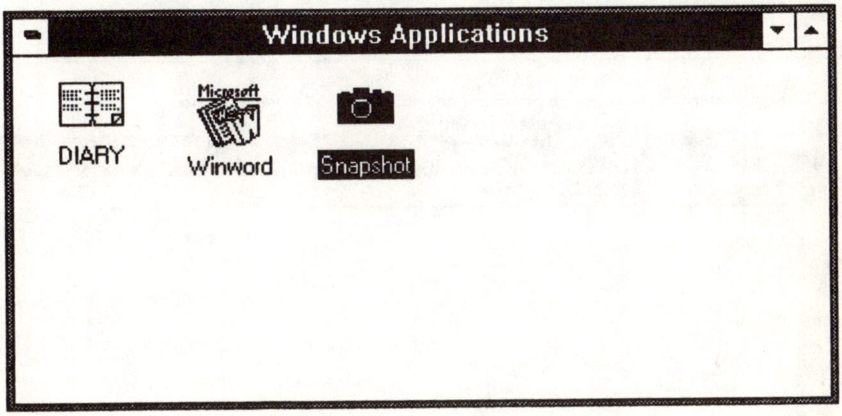

Figure 2-6. The Windows Applications Group.

RUNNING APPLICATIONS

There are several ways to run an application from Windows: select the application's icon from the group window that contains it; select a special copy of the application that is configured to operate with a specific document; use the Run... command on the Program Manager's File menu; or run the application from the DOS command line in the DOS window. What happens after you run the application is strictly dependent on what the program does and, in some cases, the mode under which Windows is running.

You can set up a non-Windows DOS application to run in a window if you are running Windows in 386 Extended Mode. Otherwise non-Windows DOS applications must use the full screen. You will learn about Windows modes in Chapter 11.

The File Manager provides several more ways for you to run an application. You will learn about the File Manager in Chapter 3.

Running a Program from a Group

You run a program from a group by opening the group window and selecting the program's icon. Open the Accessories group window and select the Notepad icon. You will see a screen similar to the one shown in Figure 2-7.

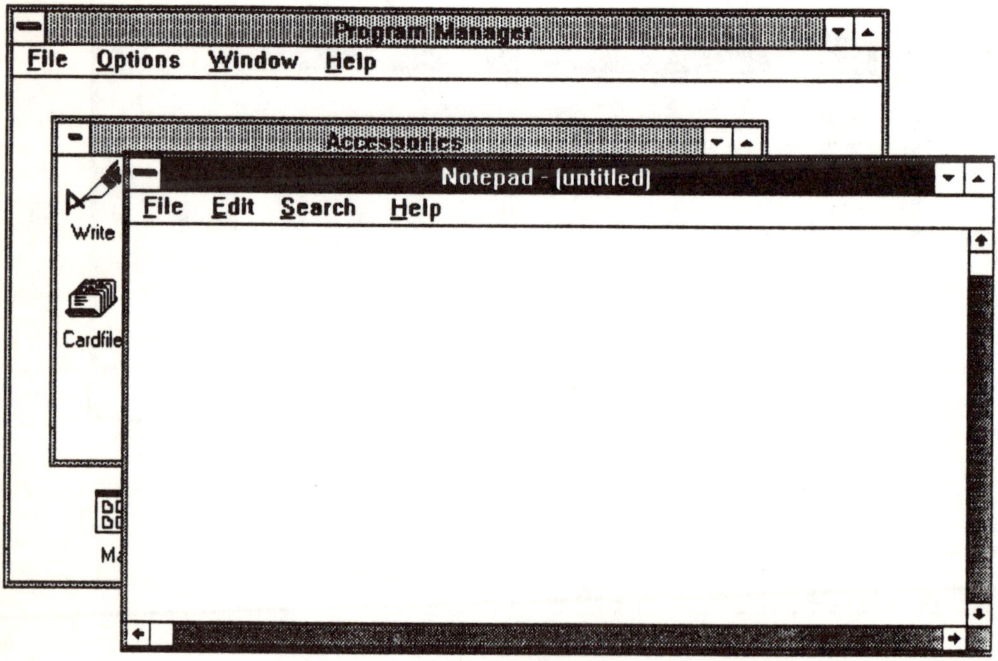

Figure 2-7. The Notepad Application.

The Program Manager is in the background, and the Notepad application window is active. The Notepad is now a running application.

The Run... Command

Select the Run... command from the File menu in the Program Manager window. You will see the Run dialogue box shown in Figure 2-8.

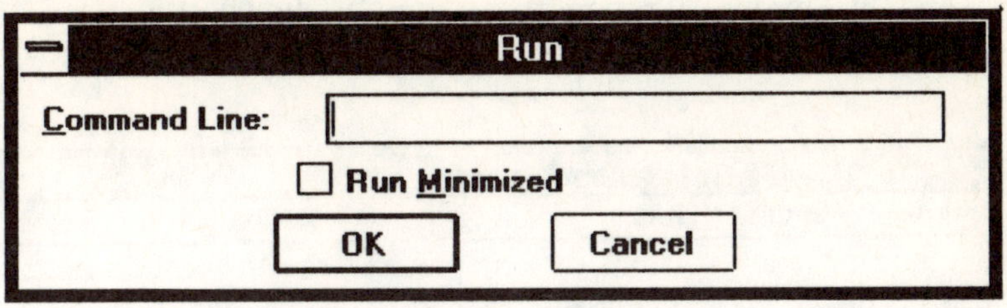

Figure 2-8. The Run Dialogue Box.

To use the Run... command you must know where the application's .COM, .EXE, or .BAT file is stored and the name of the executable file. Depending on the application, you might also need to know other things about its command line.

You use the Run... command by typing the application's command line and selecting the OK command button. If you select the Run Minimized check box, the application will begin its execution as an icon.

You can run either a Windows application or a non-Windows DOS application with the Run... command. Inasmuch as you have several of each kind installed—at least in the example environment set forward in this book—you can try running both types of application at this time.

Using Run... for a Windows Application

Type the command to execute the Windows Paintbrush program into the Run dialogue box. The command is shown in Figure 2-9.

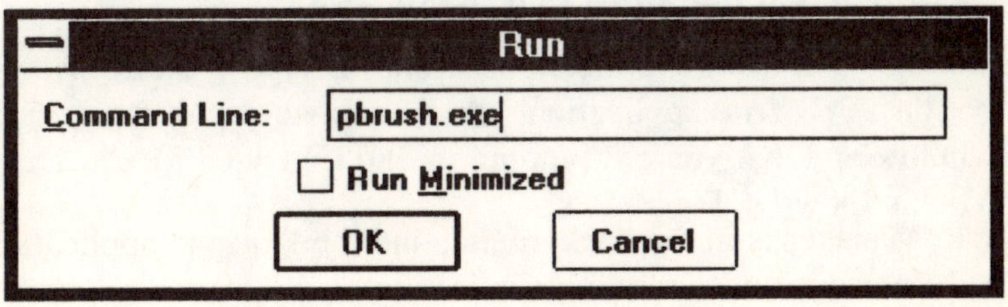

Figure 2-9. Running PBRUSH.EXE.

Select OK, and the Paintbrush program executes, as shown in Figure 2-10.

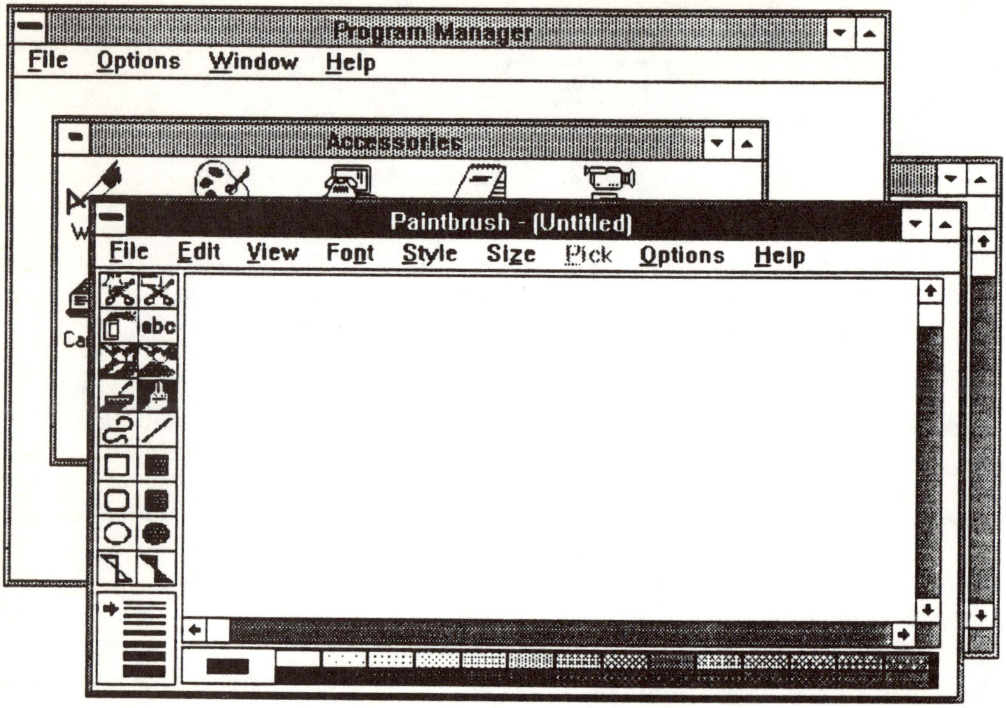

Figure 2-10. The Paintbrush Application.

Using Run... for a non-Windows DOS Application

Observe the Non-Windows Applications group in Figure 2-5. For these exercises, assume that the XY Write application, which is a word processor, is configured to run in a window and that you are running in 386 Extended Mode. The command to run XY Write is shown in Figure 2-11.

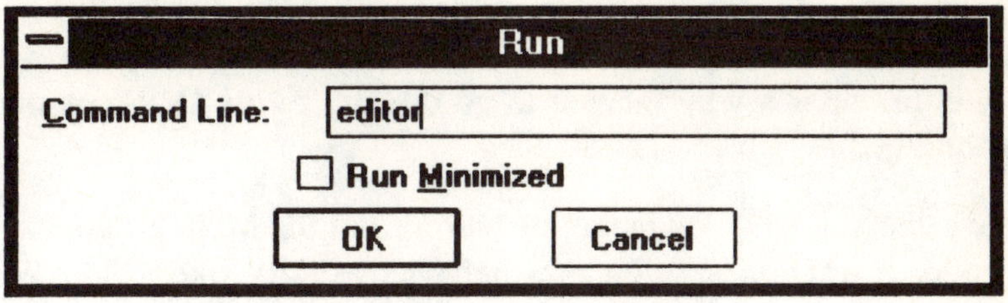

Figure 2-11. Running EDITOR.EXE.

Select OK and the XY Write Editor program executes, as shown in Figure 2-12, somewhat obscuring the screen. At this point the Notepad, the Paintbrush, and the XY Write applications are running.

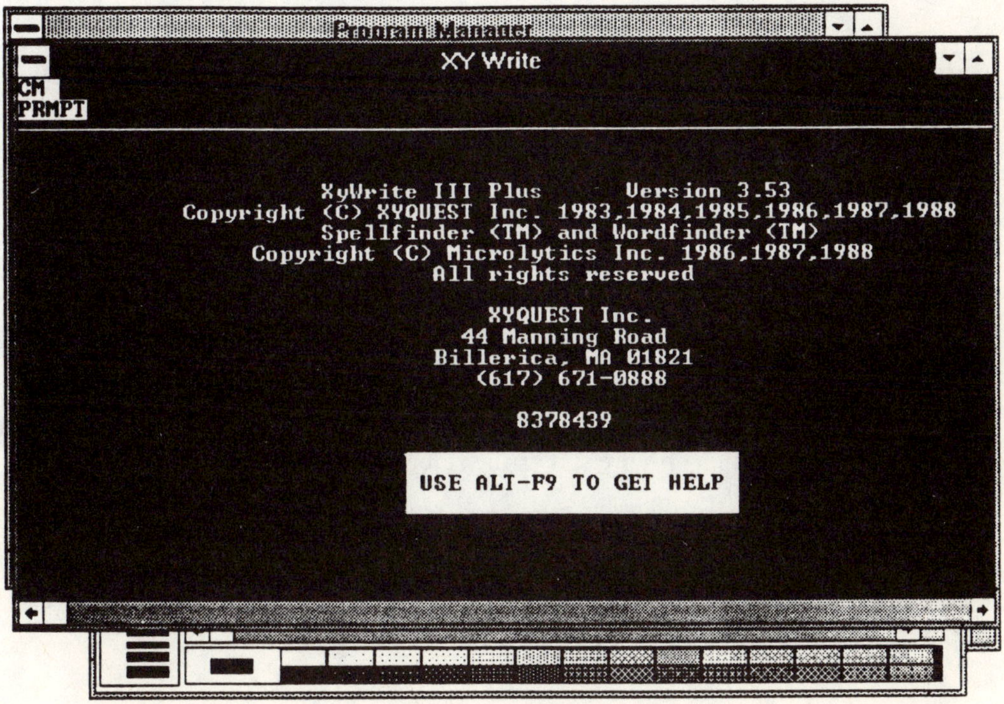

Figure 2-12. A Non-Windows DOS Application Running in a Window.

The DOS Prompt

For the next exercise, select the Program Manager window and make the Main group the active document window. The other windows move to the background. The DOS Prompt icon provides a way for you to go directly to the DOS command line from within Windows.

When you select the DOS Prompt application from the Main group, the entire screen is given over to a DOS session that behaves exactly like a non-Windows DOS computer with respect to running applications. The prompt you see is shown in Figure 2-13.

```
The IBM Personal Computer DOS
Version 3.30 (C)Copyright International Business Machines Corp 1981, 1987
             (C)Copyright Microsoft Corp 1981, 1986

C>
```

Figure 2-13. The DOS Prompt.

The difference between DOS by itself and DOS run from within Windows is that within windows you can switch between DOS and Windows applications without stopping and restarting applications, and you can have more than one DOS session active at a time.

To run a program from the DOS Prompt, you run it just as you would from DOS. Assuming that you have a DOS path to your DOS utility programs, run the DOS program EDLIN by typing its name, with a filename, on the DOS command line, as shown in Figure 2-14. The Figure shows the screen after EDLIN has begun running.

```
The IBM Personal Computer DOS
Version 3.30 (C)Copyright International Business Machines Corp 1981, 1987
         (C)Copyright Microsoft Corp 1981, 1986

C>edlin teach.doc
New file
*
```

Figure 2-14. Running EDLIN From The DOS Prompt.

MULTITASKING

If you have followed along with these exercises, you have several applications loaded into your computer, and the DOS Prompt is the current active application. The other applications are: the Notepad, the Paintbrush, the XY Write Editor program, and, of course, the Program Manager itself.

If you are running Windows in 386 Extended Mode, the other programs are running now, too, but the screen and keyboard are dedicated to the DOS Prompt. If you are not running Windows in 386 Extended Mode, the other programs are loaded and ready to go, but each one must wait for you to switch to it in order to execute. If your computer has enough memory, all the programs are resident at one time. If not, Windows swaps them in and out of its temporary disk swap files as necessary. The mechanics of operating Windows and its applications do not change because you are or are not in 386 Extended Mode. But the overall performance of your computer will be affected.

Switching Between Applications

Because you have several interactive applications running at one time, you need to be able to switch from one to the other in order to view each application's results and supply it with its next input. The Alt+Esc key is one way to switch from application to application. You can press that key to switch from the DOS Prompt of the previous exercise back to one of the windowed applications. Which one comes next depends on the sequence in which the tasks were last selected. Chances are the Program Manager is next, and you will see the screen shown in Figure 2-15.

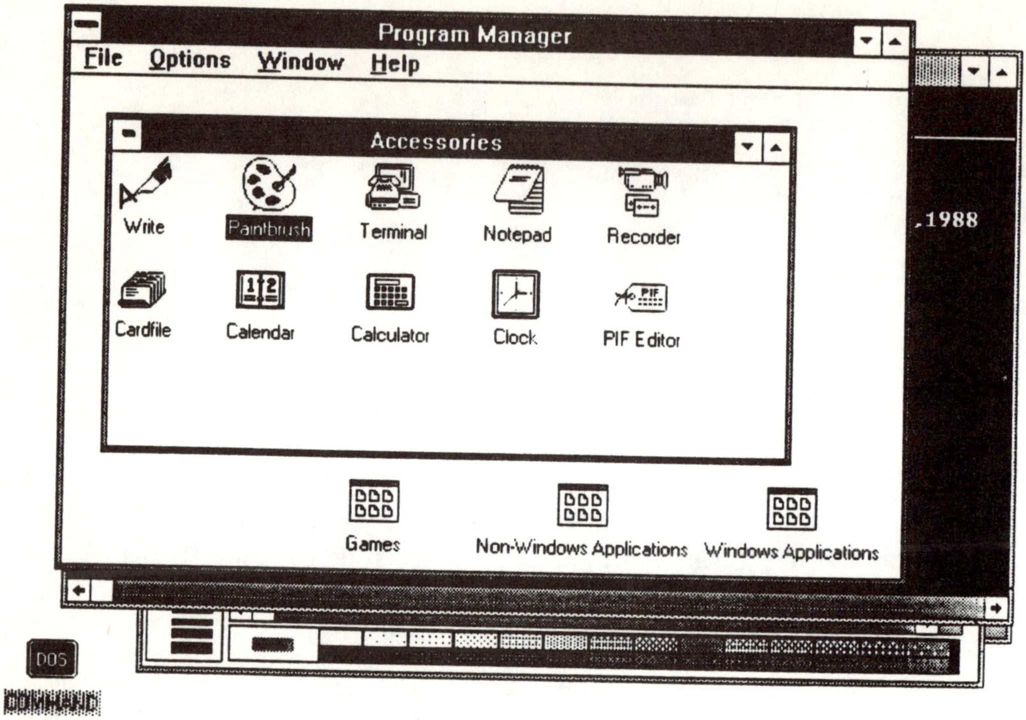

Figure 2-15. Switching Back into Windows.

Observe the DOS icon with the COMMAND label in the lower left corner of the screen. That icon indicates that a program is running that does not occupy a screen window. The program is, of course, the DOS EDLIN program that you ran from the DOS Prompt. Other programs that run as icons might have different icon symbols, but their presence as icons on the desktop indicates that they are running and not using a window at the time.

You can use the Alt+Esc key to switch from application to application now. When you get to the DOS Prompt, its label becomes highlighted, but the screen does not change to the DOS screen. The Alt+Esc key does not switch an application into a window or onto the screen when the running application is an icon.

To return to the DOS EDLIN program with the mouse, double click the DOS Prompt icon. To return with the keyboard, press Alt+Esc until the DOS icon's COMMAND label is highlighted. Next press Alt+Spacebar to open the icon's Control Menu and select the Restore command by pressing Enter. Return to the windowed applications by pressing Alt+Esc from within the DOS EDLIN session.

The Task List

The Windows task executive software maintains a Task List. While not actually a part of the Program Manager, the Task List's functions are integral to executing and monitoring the running of applications.

You can view and use the Task List in a dialogue box by pressing Ctrl+Esc or by double clicking any area of the desktop that is not occupied by a window or icon. The Task List dialogue box is shown in Figure 2-16. A task is, in this context, the same as an application.

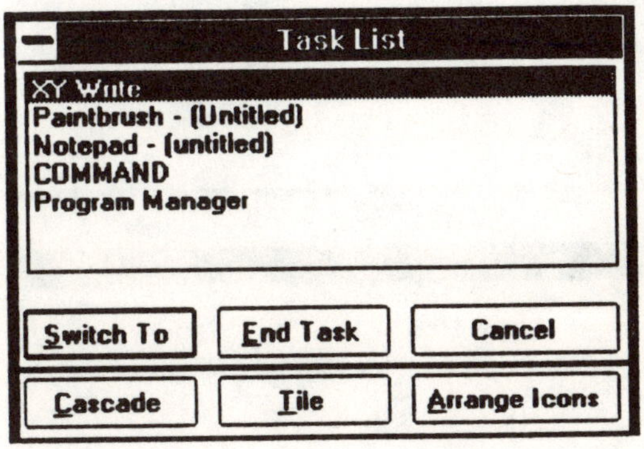

Figure 2-16. The Task List Dialogue Box.

The Task List lists all the tasks currently running and provides some commands relative to the tasks. You can move the list box cursor to a task's name and perform several operations on the task. If you double click the task name or select Switch To when the name is highlighted, the Program Manager switches to the task, and the task resumes executing. If you select End Task, the Program Manager attempts to terminate the task. The Cancel command closes the Task List. Arrange Icons rearranges the application icons at the bottom of the desktop.

The Cascade command cascades the applications windows so that the screen appears as shown in Figure 2-17.

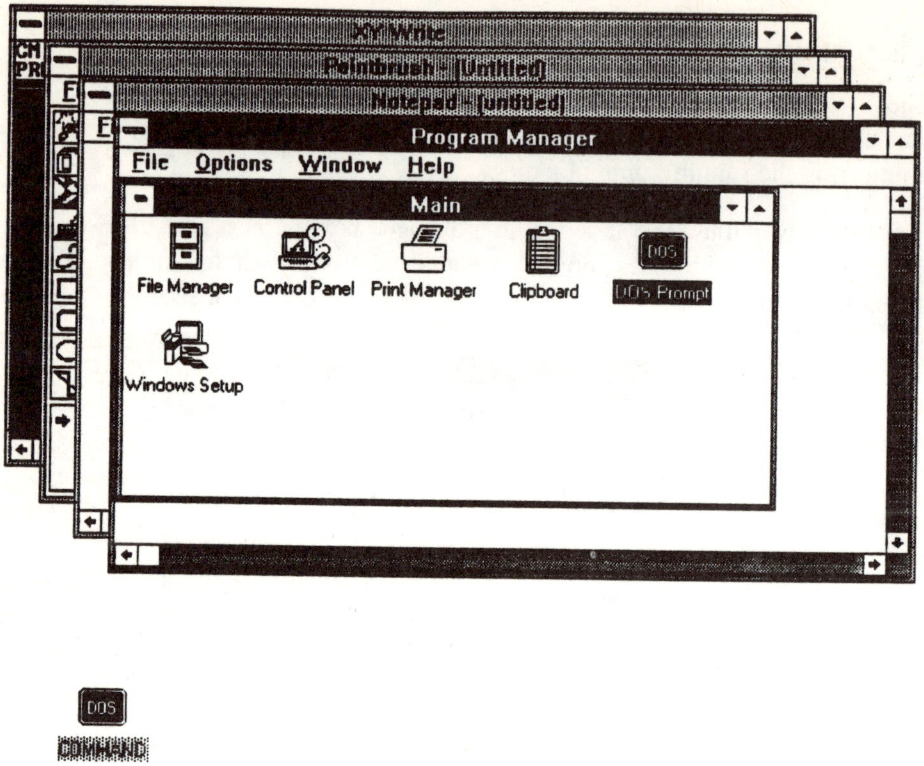

Figure 2-17. Cascaded Applications Windows.

Cascading resizes the windows to a uniform size and stacks them up so that they are all visible. The Tile Command organizes the windows into a tiled configuration, as shown in Figure 2-18. Tiled windows are arranged so that no part of any window overlaps another.

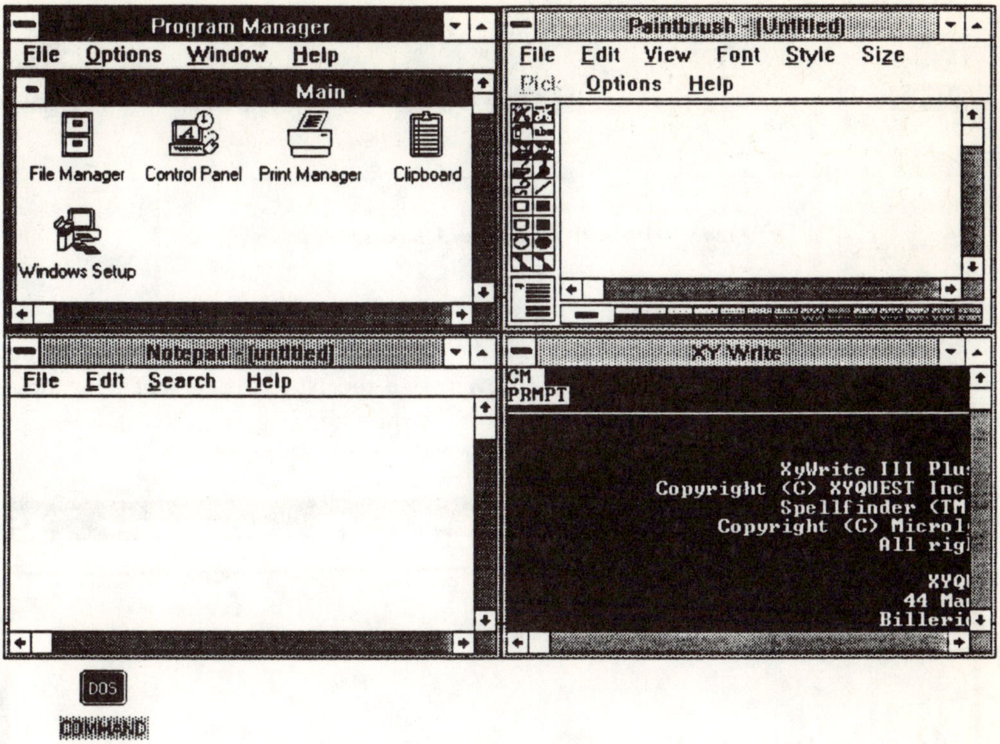

Figure 2-18. Tiled Applications Windows.

Minimizing an Application

Four of the five applications that are running in Figure 2-18 are running in applications windows. The fifth, the DOS COMMAND program, is running as an icon at the bottom of the desktop. You can minimize each running application so that it is also an icon. Click the Minimize box for each of the applications or use Alt+Esc to switch to the window; press Alt+Spacebar to call the Control Menu, and Select Minimize for each application. When you have minimized all the applications, they are all icons at the bottom of the screen, as shown in Figure 2-19.

Figure 2-19. All Applications Minimized to Icons.

You can begin to see the potential for multitasking when you go one step farther. Select the Notepad. You can double click the Notepad icon, or use Ctrl+Esc to call the Task List and select it from there. Now resize the Notepad so that it occupies most of the screen but leaves the icons visible, as shown in Figure 2-20.

Figure 2-20. One Application in a Window, the Others as Icons.

The desktop shown in Figure 2-20 represents a typical working environment. You keep the application that you use the most—in this example the Notepad—on the screen in an active window. You keep the applications that you call occasionally running as icons. When you want an application, you select it. When you are done with an application, you minimize it again, returning to an uncluttered desktop with your primary application occupying most of the screen. You used the programs from the earlier examples to illustrate this point. A more appropriate example is shown in Figure 2-21.

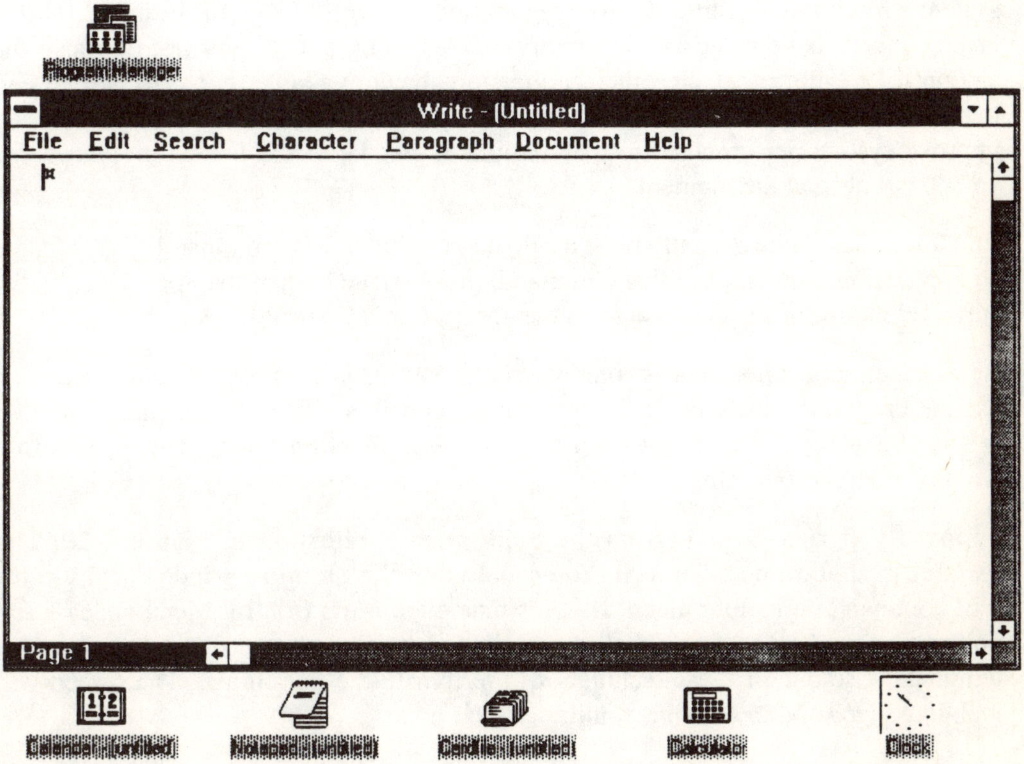

Figure 2-21. A Typical Desktop.

In this example the Write word processing application is the primary one, the Program Manager stands by as an icon at the top of the screen, and the desktop accessories are icons at the bottom. The Clock icon even keeps accurate time. You might arrange your desktop in a similar configuration each morning and work from that baseline throughout the day. Of course the applications and accessories that you would use would be ones of your personal choice.

This environment is very much like the traditional DOS environment where you load many memory-resident utilities to pop up over your main application when you need them. With Windows, however, you do not give up memory to those less frequently used utilities.

Exiting from Applications

Even though an application is an icon at the bottom of the desktop and is not using any significant screen space, it is still a running application and is using some of the system's resources just in order to hang around waiting to be used. In this respect it is very much like the old DOS memory-resident program. It does not diminish the amount of memory that the other applications have available, but it uses time and perhaps extended memory when it is swapped in and out. Sometimes you can improve system performance just by terminating some of the loaded programs that you do not need at the moment.

Windows applications usually have a File menu with an Exit command. To terminate an application, you can use this command, press Alt+F4 when the application is the current window, or select Close from the application's Control Menu.

Because an application that is running as an icon has a Control Menu too, you can use the Program Manager to exit the application if it is a Windows application. This is a convenience. You do not need to call the application up from its icon into a window in order to terminate it.

Suppose you want to exit from the Paintbrush application in Figure 2-20. The Paintbrush application is an icon. You can double click it into a window and use the Exit command on its File menu. If you single click it, its Control Menu appears and you can select Close. If its label is highlighted, you can press Ctrl-F4, and it will terminate. Use one of these techniques to terminate the Paintbrush. The screen will look like Figure 2-22, with the Paintbrush icon gone.

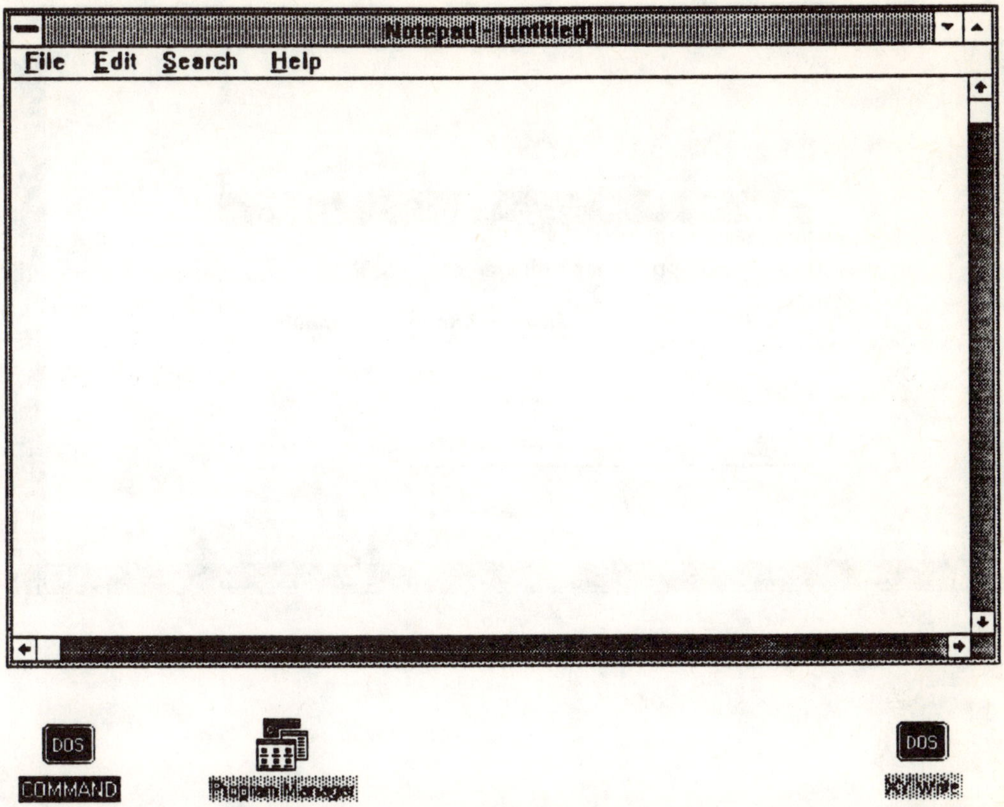

Figure 2-22. The Paintbrush Application Has Been Terminated.

You could try to terminate the Program Manager in the same way. If you do, it will try to exit from Windows as well. Try that now. You will see the usual Exit Windows dialogue box that you learned about in Chapter 1. Select OK. You will see the display shown in Figure 2-23.

The message in Figure 2-23 is telling you that the COMMAND Application is still active. The COMMAND application is the DOS Prompt application that you ran earlier to get into DOS so that you could run EDLIN. That program is still running. Its icon is in the lower left corner of the screen. Select OK to return to Figure 2-22.

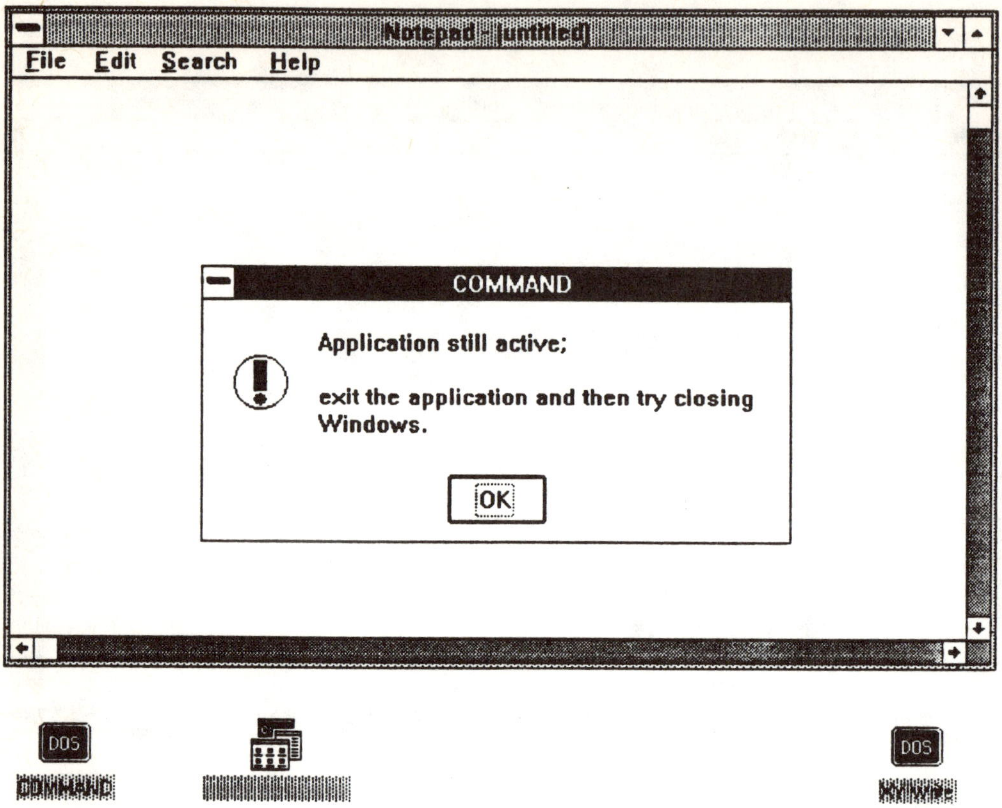

Figure 2-23. Trying To Exit the Program Manager—and Windows.

Now open the Control Menu for the DOS COMMAND icon. It looks like the one in Figure 2-24.

The Close command on the Control Menu in Figure 2-24 is not available. You can tell because the command's title is dimmer than the available ones. The only way to terminate this application is to switch into it and use its own facilities for terminating.

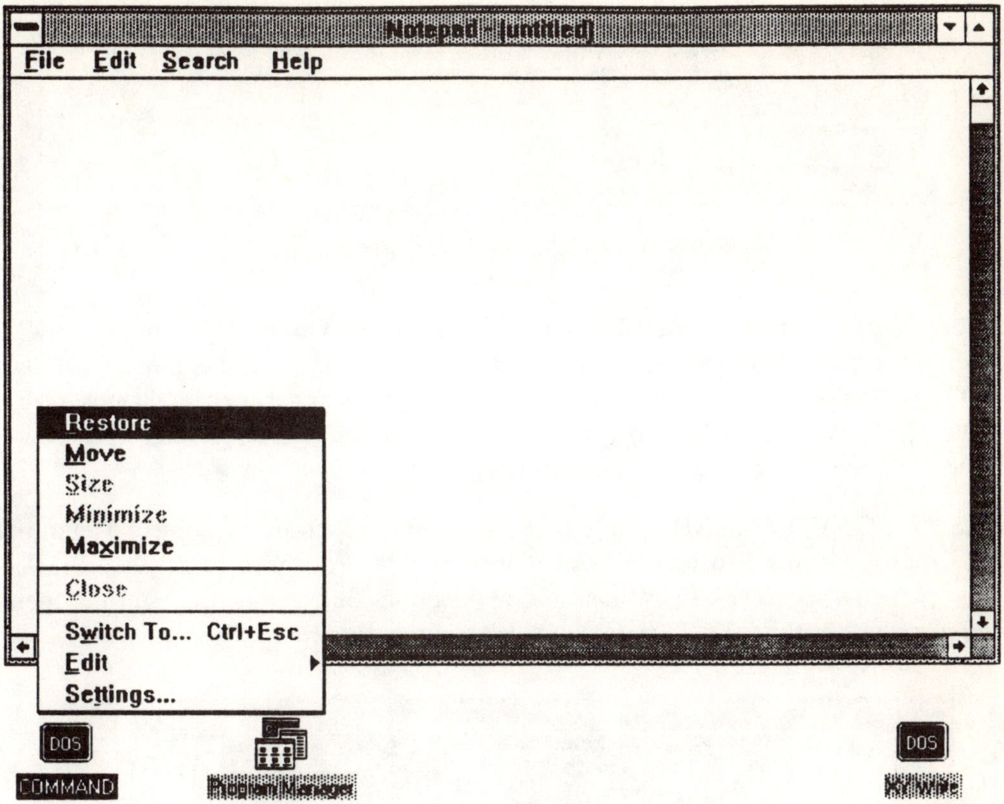

Figure 2-24. The DOS COMMAND Icon Control Menu.

With the Control Menu displayed as shown in Figure 2-24, press Enter to select Restore. Use the EDLIN Q command to quit EDLIN, answer Y to the question, and enter the DOS EXIT command to terminate the DOS session. This command sequence is shown in Figure 2-25.

```
The IBM Personal Computer DOS
Version 3.30 (C)Copyright International Business Machines Corp 1981, 1987
             (C)Copyright Microsoft Corp 1981, 1986

C>edlin teach.doc
End of input file
*q
Abort edit (Y/N)? y
C>exit
```

Figure 2-25. Terminating the EDLIN and DOS Session.

After you have terminated EDLIN and DOS, the DOS COMMAND icon goes away. Now you want to terminate XY Write. Remember that XY Write is a non-Windows DOS application that runs in a window. Also remember that you might not have a copy of XY Write installed, so you will have to follow this discussion in the book rather than running the exercise on your computer.

Like the DOS COMMAND icon, the DOS XY Write icon has a Control Menu, but the Control Menu's Close command is unavailable. You have to activate the XY Write window in order to terminate the application. Select Restore from the menu and type the XY Write QUIT command, as shown in Figure 2-26.

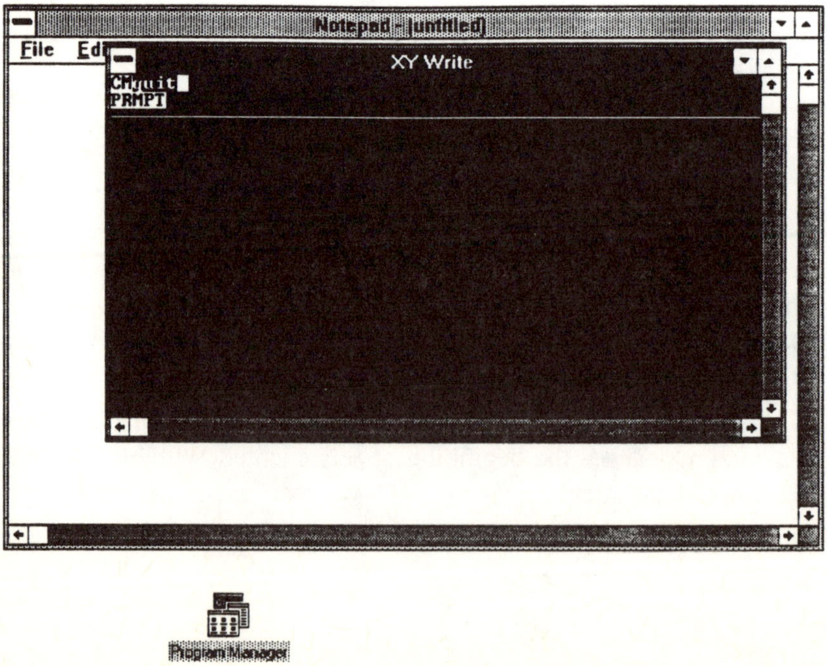

Figure 2-26. Quitting XY Write.

The only two applications remaining are the Notepad and the Program Manager. The Notepad is still a window, and the Program Manager is the only icon left at the bottom of the desktop, as shown in Figure 2-27.

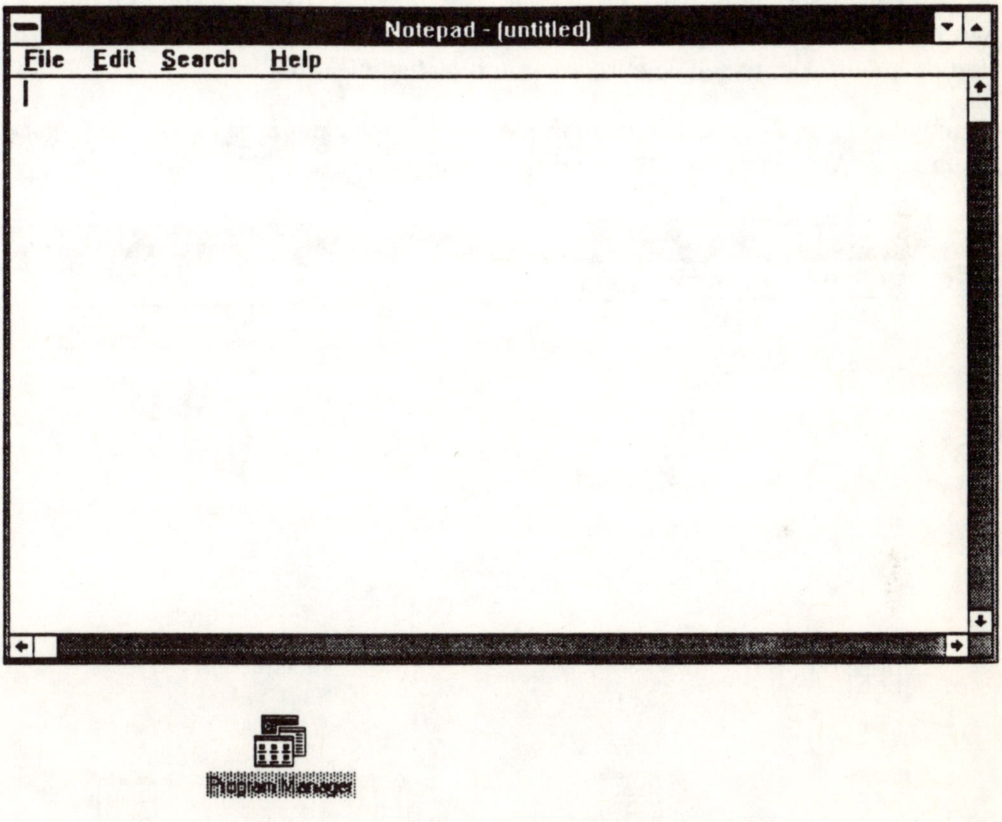

Figure 2-27. The Notepad and Program Manager.

Terminate the Notepad and open the Program Manager so that the display is similar to Figure 2-1, which appears at the beginning of this chapter. With all the shuffling of windows it is unlikely that the screen will be restored to its exact original configuration. You can try moving things around, or you might want to exit from Windows and restart it for the next series of lessons.

MANAGING GROUPS

The default Windows installation starts you out with the groups of applications that you have been working with here and in Chapter 1. It is unlikely that you will find this particular configuration suited to your taste or needs. To allow you to build your own custom organization of applications, the Program Manager supports the addition, modification, and deletion of groups and applications.

Begin with Figure 2-1 and minimize the Main group to clear away some work space. The Program Manager looks like the display shown in Figure 2-28.

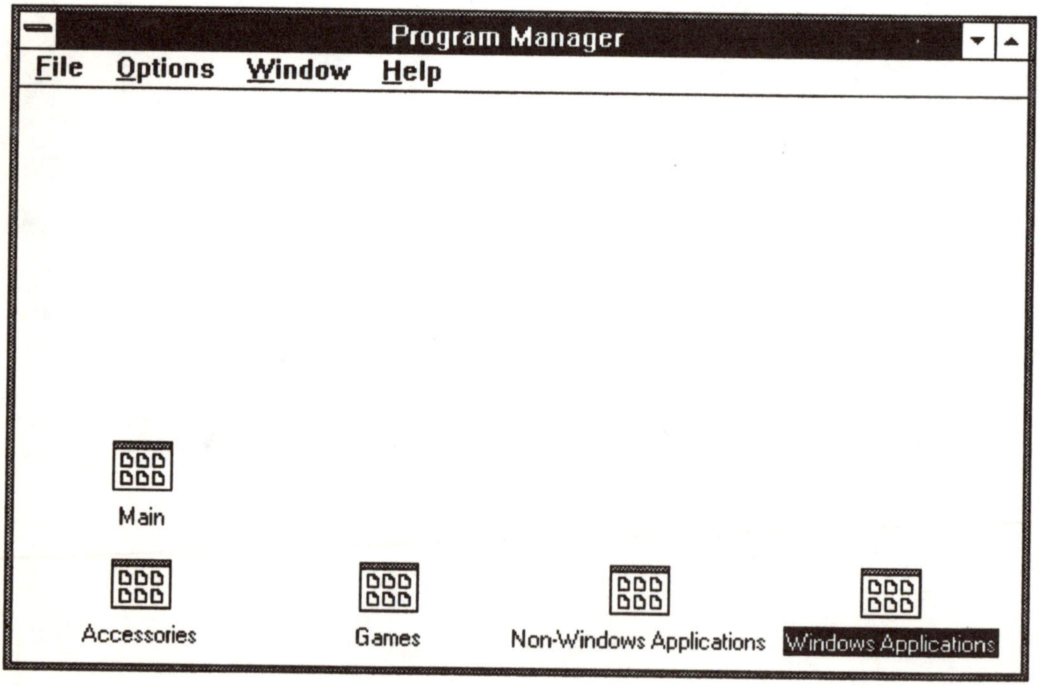

Figure 2-28. Beginning to Organize.

Adding Groups

Suppose that you keep records for a local civic organization and you want to organize the software that you use for this purpose. You have decided that you need a Civic group in your Program Manager. Open the Program Manager's File menu and select the New... command. You will see the dialogue box shown in Figure 2-29.

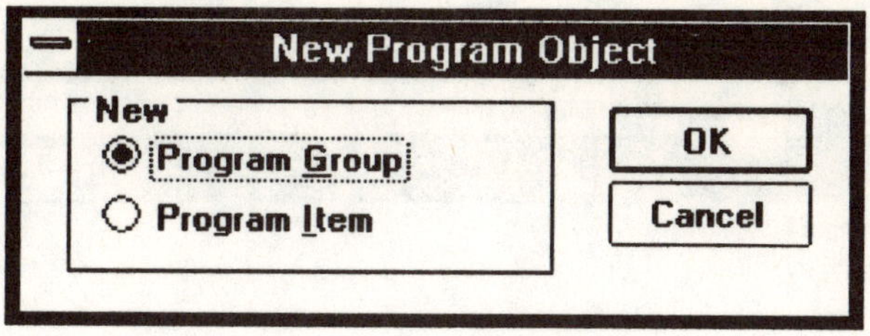

Figure 2-29. The New Program Object Dialogue Box: Groups.

The Program Group option button is already selected, so select OK. Figure 2-30 shows the next display: the Program Group Properties dialogue box.

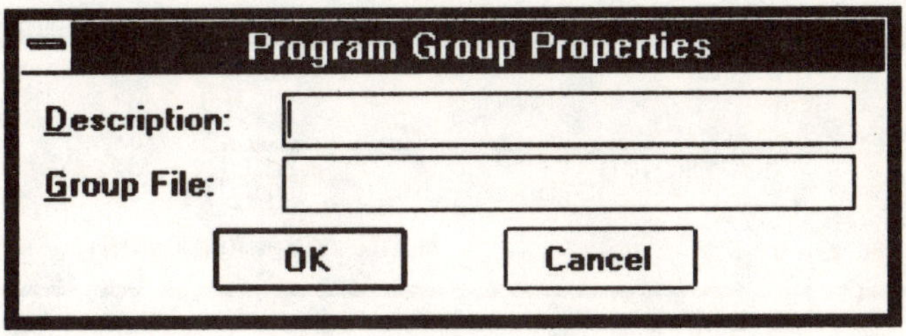

Figure 2-30. The Program Group Properties Dialogue Box.

Enter the name of your new group, Civic, into the Description field. You do not need to specify a Group File. Windows assigns a file name and remembers it for you. Select OK, and the Program Manager creates the new Civic group and opens its window, which is empty, as you can see in Figure 2-31. Minimize the Civic group to an icon.

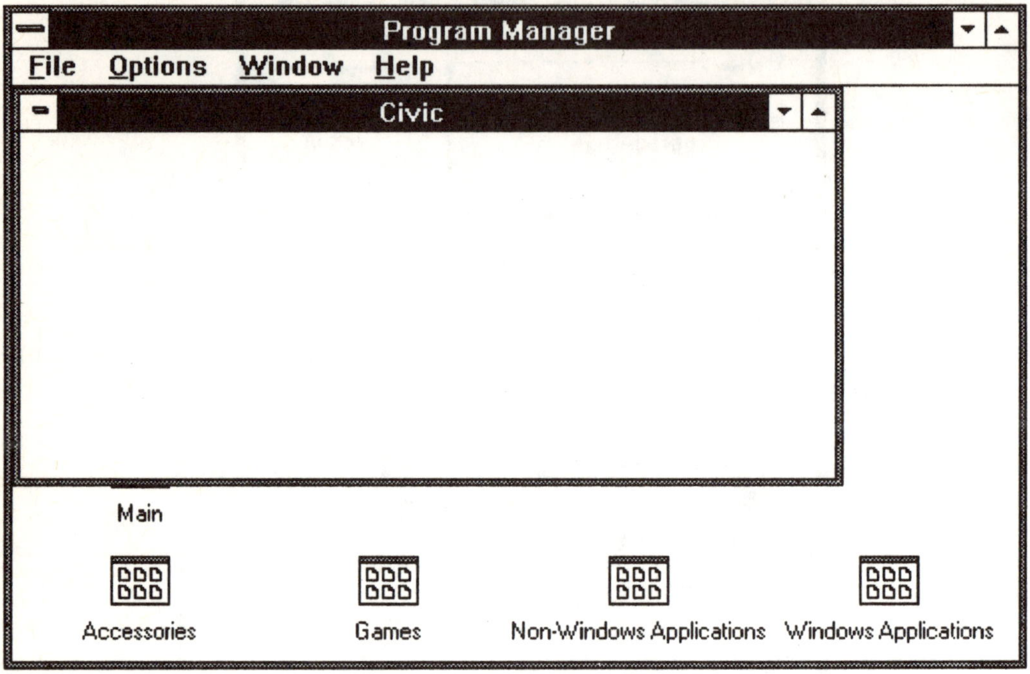

Figure 2-31. A New Empty Group Named Civic.

Deleting Groups

Suppose now that you decide that you do not need the Games group in the Program Manager. You want to delete it. Select the Games icon so that its label is highlighted and its Control Menu is not displayed. Then press Del or select Delete from the File menu. You will see the dialogue box shown in Figure 2-32.

Select Yes or No depending on whether you really meant to delete the group. For now select No. You can delete the group later if you wish.

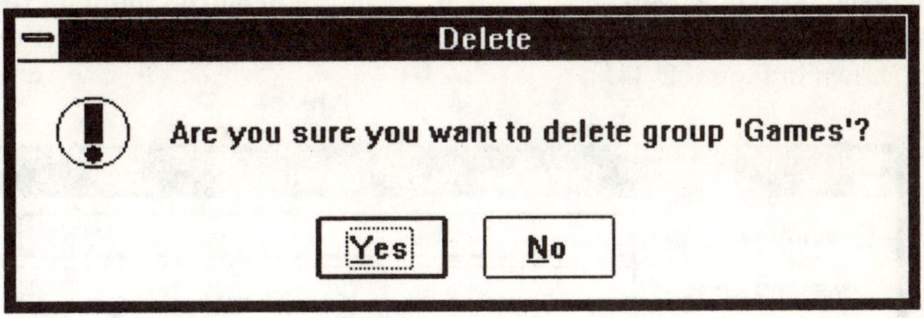

Figure 2-32. The Delete Group Dialogue Box.

Adding Applications

The Civic group still has no applications. For a group to be of use, you must install some applications into it. You can install existing Windows applications, new Windows applications that are not installed anywhere yet, non-Windows DOS applications that are already installed in another group, and new DOS applications.

Adding Windows Applications

One of your jobs is to maintain a list of members, and you decide that the Cardfile is just the application to handle the membership list. To add an application to a group, you must first activate the group's window. Select the Civic group now. Next select the New... command from the Program Manager's File menu. You will see the dialogue box shown in 2-33.

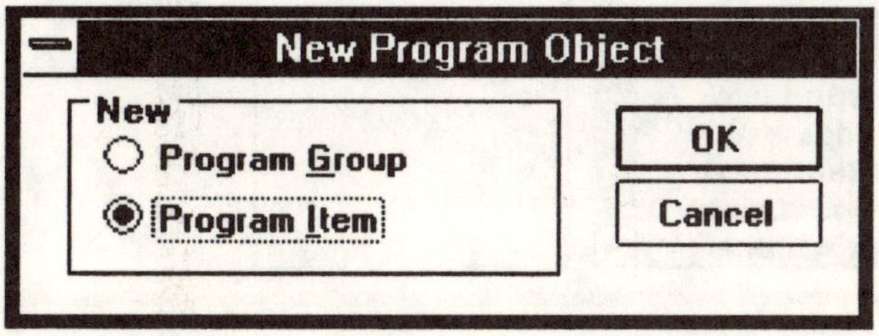

Figure 2-33. The New Program Object Dialogue Box: Applications.

The dialogue box is the same as the one in Figure 2-30 above, but the Program Item option button is selected. Select OK to see the Program Item Properties dialogue box, as shown in Figure 2-34.

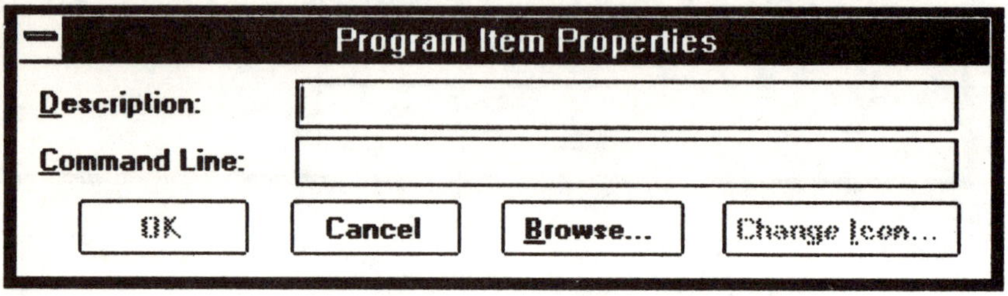

Figure 2-34. The Program Item Properties Dialogue Box.

You can enter the Description field as "Membership Roster," but you do not know the command line necessary to execute the Cardfile application. The Program Manager will help you with that. Select Browse from the dialogue box. You will see the Browse dialogue box, as shown in Figure 2-35.

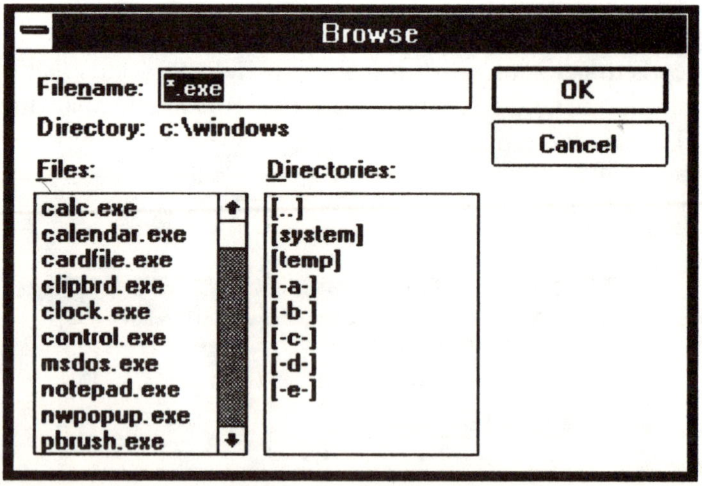

Figure 2-35. The Browse Dialogue Box.

The Browse dialogue box is a standard Windows File Open dialogue box. You learned about it in Chapter 1. For this example, you do not need to search the disk system for the program you want to install. The cardfile.exe file is in clear view. Select it by double clicking or by moving the cursor to it and selecting OK. The program's path and command appear in the Command Line field of the Program Item Properties dialogue box, as shown in Figure 2-36.

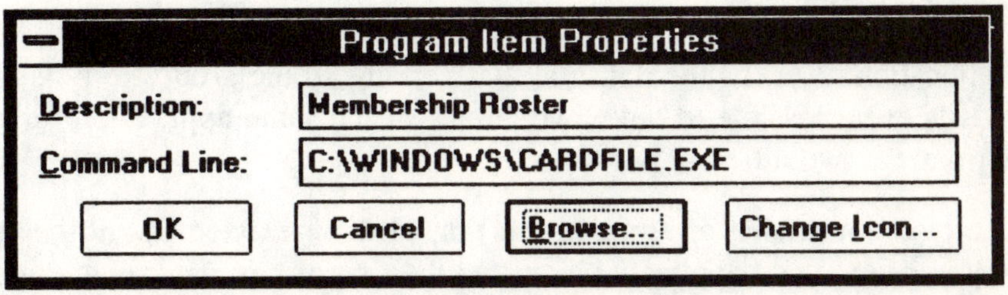

Figure 2-36. The Program Item Properties Dialogue Box Filled In.

Select OK, and the Program Manager adds the Cardfile application to the Civic group with the name Membership Roster, as shown in Figure 2-37.

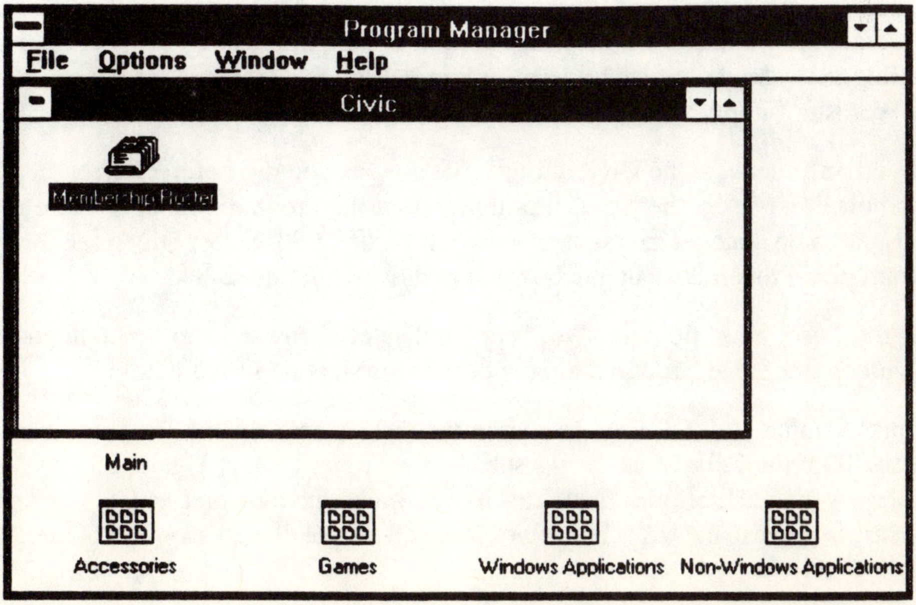

Figure 2-37. An Application Added to the Civic Group.

You must realize that even though you added the Cardfile application to the Civic group, it still exists in the Accessories group. These are not redundant records of the same application. This operation did not make a copy of all the program's files. It simply added a pointer to the program from within another group, which is a natural way to organize software. You could conceivably add the Cardfile application to several groups: one for sales leads; one for family names, addresses, and birthdays; one for maintenance records on your cars, boat, and appliances; and one for recipes.

Later you will learn how to customize these duplicate applications so that when you start an application, it opens the data file that pertains to the group from where you started it. It is even possible to have two copies of the same application running in the same group for two different purposes.

In this exercise you added an application that already existed in another group. Normally you need to add applications only to the first group. After that you simply move and copy applications between groups. You will learn that technique later.

Adding Non-Windows DOS Applications

Another of your jobs for the civic organization is as editor and publisher of the newsletter. You prefer to use Windows Write and Paintbrush to publish the newsletter, but many of the members submit articles, and they all use dependable old Wordstar. To import and edit their work, you will need Wordstar installed into your Civic group. If you have Wordstar installed as a DOS application on your hard disk, installing it is almost the same as installing a Windows application. If you do not have Wordstar, simply work through the following exercises.

First you must activate the Civic group's window as you did before. Select the Civic group now. Next select the New... command from the Program Manager's File menu. This is the same dialogue box that is shown in Figure 2-33. Select OK to see the same Program Item Properties dialogue box that is shown in Figure 2-34.

Enter the Description field as "Wordstar" and select Browse from the dialogue box. You will see the same Browse dialogue box that is shown in Figure 2-35.

For this example you will need to search the disk system for the Wordstar program. Wordstar is on the C: drive in the \ws subdirectory. Refer back to Figure 2-35 and select the [..] entry in the Directories field. This moves you to the root directory. Now select the [ws] entry to move to the \ws subdirectory. You will see the display shown in Figure 2-38.

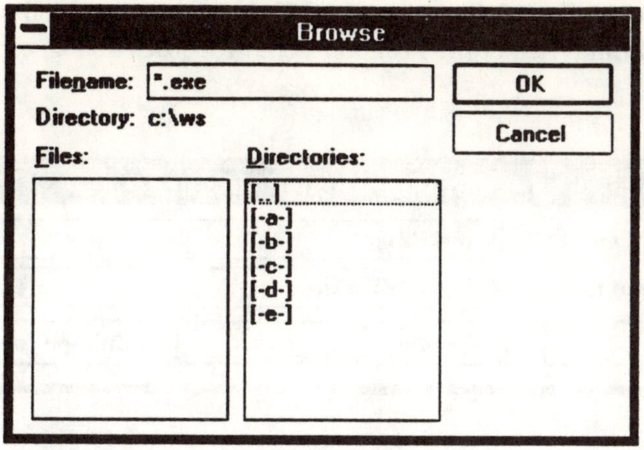

Figure 2-38. The Wordstar Subdirectory: No .EXE Files.

The \ws subdirectory appears to be empty, but that is because the Filename field has the value *.exe. Apparently there are no .exe files in Wordstar. Change the Filename field to *.* and see the display shown in Figure 2-39.

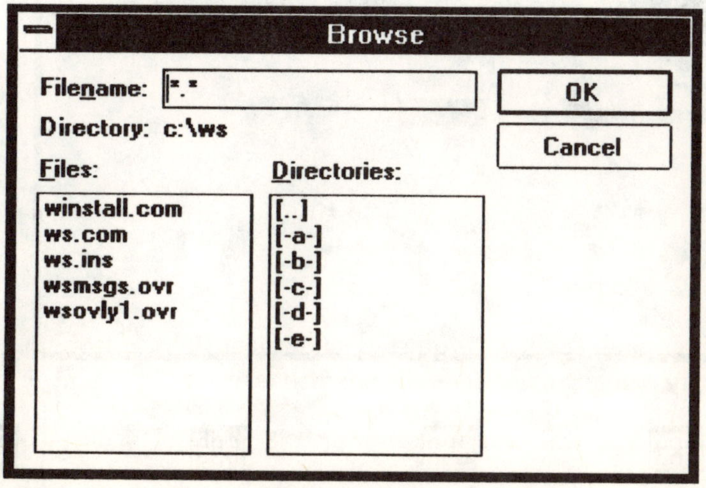

Figure 2-39. The Wordstar Subdirectory Files.

Select the ws.com entry and then select OK. The Wordstar path and command appear in the Command Line field of the Program Item Properties dialogue box, as shown in Figure 2-40.

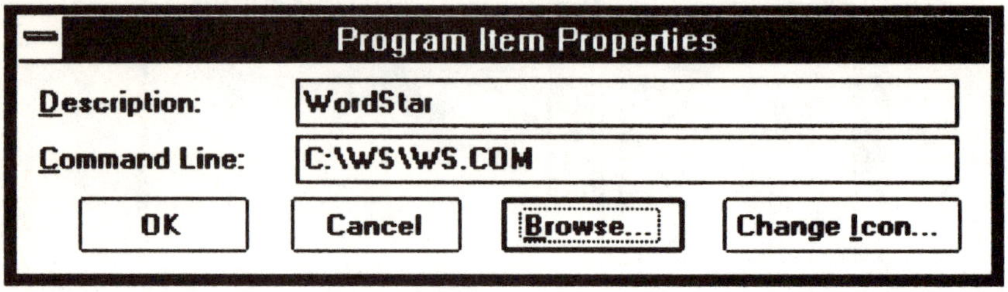

Figure 2-40. Wordstar Ready to be Installed.

Select OK, and you will see the Wordstar program installed into the Civic group, as shown in Figure 2-41.

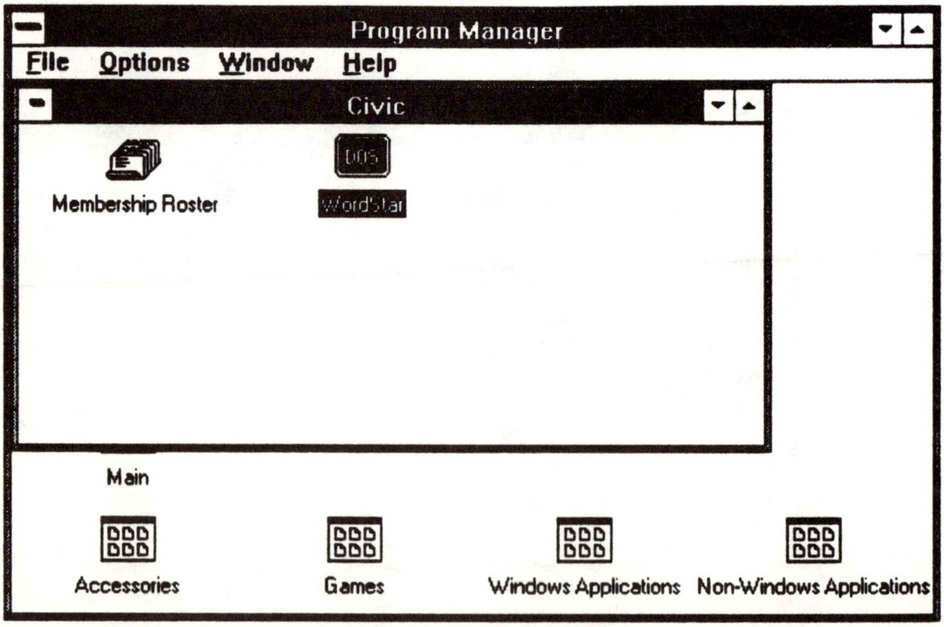

Figure 2-41. Wordstar Added to the Civic Group.

Deleting Applications

That Games group might still be bothering you. How much of it do you really need? Minimize the Civic group and activate the Games group window to see what is in it; it is shown in Figure 2-4. You decide that you might want to play Reversi from time to time, but that you do not need Solitaire, so you decide to delete it. Select the Delete command from the Program Manager's File menu. You will see the Delete dialogue box shown in Figure 2-42.

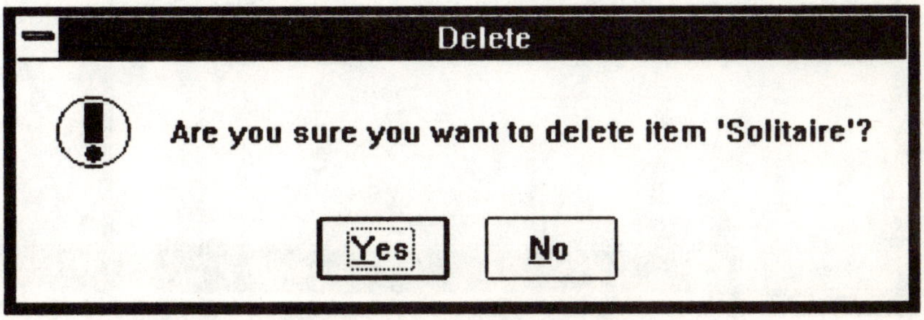

Figure 2-42. The Delete Item Dialogue Box.

This dialogue box is almost the same as the one shown in Figure 2-32, where you started to delete the Games group. What is more, both of them are displayed by selecting the Delete command on the File menu or by pressing the Del key. The difference is that when you selected Delete this time, there was a group window active. When you selected Delete before, no group window was active, but an icon was selected.

When a group window is active, the Delete command refers to the application in that window that is currently highlighted. When no group window is active, the Delete command refers to the group icon that is currently highlighted. This is an important distinction. It would not be difficult to delete one thing when you intended to delete something else, particularly when the dialogue boxes are so similar.

You can delete either of the Games if you wish. No further exercise depends on them. The illustrations in the book, however, will continue to show the Games group icon. You can minimize the Games group at this time.

Moving Applications Between Groups

Remember that you are responsible for your civic organization's newsletter. You will need the Write and Paintbrush applications for that job, so you must move them into the Civic group. First activate the Civic window and then activate the Accessories window.

Move the Accessories window down and to one side so that you can see enough of the Civic window to hold two more icons. Figure 2-43 shows how that might look.

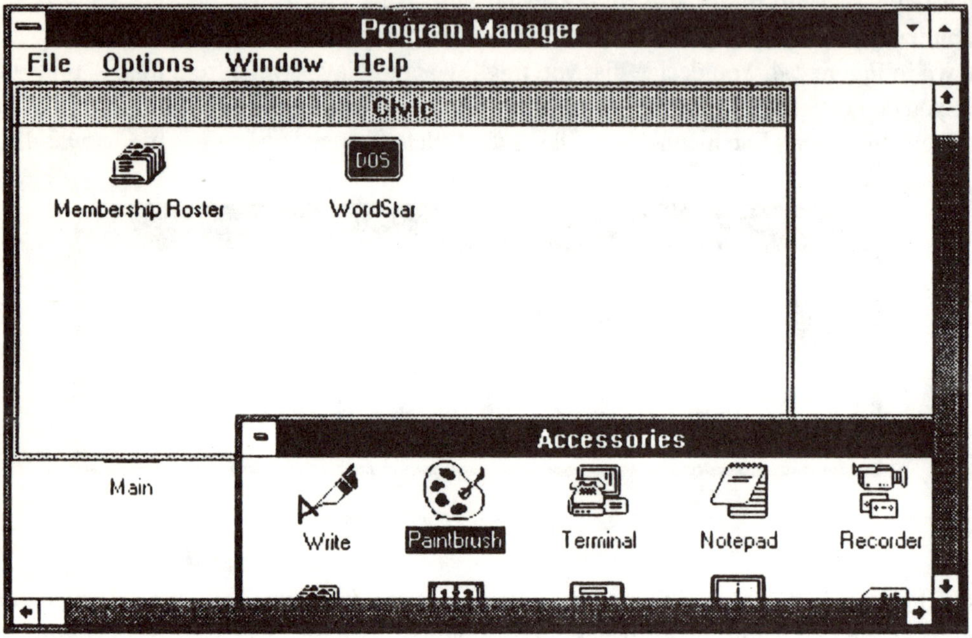

Figure 2-43. Preparing to Move Applications.

Moving an Application with the Mouse

Place the mouse cursor on the Write icon and press and hold the left button. Drag the icon from the Accessories window onto the Civic window. Release the button, and the screen will look like Figure 2-44, with the Write icon absent from the Accessories group and newly resident in the Civic group.

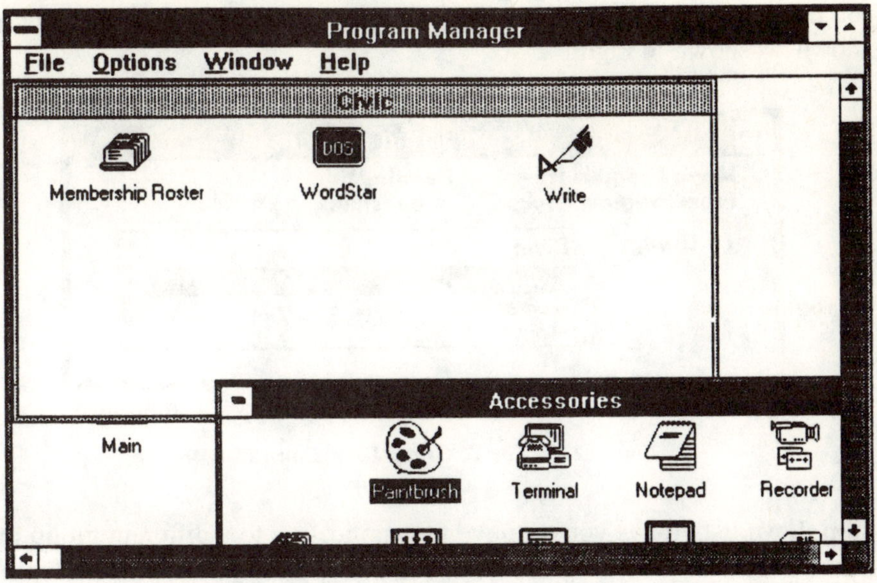

Figure 2-44. The Write Application Moved to The Civic Group.

Moving an Application with the Keyboard

Select the Paintbrush icon with the arrow keys, then open the Program Manager's File menu and select the Move... command. You will see the Move Program Item dialogue box, as shown in Figure 2-45.

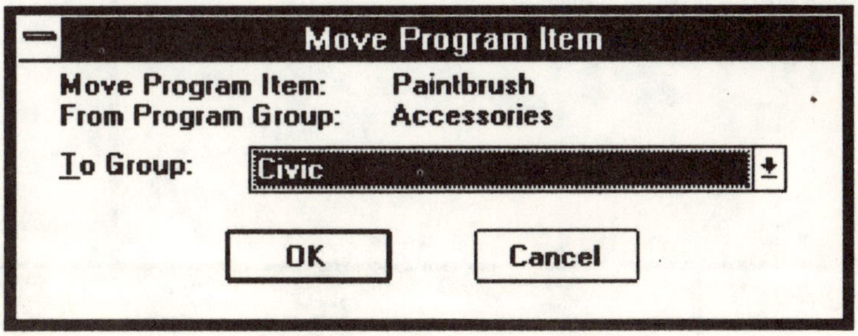

Figure 2-45. The Move Program Item Dialogue Box.

The To Group field is a drop-down list. When you select it, a list of all the groups drops down, as shown in Figure 2-46.

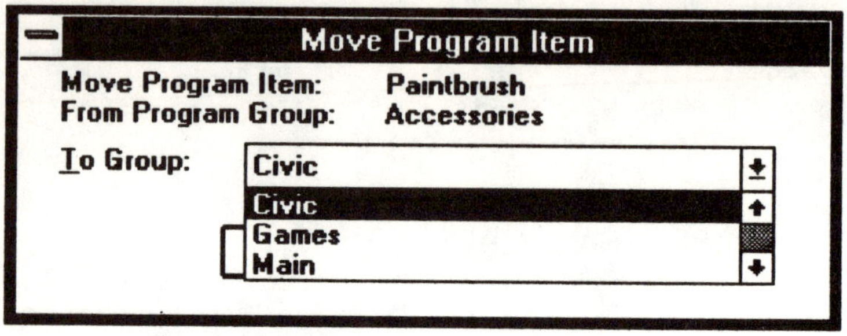

Figure 2-46. The To Group Drop-Down List.

This drop-down list allows you to move the application to a different group than the one displayed in the To Group field. For this exercise, you want the one already there, so ignore the list and select OK. This command moves the Paintbrush application from the Accessories group into the Civic group. You will see the display shown in Figure 2-47.

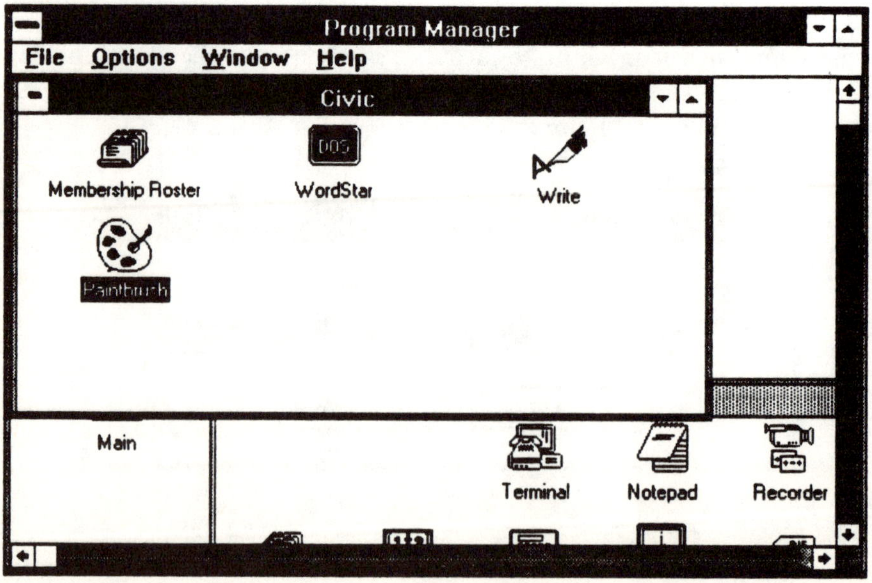

Figure 2-47. The Paintbrush Application Moved to the Civic Group.

Copying an Application to Another Group

Moving the two applications has set up the Civic group the way you want, but now you see a problem. You still want the applications in the Accessories group for other uses, and you just moved them out. The answer, of course, is to copy them back into the Accessories group.

Copying an Application with the Mouse

You copy an application with the mouse the same way that you move it, except that you hold down the Ctrl key while you drag the icon.

Try that now by dragging the Write icon from the Civic group to the Accessories group with the Ctrl key held down. Drag the icon to the lower part of the Accessories window that is visible in Figure 2-47 above. Observe that as you drag the icon you are dragging a copy. The original stays in place.

Copying an Application with the Keyboard

Copying an application with the keyboard is also much like moving an application. Select the Paintbrush icon in the Civic window with the arrow keys. Next select the Copy... command from the Program Manager's File menu. You will see the Copy Program Item dialogue box, as shown in Figure 2-48.

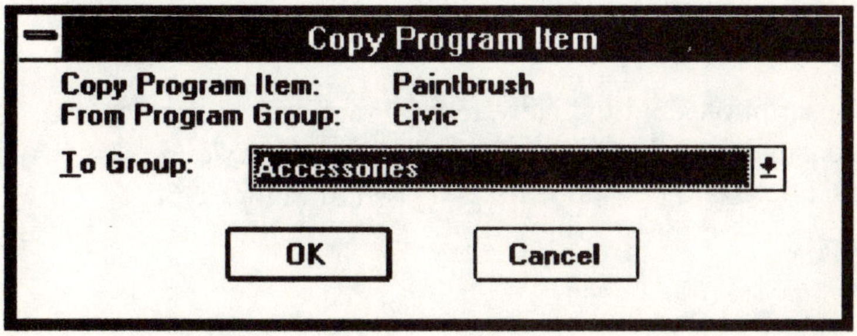

Figure 2-48. The Copy Program Item Dialogue Box.

The Copy Program Item dialogue box works like the dialogue box for moving an application. Select OK, and the Paintbrush icon is copied to the Accessories window. It might not be in view, so maximize the window and arrange the icons to your liking. Most likely the order will not be the same as before. Do not worry about that. Minimize the Accessories window to an icon and return to the Civic group window.

Changing Properties

You are not stuck with the way an application works or the way its icon appears in the group window just because you copied it from another group. You can change its description, its icon, and its command line by modifying its properties.

Changing the Icon Description

The Write and Paintbrush icons in the Civic group are not very descriptive as to their purpose. You installed them in Civic to support the newsletter, but nothing in the displays of their icons tells you that. You can change an icon's description by changing the application's properties. Select the Paintbrush icon so that its label is highlighted. Select the Properties... command from the File menu. You will see the Program Item Properties dialogue box shown in Figure 2-49.

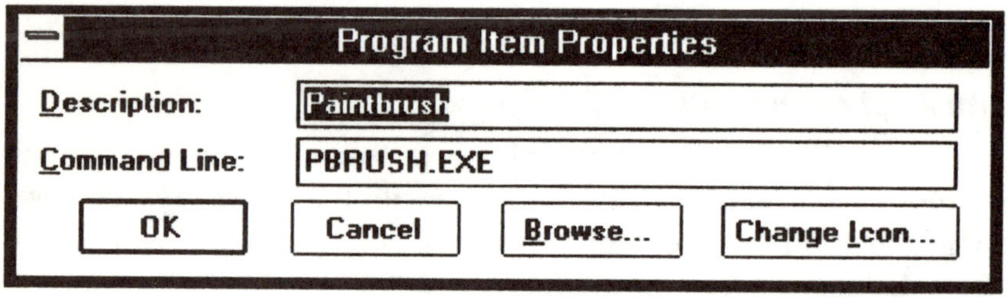

Figure 2-49. The Program Item Properties Dialogue Box.

Change the Description field to "Newsletter Graphics" and select OK. Use the same procedure to change the label on the Write icon to "Newsletter Text." With the icons renamed, the Civic group now appears as shown in Figure 2-50.

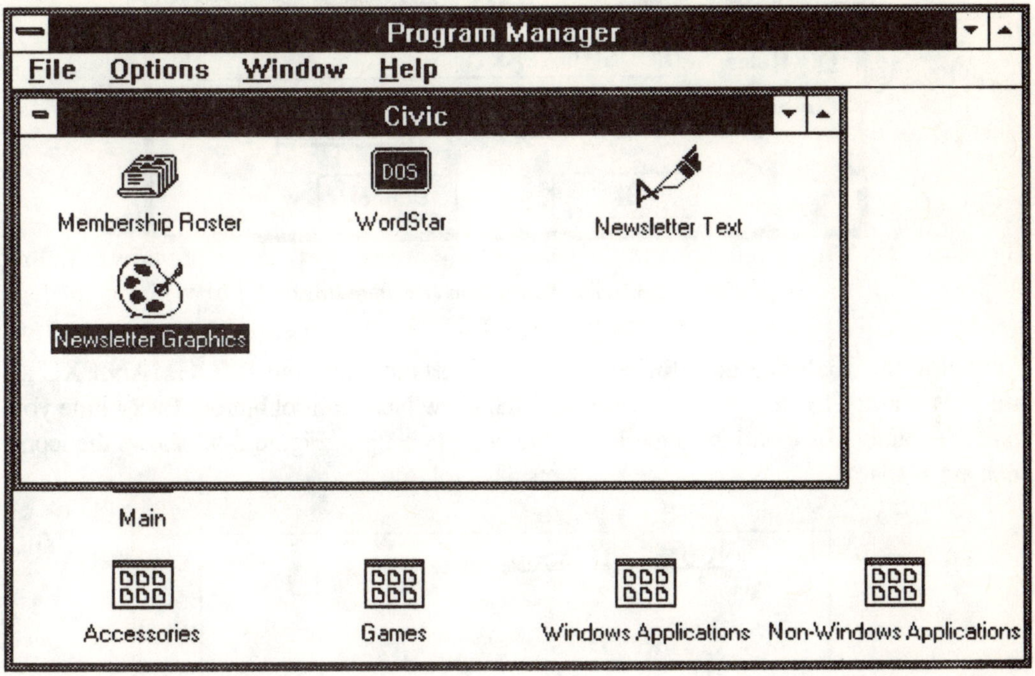

Figure 2-50. The Civic Group with Renamed Icons.

Changing the Icon

Most Windows applications are bound to an icon that the application developer designed and installed into the program. The Cardfile, Write, and Paintbrush applications all have fixed icons. The Wordstar application does not, however, because it is a DOS application. Few developers were thinking about icons and graphical operating environments when Wordstar was first designed in the 1970s.

The DOS icon indicates that Wordstar is a DOS application. But there are other icons available for DOS applications, icons that describe the nature of the application rather than the environment in which it runs. You can change the icon of a DOS application from the Program Item Properties dialogue box.

Highlight the DOS Wordstar icon and select the Properties... command from the File menu. Select the Change Icon control button from the Program Item Properties dialogue box. You will see the Select Icon dialogue box shown in Figure 2-51.

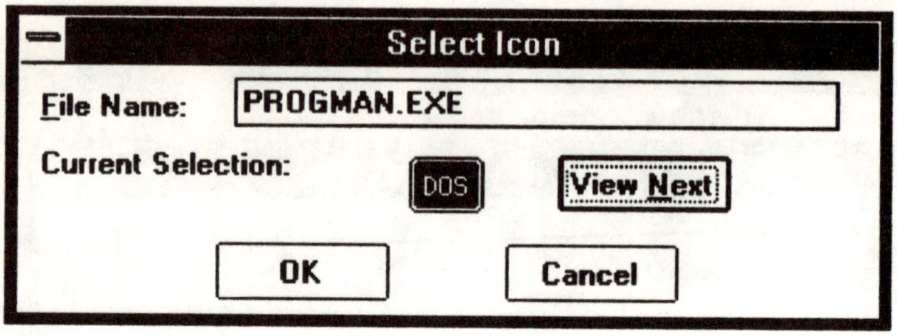

Figure 2-51. The Select Icon Dialogue Box.

Selecting this dialogue box, for some peculiar reason, calls out PROGMAN.EXE as the File Name. To change icons, you select the View Next control button. Every time you push the button the icon just to the left of the button changes. Figure 2-52 shows the icons that are available.

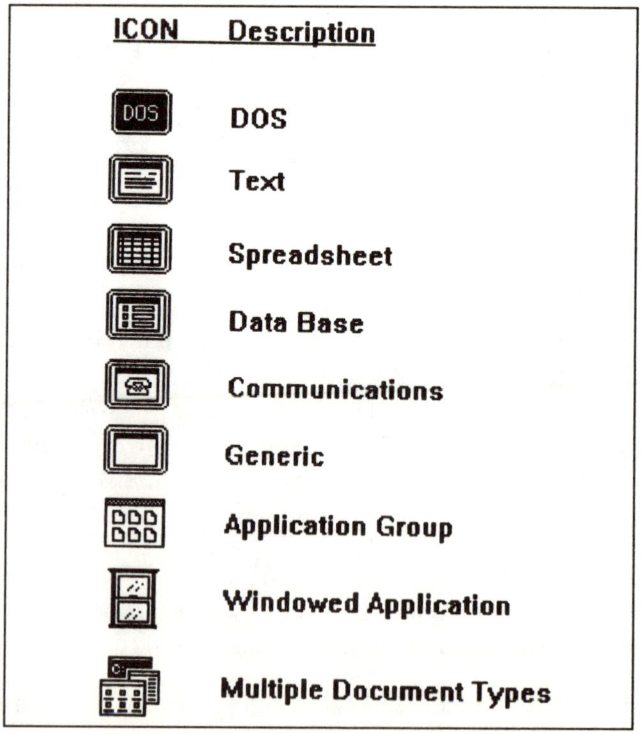

Figure 2-52. Application Icons.

Because Wordstar is a word processor, you might choose the Text icon to represent it. When that icon is in view in the Select Icon dialogue box, select OK. That selection returns you to the Program Item Properties dialogue box. Select OK there as well. The icon for the Wordstar application is now changed, as shown in Figure 2-53.

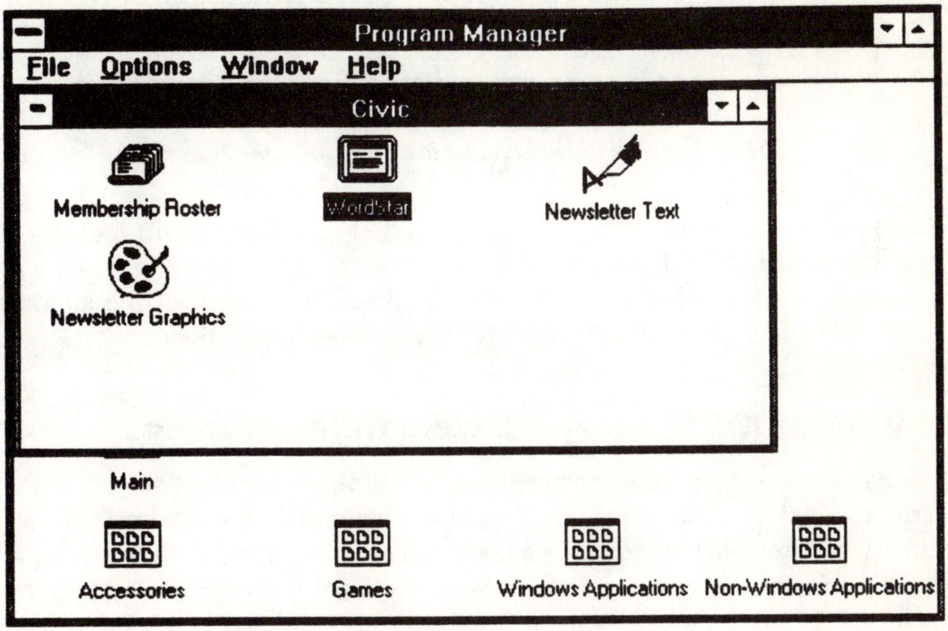

Figure 2-53. The Changed Wordstar Icon.

Running an Application with a Named Document

If you were to run the Membership Roster Cardfile application from the Civic group now, it would begin with no data base in place. You would need to use its File menu to locate and load the data base that represents your membership roster. Rather than do that every time, you can configure the Membership Roster Cardfile to load the appropriate data base each time you start the application.

Most Windows applications and many DOS applications allow you to specify a file name on the command line when you run the program. By adding the file name to the Command Line field in the Program Item Properties dialogue box, you tell the Program Manager to run the program with the specified file. Highlight the Membership Roster icon and select the Properties... command on the File menu. Add the filename "members" to the Command Line field, as shown in Figure 2-54.

Figure 2-54. A File Name Added to a Command Line Property.

When you run the Membership Roster Cardfile application, it will look for a file named MEMBERS.CRD. Because that file does not exist yet, the program will not load a file. You will need to create the file from within the Cardfile application. Chapter 10 includes a section on the Cardfile accessory application.

Running a DOS Memory-Resident Utility Program

DOS users know about the memory-resident program also called the TSR, (for "Terminate-and-Stay-Resident"). A TSR is a program that remains resident in DOS memory; you execute it by pressing a hot key. The TSR interrupts the program that is currently running and pops up over it. When you exit from the TSR, it restores the screen and returns to the program that it interrupted.

Two primary disadvantages of the TSR programs are that they occupy memory even when you are not running them and that there is no standard way of implementing them, resulting in many incompatibilities among different TSRs and programs that they interrupt. Nonetheless, some TSR programs have value to users who do not want to give them up when moving to the Windows graphical operating environment. Until the purveyors of those programs release Windows-compatible versions, the old TSRs must remain.

There are three ways to run a TSR from Windows. The first way is to load the TSR into memory before you run Windows. The disadvantages to this are: 1) The TSR's memory is not available to Windows; 2) Many TSRs do not pop up when the screen is in a graphics display mode (which is always the case when you are running Windows); and 3) Some TSRs behave in ways that are incompatible with Windows.

The second way to run a TSR is to open the DOS Prompt icon from the Main group, load the TSR, pop it up, and return to Windows by pressing Alt-Esc. The TSR is now a DOS Prompt icon at the bottom of the desktop. You can click it on whenever you want it. In this configuration the TSR uses Windows resources to remain loaded the same as any other minimized program.

The third and recommended way to run a TSR is to install it as a non-Windows DOS application—the same way you did in the section titled "Adding Non-Windows DOS Applications" earlier in this chapter. Figure 2-5 earlier in this chapter shows the Sidekick application installed into the Non-Windows Applications group. Sidekick is a TSR. If you have Sidekick, the Setup program could have installed it for you. If not, install it now to run the next exercise.

Open the Non-Windows Applications group and select Sidekick. Windows switches to a DOS full screen session, loads Sidekick, and displays the screen shown in Figure 2-55.

You can execute the TSR by pressing its hot key. You can return to Windows at any time by pressing Alt-Esc to keep the TSR running. If you are finished with the TSR and do not want to commit Windows resources to keeping it resident, pop it down and press Ctrl-C.

```
SideKick                    Version 1.56A
                          IBM-PC/XT/AT/PCjr

AST Research Version 1.56A

Copyright (C) 1984,85 BORLAND Inc.


Full System

655360 bytes total memory
512032 bytes were free
447440 bytes free


C>

              MICROSOFT WINDOWS POP-UP PROGRAM SUPPORT

     Your pop-up program is ready to run. When you have finished using
     it, press Ctrl+C to close this window and return to Windows.
```

Figure 2-55. Running a DOS Memory-Resident Program.

SUMMARY

With the completion of this chapter, you have learned enough of Windows to use it in many different ways. Now that you understand the operations of the common user interface and the Program Manager, you are ready to install and use other applications.

Chapter 3 discusses the Windows File Manager, an alternative shell to the Program Manager. You can use the File Manager to view the structure of your hard disk's subdirectories and to move, copy, and delete files. You can also use it to execute programs and format and copy diskettes.

Chapter 3

The File Manager

In Chapter 2 you learned to organize your applications into functional groups and to install different copies of the same application to operate on different documents, depending upon the nature of the group. This chapter will teach you to organize your document and program files.

The File Manager is the tool that allows you to manage your hard disk system. It provides a clear view of the subdirectory structure of your disks, allowing you to navigate between drives and among the subdirectories and files of each drive. It includes commands that move, copy, and delete single files, subdirectories, selected groups of files, and selected groups of subdirectories. You can rename your disk drive, any file, and any subdirectory. You can search for files, copy diskettes, format diskettes, and view and change the attributes of files. You can also use the File Manager to execute applications as an alternative to using the Program Manager.

You can associate document files with applications so that when you select the document or any document with the associated file name extension, the File Manager automatically executes the associated application.

SUBDIRECTORIES AND FILES

A DOS disk system consists of files and subdirectories. It is organized into a root directory with subordinate subdirectories. A subdirectory can contain files, as well as subdirectories of its own. The File Manager provides a windowed user interface for the management of the DOS subdirectory and file structure.

An Analogy: The File Cabinet

Think of your disk system as a file cabinet. The drawers are disk drives. You can remove some of the drawers (floppies), while others (hard drives) are fixed in the cabinet. A drawer, like a disk's root directory, can contain folders, which are analogous to subdirectories. You can toss paper files into the drawer without placing them in a folder. These paper files are like the files that you can store in the root directory along with the subdirectories. A folder (subdirectory) can contain paper files and other folders.

Some of the paper files in a file cabinet are forms, letters, ledgers, etc. These files are analogous to the document files in a disk subdirectory. Paper files can also be operational procedures. These files resemble applications files in your system.

Managing the Files

Just as you can throw things into a file cabinet without order or organization, you can create subdirectories and files on a disk system without giving much thought to their location and purpose. The File Manager gives you improved visibility into your file system and provides the tools to move, copy, delete, and rename things. The File Manager cannot force you to be orderly, but if you decide that you want to get organized, the File Manager provides the means to do it.

If you never pay any attention to where you store your document files, chances are you will always store them in the Windows subdirectory. Recall that in Chapter 2 you built your first Membership Roster Cardfile record. Because you specified its filename only, Windows assigned it to the current subdirectory for the current drive, which happened to be C:\WINDOWS. That practice is acceptable for these exercises, but if you continue it into your routine business, your filing system will lack order and organization.

This chapter introduces the tools for organizing your disk system. After that, it is up to you to use them.

RUNNING THE FILE MANAGER

The File Manager is a Windows application installed in the Main group. To run it you open the Main group window and select the File Manager. You will see a display similar to the one shown in Figure 3-1.

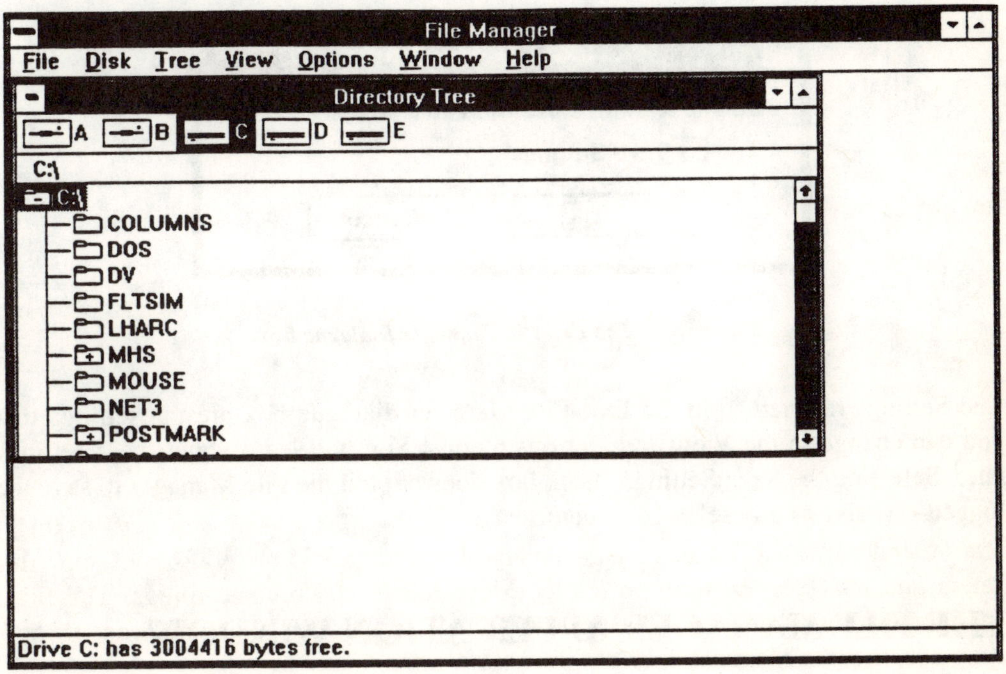

Figure 3-1. The File Manager.

The File Manager display shows the File Manager application window with the Directory Tree document window. This display is the one you see each time you execute the File Manager. The disk drive selection is the drive from which you run Windows; in Figure 3-1 it is the C drive. The directory names in the Directory Tree document window are the names of the directories on your disk system; they will, of course, be different from the ones you see in Figure 3-1.

EXITING FROM THE FILE MANAGER

You exit from the File Manager the same way you exit from any Windows application. Before you exit, the File Manager displays the Exit File Manager dialogue box shown in Figure 3-2.

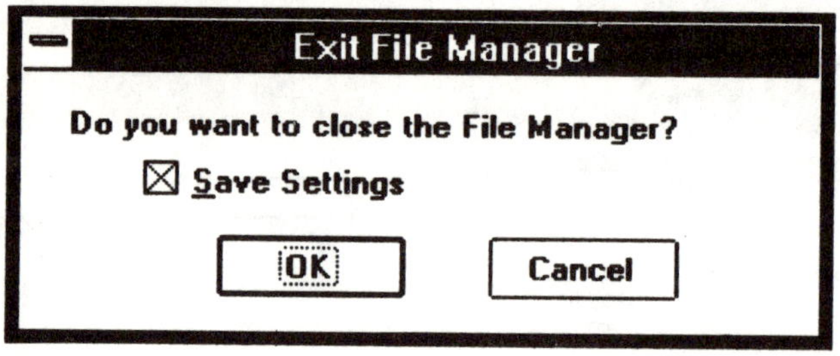

Figure 3-2. The Exit File Manager Dialogue Box.

The Settings referred to in the Exit File Manager dialogue box are the settings that you can change in the View and Options menus. You will learn about these settings later. Selecting the Save Settings check box does not tell the File Manager to save the logged-on drive or any selected directories.

THE FILE MANAGER APPLICATION WINDOW

The File Manager application window has the File Manager menu bar at the top and contains all of the File Manager's document windows and icons. The directory tree, described next, is always present—either as a window or as an icon.

The Status Bar

The bottom line of the File Manager has the status bar, which tells you how much space is available on the selected drive. You can use the status bar toggle command on the Options menu to turn the status bar on and off. When you have many directories and document windows displayed, you might need that extra line at the bottom of the window—you can get it by turning off the status bar toggle.

THE DIRECTORY TREE

The Directory Tree window displays the subdirectories in the root directories of the selected drive. The top line of the window has icons that represent the drives installed on your system.

Disk Drives

The floppy disk drives—A and B in Figure 3-1—use icons that look like a diskette drive with its diskette slot. The hard disk drives—C, D, and E in Figure 3-1—use icons that look like the front of a hard disk drive.

The current disk drive—C in Figure 3-1—is highlighted. You can change the current drive by clicking a different icon. To change drives with the keyboard, press Tab. The current drive icon is surrounded by a dotted box to indicate that you are selecting a drive. Use the left and right arrow keys to move the dotted box to the drive you want to select and press the Enter key. The File Manager reads in the directories for the new drive and displays them in the Directory Tree document window.

Directories

The folder icons in the Directory Tree document window represent directories on the disk. Observe that in Figure 3-1 the root directory, C:\, is highlighted, indicating that it is the current selected directory. If you click a different directory, it becomes highlighted. You can use the arrow keys to move the highlighting to a different directory. As you move the highlight down below the directory at the bottom of the window, the screen scrolls up. Figure 3-3 shows WINDOWS as the selected directory.

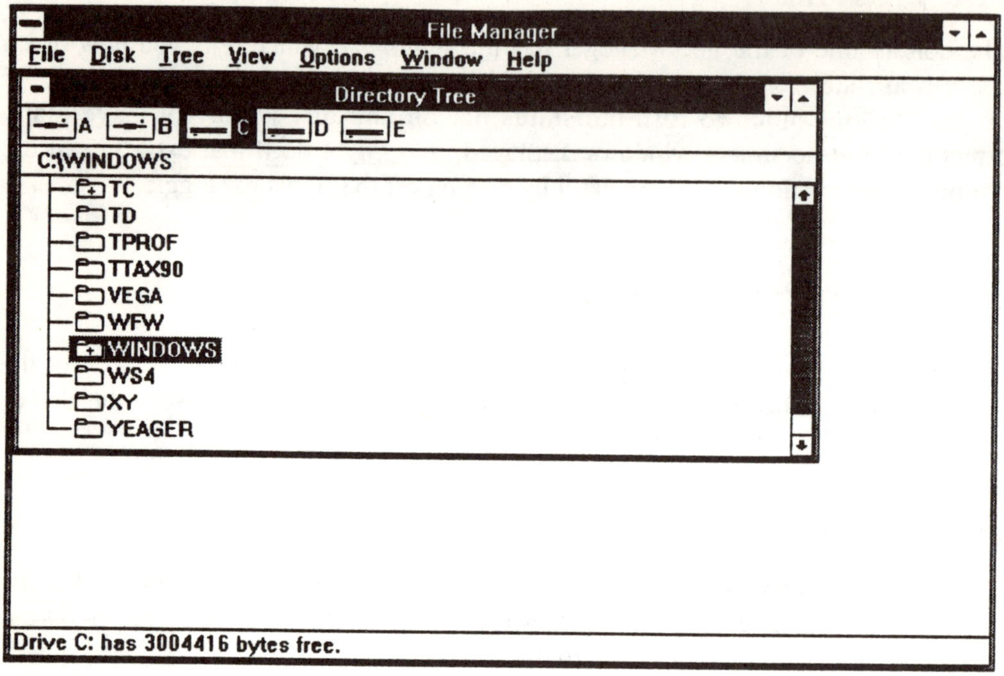

Figure 3-3. Selecting a Different Directory.

The text line just below the disk drive icons always displays the full DOS path of the current selected directory. This display is convenient in case you use the scroll bar to scroll the window so that the highlighted folder is out of view. You can always determine the selected directory from the DOS path display.

Subdirectories

The WINDOWS folder icon in Figure 3-3 has a small plus sign (+) in the icon. This plus sign means that the directory has subdirectories. If you click the plus sign or press the + key while the directory is highlighted, the directory will expand to display its subdirectories, as shown in Figure 3-4.

After you expand a directory, its plus sign changes to a minus sign (-). You can click the minus sign or press the Hyphen key to compress the subdirectories so that the display looks like Figure 3-1.

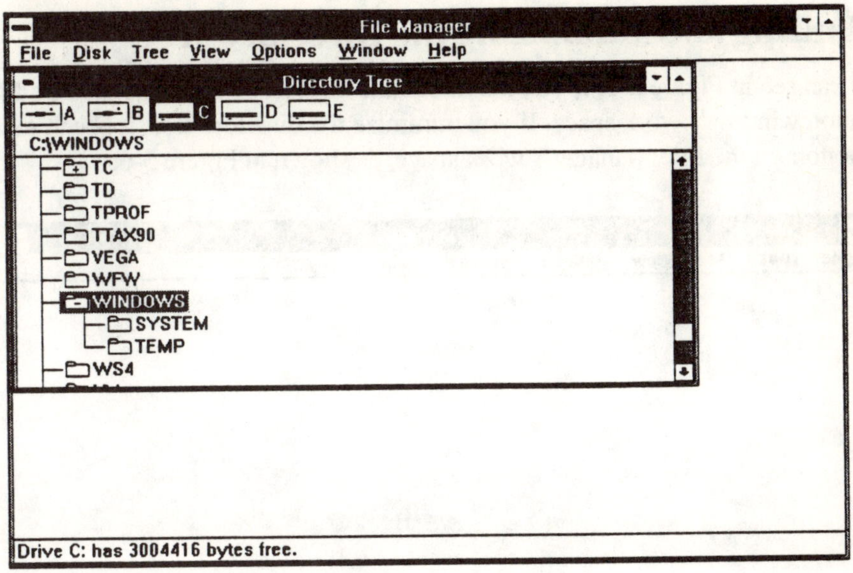

Figure 3-4. An Expanded Directory.

If you press the Ctrl+Asterisk shortcut key, you will expand every directory and subdirectory in the directory tree. Figure 3-5 shows the directory tree fully expanded and maximized to show as much of the tree as possible.

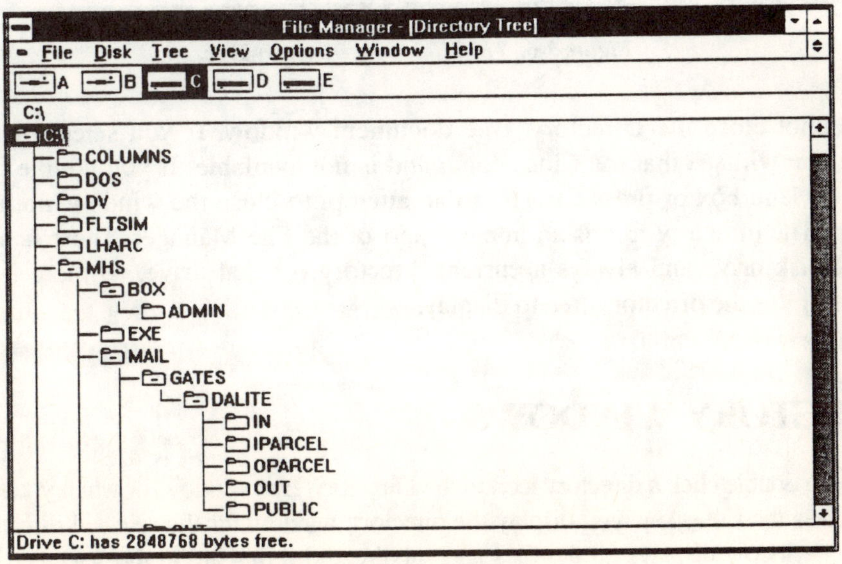

Figure 3-5. All Directories Expanded.

Maximizing and Minimizing the Directory Tree

As you can see in Figure 3-5, if you maximize the directory tree it fills the File Manager application window's work space. If you minimize the directory tree, it becomes an icon at the bottom of the File Manager's work space, as shown in Figure 3-6.

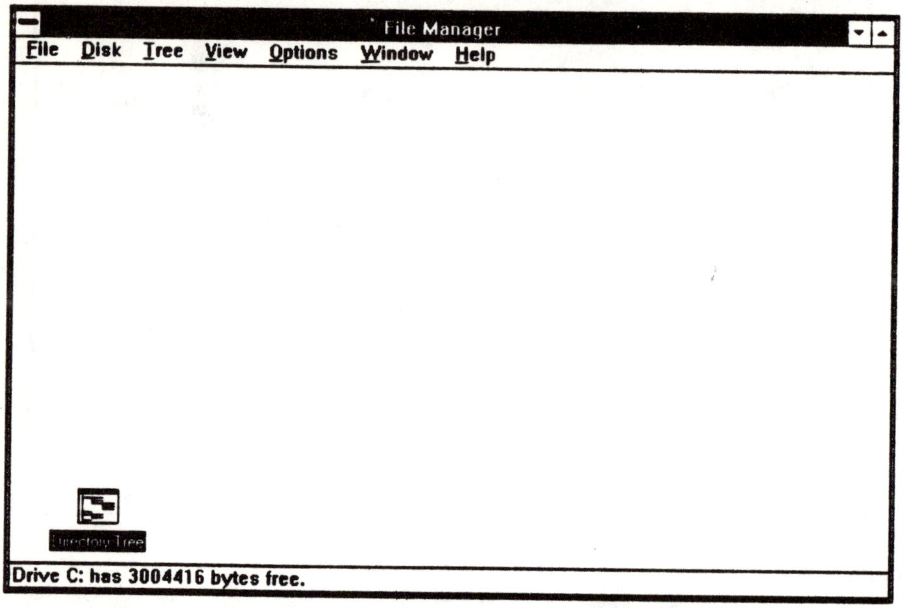

Figure 3-6. The Minimized Directory Tree.

You cannot close the Directory Tree document window. If you select its Control Menu, you will see that the Close command is not available. If you double click the Control Menu box or press Ctrl+F4 in an attempt to close the window, nothing will happen. The directory tree is an integral part of the File Manager. There is always a current disk drive and always a current directory for that drive, so there is always something for the directory tree to display.

DIRECTORY WINDOWS

When you double click a directory icon in the Directory Tree window, or when you highlight it and press the Enter key, you display the directory window for the selected directory. The directory window displays all the files and subdirectories that are in the selected directory. Figure 3-7 shows the directory window for the C:\WINDOWS directory.

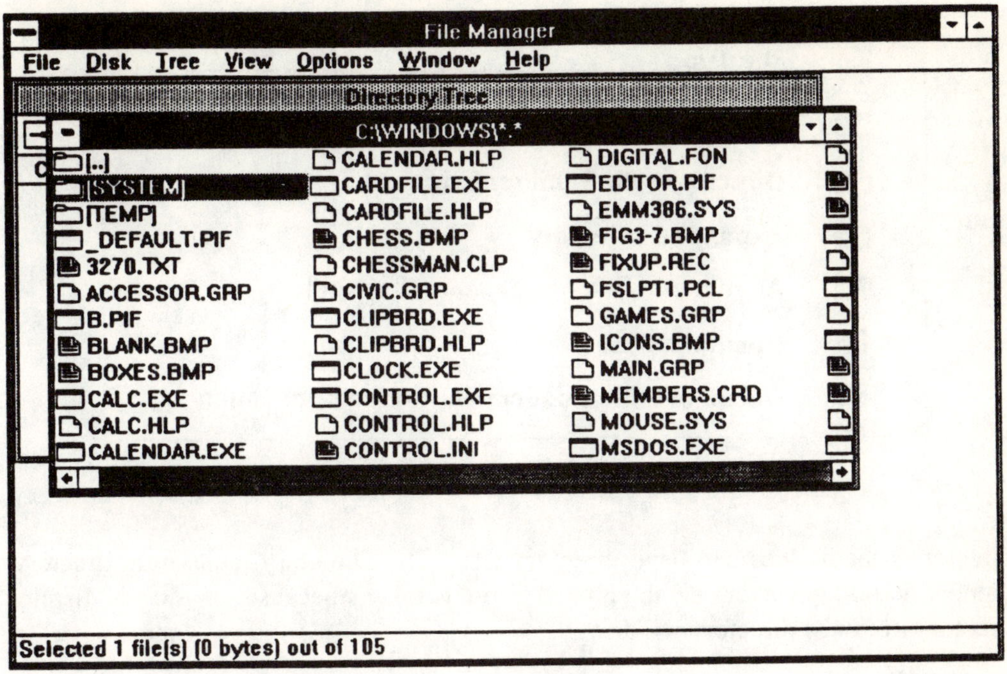

Figure 3-7. A Directory Window.

File Types

The files in Figure 3-7 use different icons depending on the type of the file. Figure 3-8 shows the icons that the File Manager uses in the directory tree and the directory windows to represent files.

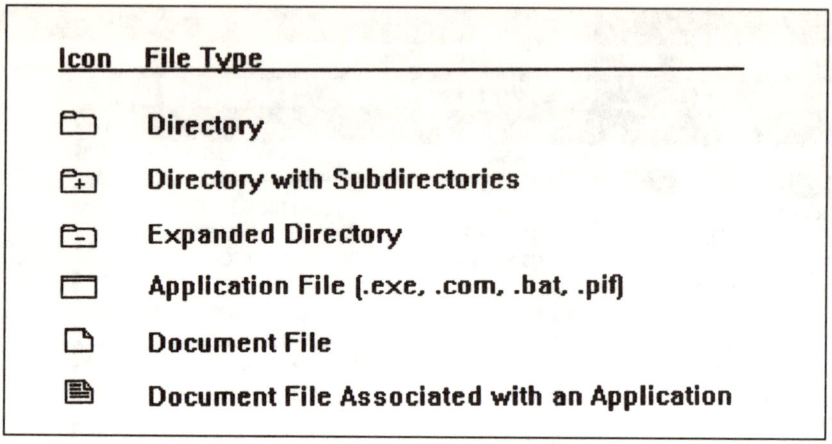

Figure 3-8. The File Manager Icons.

Directories themselves can have directory files. The Directory icons in a directory window do not, however, use the plus and minus tokens because you do not display directory trees in a directory window.

Square brackets ([]) around a filename indicate that the file is a subdirectory file. The [..] filename represents the directory that is the parent of the current subdirectory. All directories except the root directory have the [..] file as the first entry in the directory window.

The Status Bar

The File Manager status bar changes its display when you open a directory window. The status bar in Figure 3-7 shows that one file is selected and lists the file's length and the total number of files in the directory. The length of the [SYSTEM] file is zero because that file is a subdirectory. As you change the selected file, the length value in the status bar changes.

Selecting a File

You can move the highlighted file cursor around with the arrow keys or by clicking a selected file. If you press Enter or double click the file, one of several things will happen, depending on the file type.

Selecting a Subdirectory

If you select a Directory file, the File Manager will open another directory window and display the contents of the selected directory. If the directory is already open in an inactive window, the File Manager will make that window the active one. Figure 3-9 shows the C:\WINDOWS\SYSTEM subdirectory displayed in a directory window.

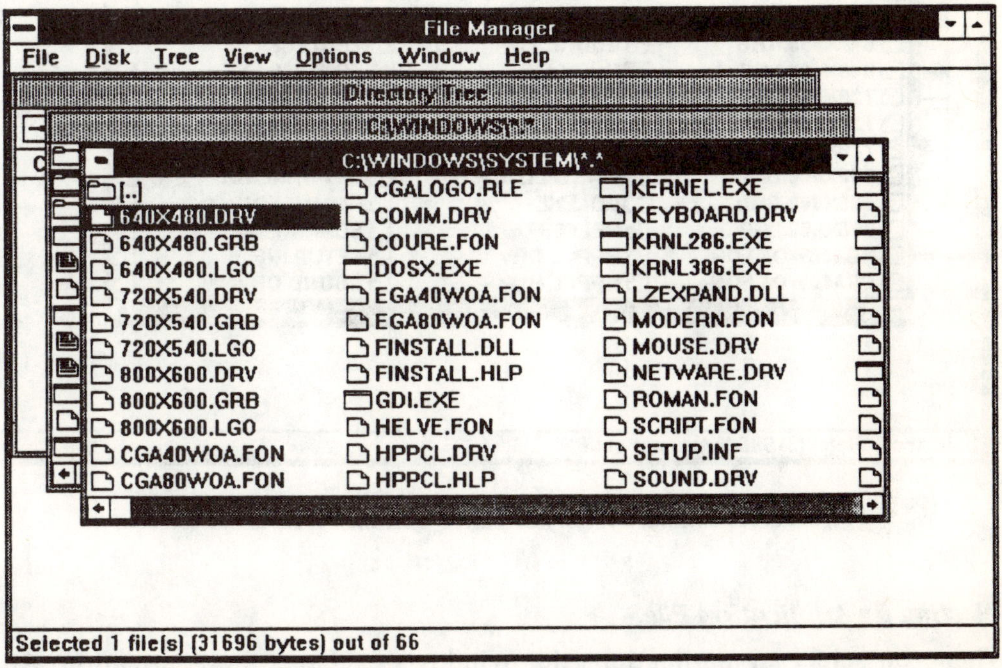

Figure 3-9. A Subdirectory Displayed in a Directory Window.

You can close the parent of a directory window without closing the directory window. From the display in Figure 3-9, select the C:\WINDOWS window as the active directory and then close it. The C:\WINDOWS\SYSTEM directory window remains open, as shown in Figure 3-10.

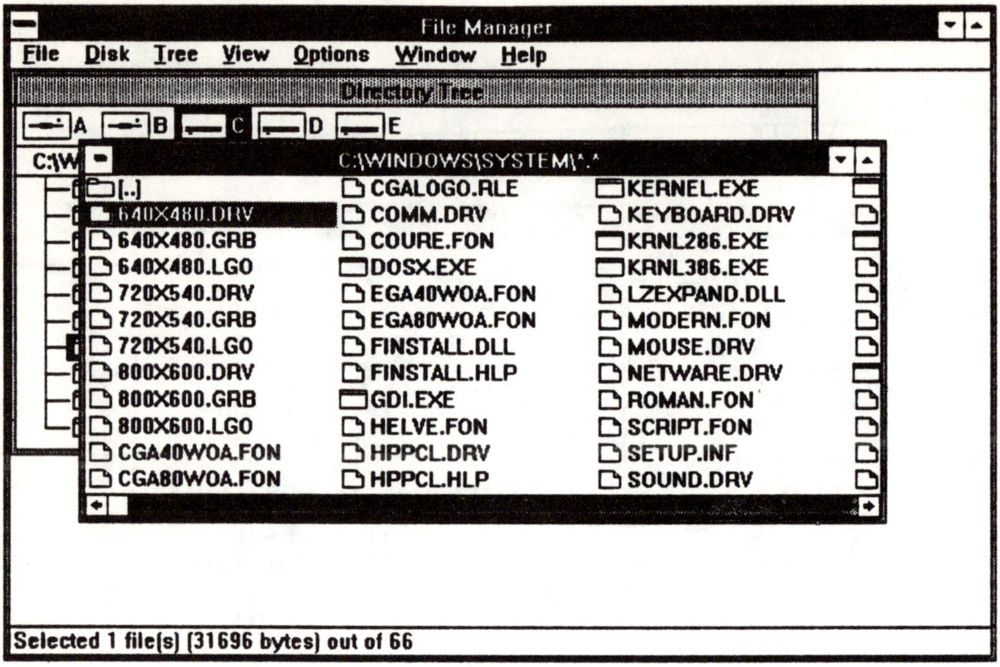

Figure 3-10. The Subdirectory Displayed After the Parent is Closed.

Selecting an Application File

When you select an application file, Windows executes the application. An application file is one that has the filename extension .EXE, .COM, .BAT, or .PIF.

Reopen the C:\WINDOWS directory window by selecting the [..] file from the C:\WINDOWS\SYSTEM directory window. Then select the file named CALC.EXE. This file is the executable file for the Windows Calculator accessory program.

The Calculator executes, as shown in Figure 3-11. Exit from the Calculator and continue.

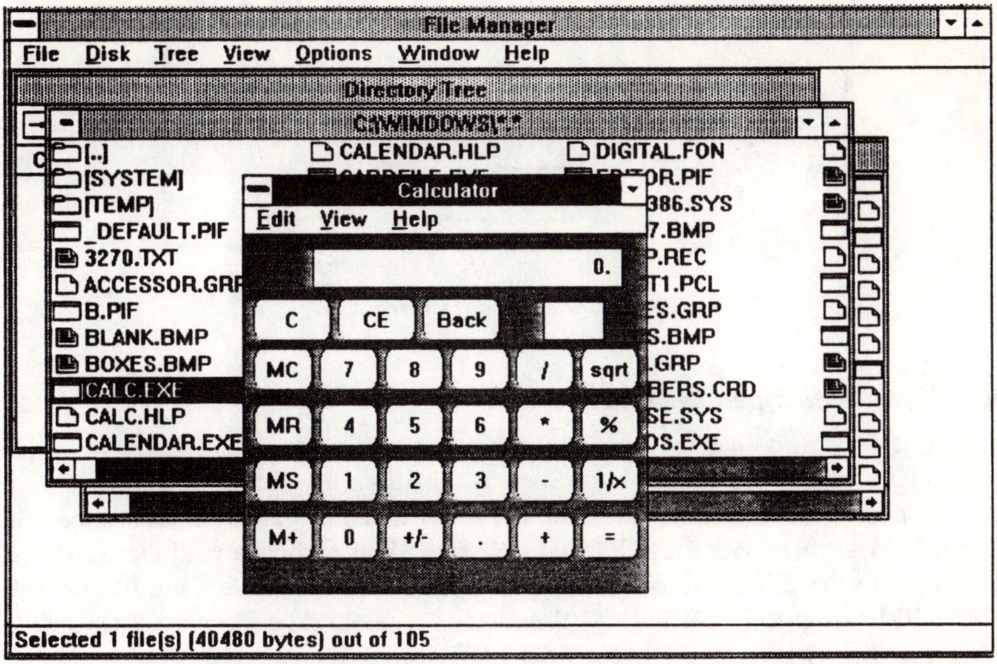

Figure 3-11. Selecting an Application File from the Directory Window.

Selecting a Document File

A document file is any file that is neither a subdirectory nor an application file. When a document file is represented by the unruled document icon, there is nothing that the File Manager can do when you select it.

Select the file named MOUSE.SYS from the C:\WINDOWS directory window. You will see the display shown in Figure 3-12.

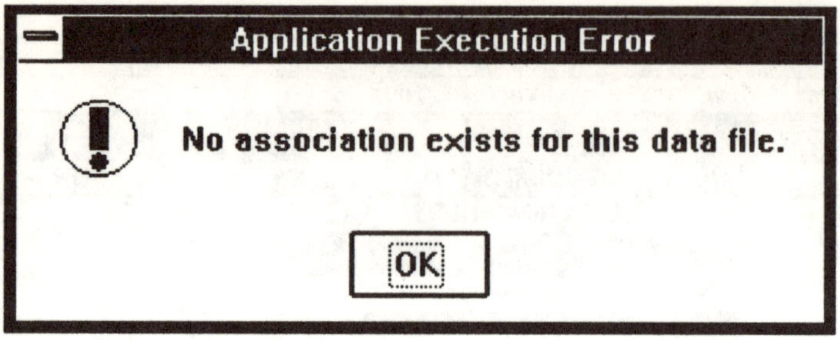

Figure 3-12. Selecting a Document File.

Selecting an Associated Document

Associated document files are ones that associate with applications. Later you will learn how to make those associations. Some associations are already made when you install Windows. For example, files with the .WRI filename extension associate with Windows Write; files with the .TXT and .INI extensions associate with the Notepad; and files with the .BMP extension associate with Paintbrush. Select the file named CHESS.BMP from the C:\WINDOWS directory window. The Paintbrush executes, and you see the window shown in Figure 3-13. Exit from the Paintbrush and continue.

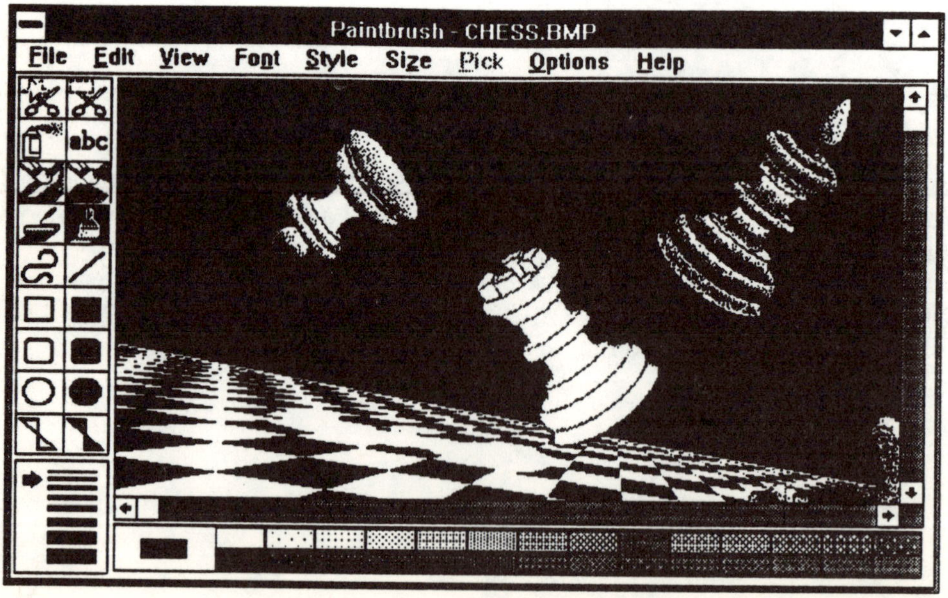

Figure 3-13. Selecting a Document that Associates with Paintbrush.

Displaying Multiple Directory Windows

You have already seen that you can open a directory and its subdirectories. But you can open other directories as well. This ability permits you to use the File Manager to move files from one place to another. You will recognize its utility when you get to the Move... command later in this chapter.

To open a second directory in another directory window, select the directory tree as the active document window. Then select another directory.

You might want the C:\WINDOWS and the C:\DOS directories open at the same time. Close the C:\WINDOWS\SYSTEM directory window, return to the directory tree, and select the C:\DOS directory. To make room in the work space, minimize the directory tree document window. Move the remaining directory window document windows around so that you can see a significant portion of both the C:\WINDOWS and C:\DOS directories. Figure 3-14 shows how the desktop might appear.

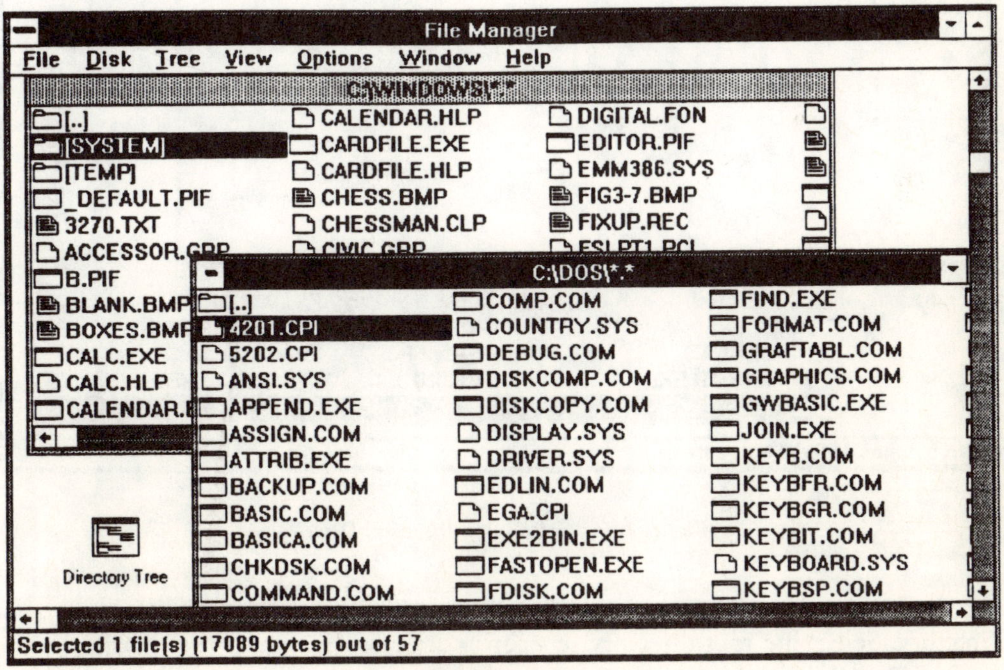

Figure 3-14. Two Opened Directory Windows.

Displaying Directory Windows for Different Drives

To copy files from one drive to another, you need directory windows open for the directories of both drives. Remember that there is only one directory tree. At the moment it is an icon at the bottom of the File Manager's work space.

Close the C:\DOS directory window, move the C:\WINDOWS directory window to the lower right corner of the work space, and reopen the directory tree. Put a diskette in the A drive and select the A drive from the top line of the directory tree. You see a display similar to the one in Figure 3-15.

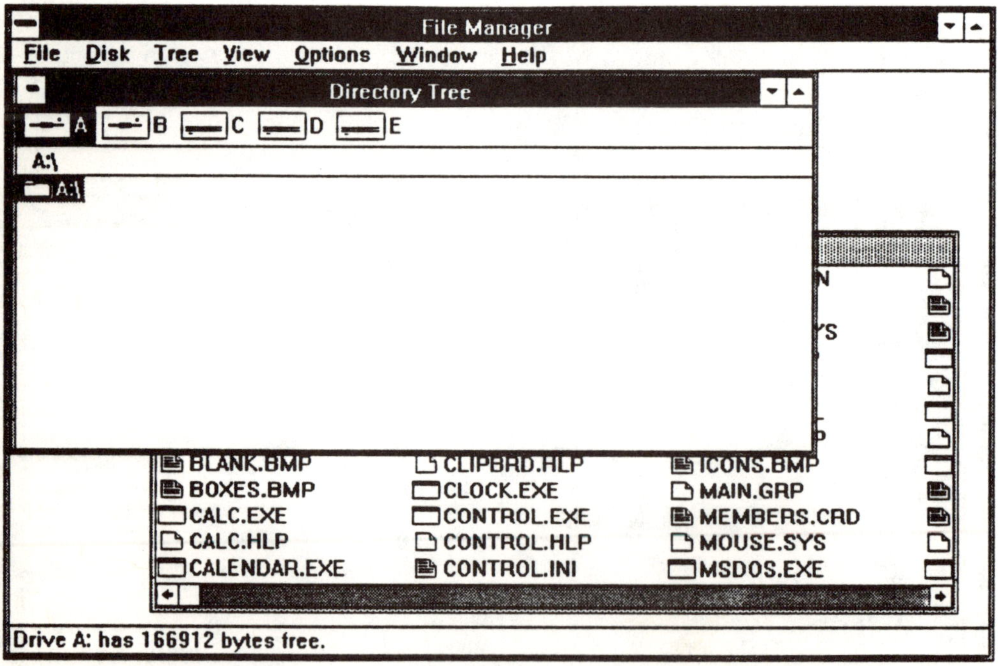

Figure 3-15. Selecting a Different Drive.

In this example the diskette in the A drive has no directories other than the root directory. Select the root directory to open a directory window. The diskette in the example has DOS and a few DOS command programs in its root directory. You can minimize the directory tree again to get it out of the way, rearrange the two directory windows, and see the File Manager set up for file copies, as shown in Figure 3-16.

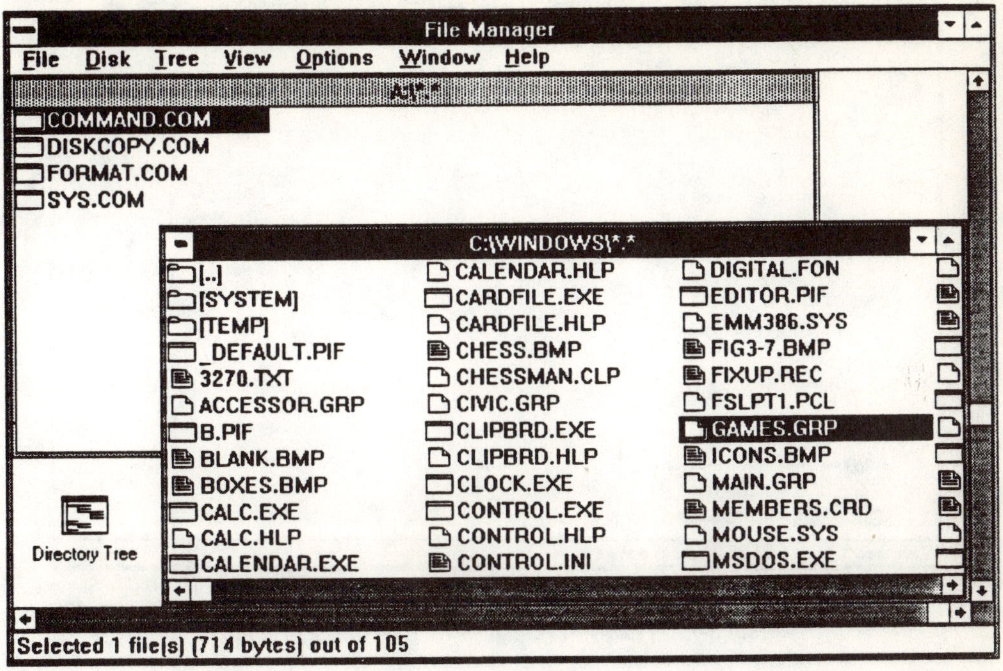

Figure 3-16. The Directory Windows for Two Different Drives.

The important feature of the File Manager window shown in Figure 3-16 is that there are two different directory windows open, with directories from different drives in them.

Minimizing Directory Windows

You can minimize directory windows to make room in the File Manager's work space. Figure 3-17 shows the File Manager with the directory tree and both open directory windows minimized.

Activate the A:\ directory window and close it. Activate the directory tree and the C:\WINDOWS directory window.

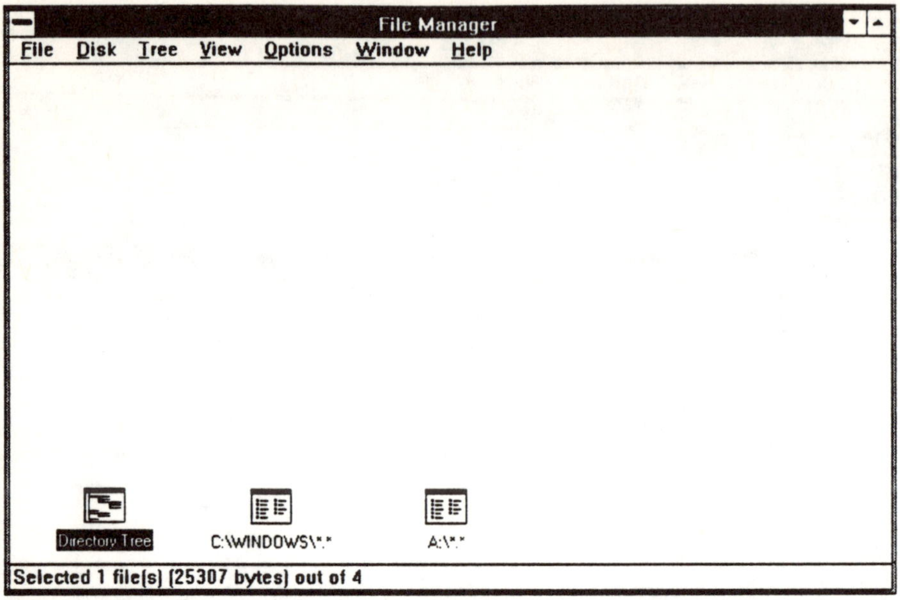

Figure 3-17. The File Manager with Everything Minimized.

NAVIGATING THE FILE MANAGER

As you have seen, you can move about freely among the disk drives, directory tree, and directory windows by using the mouse or the keyboard. The File Manager also has shortcut keys for most of the movements you can make.

Table 3-1 summarizes the shortcut keys that are not also menu commands.

Table 3-1. The File Manager Shortcut Keys.

Key	Move to	Tree	Directory
Home	First entry in the window	x	x
End	Last entry in the window	x	x
Right Arrow	Next lower subdirectory	x	
	File name to the right		x
Left Arrow	Parent directory	x	
	File name to the left		x
Up Arrow	Next higher entry	x	x
Down Arrow	Next lower entry	x	x
PgUp	Page backward	x	x
PgDn	Page forward	x	x
a,b,c,...	Entry that begins with...	x	x
Crtl+Up Arrow	Next higher entry same level	x	
Crtl+Down Arrow	Next lower entry same level	x	
Crt+A,B,C,...	Select Disk Drive	x	

MANAGING THE FILE MANAGER DISPLAYS

There are several choices you can make in the way the File Manager displays its information. These choices appear as menu toggles and commands. You can tell the File Manager to save these settings when you exit so that they will be in effect again the next time you execute the File Manager.

Upper/Lower Case

Figure 3-18 shows the File Manager's Options menu. The Lower Case command is a toggle that is currently off. The directory and file names in the directory tree and directory window are displayed in upper case.

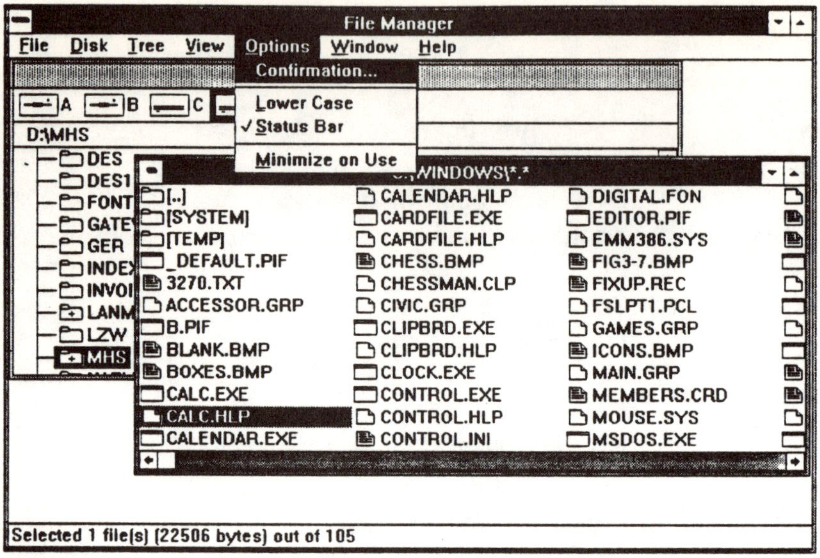

Figure 3-18. The Lower Case Toggle Off.

Figure 3-19 shows the same screen with the Lower Case toggle set on. Observe that the directory and file names in the directory tree and directory window are now displayed in lower case.

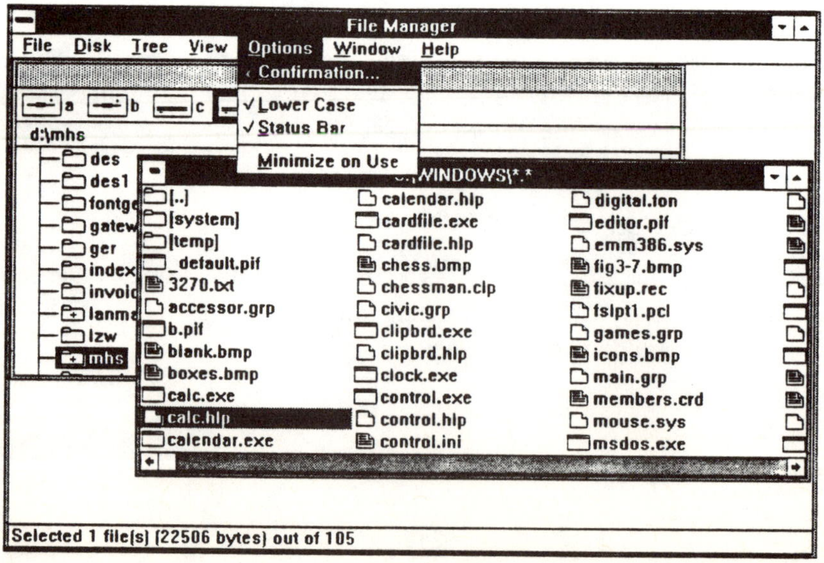

Figure 3-19. The Lower Case Toggle On.

Cascade and Tile

The Window menu includes Cascade and Tile commands. These commands work like the corresponding commands in the Program Manager. Figure 3-20 shows the File Manager with Tiled Windows.

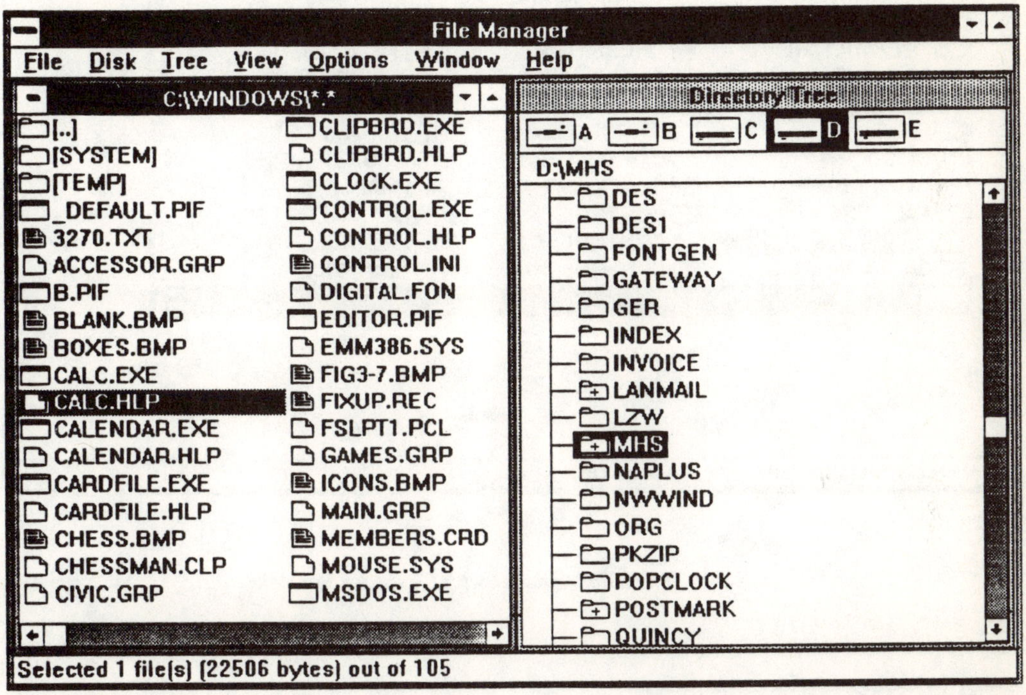

Figure 3-20. The File Manager with Tiled Windows.

Figure 3-21 shows the File Manager with Cascaded Windows.

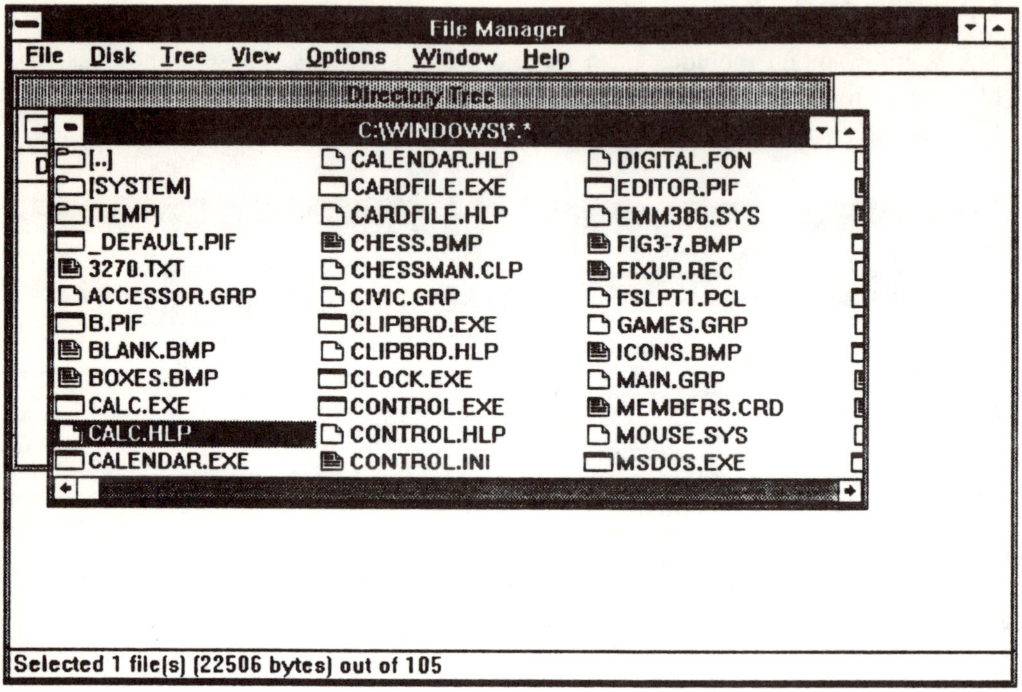

Figure 3-21. The File Manager with Cascaded Windows.

The Refresh Command

Sometimes events change what an active window is currently displaying, and the display does not get updated. If you run Windows from a network, for example, you might be looking at the contents of a directory window at the same time another user at another workstation adds or deletes a file. Your directory window does not change because your copy of Windows does not know that the change took place. The same effect occurs if a program running in the background changes the contents of the directory you are viewing.

The Refresh command on the Window menu refreshes the contents of the current window. Use it whenever you suspect that what you are looking at might not be current.

The View Menu

The File Manager's View menu has commands to control how the File Manager displays data in the directory windows. Figure 3-22 shows the View menu. In its initial configuration, the File Manager displays files in the sequence of the filename, with no other data except for the icon. The View menu allows you to modify these settings.

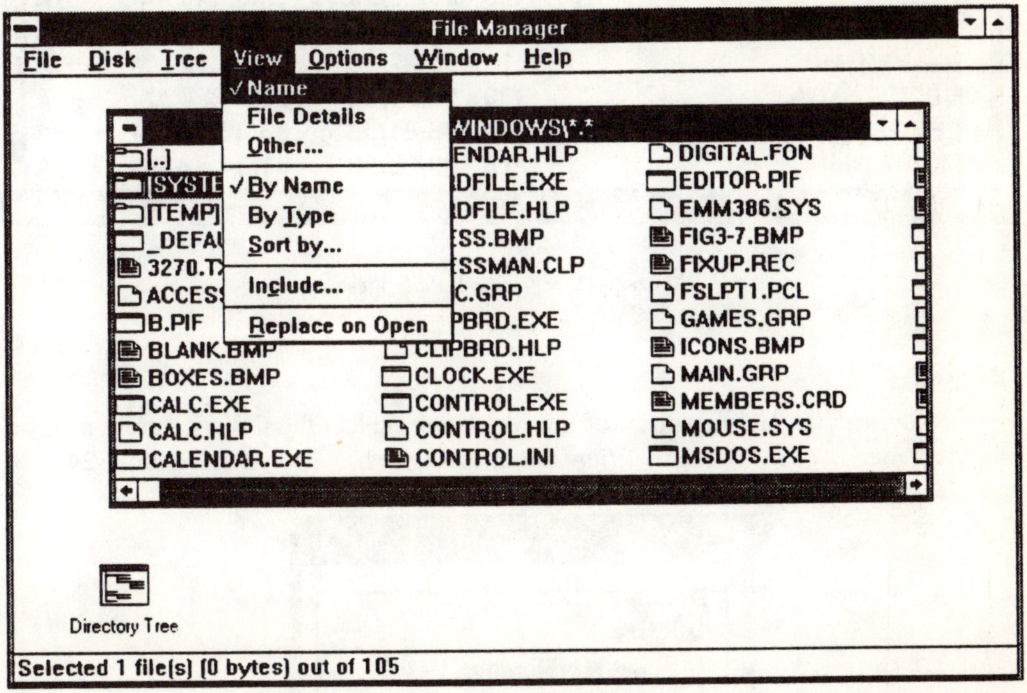

Figure 3-22. The View Menu.

Name

The Name command tells the file manager to display the file names only. This is the default setting. You use the name command to return to the default display after you have used the File Details or Others... command.

File Details

If you toggle on the File Details command, the File Manager displays not only the files' names but also their sizes, the date and time they were last written, and their DOS file attributes. Figure 3-23 shows the C:\WINDOWS directory window with the File Details view selected.

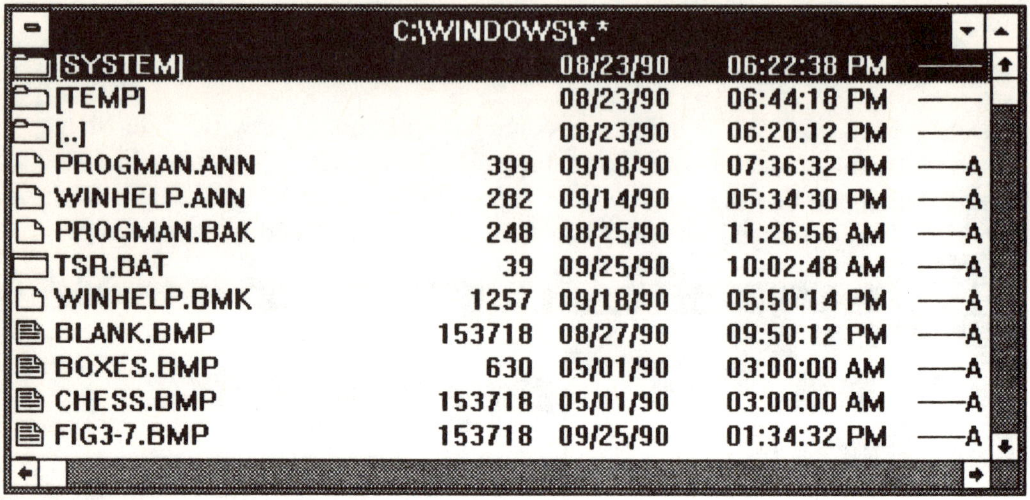

Figure 3-23. The File Details View.

Others...

If you want to view only a subset of the file details, select the Others... command on the View menu. You will see the View Other dialogue box shown in Figure 3-24.

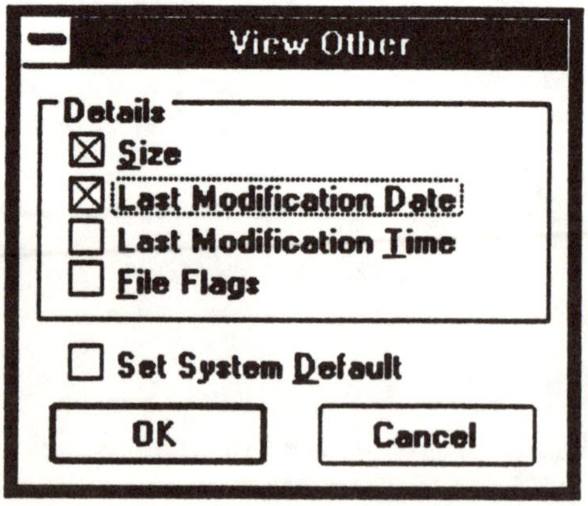

Figure 3-24. The View Other Dialogue Box.

Select the check boxes that correspond to the details you want to view. Figure 3-25 shows the directory with the size and date details selected.

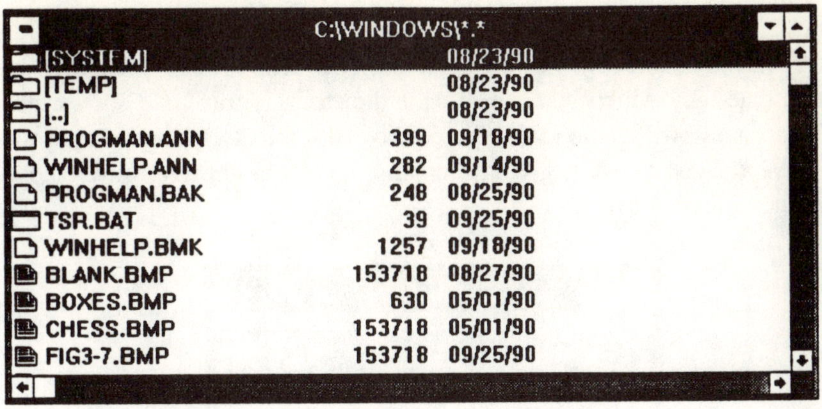

Figure 3-25. The Directory with Only the Size and Date Details Selected.

By Name

The By Name command tells the File Manager to sort the directory display by file name. This is the system default and is the way in which you are currently viewing the directory display. Use the By Name command to return to the name sort after using the By Type or Sort by... command to change the sort sequence.

By Type

The By Type command sorts the directory display by the file names' three character extensions. Figure 3-26 shows the directory sorted by file type.

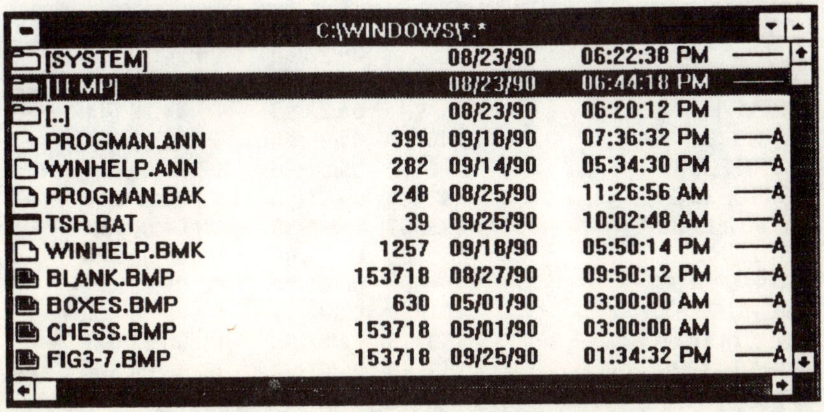

Figure 3-26. The Directory Sorted by File Type.

Sort By...

The Sort by... command allows you to select two other fields—file size and field modification date—by which you can sort the directory. Figure 3-27 shows the Sort By dialogue box that allows you to select the field by which to sort. This box permits you to select Name and Type as well, giving the same results as the By Name and By Type commands mentioned above.

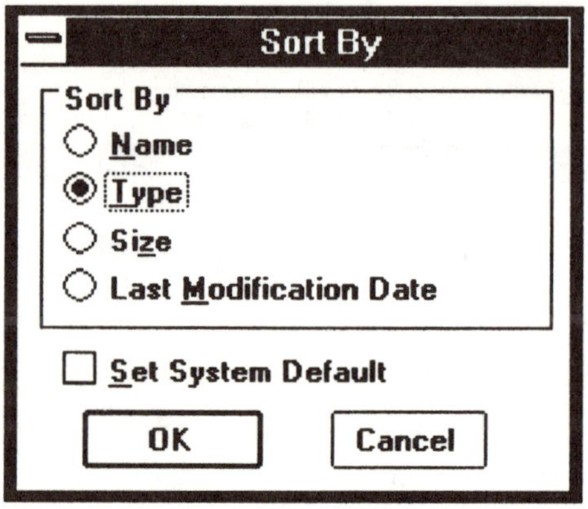

Figure 3-27. The Sort By Dialogue Box.

Figure 3-28 shows the directory sorted by file size. Observe that this type of sort displays the directory files first, followed by the application and document files with the biggest files sorted first.

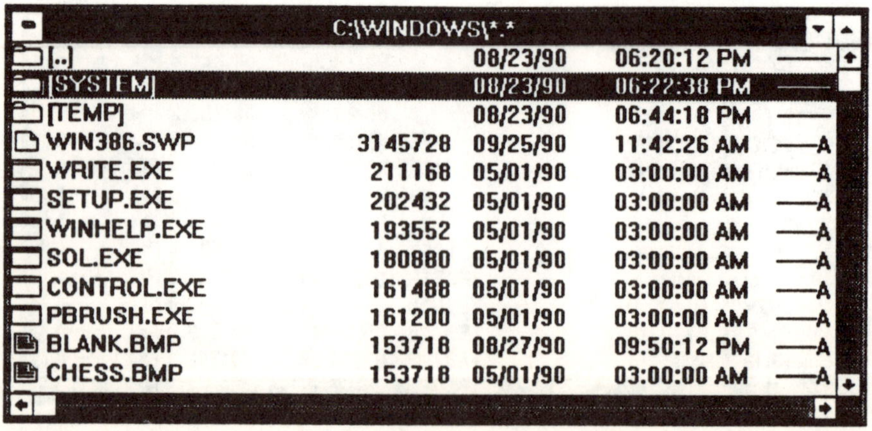

Figure 3-28. The Directory Sorted by File Size.

Include...

Directories can include many different files and file types. The Include... command allows you to further select which files will appear. You can select from the various types to which Windows assigns specific icons, and you can specify a DOS file name with wild cards to filter the files in which you are interested. Figure 3-29 shows the Include dialogue box with the file name changed to *.INI. Figure 3-30 shows the directory display of INI files.

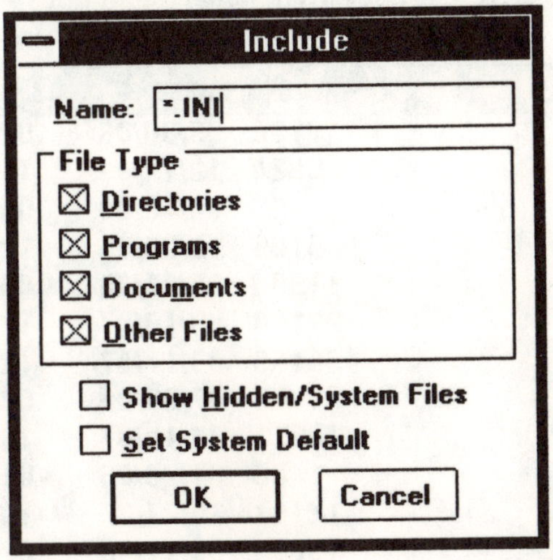

*Figure 3-29. The Include Dialogue Box with *.INI Selected.*

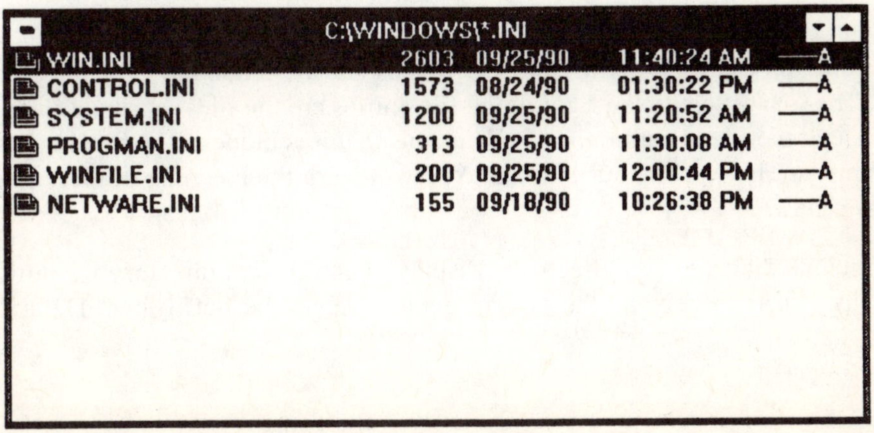

Figure 3-30. The Directory of INI Files.

If you de-select any of the File Type check boxes in the Include dialogue box, the files that correspond will not appear. The Include... command identifies Documents as those that have the ruled document icon and Other Files as those that have the unruled document icon.

The Show Hidden/System Files check box tells the File Manager to display any hidden or system files. DOS hides two system files in the root directory of a boot disk. Other applications hide files for one reason or another. Figure 3-31 shows the root directory of the C drive with Show Hidden/System Files selected.

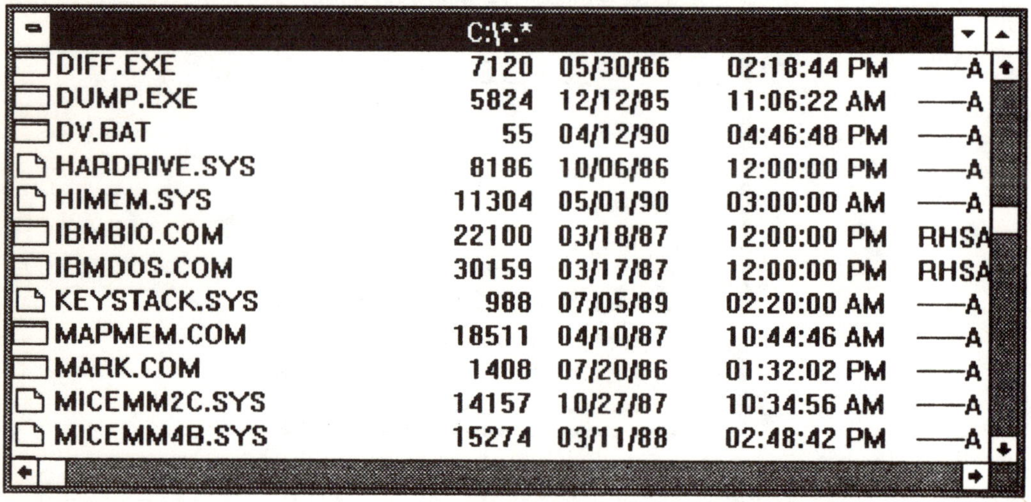

Figure 3-31. Hidden/System Files in a Directory.

The IBMBIO.COM and IBMDOS.COM files are the hidden system files that DOS uses. The four letters to the right of the file entries are the files' attribute flags. The R means that the file is read-only. The H means that it is hidden. The S identifies it as a system file. The A is the attribute bit. You will learn the meaning of these flags later in this chapter.

The Include dialogue box affects the display of the current directory window. If you want its effects to become the system default, select the Set System Default check box.

Replace on Open

Opening a large number of directory windows can clutter the File Manager's work space. If you do not need to see more than one directory at a time, you can select the Replace on Open toggle from the View menu. This toggle, when on, tells the File Manager to reuse the directory window each time you open another directory.

FILE MANAGER COMMANDS

Now that you know how to display and navigate the File Manager, you are ready to move on to the commands that allow you to manage the files on your disk system.

Creating a New Directory

The Create Directory... command on the File menu allows you to add directories to one of your disks. You can use the command while the directory tree is active or while you are working in a directory window. The new directory is subordinate to the selected directory in the directory tree or to the directory in the directory window, whichever is active.

To add a new directory to the C drive, highlight the C:\ root directory in the directory tree and then select the Create Directory... command from the File menu. You will see the Create Directory dialogue box shown in Figure 3-32.

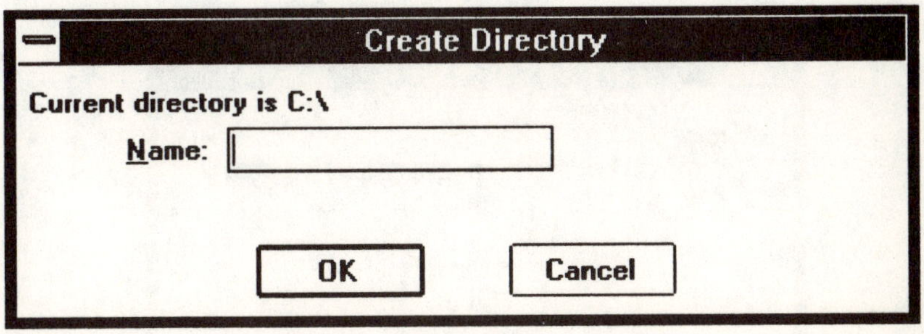

Figure 3-32. The Create Directory Dialogue Box.

Enter the name of the new directory in the Name text box and select OK. For this exercise, name the new directory EASYDIR. Figure 3-33 shows that the EASYDIR directory has been added to the C drive's root directory.

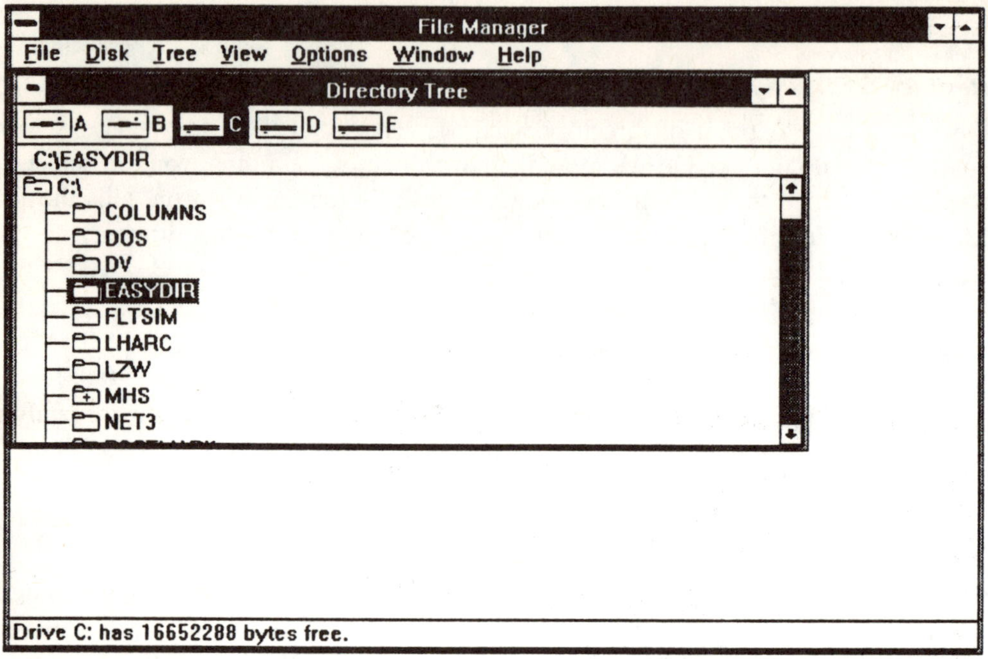

Figure 3-33. The EASYDIR Directory Added to the C Drive.

If you specify the name of an existing directory, you will see the File System Error dialogue box shown in Figure 3-34.

Figure 3-34. The File System Error Dialogue Box.

To add a subdirectory to an existing directory, either point to the existing directory in the directory tree or open a directory window with the existing directory in it. Open the EASYDIR directory you just created into a directory window and move it to the right so that you can see the EASYDIR entry in the directory tree. Select Create Directory... from the File menu, enter the name EASYSUB, and select OK.

You can see in Figure 3-35 that the EASYSUB subdirectory file entry is added to the C:\EASYDIR directory window, and the EASYDIR entry in the directory tree now has a plus (+) in its icon to indicate that it has a subdirectory.

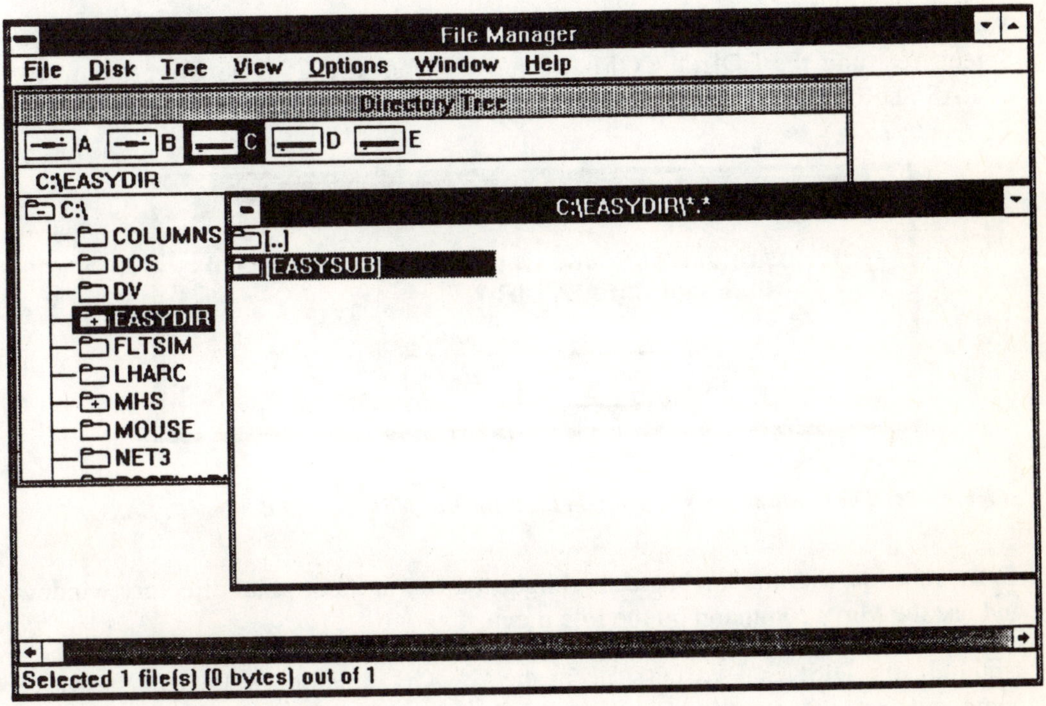

Figure 3-35. The EASYSUB Subdirectory Added to the EASYDIR Directory.

Moving and Copying

You can move or copy a file from one subdirectory to another and from one drive to another. The procedures differ slightly.

Moving a File

Open a directory window for the C:\DOS and C:\EASYDIR directories. Minimize the directory tree and move the directory windows around so you have easy access to the work space of both. To move a file, EDLIN.COM for example, click the filename and drag the icon to the destination window.

Do not drag the icon to another icon in the destination window. Drag the icon to an empty part of the window. If the window is filled with file names, drag the icon to the title bar of the destination window.

You will see the Confirm Mouse Operation dialogue box shown in Figure 3-36. Select Yes, and the EDLIN.COM file moves from the C:\DOS directory to the C:\EASYDIR directory.

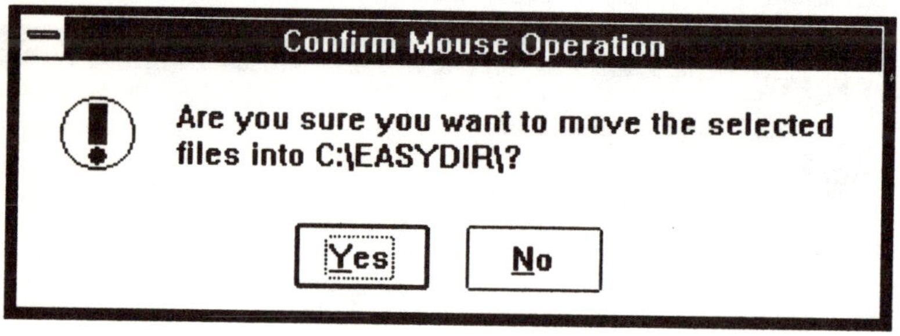

Figure 3-36. The Confirm Mouse Operation Dialogue Box for Copying Files Into C:\EASYDIR\.

To move a file with the keyboard, highlight the file in its original directory window and use the Move command on the File menu.

Highlight the DISKCOPY.COM file in the C:\DOS directory and select the Move command. You will see the Move dialogue box, as shown in Figure 3-37. You must enter the full DOS path of the directory to which you want to move the file. To move the file to the EASYDIR directory, enter C:\EASYDIR and select the Move command button.

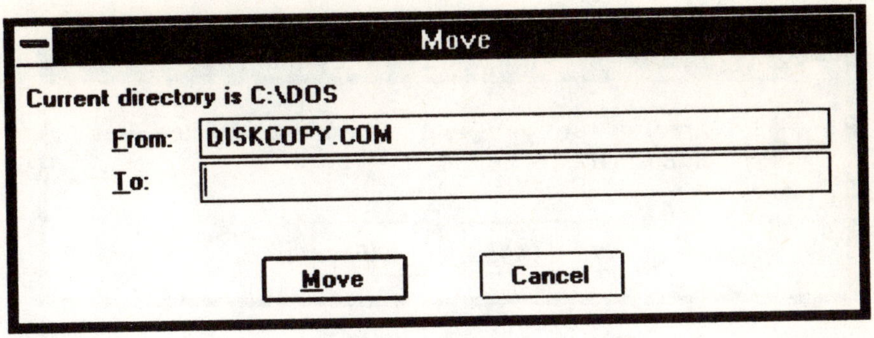

Figure 3-37. The Move Dialogue Box.

Copying Files

You do not really want to omit the EDLIN.COM and DISKCOPY.COM files from the C:\DOS directory, yet the move command deleted them from their original locations. Such is the nature of a move. So now you must copy the files from the C:\EASYDIR directory back to their original location.

To copy a file with the mouse, you use the same drag technique—but hold down the Ctrl key. Use the Ctrl+mouse technique to copy the EDLIN.COM file back into the C:\DOS directory. Hold down the Ctrl key and click on the EDLIN.COM file. Drag the icon into the destination directory. Make sure that you drag it to a blank spot and that no file in the destination directory window is outlined by a dotted box as a result of your drag. If the window is filled with file names, drag the icon to the title bar of the destination window. First release the mouse button and then the Ctrl key. You will see the Confirm Mouse Operation dialogue box shown in Figure 3-38. Select Yes to complete the copy.

To copy a file with the keyboard, you use the same procedure as you did to move a file, but with the Copy... command, rather than the Move... command, from the File menu. Use that approach to copy the DISKCOPY.COM file from the C:\EASYSUB directory window back into the C:\DOS directory window.

Figure 3-38. The Confirm Mouse Operation Dialogue Box for Copying Files into C:\DOS.

Moving and Copying to the Directory Tree

You can drag a file to a directory entry on the directory tree and move or copy it that way as well.

Moving and Copying Between Different Disk Drives

Earlier you learned how to view the directory windows of two different disk drives. To move or copy files from one drive to another, you must first open a directory window for the source and destination.

The procedures for moving and copying between drives are the same as those for moving and copying between directories on the same drive, except that they are somewhat reversed if you are using the mouse. You hold the Alt key down for moving and hold no key for copying. The idea is that you move files on the same disk more frequently than you copy them and you copy files from one disk to another more frequently than you move them, so the less routine operation in both cases requires that you hold down a key.

***

MANY USERS FIND THE REVERSAL OF THE MOVE AND COPY MOUSE PROCEDURES TO BE CONFUSING. THEY WONDER WHY THE DESIGNERS OF THE FILE MANAGER ABANDONED THE CONCEPT OF A COMMON USER INTERFACE IN THIS ONE ISOLATED AREA. NONETHELESS, THAT IS HOW THE DESIGNERS DID IT, AND YOU MUST LEARN IT THAT WAY. BY THE TIME THEY REALIZE AND ADMIT THEIR MISTAKE, WINDOWS WILL BE A DE FACTO STANDARD, AND THE CONFUSION WILL HAVE BECOME CONVENTION.

***

Select the C:\EASYDIR root directory so that it is in a directory window, put a diskette into the A drive, select the A drive, and select its A:\ root directory so that it is in a directory window. Minimize the directory tree and move the directory windows around so you can see most of both of them. Figure 3-39 shows the File Manager layout with both directory windows in view.

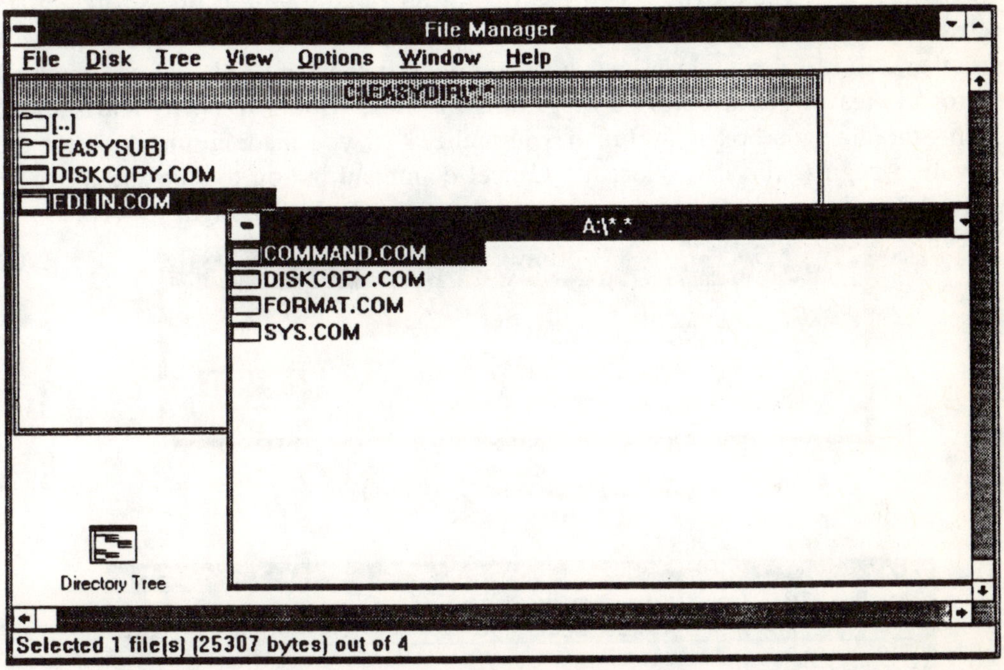

Figure 3-39. The File Manager Layout Ready to Copy a File to a Different Disk.

If you are using the keyboard, you move and copy between disks in the same way that you move and copy between directories on the same drive, so this exercise will deal with the mouse only.

To copy the EDLIN.COM file from the C:\EASYDIR directory window to the A:\ directory window, click and drag the file from one window to the other. Select the Yes command button on the Confirm Mouse Operation dialogue box, and the copy takes place.

To move the SYS.COM file from the A:\ directory window to the C:\EASYDIR directory window, hold down the Alt key, click and drag the icon, release the mouse key first, then release the Alt key. Select the Yes command button on the Confirm Mouse Operation dialogue box, and the move takes place.

Whenever you move or copy, a dialogue box—such as the one shown in Figure 3-40—appears. It goes away when the operation is completed. For short copies between fast disk drives, the dialogue box is a brief flash, and you hardly realize it was there. But for long copies—such as with long files where diskettes are involved or for copies of subdirectories or groups of files, which you will learn about soon—the dialogue box is useful. If you realize that you made a mistake after the operation begins, you can select the Cancel command button to stop the move or copy. After you have finished this exercise, the screen looks like Figure 3-41.

Figure 3-40. The Moving...Dialogue Box.

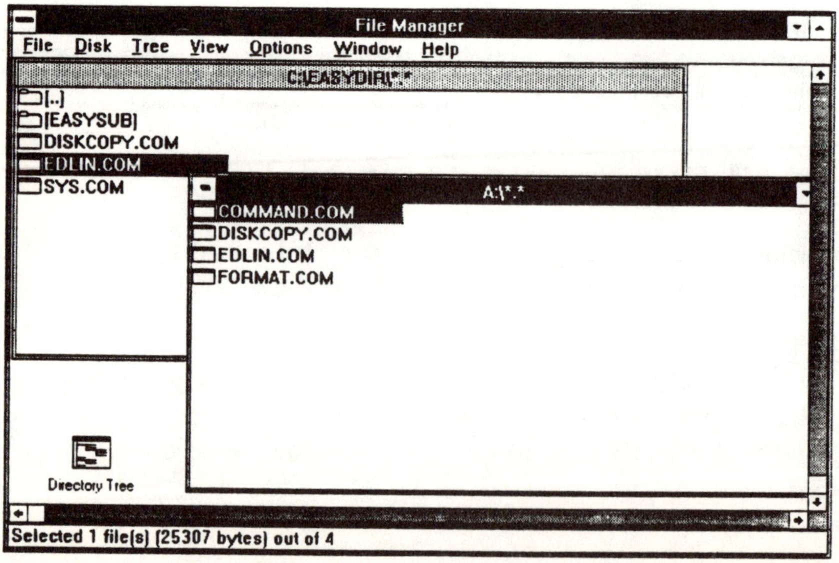

Figure 3-41. The Screen After Moves and Copies Have Been Done Between A: and C:.

Copying to an Icon

You can copy a file to an icon in the destination directory window. Drag the FORMAT.COM file from the A:\ directory window to the [EASYSUB] icon in the C:\EASYDIR directory window. Release the mouse button when the [EASYSUB] icon and filename are outlined by a dotted box. The screen displays the Confirm Mouse Operation dialogue box, as shown in Figure 3-42.

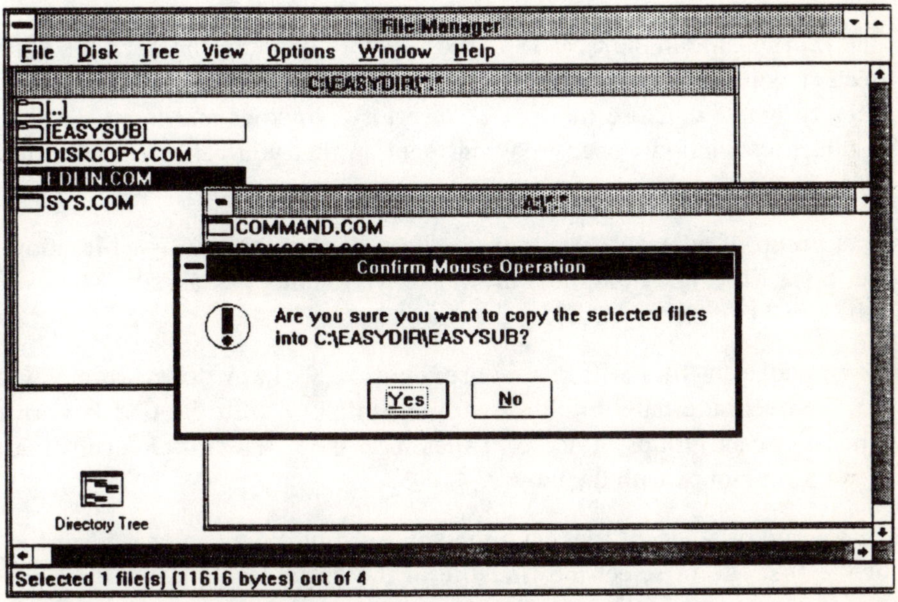

Figure 3-42. Copying a File to an Icon.

The dialogue box tells you that you are copying the selected file, FORMAT.COM in this case, to C:\EASYDIR\EASYSUB. When you select the Yes command button, FORMAT.COM is copied, and the screen once again looks like Figure 3-41.

Moving and Copying Directories

You move and copy directories by using the same procedures as you do for moving and copying files. When you move or copy a directory, three things happen: a new directory with the same name is created at the destination; all the files in the directory are moved or copied; and any subdirectories below the one you have addressed are moved and copied as well as all their files.

Starting from Figure 3-41, use one of the copy procedures to copy the [EASYSUB] directory from the C:\EASYDIR directory window to the A:\ directory window.

Marking a Group of Files

You can mark groups of files to be moved, copied, or deleted. You will learn about deleting later. The files can be contiguous or scattered, but a group is always contained within the same directory window.

Select the [..] filename in the C:\EASYDIR directory window and open it so that the root directory is in a directory window. Then select the [DOS] directory so that it is in a directory window. Close the two C: directory windows and leave the C:\DOS and A:\ directory windows open, moving them so that you can get a good look at both.

To mark a group of adjacent files with the mouse, click on the first file, move the mouse to the last file, and hold the Shift key down to click the last file. Mark several files in the C:\DOS directory window this way.

To mark non-adjacent files with the mouse, hold the Ctrl key down while you click each file. You can alternately hold down the Shift key with the Ctrl key to mark several non-adjacent groups of adjacent files. Use the C:\DOS directory window to practice marking groups with the mouse.

To mark a group of adjacent files with the keyboard, use the cursor keys or the first letter of the first file to select the first file in the group. Hold down the Shift key while you move to the last file in the group.

To mark a group of non-adjacent files with the keyboard, move the cursor to the first file and press Shift+F8. A blinking dotted outline surrounds the selected file. Use the arrow keys to move the blinking outline to the next file and press the Spacebar to select this file. You can describe an adjacent group in this way as well by moving from the selected first file to the last file in the group while holding down the Shift key. Once again, practice in the C:\DOS directory window.

Figure 3-43 shows a group of non-adjacent files marked in the C:\DOS directory window.

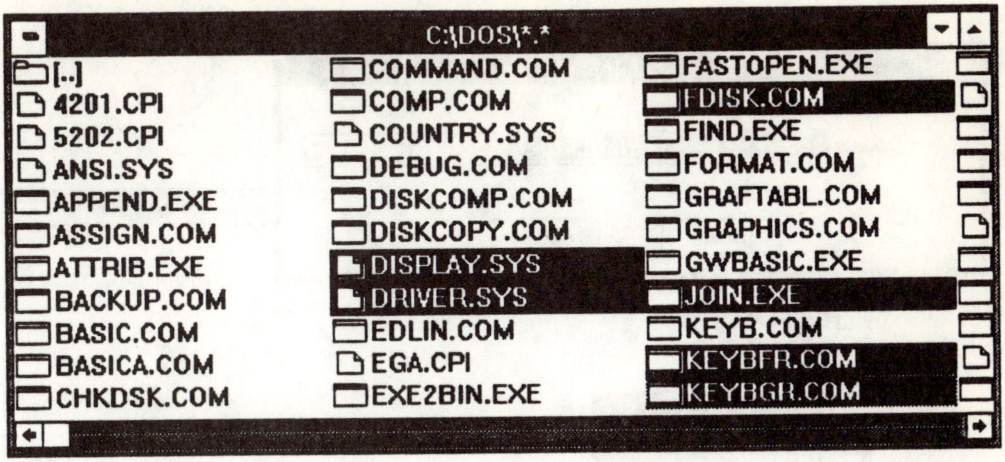

Figure 3-43. A Marked Group of Selected Files.

Moving and Copying Groups

You move and copy groups of files by using the same procedures that you use to move and copy single files. You start the mouse drag from any of the marked file names. The difference lies in the icon that you drag for a group: it resembles a stack of pages rather than the icon being dragged.

A group can include files and subdirectories. The Moving... or Copying... dialogue box that appears during the move or copy is the same one that is shown in Figure 3-40 above. The file names change as each file is moved or copied.

Deleting

You can delete a file, a directory, or a group of files by first marking them and then selecting Delete from the File menu or pressing the Del key.

Mark several files in the A:\ directory window and select Delete. You will see the Delete dialogue box shown in Figure 3-44.

The text in the Delete text box in Figure 3-44 is a list of the files in the group. You can move the cursor to the home position and horizontally scroll the text to read the entire list.

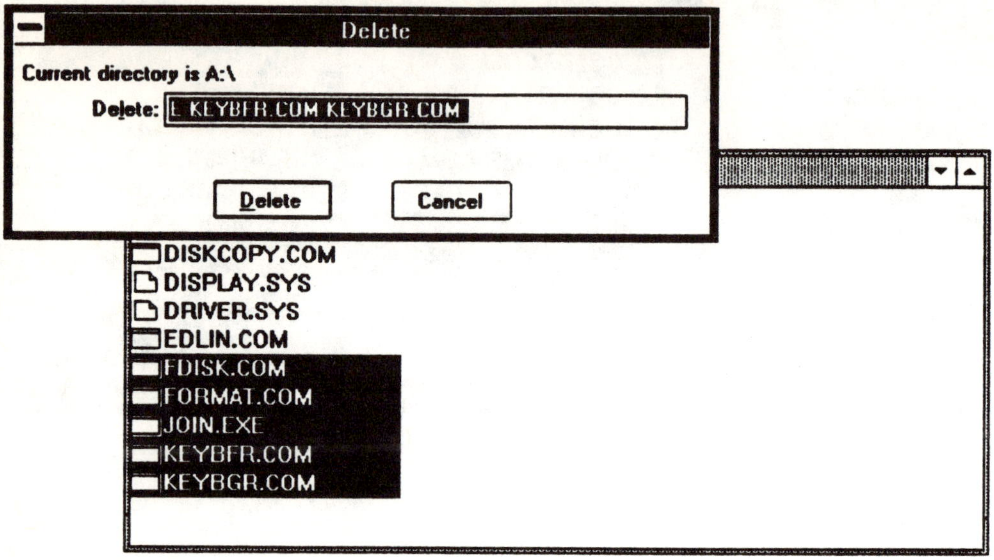

Figure 3-44. The Delete Dialogue Box.

When you select Delete to verify that the list is correct, the File Manager displays the dialogue box shown in Figure 3-45 once for each file in the list. You must select the Yes or No command button for every file. If you select the Cancel command button, the File Manager stops deleting altogether.

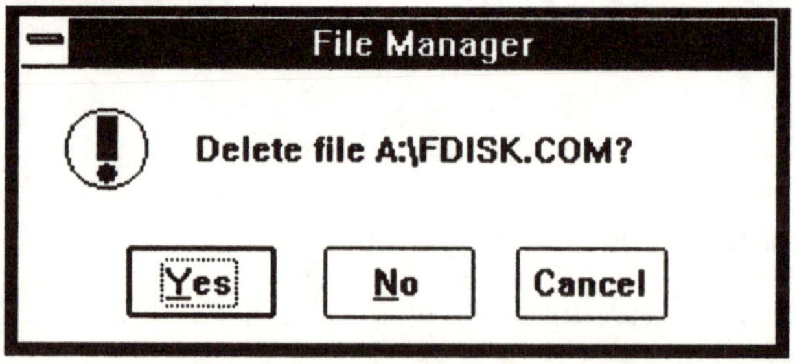

Figure 3-45. The Dialogue Box to Confirm a File Delete.

Confirmation

The business of confirming the delete of every file in a list can be annoying and time-consuming, particularly when the list is long or includes a directory or two. You can tell the File Manager not to pester you to confirm every delete if you are sure that you will always know what you are doing. The Confirmation... command on the Options menu displays the Confirmation dialogue box shown in Figure 3-46.

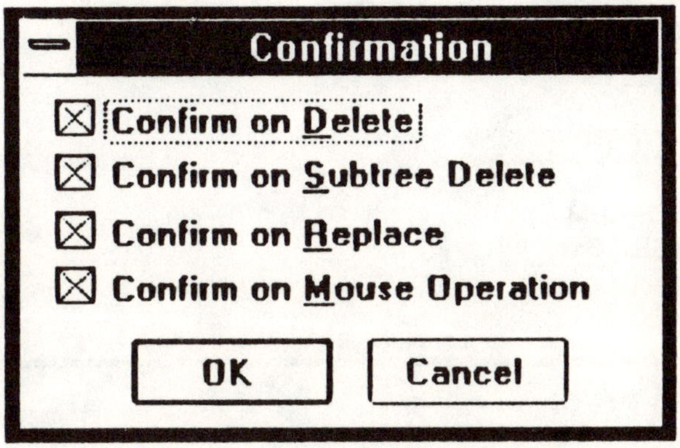

Figure 3-46. The Confirmation Dialogue Box.

The check boxes in the Confirmation dialogue box allow you to turn off the confirmation requests for deletes of files, deletes of subdirectories, replacements of existing files during a move or copy, and mouse moves or copies that bring up the Confirm Mouse Operation dialogue boxes asking you if you really mean to move or copy this or that.

If you change the settings in the Confirmation dialogue box, you can make those changes permanent when you exit from the File Manager by selecting Save Settings in the Exit File Manager dialogue box.

Renaming

Sometimes you want to change the name of a file, directory, or group. The Rename command on the File menu allows you to perform these operations.

Renaming Files and Directories

You can rename a file by selecting it and then selecting the Rename... command from the File menu. You will see the Rename dialogue box shown in Figure 3-47.

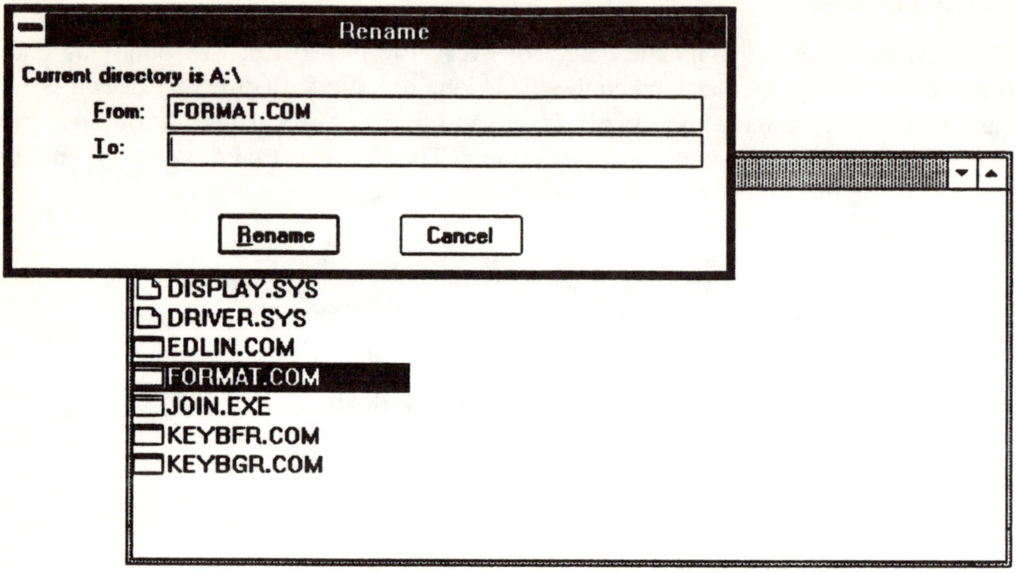

Figure 3-47. The Rename Dialogue Box.

You enter the new name of the file in the To: field. If you specify a name of an existing file in the same directory, you will see the dialogue box shown in Figure 3-48—unless you have turned off the confirmation of file replacements with the Option menu's Confirmation... command. Renaming a directory is the same as renaming a file.

Figure 3-48. The Dialogue Box to Confirm a Rename.

Renaming Groups

If you mark a group and specify a complete file name in the To: field of the Rename dialogue box, the File Manager does successive renames of each file in the group to the one name. This action effectively deletes all but the last file in the group and probably is not what you have in mind.

There is, however, a logical way to rename groups of files. Suppose you want to change the file extensions of several of the files in a group. You can mark the group and enter *.SAV, for example, in the To: field of the Rename dialogue box. Figure 3-49 illustrates this operation.

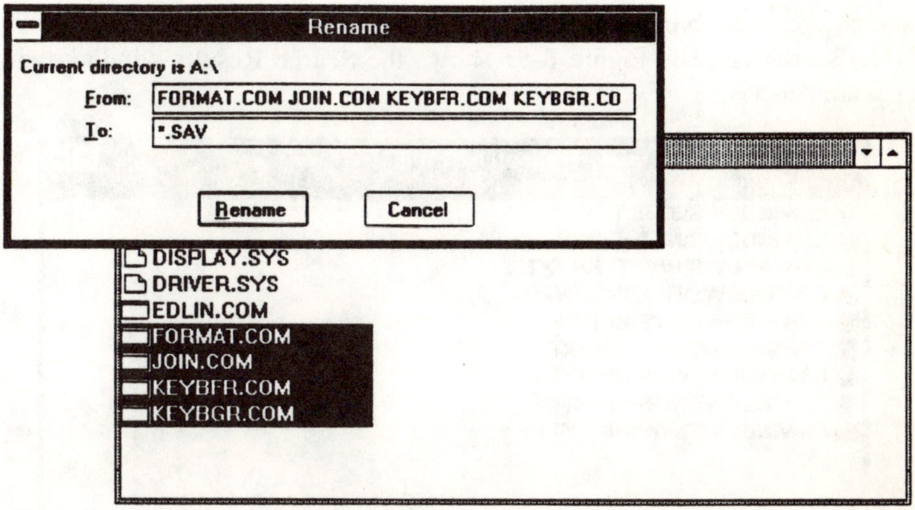

Figure 3-49. Renaming a Group.

Searching for Files

The File Manager helps you find files on your hard disk. The Search... command on the File menu allows you to search for files that match a file name specification. Suppose you want to find all the files that have the extension .TXT. Figure 3-50 shows the Search dialogue box in which you would specify the file.

You can use DOS file name wild cards in the Search For: field of the Search dialogue box. The Search Entire Disk check box tells the File Manager to search the entire current disk. If you turn the check box off, it searches only the current directory and its subdirectories.

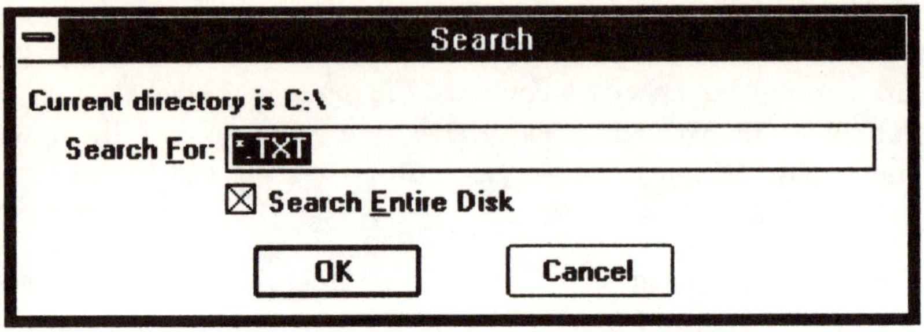

Figure 3-50. The Search Dialogue Box.

The search operation builds a Search Results window with a list of the files that match the search criteria. Figure 3-51 shows the Search Results window that the *.TXT search created.

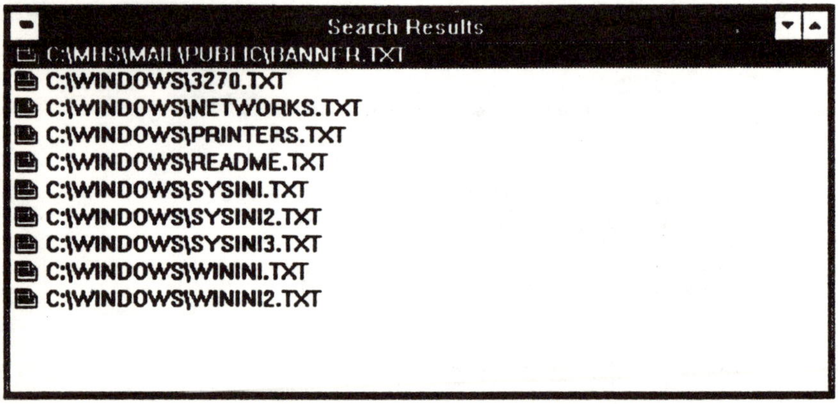

Figure 3-51. The Search Results Window.

The Search Window is like a directory window in all respects except one: you cannot move or copy files to it from other directory windows. Other than that, all the commands that work with directory windows work with the Search window.

Note that there can be only one Search window. If you do a second search without closing a prior Search window, the search results reuse the existing window.

Printing ASCII Text Files

The Print... command on the File Manager's File menu allows you to print ASCII files. ASCII files are text files without any formatting controls that are specific to an application. Many software packages come with files named READ.ME, README.DOC, or something similar. These files are usually plain ASCII text. You can print such files with the Print... command.

When you execute the Print... command, the currently selected filename appears in the Print dialogue box, as shown in Figure 3-52.

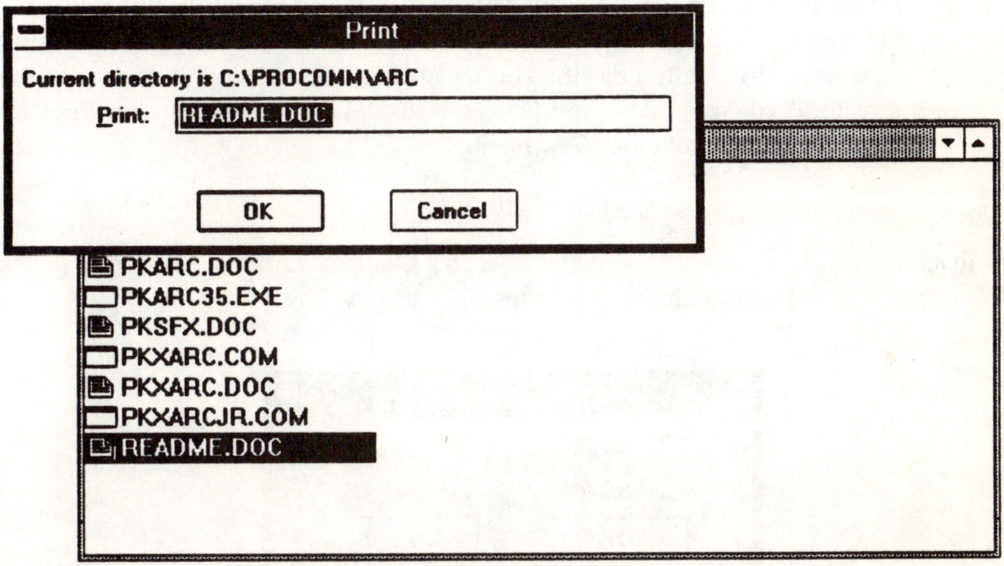

Figure 3-52. The Print Dialogue Box.

You can enter a different file name, along with its path, if the file named in the Print dialogue box is not the file you want. Select OK, and the file prints automatically. If the file you've selected is not a plain ASCII text file, the printout is likely to be unreadable. It is even possible that you could send a file to the printer that would cause the printer to behave erratically until you reset it.

Changing Attributes

Every file has four attributes associated with it that are either on or off: Read-only, Hidden, System, and Archive.

Overview of the Attributes

The Archive and System attributes are usually maintained by DOS and have no meaning to applications. A file with the System attribute belongs to DOS itself. DOS sets the Archive attribute whenever an application writes to a file. This attribute allows backup utility programs, such as BACKUP, to determine that a file has changed since the last backup operation. The BACKUP program sets the Archive attribute off when it backs up a file. If a file's Archive attribute is still off when the next BACKUP executes, the program knows that the file has not been changed and that it does not need to back up the file.

The Read-only and Hidden attributes are usually maintained by applications. When a file has the Read-only attribute set to on, you can view the file but you cannot modify or delete it. When a file has the Hidden attribute set to on, you do not see the file in a directory window unless you have selected Show Hidden/System Files on the Include dialogue box from the View menu.

Changing the Attributes of a File

With a file selected in a directory window, select the Change Attributes... command on the File menu. You will see the Change Attributes dialogue box shown in Figure 3-53.

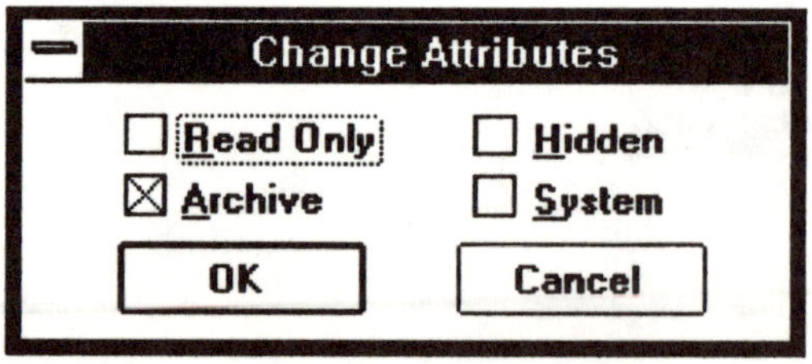

Figure 3-53. The Change Attributes Dialogue Box.

The attributes that are selected in the Change Attributes dialogue box are the ones that the file currently has set to on. You can change any of these attributes. When you select OK, the attributes take effect. If you selected Hidden, for example, the file disappears from the directory window unless you have selected Show Hidden/System Files on the Include dialogue box from the View menu.

Changing the Attributes of a Group

Assume that you renamed the group of files to *.SAV in the A:\ directory window as discussed in "Renaming Groups." Recall the window, select File Details on the View menu, and mark the .SAV files as a group. Select the Change Attributes... command from the File menu. You will see the display shown in Figure 3-54.

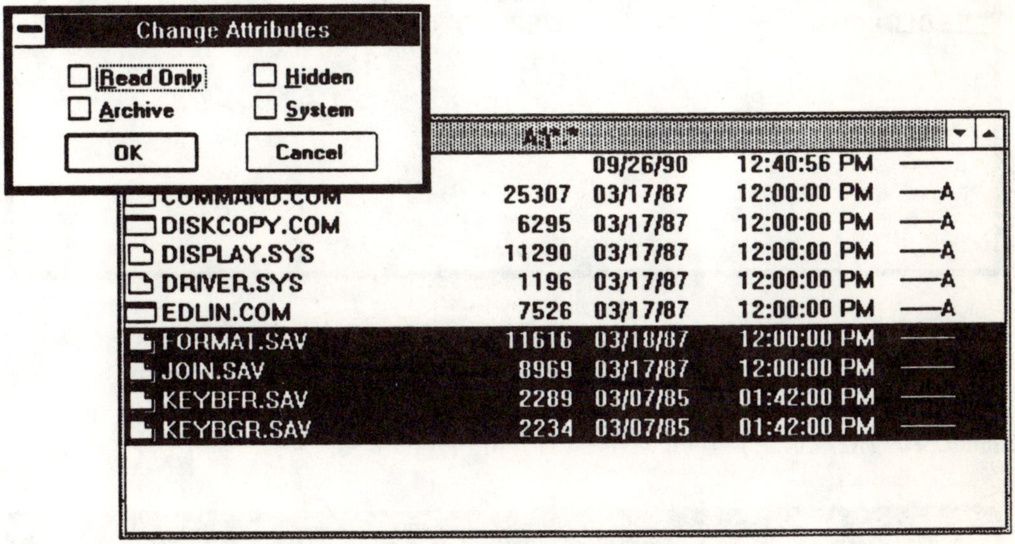

Figure 3-54. Changing the Attributes of a Group of Files.

None of the attributes is checked in Figure 3-54 because you have a group of files marked. The files might have different attributes. Select the Hidden check box in the Change Attributes dialogue box and then select OK. The A:\ directory window appears, as shown in Figure 3-55. The file group is no longer visible because you set the Hidden attribute bit for all the files in the group.

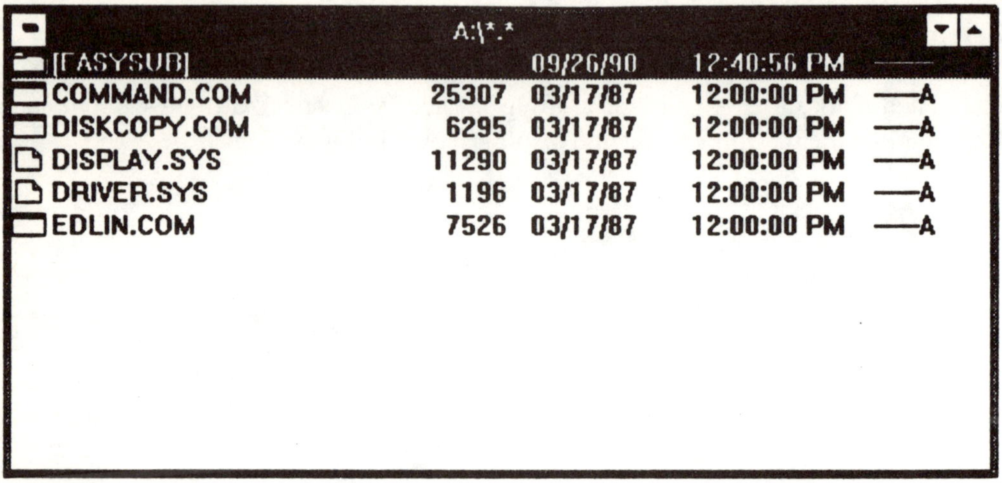

Figure 3-55. The Hidden Group of Files Out of Sight.

Now select Show Hidden/System Files on the Include dialogue box from the View menu. The files come into view, as shown in Figure 3-56.

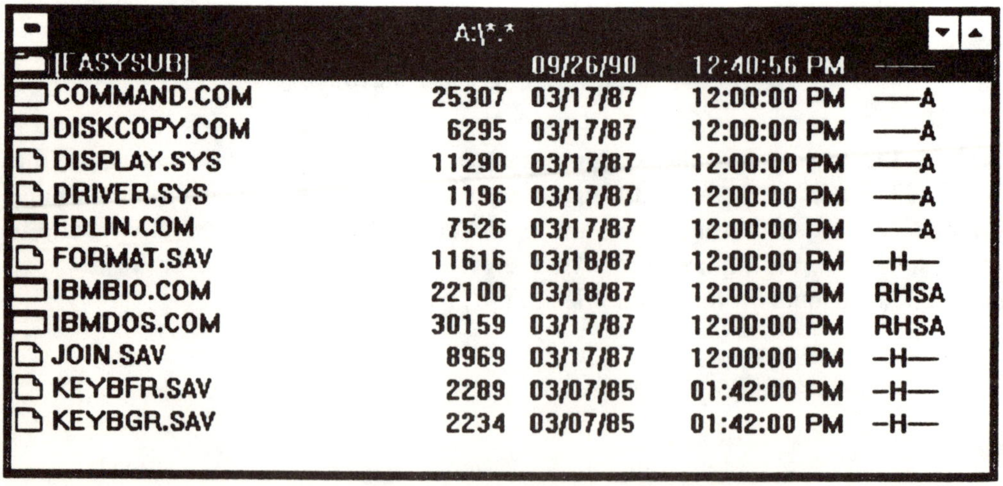

Figure 3-56. The Hidden Group of Files in View.

DISK OPERATIONS

The File Manager Disk menu provides a number of disk and diskette utility operations. You can copy, label, and format diskettes, and you can build a DOS-bootable system diskette. There are some network disk operations that you can perform as well; you will learn about them in Chapter 11.

Copying Diskettes

The Copy Diskette... command on the Disk menu allows you to copy a diskette to another drive. The two diskettes must be the same format and you must have selected a diskette drive—usually A or B—as the current drive at the top of the directory tree. If you select the Copy Diskette... command while a different kind of drive is current, you will see the error message shown in Figure 3-57.

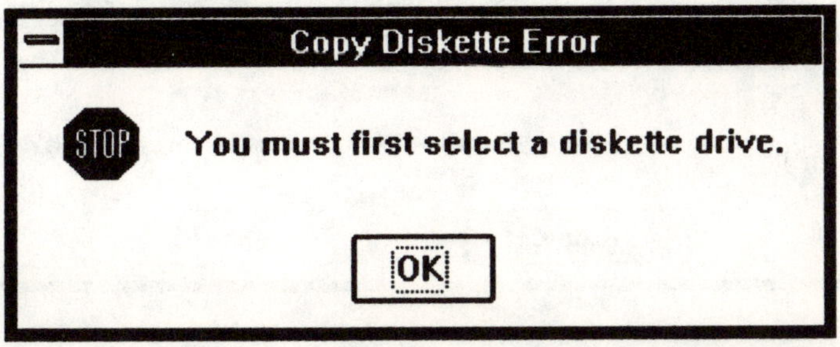

Figure 3-57. The Copy Diskette Error Message #1.

The currently selected drive is the source diskette drive for the Copy Diskette... command. With the A drive current, select the Copy Diskette... command from the Disk menu. You will see the dialogue box shown in Figure 3-58.

***

YOU CAN USE THE SAME DRIVE FOR THE SOURCE AND DESTINATION DISKETTES. THE FILE MANAGER WILL READ THE SOURCE DISKETTE INTO MEMORY AND THEN PROMPT YOU TO INSERT THE DESTINATION DISKETTE.

***

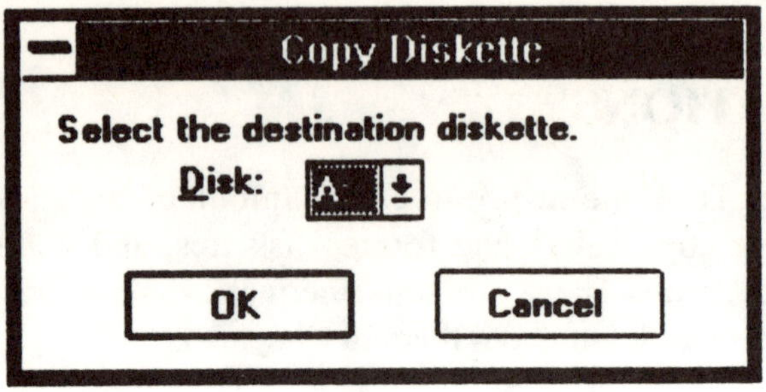

Figure 3-58. The Copy Diskette Dialogue Box #1.

The Disk field in the dialogue box is a drop-down list box. You can select it to see all the diskette drives on your system. Select one and then select OK. After you select OK, use the dialogue box shown in Figure 3-59 to verify that you want to continue. Select OK to proceed with the copy.

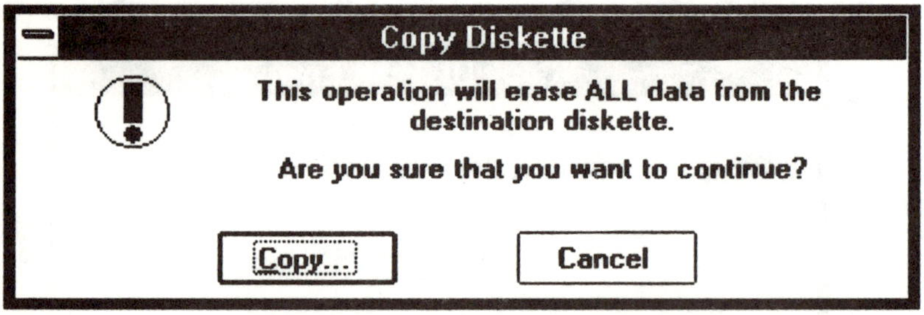

Figure 3-59. The Copy Diskette Dialogue Box #2.

First you will see the dialogue box shown in Figure 3-60. Select OK on that dialogue box.

Figure 3-60. The Copy Diskette Dialogue Box #3.

Next, if you are copying to a different diskette drive, you will see the dialogue box shown in Figure 3-61. Select OK.

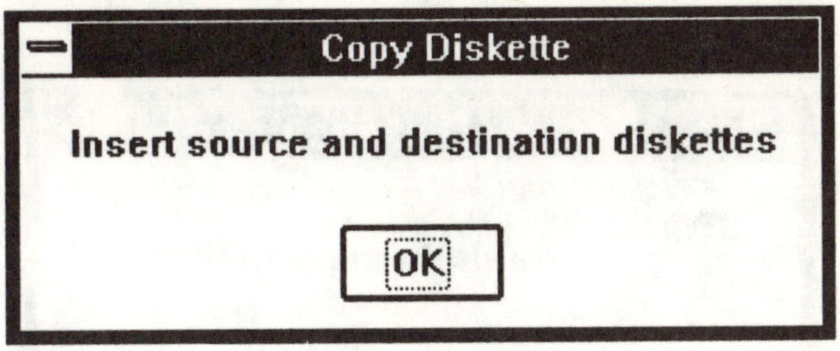

Figure 3-61. The Copy Diskette Dialogue Box #4.

While the copy operation proceeds, the dialogue box in Figure 3-62 is displayed. You can select Cancel at any time to terminate the operation.

Figure 3-62. The Copying Diskette Dialogue Box.

If you have tried to copy to an incompatible diskette format, you will see the error message shown in Figure 3-63.

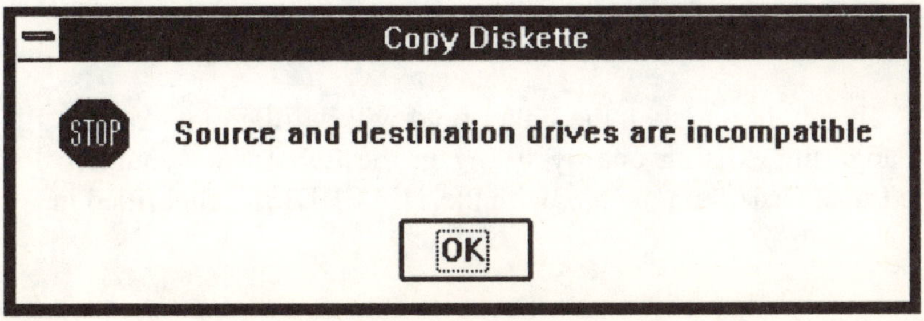

Figure 3-63. The Copy Diskette Error Message #2.

You may also encounter the error message in Figure 3-64; it tells you that the copy did not complete for any of several reasons, including your selection of Cancel during the operation.

Figure 3-64. The Copy Diskette Error Message #3.

Labeling Disks and Diskettes

Hard disks and diskettes can have labels. You can establish or change the label on the currently selected disk by using the Label Disk... command on the Disk menu. When you execute this command you see the Label Disk dialogue box shown in Figure 3-65.

Figure 3-65. The Label Disk Dialogue Box.

If the disk already has a label, the Label field will be filled in. You can fill in a new one or change the existing one by filling in the Label field yourself. Figure 3-66 shows the Label Disk dialogue box with the TEACHDISK label filled in.

Figure 3-66. The Label Disk Dialogue Box with a Label.

The next time you look at the directory tree for a disk you've labeled, you will see the label to the left of the drive and path, as shown in Figure 3-67.

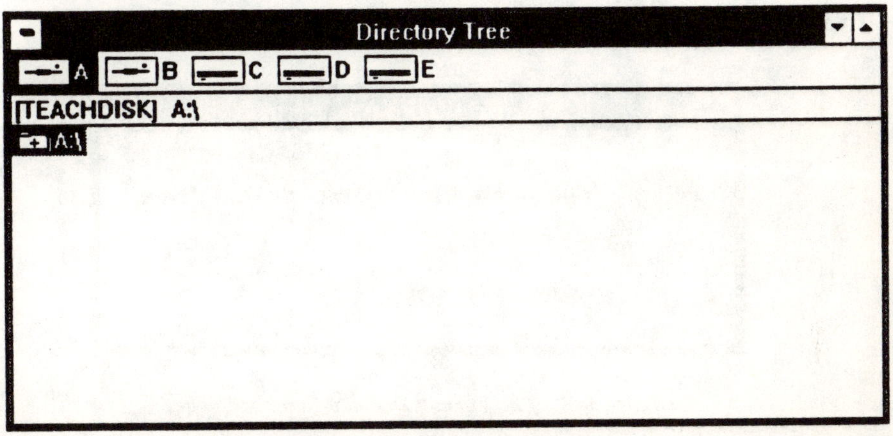

Figure 3-67. A Diskette with a Label.

Formatting Diskettes

Before you can use a diskette out of the box, you must format it. The Format Diskette... command on the File menu is for this purpose. Figure 3-68 is the Format Diskette dialogue box that you see when you select this command.

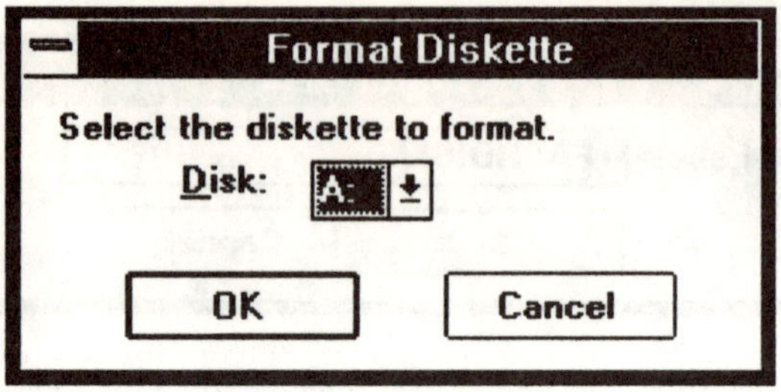

Figure 3-68. The Format Diskette Dialogue Box #1.

You cannot format the current drive. Figure 3-69 shows the error message that you get if you select the current drive from the Format Diskette dialogue box.

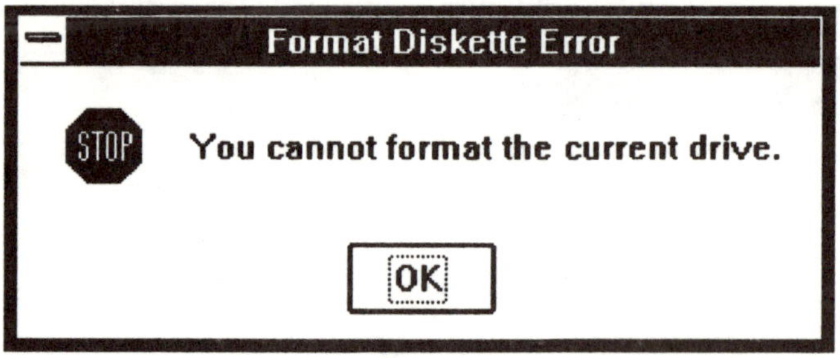

Figure 3-69. The Format Diskette Error Message.

Inasmuch as formatting wipes all data from a diskette, the File Manager asks you to verify your intentions with the dialogue box shown in Figure 3-70. Select the Format... command button to continue.

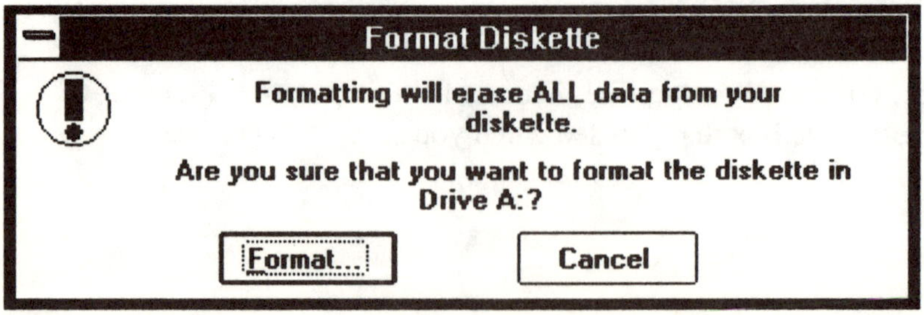

Figure 3-70. The Format Diskette Dialogue Box #2.

Figure 3-71 shows the dialogue box with which you specify your formatting options. A high density 5.25-inch diskette drive can format a 1.2 Mbyte high density diskette or a 360K diskette. A high density 3.5-inch diskette drive can format a 1.44 Mbyte high density diskette or a 720K diskette. If you select High Capacity on the dialogue box for a 3.5-inch drive and the diskette is not a 1.44 Mbyte diskette, you will get an error message. If you select High Capacity on the dialogue box for 5.25-inch drive, and the diskette is not a 1.2 Mbyte diskette, the format operation will proceed, but at a slow rate with a lot of retries; usually the format will fail before it completes.

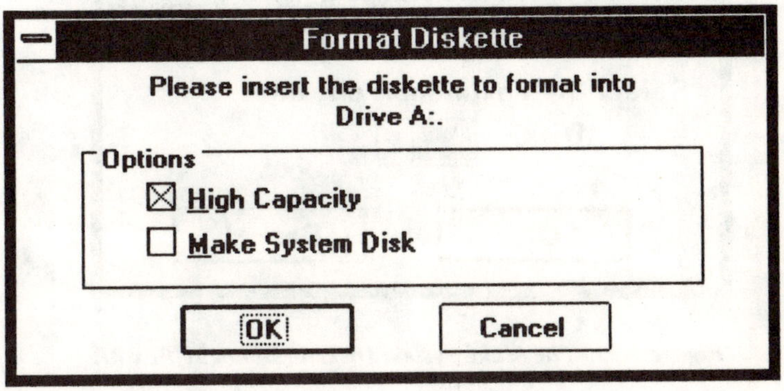

Figure 3-71. The Format Diskette Dialogue Box #3.

While the format operation is running, the dialogue box shown in Figure 3-72 is displayed. You can select Cancel at any time to stop the operation.

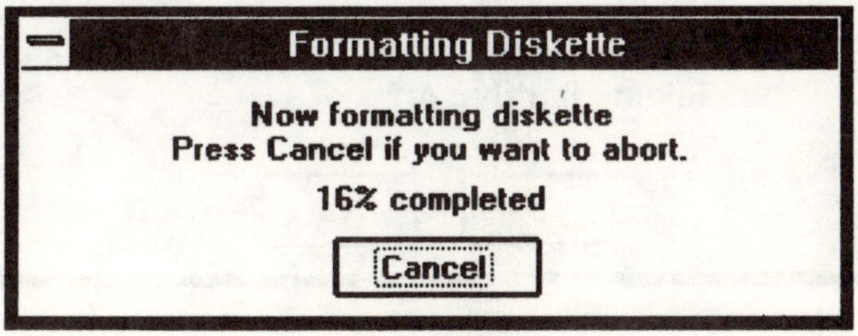

Figure 3-72. The Formatting Diskette Dialogue Box.

Making System Diskettes

Some diskettes have DOS stored on them—you can use these diskettes to boot DOS. This format supports those computers that do not boot from a hard disk. Some network work stations do not have hard disks but rather use the shared disk of the file server. The work stations boot DOS from a diskette. The Make System Diskette... command on the Disk menu allows you to copy the necessary DOS files to a diskette to make it into a DOS-bootable diskette. When you select the command you will see the dialogue box shown in Figure 3-73.

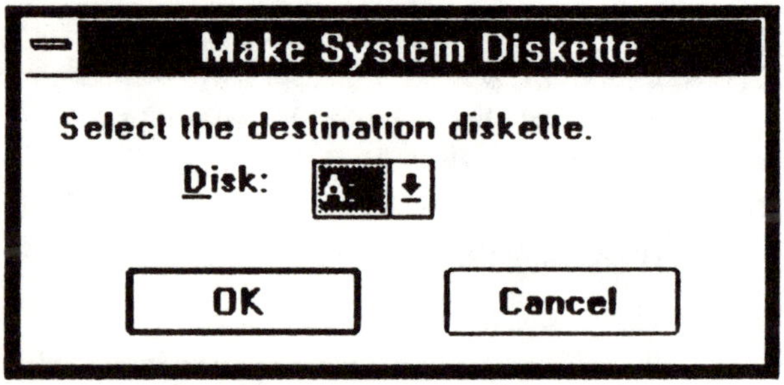

Figure 3-73. The Make System Diskette Dialogue Box #1.

Select the drive you want to make into a system diskette from the drop-down list box in the dialogue box and then select OK. You will see the dialogue box shown in Figure 3-74.

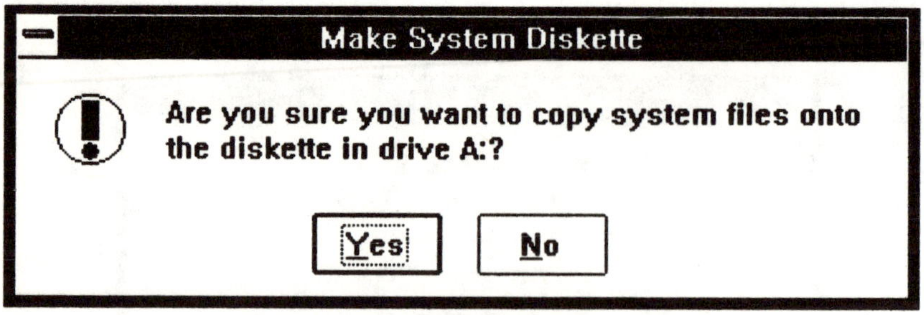

Figure 3-74. The Make System Diskette Dialogue Box #2.

Select the Yes command button from the dialogue box and the dialogue box shown in Figure 3-75 appears while the File Manager copies the DOS system files to the diskette.

Figure 3-75. The Make System Diskette Dialogue Box #3.

RUNNING APPLICATIONS FROM THE FILE MANAGER

In Chapter 2 you learned to use the Program Manager to execute programs from defined groups of applications. The File Manager offers additional ways to run programs. Any file with the Application icon is a program that you can execute. Figure 3-8, toward the beginning of this chapter, shows the File Manager icons. The Application icon resembles a window with a title bar across it. The File Manager offers several ways to start an application that has this icon.

Some applications are Windows applications, and others are not. Windows knows how to execute each one, so the effect of executing from the File Manager is the same as if you had installed the application in a Program Manager group and executed it from there.

There are two reasons for using the File Manager to execute an application. First, you might not use the program often enough to want to keep it in a Program Manager group. Second, you might want to execute the application for a specific document file that is not always the same. The File Manager allows you to associate document file types with specific applications.

Selecting Executable Files

You can execute an application simply by selecting its file name from within a directory window. Open a directory window with the C:\WINDOWS directory. Double click the CARDFILE.EXE file or move the highlight cursor to it and press Enter. The Cardfile application executes.

If you have any .PIF files, select one of them, in the same way, to execute the application with the parameters in the .PIF file. You will learn how to use the PIF Editor to create and modify .PIF files for non-Windows applications in Chapter 11. You can also use this procedure to execute .COM and .BAT files from the File Manager.

The Run... Command

The File Manager has a Run... command on the File menu. This command works exactly like the Program Manager's Run... command that you learned about in Chapter 2.

Dragging a Document to an Application

You can click on a document file and drag it to an application. This action runs the application with the document file as its input—just as if you had entered the application's and document file's names into the Run... command.

Open one directory window with the C:\ directory and another one with the C:\WINDOWS directory. Minimize the directory tree and move and scroll the directory windows around so that you can see the AUTOEXEC.BAT file in the C:\ directory and the NOTEPAD.EXE file in the C:\WINDOWS directory.

Drag the AUTOEXEC.BAT document file to the NOTEPAD.EXE application file. You will see the display shown in Figure 3-76.

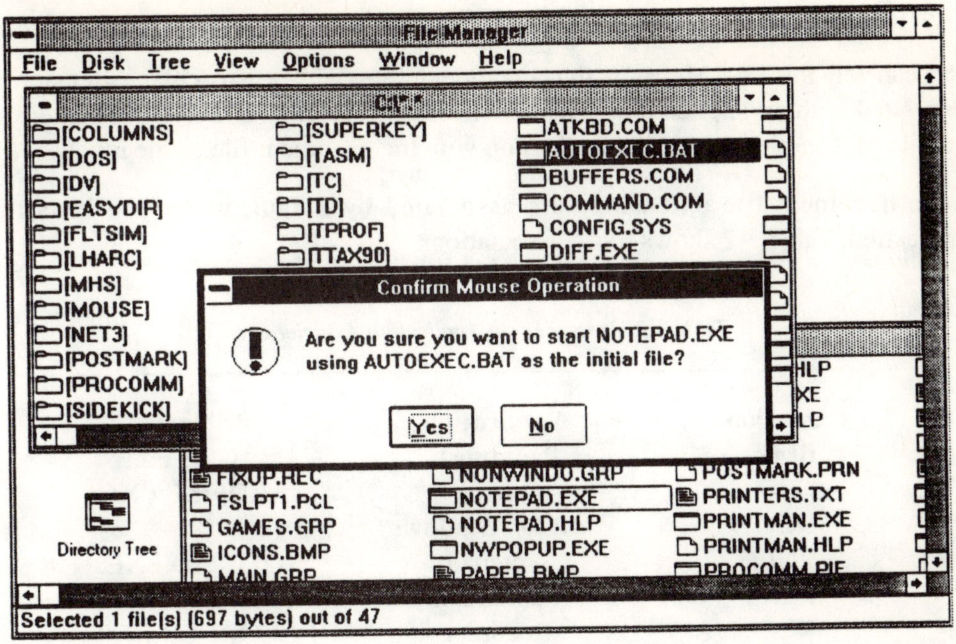

Figure 3-76. Dragging a Document to an Application.

When you select Yes, the Notepad executes with AUTOEXEC.BAT as its document file, as shown in Figure 3-77.

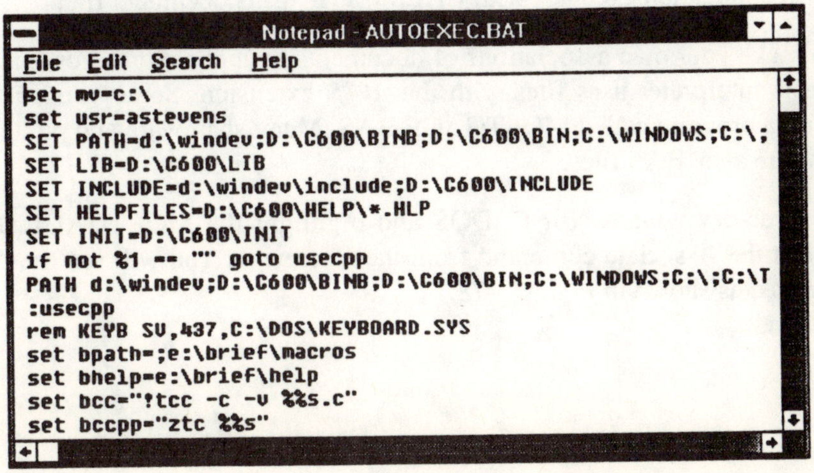

Figure 3-77. The Notepad Running with AUTOEXEC.BAT.

Associating Applications and Documents

You can tell the File Manager that document files with a particular extension are associated with an application. Then whenever you select a file with that extension, the File Manager executes the application with the document file as the input.

Some document file extensions are associated by default when you install the application. Table 3-2 shows those associations.

Table 3-2. Document to Application Associations.

Extension	Application	File Name
BMP	Paintbrush	PBRUSH.EXE
CRD	Cardfile	CARDFILE.EXE
DOC	Word for Windows*	
INI	Notepad	NOTEPAD.EXE
PCX	Paintbrush	PBRUSH.EXE
REC	Recorder	RECORDER.EXE
TXT	Notepad	NOTEPAD.EXE
WRI	Write	WRITE.EXE

* WFW is not included with Windows.

You learned and were shown in Figure 3-13 that when you select CHESS.BMP, the Paintbrush application executes with CHESS.BMP as its document file.

You can make your own associations of documents to applications. For example, the DOS Basic interpreter uses files with the .BAS extension. Some versions of DOS come with a program called MORTGAGE.BAS. Many shareware and public domain programs are also .BAS files.

Open a directory window for C:\DOS and highlight the MORTGAGE.BAS file. Then select the Associate command from the File menu. You will see the Associate dialogue box, as shown in Figure 3-78.

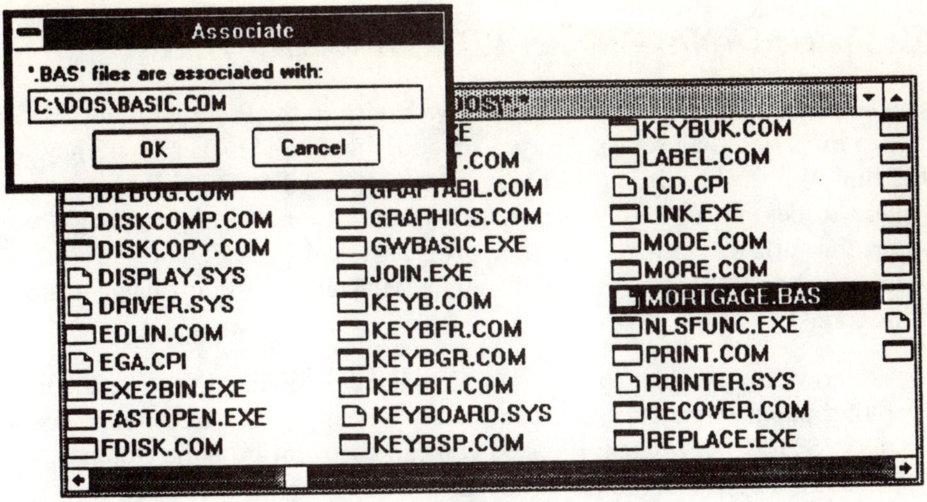

Figure 3-78. The Associate Dialogue Box.

By highlighting the MORTGAGE.BAS program you told the Associate command what kind of files you want to associate with the Basic interpreter. Fill in the path and name of the Basic interpreter file, as shown in Figure 3-78, and select OK. Figure 3-79 shows that the MORTGAGE.BAS file now has an Associated Document icon, which means that when you select it you will run an application. If you double click the file now, you will run the Basic application with MORTGAGE.BAS as the input file.

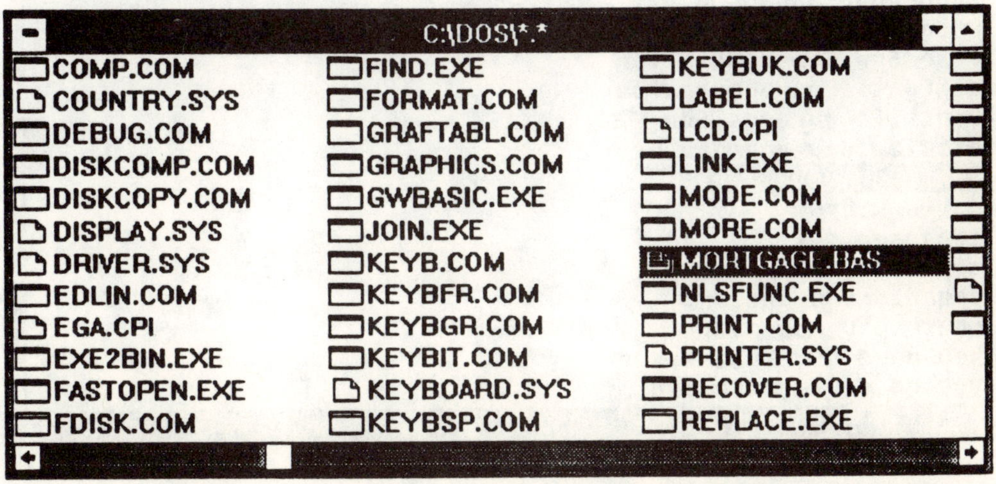

Figure 3-79. MORTGAGE.BAS Associated with an Application.

THE FILE MANAGER AS THE DEFAULT SHELL

As you learned in Chapters 1 and 2, Windows begins in the Program Manager. Some users, however, find themselves always executing the File Manager first. They would prefer that Windows begins that way. You can modify the Windows startup procedure to begin with any program you want, although it should begin with a program that allows you to run other programs and look at your files. Such a program is called a "shell," and the Program Manager and File Manager are both shell programs.

When Windows begins running it reads a file called SYSTEM.INI to load a number of operating parameters. One of those parameters specifies the name of the shell program. SYSTEM.INI is a text file, and you can change it from the Notepad. Figure 3-80 shows the file loaded into the Notepad.

Because INI files are associated with the Notepad all you need to do to get at the file is to double click it. The line you are interested in is highlighted in Figure 3-80. To direct Windows to load the File Manager as the shell, change the line to read:

shell=winfile.exe

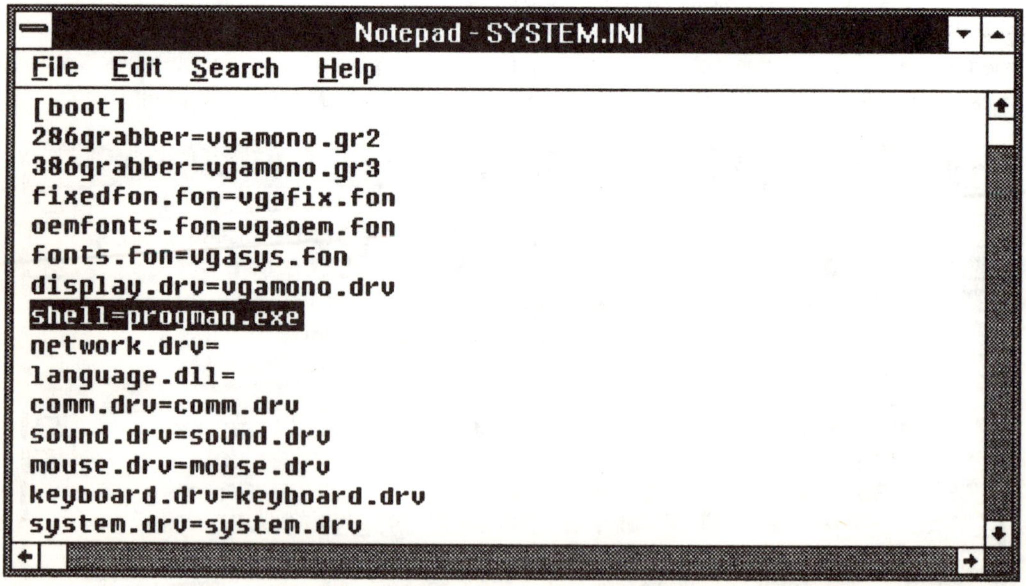

Figure 3-80. The SYSTEM.INI File.

With the line changed to the new value, save the file by selecting the Save command on the Notepad's File menu. Exit from Windows and reload it. Windows starts running in the File Manager. The only remnant of the Program Manager is the fact that you can still use the Task List, which is actually not a part of the Program Manager but is an integral part of the Windows multitasking executive.

SUMMARY

With a sound understanding of the Program Manager and File Manager, you are ready to learn how Windows uses the Clipboard to support the exchange of data between applications. Chapter 4 introduces the Clipboard and teaches you the many ways you can use it with Windows and DOS programs.

Chapter 4

The Clipboard

The Clipboard is an integral part of the multi-program Windows environment. It is a method by which applications exchange text and graphics data under your control.

HOW THE CLIPBOARD WORKS

To transfer data from one program to another, you tell the sending program to write the data to the Clipboard, then you tell the receiving program to read the data from the Clipboard. The Clipboard remembers its contents until you delete them, copy other data to the Clipboard, or exit from Windows. It helps to examine the circumstances under which you would want to transfer data from one application to another. Consider the following examples.

Suppose that you are using the Notepad to write a memo to one of the civic organization's members. You can call up the Cardfile record for that member, copy the member's name and address into the Clipboard, return to the Notepad, and paste the name and address from the Clipboard into the memo.

As another example, it is common practice to prepare graphics illustrations in one program—Paintbrush for example—and integrate them into a document with your word processor. The clipboard offers a way to move the illustrations from the composition software to the document preparation program.

You might also want to include the rows and columns of a spreadsheet in a report. By using the Clipboard, you can move the required information from the spreadsheet program into the word processor document even if the two programs use incompatible file formats.

***

SOME PROGRAMS USE THE CLIPBOARD TO EXCHANGE DATA WITHOUT YOUR INTERVENTION. YOU SHOULD BE AWARE OF THIS POSSIBILITY SO THAT YOU WILL NOT BE SURPRISED IF YOU FIND THAT EVERY NOW AND THEN THE CLIPBOARD CONTAINS DATA OTHER THAN WHAT YOU EXPECTED.

***

Sending data to the Clipboard is called "cutting" and "copying." An application that can cut or copy first marks the block of text or graphics to be cut or copied. Cutting implies that the data block is deleted from the sending application when it is transferred to the Clipboard. Copying implies that the sending application retains its copy of the data block, transferring a copy of it to the Clipboard.

The Clipboard holds either text or graphics images at any one time; the format depends on the sending application. If the sending application is a graphics application, such as Paintbrush, the Clipboard's contents will be a graphics image. If the sending application is a text application, such as Notepad, the Clipboard's contents will be text.

Receiving data from the Clipboard into an application is called "pasting." You paste text Clipboard data into a program that processes text, and you paste graphics Clipboard data into a program that processes graphics. A text-only application, such as the Notepad, cannot paste graphics data from the Clipboard. If the Clipboard contains graphics data, it appears to be empty to a text-only application. Likewise a graphics-only application cannot paste text data from the Clipboard.

Some applications can process both text and graphics. Windows Write is such an application. If the Clipboard contains text, Write pastes text into the document. If the Clipboard contains graphics, Write pastes graphics into the document. When cutting or copying, Write first marks a block which must be all text or all graphics. The format you mark determines the format that the Clipboard receives.

***

Do not confuse the text you see in some Paintbrush images with the Clipboard's concept of text versus graphics. Text in a graphics-only application is really a graphical representation of the letters and numbers. Even though it appears to be text on the screen, it is internally represented as a graphics image.

***

Non-Windows DOS applications can exchange only text with the Clipboard. If the DOS application runs in a window—386 Extended Mode only—you can transfer selected blocks of text to the Clipboard. If the application runs full-screen, you must transfer the entire screen to the Clipboard. Pasting into a DOS application works only with unformatted text. The paste operation transmits the data as if the Clipboard was typing into the application.

The Clipboard is a Windows application with an icon in the Main group. Besides cutting, copying, and pasting, you can run the Clipboard to view its contents, save the current Clipboard to a file, and load a previously saved Clipboard file.

For the exercises that follow, you will use some of the applications to which you have already been exposed. Although the details of these applications are presented later in the book, you will use subsets of their features to learn about the Clipboard. Other exercises will use the XY Write and Wordstar examples. If you do not have these programs, you can follow along in the book.

Sending Applications Data to the Clipboard

You use the Cut or Copy commands from the File menus of Windows applications to send data to the Clipboard. You use other means to send data from non-Windows DOS applications. The procedures for sending text and graphics are quite similar.

Sending Text to the Clipboard from a Windows Application

Begin by executing the Notepad from the Accessories Group. Type some text into the Notepad, as shown in Figure 4-1. Type any text you want, not necessarily the text in the figure.

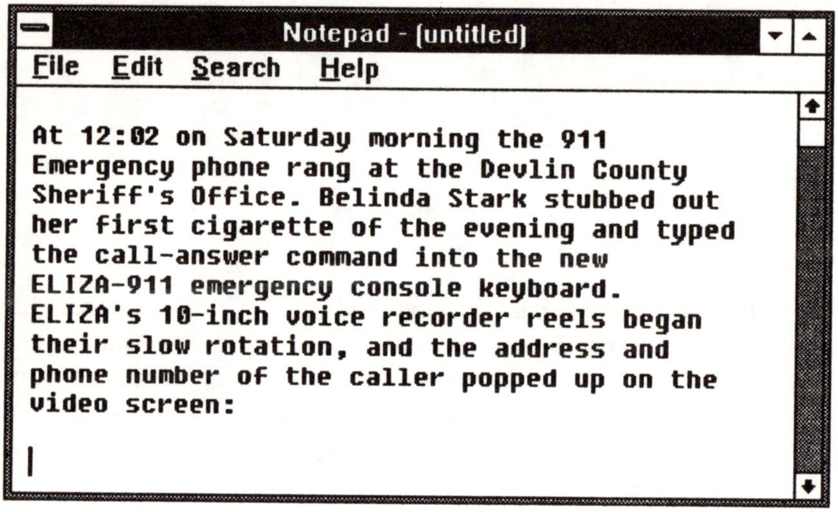

Figure 4-1. The Notepad with Some Text.

To send text to the Clipboard, you must mark it. To mark text with the mouse, move the cursor to the first character of the block, hold down the left mouse button, and drag the cursor to the last character of the block. As you move the mouse, the text is highlighted to indicate the range of the marked block.

To mark text with the keyboard, move the keyboard cursor to the first character of the block. Hold down the Shift key and move the cursor with the arrow keys. As you move the cursor, the text is highlighted to indicate the range of the marked block.

Figure 4-2 shows the Notepad with a marked block.

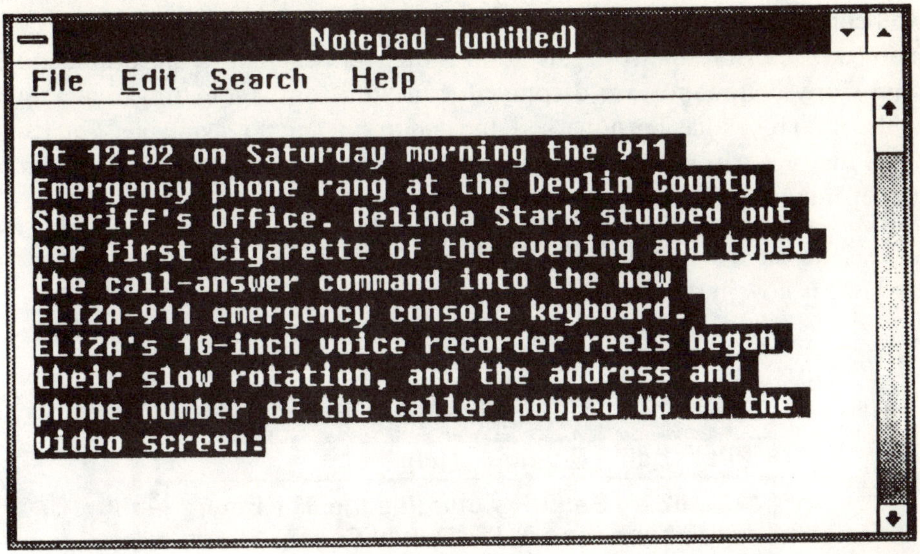

Figure 4-2. A Marked Block of Text.

To copy the marked block to the Clipboard, select the Copy command from the Notepad's Edit menu, as shown in Figure 4-3.

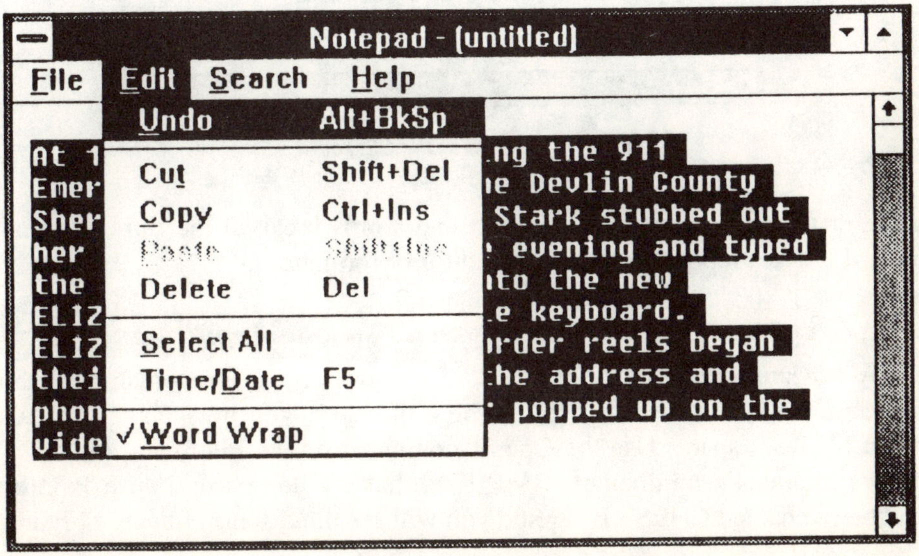

Figure 4-3. The Notepad's Edit Menu.

The Cut command has the same effect as the Copy command, except that Cut deletes the marked block from the Notepad when it transfers the text to the Clipboard. The Cut and Copy commands are displayed in a bold font, indicating that they are available. If no block has been marked, the commands are not available. You can use the Ctrl+Ins or Ctrl-Del shortcut keys to execute the Copy and Cut commands without opening the menu.

If you execute the Clipboard application from the Main group, you will see that the selected text is now in the Clipboard, as shown in Figure 4-4.

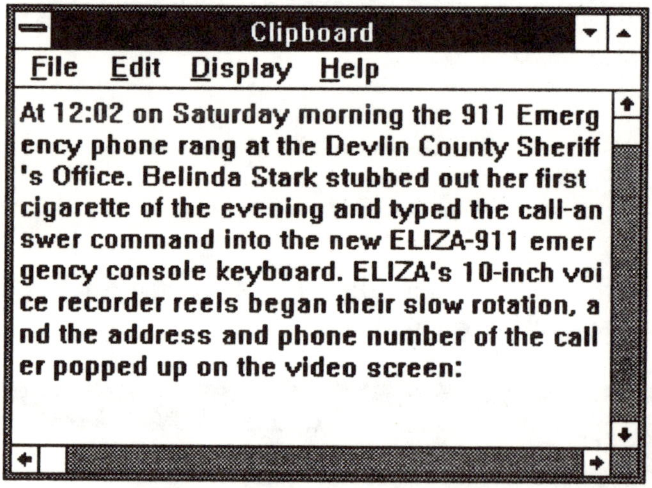

Figure 4-4. Text in the Clipboard.

Observe that the text is unformatted and that words break at the right margin. The Clipboard is a text repository, not a text editor or formatter.

Sending Graphics to the Clipboard from a Windows Application

Begin by executing Paintbrush from the Accessories group. Paintbrush is a graphics application. To send graphics data to the Clipboard, you must have a picture in Paintbrush's work space. Use the Open... command on the File menu to find a file. Windows includes a number of .BMP files that are compatible with Paintbrush. Select the file named CHESS.BMP and you will see the display shown in Figure 4-5.

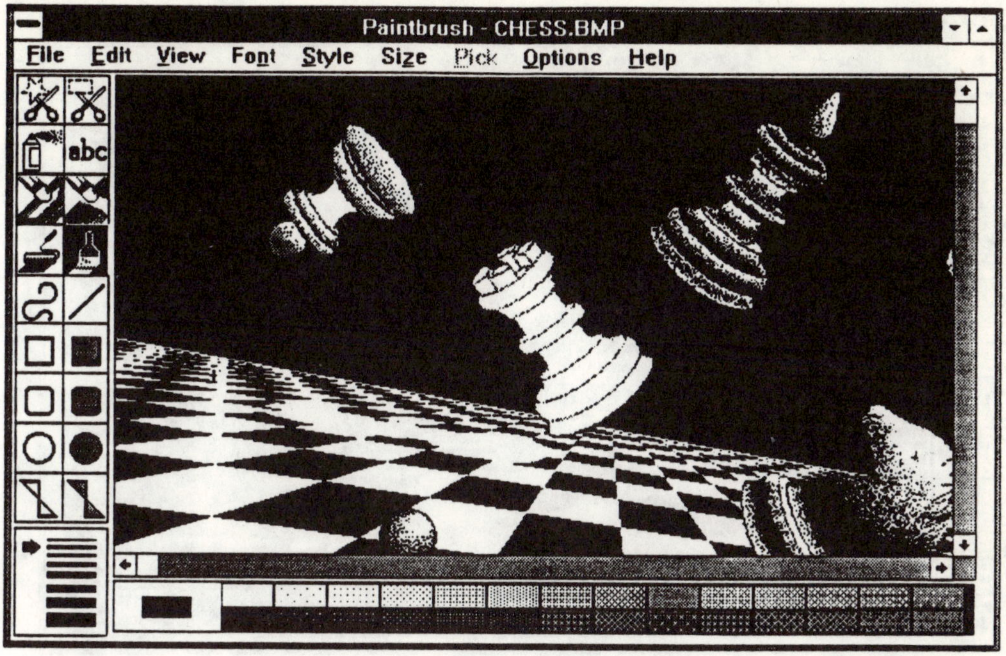

Figure 4-5. The Paintbrush with Some Graphics.

To transfer graphics data to the Clipboard, you must mark a block. To mark a graphics block, move the mouse cursor to one corner of the block and drag the cursor to the opposite corner.

The display shows a dotted rectangle to describe the block. When you have the block where you want it, release the mouse button. If you don't like the way the block turned out, click the mouse button outside of the block and start over.

Figure 4-6 shows the picture with one of the chessmen marked as a graphics block.

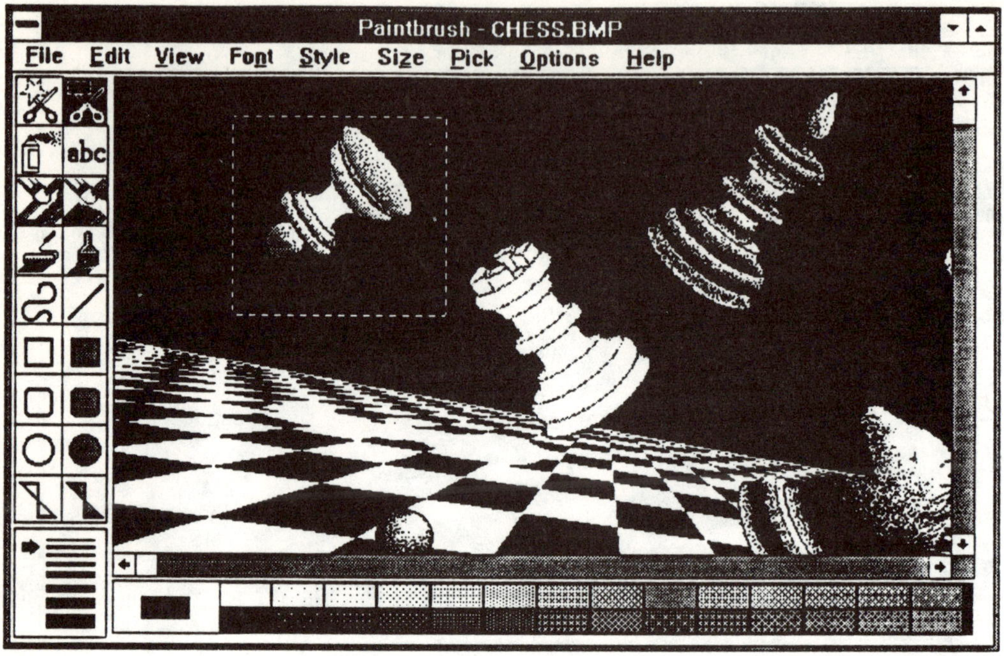

Figure 4-6. A Marked Graphics Block.

With the graphics block marked, select Copy from the Edit menu or press Ctrl-Ins. If you open the Clipboard application now, you will see that the selected chessman is there, as shown in Figure 4-7.

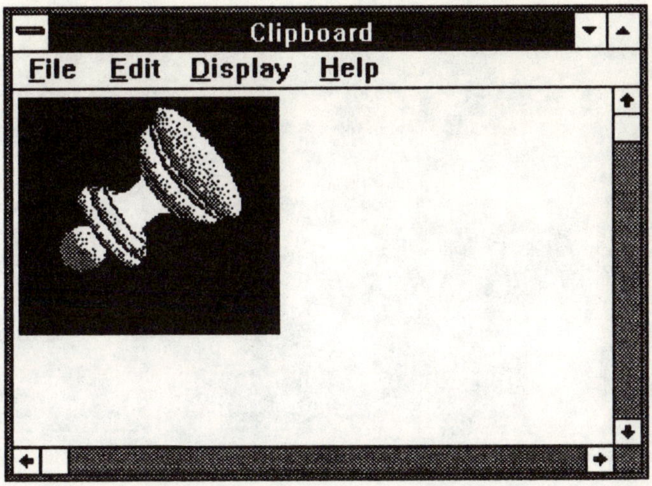

Figure 4-7. Graphics in the Clipboard.

Sending Text to the Clipboard from a DOS Application Running in a Window

In the examples above, you had a DOS application, XY Write, running in a window. XY Write is a word processor, and you can use it to see how to send text from such an application to the Clipboard. Figure 4-8 shows the XY Write application with some text in it.

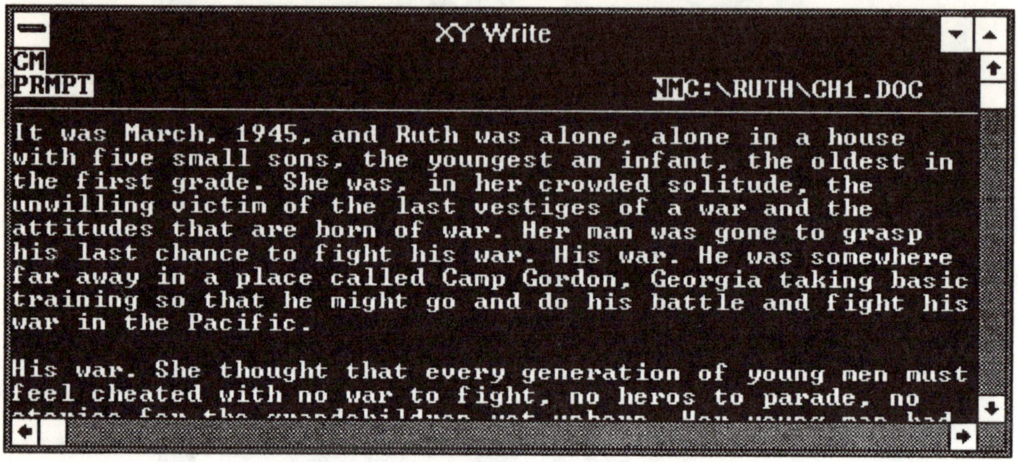

Figure 4-8. The XY Write Window With Text.

You send text from XY Write to the Clipboard differently than you sent it from the Notepad. The Notepad, being a Windows application, has its own built-in Cut and Copy commands; DOS applications do not. A window that runs a DOS application, however, has its own version of the Control Menu with extra commands that support Clipboard operations.

First you must mark a block of text. You can move the mouse cursor to a corner of the block of text and drag the cursor to the opposite corner. The text block appears in reverse video. To turn the block off, press the right mouse button.

To mark a block of text with the keyboard, select the Edit command from the window's Control Menu. You will see the Edit menu, as shown in Figure 4-9. The Copy command on the Edit menu is not available because no text block is marked yet.

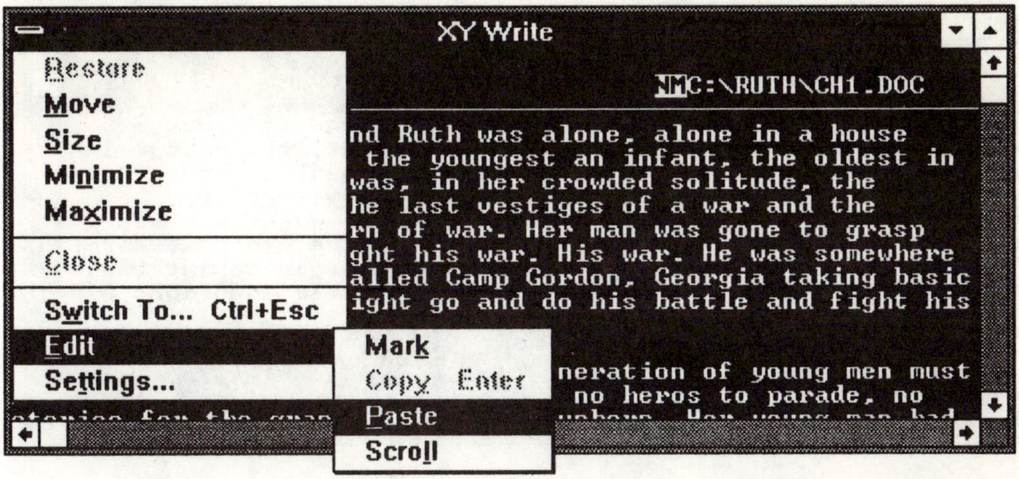

Figure 4-9. The Control Menu's Edit Menu.

Select Mark on the Edit menu. The menus disappear, and a blinking cursor appears in the upper left corner of the window.

Move the blinking cursor to the upper left corner of the block of text you want to transfer to the Clipboard. Hold down the Shift key and use the arrow keys to move the cursor and describe the block. Figure 4-10 shows the XY Write window with a block of text defined.

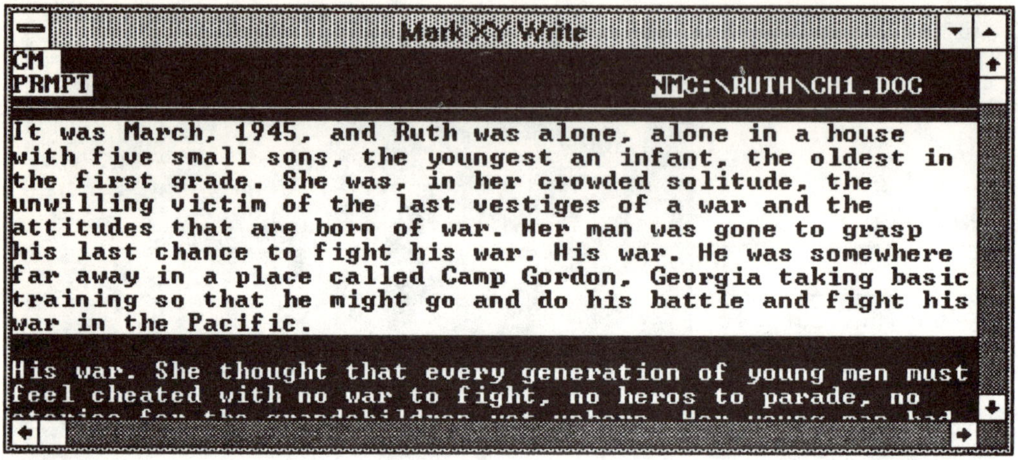

Figure 4-10. Text Marked in a DOS Application Window.

With the text block marked, select the Edit menu from the Control Menu. Figure 4-11 shows the Edit menu selected, with the text block defined under it.

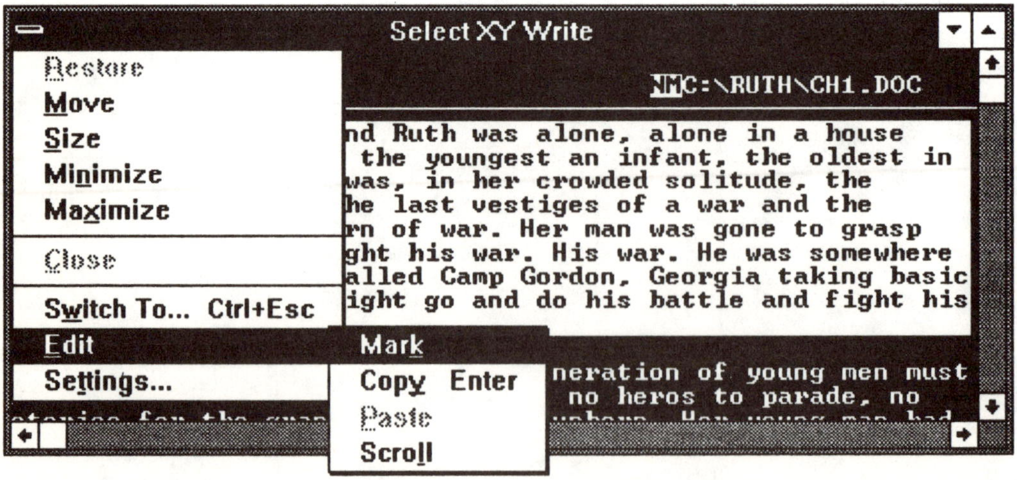

Figure 4-11. The Edit Menu with Copy Available.

The Copy command is now available, so you can select it. The Copy command copies the marked block to the Clipboard and unmarks the block. There is no Cut command on the Edit menu because the Program Manager does not know how to tell the application to delete text.

If you run the Clipboard application now, you will see the text that was copied there, as shown in Figure 4-12. If you are running the XY Write program along with these exercises, use its QUIT command to terminate it before proceeding to the next exercise.

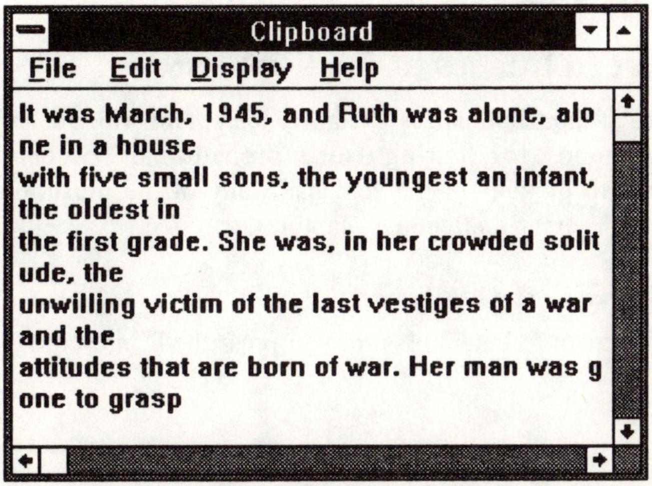

Figure 4-12. Text in the Clipboard.

Sending Text to the Clipboard from a DOS Application Running Full-Screen

The Wordstar application that you added to the Civic group in Chapter 2 runs in full-screen mode—when you run the application, it takes over the entire screen. Applications that run in full-screen mode cannot send selected blocks to the Clipboard. They can, however, send the entire text screen.

To send a text screen to the Clipboard from a full-screen DOS application, press the Print Screen key. When you return to Windows from the DOS application, the Clipboard contains the application's text screen image. You cannot, however, send the screen image of a DOS application that itself uses graphics displays.

Sending Screen Images to the Clipboard

A useful feature of the Clipboard is its ability to capture window and screen images. This feature is handy for writing user's procedures. You can illustrate your documentation with pictures of the screens. Many of the illustrations in this book were prepared with screen and window captures.

Sending the Screen to the Clipboard

To send the full screen to the Clipboard, you press the Print Screen key. Figure 4-13 shows a typical desktop.

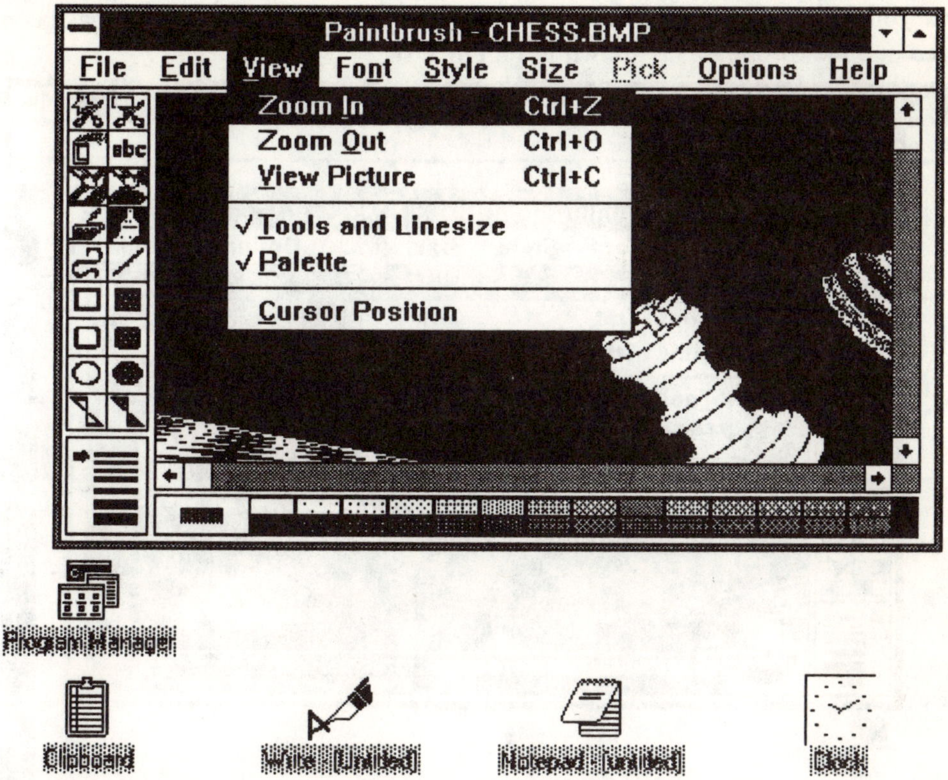

Figure 4-13. A Typical Desktop.

When you press the Print Screen key from the desktop shown in Figure 4-13 and then execute the clipboard application, you will see that the entire desktop has been captured into the Clipboard, as shown in Figure 4-14.

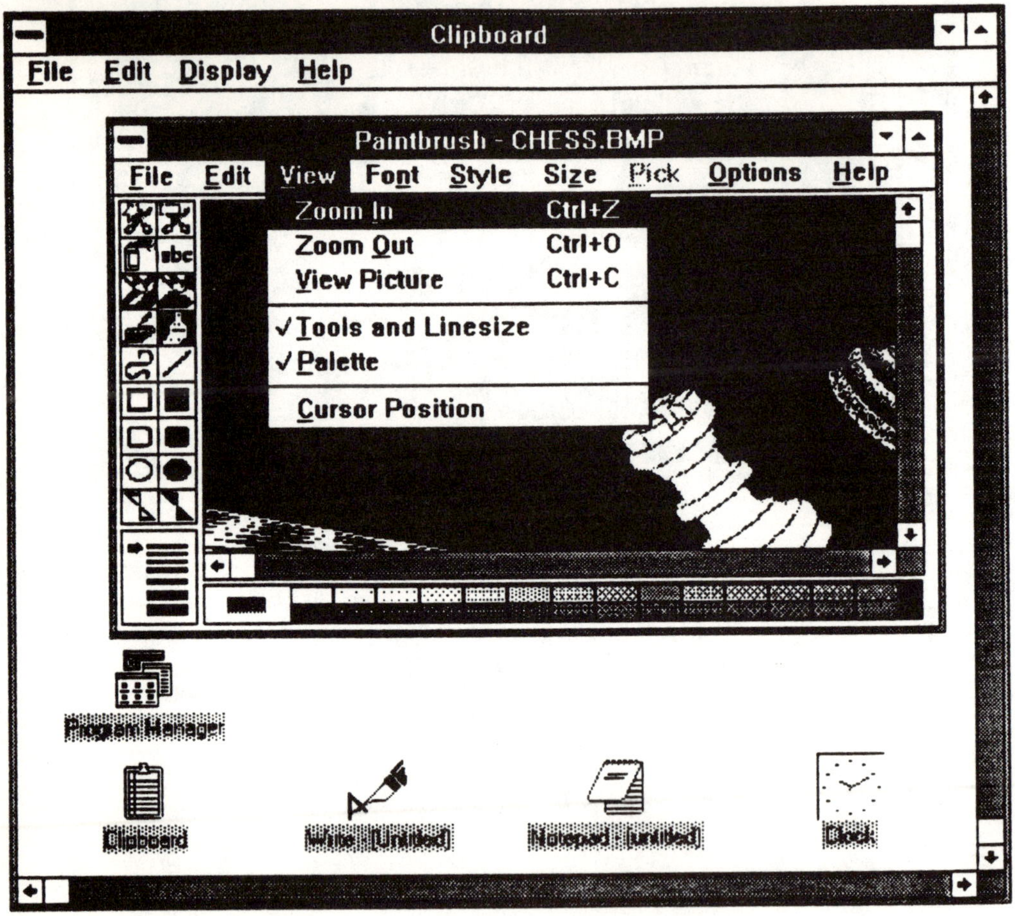

Figure 4-14. A Screen Captured to the Clipboard.

Sending the Current Window to the Clipboard

Often your desktop is cluttered with icons and inactive windows, and you want to capture only the current window. To send the current window to the Clipboard, you press the Alt+Print Screen key. Figure 4-15 shows a typical cluttered desktop.

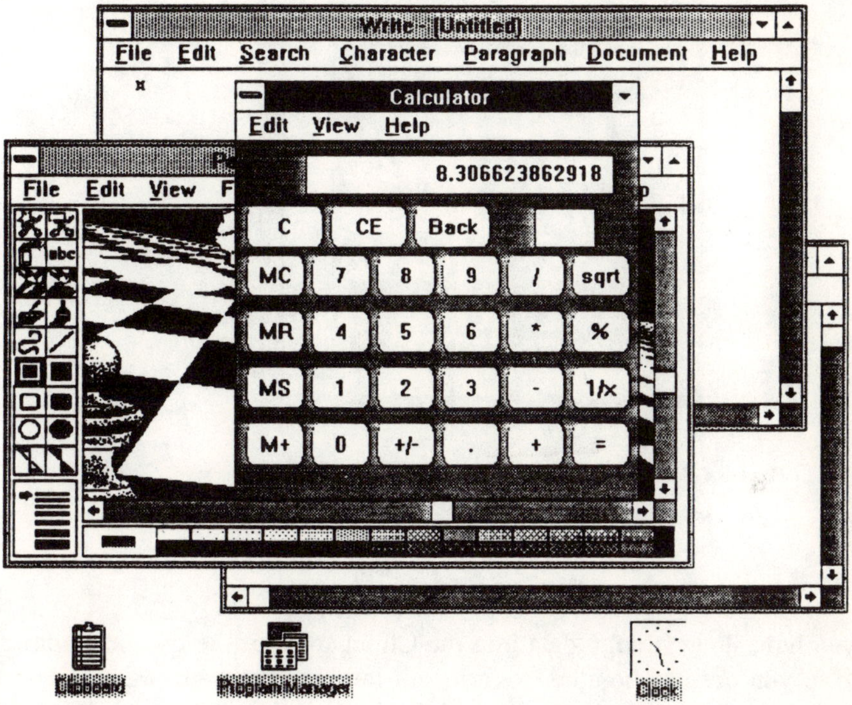

Figure 4-15. A Typical Cluttered Desktop.

When you press the Alt+Print Screen key from the desktop shown in Figure 4-15 and then execute the clipboard application, you will see that the current window, the Calculator, has been captured into the Clipboard, as shown in Figure 4-16.

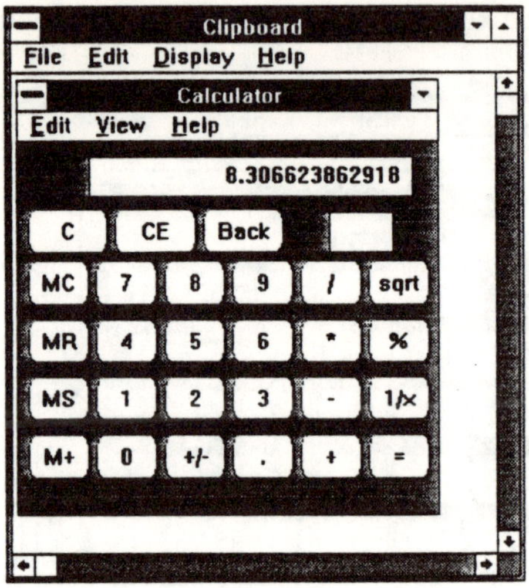

Figure 4-16. The Current Window Captured to the Clipboard.

Pasting Data from the Clipboard

So far all you have done is copy data into the Clipboard. For the text or graphics to be of any use, you need to be able to get it out into another application. Clear the clutter from your desktop and open the Membership Roster Cardfile application from your Civic group. You will get a Change Disk message telling you that the program cannot find MEMBERS.CRD. That is because you have not yet built the file. Select the Cancel control button to get past the message.

You need to add a record to the Cardfile in order to use it. Type a name and address on the first card, as shown in Figure 4-17.

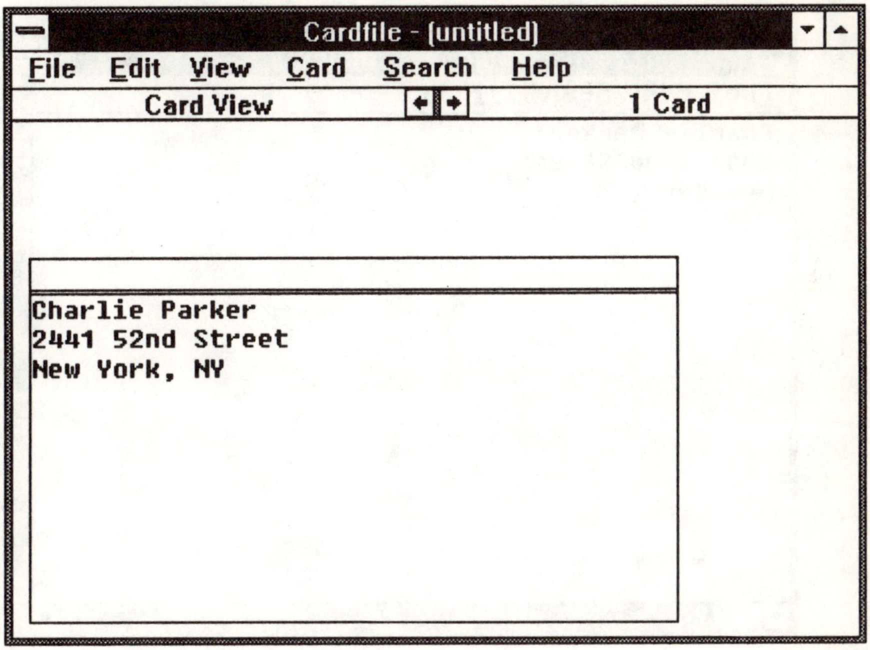

Figure 4-17. A Cardfile Record with Some Text.

Select the Save As... command from the File menu and type "members" into the Filename field of the File Save As dialogue box that appeared when you selected the Save As... command. Select OK on the dialogue box to build the first record into your membership roster. From now on, when you use the Membership Roster a record will be there.

Pasting Text from the Clipboard to a Windows Application

Now suppose that you are using the Notepad to write a memo to the person who is named on this card. Mark the name and address text the way you learned earlier in this chapter and select Copy from the Edit menu—this puts the name and address into the Clipboard. You can exit from the Membership Roster Cardfile application now.

Select the Notepad from the Accessories group. You will see a blank Notepad window just like you've seen before. Press Shift+Ins or select Paste from the Edit menu. The Name and Address appear on the Notepad, as shown in Figure 4-18.

Figure 4-18. Text Pasted from the Clipboard to the Notepad.

Pasting Graphics from the Clipboard to a Windows Application

Suppose that you want to include a picture in the letter you are writing. The Notepad cannot handle graphics, but Windows Write can. Close the Notepad, open the Write application, and select Paste from the Edit menu to paste the text of the name and address on the screen, as shown in Figure 4-19.

Figure 4-19. The Name and Address Pasted into a Write Document.

Open the Paintbrush and open the CHESS.BMP file, just as you did in an earlier exercise. Mark one of the chessmen and copy it to the Clipboard. Exit from the Paintbrush and return to Write. Select Paste from the Edit menu and watch the picture you saved come into your document, as shown in Figure 4-20.

Figure 4-20. A Picture Pasted into a Write Document.

Pasting from the Clipboard to a non-Windows DOS Application Running in a Window

Open your Membership Roster Cardfile and copy the name and address into the Clipboard again. Close the Cardfile application.

If you do not have the XY Write application installed to run in a Window, simply follow along with this exercise in the book. Open the XY Write application from the Non-Windows Applications group. In order for XY Write to allow you to enter data, you must name a new document. Type "new test.doc" on the XY Write command line—this puts XY Write into a mode that allows text entry.

Select the Edit menu from the Control Menu, as shown in Figure 4-21.

Figure 4-21. The Edit Menu for a Non-Windows DOS Application in a Window.

Select the Paste command and observe that the text is pasted into the non-Windows DOS application, as shown in Figure 4-22.

Figure 4-22. Text Pasted into a Non-Windows DOS Application in a Window.

Pasting from the Clipboard to a non-Windows DOS Application Running Full-Screen

To paste into a non-Windows DOS application that is running full-screen you must first use Alt+Esc to return to Windows. The non-Windows DOS application appears as an icon at the bottom of the screen. Open the Control Menu for that icon and select the Edit menu and the Paste command, as shown in Figure 4-23. When you return to the DOS application, you will see that the Clipboard text is in the application as if you had typed it there yourself.

Figure 4-23. The Edit Menu for a Full-Screen Non-Windows DOS Application.

Saving and Reloading Clipboard Files

The Clipboard application has a File menu that allows you to save the Clipboard's contents and load a previously saved file into the Clipboard. Figure 4-24 shows that menu. It works just like the other File menus you have learned.

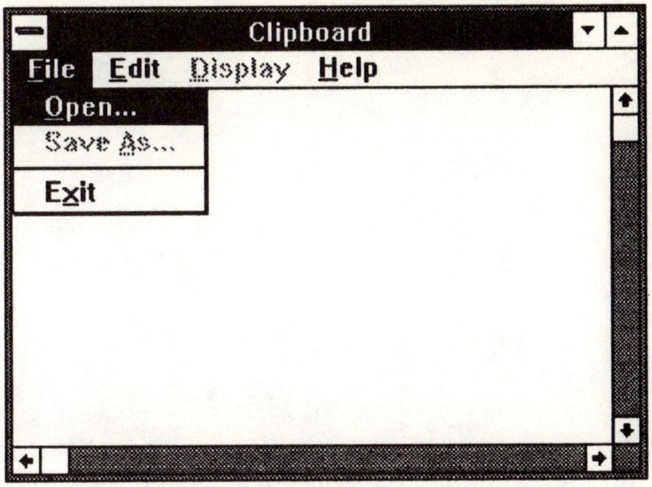

Figure 4-24. The Clipboard's File Menu.

SUMMARY

With the Clipboard as one of your tools, you can now freely exchange data between your applications. Your knowledge encompasses the Windows graphical operating environment, the Program Manager, and the File Manager.

Chapter 5 moves you one step closer to your mastery of this fascinating operating environment. In this chapter you will learn how to use the Control Panel to maintain the operating parameters that allow your computer to make the most of its hardware, and you will discover how to customize the appearance of Windows to suit your own taste.

Chapter 5

The Control Panel

The Control Panel is an application in the Program Manager's Main group. You use it to manage the appearance of your desktop and certain characteristics of the hardware and the operating environment.

***

If you decide to run programs from the File Manager rather than the Program Manager, address the Control Panel as CONTROL.EXE, a file in the WINDOWS directory on the drive where you installed Windows.

***

Figure 5-1 shows the Control Panel application window. It contains an icon for each of the items you manage with the Control Panel. When you select an icon, you execute a process that controls one of the Control Panel functions. The following sections address those processes.

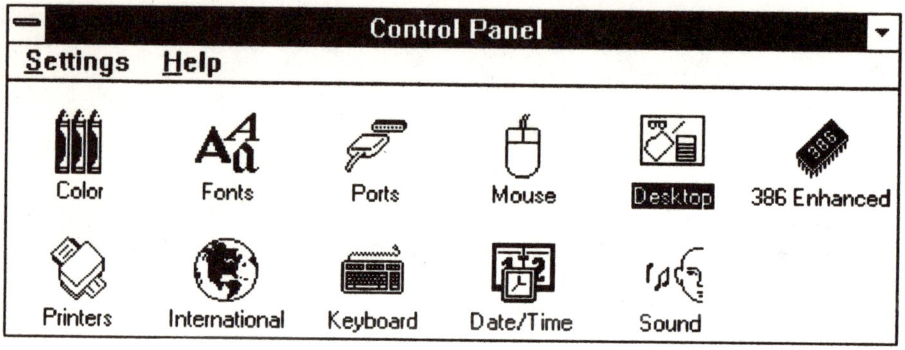

Figure 5-1. The Control Panel Application Window.

COLOR

The control panel provides you with a great breadth of color control—the black and white examples in this book hardly do this capacity justice. You can make dramatic changes in the appearance of your desktop, particularly if you have a color VGA monitor. You can change the color scheme of the desktop components, selecting from a set of defined schemes or building your own scheme by selecting from a color palette. You can even create your own colors. You change colors by selecting the Color icon on the Control Panel. Figure 5-2 shows the Color dialogue box that you see when you select this icon.

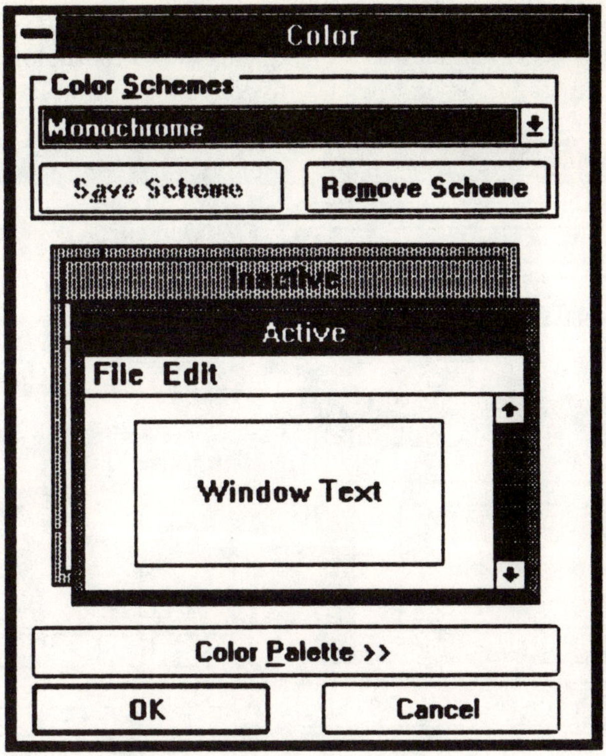

Figure 5-2. The Color Dialogue Box.

Selecting a Color Scheme

The Color Schemes field is a drop-down list box that records the names of the defined color schemes. You can select a scheme from this box, use the Remove Schemes control button to delete a scheme from the list, or build your own scheme and add it to the list.

The stacked windows in the display represent the components of the Desktop. As you try different schemes, the colors in this display change to allow you to view the effects of your changes.

Constructing a Custom Color Scheme

The Color Palette >> Command Button expands the Color dialogue box, as shown in Figure 5-3. This dialogue box allows you to construct custom color schemes.

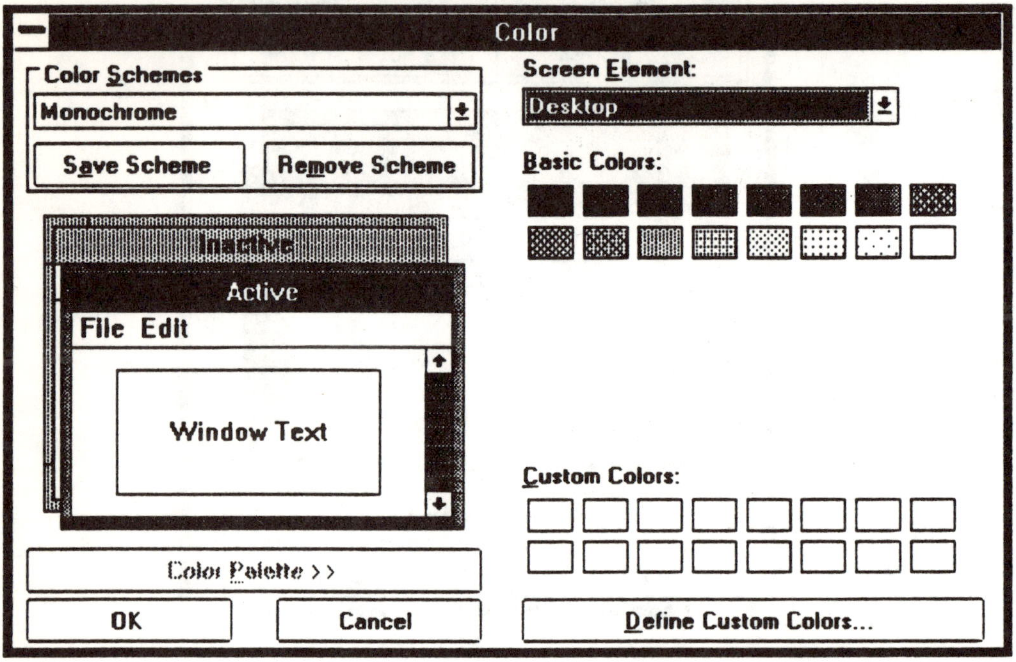

Figure 5-3. The Color Palette Dialogue Box.

The Screen Element field is a drop-down list box that lists the components of the desktop. You select one of the items in this box to identify the component for which you will select a color. The Basic Colors field is an array of blocks with color selections in them. You can click one of the blocks to assign that color to the current selected screen element. You can also Tab to the field and use the arrow keys to select one of the boxes. When a dotted outline surrounds the box you want, press the Spacebar to assign that color.

Building a Custom Color

The Custom Colors field is an array of white boxes. You can build custom colors into one of the boxes and assign it to the current selected screen element. To build a custom color, first select the box—just as you selected one of the Basic Colors boxes. Then select the Define Custom Colors... command button. You will see the Custom Color Selector dialogue box shown in Figure 5-4.

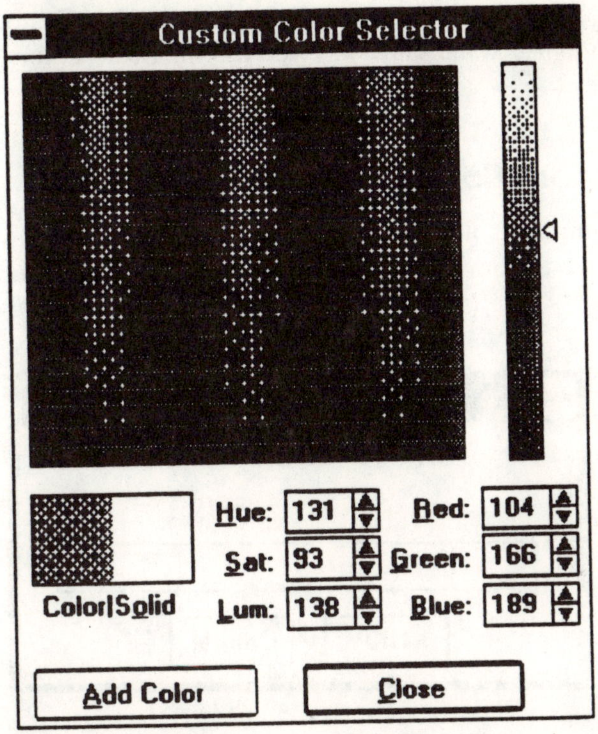

Figure 5-4. The Custom Color Selector Dialogue Box.

The Custom Color Selector dialogue box shows a window with a two-axis color spectrum and a cross-hair cursor. The cursor controls the hue and saturation of the color. Moving the cursor right and left increases and decreases the hue, while moving it up and down increases and decreases the saturation. You can move the cursor by dragging it with the mouse or by changing the values in the Hue and Sat fields. The vertical bar to the right of the spectrum window controls luminance. You move its pointer up and down either by using the mouse or by changing the value in the Lum field.

The Color|Solid box shows the effective color and its solid color component. When the color is one you like, select the Add Color Command Button to add that color to the selected Custom Colors box. Select another Custom Colors box and build another color. When you have built all the colors you want, select the Close control button on the Custom Color Selector dialogue box. The Custom Colors are now available for you to use in the same way you use the Basic Colors in building a color scheme.

Saving a Custom Color Scheme

When your customized color scheme is complete, select the Save Scheme control button. You will see the Save Scheme dialogue box shown in Figure 5-5.

Figure 5-5. The Save Scheme Dialogue Box.

Enter a name for the color scheme. The name you enter is added to the Color Schemes drop-down list and selected as the current color scheme.

Installing a Color Scheme into the Windows Desktop

When you have named the scheme you want at the top of the Color Schemes drop-down list box, select OK. The new color scheme is now in effect on your desktop.

FONTS

The Control Panel allows you to install and delete screen fonts in the graphical user interface. Fonts are descriptions of typefaces as they relate to printing. Your printer already knows how to print the fonts in its repertoire. Windows, however, needs to know how to display the same fonts on the screen so that your documents on the screen resemble the way they will print.

When you installed your printer during the installation of Windows, the printer installation procedure added the fonts that the printer can print. You can, however, enhance some printers with additional fonts not known to Windows. You can also use a printer that is unknown to the original distribution of Windows. Often the vendors of these printers and fonts will supply screen fonts as well. These are the fonts that you can add with the Fonts function of the Control Panel.

Viewing the Installed Fonts

When you select the Fonts icon from the Control Panel, you see the Fonts dialogue box shown in Figure 5-6.

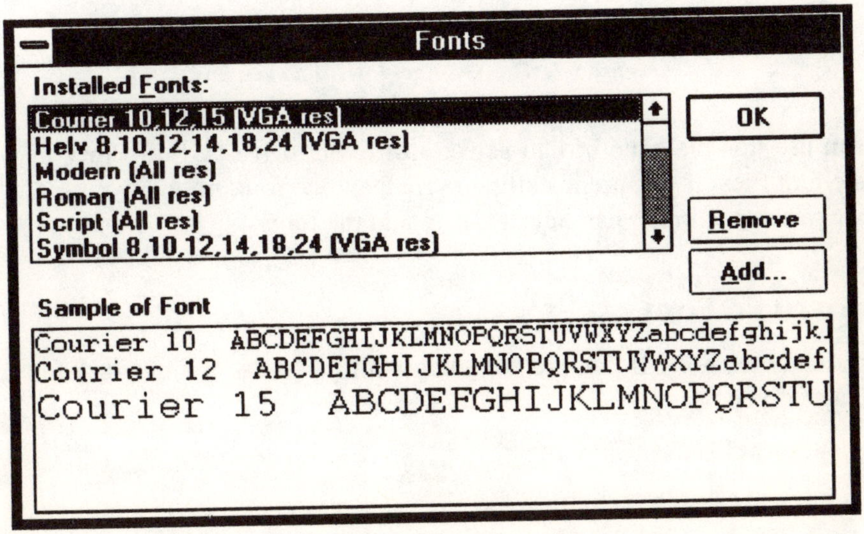

Figure 5-6. The Fonts Dialogue Box.

The Installed Fonts list box shows the fonts that are currently installed. The Sample of Font list box shows what the font looks like on the screen. If the font is available in several sizes, the sample shows them all.

Adding a Font

The Add... Command Button allows you to add a font. Fonts are distributed as files with the .FON extension. You usually get them on diskettes from their vendors. When you select the Add... command button, you see the Add Font Files dialogue box shown in Figure 5-7.

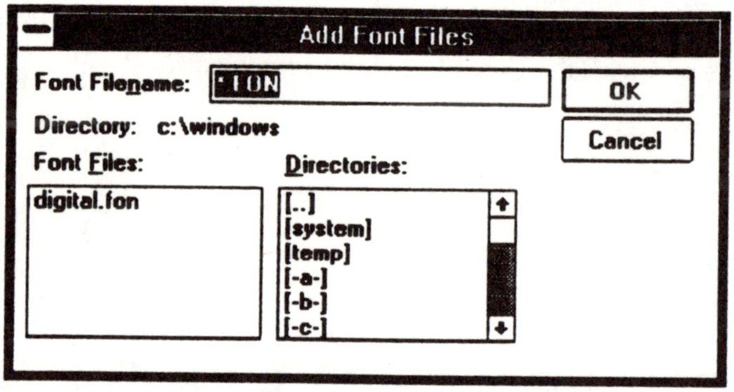

Figure 5-7. The Add Font Files Dialogue Box.

You can use this dialogue box to select a different drive and directory in which to find the font files. If you are installing more than one font, hold down the Ctrl key as you click each one in the list. Select OK to add the fonts.

Removing a Font

Fonts occupy memory. If you are not using a font, you can remove it. You can add it again later if you need it.

***

DO NOT REMOVE THE HELV FONT SET. WINDOWS USES IT FOR ITS OWN DISPLAYS.

***

To remove a font, point to it in the Installed Fonts list and select the Remove command. You will see the Control Panel dialogue box shown in Figure 5-8.

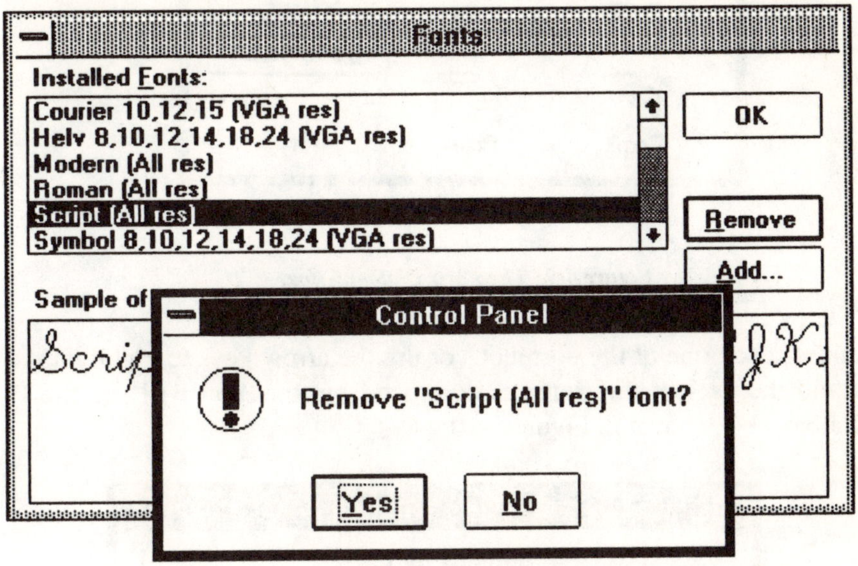

Figure 5-8. The Control Panel Dialogue Box to Remove a Font.

PORTS

The Control Panel lets you define the initial values of your communications ports. The communications ports—COM1 through COM4—are the hardware input/output devices that allow you to connect modems, other computers, printers that have serial rather than parallel interfaces, and video terminals. Each of these connections requires that certain configuration items be established. The values of these configuration items are usually specified in the documentation that accompanies either the hardware device to which you connect the COM port or the software program that uses it.

When you select the Ports icon on the Control Panel, you will see the Ports dialogue box shown in Figure 5-9.

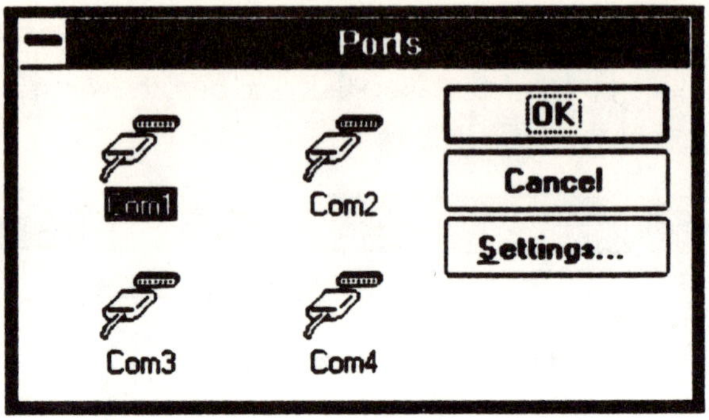

Figure 5-9. The Ports Dialogue Box.

You can double click one of the port icons or use the arrow keys to highlight the one you want and then select the Settings command button. You will see the Ports-Settings dialogue box shown in Figure 5-10.

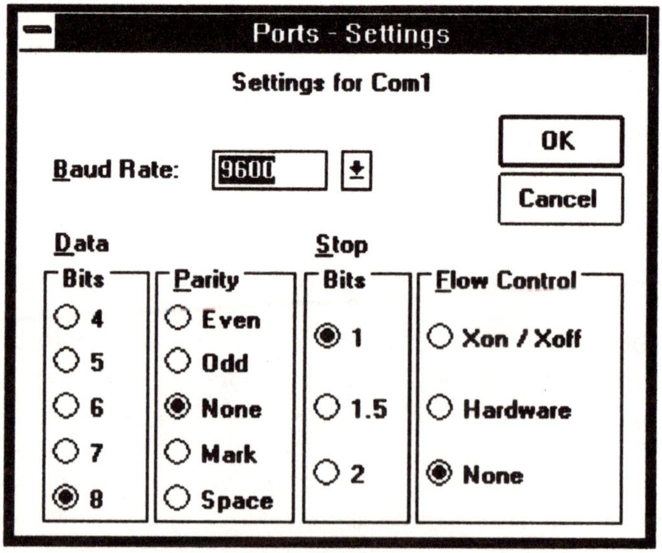

Figure 5-10. The Ports-Settings Dialogue Box.

The Baud Rate field is a drop-down list box that allows you to select from the baud rates available to the port. The baud rate must match that of the device connected to the port. If you are communicating with a remote computer through a modem, the baud rate must match that of the remote computer. The other fields are option buttons, each of which must match the same options of the device at the other end of the communications connection.

MOUSE

You can train your mouse from the Control Panel's Mouse function. Double click the Mouse icon in the Control Panel. You will see the Mouse dialogue box shown in Figure 5-11.

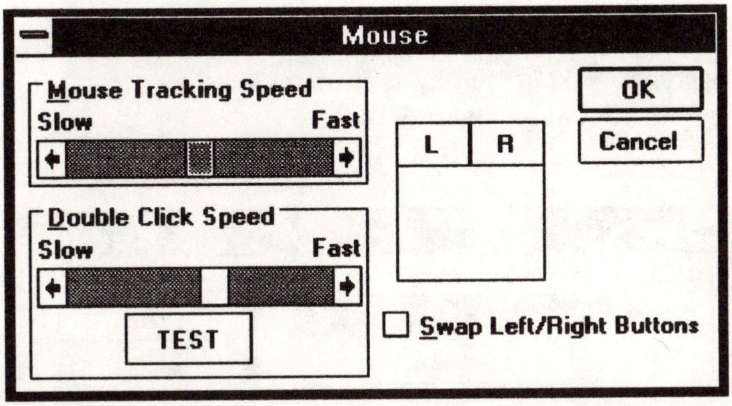

Figure 5-11. The Mouse Dialogue Box.

The Mouse Tracking Speed scroll bar adjusts the sensitivity of the mouse. The faster the setting you choose, the farther the cursor moves across the screen in relation to the distance you move the mouse across your desk. As you change the setting, the mouse changes its behavior. You can test the setting as you change it.

The Double Click Speed scroll bar adjusts the interval of time between clicks that the mouse software uses to discern a double click from two independent single clicks. The faster settings shorten the interval. The Test button allows you to test the setting; it changes color when you double click it.

The L/R boxes enable you to test the mouse buttons to make sure they work. When you press a mouse button, the corresponding box changes color, returning to its original color when you release the button. You can use the Swap Left/Right Buttons check box to reverse the meaning of the left and right buttons.

When the mouse behaves the way you want it to, select OK. If you want to ignore your changes and return to the mouse's original behavior, select Cancel.

DESKTOP

The Desktop icon in the Control Panel allows you to change the pattern that the desktop uses for its background display, the rate that the keyboard cursor blinks, the spacing of icons and windows, and the width of a window's borders.

When you select the Desktop icon in the Control Panel window, you will see the Desktop dialogue box shown in Figure 5-12.

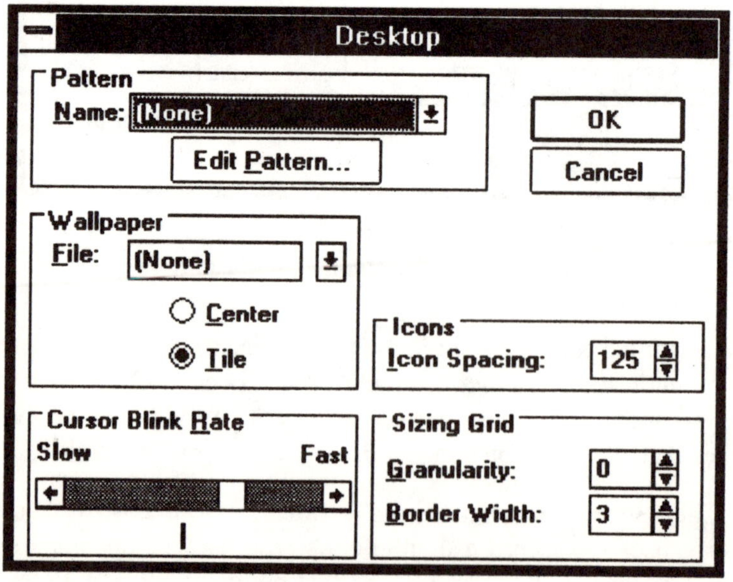

Figure 5-12. The Desktop Dialogue Box.

The Desktop Pattern

The Pattern field on the Desktop dialogue box specifies one of a number of small patterns that combine to describe the background of the desktop. The field is a drop-down list. Figure 5-13 shows the list dropped down and the Boxes pattern selected.

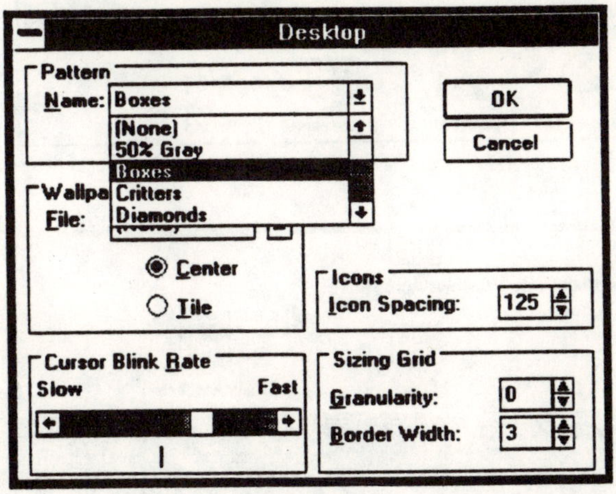

Figure 5-13. The Pattern Drop-Down List.

If you select the Boxes pattern and then select OK in the Desktop dialogue box, the Boxes pattern will fill the desktop, and the screen will look like Figure 5-14.

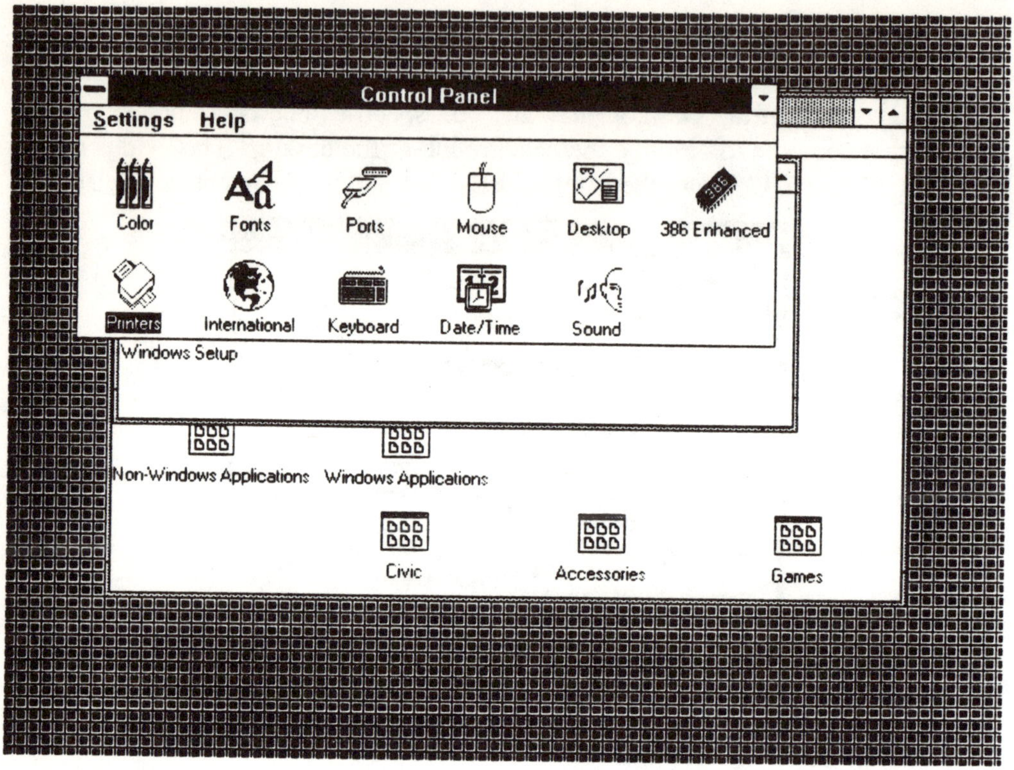

Figure 5-14. Boxes as a Pattern.

Editing a Pattern

Patterns are made up of small graphics boxes that connect side-by-side and up-and-down. You can select one of the patterns and edit it by selecting the Edit Pattern... command button. You will see the Desktop-Edit Pattern dialogue box, as shown in Figure 5-15.

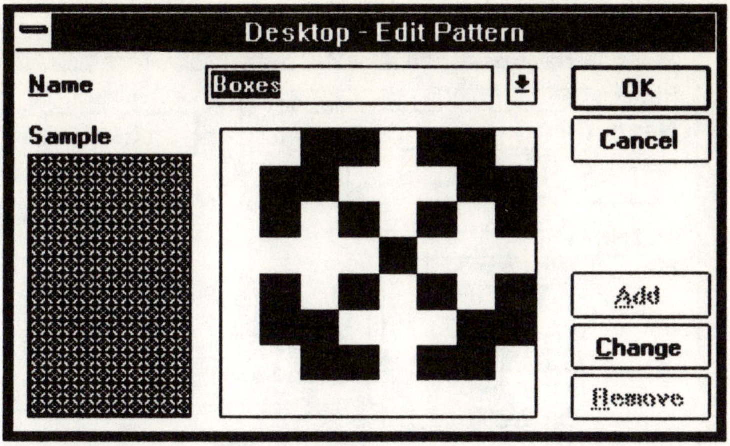

Figure 5-15. The Desktop-Edit Pattern Dialogue Box.

A pattern is an eight-by-eight array of pixels (picture elements). The dialogue box includes an exploded copy of the pattern. You can set the pixels on and off by clicking them, thereby forming a new pattern. The Sample window to the left of the pattern shows how the pattern will form into the desktop pattern if you use it. The Name field is a drop-down list that lets you select from the existing patterns.

Using Wallpaper for the Desktop

You can use a .BMP file, rather than a pattern, to form the desktop. This approach is called "wallpaper." Figure 5-16 shows how you can use the Wallpaper File drop-down list to select from the .BMP files that are available.

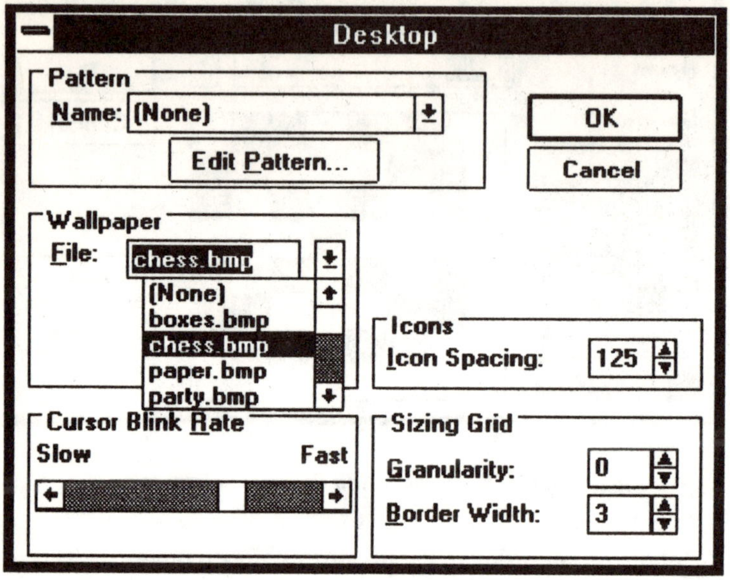

Figure 5-16. Selecting Wallpaper.

If you were to choose the CHESS.BMP file that comes with Windows, for example, your desktop would look like Figure 5-17.

Figure 5-17. Chessmen as the Wallpaper.

Some .BMP files contain bitmaps that do not fill the screen. The PYRAMID.BMP file that comes with Windows is such a bitmap. The Tile option button causes those bitmaps to repeat themselves.

Wallpaper files can come from many sources. A file that you can load into the Paintbrush application can become a wallpaper file. Some users load scanned photographs of their family. Others download wallpaper files from electronic bulletin boards.

Controlling the Keyboard Cursor Blink Rate

The Desktop dialogue window includes a scroll bar that lets you change the rate at which the keyboard cursor blinks. The blinking cursor just below the scroll bar changes its rate to reflect the changes you are making.

Setting Icon Spacing

You have no doubt seen that some icons collide, particularly if their labels are long. You use the Icon Spacing value to increase or decrease the distance that Windows puts between icons when they are spaced out. The Windows installation that prepared the examples in this book used a spacing of 125. The default spacing is 75.

The Grid

When you move windows and icons around, they move smoothly anywhere you drag them, as long as the Granularity value is zero. If you change this value, you describe a grid, and the windows and icons tend to snap to coordinates that align with this grid.

Setting the Border Width

The Border Width field changes the width of windows that have borders. The default is 3, but you can experiment with this value. Figure 5-18 shows the Program Manager's application window when the border value is set to 15.

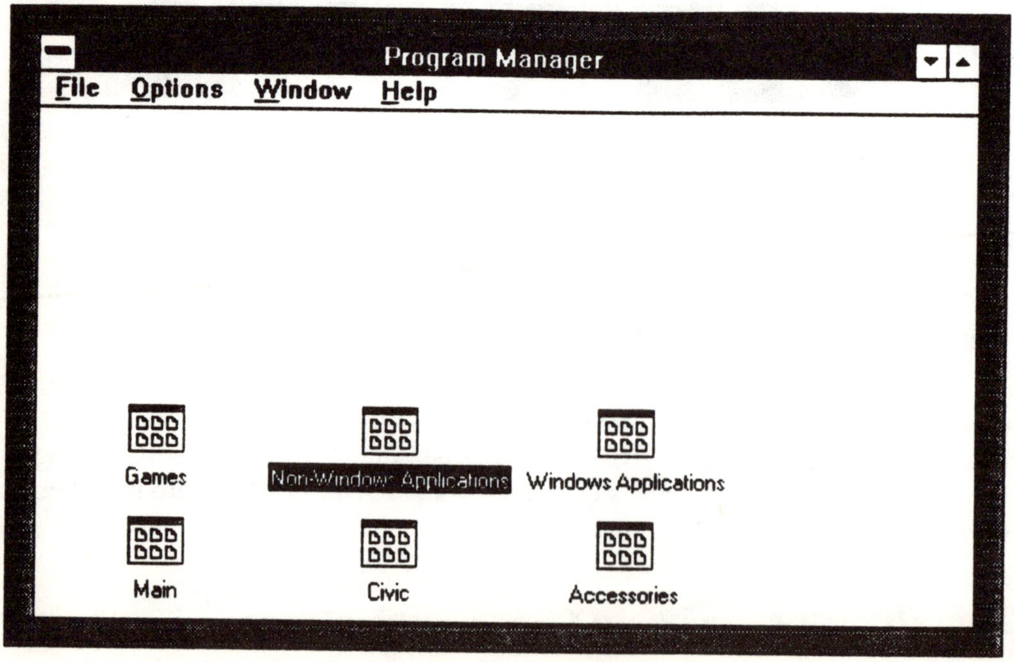

Figure 5-18. Fat Borders.

PRINTERS

You can configure and add printers to your system by selecting the Printers icon from the Control Panel. When you select this icon you will see the Printers Dialogue Box shown in Figure 5-19.

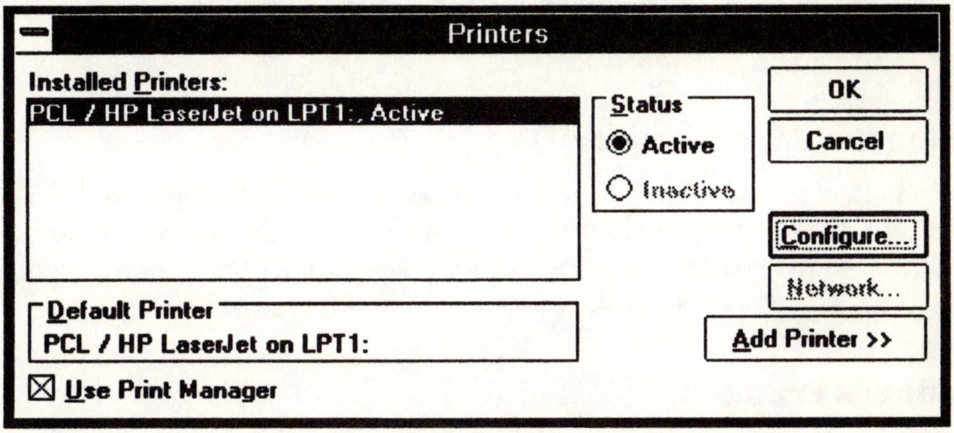

Figure 5-19. The Printers Dialogue Box.

The Installed Printers list box lists the printers that you installed either when you installed Windows or through an earlier use of the Control Panel. The Default Printer field specifies which of the installed printers is currently in use. When you print from an application, output goes to the default printer. You may have several printers installed, but only one of them is the default printer at a time.

Selecting the Default Printer

You select the default printer by double clicking its entry in the Installed Printers list or by selecting that entry with the arrow keys and pressing the Alt+D keys. The default printer must be active. The procedure for making a printer active is described in the next section.

Making the Printer Active

The Printers dialogue box has status option buttons with the values Active and Inactive. An installed printer is assigned to a printer port, as you will soon see. When you have assigned more than one printer to the same port—if you were using an external printer selection switch, for example—only one of them can be active at a time. If only one printer is assigned to a port, that printer is always active.

***

DO NOT CONFUSE AN ACTIVE PRINTER WITH THE DEFAULT PRINTER. MOST WINDOWS APPLICATIONS SIMPLY PRINT TO THE DEFAULT PRINTER. YOU SPECIFY THE PRINTER TO WHICH AN APPLICATION PRINTS WITH THE DEFAULT PRINTER SETTING, AS DESCRIBED ABOVE. THE ACTIVE/INACTIVE OPTION BUTTONS MERELY TELL WINDOWS WHICH PRINTER IS CURRENTLY CONNECTED TO A SHARED PORT.

***

Using the Print Manager

The Use Print Manager check box tells Windows to use the Print Manager to queue print jobs. Chapter 6 discusses the Print Manager. You will usually want to use it because it allows you to do other work in the same application or to exit from the application while the printer is still printing.

Adding a Printer

To add a printer you select the Add Printer >> command button. The Printers dialogue box expands to include the List of Printers list box. This box lists the printers that Windows can install, as shown in Figure 5-20.

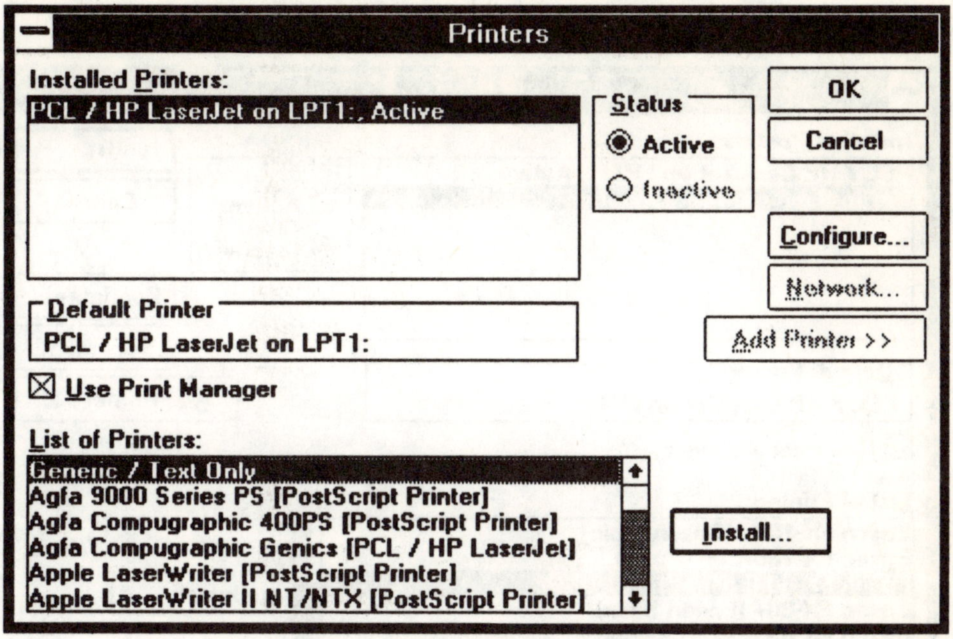

Figure 5-20. Installing a Printer.

Installing the Printer Driver Software

Move the list box cursor to the printer you want to install and select the Install... command button. Windows must load the printer driver software for the selected printer, so it displays the dialogue box shown in Figure 5-21. You will see the printer added to the Installed Printers list, as shown in Figure 5-22.

Figure 5-21. Loading a Printer Driver.

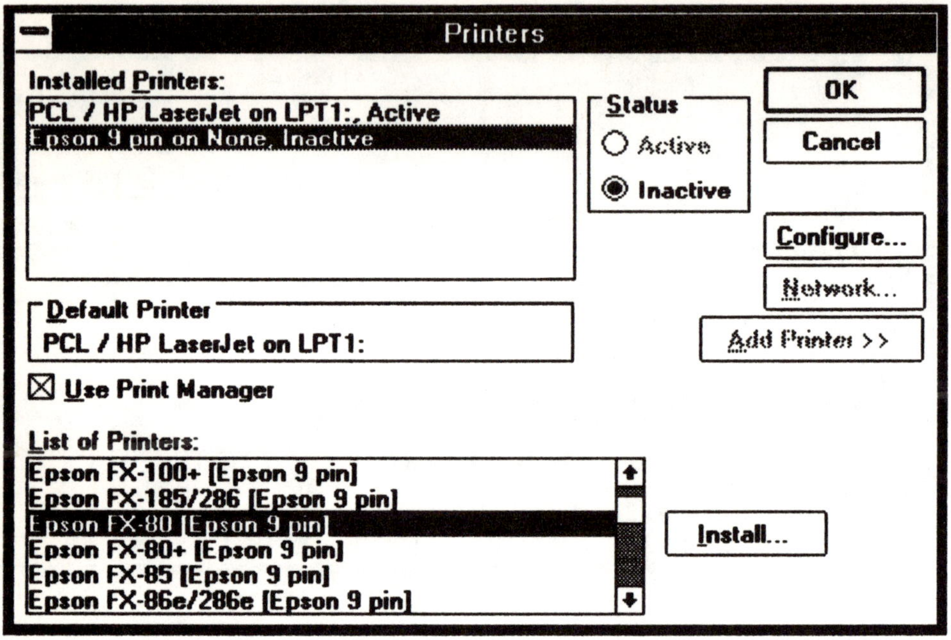

Figure 5-22. The Printer Added to the Installed Printers List.

Printer Groups

Many printers on the list are in a printer group. The name of the group appears in square brackets after the name of the printer. The selected printer in Figure 5-22 is in a group. The Installed Printers list identifies the group. Printers in a group share the same printer driver software. You will identify the specific printer later when you set up the printer.

Selecting a Printer Port

The new printer is specified as being "on None" and inactive. A printer must be connected to a printer port or its output must be directed to a file. Select the Configure... command button. You will see the Printers-Configure dialogue box shown in Figure 5-23.

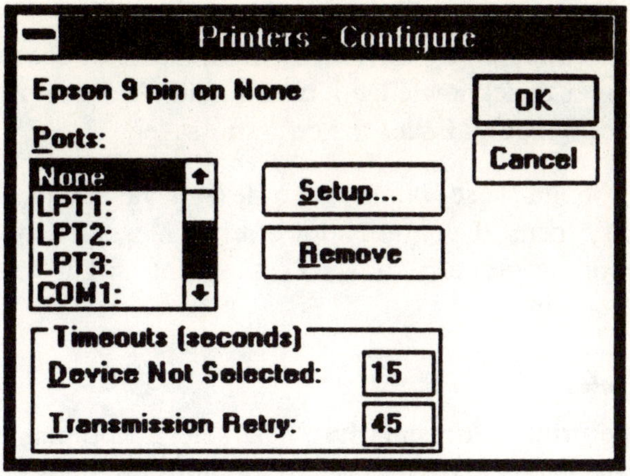

Figure 5-23. The Printers - Configure Dialogue Box.

The Ports list box lists the ports to which the printer can be connected. The ports are:

- three parallel ports—LPT1, 2, and 3
- four serial ports—COM1, 2, 3, and 4
- EPT—for printers such as the IBM Personal Pageprinter
- FILE—for printing to a file
- LPT1.OS2 and LPT2.OS2—for running Windows within OS/2
- files in the WINDOWS directory—with an extension of .PRN

If you select FILE, the Print Manager will prompt you to name a file every time an application prints to the printer you are configuring in this procedure. If you select a file name with the .PRN extension, the printed output always goes to that file. You will see the .PRN filenames in the Ports list box only if such files exist in the WINDOWS directory. The port that you select will appear along with th printer name in the Installed Printers list.

Timeouts

You can specify two timeout values for the printer from the Printers-Configure dialogue box. The Device Not Selected timeout is the number of seconds that Windows will wait for the printer to be ready before it displays a Not Ready error message. The Transmission Retry timeout is the number of seconds that Windows will wait for the printer to acknowledge a transmission before it tries a second time; after a second failure, Windows issues the error message.

When would you change these values? The default values usually work, so you rarely need to modify them. If you get a lot of error messages when you know that the printer is functioning properly, however, then you might need to increase the values.

Setting Up the Printer

You must set up the printer, particularly if you select a printer that is in a printer group. The procedure varies between printers because different printers and groups have different options. In any case, though, you choose the Setup command button from the Printers-Configure dialogue box. Figure 5-24 shows the Setup dialogue box for one printer.

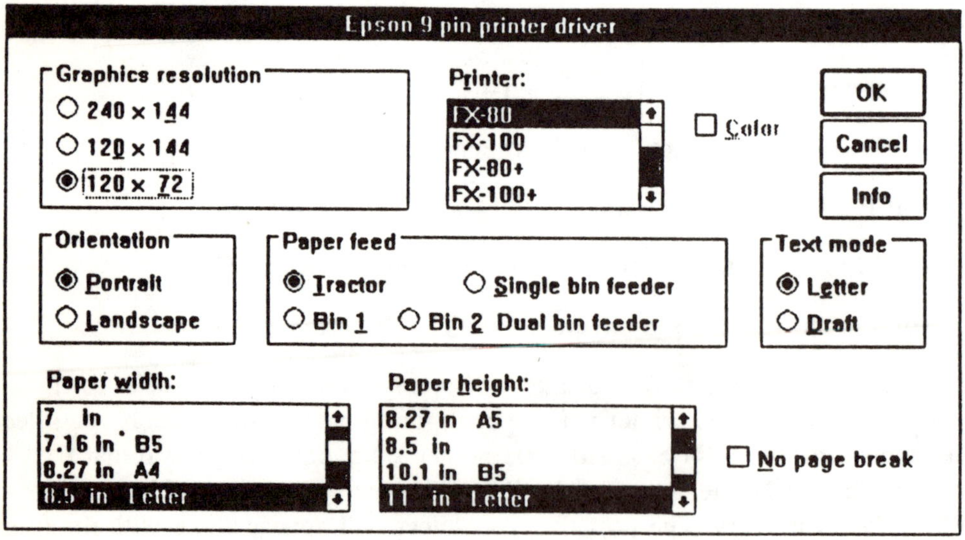

Figure 5-24. Setting Up a Printer.

Printer group setup procedures require that you select the specific printer from the group. The dialogue boxes differ in format, but most have a list box or drop-down list box from which you select the printer. When the setup is complete, select the OK command button.

Many Windows applications also include a Printer Setup... command on their File menu. This command displays the Printer Setup dialogue box, as shown in Figure 5-25.

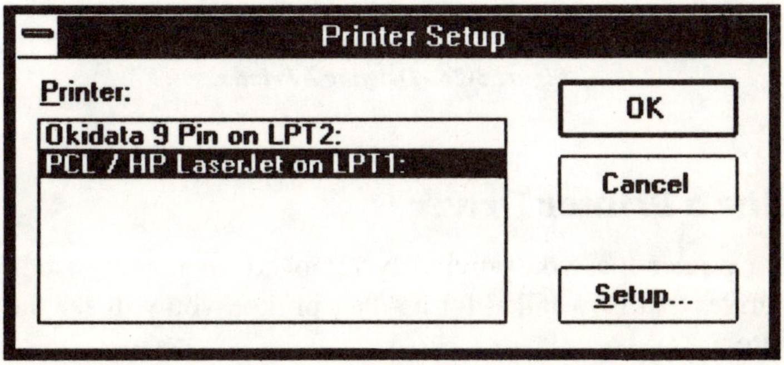

Figure 5-25. The Printer Setup Dialogue Box.

You can select the default printer from the Printer Setup dialogue box, and you can select the Setup... command button, which displays the unique setup dialogue box for the selected printer. You do not need to suspend the application and call the Control Panel in order to change the printer setup.

Removing a Printer

You can delete a printer from the Installed Printers list by selecting the Configure... command button and then selecting the Remove command button from the Printers-Configure dialogue box. If you do this you will see the dialogue box shown in Figure 5-26.

Figure 5-26. Deleting a Printer.

Re-Installing a Printer Driver

If you install a printer that you previously removed, or if you install a printer that uses a group driver that is installed for another printer, you will see the dialogue box shown in Figure 5-27.

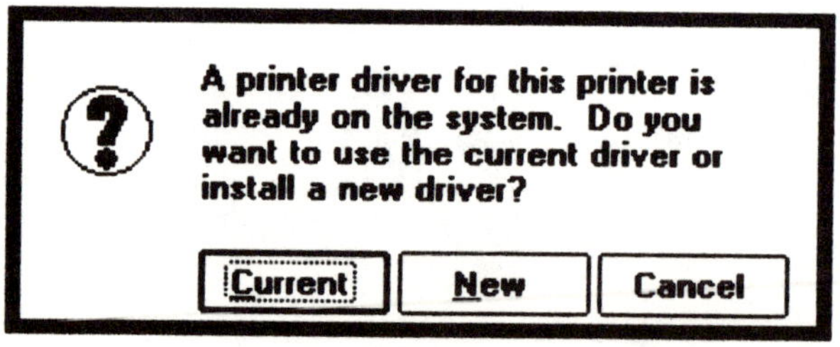

Figure 5-27. Re-installing a Printer Driver.

In most cases you will want to select the Current command button. If not, you will know that and will know why and what to do—usually as the result of some special instructions that accompanied the printer and/or the driver when you acquired it.

INTERNATIONAL CONVENTIONS

The Control Panel's International icon allows you to change the characteristics of your system to match the conventions of different countries. When you select the International icon, you see the International dialogue box shown in Figure 5-28.

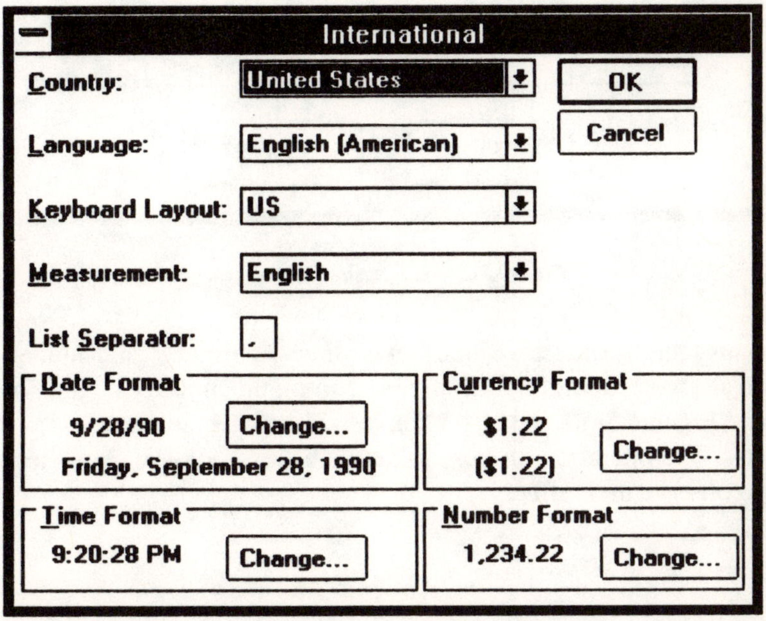

Figure 5-28. The International Dialogue Box.

The Country, Language, Keyboard Layout, and Measurement fields are drop-down list boxes that allow you to select the conventions that match your environment. If you change languages you will see the dialogue box shown in Figure 5-29.

Figure 5-29. Changing Languages.

You can change the format in which dates, times, currency, and numerical values appear with the corresponding Change... command buttons in the International dialogue box. Figures 5-30, 5-31, 5-32, and 5-33 are the dialogue boxes that control these displays. The operation of these dialogue boxes is typical. You can experiment with them to observe their effects.

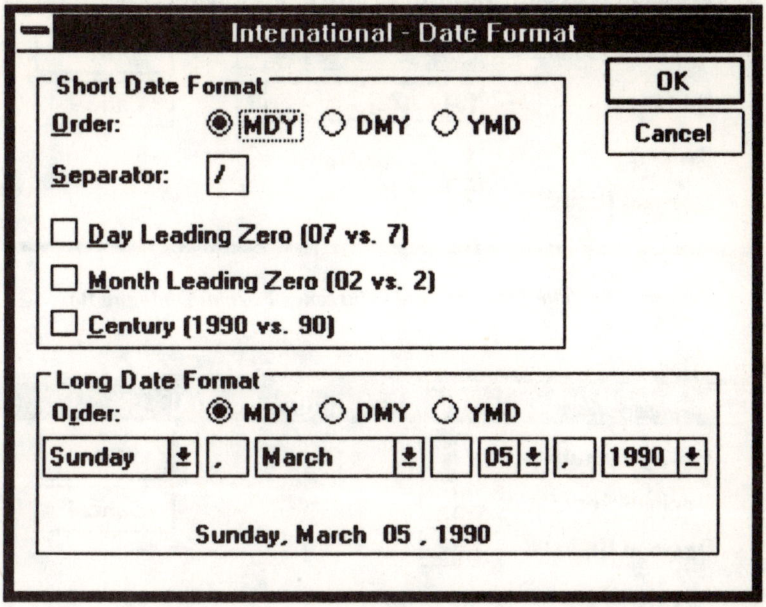

Figure 5-30. The International - Date Format Dialogue Box.

Figure 5-31. The International - Time Format Dialogue Box.

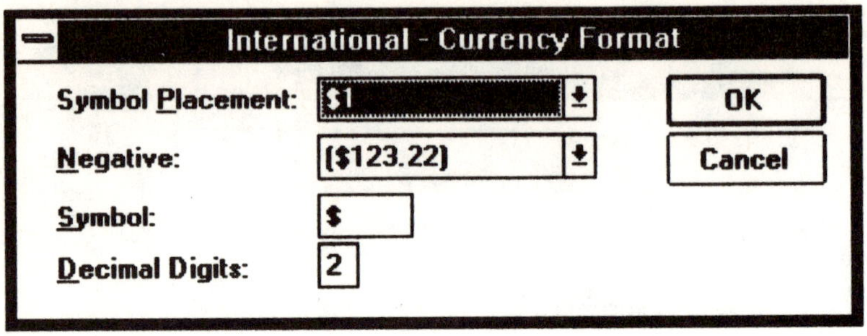

Figure 5-32. The International - Currency Format Dialogue Box.

Figure 5-33. The International - Number Format Dialogue Box.

***

CHANGING THE INTERNATIONAL SETTINGS DOES NOT GUARANTEE THAT EVERY APPLICATION WILL BE AUTOMATICALLY TRANSLATED. ONLY THOSE APPLICATIONS THAT INCLUDE THE NECESSARY TRANSLATION FILES CAN CONFORM.

***

KEYBOARD

The Keyboard icon on the Control Panel allows you to modify the keyboard's "typematic" rate—the speed at which the keyboard repeats when you hold a key down. Figure 5-34 shows the Keyboard Dialogue Box.

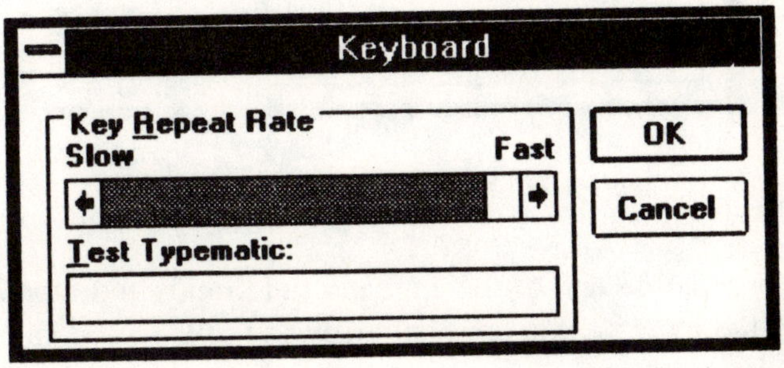

Figure 5-34. The Keyboard Dialogue Box.

To modify the typematic rate, move the Key Repeat Rate scroll box between the fast and slow settings. Tab to the Test Typematic text box and test the rate by holding down a key. Select OK when you are satisfied with the new rate or select Cancel to ignore any changes and return to the previous rate.

DATE AND TIME

The Date/Time icon on the Control Panel lets you change the system clock and calendar. Figure 5-35 is the Date & Time dialogue box that you use to change those settings.

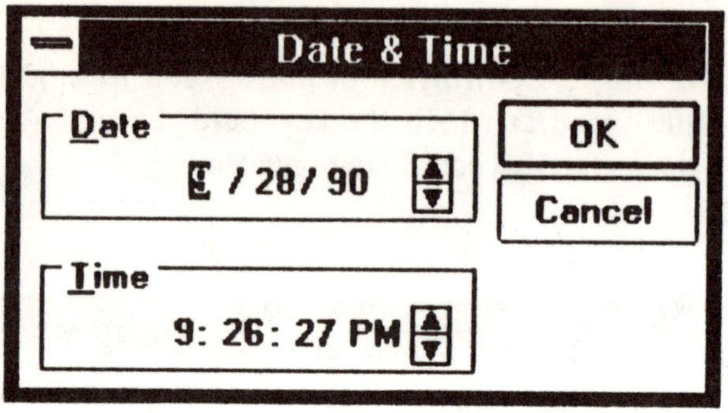

Figure 5-35. The Date & Time Dialogue Box.

You can Tab to or click on one of the date and time fields and type in the new value, or you can click the increment/decrement arrows to change the values. Select OK to record the new date and time or select Cancel to ignore your changes and retain the original clock and calendar settings.

SOUND

Windows beeps at you to get your attention for such events as error messages. These beeps can be annoying, particularly if you have close neighbors in your office. They can also be misleading if you and your coworkers sit near one another and everyone uses Windows. Every beep from every computer sounds like it comes from yours.

You can turn off the beeps if they are bothering you. The Sound icon on the Control Panel allows you to do this. When you select this icon, you will see that the Sound dialogue box includes a Warning Beep check box, as shown in Figure 5-36. This check box controls whether or not Windows beeps at you.

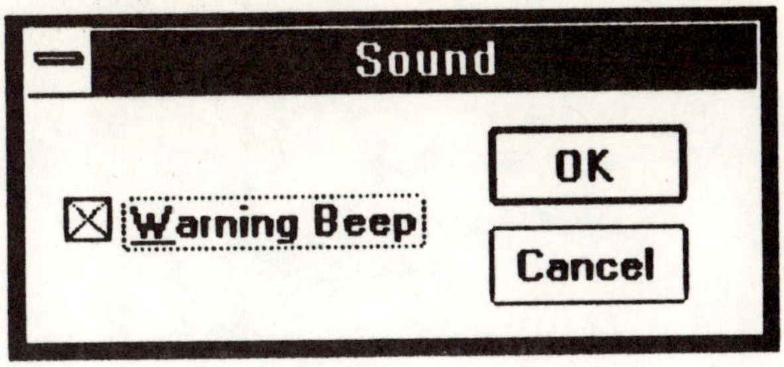

Figure 5-36. The Sound Dialogue Box.

OTHER CONTROL PANEL ICONS

If you are running in 386 enhanced mode, you will see the 386 Enhanced icon on the Control Panel. If you are on a network, you will see the Network icon on the Control Panel. These icons allow you to do some advanced operations. You will learn about them in Chapter 11.

SUMMARY

You know Windows well by now. You should be able to run most Windows applications without assistance because you understand the Windows common user interface and can manage your applications, data files, and system with the Program Manager, File Manager, and Control Panel. Chapter 6 teaches you about the Print Manager, the program that queues and manages your print jobs.

Chapter 6

The Print Manager

When you print a report or graphic from a Windows application, the print job is managed by the Print Manager. The Print Manager accepts print jobs, places them in printer-related queues, and prints them from the background while you are doing other work. In addition to intercepting, queuing, and printing the print jobs, the Print Manager provides a Windows interface with which you manage the queues and printers.

PRINTING FROM A WINDOWS APPLICATION

When you print from a Windows application, the application directs the output to the default printer, as selected in the Control Panel. While the application is generating the printer output, the dialogue box shown in Figure 6-1 is displayed.

Figure 6-1. Printing from an Application.

***

You will often hear programs such as the Print Manager called "spoolers" and background printing called "spooling." These terms originated in the so-called second generation of computers. Multitasking was used then to read card decks and print reports at the same time that other programs were processing applications. SPOOL was an acronym for Simultaneous Peripheral Operation On Line.

***

You can terminate a print job by selecting the Cancel command button from the dialogue box, or you can wait until the printing operation completes.

Printing With the Print Manager

If you have elected to use the Print Manager by selecting the Use Print Manager check box in the Control Panel's Printers dialogue box, then the output that an application directs to a printer goes to the Print Manager, which collects the print output into a queue.

The dialogue box shown in Figure 6-1 is displayed while the Print Manager is receiving output from the application. The application is free to continue after the Print Manager has collected and copied the output to the queue.

***

You should use the Print Manager to queue printer data when you have long reports or high density graphics to print and when the length of print data exceeds the buffering capability of your printer. You can generally use the Print Manager at all times with little or no compromise to your productivity.

***

Printing Directly to the Printer

If you have elected not to use the Print Manager by not selecting the Use Print Manager check box in the Control Panel's Printers dialogue box, then the output that an application directs to a printer goes directly to the printer.

When you print directly to the printer, the dialogue box shown in Figure 6-1 remains on the screen for as long as it takes to print the output. You cannot return to the application to do other work, and you cannot terminate the application. If the printer is slow and the output is long, you will be stuck for a while. You can call a different application and work with it, but the current application is dedicated to driving the printer until the output is done.

***

You should print directly to the printer, bypassing the Print Manager, only when your printer can accept data faster than the Print Manager can write it to a queue and when the volume of your print data does not create a bottleneck.

***

PRINTING FROM NON-WINDOWS APPLICATIONS

DOS programs use their own printer management. Some simply print to the DOS standard logical print device, others give you a choice of printer ports. Some even use queuing mechanisms similar to those of the Print Manager. When you run a DOS application from Windows, however, that application does not use the Print Manager. Even worse, if the Print Manager is printing for a Windows application, and you begin to print from a DOS application at the same time, your printed output will probably be jumbled. If you are mixing DOS and Windows applications that print, you should tell the Print Manager to pause all printers until you are certain that the DOS applications are not printing.

RUNNING THE PRINT MANAGER

The Print Manager is a Windows application. You can execute it from the Program Manager's Main group. If you do not execute the Print Manager yourself, Windows will execute it the first time an application prints through it.

***

IF YOU DECIDE TO RUN PROGRAMS FROM THE FILE MANAGER RATHER THAN THE PROGRAM MANAGER, ADDRESS THE PRINT MANAGER AS PRINTMAN.EXE, A FILE IN THE WINDOWS DIRECTORY ON THE DRIVE WHERE YOU INSTALLED WINDOWS.

***

When Windows executes the Print Manager, it comes up in its minimized state as an icon at the bottom of the desktop. The Print Manager then terminates itself when the last print job is done. Figure 6-2 shows the Print Manager icon.

Figure 6-2. The Print Manager Icon.

When you execute the Print Manager yourself, it continues running until you terminate it.

USING THE PRINT MANAGER APPLICATION

Figure 6-3 shows the Print Manager application window. A printer can be idle (with no jobs queued), paused, or printing. The hand icon to the left of the printer's name and the [Paused] tag to the right tell you the printer is paused. If the printer is printing, the icon is a tiny printer. If the printer is idle, there is no icon. Figure 6-3 shows two printers installed, each with four print jobs queued. Both printers are paused.

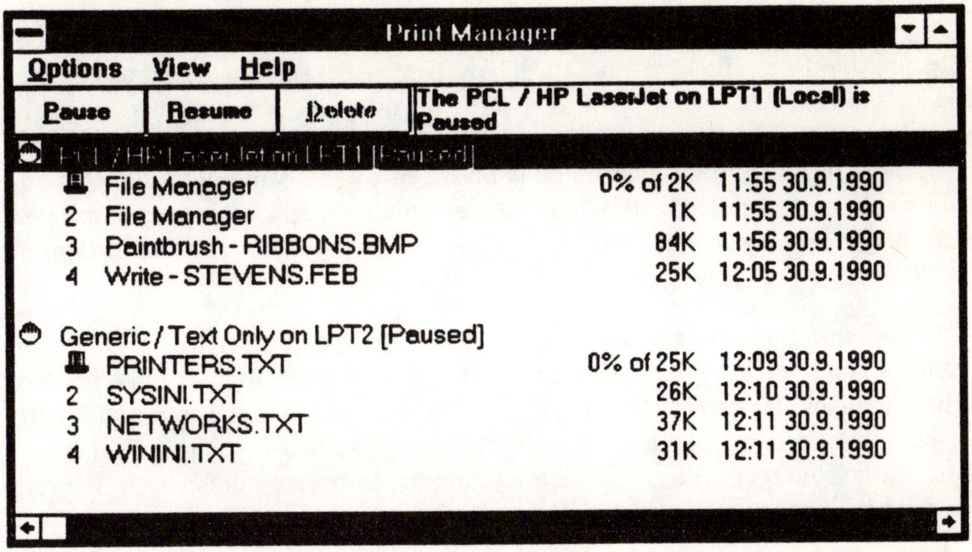

Figure 6-3. The Print Manager Application Window.

The lists of print jobs are numbered according to their place in the queue. The first entry in the queue has the printer icon instead of a number to indicate that it is the job being printed.

***

The names assigned to print jobs vary, depending on the application that printed them—you do not always find consistency in a common user interface. The first two jobs in the first list in Figure 6-3, for example, are named simply "File Manager." That is the name that the File Manager assigns to print jobs when you use its Print... command to print an ASCII file. The Paintbrush application assigns its own name followed by the name of the file it is printing. You can see that the Notepad assigns only the name of the file to the print job; it printed the four files in the second list shown in Figure 6-3.

***

Pausing and Resuming a Printer

You pause a printer by moving the highlight cursor to the printer to be paused and selecting the Pause function button. If you pause an idle printer, it goes into pause mode, and any subsequent print jobs wait. If you pause a printer that is printing a print job, it stops in the middle of that job and waits. There are three indications that a printer is paused: the printer name is preceded by the hand icon; the [Paused] tag follows the printer name; and, when you have the highlight cursor on the printer, the information display to the right of the function buttons tells you that the printer is paused.

You resume a paused printer by moving the highlight cursor to the printer to be resumed and selecting the Resume function button. If there are jobs to be printed, the printer icon and [Printing] tag surround the printer name, and the information display to the right of the function buttons tells you that the printer is printing. If there are no jobs, there is no icon, the tag says [Idle], and the information display to the right of the function buttons tells you that the printer is idle.

When the Printer is Not Ready

If the Print Manager is printing a job and the printer becomes not ready—perhaps it is out of paper, or perhaps you took it off line, for example—you will see the error message shown in Figure 6-4.

Figure 6-4. A Printer Error Message.

When you select OK, the printer status tag becomes [STALLED] and the Print Manager stops trying to print until you select Resume again.

Deleting a Print Job

You can delete a print job by moving the highlight cursor to the job's queue entry and selecting Delete. You will see the dialogue box shown in Figure 6-5. Select OK to delete the job.

Figure 6-5. Deleting a Print Job.

***

IF YOU DELETE THE JOB AT THE TOP OF THE QUEUE—THE ONE THAT IS PRINTING—YOU MIGHT HAVE TO RESET YOUR PRINTER, PARTICULARLY IF THE JOB INVOLVES GRAPHICS. SOME PRINTERS CANNOT RECOVER BY THEMSELVES FROM AN INTERRUPTED STREAM OF GRAPHICS DATA. YOU MIGHT HAVE TO POWER THE PRINTER DOWN AND UP TO RESET IT.

***

Reordering the Queue

You can change the order of the jobs in the queue by moving any job entry other than the first to any new location other than the first. To move a job with the mouse, click and drag a queue entry to its new location. To move a job with the keyboard, move the highlight cursor to the job with the arrow keys. Then hold down the Ctrl key and move the dotted outline to the new position. When you release the Ctrl key, the job entry moves.

Assigning Print Manager Priority

The processing priority controls how the Print Manager shares the computer's processor with the other applications that are running. The Print Manager Options menu, shown in Figure 6-6, has three commands that allow you to modify the processing priority: Low Priority, Medium Priority, and High Priority. These commands are mutually exclusive toggles—only one can be in effect. The current priority is indicated by a check mark next to its command on the menu.

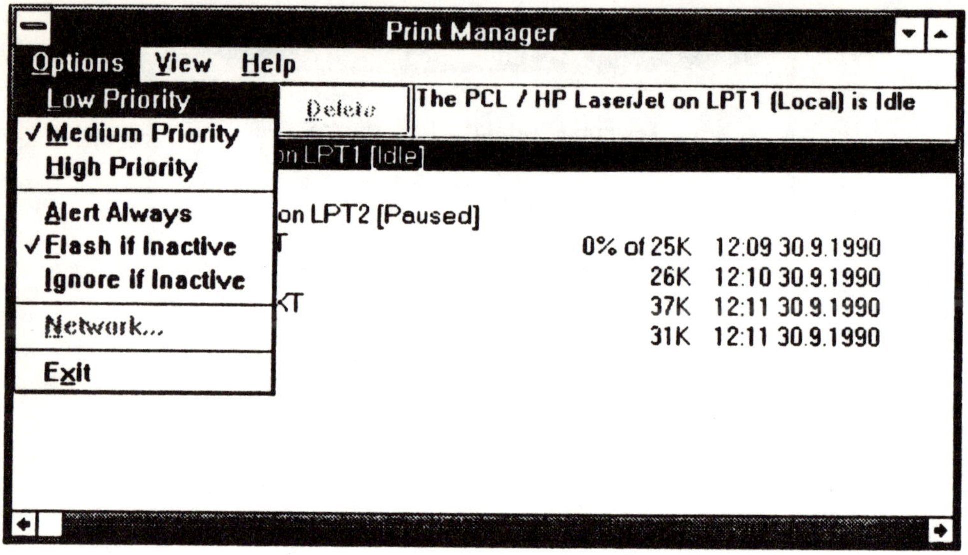

Figure 6-6. The Print Manager Options Menu.

By default, the Print Manager runs at medium priority, which means that the Print Manager and other applications share the processor equally. Low priority gives the other programs a larger share, and high priority gives the Print Manager a higher share.

If your jobs are not printing fast enough, give the Print Manager high priority. If your jobs are printing fine, but your other applications are sluggish, give the Print Manager a low priority.

Specifying How The Print Manager Alerts You

The Print Manager can interrupt whatever you are doing to tell you that the printer needs attention. If the printer is in an error state, the Print Manager will always interrupt you with an error message. But other interruptions are routine. Your printer might be set up to pause between pages, for example. You can control how the Print Manager alerts you to these routine conditions.

The Options menu contains three mutually exclusive toggle commands: Alert Always, Flash if Inactive, and Ignore if Inactive. When you select Alert Always, the Print Manager displays alert messages regardless of whether the Print Manager application window is active. If you select one of the other two commands, the Print Manager displays alert messages only if the Print Manager application window is active. If you select Flash if Inactive, the Print Manager's icon flashes if the Print Manager is minimized. If the Print Manager window is simply inactive, the title bar of the window flashes. If you select Ignore if Inactive, you won't get any notice of the condition until you activate the Print Manager application window.

Controlling The Queue Displays

The Print Manager View menu, shown in Figure 6-7, has two toggle commands to control the queue displays. You can turn off the time and date display as well as the file size display with these commands. The only reason to turn them off, however, is if you want to resize the Print Manager application window.

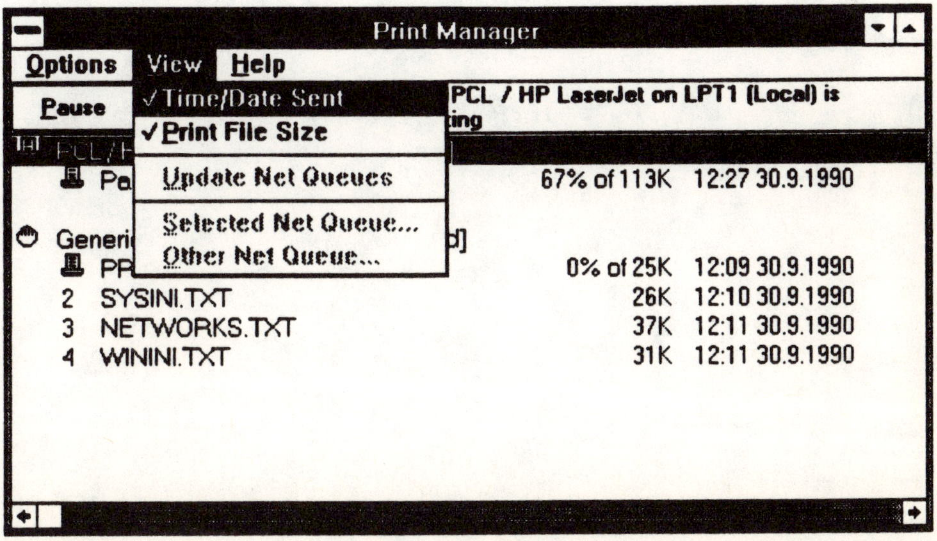

Figure 6-7. The Print Manger View Menu.

SUMMARY

This chapter ends your introductory tutorial. You now know how to use Windows and make it do what you want. The next four chapters discuss the applications and accessory programs that come with Windows. You will learn to use each of these features—from the simple Clock to the complex Recorder. You will also explore word processing and graphics. Finally, in Chapter 11, you will become a Windows power user.

Chapter 7

Word Processing: Windows Write

Windows Write is a word processing application found in the Program Manager's Accessories group. With it you can write memos, letters, documents, and publications that integrate text and graphics. Write is not a high-end word processor—like Word for Windows, WordPerfect, and others—and it is not a powerful desktop publisher—like PageMaker—but it is sufficient for the small word processing applications of most homes and offices.

TYPING A DOCUMENT

When you start Write, you will see the Write application window shown in Figure 7-1. The small four-pointed star in the upper left corner of the Write work space marks the end of the document. At first that mark is at the beginning because the document has nothing in it. As you enter data into the document, the mark moves forward.

Figure 7-1. The Write Application Window.

***

Beginning with this chapter, you will see fewer illustrations that walk you step-by-step through exercises. By now you know what to expect in the Windows common user interface. You know how to run a program, select a command from a menu, and change the value of a field in a dialogue box without needing to see the details of every display in an example. If something confuses you or you have forgotten how something works, return to Chapter 1 for a refresher.

***

The vertical bar to the immediate left of the star is the keyboard cursor. That is where you will type text or insert graphics. You can move the cursor around within the document after you enter some text by using the mouse or the keyboard.

***

IF YOU DECIDE TO RUN PROGRAMS FROM THE FILE MANAGER RATHER THAN THE PROGRAM MANAGER, ADDRESS WRITE AS WRITE.EXE, A FILE IN THE WINDOWS DIRECTORY ON THE DRIVE WHERE YOU INSTALLED WINDOWS. WRITE IS ASSOCIATED WITH FILES THAT HAVE THE .WRI EXTENSION, SO YOU CAN EXECUTE IT BY SELECTING ONE OF THOSE FILES FROM THE FILE MANAGER AS WELL.

***

Margins

Type some text into the document. The first thing you might notice is that the lines go well beyond the right margin of the window before a word wraps around, as shown in Figure 7-2.

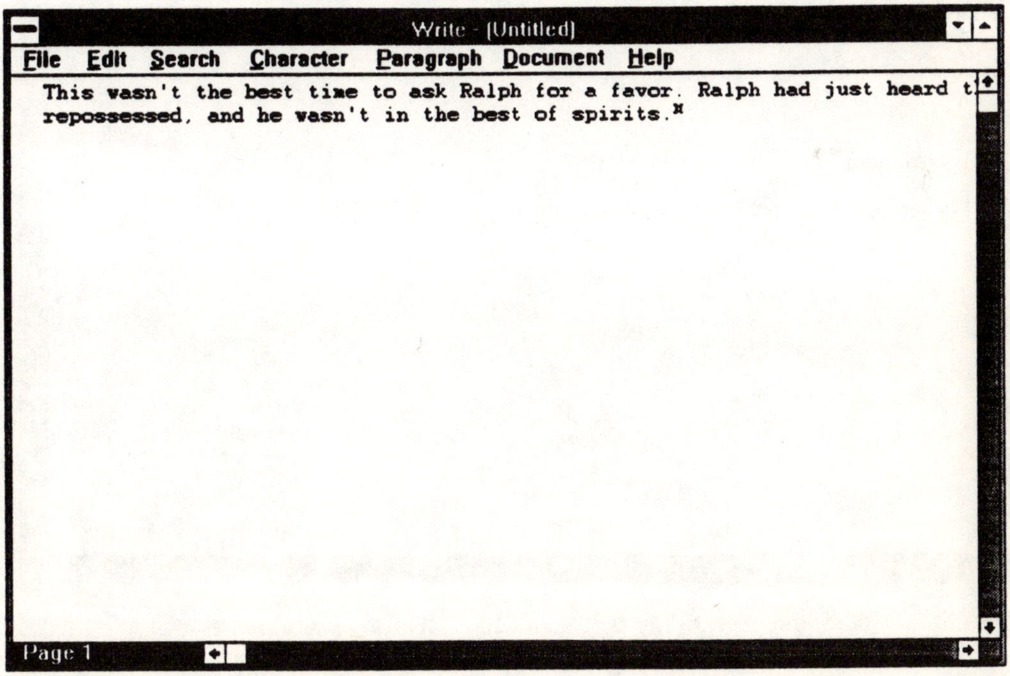

Figure 7-2. Text Exceeding the Window Width.

Write orients its display to the printed page, trying to show the document on the screen as it will appear on paper. The initial right and left page margins are set to 1.25 inches on 8.5 x 11 paper, and the default screen font for some printers needs more than a window's width to display 6 inches of text.

Most people prefer to view the entire line when they type. Write's horizontal scrolling refreshes the screen in an uncomfortable way whenever you type on the part of the line that is beyond the right border of the Window. One way to solve this problem is to change the margin so that all the text is on the screen. To do this, select the Page Layout command from the Document menu. You will see a Page Layout dialogue box. If you change the right margin of the document from 1.25 inches to 3 inches, the document will appear as shown in Figure 7-3. Before you print the document you can set the margin back to 1.25 inches.

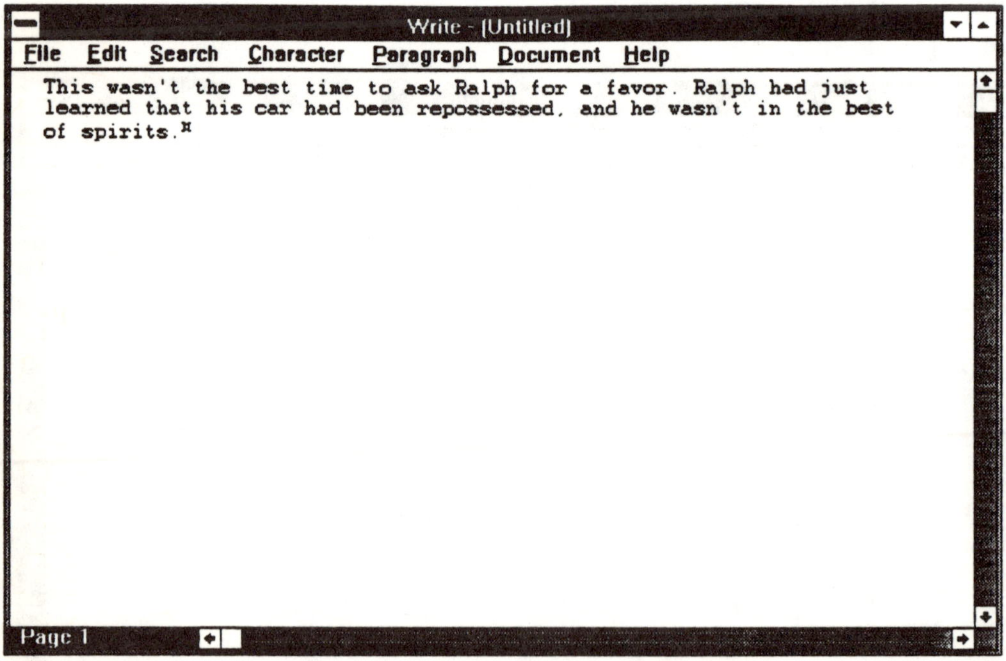

Figure 7-3. The Document with a 3-inch Right Margin.

Another possible solution is to change the right indent value to one that brings all the text into view. You will learn about indenting paragraphs later in this chapter.

Non-Default Document Formats

Write does not allow you to modify its default values, and you might naturally protest that you do not want to step through those margin-setting measures every time you begin a new document. There are four solutions to this problem.

Recording the Margin Command

You can record the steps necessary to change the margin as a Recorder Macro. Then whenever you start a new document, you can make the change with a single keystroke. Chapter 10 will show you how to do that.

Installing the Generic Printer

You can install the Generic/Text Only printer driver from the Control Panel. Although you might not have such a printer, its default font displays 6-inch lines that fall well within the borders of the Write window, even when you have reduced the window to a smaller size. Figure 7-4 shows the same document that was shown in Figure 7-3 as displayed for the Generic/Text Only printer.

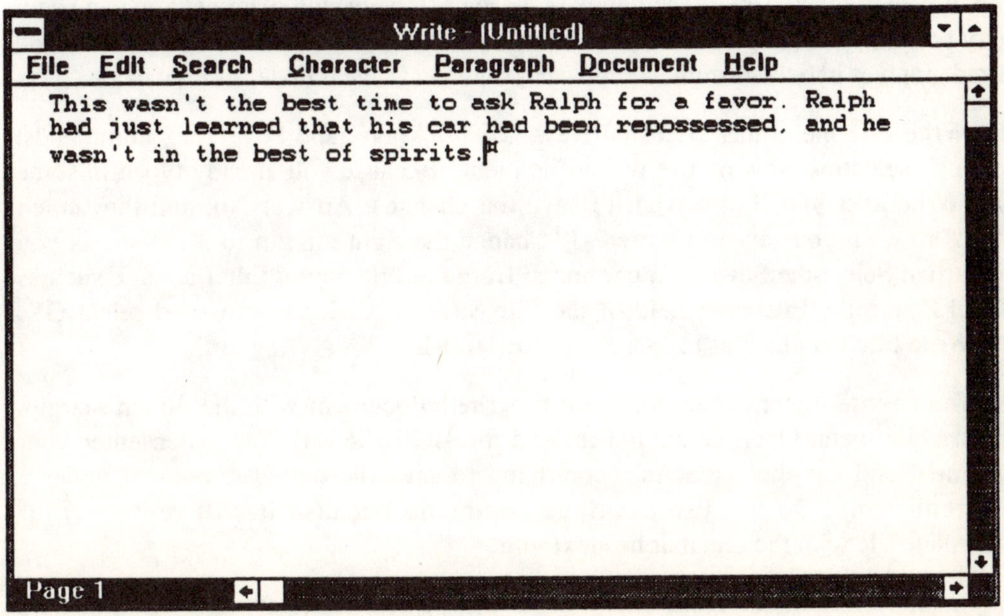

Figure 7-4. The Document with the Generic/Text Only Printer.

Notice that the fonts appear the same on the screen for the two printers in the examples. Windows uses the screen font that most closely approximates what it knows to be the printer font. In this case it uses the same screen font for different printer character widths. To compensate, it stretches or compresses the displayed paper width.

You can select the generic printer from the Printer Setup command on the File menu and keep it in effect while you are typing. This selection affects the Write session only. Other applications that might be printing in the background will still print to the default printer. When you are ready to print your Write document, you can select the correct printer.

A disadvantage to this solution is that the generic printer definition might not support your printer's fonts. You will have to change printer selections and modify the font settings for italics, headlines, etc., after you are done entering the text.

Building a Boilerplate Document

The third solution is to prepare a boilerplate document that has all the settings you want with respect to fonts, paragraph alignment, headers, footers, and margins. You can begin every session by loading the boilerplate document. Then, when you have typed text and pasted graphics into the document, you can print it and save it under its own name.

The Write File menu has the usual New, Open..., Save, and Save As... commands. Begin by selecting New on the Write File menu. Because you already typed in some text, Write asks you if you want to save the changes. Answer No, and the screen returns to what you saw in Figure 7-1. Change the right margin to 3 inches, as you did earlier. Select the Save As... command from the File menu. Enter a name such as BOILER into the Filename field of the File Save As dialogue box, and select OK. The Write title bar changes to Write-BOILER.WRI.

Exit from Write. Later, when you want to write a document with the 3-inch margin, use the File menu Open command to load the BOILER.WRI file. Then enter your document and use the Save As... command to save the edited document under a different name. Do not use the Save command because it will replace your boilerplate file with the one that has text in it.

As you may remember from Chapters 2 and 3, you can start applications with defined documents loaded. You can start Write with your boilerplate document. You can even have several such boilerplates and install a different copy of Write in the Program Manager for each one. You can execute Write from the File Manager by selecting the appropriate .WRI boilerplate file as well.

Using Notepad for Text and Write for Document Preparation

The fourth solution is to key in your text with the Notepad accessory, which you will learn in Chapter 10. You can then use Write to integrate text and graphics and to manage the page layout and document formats.

Moving Around in the Document

Start over again and begin a new document. After you have some text typed in, try moving the cursor around in the text that you have entered. Table 7-1 lists the keystrokes that move the cursor.

Table 7-1. Write Cursor Movement Keystrokes.

Keystroke	Moves the Cursor
Up, Down, Left, Right	one character position
Ctrl+Right/Left	one word right and left
Pad 5+Right/Left	one sentence right and left *
Home, End	to the beginning and end of the line
Pad 5+Up/Down	to the previous and next paragraph
Ctrl+PgUp/PgDn	to the top and bottom of the window
Pad 5+PgUp/PgDn	to the previous and next page **
Ctrl+Home/End	to the beginning and end of the document

* Pad 5 is the 5 on the numeric keypad
** works only after Repaginate command or you have printed the document

MARKING TEXT

Many of the Write commands operate on a marked block of text. You can mark text in the usual ways, as explained in Chapter 4. If you have a mouse, Write provides additional methods to mark text. When you move the mouse cursor to the left margin of the text, the cursor changes to a diagonal arrow that points to the upper right. When the cursor has this form, you can mark text in several ways. Table 7-2 outlines these operations.

Table 7-2. Marking Text from the Left Margin.

To Mark	Do This
A line	Click once with the mouse cursor at the line
Adjacent lines	Click the first line and drag the cursor to the last. Or mark the first line, move to the last line, hold the Shift key down and click.
A paragraph	Put the cursor next to any line and double click.
The document	Hold the Ctrl key down and click.

MOVING AND COPYING TEXT

You move and copy blocks of text by marking the block and then cutting or copying the text to the Clipboard and pasting it into its new location.

DELETING TEXT

You can delete a marked block of text by pressing the Del key. The Undo command on the Edit menu recovers the most recently deleted block of text.

SEARCHING FOR TEXT

Write has commands that allow you to search the document for a match on a text string. You can also tell Write to replace instances of a text string with a substitute text string.

Search

You can search a document for text by using the Find... command on the Search menu. A search proceeds through the entire document from the current location to the end, wrapping around to the beginning and back to the current location. If you have a block of text marked, however, the search involves only the marked block.

You enter the word or phrase for which you are searching in the Find dialogue box shown in Figure 7-5.

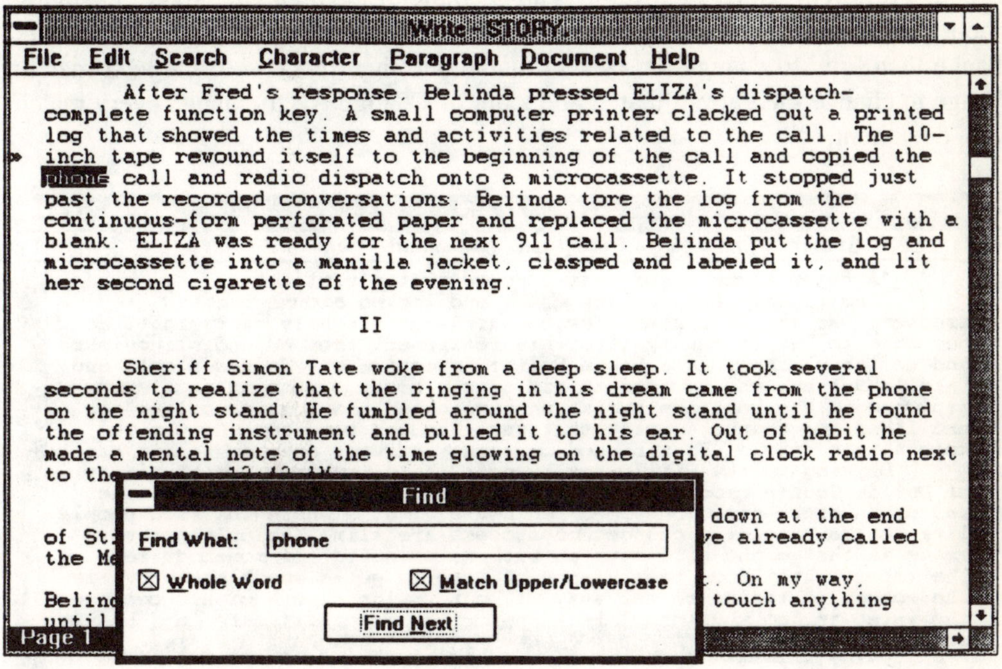

Figure 7-5. Searching for Text.

The Whole Word check box specifies that you want matches on whole words only. If you check this box, a search for the word "phone," for example, will not match the word "phonetic." If you select the Match Upper/Lowercase check box, the match will occur only if the text and the Find What text box are in exactly the same case.

When you have found the word for which you are searching, you can use the Find Next command button to find subsequent instances of the word. You can also use the Repeat Last Find (F3) command on the Search menu to repeat the find after the dialogue box is gone.

The Find dialogue box remains in view even when it is no longer the active window. To erase the Find dialogue box, activate it and press Esc or choose Close on its Control Menu.

Change Text

The Change... command on the File menu allows you to change instances of a text string to a different string. Figure 7-6 is an example of the dialogue box for changing "phone" to "telephone." You can select Find Next to proceed to the next match; Change then Find to change the current match and then proceed to the next match; Change to change the current match and stop; or Change All to change every match in the document.

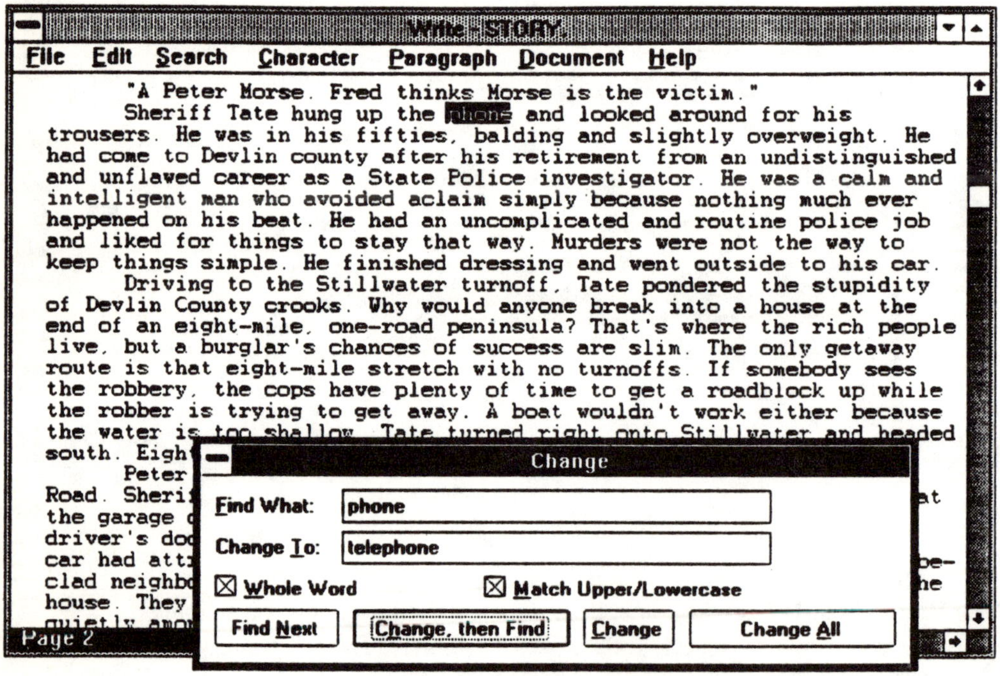

Figure 7-6. Changing Text.

The Change dialogue box remains in view even when it is no longer the active window. To erase the Change dialogue box, activate it and press Esc or choose Close on its Control Menu.

Wild Cards

You can use wild card characters, white space indicators, and control characters in your search text string. Table 7-3 identifies the control characters.

Table 7-3. Control Characters in a Search String.

Enter	To Search For
?	any character (The string "b?ck" matches back, beck, etc.)
^w	a space
^t	a tab
^p	a paragraph mark
^d	a page break

FORMATS AND LAYOUTS

Write gives you control over the format and appearance of a document, within your printer's abilities. You can change fonts, justify the text, change the spacing and indentation, add headers and footers, use tabs, control page numbers, and set the margins.

Characters and Fonts

The Character menu has a number of selections that allow you to control the character set in your document. You can choose from a number of character enhancements, fonts, and sizes. When you make a selection, it affects a marked block of text or, if no block is marked, the typing that follows. Selecting one of these commands has an effect only if your printer supports that effect. The Normal command resets all the other commands to their default settings.

Character Enhancement

The first group of character commands after Normal enables you to enhance the appearance of text. The commands in this group are Bold, Italic, Underline, Superscript, and Subscript. Superscript and Subscript are mutually exclusive.

Common Fonts

The second group of commands allows you to choose from the most commonly used fonts on your printer. The names of these commands vary from printer to printer.

Font Sizes

Fonts are available in different sizes. The Reduce Font and Enlarge Font commands affect the font's point size. Not all fonts have all the same sizes, however. The Reduce Font and Enlarge Font commands step through the sizes available to the current font.

Other Fonts

The last command on the Character menu is the Fonts... command. It allows you to choose from the other fonts that are available to the printer and to select the size from those available for the selected font. Figure 7-7 shows a typical Fonts dialogue box.

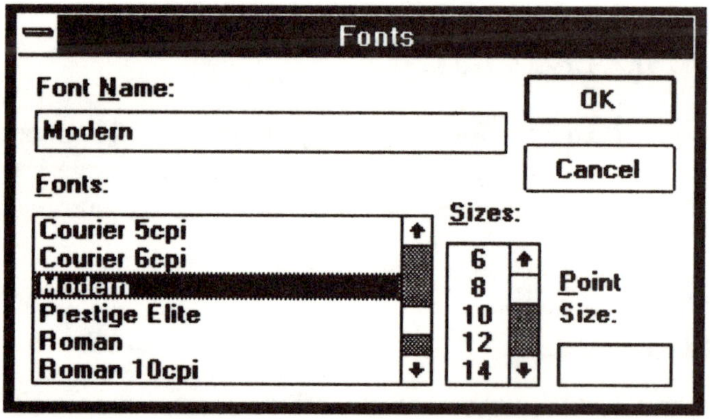

Figure 7-7. The Fonts Dialogue Box.

Paragraphs

The Paragraph menu has commands that affect the format of a selected paragraph or paragraphs. If you want to change a single paragraph, put the keyboard cursor inside that paragraph. If you want to change several paragraphs, mark them as a block. The Normal command resets all the other commands to their default settings.

Paragraph Alignment

The first group of paragraph commands after Normal controls the alignment of paragraphs. These commands are mutually exclusive.

The Left command aligns the text on the left margin with a ragged right margin—this is the default setting.

The Centered command aligns each line in the center of the page. You might use the Centered command to center the text of your letterhead.

The Right command aligns the text on the right margin with a jagged left margin. Some business stationery lists the names and titles of the partners in a right-justified fashion.

The Justified command spreads out the text so that it is justified at both margins like a newspaper column.

Figure 7-8 shows examples of the use of these commands.

Figure 7-8. A Document with Different Text Justifications.

Spacing

The spacing commands on the Paragraph menu allow you to use single, one and a half, and double spacing in different parts of the document. If your printer does not support the spacing you choose, Write will not modify the text on the screen.

Indenting

The Indents... command on the Paragraph menu allows you to specify automatic indenting. Figure 7-9 shows the Indents dialogue box.

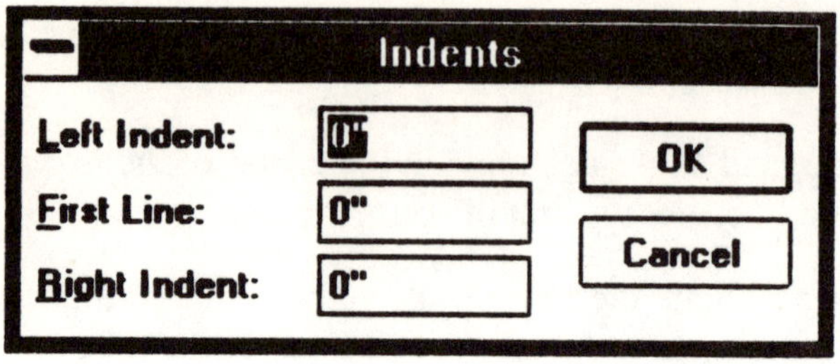

Figure 7-9. The Indents Dialogue Box.

There are three ways to change the indenting for the current paragraph. You can tell Write to: 1) indent the left side of an entire paragraph a specified distance from the left margin; 2) do the same for the right margin; or 3) indent the first line of a paragraph a specified distance from the left edge of the rest of the paragraph.

Figure 7-10 shows how you can use an indented paragraph and italics to offset a paragraph. In the example, the center paragraph has left and right indent values of 0.25 inches and is italicized from the Character menu.

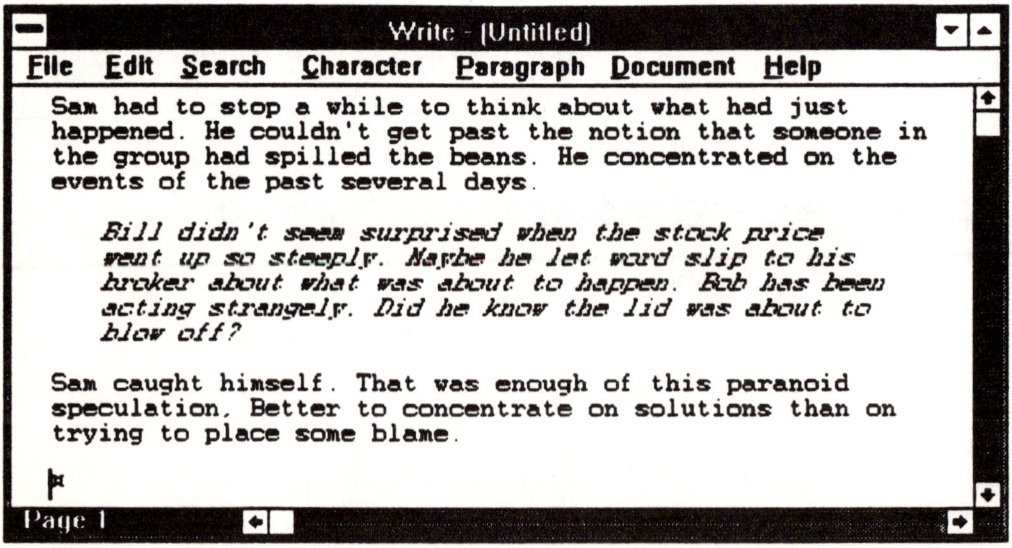

Figure 7-10. An Indented, Italicized Paragraph.

Headers and Footers

A header is a body of text that prints at the top of every page of the document except, possibly, the first page. A footer is a body of text that prints at the bottom of every page. You can use the Header... and Footer... commands on the Document menu to describe the content and format of a document's header and footer.

Headers

Figure 7-11 shows the document window and dialogue box that allow you to compose a header for your document.

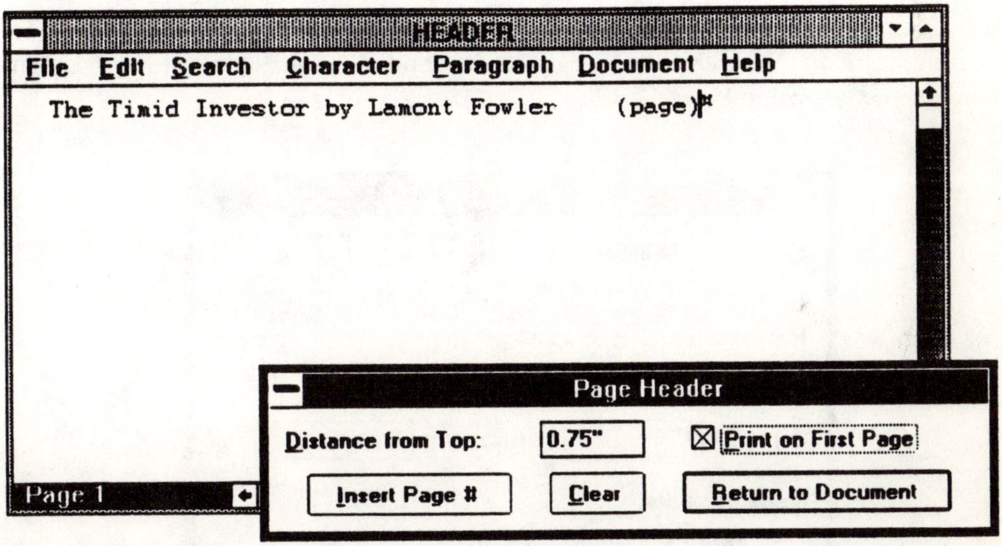

Figure 7-11. The Document Header.

The HEADER document window is a second Write document window. Even when the Page Header dialogue box is inactive, it overlaps the HEADER document window. You can use the Page Header dialogue box to specify how far from the top margin of the page you want the header to begin. You can also specify whether or not you want the header to print on the first page. Many documents use the first page as a title page and do not print the header there. If you select the Insert Page # command button, the (page) label appears in the header text at the current cursor position, as shown in Figure 7-11. This is where the page number will print in the header on every page.

Select the Clear command button to clear the header. If you make no other changes, the document will have no header. Select the Return to Document command button when the header is the way you want it. Do not try to close the HEADER document window unless you want to exit from Write.

Footers

Page footers work just like page headers except that you specify the distance from the bottom margin rather than the top.

Page Layout

You can control the page layout by selecting the Page Layout... command on the Document menu. When you select this command, you will see the Page Layout dialogue box shown in Figure 7-12.

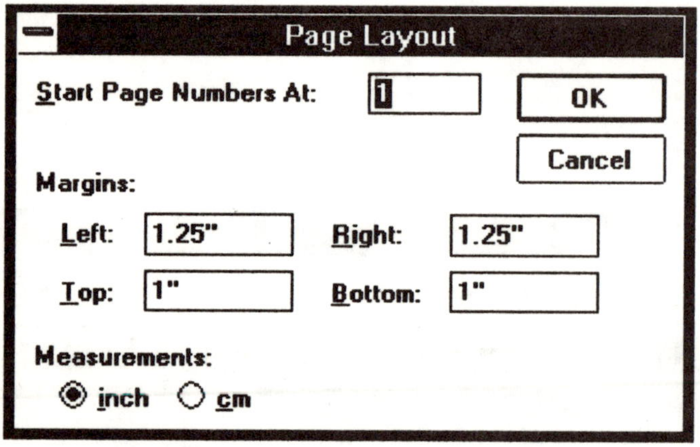

Figure 7-12. The Page Layout Dialogue Box.

The first field in this dialogue box allows you to change the first page number of the document. You would use this feature, for example, for printing a file that was one of several chapters in a document. You cannot use this feature to generate page numbers that follow the format 1-1 or 1.1. You can, however, include the 1- or 1. in the header or footer and follow it with the (page) insertion token.

The four margin fields control the margins that Write prints. Some printers have built-in margin controls, so you might need to set the left and top margins to zero.

You can specify whether the measurements used throughout Write are in centimeters or in inches by selecting the Measurements option button.

Tabs

The default for tabs in a Write document is two to the inch, but you can set overriding tab positions. There are regular tabs and decimal tabs. A regular tab works like one on a typewriter. A decimal tab is for entering numbers with decimal places—the characters you type go to the left of the decimal point until you type the decimal point itself, then the characters go to the right of the decimal point.

There are two ways to set tabs. One way is to use the Tab command on the Document menu. The other way is to use the Ruler, which has other functions as well. You will learn about the ruler in the next section.

Figure 7-13 shows the Tabs dialogue box for a report with tab stops set at 0.5 inches and at 3 inches. The tab at 3 inches is a decimal tab.

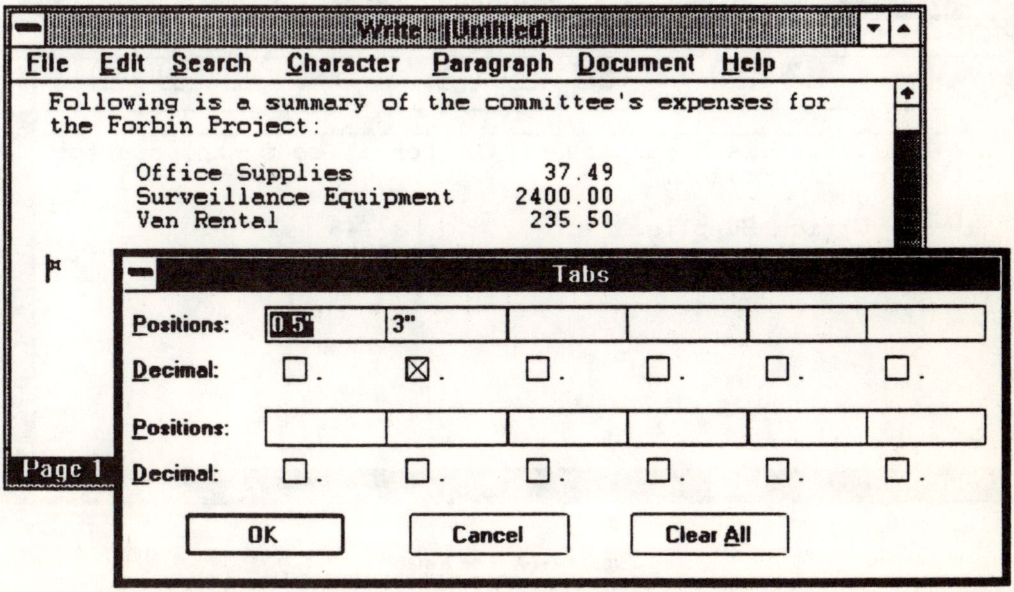

Figure 7-13. Setting Tabs.

Tabs are not associated with specific paragraphs the way spacing, indenting, and alignment are. The tab setting applies to the entire document.

The Ruler

Write displays a Ruler at the top of the window. If you have a mouse you can use the Ruler to change the format. The Ruler supports several of the operations you just learned. Besides letting you view and change the tab and indent settings, the Ruler also includes icons that allow you to click on the spacing and alignment of the document.

Displaying the Ruler

You display the ruler by selecting the Ruler On command on the Document menu. The Ruler On command is a toggle—it becomes the Ruler Off command when you are displaying the Ruler. Figure 7-14 shows the Ruler being displayed for a document.

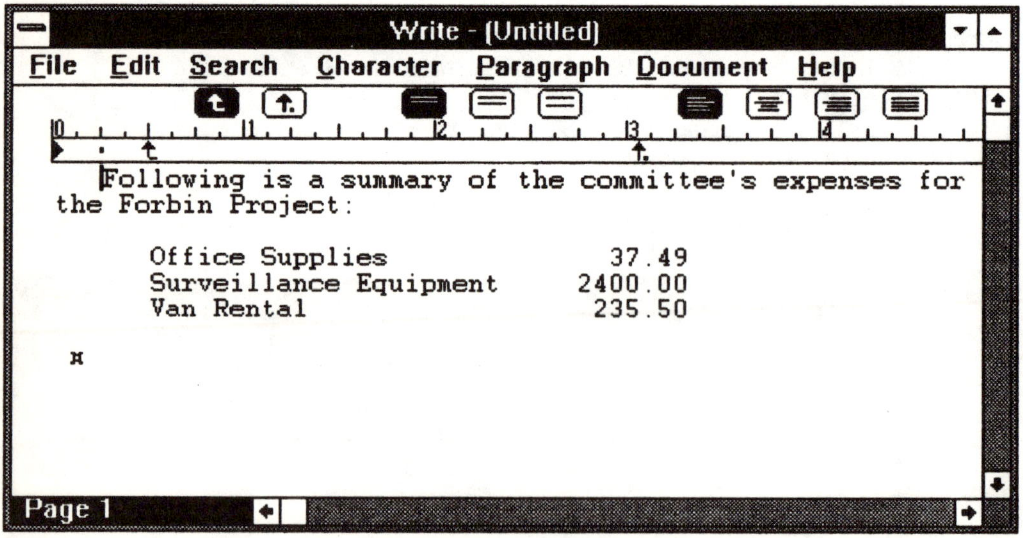

Figure 7-14. The Ruler.

The ruled line shows measurements in inches or centimeters, depending on which unit you chose in Page Layout. The ruled line begins at 0, which corresponds to the left margin of the page. A format line appears directly below the ruled line; it shows you where the tabs and indent markers are set.

Indenting with the Ruler

The right-pointing arrowhead at the left end of the format line is the left indent marker. The small dot just to its right is the first line indent marker. If the left indent and first line indent markers occupy the same space, the dot is white inside the black arrowhead. There is also a left-pointing arrowhead that marks the right indent, but it is off-screen in the figure.

You can move the indent markers by dragging them with the mouse cursor, although the first line marker will not go to the left of the left indent marker.

Changing Tabs with the Ruler

The upward pointing arrow with the curled shaft, at the 0.5-inch mark, is a tab. The arrow with the straight shaft and the small dot next to it, at the 3-inch mark, is a decimal tab.

You can set either kind of tab by clicking its corresponding icon above the ruled line and then clicking in the format line where you want the tab to appear. You delete a tab by dragging it off the left end of the format line.

Changing Spacing with the Ruler

The three icons in the center of the space just above the ruled line select single, one and one-half, and double spacing. Place the keyboard cursor inside the paragraph you want to change and click the spacing you want. As you move the keyboard cursor from paragraph to paragraph, the spacing icon that is in effect is highlighted.

Changing Paragraph Alignment with the Ruler

The four icons at the right of the space just above the ruled line select left alignment, center alignment, right alignment, and justification. Place the keyboard cursor inside the paragraph you want to change and click the alignment you want. As you move the keyboard cursor from paragraph to paragraph, the alignment icon that is in effect is highlighted.

GRAPHICS

You can integrate text and graphics into a Write document. Graphics come from the Clipboard. You cannot read a graphics file directly into Write. A picture occupies the entire width of the page, regardless of the width of the picture itself. You cannot enter text on a line to the right or left of a picture.

Do not expect to use the applications and accessories that come with Windows for any serious desktop publishing. The facilities for mixing text and graphics are minimal—it is easy to believe that these tools can do much more than they can.

Inserting a Picture

Assume that you have a picture that you composed in Paintbrush and that looks like the picture in Figure 7-15. You will learn about composing such pictures in Chapter 8.

Figure 7-15. A Picture for a Document.

Now suppose that you want to use that picture as the letterhead for your document. To transfer a picture into a Write document, you must first get the picture into the Clipboard. Point the mouse at the top right scissors icon—the one that has a dashed rectangle. That icon represents the Paintbrush tool for defining rectangular areas on the screen. Click the mouse to select the tool and move the mouse cursor into the picture area. The mouse cursor will change to a crosshair. Select the part of the picture to send to the Clipboard by starting in the upper left corner, holding down the left mouse button, dragging the dashed rectangular outline to the lower right corner, and releasing the button. If the outline does not adequately circumscribe the picture, try again. When the outline surrounds the border in the picture, select Cut on the Edit menu. The picture is now in the Clipboard.

Start the Write application and begin a new document. You insert pictures into a Write document where the keyboard cursor is positioned. A picture occupies the full width of the page regardless of the picture's actual width, so if the cursor is inside some text, inserting a picture will split the text.

Inasmuch as the picture is to be the letterhead, you want it at the beginning of the document, so leave the cursor at the beginning and select Paste from the Edit menu. The picture will appear at the beginning of the document, as shown in Figure 7-16.

Figure 7-16. A Picture Inserted into a Write Document.

Selecting a Picture

The picture that you pasted into the document is too big to be a letterhead. You can size and move a picture within a document, but first you must select it. To select a picture with the mouse, move the mouse cursor inside the picture and click the left button. To de-select a picture, click outside of the picture. To select and de-select a picture with the keyboard, use the up and down arrow keys to move in and out of the picture area. A selected picture displays in reverse video, as shown in Figure 7-17.

Figure 7-17. A Selected Picture.

Sizing a Picture

To size a picture, select it and then select the Size Picture command from the Edit menu. A dotted outline appears around the picture, and a square box appears at the center of the picture. The idea is to use the box to modify the shape and size of the outline—when the outline is the size and shape that you want the picture to be, you are done. This procedure is cantankerous, however, and requires practice and patience.

One method for sizing a picture is to place the box at the lower right corner of the screen. Move the box with the cursor, but do not click yet. You can also move the box to the right border with the right arrow key and then to the bottom right corner with the down arrow key. Sometimes this movement shrinks the outline's width too much, however, and you cannot move the box to the right. You must move the box around and watch the outline change. When the size is where you want it, click the mouse or press the Enter key.

Sometimes you will find success by stretching or shrinking the outline in one direction and clicking and then selecting the Size command to stretch or shrink in the other direction.

The outline sometimes snaps out of reach and nothing seems to work. This behavior seems to indicate that Write has only enough memory for certain sizing limits, and the outline will not let you exceed them. You can press Esc to start over.

If you do not maintain the same aspect ratio of the original picture, the new size will be distorted. You can select Undo from the Edit menu to return to the original size and start over.

The lower left corner of the Write window displays the values 1.0X/1.0Y. These are the X/Y ratios of the sized picture to the original. As you change the size, these values also change. If you keep the two numbers the same, the aspect ratio will be close to correct.

Figure 7-18 shows the picture sized smaller for the letterhead. If you are not sure whether the size is correct, print the document to see how it looks on paper.

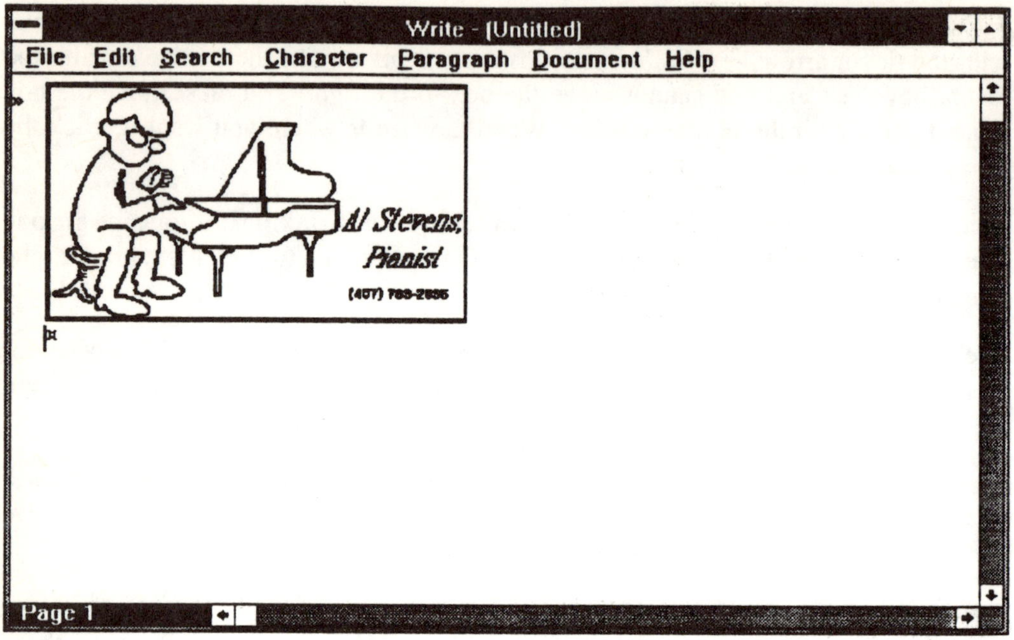

Figure 7-18. The Picture Shrunk.

Moving a Picture

You can move a picture horizontally across the page by selecting the picture and then selecting the Move Picture command from the Edit menu. The same dotted outline and box appear as do when you size a picture. Move the outline right and left with the mouse or use the right and left arrow keys. When the outline is where you want the picture to be, click the mouse or press the Enter key. Figure 7-19 shows the picture moved to the center of the page.

Figure 7-19. The Picture Moved.

***

WITH THE LETTERHEAD PICTURE AT THE CORRECT SIZE AND IN THE CORRECT POSITION, YOU MIGHT WANT TO SAVE THE DOCUMENT IN A FILE AS BOILER PLATE LETTERHEAD STATIONERY. THAT WAY IT WILL ALWAYS BE AVAILABLE FOR USE IN PREPARING OTHER DOCUMENTS.

***

To move a picture vertically within a document, select it, cut it to the Clipboard, move the keyboard cursor to where you want the picture, and paste the picture into its new position.

Adding Text

Adding text is simply a matter of typing. Select a font and type the body of your letter below the letterhead. Figure 7-20 shows the document with some text added.

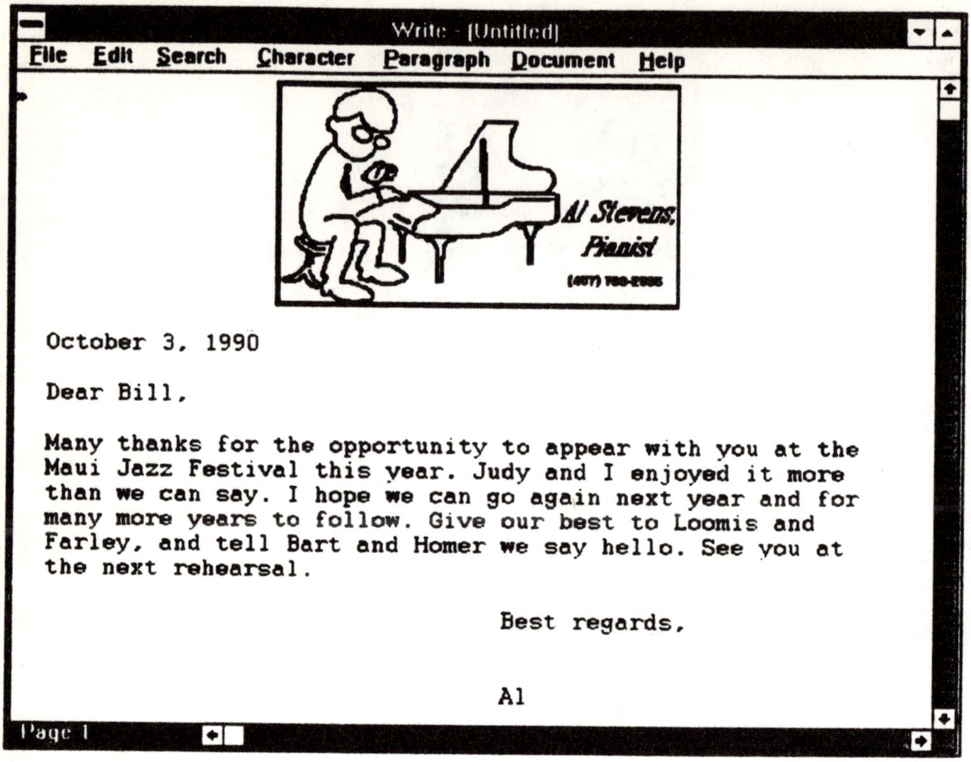

Figure 7-20. Text Added.

The picture in these examples looks a bit ragged on the screen after you shrink it down. Figure 7-21 shows the letter printed on a laser printer that has 300 dots-per-inch resolution—you can see that the printed rendition is much better.

October 3, 1990

Dear Bill,

Many thanks for the opportunity to appear with you at the Maui Jazz Festival this year. Judy and I enjoyed it more than we can say. I hope we can go again next year and for many more years to follow. Give our best to Loomis and Farley, and tell Bart and Homer we say hello. See you at the next rehearsal.

Best regards,

Al

Figure 7-21. The Picture Printed.

Deleting a Picture

You can delete a picture by selecting it and pressing the Del key. If, after you delete the picture, you decide that you didn't want to delete it after all, you can select Undo on the Edit menu to get the picture back. Another way to delete is to select and cut the picture to the Clipboard. That way you capture the picture at the same time that you delete it.

PAGINATION

When you print a document, Write changes pages according to the margins in the page layout and the length of the paper, as defined in your printer setup. Write also breaks pages one line early if the last line on the page will be the first line of a paragraph or if the first line on the next page will be the last line of a paragraph.

Inserting Page Breaks

Sometimes you want to force a page break where one might not otherwise occur. Perhaps, for example, every major heading in a document should start on a new page. To insert a page break, put the keyboard cursor where you want the break to occur and press Ctrl+Enter. Write displays a dotted line where the page break will occur.

Repaginating the Document

You can tell Write to indicate where the page breaks will occur by using the Repaginate... command on the File menu. Figure 7-22 shows the Repaginate Document dialogue box. When you select OK, the page breaks appear as a small >> symbol in the left margin of the document.

Figure 7-22. The Repaginate Document Dialogue Box.

Confirming Page Breaks

The Confirm Page Breaks check box on the Repaginate Document dialogue box specifies that you want to confirm the page breaks as Write assigns them. Figure 7-23 is the Repaginating Document dialogue box that you use to confirm or change a page break.

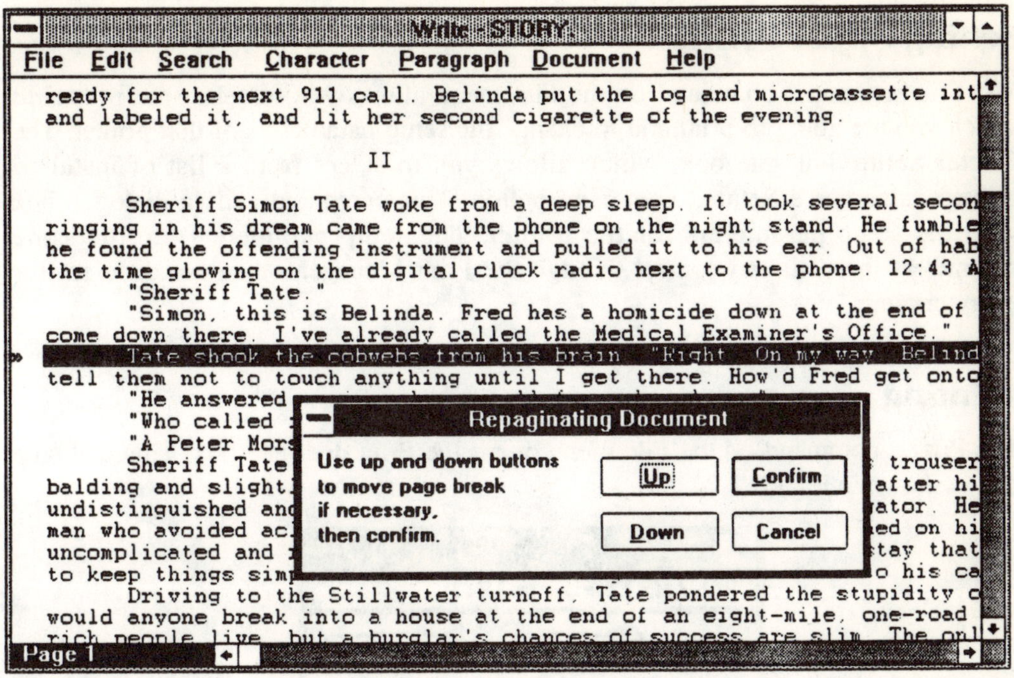

Figure 7-23. Confirming a Page Break.

You can use the Up and Down command buttons to move the page break among the lines above where Write has decided to place it. When you have the page break where you want it, select the Confirm command button, and the re-pagination continues to the next page break. If you select the Cancel command button, re-pagination stops and you can edit the document.

PRINTING THE DOCUMENT

The Write File menu has Print... and Printer Setup... commands that allow you to print your document.

Setting Up the Printer

The Printer Setup... command on the File menu allows you to select the printer to which you are going to print and to change the setup parameters of that printer. The Printer Setup dialogue box, which allows you to select from a list of installed printers, also has a Setup... command button. This command calls a dialogue box with the setup parameters for the printer. The setup parameters are the same parameters that you can control through the Print Manager—they are different for every printer.

Printing

The Print... command on the File menu opens the Print dialogue box. This dialogue box is shown in Figure 7-24.

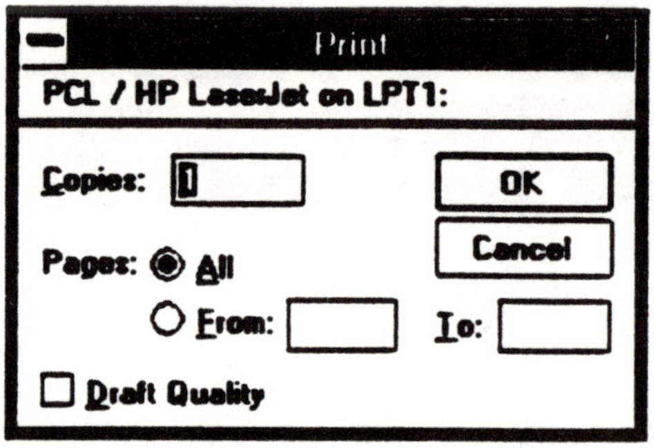

Figure 7-24. The Print Dialogue Box.

You can select the number of copies and specify whether you want to print all or just a selected range of pages from the document. If your printer has draft and proof modes, you can select one of them by using the Draft Quality check box.

SUMMARY

Windows Write is a small but powerful word processor that can support the word processing needs of many users. In this chapter you learned to integrate graphics from another application into a Write document. Chapter 8 introduces Windows Paintbrush, a graphics composition program that you can use to prepare pictures.

Chapter 8

Graphics: Paintbrush

Paintbrush is an application in the Program Manager's Accessories group. The Windows Paintbrush is a graphics composition tool that you use to construct pictures. You can build these pictures to integrate into documents, as you learned in Chapter 7. You can also use the pictures by themselves, perhaps in presentations.

The artwork for the pictures you create can come from several places. It can come from compatible picture files that are available commercially or from photographs and illustrations that you load into your computer with a scanner device. You can also capture the graphic displays of other programs. Your artwork can even be original creations that you compose with the Paintbrush design tools.

No book can teach you to be a creative designer. You can learn the tools and techniques that Paintbrush offers, but how you use them is a function of your own artistic bent. You will see many wonderful and imaginative designs in books and magazine articles that describe Paintbrush and similar programs. Many of those pictures were composed by professional illustrators—others are the work of talented amateurs. If your first efforts do not measure up to the examples you find in published works, keep trying. With effort you can master the art of interactive graphics design.

***

If you decide to run programs from the File Manager rather than the Program Manager, address Paintbrush as PBRUSH.EXE, a file in the WINDOWS directory on the drive where you installed Windows. Inasmuch as paintbrush is associated with files that have the .BMP and .PCX extensions, you can also execute it by selecting one of those files from the File Manager.

***

USING PAINTBRUSH WITHOUT A MOUSE

Although all the Paintbrush functions are available to users who have no mouse, using Paintbrush with the keyboard is pure agony. There are keyboard substitutes for mouse actions, as shown in Table 8-1, but progress is painfully slow. If you intend to use your computer for graphics design, the cost of a mouse is a good investment—regardless of which program you use.

Table 8-1. Keyboard Substitutes for Mouse Operations.

Mouse Operation	Keystroke
Click left button	Ins
Click right button	Del
Double-click left button	F9+Ins
Double-click right button	F9+Del

THE PAINTBRUSH

Figure 8-1 shows the Paintbrush application window. You build pictures interactively inside the work space of the window by using the tools and the palette.

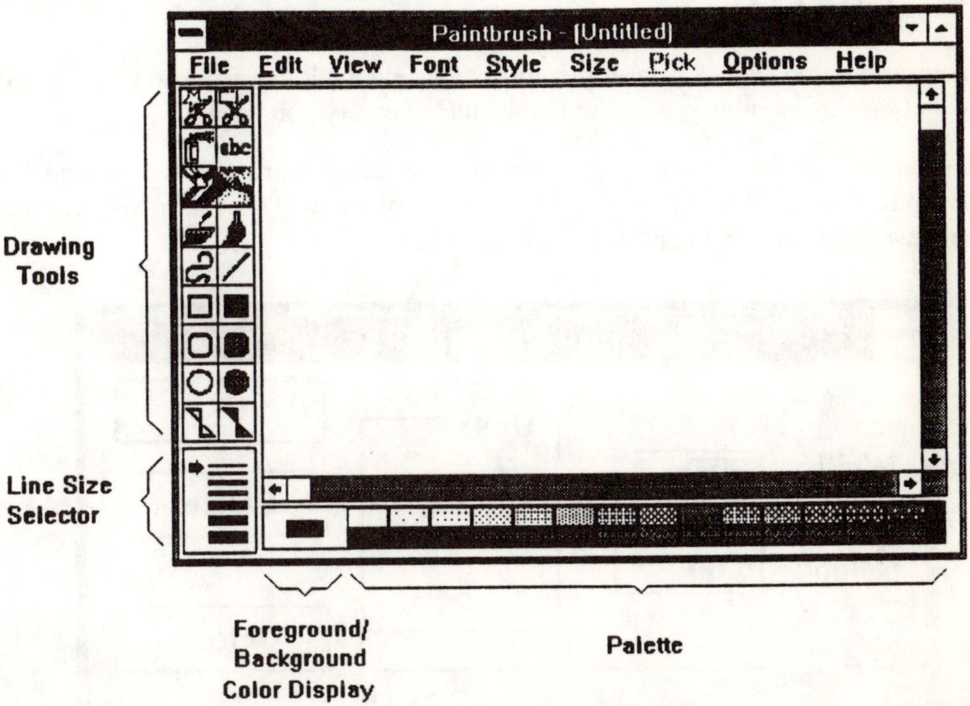

Figure 8-1. The Paintbrush Application Window.

The boxed icons along the left edge of the window are the tools. Each tool selects a drawing function. You select a tool by clicking its icon.

The cursor changes shape as you move it around the window. Outside the work space, the cursor is the familiar upward left slanting arrow. Inside the work space, the cursor assumes a shape that represents the currently selected tool.

The Line Size Selector in the lower left corner of the window selects the width of the lines that you draw; the size of the eraser's effective sweep; the width of the borders for shapes you draw; and the width of the air brush's pattern.

The Foreground/Background Color Display shows the colors for a picture's foreground and background. You select colors from the Palette that appears along the bottom edge of the window.

PICTURE SIZE

Paintbrush works with a default picture size. The default varies, depending on what kind of display monitor you use and how much memory you have.

You can change the default size by selecting the Image Attributes... command from the Options menu. When you select this command, you will see the Image Attributes dialogue box shown in Figure 8-2.

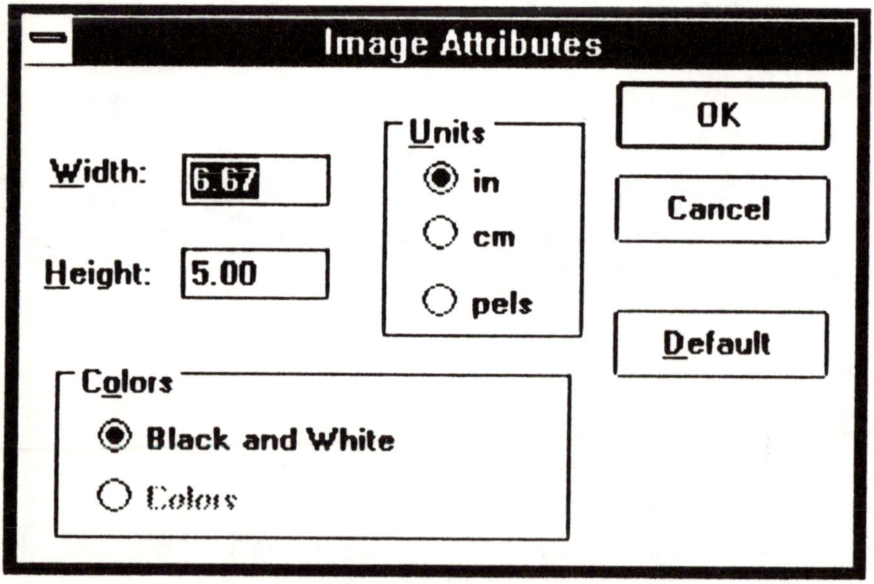

Figure 8-2. The Image Attributes Dialogue Box.

The Height and Width text boxes specify the dimensions of the image area. You can specify that the dimensions be expressed in inches, centimeters, or pixels by selecting one of the Units option buttons. If the picture is to be in black and white, you should also select the Black and White option button.

The Default command button returns the settings to their original default values.

PICTURE ATTRIBUTES

There are several attributes that affect how the various tools operate. When you change an attribute, the tools that it affects will then work differently.

Line Size

As mentioned above, the Line Size Selector is the box in the lower left corner of the Paintbrush application window. It has a stack of horizontal lines of graduated widths. You select a thicker line in the selector to tell Paintbrush to draw and spray thicker lines and to erase wider areas. To select a line size, point the mouse cursor at one of the selector's lines and click.

Brush Shapes

The Brush Shapes command on the Options menu allows you to select the shape of a line drawn by the Brush tool. Figure 8-3 shows the Brush Shapes dialogue box that appears when you select this command. As a shortcut you can double click the brush tool icon to select the Brush Shapes command.

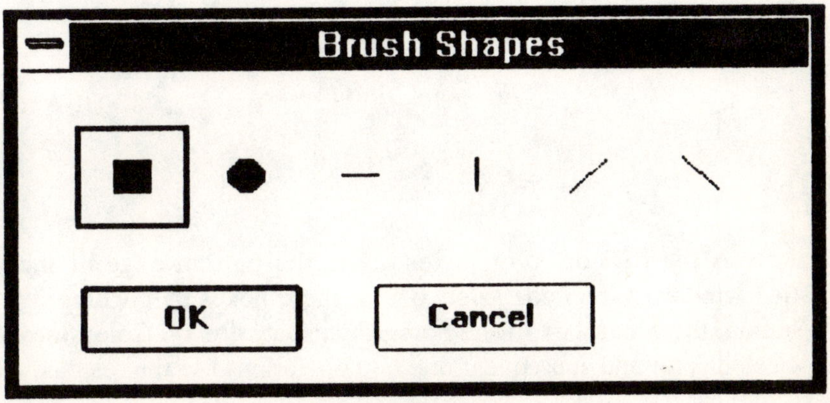

Figure 8-3. The Brush Shapes Dialogue Box.

There are six brush shapes from which to select. The default brush shape is a square box. The square outline that surrounds it indicates that it is currently selected. Click a different shape to select it. The outline will move around your selection. Select OK when you have selected the desired shape.

Figure 8-4 shows the effects of the various brush shapes.

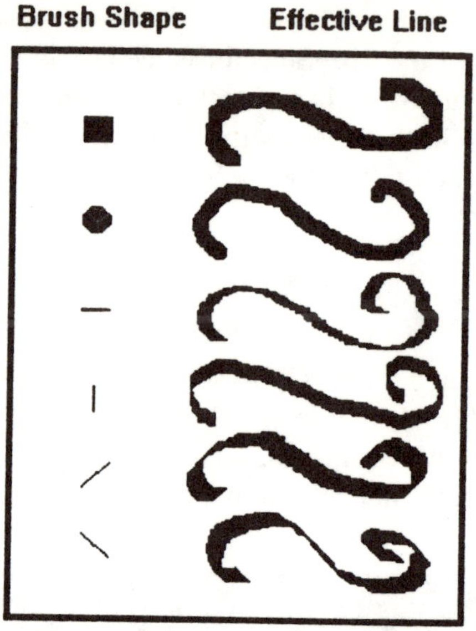

Figure 8-4. Brush Shapes.

Palette

The palette is the row of color boxes along the bottom edge of the Paintbrush application window. When you select one of these boxes by clicking it with the left mouse button, the center box of the Foreground/Background Color Selector changes to the selected color and subsequent drawing operations use the selected color.

To change the background color, select a color with the right mouse button. This does not change the background for the current picture, but it does change how some of the tools work. The background color is the border color for filled boxes, circles, and polygons. When you select New from the File menu, the current background color becomes the background for the new picture.

DRAWING TOOLS

The drawing tools are the icons that are displayed along the left edge of the Paintbrush application window. Only one of these tools is active at a time. You select one of them by clicking its icon. Figure 8-5 shows the icons and the names of the tools that they represent.

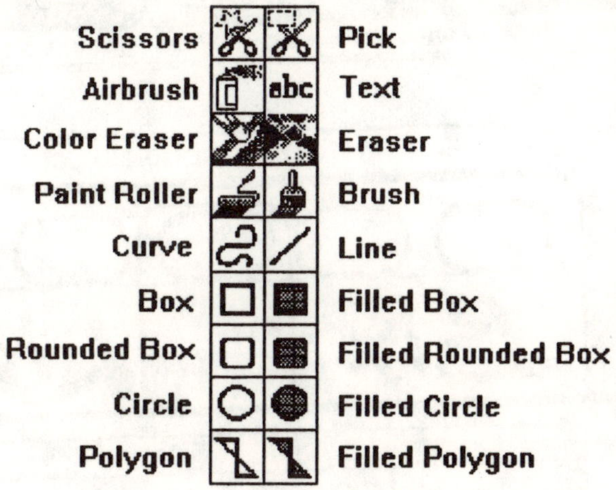

Figure 8-5. The Drawing Tool Icons.

Scissors and Pick

You use the scissors and pick to outline an area of your picture. This defined area is called a "cutout." The scissors tool allows you to draw a freehand outline around the cutout. The pick tool allows you to draw a rectangular outline around the cutout.

After you have outlined a cutout, you can do several image manipulation operations on it. Those operations are described below under "Image Manipulation."

When you have a cutout defined, the Clipboard's Cut and Copy commands on the Edit menu are enabled. You use these commands to send the cutout to the Clipboard, as you learned in Chapter 4. If you are not using the Clipboard for data exchange with another program at the time, the Cut command is a convenient way to delete large areas of the picture without using the eraser tool.

Airbrush

The airbrush tool emulates a paint spray can. You select a foreground color and a line size and then move the mouse cursor around, holding the left button down to spray a pattern. The subway decoration in Figure 8-6 was sprayed with the airbrush.

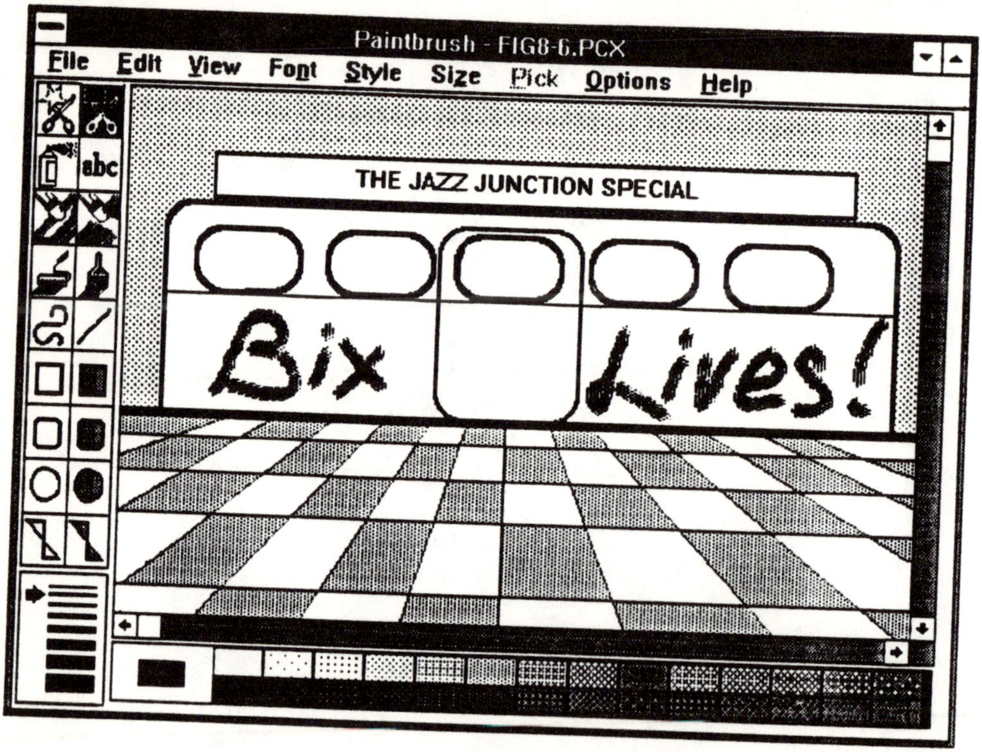

Figure 8-6. Airbrush Graffiti.

Text

The Text tool allows you to type text of various fonts, styles, and sizes into your picture. The sign on top of the subway in Figure 8-6 is an example of text entry. You will learn about text and characters later in this chapter.

Erasers

There are two erasers: the regular eraser and the color eraser. The regular eraser tool erases the area of the picture under the eraser cursor, which is a square box. You move the mouse cursor across the picture and hold down the left button to erase. The size of the eraser box is controlled by the Line Size Selector.

You can drag the color eraser tool across the screen the same way you do the regular eraser, but the color eraser changes a selected color to another color rather than erasing. To specify the color to change, select it as the foreground color. To specify the new color, select it as the background color. To change all occurrences of the selected foreground color to the background color within the visible part of the drawing area, double click the color eraser tool.

Paint Roller

The paint roller tool fills an area with the selected foreground color. It spreads the color out, stopping when it hits the border's edge. The back wall and tiles in the subway picture in Figure 8-6 were filled in with the paint roller.

If the paint roller finds a break in the border of a form you are trying to fill, it will leak through and fill adjacent forms. Use the Undo command on the Edit menu to undo the fill and try again.

Brush

You use the brush tool to draw freehand. The brush shape and the line size both affect the lines that you draw. Figure 8-7 is an example of a picture of a cowboy that was drawn entirely with the brush.

Figure 8-7. Drawing with the Brush.

Line

The line tool lets you draw straight lines. You select the line size and foreground color, move the mouse to the starting point of the line, and press and hold the left mouse button. Then you drag the other end of the line to where you want it. Figure 8-8 is a wire-frame airport drawing made entirely from lines.

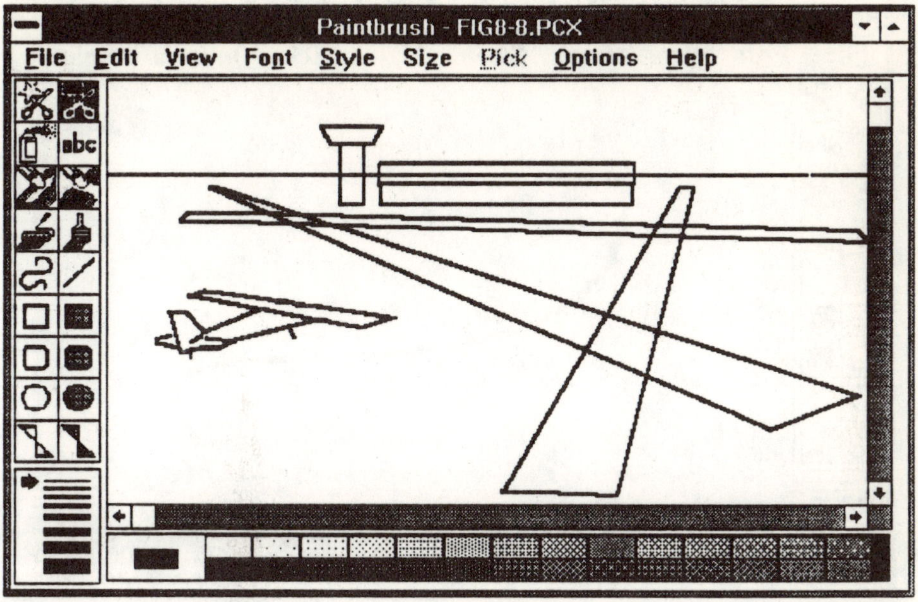

Figure 8-8. Lines.

Curve

The curve tool lets you draw a line in the work space and then distort it to form a curve. You move the mouse cursor to the beginning of the line and press and hold the left button, then you drag to the other end. When you release the button, you have drawn a straight line. You can then move the mouse cursor elsewhere on the screen and hold down the left button. The line will warp toward the mouse cursor. As long as you hold down the button, you can move the mouse to form the curve in different ways and directions. You can then release the button, move to a second location and warp some more. When you release the button the second time, you have defined the curve and it becomes a part of the drawing.

Figure 8-9 is an example of a curve drawn with the curve tool. The curve tool draws a much smoother curve than you could with the brush tool, and that is its advantage. It does, however, take some practice to get used to how the curve tool works so that you can draw a curve with a predictable shape.

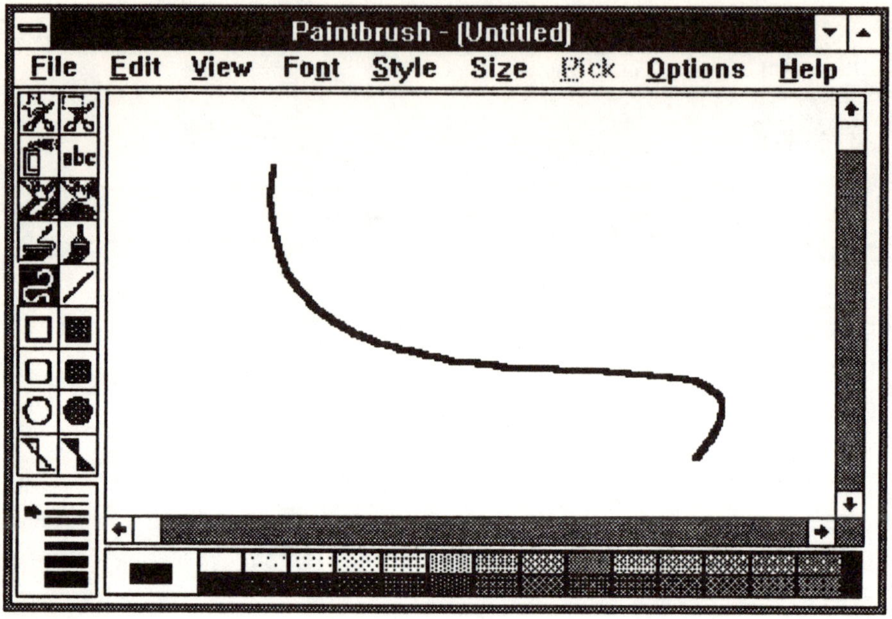

Figure 8-9. A Curve.

Boxes

You can draw four kinds of boxes. The box and rounded box tools draw a box outline without changing the part of the picture that is inside the box. The outline uses the foreground color. The filled box and filled rounded box tools draw the boxes using the background color as a frame and the foreground color to fill the box. Figure 8-10 shows a random collection of boxes.

Figure 8-10. Boxes.

Circles

The circles and filled circles tools allow you to draw circles and ellipses. The filled circles tool draws the circle using the background color as a frame and the foreground color to fill the circle. The clown in Figure 8-11 is made entirely from circles and ellipses.

Figure 8-11. Circles.

Polygons

The polygon and filled polygon tools allow you to draw polygons. After selecting the line size and colors, you select the tool and move the mouse cursor to the start of your polygon. Press the left mouse button and drag the cursor to the end of the first side of the polygon.

When you release the button, the first side of the polygon appears. Move the mouse cursor to the end of the second side and click. A line appears, running from the end of the first side to the current position of the mouse cursor. Repeat this step until you are ready to terminate a line at the starting point of the first side. When you release the mouse button this time, the complete polygon appears.

The pyramids, pit, building, and ship in Figure 8-12 were created with polygons.

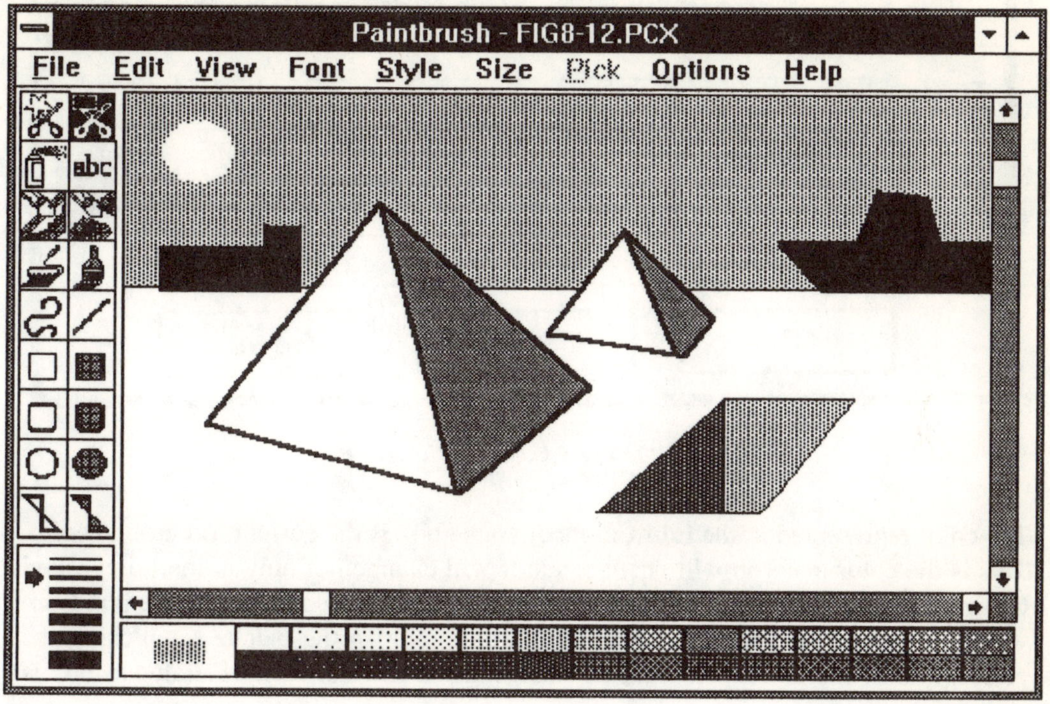

Figure 8-12. Polygons.

MAKING NEW COLORS

The Palette at the bottom of the Paintbrush application window describes 28 colors. Any of them can be the foreground or background color for your picture. You can modify any or all of the colors, thus defining your own custom palette. You can save that palette definition in a file and retrieve it later for subsequent use.

Changing a Color

Select the Edit Colors command on the Options menu. You will see the Edit Colors dialogue box shown in Figure 8-13. As a shortcut you can double click any of the color boxes at any time to execute the Edit Colors command.

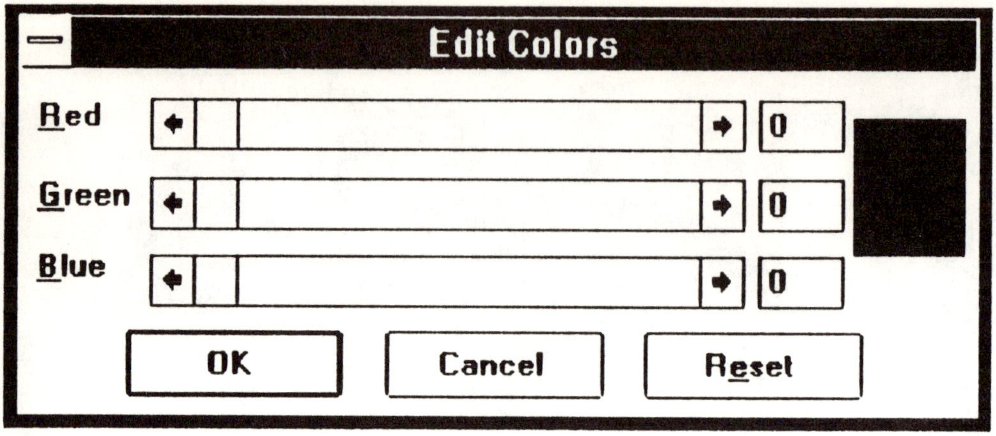

Figure 8-13. The Edit Colors Dialogue Box.

The color represented in the Edit Colors dialogue box is the current foreground color. This is the color that you will change, and it will change not only in the Foreground Color Display in the lower left corner of the window but also in the palette box from which you chose it. You can change a different color in the palette by clicking the palette box of the color you want to change while the Edit Colors dialogue box is still active.

To change the color, move the scroll boxes for the red, green, and blue components of the color. You can drag the boxes, click their scroll buttons, or type new numbers into the text boxes that show the relative value—from 0 to 255—of each color component.

Some combinations of values give a solid color, while others add texture. When the three values are combinations of 0, 64, 128, 192, or 255, you usually get a solid color. The default palette for a color system consists of colors with only these values. With other combinations you get a textured color. As you change the values, the sample color in the box at the right end of the dialogue box changes so you can see the effective color.

If you have selected Black and White in the Image Attributes command box on the Options menu, each color in the palette has three components with the same value. When you change the value of one of the components in such a monochrome palette, the values of the other two components change along with it.

When you've created the color you want, select OK. To change a color to its original value, select Reset. Select Cancel to leave the color the way it was when you executed the Edit Colors command. You can change any or all of the colors in the palette by using the procedure you just learned.

Recording and Retrieving a Palette File

The Save Colors... command on the Options menu allows you to save the current palette in a named file with the extension .PAL. Later you can use the Get Colors... command to select from among the palettes that you have stored.

TEXT

The "abc" tool icon allows you to enter text into your picture. When you select that icon, you can move the mouse cursor to a location, click to identify the position of the first character, and begin typing. The first character position becomes the left margin of the text you type. If you press the Enter key, the text cursor moves to the next line at the left margin.

The text is treated as a text entry for as long as you type and do not select a different tool icon or move the text cursor with the mouse. When you take one of these actions, the text is anchored into the picture and becomes a part of the graphics.

Fonts

There are nine fonts that you can select from the Font menu. Figure 8-14 shows how each of these fonts appears on the screen.

Figure 8-14. Fonts.

If you change fonts while you are still typing, the entire body of text changes to the new font. Once the text has been anchored, you cannot change its font.

Character Style

The Style menu has several character styles that you can select for text in a picture. The Normal command turns the other styles off—use this command to reset everything. The Bold, Italic, and Underline styles are toggle commands. When they are in effect, a check mark appears to the left of the command name in the menu. You can select any combination of these three commands.

The Outline and Shadow styles are mutually exclusive. The Outline style displays the character as an outline of the background color against the foreground color in the center of each character. For the Outline style to have any effect, you must change the foreground and background colors. The Shadow style displays the characters formed in the foreground color with a shadow made of the background color. As with the Outline style, you must change the foreground and background colors in order for the Shadow style to have any effect. Figure 8-15 illustrates the various character styles.

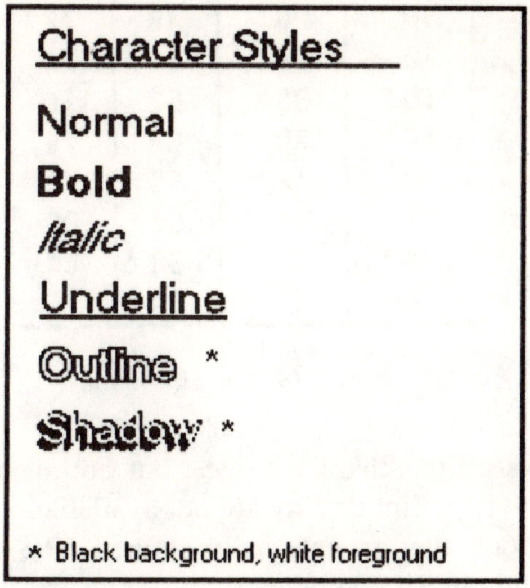

Figure 8-15. Character Styles.

If you change character styles while you are still typing, the entire body of text changes to the new style. Once the text has been anchored, you cannot change its style.

Character Size

The Size menu displays the character sizes that are available for the current font. Figure 8-16 shows the Size menu.

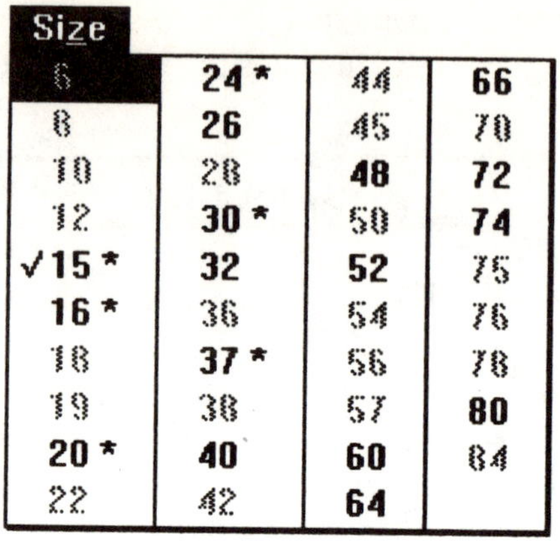

Figure 8-16. The Size Menu.

The Size menu shows all the character sizes, but not all of them are available on every font. The sizes with a dim display are not available. The sizes with an asterisk represent individual fonts that are internally defined. The sizes without an asterisk represent fonts that Paintbrush computes from one of the defined fonts of a nearby size. You should see no difference when you use the two kinds of available character sizes. Figure 8-17 shows typical character sizes.

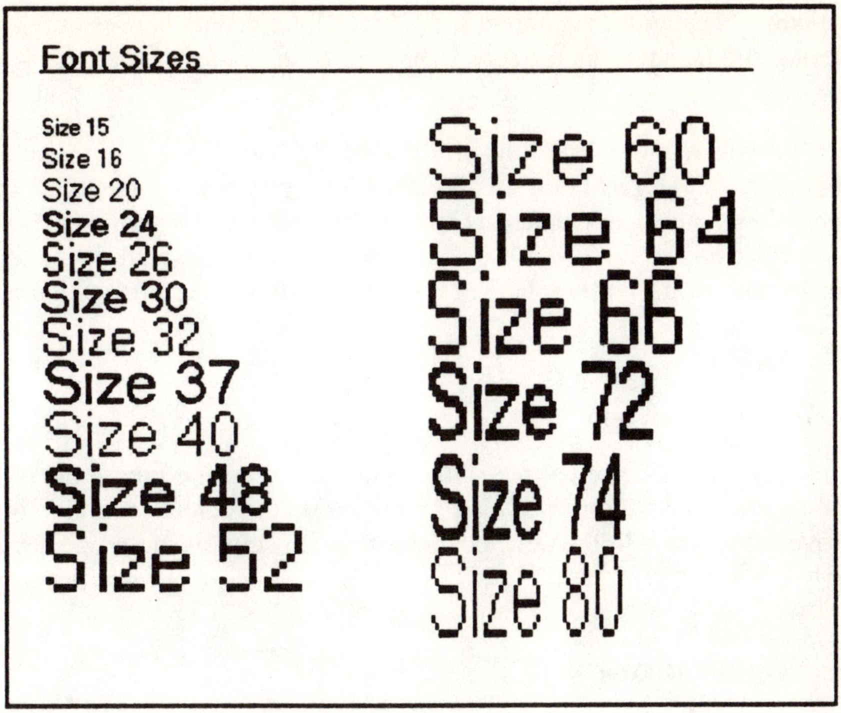

Figure 8-17. Character Sizes.

If you change the character size while you are still typing, the entire body of text changes to the new size. Once the text has been anchored, you cannot change its size.

IMAGE MANIPULATION

Paintbrush has several operations that allow you to manipulate a picture to achieve certain effects. All these operations use a cutout that you define with the scissors or pick tool.

Moving a Cutout

Move the mouse cursor inside the cutout. Hold the left mouse button down and drag the cutout to its new location. The dashed outline that defines the cutout disappears so that you can see the movement occur.

As you move the picture, you might see some color bleeding between the cutout you are moving and the areas on the screen through which you move it; a lot will depend on the colors.

A black on white image superimposes the cutout over the receiving area without removing any of the receiving area's detail, except where elements of the image intersect. This kind of movement is called "transparent" movement. You can also move a cutout opaquely by using the right mouse button instead of the left. If you use this technique, the entire image of the cutout will replace the location where you move it.

Copying a Cutout

To copy a cutout, hold down the Shift key as you drag the mouse away from the original cutout. This action causes the image inside the cutout to remain in place as you move a copy of it to the new location. You can copy a cutout transparently and opaquely as well.

Sweeping a Cutout

If you hold down the Ctrl key while you move a cutout, the cutout sweeps across the screen, repeating copies of itself. The faster you drag it, the further apart the copies will be. You can space them even further apart by tapping the Ctrl key as you drag the cutout. If you sweep with the left mouse button, the swept copies will be transparent. If you use the right mouse button, the copies will be opaque. Figure 8-18 is an example of both kinds of sweeping.

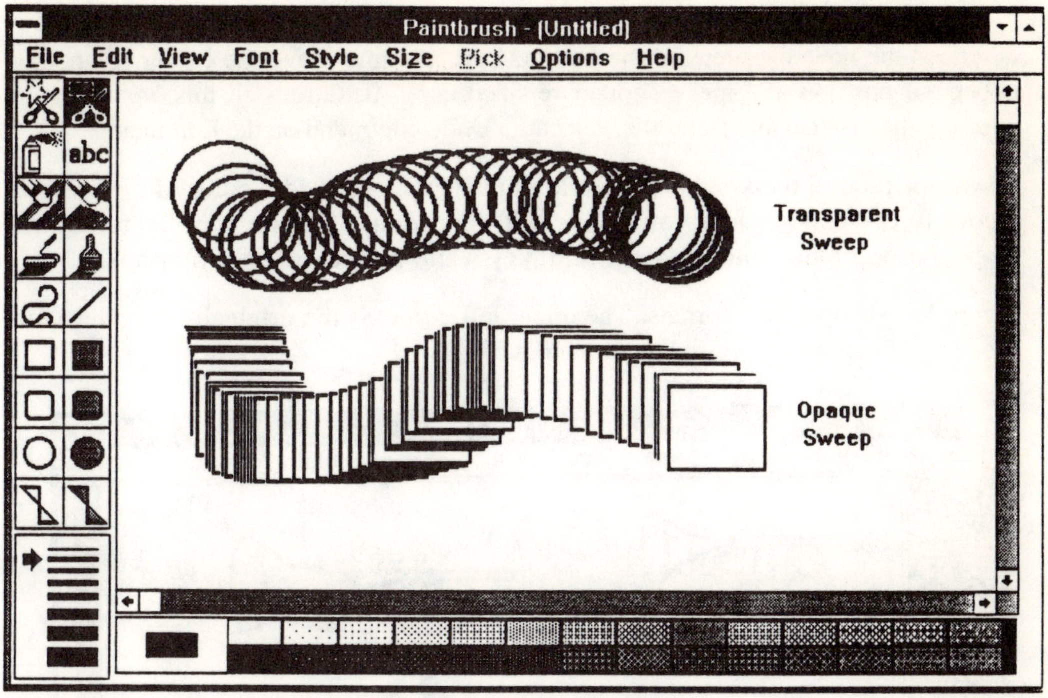

Figure 8-18. Sweeping.

Sizing

Defining a cutout enables the Pick menu, on which you will find commands to flip and size the cutout, tilt it, and change it to inverse video.

The Clear command toggle tells the other commands on the Pick menu to make the change and clear the original copy; usually that is what you want to do.

The Shrink + Grow command on the Pick menu allows you to change the size of the cutout. First you define the cutout. Then, unless you are retaining the original and making a sized copy, it is a good idea to select the Clear command toggle so that it has a check mark next to it on the menu. Then select Shrink + Grow. You will be back in the Paintbrush work space with the crosshair cursor, and the cutout's outline will be gone. Move the cursor to the upper left corner of where you want to place the newly sized cutout. Then hold down the left mouse button and drag the cursor to the lower right corner of the sized cutout. The dotted outline will follow along. When the outline describes the new size, release the button. You can now move the cursor to another upper left position and make another re-sized copy. If, during all this, you want to return to the original and start over, select the Undo command on the Edit menu.

The shape ratio of the sized copies follows the height and width ratios of the original cutout to the new outline you define with the mouse. If you want to retain the original aspect ratio, hold down the Shift key while you describe the new box.

Figure 8-19 shows four cornets. The upper left cornet is the original—the others are products of the Shrink + Grow command.

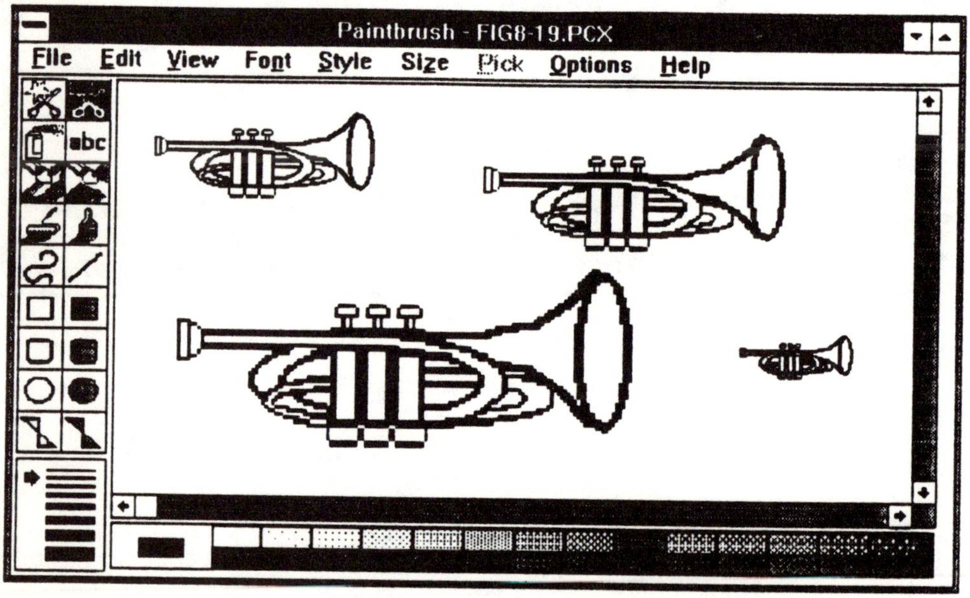

Figure 8-19. Sizing.

Flipping

The Flip Horizontal and Flip Vertical commands on the Pick menu change the horizontal and vertical orientation of the cutout. The Clear command has no effect on these two commands because they take effect in the same space occupied by the original cutout.

Figure 8-20 shows the effect of flipping. Paintbrush has no rotate command, so there is no way to stand the cornet in Figure 8-20 on end.

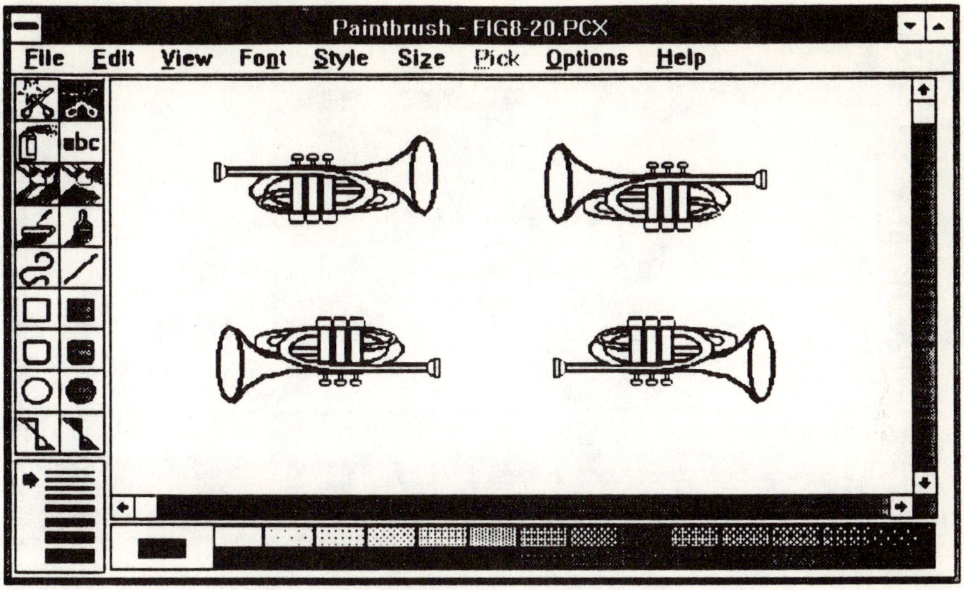

Figure 8-20. Flipping.

Tilting

The Tilt command on the Pick menu allows you to tilt a cutout forward or backward. When you select the Tilt command, you are returned to the work space—the crosshair cursor appears, but the cutout outline is gone. Move the cursor to the upper left corner where the tilted copy will be and press the left button to display the outline of the tilted cutout. As you move the cursor to the left and right, the base of the tilting cutout outline moves left and right while its top stays in place. When the outline appears the way you want it, release the mouse button. You can move the mouse to a different upper left corner and repeat the tilt. To return to your original starting place use the Undo command on the Edit menu. Select any tool or menu to lock the tilted cutouts in place.

Figure 8-21 shows a car apparently standing still. Figure 8-22 shows the same car with the illusion of motion added. By tilting the car forward and adding some horizontal lines, dust, and exhaust, the car has been made to appear to be speeding along. Observe how the tilting process also modifies the color texture of the auto body and tires.

Figure 8-21. An Immobile Automobile.

Figure 8-22. A Speeding Car.

Inverse

The Inverse command on the Pick menu reverses the foreground and background colors of the cutout. Figure 8-23 shows a scanned hand drawing of a piano. Figure 8-24 is the same drawing after the Inverse command was used.

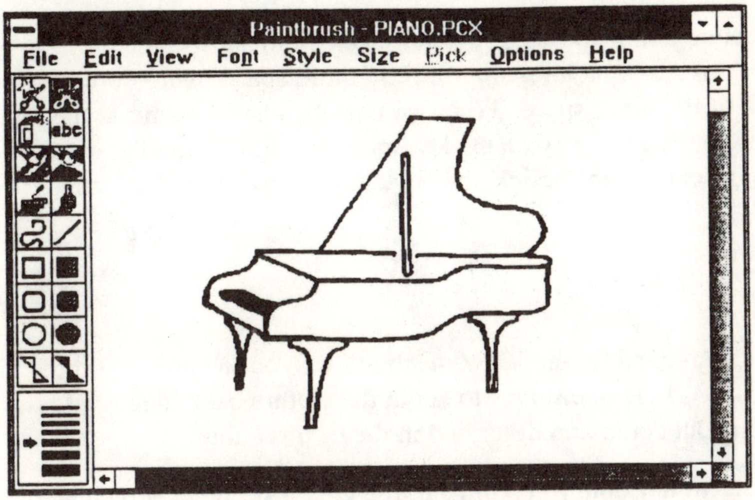

Figure 8-23. A Scanned Drawing.

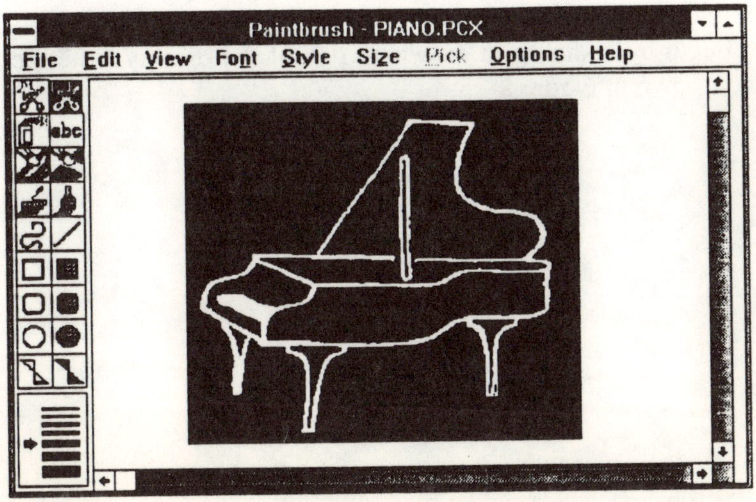

Figure 8-24. An Inverse Drawing.

VIEWS

The Views menu offers several different techniques for looking at a picture.

Viewing a Picture

The View Picture command uses the entire screen to show a picture. This command is useful for looking at pictures that occupy more space than you can see inside the viewing area of the work space. When you are finished looking at the picture, press either a mouse button or a key on the keyboard to return to the Paintbrush display. As a shortcut you can double click the pick tool icon to execute the View Picture command.

Zoom In

The Zoom In command on the View menu allows you to zoom in on the picture and do some detail work. It also serves to zoom the picture back to normal after you have used the Zoom Out command described in the next section.

When you select the Zoom In command, the cursor becomes a rectangle. You move the cursor to the position that you want to see in more detail and click.

Refer back to the airport design in Figure 8-8. Suppose you want to modify it by removing the intersecting lines on the runways and buildings and adding wheels to the airplane. Begin by zooming in on where two of the runways intersect. You will see the display shown in Figure 8-25.

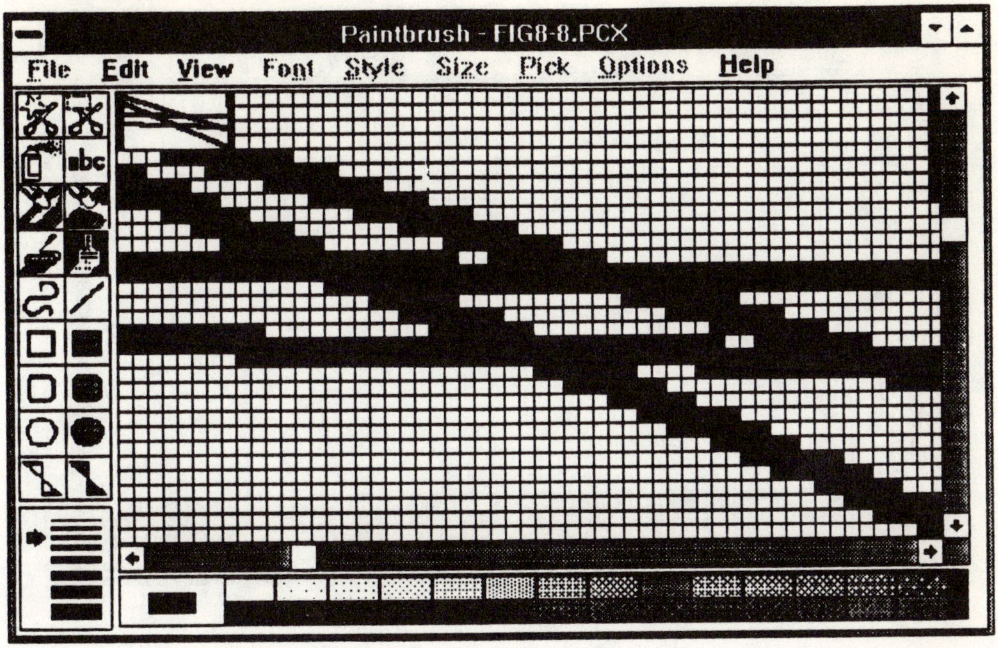

Figure 8-25. Zooming in on a Picture.

The picture in Figure 8-25 is the zoomed-in area magnified several times so that you can see each individual pixel (picture element). The small detail in the upper left corner of the work space shows the zoomed-in area as it normally appears.

You edit the image in a zoomed-in area by turning pixels on and off. You turn a pixel on by pointing the mouse cursor at it and clicking the left button; the right button turns the pixel off. You can watch your progress by looking at the detail picture.

The scroll bars allow you to move the zoomed-in area around as you make changes. If you want to undo the changes you made since zooming in, use the Undo command on the Edit menu.

When you are done with your zoomed-in pixel changes, use the Zoom Out command to return to the normal Paintbrush view. You can then zoom in on another area and make more changes.

Figure 8-26 shows the airport with the changes made.

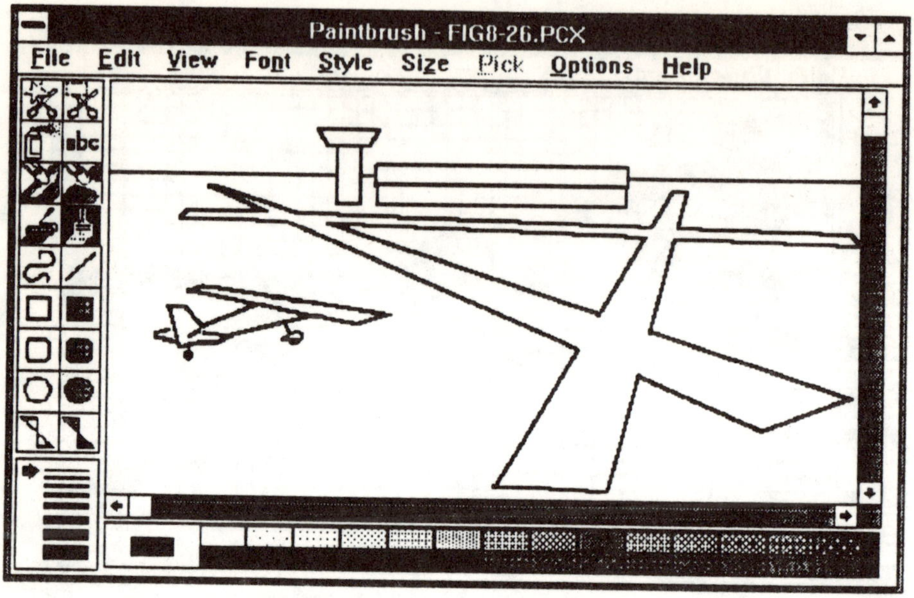

Figure 8-26. The Modified Airport.

Zoom Out

The Zoom Out command zooms the picture out so that the entire image area is visible within the work space. When you have zoomed out a picture, only a few of the Paintbrush actions are enabled, and the pick tool is the only tool you can use. You can define an outline, but the only thing you can do with it is cut or copy it to the Clipboard with the Cut and Copy commands or copy it to a file with the Copy To... command. Those commands are on the Edit menu.

Figure 8-27 shows the airport picture zoomed out with an outline defined and ready to copy or cut.

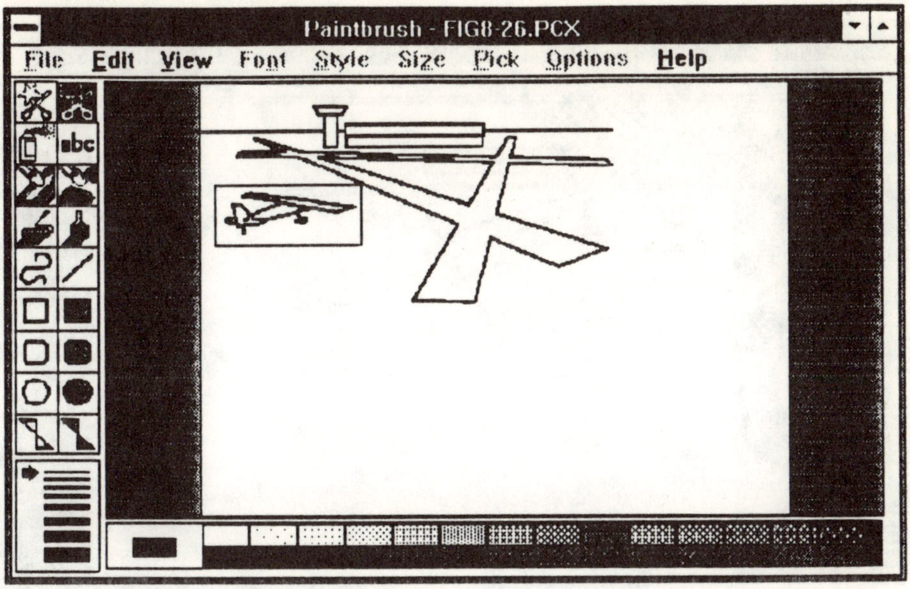

Figure 8-27. A Picture Zoomed Out with an Outline Defined.

If you paste from the Clipboard or a file in the normal viewing configuration, the paste operation clips—or truncates—any part of the pasted picture that does not fit within the viewed work space. In other words screen and window size affect the size of a pasted image. To allow the paste to affect the entire picture area, you must paste while you have zoomed out the picture.

When you have zoomed out the picture and you select Paste or Paste From... on the Edit menu, a crosshatch pattern appears in the upper left corner of the picture. The pattern is the size of the image that is about to be pasted. In Figure 8-28 you have copied the airplane to the Clipboard, zoomed out, and selected the Paste command.

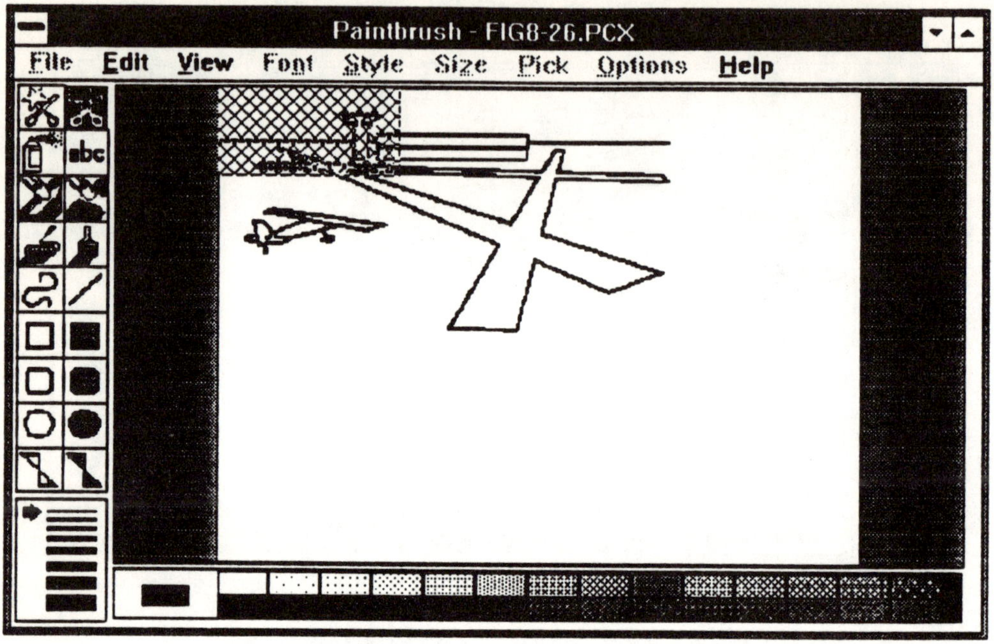

Figure 8-28. Pasting from the Clipboard.

The crosshatch pattern in the upper left corner of the work space indicates where the pasted image will go. You can move it around on the picture by dragging it with the mouse. When you have it where you want it, move the cursor out of the crosshatch and click or select the Paste command again. Figure 8-29 shows the new airplane pasted in place.

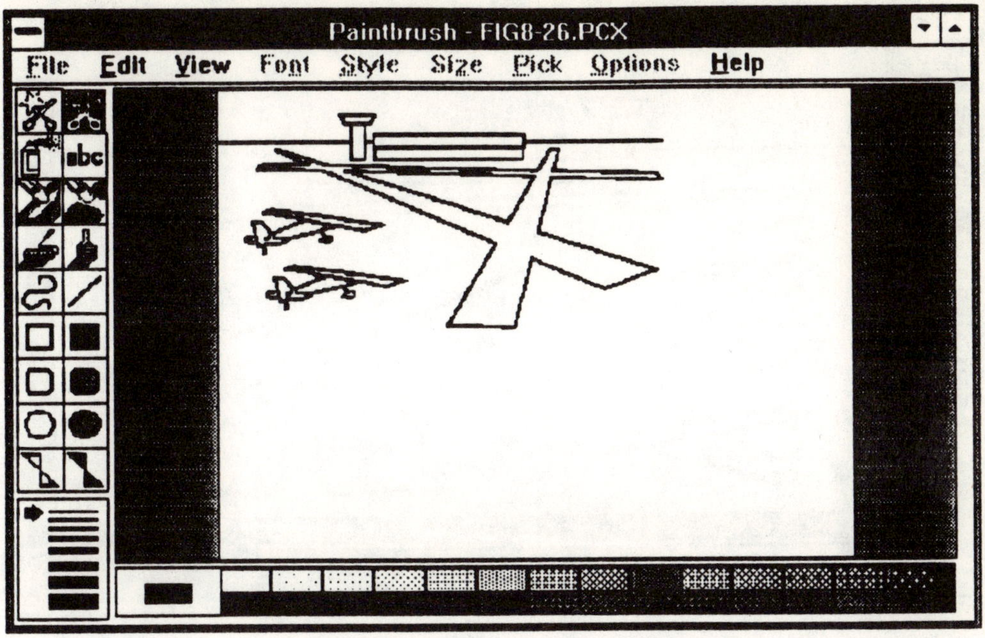

Figure 8-29. A Second Airplane Pasted In.

Figure 8-30 shows how you can populate the airport can be populated with a fleet of airplanes by using several pastes of the airplane and by using the Shrink + Grow command to add perspective.

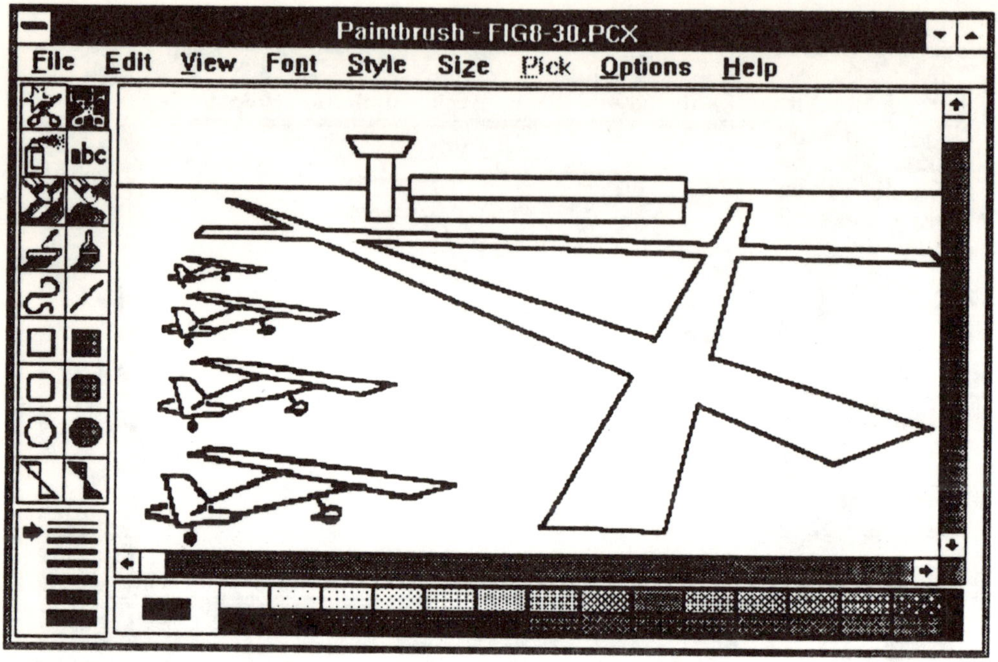

Figure 8-30. The Fleet.

Suppressing the Tools and Palette

The Tools, Linesize, and Palette toggle commands on the View menu allow you to remove the corresponding components of the Paintbrush screen in order to obtain a larger work space.

Displaying the Cursor Position

The Cursor Position command on the View menu displays the cursor X/Y coordinates as two numbers in a small window in the upper right corner of the Paintbrush application window. The first number is the left-to-right X coordinate—it ranges from 0 at the left edge of the work space to 622 at the right. The second number is the top-to-bottom Y coordinate—it ranges from 0 at the top of the work space to 424 at the bottom.

FILES

You retain your pictures in files, and you might get pictures from other sources that distribute them in files. There are several formats for storing graphics images, and you can read and write all of them. The file extension identifies these formats. The .BMP format is used for Windows wallpaper. The other format is the .PCX file. You should avoid using .BMP files other than for defining wallpaper files. They require much more disk space than the PCX file, and they take a lot longer to read into memory.

Loading an Existing File

You load an existing picture file into Paintbrush by using the Open... command on the File menu. Figure 8-31 shows the File Open dialogue box.

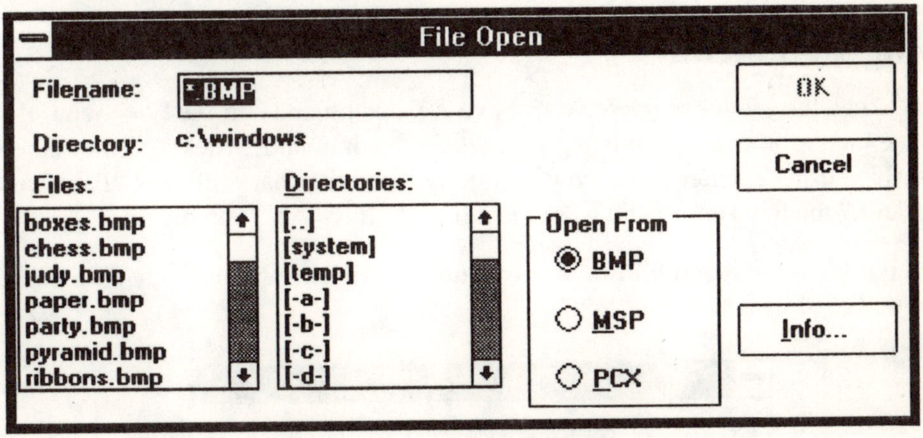

Figure 8-31. The File Open Dialogue Box.

Use the Open From option buttons to select the kind of file you are going to retrieve. The MSP file type is an older Windows format that Windows 3.0 supports only for compatibility.

The Info... command button tells you the dimensions of the file in the Picture Information dialogue box shown in Figure 8-32.

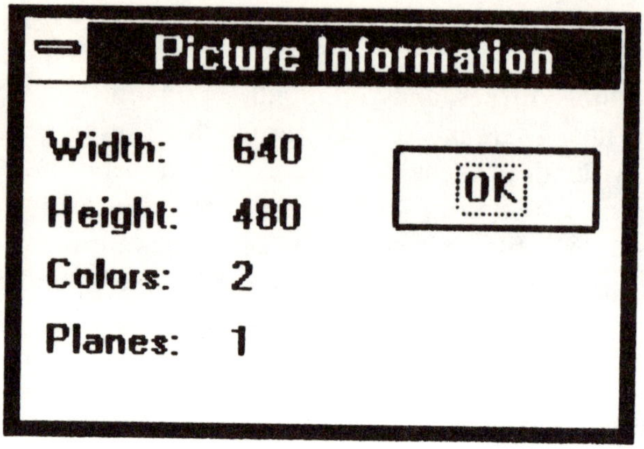

Figure 8-32. The Picture Information Dialogue Box.

Saving Your Picture

To save a picture, you use the Save or Save As... commands on the File menu. If you read the picture in from an existing file, the Save command writes it to the same file name. If you have generated a new picture and the title bar still says "Paintbrush - (Untitled)," the Save command works just like the Save As... command.

The Save As... command allows you to name the file. It produces the File Save As dialogue box shown in Figure 8-33.

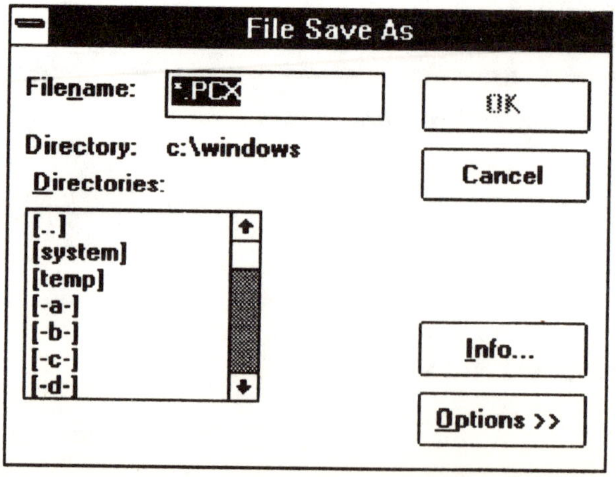

Figure 8-33. The File Save As Dialogue Box.

The Filename field lists *.PCX or *.BMP, depending on which file format you have most recently used; you must provide the file name.

Simply changing the file name's extension is not enough to get the file format you want. You must select the Options >> command button. Figure 8-34 shows the dialogue box expanded to include the save options.

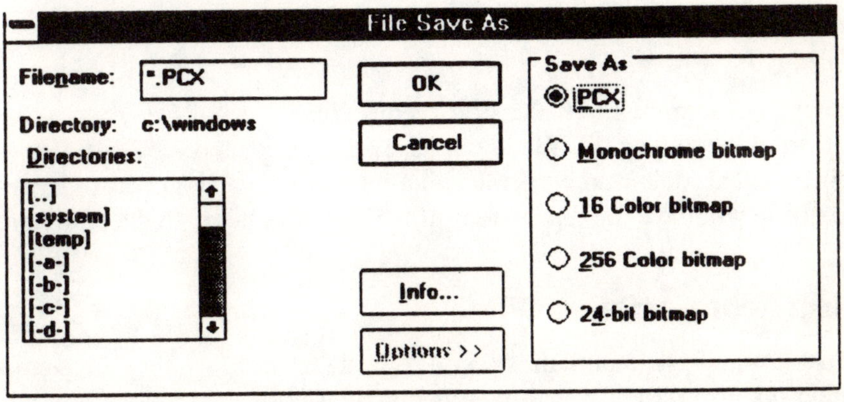

Figure 8-34. The Save Options.

Select the option button that represents the correct format. The Info... command button tells you the dimensions of the file in the same Picture Information dialogue box that you saw in Figure 8-32. You can view this box during a Save As... only if you originally loaded the file you are saving or if you have saved it at least once before in the same Paintbrush session.

***

You can execute the Save or Save As... process after you select the New command or the Open... command or attempt to exit from Paintbrush without having saved a picture that you have modified. A dialogue box will ask if you want to save the current image. If you answer Yes, the Save As... or Save process takes over. The Save As... process runs if the picture is still untitled; otherwise the Save process runs.

***

Starting a New Picture

You start a new picture when you execute Paintbrush—unless you call it from the File Manager by selecting a .PCX or .BMP file. You can change to a new picture after starting or loading a different picture by selecting the New command on the File menu. As a shortcut you can double click the eraser tool icon to execute the New command.

Copying to a File

The Copy To... command on the Edit menu allows you to Copy a cutout to a file rather than to the Clipboard. When you issue this command, you will get a Copy To dialogue box that looks and works just like the Save To dialogue box, except that the copied image will have the dimensions of the cutout rather than the entire picture.

Pasting From Another File

The Paste From... command allows you to paste an image into your picture from a file rather than from the Clipboard. When you issue this command, you will get the Paste From dialogue box, which looks and works just like the File Open dialogue box. The difference is that when you use the Paste From... command the image in the file is pasted into the current picture. When you open a file, the image dimensions are that of the file. When you paste from a file, you can paste a smaller image into a larger picture, or vice versa.

PRINTING

If you have a printer with graphics capabilities installed, you can print your pictures from within Paintbrush. There are commands to set up the page format, set up the printer, and print the picture.

Page Setup

Figure 8-35 shows the Page Setup dialogue box. In this box you can specify the four margins for the picture, as well as brief header and footer text to print along with the picture.

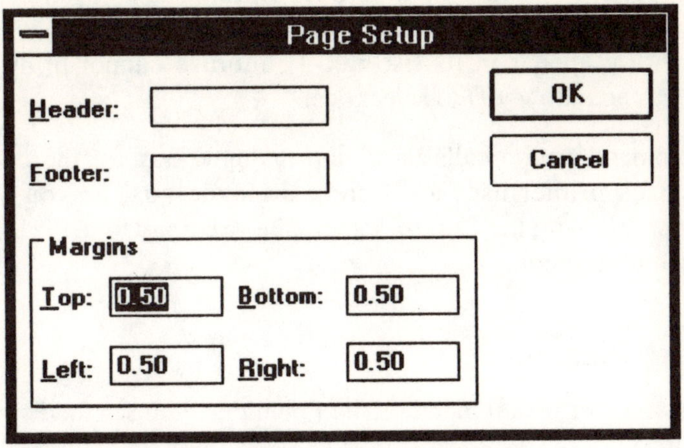

Figure 8-35. The Page Setup Dialogue Box.

Printer Setup

Paintbrush has a Printer Setup command on the File menu. It displays the Printer Setup dialogue box shown in Figure 8-36.

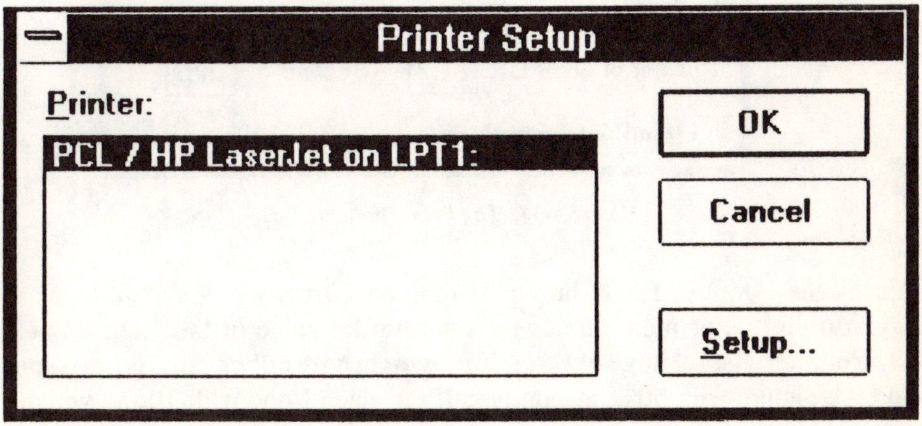

Figure 8-36. The Printer Setup Dialogue Box.

The difference between this Printer Setup dialogue box and those of other applications, such as Windows Write, is that only the installed printers that have graphics capability appear in its list box. Paintbrush cannot print to a text-only printer, so it does not allow you to select one.

The Setup command button calls the Setup dialogue box for the printer you have highlighted. Each printer uses a different dialogue box, as you saw when you installed your printer with the Control Panel. See "Setting Up the Printer" in Chapter 5 for additional information.

Printing the Picture

When you select the Print command on the File menu, you see the Print dialogue box shown in Figure 8-37.

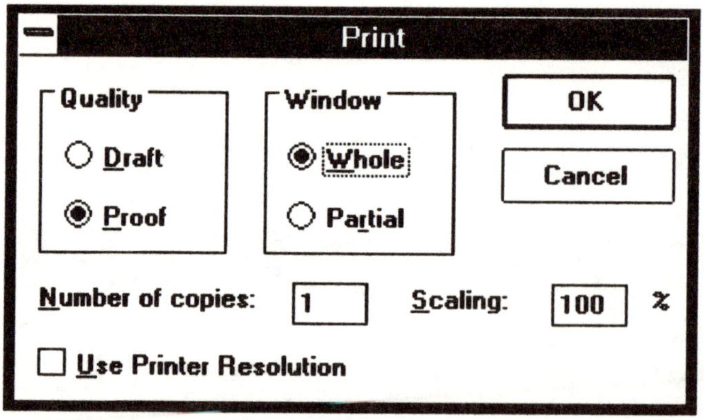

Figure 8-37. The Print Dialogue Box.

You can select Draft or Proof, but the two options usually produce the same picture. You can print one or more copies by entering the value in the Number of Copies field. You can also change the scaling, which will either enlarge or reduce the picture. A picture with 50% scaling is half the size of one with 100%, which is half the size of one with 200%.

The Whole and Partial options indicate whether you want to print the entire picture or a cutout portion of it. If you select Partial, you will see a display like the one shown in Figure 8-38 after you select OK on the Print dialogue box to print the picture. Use the cursor to describe a cutout to be printed as the partial picture.

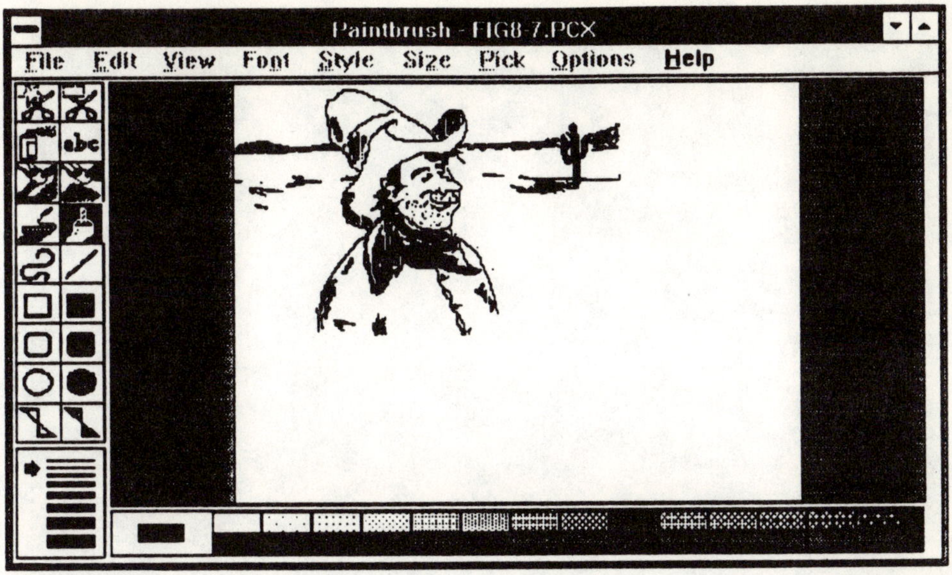

Figure 8-38. Partial Printing.

WALLPAPER

If you save a picture as a .BMP file, you can use the Control Panel to install it into your desktop as wallpaper. Chapter 5 explains how to install wallpaper. A unique wallpaper file is the ultimate personal expression. By using high-resolution scanners, the libraries of clip art, custom graphics files that you can download from on-line services and bulletin boards, and the tools of the Paintbrush, you can decorate your Windows desktop with the wallpaper of your choice. Figure 8-39 shows the wallpaper that greets me each day.

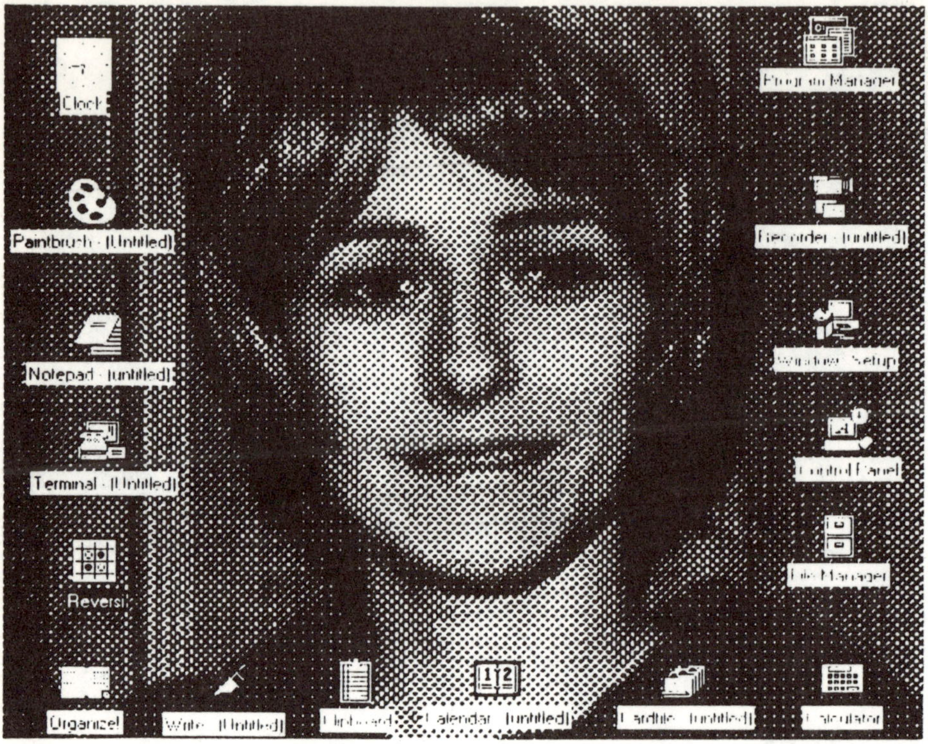

Figure 8-39. Sample Wallpaper: Judy in Windowland.

SUMMARY

With the promise of wallpaper that you can download from on-line services and bulletin boards, you might well ask how you go about getting this wallpaper. The first step is to have a communications program. Chapter 9 discusses Windows Terminal, the communications program that comes with Windows.

Chapter 9

Communications: Terminal

The Windows Terminal program is a small communications program that allows you to connect your computer to on-line services, electronic bulletin boards, and other computers. You use a modem when you connect to on-line services and bulletin boards. You can also use a modem to connect to another computer or, if the other computer is nearby, you can connect to it directly.

Figure 9-1 illustrates a typical computer-to-computer connection. Both computers have external modems that are connected to the phone line. When one computer dials the phone number of the other, the other computer answers the phone, and the connection is complete.

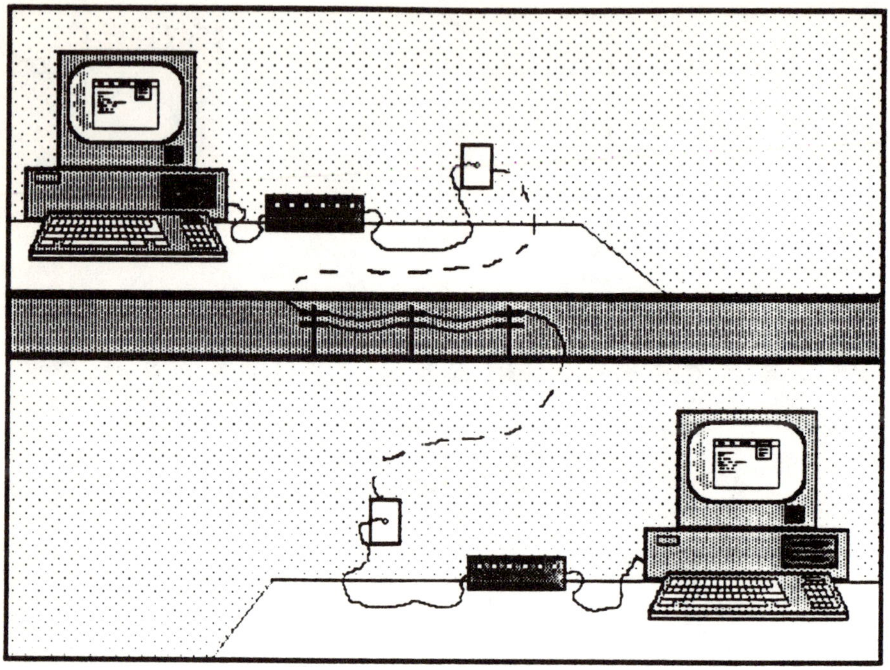

Figure 9-1. Connecting Two Computers.

THE MODEM

A modem is a device that translates the data signals that the computer sends to its serial communications port into tones that telephone lines can carry. This translation is called "modulation." In the other direction, the modem translates, or "demodulates," the tones that it receives from a remote modem into data signals that the computer can read through its serial communications port. The name "modem" means "modulator-demodulator."

Besides translating signals, the modem handles other chores for the computer. It dials and answers the phone, senses the busy signal, and notifies the calling computer when the remote computer's modem has answered.

A modem can be an external device, as shown in Figure 9-1, or it can be installed internally in your computer.

COORDINATING CONNECTIONS

Getting one computer to call another, getting the other computer to answer the phone, and then getting both computers to exchange data in a meaningful way requires a good deal of complex technical coordination. It is the job of a communications program, such as Terminal, to automate that coordination, but it is your responsibility to provide the parameters that make it possible. Terminal has many parameters for you to set. Do not feel intimidated by the extent of the information you must provide, even if you are a newcomer to computer communications. This chapter will explain the basics and lead you through each step of the process.

Every computer connection has its own set of parameters that you must define to Terminal in order to successfully make the connection. For example, you might routinely call any of these or similar systems:

- MCI Mail—for electronic mail
- CompuServe—to participate in special interest forum discussions
- Numerous bulletin board services—to upload and download free and shareware software
- A friend's personal computer—to chat and exchange files
- Your employer's computer—to do some work from home

Each one of these connections has a set of communications parameters and interactive protocols. Fortunately for you, Terminal allows you to record the unique information about each service you call into a file so that you do not need to enter the parameters every time you make a connection. This chapter will walk you through some typical sessions.

Regardless of the kind of system you call with Terminal, you are calling a computer. On-line services such as CompuServe, Genie, BIX, and Prodigy are big computers that are far away and have many modems for handling large numbers of subscribers at once. Often you gain access to these services by calling a local time sharing network such as Tymnet or Telenet—these, too, are computers. Electronic bulletin boards are commonly operated as free services by individuals who dedicate a second phone line to a personal computer and install public domain bulletin board software.

RUNNING TERMINAL

Terminal is an application in the Program Manager's Accessories group. When you run it, you see the Terminal applications window shown in Figure 9-2.

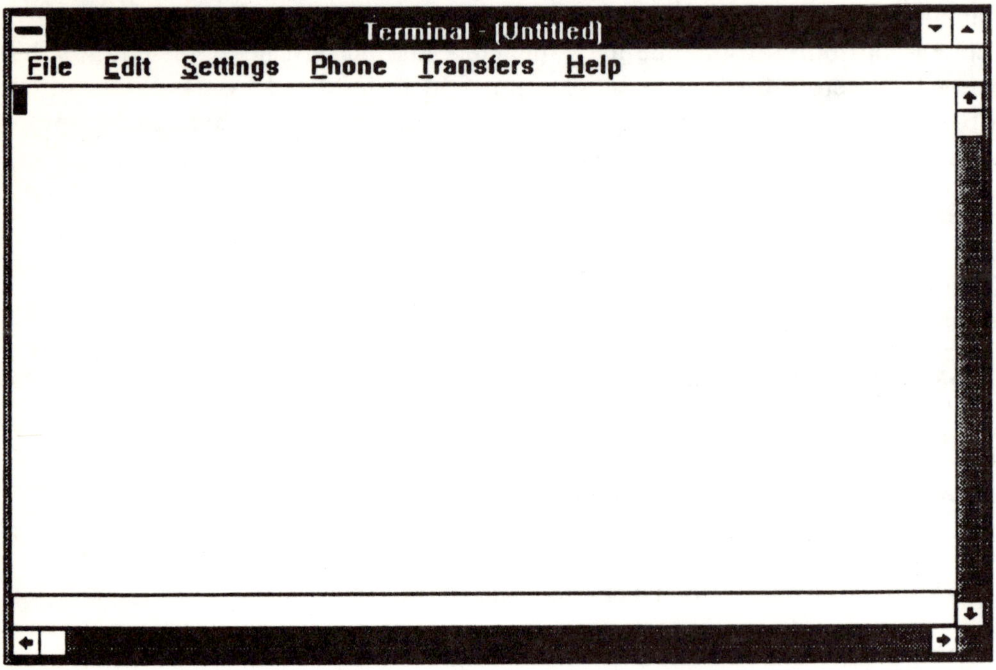

Figure 9-2. The Terminal Applications Window.

***

IF YOU DECIDE TO RUN PROGRAMS FROM THE FILE MANAGER RATHER THAN THE PROGRAM MANAGER, ADDRESS TERMINAL AS TERMINAL.EXE, A FILE IN THE WINDOWS DIRECTORY ON THE DRIVE WHERE YOU INSTALLED WINDOWS. TERMINAL IS ASSOCIATED WITH FILES THAT HAVE THE .TRM EXTENSION, SO YOU CAN ALSO EXECUTE IT BY SELECTING ONE OF THOSE FILES FROM THE FILE MANAGER.

***

The blinking box cursor in the upper left corner of the Terminal work space is the communications cursor. If you start typing now, the characters you type will be sent to the selected communications port. Depending on what device is connected to that port and how the device configures itself when you power up, you might see the characters you type echoed on the screen. Regardless of what you see when you type, you are transmitting those characters to the communications port—whether or not anything is connected to it. You will learn what a communications port is later in this chapter.

The Terminal window's work space is itself a window into a buffer. As you send and receive lines of text, they appear in the work space. When you get to the bottom of the work space, the text at the top scrolls out of sight. The scrolled-off text is not lost. You can use the vertical scroll bar to view it. The buffer can hold a maximum number of lines, however; when that number is reached, the text at the top of the buffer is lost. You can control the buffer size with one of the Terminal settings described later in this chapter.

SETTING PARAMETERS

In order to call another computer, you must set the values of a number of parameters. These parameters range in complexity from the simple—such as the telephone number—to the arcane—such as the number of stop bits. Although the number and scope of these parameters might dazzle the newcomer, the parameters are industry standards, and you should have little trouble finding out what they are for a given setup. Some of them—such as the communications port and the modem commands—are related to your hardware. Others—such as the baud rate—depend on settings required by the computer you are going to call. You set parameters from the Settings menu, which includes commands for several parameter categories.

Phone Number

The Phone Number... command on the Settings menu allows you to define and change the phone number that Terminal is going to call. The command displays the Phone Number dialogue box shown in Figure 9-3.

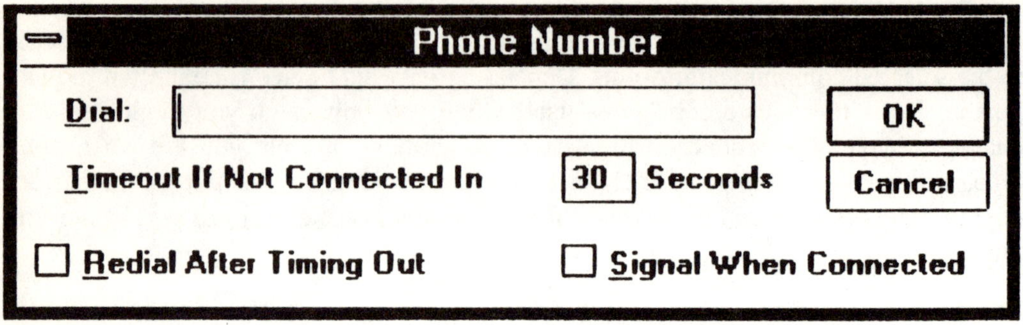

Figure 9-3. The Phone Number Dialogue Box.

Enter the phone number of the computer you are going to call. You can enter punctuation and spaces to make the number more readable, for example: 1-(800) 123-4567.

If you are dialing from a phone connected to a switchboard—such as one you might find in an office or hotel—you might need a pause after an initial access digit to gain access to the outside line. You can insert a comma in the phone number to cause the dialing to delay two seconds, for example: 9,123-4567.

The Timeout If Not Connected In field in the Phone Number dialogue box allows you to specify the number of seconds to wait for an answer. The Redial After Timing Out check box tells Terminal to try again if there is no answer after the timeout.

The Signal When Connected check box tells Terminal to sound an audible signal when a successful connection is made. Many bulletin board systems are extremely busy, and you get a busy signal every time you call. You can tell Terminal to retry every minute, for example, and signal you when the call goes through.

Terminal Emulation

You call a remote computer to use the software in that computer. Sometimes the software in the other computer expects to be called by a particular kind of terminal device. The remote software sends commands to the local terminal to tell it to clear the screen, position the cursor, display colors, and so on. By using the protocols of a known terminal, the software can manage the screen of the terminal and generate visually effective displays.

Most bulletin board systems and on-line services direct their displays to a common denominator: the generic TTY device. They use no special screen-formatting commands so that they can communicate with the largest number of users. But some services, the FIDO network for example, allow a user to specify that he or she uses a particular terminal. FIDO uses the special commands of the ANSI standard terminal if it knows you have one, but other computers you call might simply require a specific terminal. If you don't have the required terminal, your communications program must be able to emulate it.

Terminal can provide generic TTY terminal emulation and it can emulate two popular terminal devices that are used by many on-line services. The Terminal Emulation... command on the Settings menu allows you to tell Terminal which terminal device to emulate. Figure 9-4 shows the Terminal Emulation dialogue box that appears when you select this command. The example sessions in this chapter work with any of the selections.

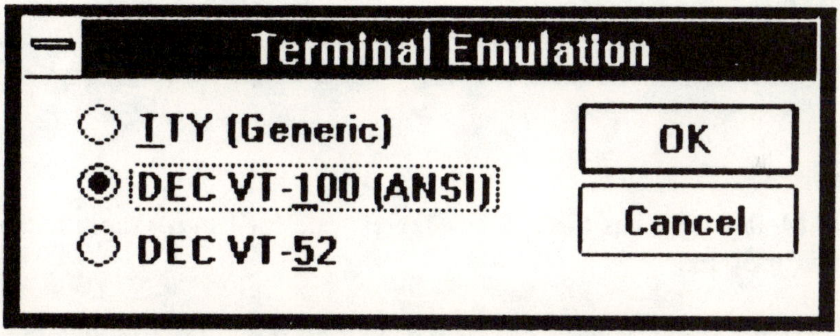

Figure 9-4. The Terminal Emulation Dialogue Box.

Terminal Preferences

There are a number of different ways you can set up Terminal to talk to another computer. The Terminal Preferences... command on the Settings menu allows you to set these preferences. Figure 9-5 shows the Terminal Preferences dialogue box that appears when you select this command.

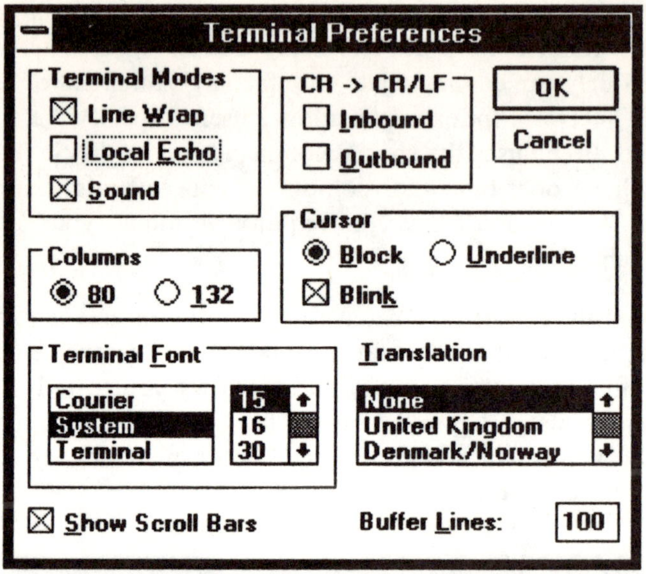

Figure 9-5. The Terminal Preferences Dialogue Box.

Terminal Modes

The Terminal Modes field has three check boxes: one for Line Wrap, one for Local Echo, and one for Sound.

Line Wrap. Set the Line Wrap check box on so that if the remote computer sends lines that are longer than the number of columns you specify, Terminal will continue the input line on the next line in its work space instead of truncating the excess characters.

Local Echo. Set Local Echo on if the characters you type to the other computer do not appear on your screen. Here is how this feature usually works.

When you call another computer and send it a keystroke, the other computer receives it and sends it back to your computer. This returned character is called an "echo." Because Terminal displays every character it receives, the echoed character appears on the screen just after you type it. The relationship between the computers is one of "originator" and "answerer." The answerer echoes the characters of the originator.

Before you call another computer, and if there is a modem connected to your communications port, the keys you type go to the modem. As initially configured by

Terminal, a Hayes-compatible modem echoes the command characters it receives back to Terminal and they, too, appear on the screen. The modem stops echoing when the connection is complete because it assumes that the answering computer will take over.

This echoing behavior of the remote computer is a part of what is called "full duplex" operation. If the documentation—assuming there is some—for connecting to the remote computer specifies that it uses full duplex operation, leave the Local Echo option button off—this is its default setting. If the documentation specifies "half duplex," set the Local Echo option on.

In the absence of any documentation from the remote computer, begin by assuming that it uses full duplex; most systems do. If you believe you have the computers properly connected and you do not see the characters you type being displayed as you type them, try setting the Local Echo option on. On the other hand, you could have Local Echo set on and see each keystroke echoed twice, for example: HHeelloo,, DDoollyy.. In that case, turn off the Local Echo option.

***

Many on-line services and bulletin boards require you to enter a password. They intentionally do not echo the password you type to protect you from revealing your password to a passerby who happens to look over your shoulder when you type it. Do not make any decisions about Local Echo based on the behavior of Terminal while you enter a password.

***

Sound. The remote computer might send you the ASCII BEL character. This character was used in the times of the Teletype device to ring a small brass bell on the device to get the operator's attention. With the Sound check box turned on, Terminal will beep an audible alarm if the remote computer sends the BEL character.

***

If you want to ring the bell of the remote computer once you are connected, type Ctrl+G to send the BEL character.

***

CR -> CR/LF

The CR -> CR/LF field has an Inbound and an Outbound check box. The CR acronym means "carriage return," a typewriter term, and it has come to mean what is now usually labeled as the Enter key on a personal computer. The LF acronym means "line feed."

When Terminal receives characters, it displays them on the screen at the current cursor position, advancing the cursor one position for each character received. When Terminal receives a carriage return character, it moves the cursor to the left margin of the current line. When Terminal receives a line feed, it moves the cursor one line down but does not change the column.

The Inbound check box tells Terminal to add a line feed every time it receives a carriage return. If the remote terminal sends you exactly what its user types, and its user types only the Enter key at the end of every line, each line will overwrite the one that preceded it. In that case you need to add a line feed to the inbound text, so you would select the Inbound check box.

The outbound check box tells Terminal to add a line feed to the output data stream every time you type the Enter key. This can get confusing. If you add inbound line feeds and the user at the remote computer adds outbound line feeds, you will get two line feeds for every line, and your screen will be double-spaced.

The same thing will happen to the other person if you add outbound line feeds and she or he adds inbound line feeds.

What's more, if you do not add outbound line feeds, and the remote user adds inbound line feeds, the remote computer might or might not echo the added line feeds. The remote user will see the lines you type properly, but you will not—your lines will overwrite themselves locally.

What to do? Agree with the party at the other end that you will both add outbound line feeds. If you do that, everything should work correctly, and you will be compatible with most unattended on-line services and bulletin boards where the operation of the software is fixed.

If, however, you begin to see double spacing or line overwriting where you do not expect them, turn the options on and off until things straighten out.

Columns

You can tell Terminal to use 80 or 132 columns as its terminal width. This value determines the width of the work space and the position at which Terminal truncates or wraps lines.

Cursor

The Terminal cursor can be a block or an underline, and it can blink or not, depending on your preference. The default is a blinking block.

Translation

The Translation list box in the Terminal Preference dialogue box tells Terminal to translate the characters to the character sets used by other countries. Only change this setting if the remote system recognizes the character set you select.

Show Scroll Bars

You can choose not to show the scroll bars if you do not need to scroll the work space. You would do this to dedicate more of the screen to the work space. The Show Scroll Bars check box in the Terminal Preference dialogue box manages this option.

Buffer Lines

The Terminal application buffers the lines it receives, but it keeps only a specified number of lines in the buffer. After you exceed that number, the top-most line is lost when a new line comes in. The default number of buffered lines is 100. You can set the number of lines from 25 to 400 by entering a value in the Buffer Lines field in the Terminal Preference dialogue box.

Terminal Font

Terminal can display the characters you receive in the Courier, System, or Terminal font and in many sizes. You select the font and its size with the Terminal Font field in the Terminal Preferences dialogue box.

Figure 9-6 shows a typical dialing sequence in the work space with a 30-point font. The font and its size do not affect the size of the Terminal buffer; they affect only the display.

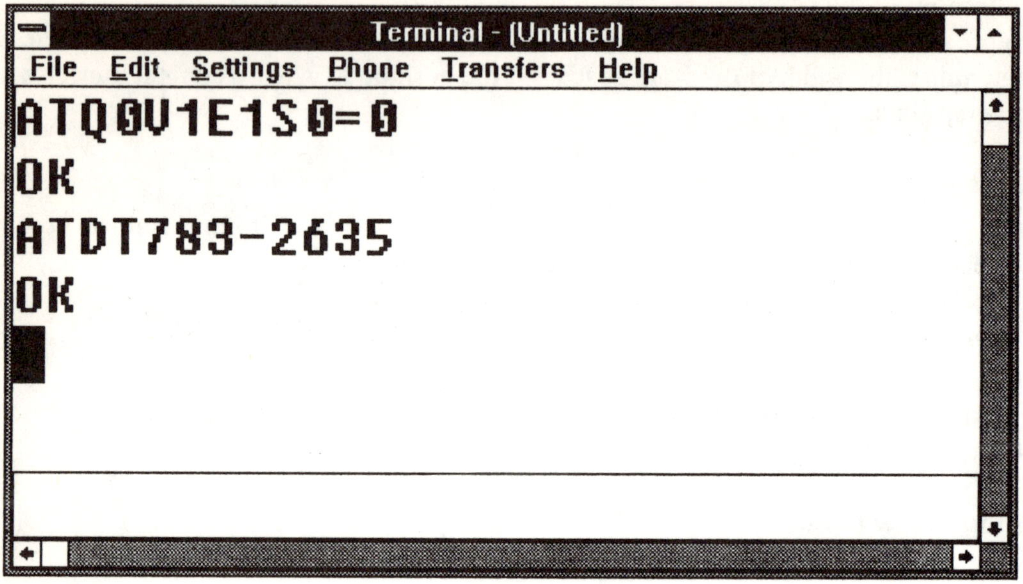

Figure 9-6. Enlarged Characters.

Function Keys

A typical dialogue with an on-line service or bulletin board includes a number of routine data entries that you make. For example, many services ask you to enter your name or an identification code. Then they prompt you for a password, which you must enter to gain access to the service.

Depending on how you use the service, there might be commands that you need to enter to navigate throughout the service's menu and command structure. Some services provide a novice command set for newcomers to the service and an expert command set for those who know their way around the menus. Once you know the terse expert commands, you can use them to reduce connect and long-distance charges.

There will also be other text and command strings that you enter repeatedly. You might, for example, have a personalized salutation or signature for messages you send to other users of the service. The world of on-line users has its own language of acronyms and symbols with special meanings: IMHO means "in my humble opinion;" BTW means "by the way;" ROFL means "rolling on the floor laughing;"

the :-) symbol is a grin; the :-(symbol is a frown; for indifference you use the :-| symbol; if you wear glasses and have a big nose your grin might be the 8^) symbol; and so on.

Assigning Function Keys

You can assign any of the routine text entries discussed in the previous section to the Terminal function keys by selecting the Function Keys... command on the Settings menu. Figure 9-7 shows the Function Keys dialogue box with some values entered.

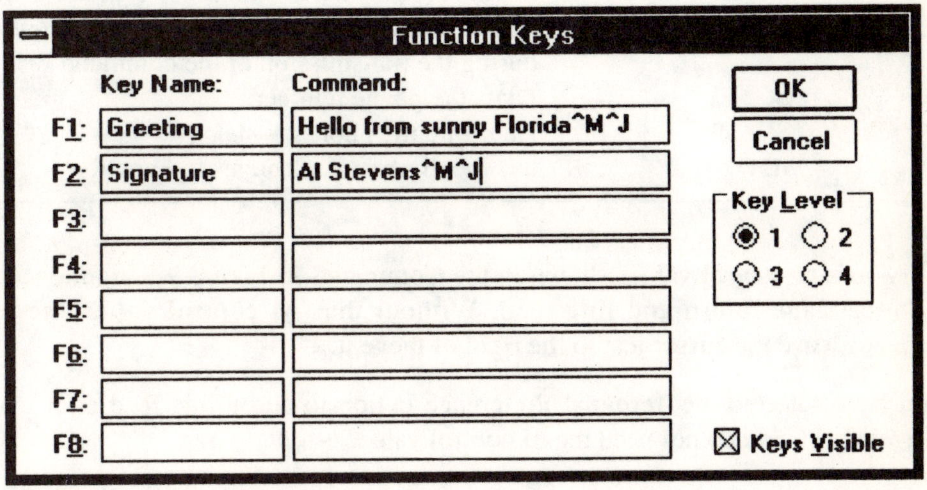

Figure 9-7. The Function Keys Dialogue Box.

There are eight function keys and four levels. Each level is a separate set of eight keys that you can assign. You type a name for the function key into the Key Name field and the text value into the Command field. When you select the function key, Terminal transmits the command text string. A command string can be text for the remote computer or a command to your modem.

Besides text values, you can put control values into the Command field for different effects. A control value is prefixed with the caret (^) character so that Terminal can recognize it. Table 9-1 shows the valid control values.

Table 9-1. Function Key Command Control Values.

Value	Purpose
^A - ^Z	Sends the associated control byte to the remote computer
^A = 1, ^B = 2 ... ^Z = 26	These values are the binary values 1, 2 ... 26, not the ASCII character strings "1", "2" ... "26"
^$Dnn	nn is a number. Causes a delay for nn seconds during the transmission of the command
^$C	Dials the phone number.
^$H	Hangs up the phone.
^$Ln	n is the digit 1 - 4. Changes to Function

The ^M and ^J control values shown in the Commands in Figure 9-7 are the values for the carriage return and line feed. Without the ^M control value, the text commands leave the cursor just to the right of the text.

If you have selected the Terminal Preference option to add a line feed after every carriage return, you do not need the ^J control value.

Displaying the Function Keys

If you select the Keys Visible check box, the Function keys will appear at the bottom of the Terminal applications window—if the Show/Hide Function Keys command in the Settings menu is set to Show. You show and hide the function keys during a session by using the Show/Hide Function keys command.

Figure 9-8 shows the function keys visible in the Terminal application window.

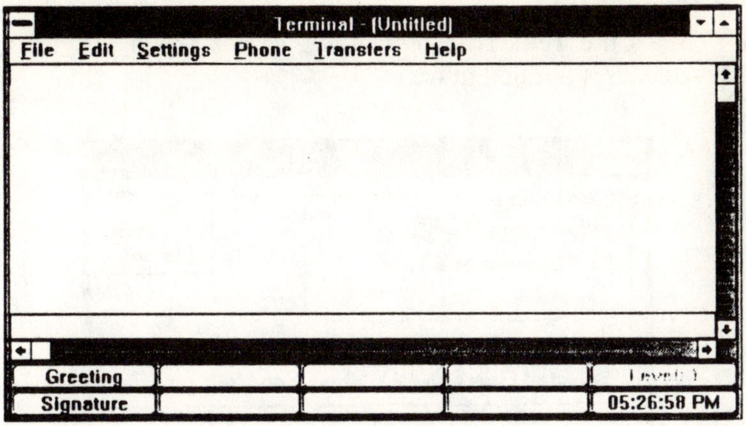

Figure 9-8. The Function Keys in View.

Selecting Function Keys

You can select a function key by clicking it with the mouse or by pressing Ctrl+Alt+ the keyboard function key associated with the command. Refer back to Figure 9-7 to see the keyboard equivalent function keys. For example, you can select the Greeting function key in Figure 9-8 by clicking it or by pressing Ctrl+Alt+F1. Ctrl+Alt+F2 selects the Signature function key. The keystroke selections work whether you have displayed the function keys in the window or not. Later exercises will use function keys to automate certain aspects of on-line operations.

Text Transfers

The Text Transfers... command on the Settings menu allows you to specify how you wish to send and receive text files between your computer and the remote computer. Text files are those files with only ASCII text characters in them. A file that you generate with the Notepad is a text file. Write files are not text files because they have format control values embedded in them, and these values are not always ASCII text. Files that are not ASCII text are binary files, which you will learn about later.

When a computer sends a text file to another computer, it needs some form of control to assure that the file transmits with a minimum of error. Because a text transfer has no error-correcting protocol, you need to establish ways that the two computers can synchronize their exchange. It would not do, for example, for the transmitting computer to keep transmitting when the receiving computer needs to stop receiving for a moment, perhaps to write the text to a disk file.

Standard Flow Control

Figure 9-9 shows the Text Transfers dialogue box when you have selected the Standard Flow Control option button.

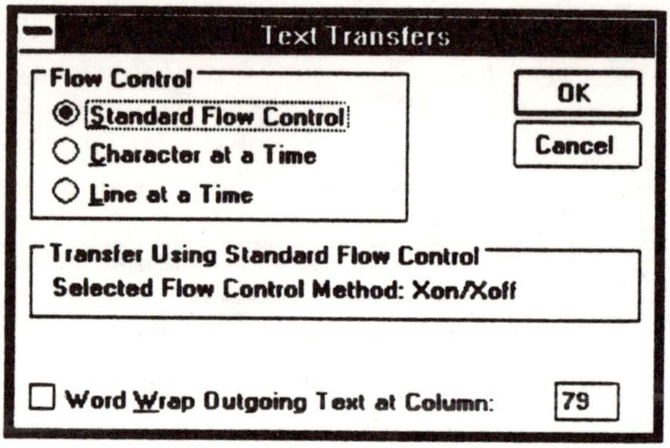

Figure 9-9. The Standard Flow Control Text Transfers Dialogue Box.

The standard flow control will be either Xon/Xoff, Hardware, or None, depending on how you set the Flow Control parameter for the Communications command discussed later. The Standard Flow Control option is the one most often selected for text file transfers.

Character at a Time

Figure 9-10 shows the Text Transfers dialogue box when you have selected the Character at a Time option button.

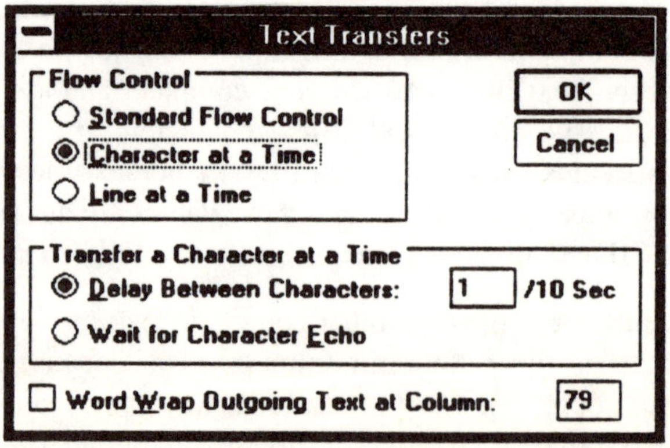

Figure 9-10. The Character at a Time Text Transfers Dialogue Box.

If you decide to transmit characters one at a time, you can manage the data flow in one of two ways. First, you can select the Delay Between Characters option button to specify a delay period between characters in tenths of a second. The Terminal transmission sends a character and then waits the specified amount of time before sending another. This method gives the receiver time to do something meaningful with the data stream during the delays between character transmissions.

The other way to manage data flow is to select the Wait for Character Echo option button. This option tells Terminal to send a character and then to wait for the receiving computer to echo it back before sending another one. This technique assumes that the receiver is in full duplex mode and that when it echoes a character it is telling your computer that it can receive another character. Some communications programs, however, do not echo the text they receive during a file transfer—this option would not work with such programs.

Line at a Time

Figure 9-11 shows the Text Transfers dialogue box when you have selected the Line at a Time option button.

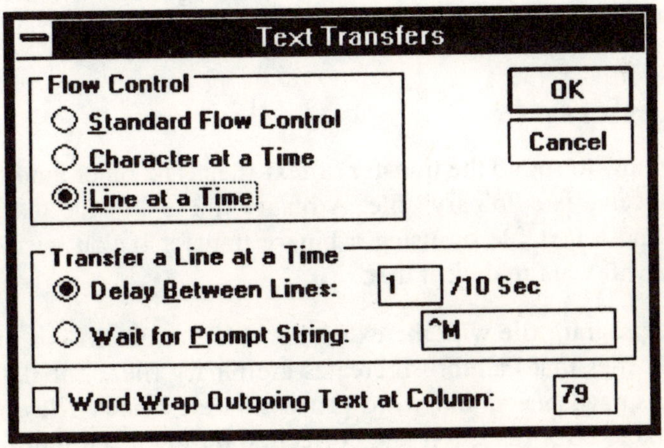

Figure 9-11. The Line at a Time Text Transfers Dialogue Box.

The Line at a Time option allows Terminal to transmit the text file in bursts of one line. A line consists of the characters from the first character in the left margin to the terminating carriage return.

If you decide to transmit text a line at a time, you can manage the data flow in one of two ways. First, you can select the Delay Between Lines option button to specify a delay period between lines in tenths of a second. The Terminal transmission sends a line and then waits the specified amount of time before sending another. This method supposedly gives the receiver time to do something meaningful with the data stream during the delays between line transmissions.

The other way to manage data flow is to select the Wait for Prompt String option button. This option tells Terminal to send a line and then wait for the receiving computer to transmit a specified prompt string before sending another one. This technique assumes that the receiver transmits some kind of prompting string and that when it does, it is telling your computer that it can receive another line of text. If the receiver is in full duplex mode you can specify the carriage return that you know the receiver will echo at the end of the line. The ^M in the Wait for Prompt String text box represents a carriage return. Some communications programs, however, do not echo the text they receive during a file transfer—this option would not work with such programs.

Word Wrap

If you select the Word Wrap Outgoing Text at Column check box, you can specify a column number where Terminal will insert a carriage return if the text in a line reaches the column.

Binary Transfers

You now know how to set up the transfer of text files. The other kind of file that you will send and receive is a "binary" file. A binary file is any file that is not text. In fact, you can send a text file by using a binary transfer if you wish, and there are times when you will want to do just that.

Any executable program file with the extension .EXE or .COM is a binary file. The .BMP and .PCX files that Paintbrush creates are binary files. The data files of data base programs, spreadsheets, and word processors are binary files. Any time you need highly reliable error detection and correction during a file transfer, you should use a binary file transfer.

You set up your binary file transfers by selecting the Binary Transfers... command on the Settings menu. Figure 9-12 shows the Binary Transfers dialogue box that appears when you select this command.

Figure 9-12. The Binary Transfers Dialogue Box.

The selections in the Binary Files Transfers box are file transfer protocols that your computer and the remote computer can use to exchange binary files. Terminal supports two such protocols.

XModem/CRC

The XModem/CRC protocol is one that you can use when you have eight data bits selected in the Communications parameters. The Communications parameters are discussed in more detail in the next section. You cannot use XModem/CRC if you are using seven or fewer data bits. Some time-sharing networks, through which you might gain access to on-line services, require seven-bit data formats. You also cannot use XModem/CRC if the remote computer's software does not support it. Some implementations of the XModem use the XModem/Checksum protocol, which is usually just called XModem. The Terminal XModem/CRC protocol can sense when the other computer does not use the more advanced CRC version and will adjust itself to the checksum version.

Kermit

Kermit is a file transfer protocol—named after the frog—that works with either seven- or eight-bit data formats. Kermit is more tolerant than XModem of the time delays that characterize connections through time share networks during peak hours, so it is often the protocol of choice. As with XModem, you must make sure that the computer at the other end supports Kermit before you can use it.

Communications Parameters

Communication between two computers requires that the computers use common communication parameters. Proper use of your communications hardware—the serial port and the modem—requires that you configure communications parameters as well. You set these parameters by selecting the Communications... command on the Settings menu and entering the correct values into the Communications dialogue box shown in Figure 9-13. Some of the communications parameter values are common to both computers; others reflect the local computer's hardware.

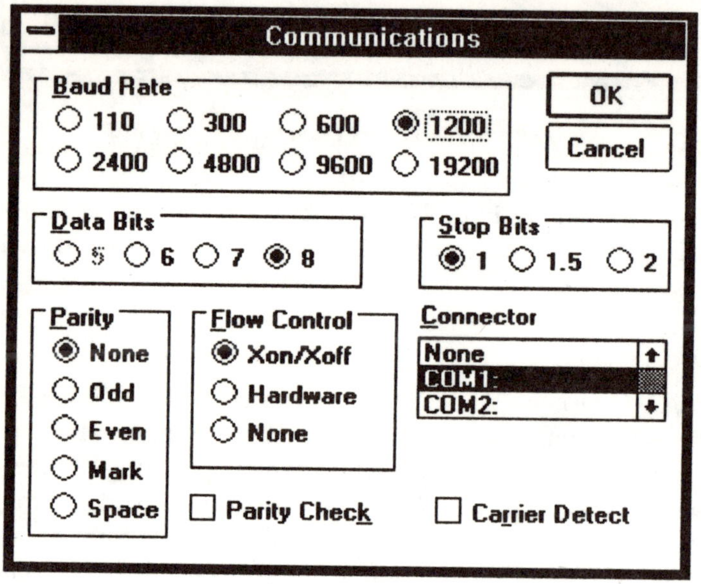

Figure 9-13. The Communications Dialogue Box.

Common Communications Parameters

You set the common communications parameters after determining the compatible values of the other computer. These values are not difficult to determine. An on-line service or a bulletin board must provide information that tells you what they should be. A typical specification looks like this: 2400,N,8,1. This specification means: 2400 baud, no parity, 8 data bits, 1 stop bit. You will learn what these things mean in the sections that follow.

Baud Rate. The baud rate is the rate at which the computers transmit characters. It is expressed in bits per second. Typical baud rates are 110, 300, 600, 1200, 2400, 4800, 9600, and 19200. The most common ones in use today among personal computer users are 1200 and 2400. A modem can transmit both at a maximum baud rate and at the rates less than its maximum. If you have a 2400 baud modem, for example, it can usually transmit and receive at 300, 600, 1200, and 2400 baud.

The baud rate is not a function of the modem. The modem accepts commands at whatever baud rate the computer sends them, and it passes data through at the baud rate of the sending computer.

A remote service can usually accept calls from computers at baud rates lower than the published rate; the published rate is the maximum. For example, you can use your 1200 baud modem to call a service that supports 2400 baud. The service senses your computer's baud rate and adjusts its own rate accordingly.

Data Bits. The computer sends its data characters through the serial port a bit at a time. The receiving computer receives those bits just as they were sent from the sender. The receiver needs a way to find the characters from what would otherwise appear to be a string of random bits. Therefore, the sender frames each character by surrounding its data bits with start and stop bits. There are seven or eight data bits, depending on the nature of the transmission. Both computers should agree on the number of data bits. The rule is this: if the on-line service asks for eight data bits, select the 8 option button in the Data Bits field; if it wants seven, select 7. The Data Bits field also allows you to specify five or six data bits, but these values are rarely used.

Parity. Immediately following the data bits is the parity bit—if one is required. Usually you will have a parity bit if there are only seven data bits. When you have eight data bits, you usually select the None option button in the Parity field. If there is a parity bit, it can be set to Odd, Even, Mark, or Space. If it is Odd, the transmitting system will set its value to one or zero, whichever is required so that there are an odd number of one bits in the bit stream. If the parity bit is to be Even, the transmitting system will set its value to one or zero, whichever is required so that there are an even number of one bits in the bit stream. If the parity bit is set to Mark or Space, the transmitting system will set all parity bits to zero or one, irrespective of parity.

Stop Bits. The presence of stop bits allows the receiver to wait for a polarity change to the start bits so it can synchronize itself to the next character in the stream. One stop bit is usually used. You will see 1.5 or two stop bits required by some systems, usually at the slower baud rates.

Flow Control. The Flow Control field allows you to specify the method that the receiving computer uses to tell the sending computer to stop sending characters during a text file transfer. The software protocols of the binary file transfers take care of flow control, so you do not need to worry about them for binary file transfers.

When you are transmitting and receiving text through a modem, your flow control will usually be Xon/Xoff. Here is how Xon/Xoff works. The transmitting computer begins to transmit characters that the receiving computer collects. There comes a time when the receiving computer must do something with the characters it has collected so far; usually it writes them to a disk file. This activity takes time away from the computer's ability to continue to read the characters that the transmitter is sending, so the receiver sends the ASCII XOF (Ctrl+S) character to the transmitter to tell it to stop sending. When the transmitter sees the XOF character come into its own input buffer, it stops transmitting and watches for more input. When the receiver is ready to receive text again, it sends the XON (Ctrl+Q) character to the transmitter. When the transmitter receives the XON character, it resumes transmitting data characters.

The Hardware Flow Control option button specifies that the receiving device will tell the transmitter to stop transmitting by asserting certain electrical signals at the serial port. A modem can assert these signals, but there is no way for the remote computer to tell the local modem to do so. Therefore, you use the Hardware option only when you are connecting to another computer locally without using a modem and then only when both computers have compatible serial ports and software to drive them.

You can select None as the text file transfer flow control if the computers do not use any flow control. When the receiver has no way to tell the transmitter to stand by, you have a good chance of losing some characters in the stream. The sender will continue to transmit beyond the receiver's ability to deal with the data. You can take this path when the baud rate is slow enough—usually 300 to 1200 baud—that the sender has no way of outrunning the receiver or when you use one of the time delays in your Text Transfers dialogue box.

Local Communications Parameters

These parameters are related to your communications hardware and how you use it and are not necessarily the same as those of the remote computer.

Connector. The Connector field in the Communications dialogue box is where you tell Terminal which of the communications ports—COM1, COM2, COM3, or COM4—you are using for modem communications. Most PCs and ATs have one or two communications ports: COM1 and COM2. More recent machines can have COM3 and COM4 as well.

Communications ports transmit characters in a serial stream with format and voltage levels that are defined by a standard specification—called RS-232-C. You will hear these devices referred to by any of these names: communications ports, RS-232 ports, RS-232-C ports, serial ports, auxiliary ports, the AUX devices, COM1, COM2, etc.

If you have an internal modem, it will use one of the communication port assignments. If you have an external modem, you will connect it to one of the ports with a serial cable. If you connect your computer directly to another computer, it will be with a null modem cable (discussed later), connecting a serial port of one computer to the other.

***

ODDLY, THE WINDOWS USER'S GUIDE TELLS YOU TO SPECIFY NONE FOR THE CONNECTOR PARAMETER IF YOU ARE CONNECTING DIRECTLY TO ANOTHER COMPUTER THROUGH A NULL MODEM CABLE. THIS GUIDANCE IS INCORRECT. IF YOU SPECIFY NONE, THE CONNECTION WILL NOT WORK BECAUSE SUCH CONNECTIONS USE COMMUNICATIONS PORTS IN THE SAME WAY THAT MODEM CONNECTIONS DO. IN FACT, THERE SEEMS TO BE NO REAL USE FOR THE NONE SELECTION. WITHOUT A COMMUNICATIONS PORT, TERMINAL IS USELESS—IT PERFORMS NO USEFUL FUNCTION BY ITSELF.

***

Parity Check. If you are using the Odd or Even parity format and Terminal sees a parity error in the input, it will display the character as a question mark (?) unless you select the Parity Check check box. If you select the Parity Check box, Terminal will then display the character as it was received, which might make sense to you. Then again it might not. It depends on whether the parity error was in the parity bit itself or one of the data bits.

Carrier Detect. Usually the modem tells Terminal that it has made a successful connection with a remote computer by sending a string that starts with the word "CONNECT." The modem knows that the connection is complete because the remote computer transmits a continuous high-frequency tone to say that it is on line. This tone is called the "carrier signal."

There is a serial port signal that indicates that the modem is detecting the carrier signal. You can tell Terminal to watch that signal instead of waiting for the CONNECT message by selecting the Carrier Detect check box. You do this if you are using a modem that does not supply the CONNECT message. Older 300 baud acoustic couplers are typical of the modems that require the software to monitor the carrier detect signal.

Modem Commands

The Modem Commands... command on the Settings menu displays the Modem Commands dialogue box shown in Figure 9-14.

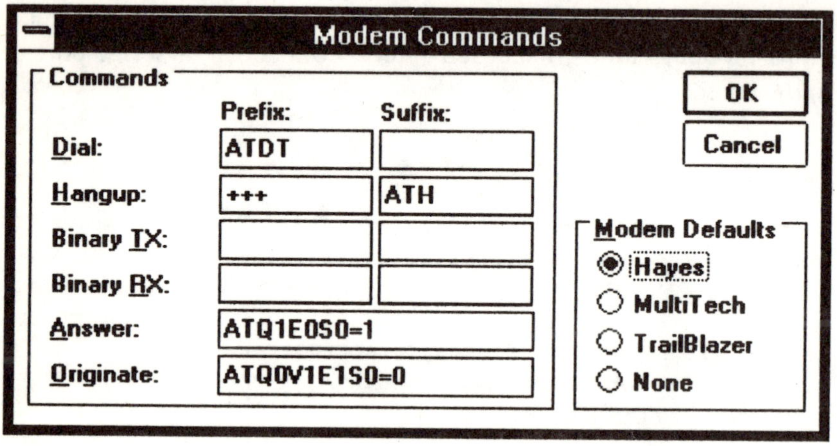

Figure 9-14. The Modem Commands Dialogue Box.

Modem commands are strings of text that, when you are not connected to another computer and you send them to the modem, direct the modem to take some action. You will seldom need to change the modem commands.

If you do not have touch tone dialing, you will need to change the Dial Prefix from ATDT to ATDP. Other than that, the modem default commands should work fine. Your modem's user's guide defines the modem's complete command set. Refer to it if you want to change the way the modem works.

SAVING AND RESTORING PARAMETERS

Once you have all your parameters set the way you need them for a particular connection, you should save them in a file. You can have separate files for every computer and service you call, each one with its own phone number, terminal settings, communications settings, modem settings, function keys, and file transfer settings.

The Terminal File menu has the usual New, Open, Save, and Save As... commands. By convention, Terminal settings files have the .TRM extension.

PRINTING THE ON-LINE SESSION

The File menu has a Printer Setup... command similar to those you learned about with Write and the Paintbrush, but it does not have a Print command. That is because you do not print files or pictures from Terminal; you print on-line sessions. The Printer Echo toggle command on the Settings menu causes everything received by Terminal, except file transfers, to be echoed to the printer.

TIMING THE ON-LINE SESSION

If you look back at Figure 9-8, you will see that Terminal displays the time of day in the lower right corner of the screen among the function keys. You can change that display to an elapsed-time timer by selecting the Timer Mode toggle command on the Settings menu. The timer starts at 00:00:00 when you first select it and proceeds to tick off the seconds. When you make a connection, the timer restarts at zero so you can keep watch on the length of time you have been on line. When you hang up, the timer reverts to the time of day.

CALLING ANOTHER COMPUTER

To call another computer, set all the parameters to match the remote computer, fill in the phone number, and dial.

Dialing

Select the Dial command on the Phone menu. You will see the Terminal dialogue box shown in Figure 9-15.

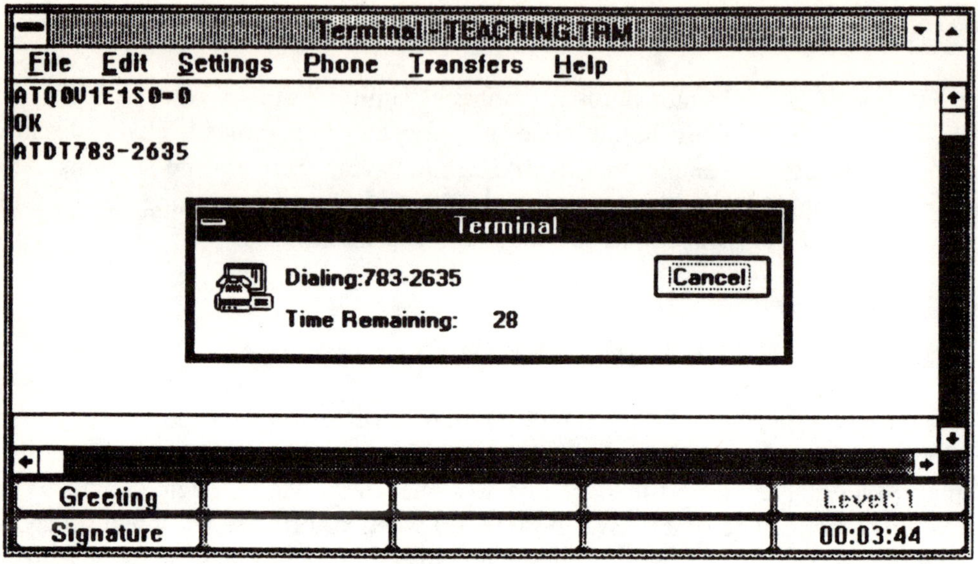

Figure 9-15. Dialing.

***

IF YOU HAVE NOT ENTERED A PHONE NUMBER AND YOU SELECT THE DIAL COMMAND, TERMINAL DISPLAYS THE PHONE NUMBER DIALOGUE BOX THAT YOU SAW IN FIGURE 9-3 EARLIER. YOU MUST FILL IT IN BEFORE TERMINAL CAN DIAL THE PHONE.

***

Observe the displays in the Terminal work space in Figure 9-15. The first line is the modem command to tell the modem that you are going to originate a call. If you look at the Modem Commands dialogue box in Figure 9-14, you will see that the Originate string matches the first line in the work space.

The second line says OK—that is the modem's answer, saying that it received the originate string.

The third line is the modem's Dial command. The ATDT prefix appears first, followed by the phone number.

No Answer or Busy

While Terminal is dialing and afterwards while it is waiting for an answer, the Time Remaining display in the Terminal dialogue box counts down starting from the value you set in the Phone Number dialogue box. If the time remaining reaches zero, and you have selected Redial After Timing Out in the Phone Number dialogue box, Terminal will reset the count, redial the number, and start over. If you have not selected the redial option, the Terminal dialogue box will go away, and the Terminal application window will look like Figure 9-16.

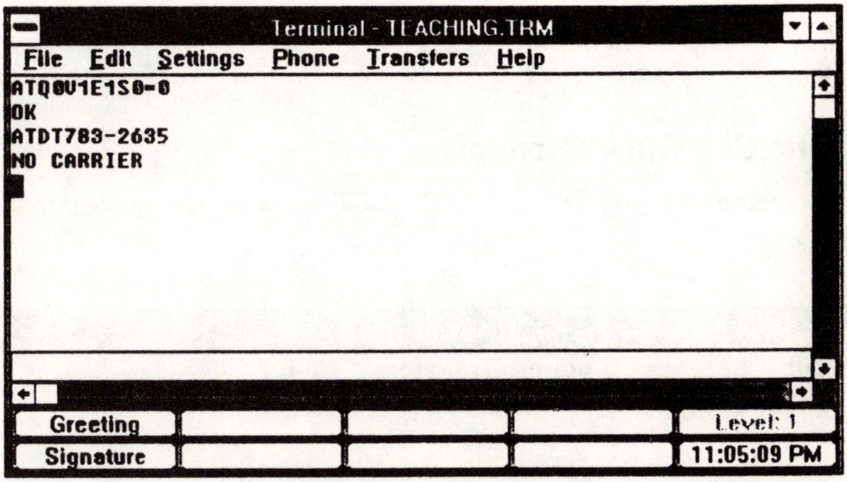

Figure 9-16. No Answer.

The NO CARRIER message in the work space shown in Figure 9-16 came from the modem to tell the you that the remote computer did not answer. If the line had been busy, you would have seen a BUSY message instead of NO CARRIER.

If you accidentally call the wrong number and someone answers, some modems will display a VOICE message. You can hear the person answer through the modem's speaker, but you cannot talk to them. Their phone will be dead, and they will probably get mad and hang up.

***

Every now and then people get called by computers. The computer usually hangs up as soon as it recognizes a voice. Perhaps you've received such calls. You say, "Hello," and hear what appears to be a dead connection followed by a click when the computer hangs up. This annoyance can be caused by someone who has entered the wrong phone number into a communications program. It might also be the work of some computer snoop who programs a computer to scan through all the possible local phone numbers in search of computers to break into. Such programs recognize the carrier signal, hang up, and record the number for the snoop to try later. There are also such programs that scan in a similar fashion looking for FAX machines to send unsolicited junk mail to.

***

When the Call Goes Through

If the call is successful, you will see a CONNECT message such as the one shown in Figure 9-17.

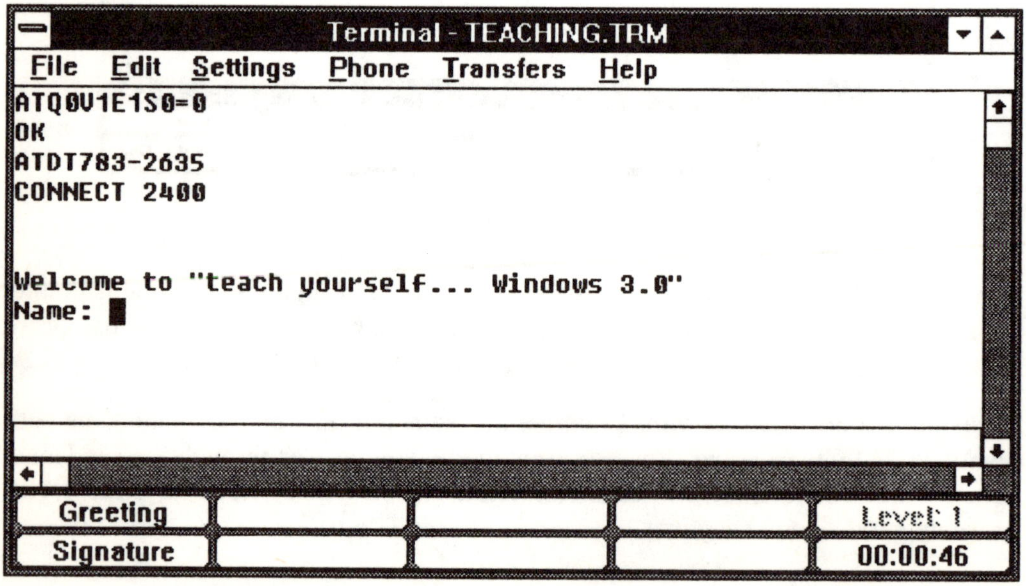

Figure 9-17. A Successful Connection.

What follows the CONNECT message depends on the program that is running in the remote computer. The example in Figure 9-17 is typical of many private bulletin board systems.

Your next step would be to enter your name and perhaps a password. The system might display a text menu of choices. You can pick up electronic mail messages that others have left for you, leave messages for them, upload files to the service, and download files that others have contributed.

If you are calling the computer of a friend, the two of you might chat and exchange files. If you are calling one of the major on-line services, you might exchange electronic mail with other subscribers, use the service's research facilities, read product reviews, order products, watch the stock market, get weather reports, make airline reservations, or file your own flight plan.

When You Are Done

The system you call might have a Goodbye or OFF command that you use to tell it you are signing off. Wait until it has told you that is disconnecting and you see the modem's NO CARRIER message, then select the Hangup command on the Phone menu. Unless you follow this procedure, Terminal will not allow you to dial another number.

CALLING A BULLETIN BOARD SYSTEM (BBS)

In the examples that follow you will call a bulletin board system—called the BBS. The bulletin board is the host mode of Procomm, a shareware DOS communications program. Procomm's host mode has some of the features of bulletin board software. You can upload and download files and chat with the user of the Procomm program.

The parameters for communicating with the BBS are mostly the defaults set by Terminal. Of course you need to enter the phone number and the baud rate of your modem. For convenience, the user name and password are function keys. You selected the XModem/CRC file transfer protocol as your default. You saved these few unique settings in a file named BBS.TRM.

***

Conventional wisdom holds that recording passwords in a system file is an invitation to burglary. You should exercise prudence in this practice. If your system is essentially closed—perhaps at home—then you can indulge yourself in the convenience of using function keys to send passwords. That way, if you use a lot of on-line services and bulletin boards, you do not have to remember all those passwords. It would definitely be imprudent to use the same password for all your accounts.

***

A hint: Add a Connections applications group to the Program Manager. Install copies of Terminal in the group with the names of the services and BBSs in the Program Item Properties Description fields. Put the names of the .TRM files into the Command Line field of the properties. Then you can simply click onto the particular service you want to call.

Figure 9-18 shows your computer screen after you have called and signed onto the BBS.

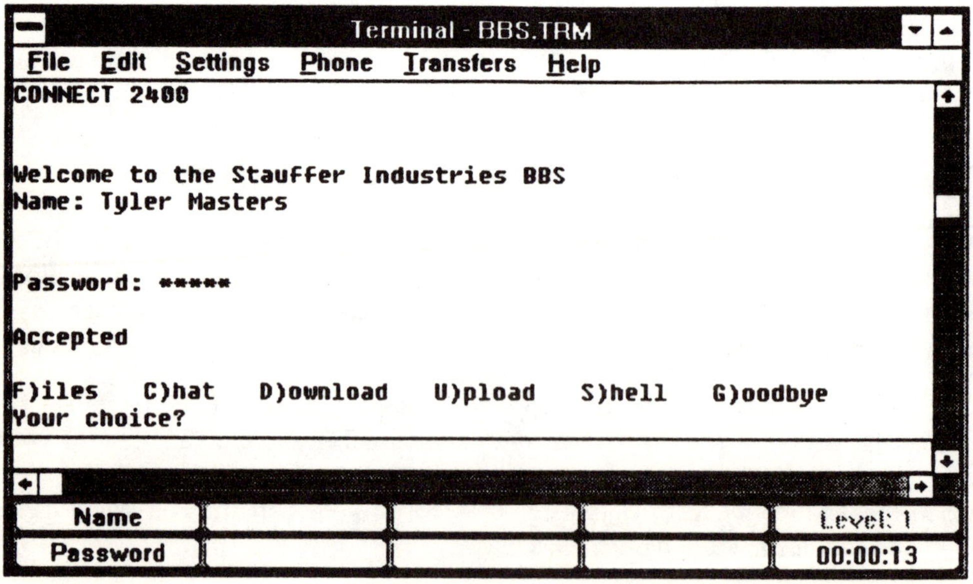

Figure 9-18. Calling a BBS.

Keep in mind that the dialogues you see in the work space are those of the remote computer's software—in this case the Procomm program, which is not a part of Windows. These examples use Procomm because it is simple and typical. The lessons to be learned are in the Terminal procedures that allow you to use the facilities of the remote computer.

Chatting With the Other User

Once you are signed on, you can type characters to the remote computer. The Procomm program has given you a menu. To chat with the user at the other end, type C. When the user answers, you can freely exchange text by typing. It is a good idea to size the Terminal applications window to its longest height so that you can view as much of the conversation as possible at one time. Remember that you can use the scroll bars to look at anything in the buffer that might have scrolled off. You can also hide the function keys to gain some additional viewing area.

Figure 9-19 shows your screen after you have selected the Procomm chat mode. The user at the other end has heard the page and come on line.

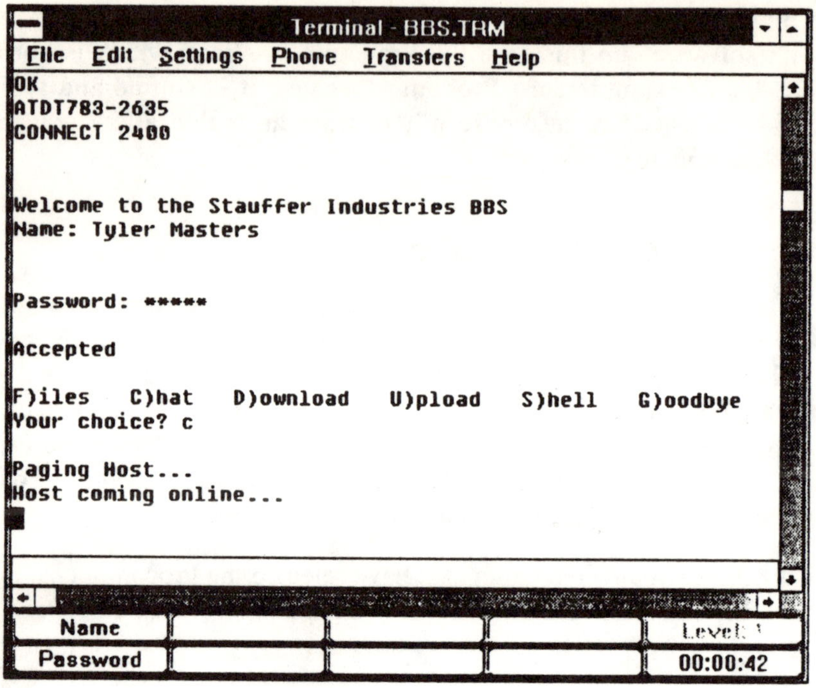

Figure 9-19. Paging the Host.

Figure 9-20 shows your computer screen as you and the other user chat. The shaded areas in the figure show where you have entered text and whether the text came from your typing or a function key. The shading does not appear in the Terminal window; rather, it serves to highlight the text in the illustration. The shadowed boxes and arrows are part of the illustration, too; they do not appear on your screen.

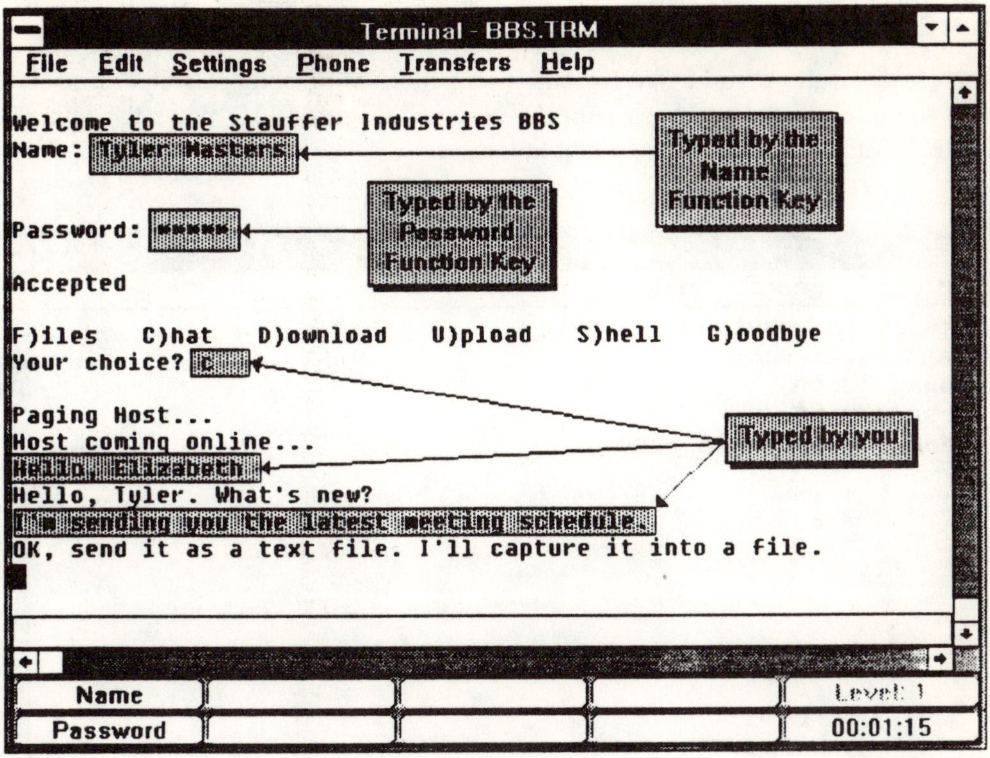

Figure 9-20. Chatting.

Transferring Files

One of the benefits of calling other computers is that you can easily exchange program and data files with the users of those other computers. If you exchange messages with the other users, you can compose your messages in Notepad while you are off-line, and upload them as files once you have made the connection. This approach has two advantages. The first advantage is that the editors that on-line services use are usually primitive line editors without many features. The second advantage is that uploading long messages instead of typing them on line can save connect time and, perhaps, charges.

You can send and receive text and binary files to and from the remote computer.

Sending Text Files

In the conversation, you agree to send a text file: the meeting schedule. You have built this file off line, perhaps with the Notepad. Figure 9-21 shows the text file, SCHEDULE.TXT, that you are going to transfer.

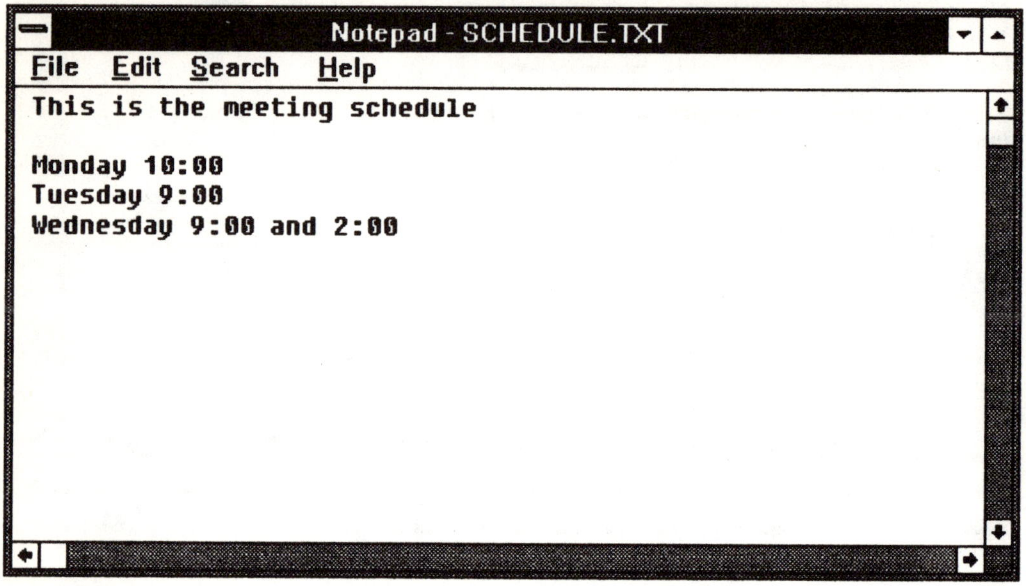

Figure 9-21. A Text File to Transfer.

To send a text file, select the Send Text File... command on the Transfers menu. You will see the Send Text File dialogue box. As shown in Figure 9-22, you have entered the name of the SCHEDULE.TXT file.

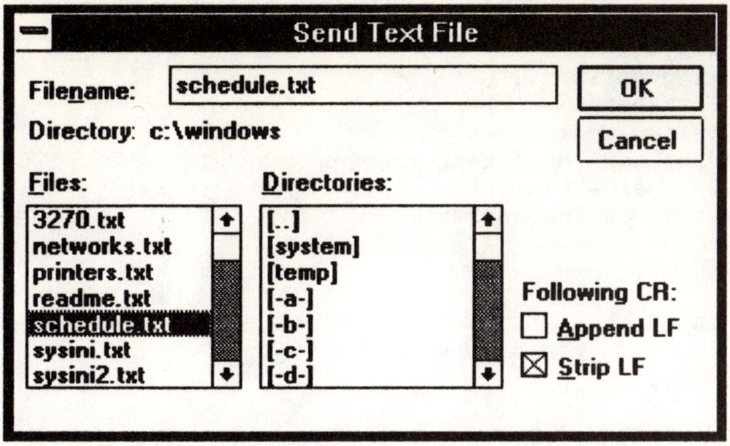

Figure 9-22. The Send Text File Dialogue Box.

When you select OK in the dialogue box, Terminal sends the text file just as if you typed it. The remote computer echoes it, and you see it on your screen, as shown in Figure 9-23.

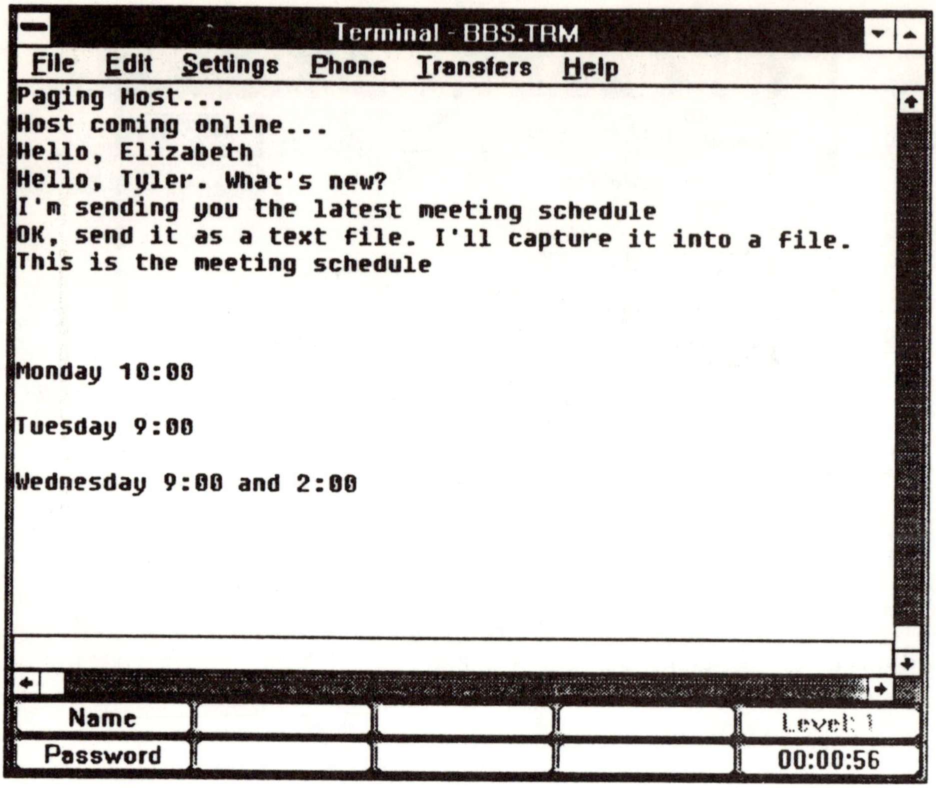

Figure 9-23. Sending a Text File.

Sending Binary Files

After you send the text file, the user at the other end exits from the chat mode, and you get the Procomm menu again. You want to send a picture file from Paintbrush to the other end, and you must use a binary transfer for that. You tell the other computer that you are uploading the file COMPUTER.PCX by using the XModem protocol. The other computer tells you to begin your transfer procedure. You select the Send Binary File... command on the Transfers menu. The command displays the Send Binary File dialogue box shown in Figure 9-24. The figure shows that you have already selected the COMPUTER.PCX file name.

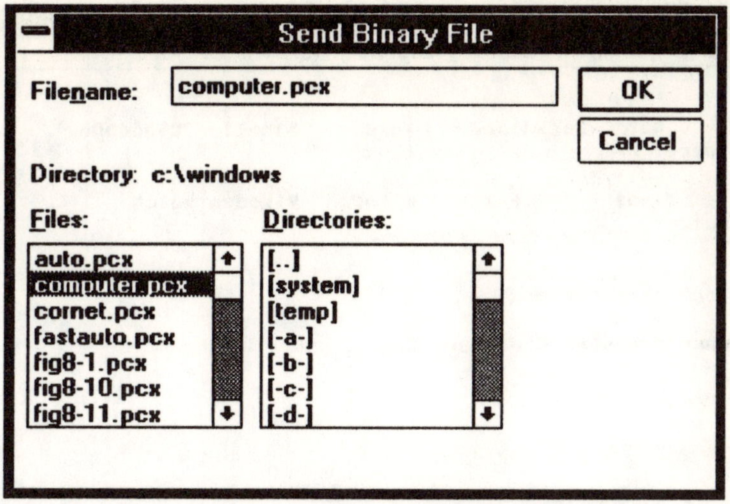

Figure 9-24. The Send Binary File Dialogue Box.

When you select OK on the dialogue box, Terminal begins sending the file. Figure 9-25 shows how the Terminal screen appears while it is sending a binary file.

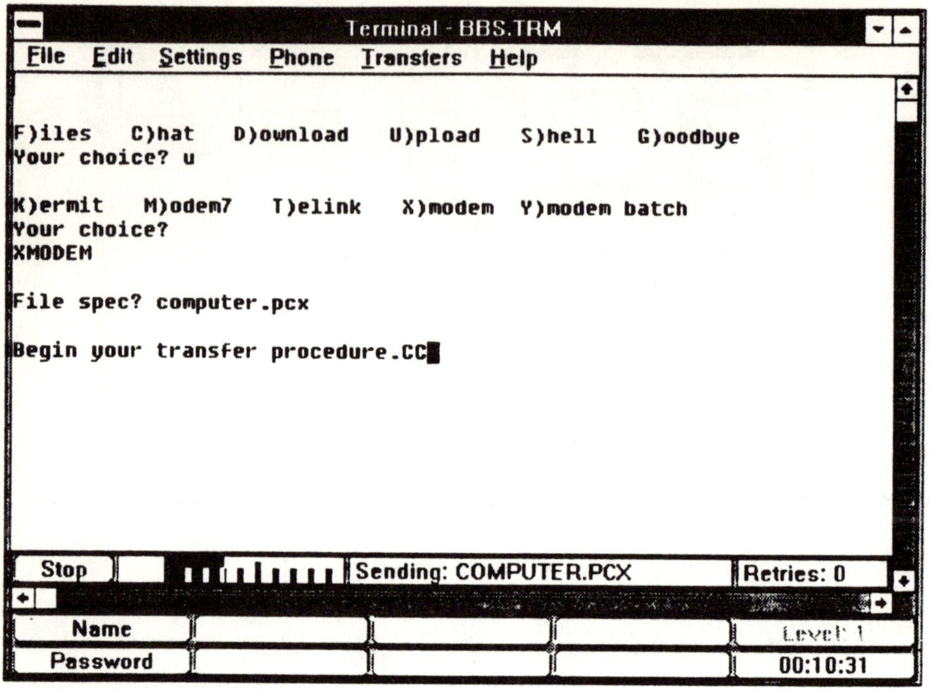

Figure 9-25. Sending a Binary File.

The work space in Figure 9-25 still shows the dialogue box that you used to tell the remote computer a file was coming. The bottom of the window has four new displays. The Stop function button allows you to terminate the transmission in the middle. The ruled scale has a reverse video bar that moves from left to right to indicate the progress of the transmission. The Sending field identifies the file that you are sending. The Retries field shows the number of retries that Terminal has made during the transmission. If this number is high, you might be getting a lot of interference in the phone lines, and you might want to stop the transfer and try it again another time.

Receiving Binary Files

You use the Procomm F)iles menu option to see what files are in Procomm's BBS area and to see the display shown in Figure 9-26.

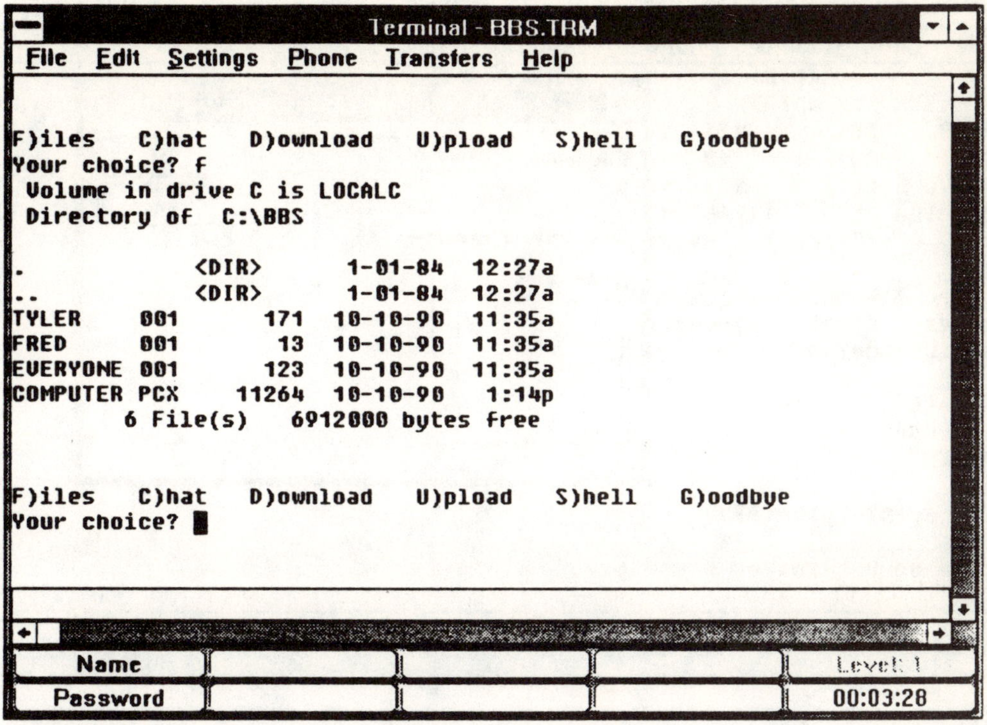

Figure 9-26. A Directory of the Remote Files.

Note that the directory in Figure 9-26 looks just like a DOS directory listing. Procomm is a DOS program that is running in a remote DOS computer—it uses the DOS DIR command to send you a directory of the files you can see. If the directory is longer and scrolls off your screen before you can read it all, you can use the scroll bars to read the scrolled-off portion.

One of the files is named TYLER.001. According to a convention agreed to between the remote user and callers to her BBS—this user, the callers, and their agreement being a totally fictional setup contrived for the purposes of these exercises—that file is for you. To download the file, you first tell the remote computer that you are going to use XModem. The remote computer tells you to begin your transfer procedure. You select the Receive Binary File... command on the Transfers menu and see the Receive Binary File dialogue box shown in Figure 9-27. In the figure you have already named the file you are going to receive.

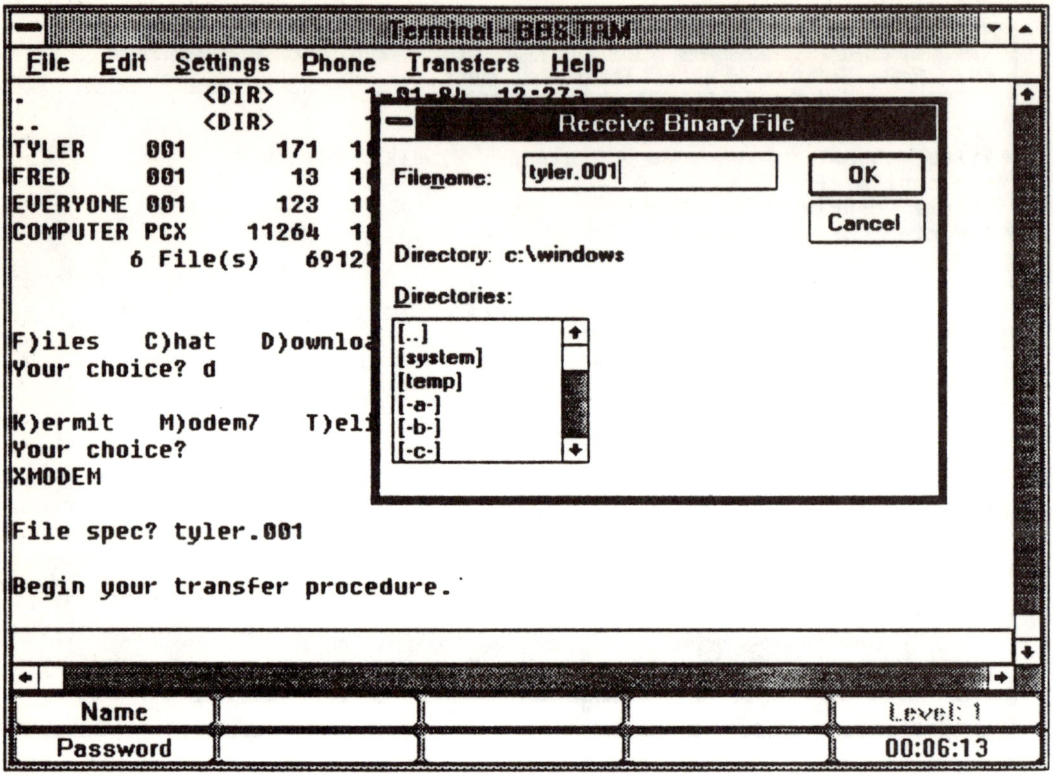

Figure 9-27. The Receive Binary File Dialogue Box.

While the binary file is transferring into your computer, Terminal displays additional information at the bottom of the window, as shown in Figure 9-28.

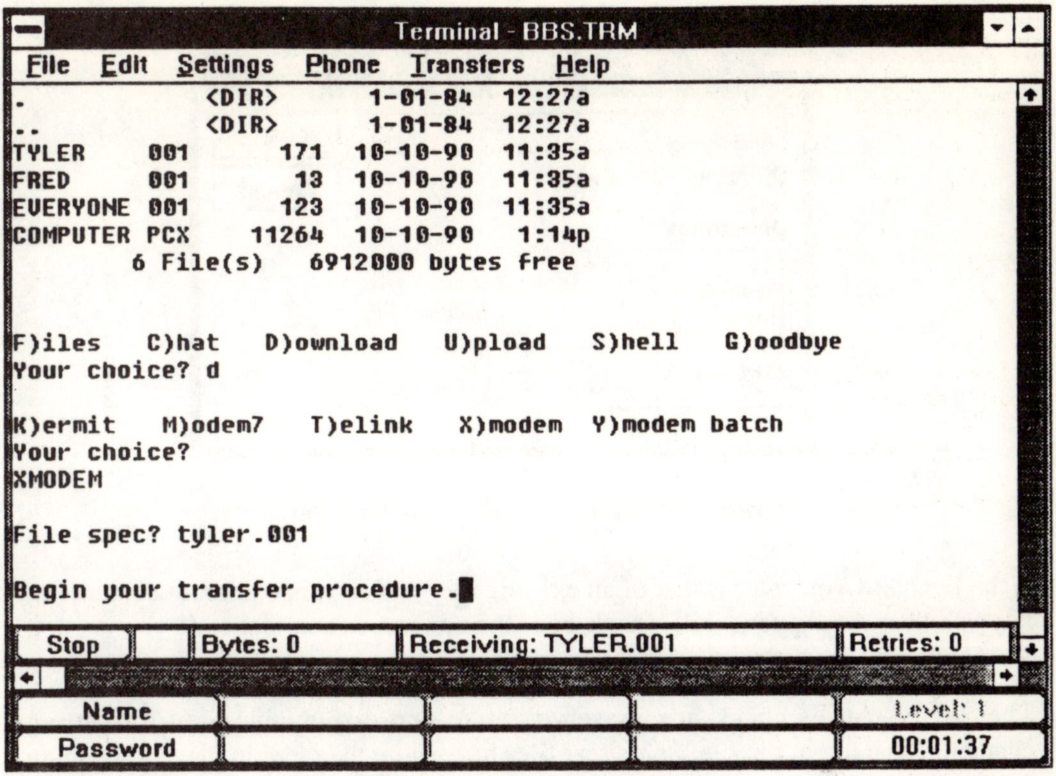

Figure 9-28. Receiving a Binary File.

The Stop function button allows you to terminate the reception in midstream. The Bytes count tells you how many bytes have been received so far. The Receiving field names the file that you are receiving, and the Retries field is the number of retries so far.

Receiving Text Files

Procomm does not have a text option for downloading files to you from its host mode, but other systems you call will. Before the remote computer begins sending a text file, select Receive Text File on the Transfers menu. Select the appropriate drive and directory and enter the file name in the Receive Text File dialogue box shown in Figure 9-29.

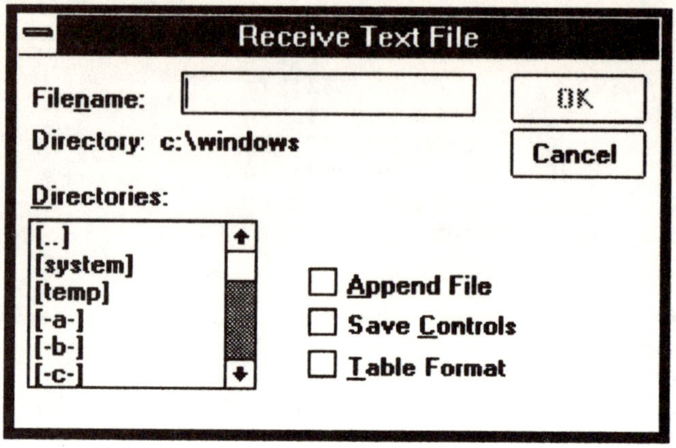

Figure 9-29. The Receive Text File Dialogue Box.

If the file name you enter is that of an existing file, you can append to it or replace it. If you select the Append File check box, the append is automatic. If you do not, Terminal will ask you to verify that you are replacing an existing file.

The Save Controls check box preserves some non-displayable, non-formatting characters that are in the file. Some text files have more than text in them, depending on the software that generated the files. This option preserves most of those control values.

The Table Format check box tells Terminal to replace strings of spaces with Tab characters.

When you are ready to receive, select OK. You will see the screen shown in Figure 9-30.

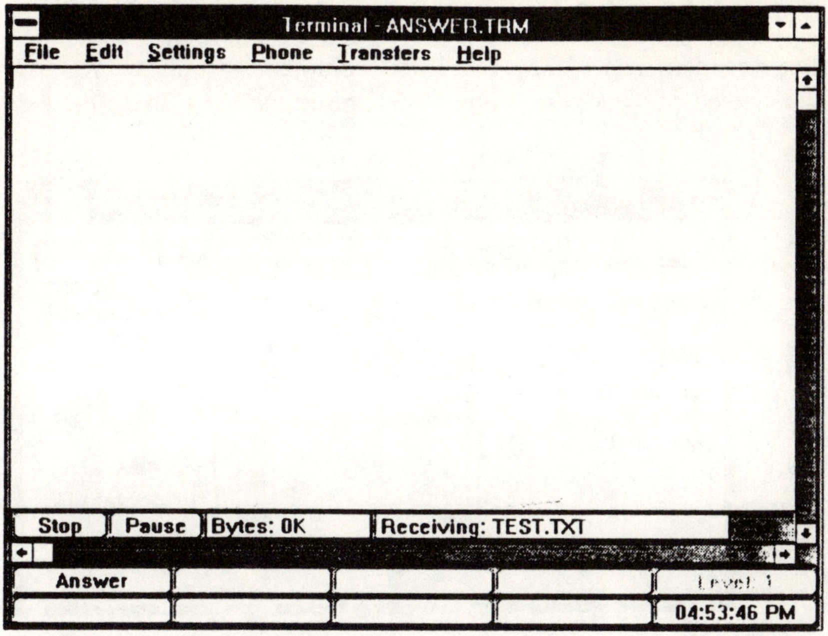

Figure 9-30. Receiving a Text File.

The remote computer may begin sending the text file now. You can click the Stop function button to terminate the transfer, or you can click the Pause button to temporarily pause it. The Pause button changes to a Resume button that you use to resume the transfer. The Bytes field displays the number of characters received so far, and the Receiving field identifies the name of the file you are receiving.

During the reception, the text is displayed on the screen. It might appear with each line overwriting the previous one, which means that the file has carriage returns without line feeds. In that case, stop the transfer with the Stop button, turn on the CR -> CR/LF Inbound check box in the Terminal Preferences dialogue box, and transfer the file again.

When the text file has completed transferring, select the Stop function button at the bottom of the window's work space.

VIEWING TEXT FILES

The Transfers menu has a View Text File... command that allows you to select a text file to be viewed on the screen. Figure 9-31 shows the View Text File dialogue box.

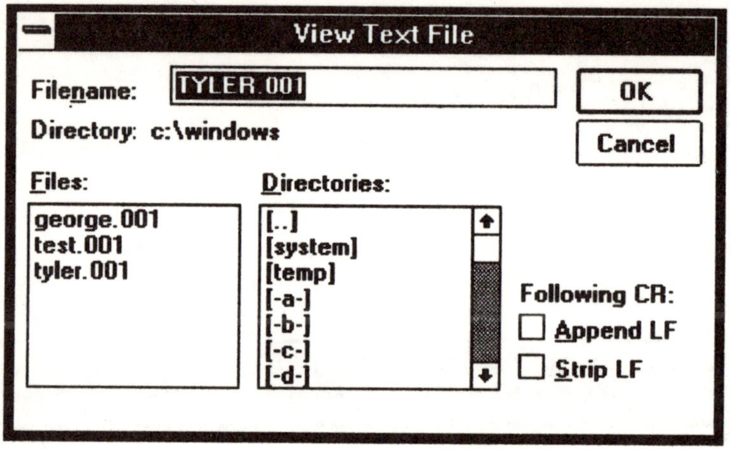

Figure 9-31. The View Text File Dialogue Box.

If you have just downloaded a text file, its name appears in the dialogue box's Filename field by default, and any other files with the same extension appear in the Files list box. If you downloaded a text file without line feeds and you wish to view it but not to transfer it again, you can select the Append LF check box.

If you downloaded a file that has line feeds and you are adding line feeds as well, the file will have an extra blank line for every line in the original. You can use the Strip LF check box to strip the extra line feeds when you display the file.

Viewing a text file writes it into the work space of the Terminal window just as if you had received it from the remote computer. Figure 9-32 shows how the screen appears while you are viewing the PRINTERS.TXT file that comes with Windows 3.0.

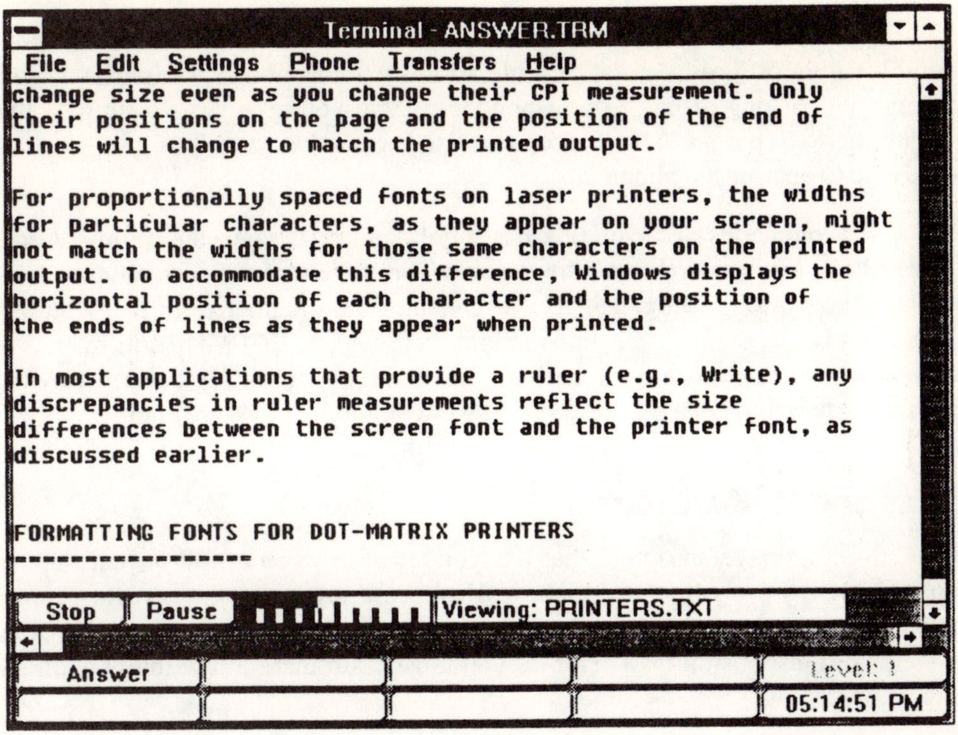

Figure 9-32. Viewing a Text File.

The ruler bar at the bottom of the screen moves from left to right to track your progress through the file. As it is displayed, the file continues to scroll off the top of the window. You can select the Pause function button at the bottom of the window. If you do so, the display will stop, the Pause function button will become a Resume function button, and you will be able to use the scroll bars to view the upper parts of the file that have scrolled out of sight. You can select the Resume function button to continue viewing the file.

USING TERMINAL TO ANSWER THE PHONE

Windows does not provide a way for Terminal to be the answering computer. Suppose you and a friend both use Terminal and you want to connect your computers. One of you must call the other, and that means that one of your communications programs must be able to answer the phone. Or perhaps your agreement with a long distance correspondent is that you take turns calling so that you share the toll charges. That agreement also means that your Terminal program must be able to answer the phone.

The Modem Commands dialogue box has a field called Answer, but Terminal does not have a built-in command that allows you to use it. Few of the currently available books about Windows 3.0 explain this discrepancy, and neither does the Windows 3.0 User's Guide. It seems to be an oversight, perhaps one that Microsoft intends to correct in a future version of Terminal. Until then, you can use the following procedures to turn Terminal into an auto-answer communications program.

Echoes and Half-Duplex

Terminal does not have an option that lets you tell it to work in full or half duplex. Because it always expects to be the calling computer, it expects the remote answering computer to echo the characters that Terminal transmits, but it shares no such reciprocal responsibility. Therefore you must coordinate a few things with the calling computer.

Because Terminal does not echo the characters it receives, the remote calling computer must echo its own characters as it sends them. Because you are using Terminal as the answering computer, however, the remote computer expects to be treated like a terminal and will not echo the characters your computer sends—your computer must echo its own.

Adding Line Feeds

You and the remote user might have to play with the line feed option to see what works best. In Terminal you should set the Outbound option in the Terminal Preferences CR -> CR/LF field and leave the Inbound option off. The user of the remote computer should do the same.

Building an Auto-Answer Settings File

Once you have a working configuration defined, save it for future use. The procedures that follow work for most connections where Terminal must answer the phone.

Auto-Answer Parameters

In the Terminal Preferences dialogue box, set the Local Echo check box on. Set the Inbound CR -> CR/LF check box off and the Outbound option on.

Set your file transfer and communications parameters according to your preferences. Those who call your computer must comply or you must agree to change your settings when a caller needs something different.

The Answer Function Key

Assign the name "Answer" to the Key Name field of the F1 function key. Enter this text value into its Command box:

ATQ1E0S0=1^M

This string is the command that tells the modem to prepare to answer the phone. It comes from the Answer field of the Modem Commands dialogue box when the Hayes modem is selected. If you use one of the other modems, use its Answer string. Be sure to follow it with the ^M sequence to send the carriage return character at the end of the command.

The Reset Function Key

Assign the name "Reset" to the Key Name field of the F2 function key. Enter this text value into its Command box:

^$HATQ0E1V1S0=0^M

This string is the command that tells the modem to hang up and return to originate mode so that it will no longer answer the phone. The command begins with the ^$H sequence to hang up the phone. That sequence is followed by a string taken from the Originate field of the Modem Commands dialogue box when the Hayes modem is selected. If you use one of the other modems, use its Originate string. Be sure to follow the command with the ^M sequence to send the carriage return character at the end. Save the file with the name ANSWER.TRM.

Answering the Phone

Because Terminal was not intended to act as a host, it has no provision for hosting a caller in an unattended session. When someone calls, you must be around to deal with them personally. When you are ready to accept calls, start Terminal with the ANSWER.TRM file loaded. Select the Answer function key and wait for a call.

Terminal will not tell you that someone has called. If your modem has a loud enough speaker and you are in the same room, you will hear the carrier signal. It will sound until both computers know that the connection is complete.

You can tell your caller to send several Ctrl+G keystrokes to get your attention. That will cause Terminal to sound your computer's audible alarm unless you turned off the Sound check box in the Terminal Preferences dialogue box. After you have answered the phone, you and the caller can freely type messages back and forth.

Exchanging Files

To transfer files in the answer mode, you must agree that the receiver will prepare to receive the file before the sender starts sending it; otherwise the receiver's software will treat the incoming data as conversational text to display on the screen. Other than that consideration, file transfers work just as you have learned them.

Hanging Up

If you want Terminal to answer more calls, select the Hangup command on the Phone menu. If you want to return your phone line to normal operation, select the Reset function key that you defined earlier. If you do not select Reset, the next caller to your line will be greeted by the high-pitched carrier signal, which will continue for a while after they hang up.

CONNECTING DIRECTLY TO ANOTHER COMPUTER

When you connect your computer directly to another computer, you do so with a cable that connects the serial port of one computer to that of another. The cable is called a "null modem" because it does the job of both modems and the telephone system as long as the two computers are relatively close to one another. Two computers connected by a null modem can communicate at speeds much greater than those supported by modems. Terminal allows you to use up to 19200 baud, but other applications have successfully transmitted data through a null modem cable at much greater speeds. You can get a null modem cable at Radio Shack or your computer store.

Assume that you are using Terminal in both computers. You must configure the settings of both computers for compatible communications. You do not need a phone number or any particular terminal emulation. Set Local Echo and Outbound CR -> CR/LF on in both computers. Set Inbound CR -> CR/LF off in both computers. You might as well use 19200 baud because that is the fastest rate that Terminal supports. For flow control you can use either Xon/Xoff or, if the null modem cable supports it, the Hardware setting.

When you start Terminal in both computers, you should be able to type at one keyboard and see the characters on both screens. File transfers work the same as they do when you connect through a modem, except that they are faster, due to the higher baud rate.

If you are using Terminal to connect your PC to a mainframe or minicomputer, set the Terminal settings to match those of the host computer. When you run Terminal, you should be connected to the host as if you were using an actual terminal device instead of a PC or AT running Windows and Terminal. As with the other uses, if you regularly use Terminal to connect directly to another computer, you should record a file of the Terminal settings.

EDITING AND THE CLIPBOARD

The Clipboard has special uses in Terminal. You can use it to transfer information that came from the remote computer to another application, and you can use it to send information from another application to the remote computer.

Copying to the Clipboard

You can copy data from the Terminal's buffer to the Clipboard by marking the data and selecting the Copy command on the Edit menu. You mark data with the mouse or keyboard just as you mark it in other applications. To mark data with the mouse, hold down the left button and drag the mouse cursor from the start of the copy block to the end. Release the button at the end. To mark data with the keyboard, use the arrow keys to move the vertical bar cursor to the start of the block. Hold down the shift key while you move the cursor to the end of the block. You can also use the Select All command on the Edit menu to select all the text that is in the Terminal buffer.

With the block marked, select the Copy command from the Edit menu. The marked text is copied into the Clipboard. You can now call another application and paste the Clipboard text into that application's work space.

Pasting from the Clipboard

The Paste command on the Edit menu transmits what is in the Clipboard to the remote computer. You can use this feature to transmit data from other applications. Copy the data from the other application into the Clipboard, then return to Terminal and use the Paste command on the Edit menu to transmit the Clipboard data to the remote computer.

Sending Marked Data

You can mark a block of data in the Terminal buffer to send to the remote computer. Mark the block just as you did earlier for the Copy command, then use the Send command on the Edit menu to transmit the marked data to the remote computer. You use this feature when you want to forward the contents of a communication to another computer. After the first communication is over, call the second remote computer, mark the text of the first communication, and use the Send command to forward it.

Clearing the Buffer

The Clear Buffer command on the Edit menu clears the Terminal buffer of all text.

SUMMARY

Do not allow anyone to tell you that learning inter-computer communications is a snap. It can be reasonably easy once you have the routine procedures in place and recorded into files of Terminal settings. But every new connection can add wrinkles to the process. This chapter has covered the basics of using Terminal. Chapter 10 provides detailed descriptions of the accessories that Windows provides: the Calculator, the Notepad, the Cardfile, the Clock, the Calendar, and the Recorder.

Chapter 10

Accessories

This chapter describes some of the accessory programs that come with Windows. You will find these accessories in the Program Manager's Accessories group. You have already learned about the Write, Paintbrush, and Terminal accessories—there are chapters on each of these accessories earlier in the book. This chapter discusses six more accessories: the Clock, the Notepad, the Calendar, the Cardfile, the Recorder, and the Calculator. Chapter 11 describes the final accessory: the PIF Editor.

You can execute these accessories from the File Manager by selecting the program files or associated document files shown in Table 10-1.

Table 10-1. Accessories Program and Document Files.

Accessory	Program File Name	Document File Extensions
Clock	CLOCK.EXE	(none)
Notepad	NOTEPAD.EXE	*.TXT, *.INI
Calendar	CALENDAR.EXE	*.CAL
Cardfile	CARDFILE.EXE	*.CRD
Recorder	RECORDER.EXE	*.REC
Calculator	CALC.EXE	(none)

THE CLOCK ACCESSORY

The Clock accessory displays a time-of-day clock on the screen. Figure 10-1 shows the clock display.

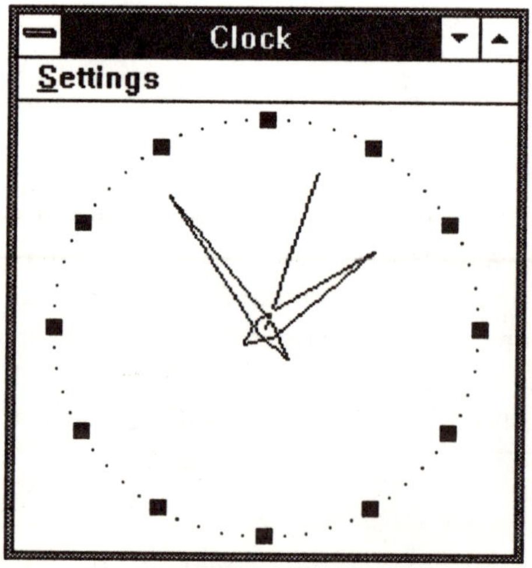

Figure 10-1. The Analog Clock.

The Settings menu allows you to select from two clock formats: the Analog display, which is shown in Figure 10-1, and the Digital display, which is shown in Figure 10-2.

Figure 10-2. The Digital Clock.

When you minimize either clock format, it becomes an icon that continues to give the time—but only down to the minute, rather than down to the second as with the maximized display. Figure 10-3 shows the two clock icons. You might keep whichever format you prefer as an icon, maximizing it only when you need to know the time down to the second. You do not set the clock's time from the Clock accessory program, rather you use the Control Panel to do this.

Figure 10-3. The Clock Icons.

THE NOTEPAD ACCESSORY

The Notepad Accessory is a text editor capable of small word processing tasks. Many users find that it contains all the word processing they need. Others use it for memos and short letters, preferring to use Write, Word for Windows, or some other more powerful word processor for document preparation. You have used Notepad in some of the exercises in previous chapters, so it is not new to you. Figure 10-4 shows the Notepad application window.

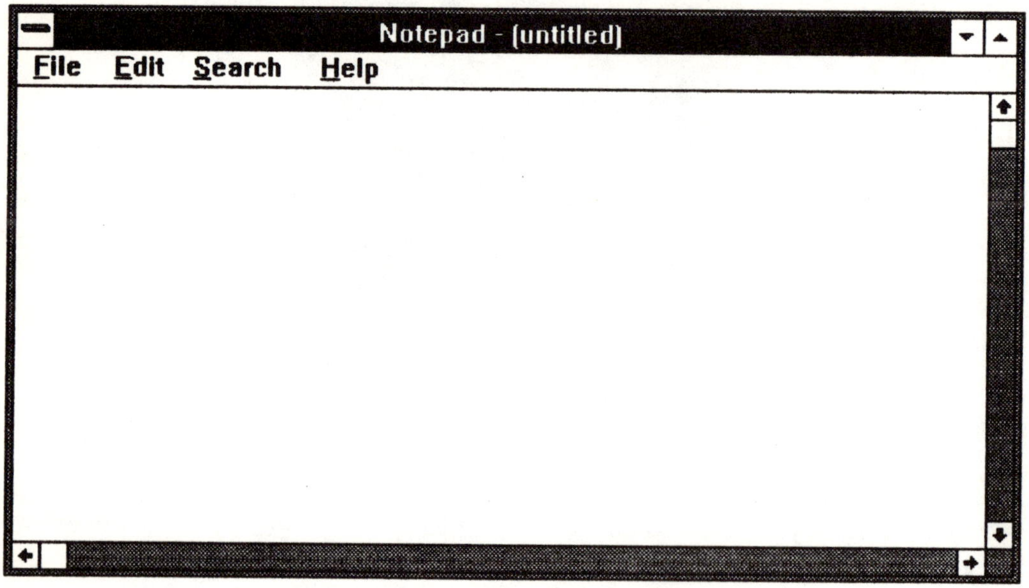

Figure 10-4. The Notepad Application Window.

Notepad Files

Notepad can support text files of up to about 50,000 characters. The About Notepad... command on the Help menu tells you the size of the current document. The File menu has the usual New, Open, Save, and Save As... commands. The default file extension is .TXT—you can use the File Manager to run Notepad by selecting any .TXT file. Notepad will also run if you select a .INI file—.INI is the extension for the initialization files that Windows uses. Those files are ASCII text, and you can use Notepad to view or change any of them. Each of these files has a corresponding .TXT file that explains the entries in the .INI file.

Entering Text

You enter text into the Notepad by typing. The Word Wrap command toggle on the Edit menu tells Notepad to wrap words at the right window border, keeping all of your text in view. You will want to use that option if you are typing a letter, memo, or document. The paragraphs reform themselves as you change the size of the window. When Word Wrap is on, the horizontal scroll bar goes away. Word Wrap is off by default when you first run Notepad. The Enter key defines the end of a paragraph.

Moving Around in the Text

You can move the cursor to a point in the text file by moving the mouse cursor to the desired location and clicking. You can also use the keyboard to move the cursor. Table 10-2 shows the keystrokes that move the cursor.

Table 10-2. Cursor Movement Keys.

Keystroke	Movement
Up and down arrow keys	Up and down one line
Right and left arrow keys	Right and left one character
Ctrl+right/left arrow	Right and left one word
Home/End	Beginning and end of the line
PgUp/PgDn	Previous and next screen
Ctrl+Home/End	Beginning and End of the file

Selecting Text

You can select blocks of text for cutting and copying to the Clipboard or for deleting from the file. To select text with the mouse, click the first character of the block and hold down the left button while you drag the cursor to the end of the block. The highlighted text displays in reverse video. Use the keys in Table 10-2 while you hold down the Shift key to select a block of text with the keyboard.

The Select All command on the Edit menu selects all the text in the file. To de-select a marked block, click the cursor once or press an arrow key.

Deleting Text

When you have selected a block of text, the Del or backspace key deletes the block. Pressing a character key deletes the block and inserts the character. You can use the Undo command on the Edit menu to undo the most recent delete.

When no block is marked, the Del key deletes text one character at a time to the right of the cursor. The backspace key deletes text one character at a time to the left of the cursor.

Cut, Copy, and Paste

The Cut and Copy commands on the Edit menu cut and copy the selected block of text to the Clipboard. The Paste command pastes the current text contents of the Clipboard into the file, beginning at the current cursor location.

Searching a Text File

You can search a file for a string value. The Find command on the Search menu opens the Find dialogue box shown in Figure 10-5.

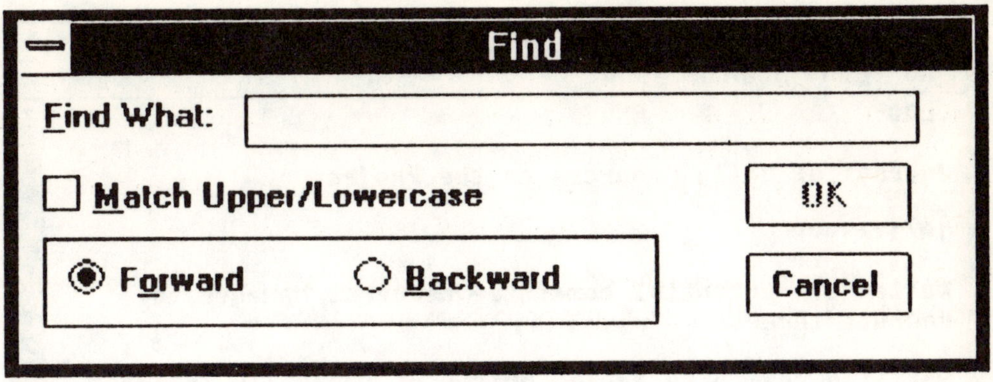

Figure 10-5. The Find Dialogue Box.

Enter the text you wish to find in the Find What field. If you want to have the search match your entry exactly with regard to upper and lower case letters, select the Match Upper/Lowercase check box. The Forward and Backward option buttons specify the direction you want to search, starting at the current cursor location. A search proceeds forward to the end of the file or backward to the beginning of the file.

If Notepad does not find the text, it displays an error message. If it finds the text, it stops searching and marks the text. The Find Next command on the Search menu continues the search from the point of the last text that was found, continuing in the direction you originally selected.

Date-Stamping a File

The Time/Date command on the Edit menu inserts the current date into the text at the current cursor position. If you put the text value .LOG into a file beginning in the left margin of the first line, Notepad will append the current date onto the file and position the cursor on the next line after the date every time you open the file. This feature allows you to define a diary or journal file that always date-stamps your entries.

Figure 10-6 shows the beginning of a personal journal that uses the .LOG convention.

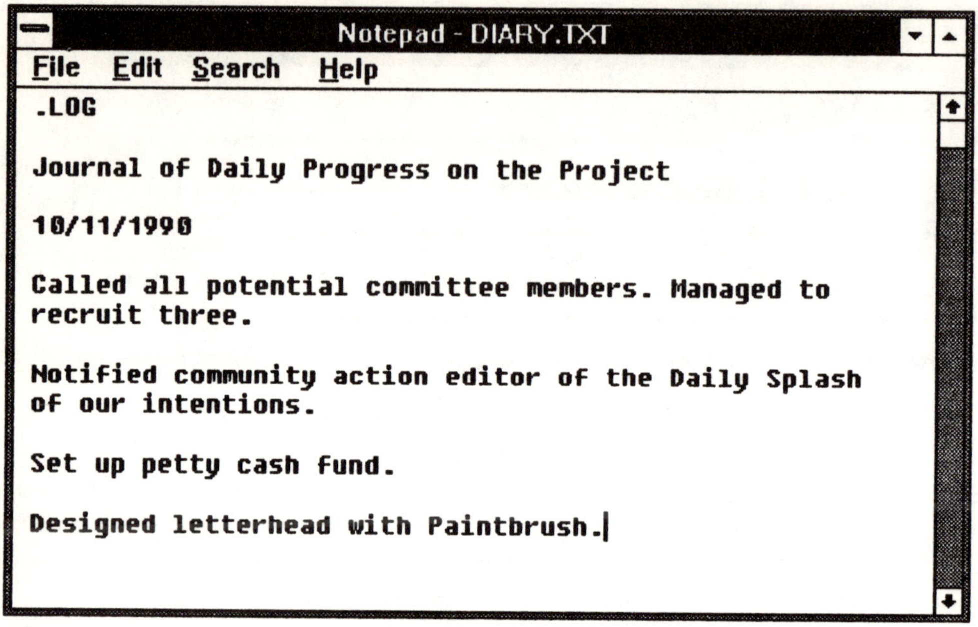

Figure 10-6. Using the .LOG Convention.

***

The Windows User's Guide says that the Time/Date command and the .LOG convention insert both the time and the date into the file, but they do not—at least not in the first release of Windows 3. They insert the date only.

***

Printing

The Notepad's Edit menu has the usual Print and Printer Setup commands. You can use the Page Setup... command to design the format of the printout of the text file. Figure 10-7 shows the Page Setup dialogue box that appears when you select this command.

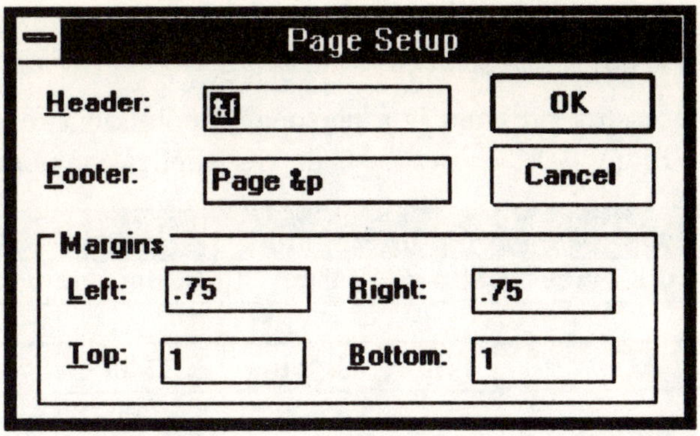

Figure 10-7. The Page Setup Dialogue Box.

You can change the four margin values by entering the new values into the Left, Right, Top, and Bottom Margin fields. You can also enter text and certain symbols into the Header and Footer fields. Table 10-3 shows the symbols that insert run-time values into the header and footer.

Table 10-3. Notepad Header and Footer Symbols.

Symbol	Inserts
&t	Time
&d	Date
&p	Page number
&f.	Name of the file
&	Text that follows the symbol is justified left
&r.	Text that follows the symbol is justified right
&c.	Text that follows the symbol is centered

THE CALENDAR ACCESSORY

The Calendar accessory program is a personal appointment or scheduling calendar and alarm clock. Figure 10-8 shows the Calendar application window.

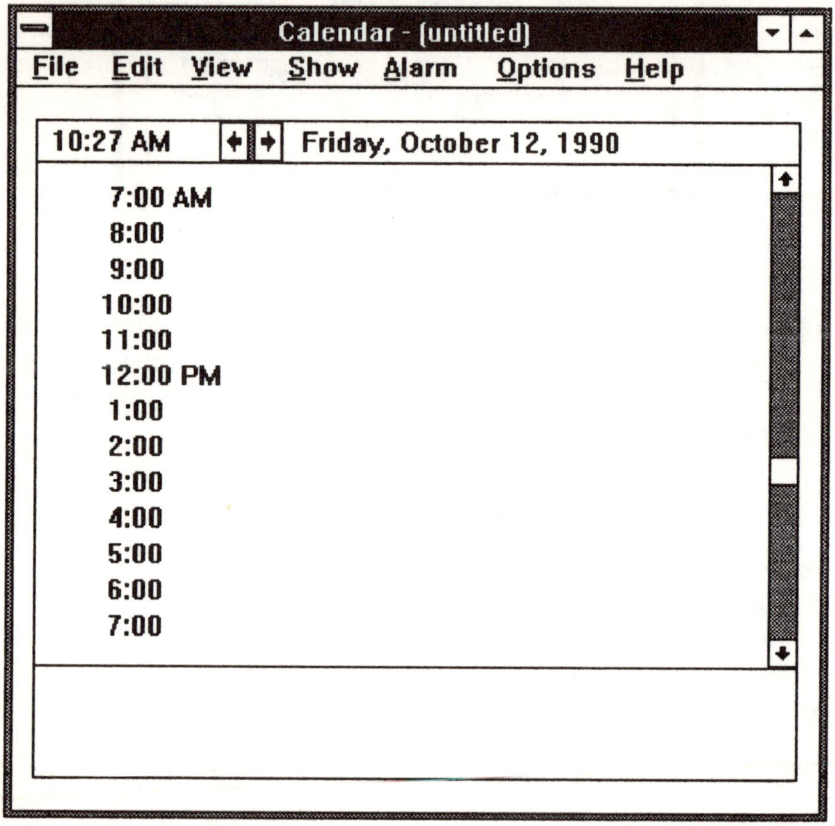

Figure 10-8. The Calendar Application Window.

You can use Calendar as a personal scheduler and as a scheduler for resources. You might use one copy of Calendar for your appointments and others to maintain the scheduled use of company resources such as conference rooms, overhead projectors, and company cars. A lawyer or consultant, for example, can use Calendar to record time spent on jobs and with clients.

If you are in the business of contracting labor—such as a music-booking agent, a temporary office help company, or a job shop—you can use separate copies of Calendar for your employees' schedules. Your work force can then use Calendar as time cards.

If you are a piano teacher, you can use Calendar to schedule students. You can also use Calendar to record birthdays or to schedule virtually anything that is based on date and time.

The Day's Schedule

When you start Calendar, it displays the current day's schedule. The time displayed is the current time, and Calendar keeps it updated. The schedule contains entries for each hour, although you will learn how to change the intervals. The default display starts with 7:00 AM as the first entry; you can scroll to the entries that precede that time. You will learn how to change the time that displays at the top when you view a calendar later in this chapter.

The bottom of the Calendar is a scratch pad where you can enter notes about the day's schedule. You make entries by typing them in. An entry's length can exceed the space given it on its time line in the schedule; it scrolls horizontally. You can move the cursor to new entries or the scratch pad by clicking where you want to type or by using the keyboard.

The right and left arrows at the top of the window are mouse function buttons that move to the previous and next day in the Calendar.

Table 10-4 lists the keystrokes that move the cursor, while Figure 10-9 shows a typical day in a Calendar's schedule.

Table 10-4. Calendar Keys (Day View).

Key	Movement
Up/Down arrow	Up and down the time entries
Enter	Next entry down
Home/End	Beginning/end of the current entry
PgUp/PgDn	Page through the day
Ctrl+Home/End	Start time/start time + 12 hours
Tab	To the scratch pad and back
Ctrl+PgUp/PgDn	To the previous/next day

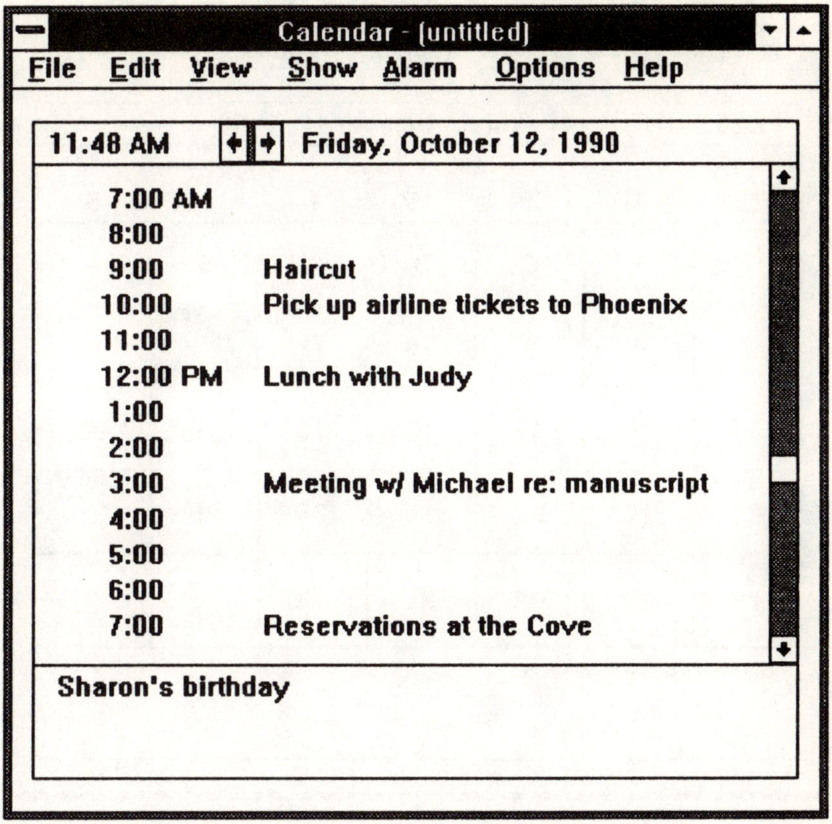

Figure 10-9. A Typical Day in a Calendar's Schedule.

Viewing the Month

To view the month, select the Month command on the View menu. Figure 10-10 shows the month view.

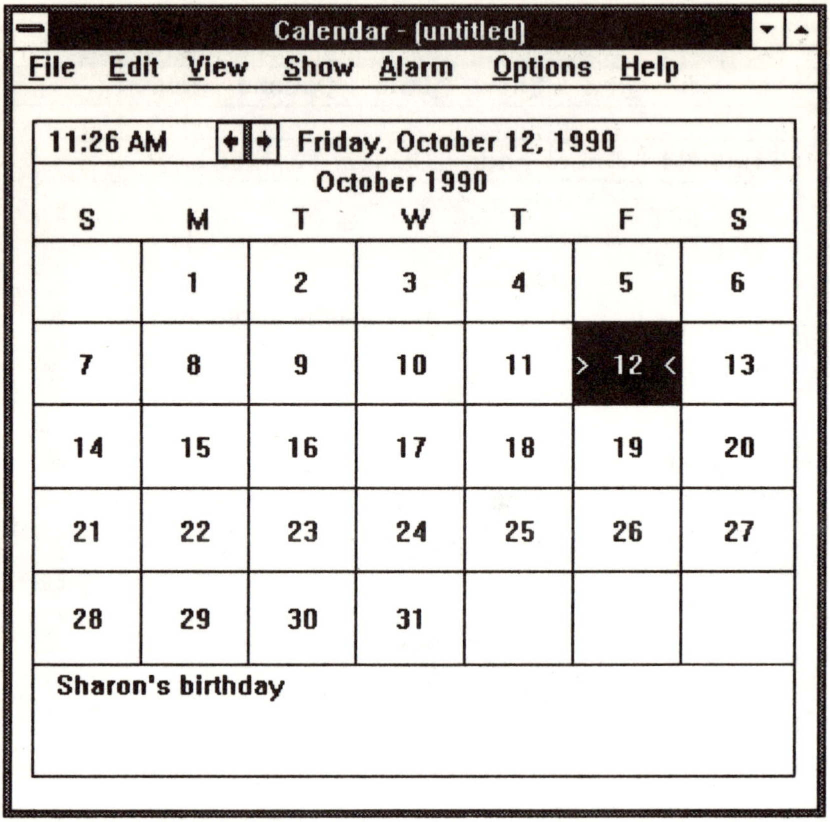

Figure 10-10. The Calendar in Month View.

You can use the keyboard or the mouse to move around in the month view. Table 10-5 lists the keystrokes for doing this.

Table 10-5. Calendar Keys (Month View).

Key	Movement
Arrow keys	Up and down, right and left, day to day
Enter	Select day view
PgUp/PgDn	Previous/next month
Tab	To the scratch pad and back

If you use the arrow keys to move beyond the first or last day of the month, you will move to the previous or the next month. If you double click a day, you will select the day view for that day.

As you move from day to day, you see the scratch pad entries for the selected date. The month view, along with the scratch pad, are handy holiday and birthday calendars.

Marking Days

You can mark days in the month by selecting the Mark command on the Options menu. Figure 10-11 shows the Day Markings dialogue box that appears when you select this command.

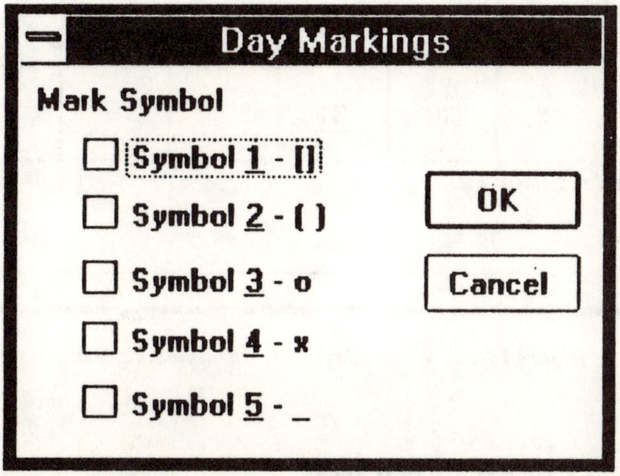

Figure 10-11. The Day Markings Dialogue Box.

Each day's check box contains a different style of mark. You can choose any or all of the styles to mark the currently selected day. For example, you might use one symbol for holidays, another for paydays, another for oil changes, and so on. Figure 10-12 shows the Wednesdays with one symbol each. The first day of the month has all the symbols.

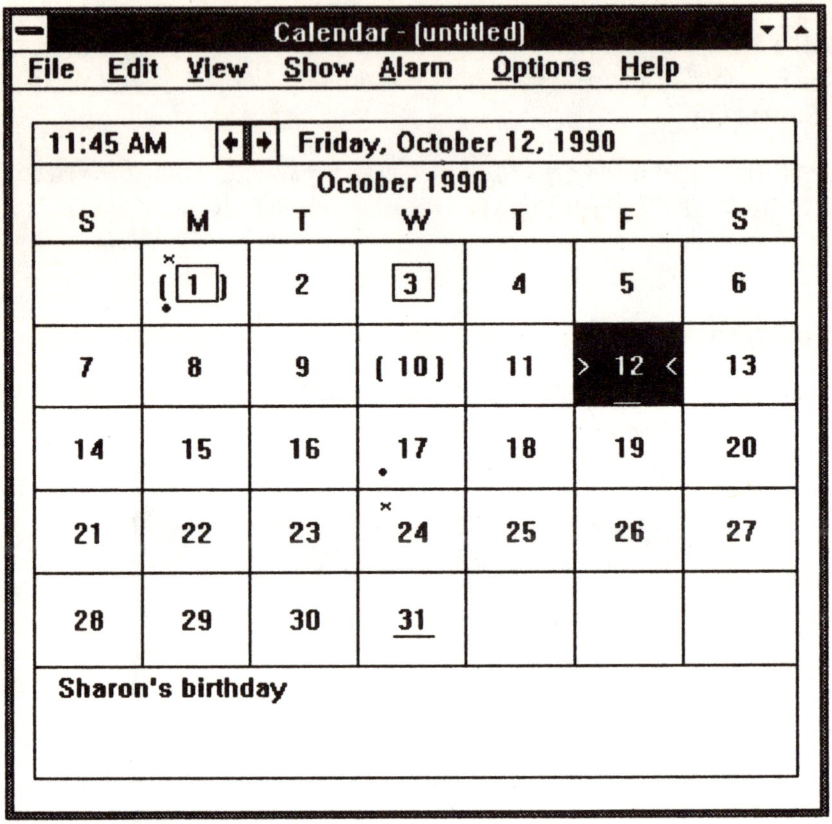

Figure 10-12. Wednesdays with One Symbol Each.

Changing the Day View Format

By default, the Calendar displays its time entries for a day in one-hour intervals, uses a 12-hour clock, and displays a start time of 7:00 AM. You can change these settings by selecting the Day Settings... command on the Options menu. Figure 10-13 shows the Day Settings dialogue box that appears when you select this command.

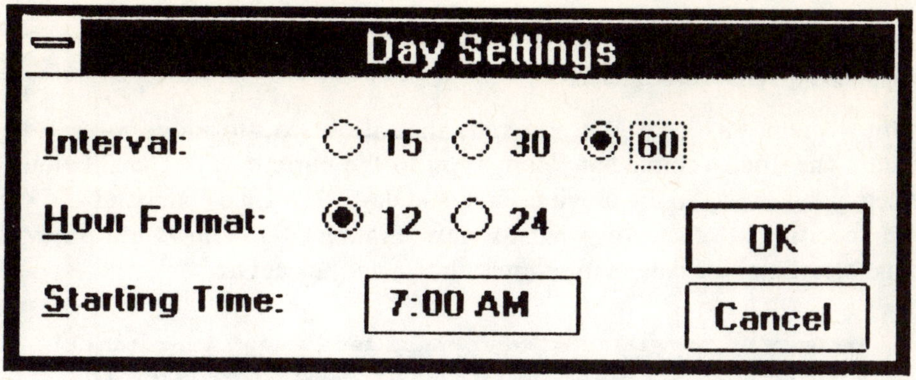

Figure 10-13. The Day Settings Dialogue Box.

Select the Interval option button that represents the time intervals for your daily schedule, then select the 12 or 24 hour time representation. Enter the starting time that you want to appear when you first see a day view.

Inserting or Deleting a Special Time

The Special Time command on the Options menu allows you to specify a time other than one of the intervals. This new time interval appears on the calendar only on the currently selected day. Figure 10-14 shows the Special Time dialogue box.

Figure 10-14. The Special Time Dialogue Box.

You can use the Special Time command to delete a special time, but you cannot delete one of the normal intervals. If you select the command while the Calendar cursor is on a special time entry, the dialogue box comes up with the special time already entered.

Navigating the Calendar

The Show menu has several commands that allow you to move around in the Calendar. The Today command returns you to the current day. The Previous and Next commands move to the previous and next days. The Date command allows you enter a specific date that you want to view. Figure 10-15 shows the Show Date dialogue box. Enter the date in the format shown and select OK.

Figure 10-15. The Show Date Dialogue Box.

The Alarm Clock

The Calendar, not the Clock, is your Windows alarm clock because it can remind you of an appointment. To set an alarm, move the cursor to the time on the day you want to be alerted and select the Set command on the Alarm menu. A small bell icon appears in the left margin of the selected time entry, as shown in Figure 10-16.

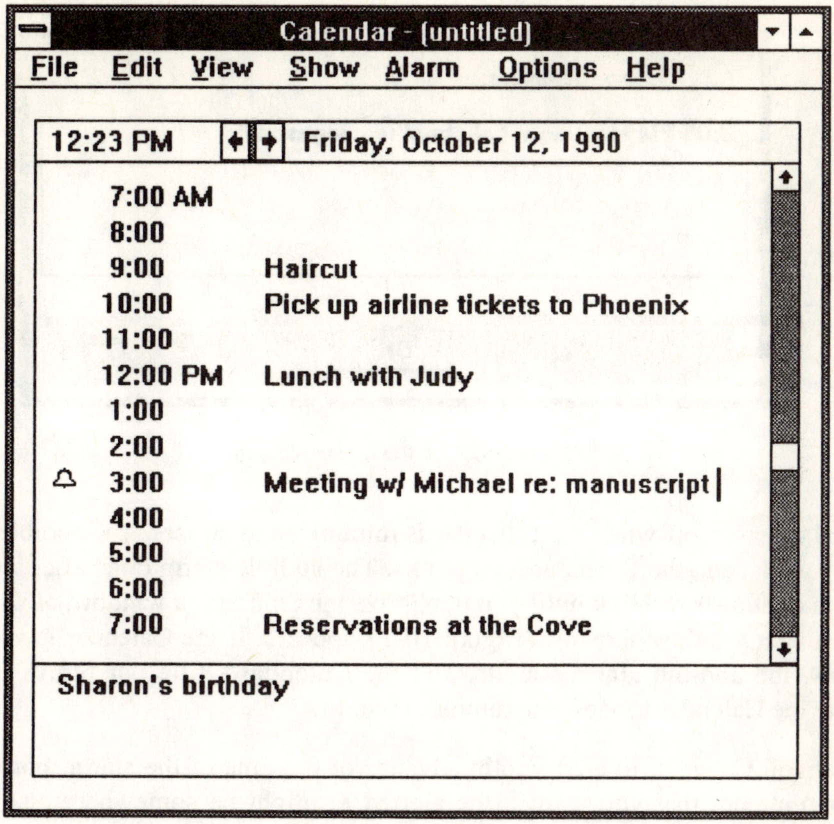

Figure 10-16. The Bell Icon on a Selected Time Entry.

If the alarm goes off while you are working in the Calendar, an audible beeping alarm sounds, and a reminder window appears, as shown in Figure 10-17.

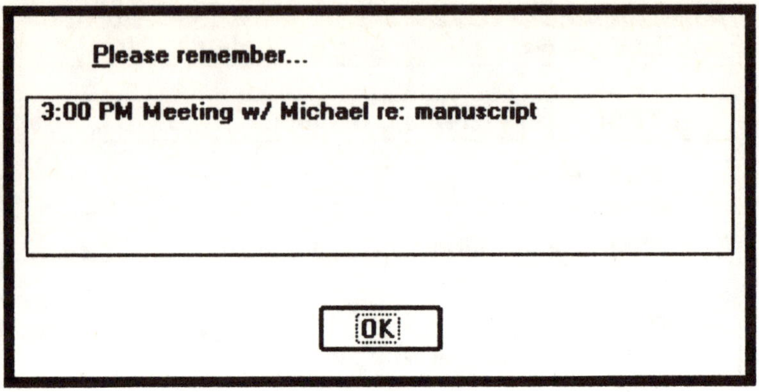

Figure 10-17. A Reminder Window.

If the alarm goes off when the Calendar is minimized to an icon, the audible beeping alarm sounds, and the Calendar icon blinks. The audible alarm quits after a time, but the icon continues to blink until you maximize the icon into a window, at which time the reminder window shown in Figure 10-17 appears. If the Calendar is an inactive window, the audible alarm sounds, and the Calendar's title bar blinks until you activate the Calendar to view the reminder window.

You can tell Calendar to alert you in advance of the time of the alarm. For example, the appointment that you want to be alerted to might be somewhere else and you need time to get there. The Controls... command on the Alarm menu allows you to specify up to 10 minutes advance time for the alarm. Figure 10-18 shows the Alarm Controls dialogue box that appears when you select this command.

Figure 10-18. The Alarm Controls Dialogue Box.

You can also use the Sound check box on the Alarm Controls dialogue box to suppress the audible part of the alarm.

To clear an alarm, move to the time entry and select the Set command again.

Removing Calendar Entries

The Remove... command on the Edit menu allows you to delete a range of appointments by specifying the begin and end dates. Figure 10-19 shows the Remove dialogue box. Enter the From and To dates and select OK.

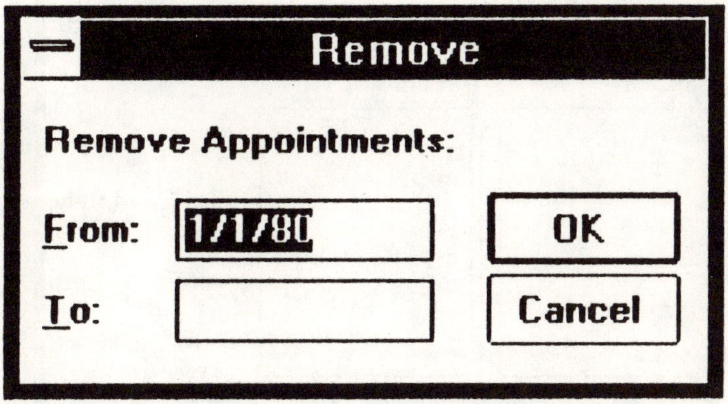

Figure 10-19. The Remove Dialogue Box.

The Calendar and the Clipboard

You can select the text of a Calendar entry and cut or copy it to the clipboard. You can then paste the contents of the Clipboard into an entry. Mark the text with the mouse or keyboard the same way you do in other applications and use the Cut, Copy, and Paste commands on the Edit menu.

Files

The File menu is the same as Notepad's File menu—it includes the New, Open..., Save, and Save As... commands. You can maintain several calendars by saving each one in its own file. The default file name extension is .CAL. This extension is associated with the Calendar application in the File Manager; you can execute Calendar by selecting a .CAL file.

Figure 10-20 shows the Calendar's File Open dialogue box. It differs from other File Open dialogue boxes in that is has a Read Only check box. If you select this check box, Calendar will not allow you to make any changes to the file. This option is for convenience rather than for security. You might use it if you know that you are viewing a Calendar that someone else maintains.

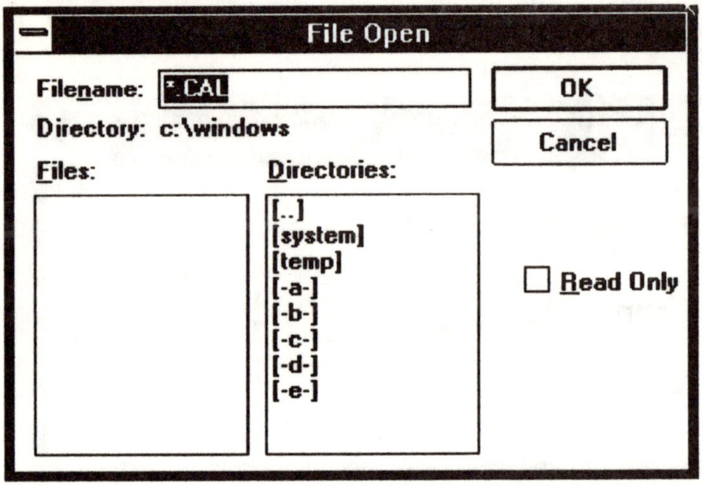

Figure 10-20. The Calendar's File Open Dialogue Box.

Printing

The File menu is the same as Notepad's File menu—it includes the Print..., Page Setup..., and Printer Setup... commands. The Print... command works differently than the Print commands of other applications, however; it displays the Print dialogue box shown in Figure 10-21.

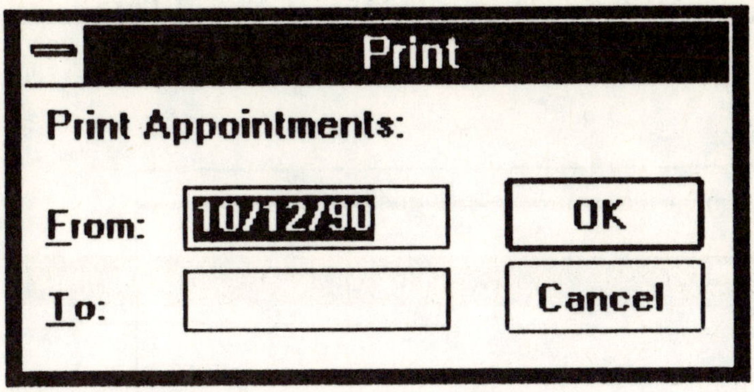

Figure 10-21. The Calendar's Print Dialogue Box.

Enter the range of dates for the appointments you want to print. If you do not change anything in the From and To fields, Calendar will print the schedule for only the current day.

THE CARDFILE ACCESSORY

Cardfile is an application for storing information in what resembles 3x5 card format. You can store text and pictures, retrieve the records by searching, and print the contents of the cards. Figure 10-22 shows the Cardfile application window.

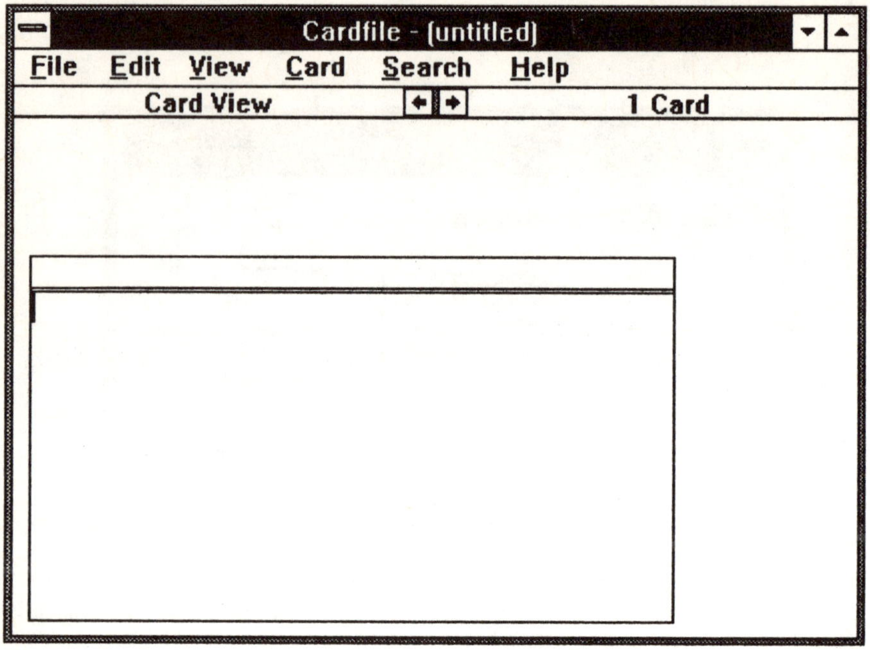

Figure 10-22. The Cardfile Application Window.

The rectangle that appears in the lower left corner of the Cardfile work space is the card itself. The first line of the card is the index line, and the rest of the card is the information area. You can type text into the index line, and you can type or paste text and paste pictures into the information area. Although you can change the size of the Cardfile application window, the size of the card does not change.

When you first start Cardfile there are no cards in the file. In Chapter 2, you used Cardfile to help learn about the Program Manager, and you built a small card data base with one card in it. This chapter will teach you to build a larger data base and introduce you to other uses for Cardfile.

Uses for Cardfile

You can use Cardfile for most applications that require storage and retrieval of small text entries or pictures. You can store sales prospects, recipes, your Christmas card list, scanned snapshots, and so on.

Building a Cardfile Data Base

The first card in every Cardfile is empty. To start a data base, you must put something in it. Every card has an index area that contains the text by which Cardfile sorts the file. In a name and address file, the index is usually the name. To enter the index for the first blank card, select the Index... command from the Edit menu. You will see the Index dialogue box shown in Figure 10-23.

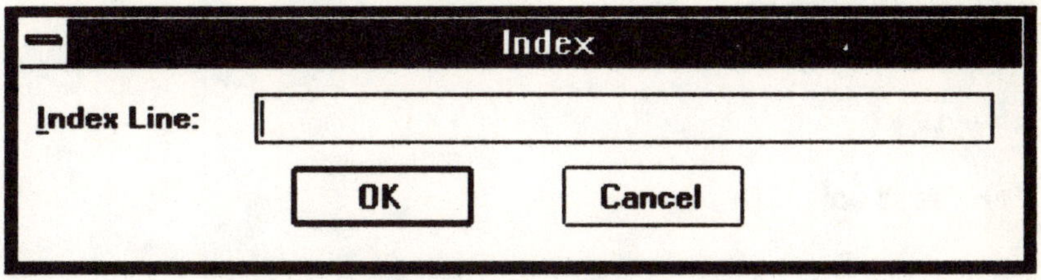

Figure 10-23. The Index Dialogue Box.

Enter a name into the dialogue box and select OK. For a well-ordered name and address file, enter the last name first. The name you enter will appear in the index line of the card, and the cursor will be in the card's information area. Enter the address, phone number, and any other relevant information about the person. For example, if this file is for employees, you might include the social security number and job title. Figure 10-24 shows a card with an index and some information entered. That's all you have to do to build the first card. It is in the Cardfile data base now. Although you have not named or saved the file, the card is in memory.

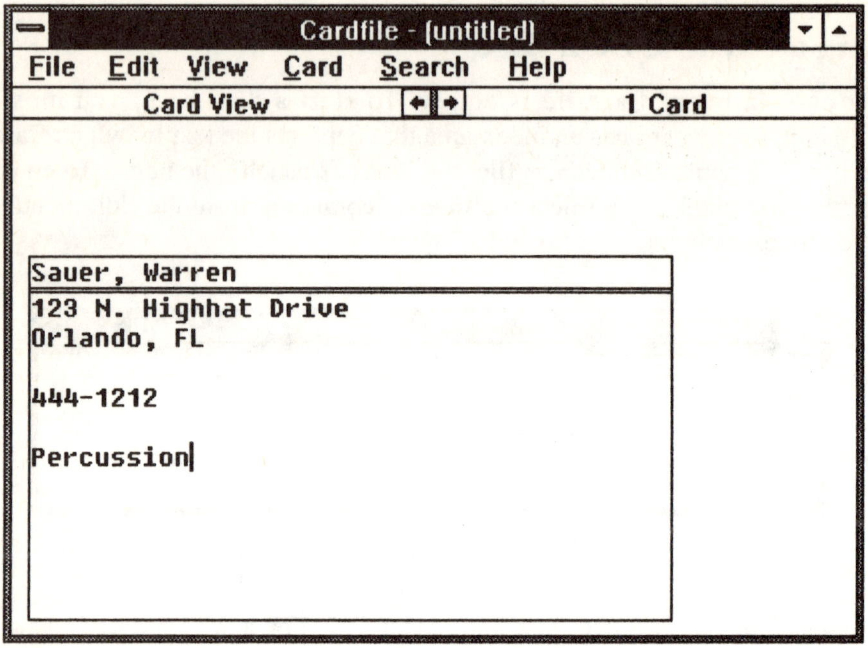

Figure 10-24. A Card with an Index and Some Information Entered.

To add more cards to the file, select the Add... command on the Card menu. When you select this command you see the Add dialogue box shown in Figure 10-25.

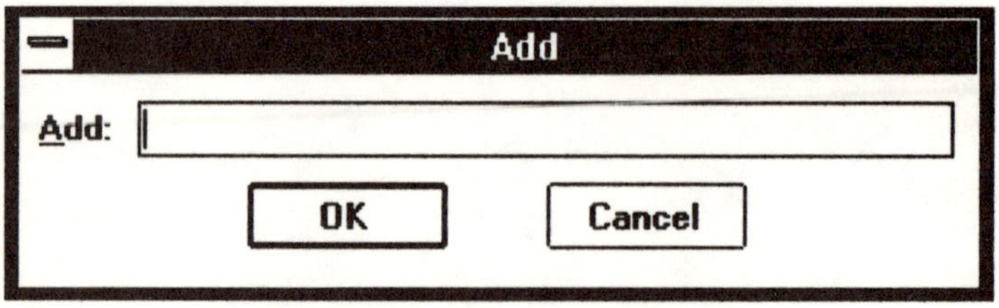

Figure 10-25. The Add Dialogue Box.

The Add dialogue box looks a lot like the Index dialogue box. It also serves the same purpose as the Index dialogue box when you are adding new cards to an existing file. The Index dialogue box's first purpose is to supply the index line for the first card in an empty file. Subsequently, you use the Index dialogue box when you want to change the index lines for existing cards.

Enter a name into the Add dialogue box and select OK. The first card moves back, and the new card is at the front of the stack, ready for an address, as shown in Figure 10-26.

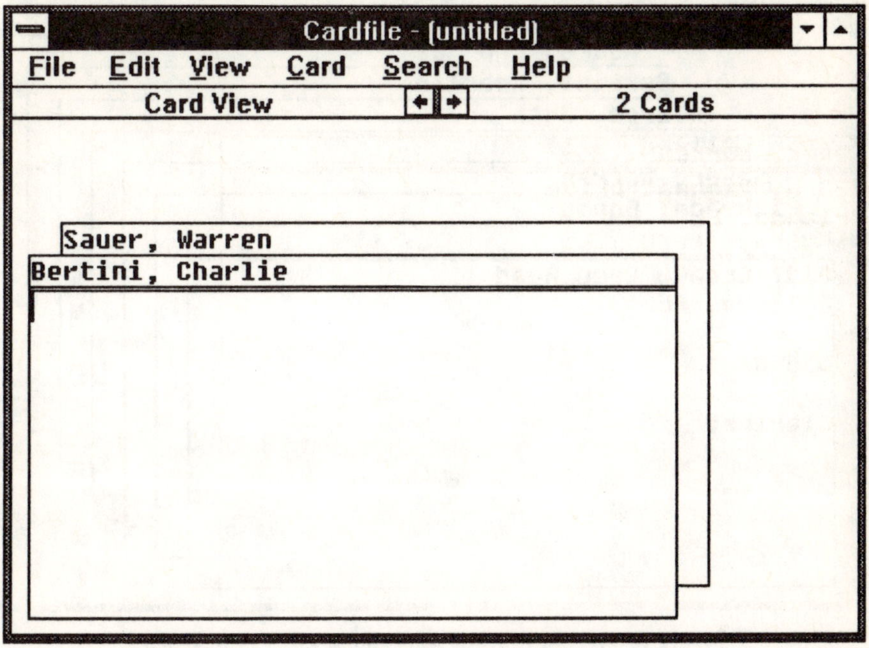

Figure 10-26. A Name Entered into the Add Dialogue Box.

Enter an address into the information area of the second card. Add several more cards to the file by using the Add... command. When you are done adding cards, the Cardfile application window will look like Figure 10-27.

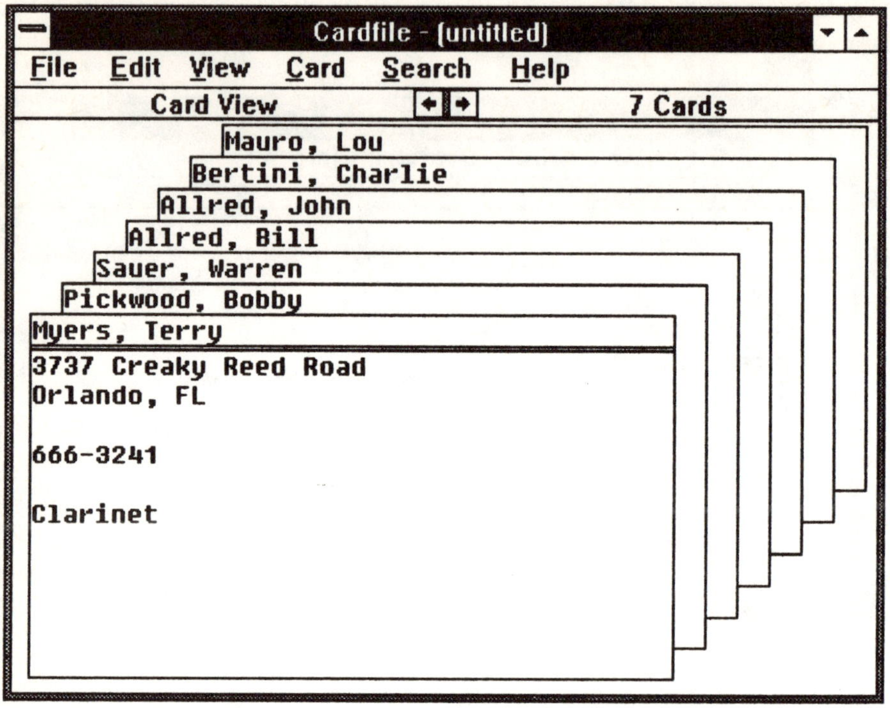

Figure 10-27. The Cardfile Application with Cards Added.

The file in Figure 10-27 has only seven cards in it. In actual use, a Cardfile data base will grow much larger, and you will not be able to see all the cards in the stack as you can now. You can expand the size of the application window to see more of the cards, but most data bases will be too big to fit into the window. To view other cards you must move around in the data base.

Moving around in a Cardfile Data Base

Cardfile keeps cards sorted by the index line. The card at the front of the stack is always the current one. You can use the mouse to select a card that is in view by clicking its index line. When you do this, the card comes to the front of the stack. You can click on the two arrows that are in the line just below the menu bar to move back and forward one card.

Table 10-6 shows the keystrokes for moving around in a Cardfile data base.

Table 10-6. Cardfile Keys.

Key	Function
PgUp/PgDn	Previous/next card
Ctrl+Home/End	First/last card in the file
Ctrl+letter	Card with index starting with letter

Later in this chapter you will learn to search a Cardfile data base for cards that match specified text strings.

Editing

You can use most of the standard editing techniques—including copying, cutting, pasting, and deleting text—in the Cardfile information area. You mark text by dragging the mouse cursor across the text or by holding the Shift key down while you move the keyboard cursor with the arrow keys.

Deleting Text

To delete a marked block of text from the information area, press the Del key.

Undo

The Undo command on the Edit menu undoes the most recently deleted block.

Restore

The Restore command on the edit menu restores any changes you have made to the current card since you moved it to the top of the stack. Restore does not restore changes made prior to the last save of the file, however.

Cutting, Copying, and Pasting Text

The Edit menu's Cut, Copy, and Paste commands work just as they do in other applications. You can cut or copy a marked block of text in the information area to the Clipboard, and you can Paste text from the Clipboard to the information area.

Saving the Data Base

The File menu has the usual New, Open..., Save, and Save As... commands. These commands use the default file name extension .CRD for a Cardfile data base. For these exercises, save the data base with the name ALLSTARS.

The List View

The View menu allows you to switch between the Card View, which is the default, and the List View, which lists the cards by their index line. Figure 10-28 shows the Cardfile list view.

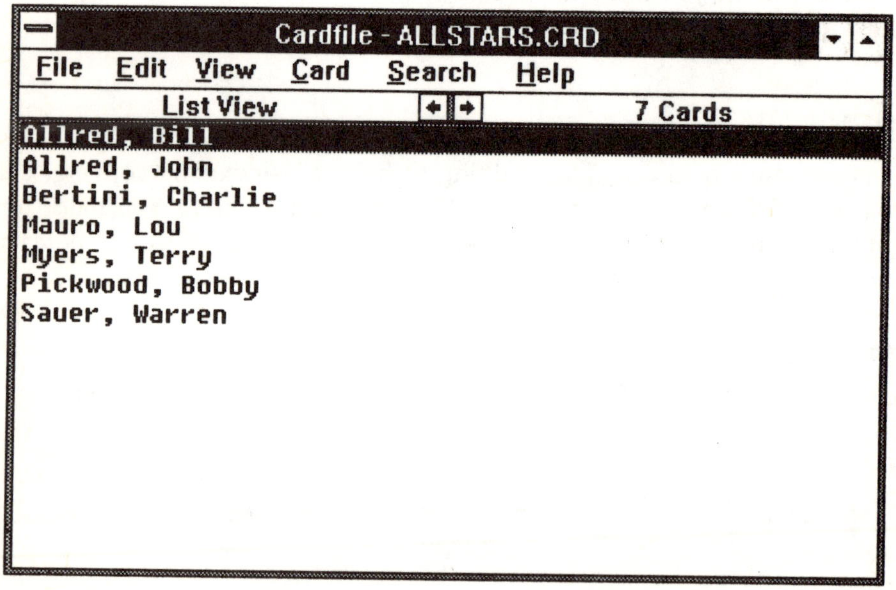

Figure 10-28. The Cardfile List View.

The list view allows you to see more of the cards in the stack. It always displays the cards in sequence, with the first card in the file at the top of the list. You can move the highlight bar to a card either by using the arrow keys or by clicking the highlight bar. If the number of cards exceeds the height of the window's work space, the window will have a vertical scroll bar. If you double click an entry, Cardfile will open the Index dialogue box for you to change the index value. You saw the Index dialogue box in Figure 10-23.

If you put the highlight bar on an entry in the list and change to Card view, the card for the highlighted entry will be at the top of the stack.

Searching

If you are in the Card View, you can search the Cardfile data base for a match on a text string by using the Find... command on the Search menu. Figure 10-29 shows the Find dialogue box that appears when you select this command.

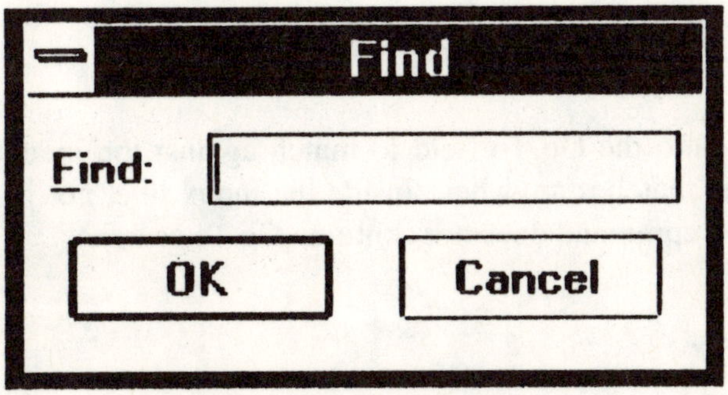

Figure 10-29. The Find Dialogue Box.

Enter the text for which you want to search in the Find field and select OK. When Cardfile finds a match on the text, it brings the matching card to the top of the stack and highlights the matching text. The search matches a string regardless of upper/lower case and does not include the index line in the search. You can use the Find Next command on the Search menu to continue the search to the next matching card.

To search for matches on the index line, use the Go To... command on the Search menu. The Go To... command works in both the Card View and the List View. Figure 10-30 shows the Go To dialogue box.

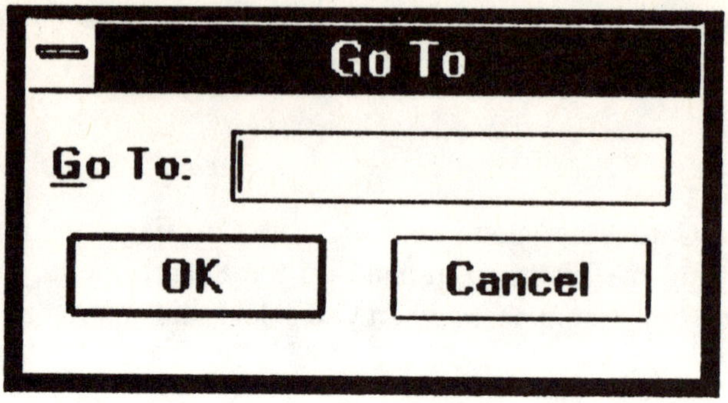

Figure 10-30. The Go To Dialogue Box.

Enter some text into the Go To field to match against the index lines in the cards. The search string matches anywhere inside the index line, not just at the beginning, but the Find Next command does not continue Go To searches.

Pictures

The Picture toggle command on the Edit menu allows you to paste a picture from the Clipboard to the card. Figure 10-31 shows one use for this feature.

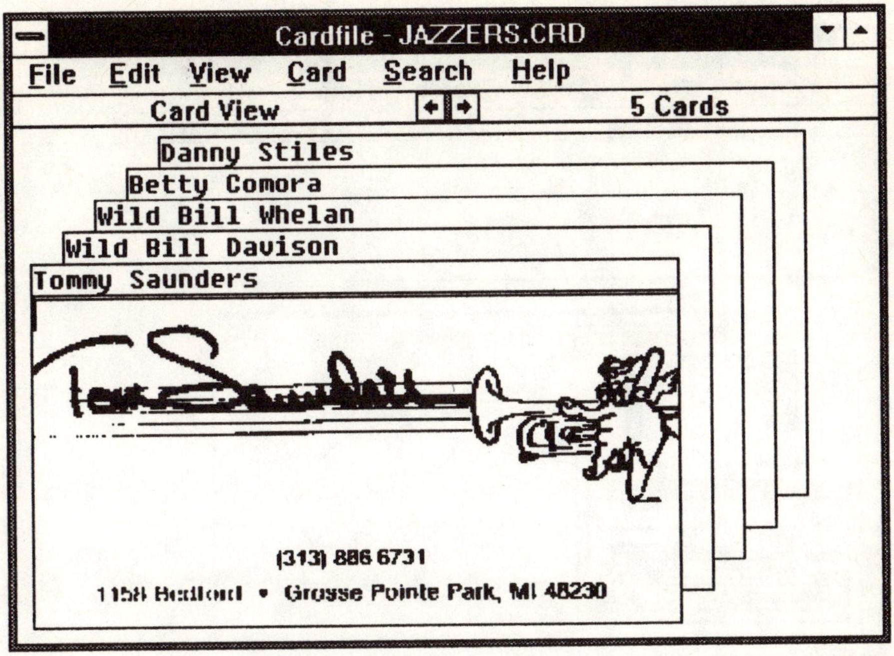

Figure 10-31. Using the Picture Command: the JAZZERS.CRD Data Base.

The JAZZERS.CRD data base in Figure 10-31 is made up of business cards that were scanned into Windows, copied to the Clipboard, and pasted into the Cardfile data base. You need a scanner device and Windows-compatible scanning software for such an application.

Pasting Pictures

You can use Cardfile to store clip art that you design with Paintbrush, scan into Windows, or acquire as .PCX files from other sources. Each item of clip art can have its own card. When you want to use a piece of clip art in a design, copy the picture from the Cardfile data base to the Clipboard and paste it into your artwork.

To paste a picture into a card, select the Picture toggle command on the Edit menu. The cursor changes to a small rectangle to indicate that Cardfile is in picture mode. Paste the picture into the card and use the mouse or the arrow keys to move it to where you want it. Figure 10-32 shows a card with a Paintbrush clip art picture pasted onto it.

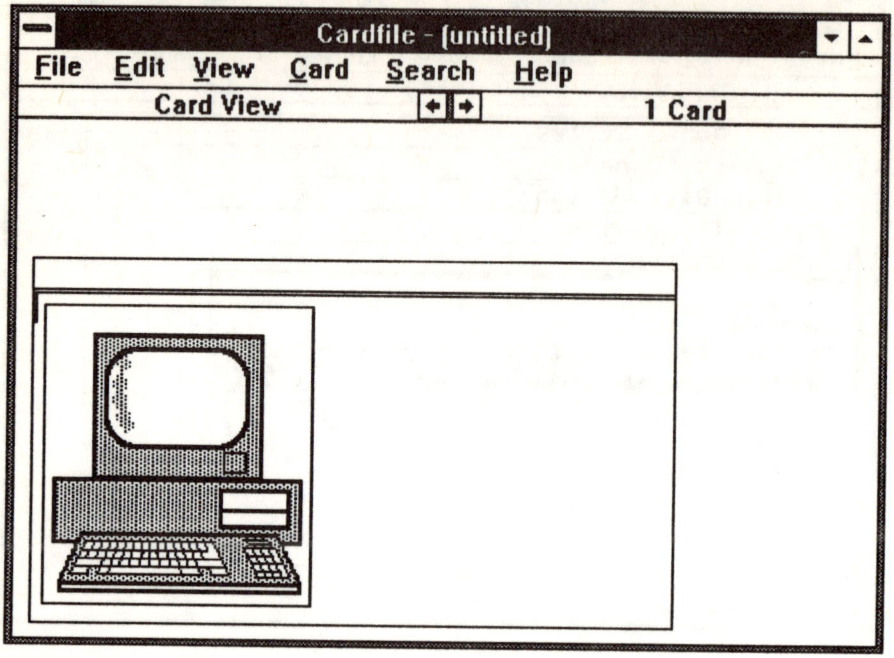

Figure 10-32. A Card with a Picture.

Mixing Text and Graphics

You can mix text and graphics in a Cardfile card. After you have pasted the picture onto the card, move the picture to a part of the card where you will not be entering text. Put the card back into text mode by selecting the Text command on the Edit menu. Then you can type any text you like. If you type over the picture, the text and picture intermingle, but they do not interfere with one another. Figure 10-33 shows some text added to the card that already has a clip art picture.

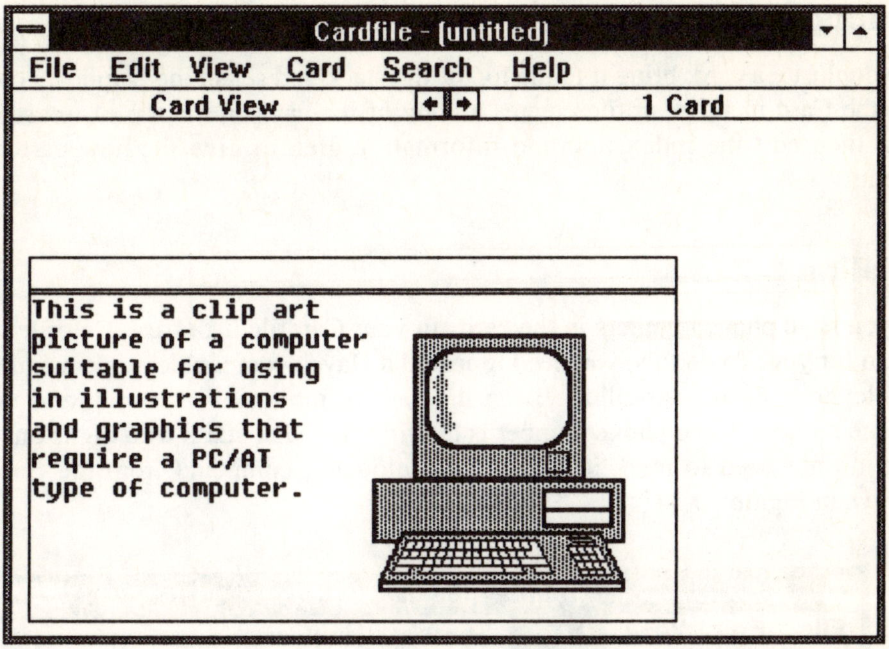

Figure 10-33. Text Added to a Card with a Picture.

Cutting and Copying Pictures

As long as a card is in picture mode, you can cut or copy its picture to the Clipboard. To put the card into picture mode, select the Picture command on the Edit menu.

Picture Sizes

A card can record a picture that is much bigger than the visible area of the card. If Cardfile is in picture mode, you can drag the picture around inside the card as well as copy it to the Clipboard.

Deleting a Card

To delete a card, bring it to the top of the stack and select the Delete command on the Card menu.

Duplicating a Card

To duplicate a card, bring it to the top of the stack and select the Duplicate command on the Card menu. Cardfile creates a copy of the card on the top of the stack. You can then edit the index line and information area to give the new card its own identity.

Dialing

If you have phone numbers in the cards in your Cardfile data base, Cardfile will dial them for you. To do this, you need to install a Hayes-compatible modem and connect a telephone to the same line. Bring the card to the top of the stack and mark the phone number. If the phone number is the first field that starts with digits on the card you do not need to mark it. Select the Autodial... command from the Card menu shown in Figure 10-34.

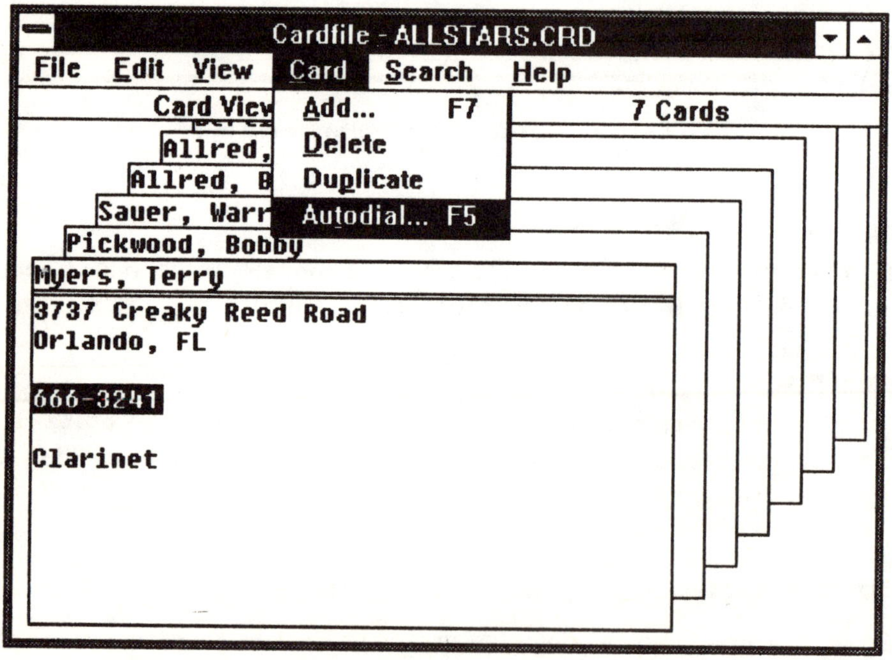

Figure 10-34. The Card Menu.

You will see the Autodial dialogue box shown in Figure 10-35.

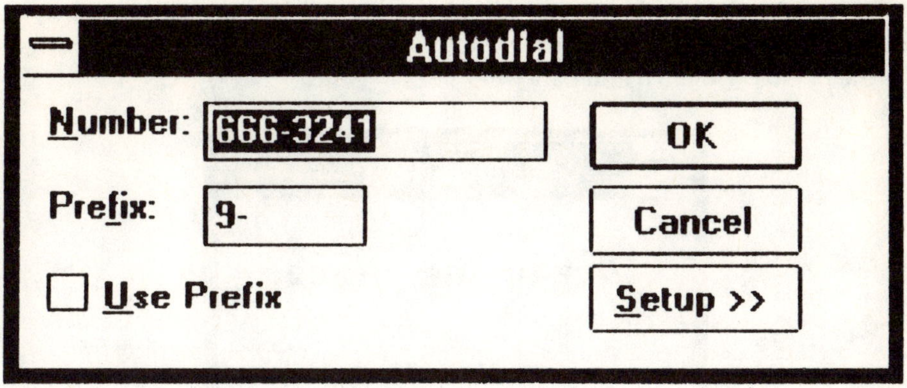

Figure 10-35. The Autodial Dialogue Box.

You can enter a dialing prefix if your telephone requires one. In order for Cardfile to dial the prefix, you must select the Use Prefix check box. Select the Setup >> command button to see the Setup part of the Autodial dialogue box shown in Figure 10-36.

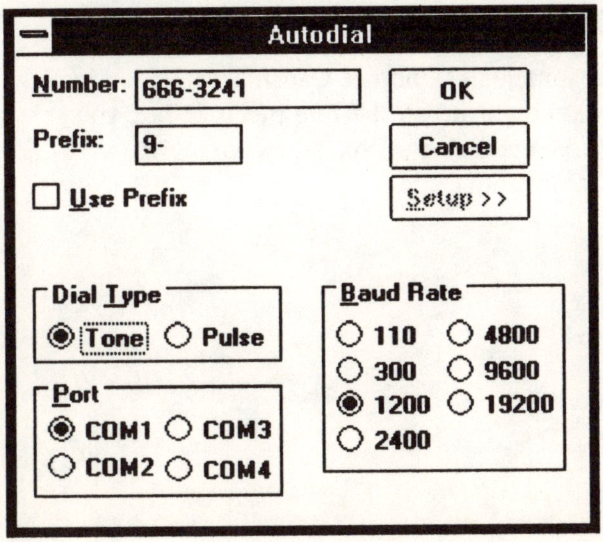

Figure 10-36. The Setup Portion of the Autodial Dialogue Box.

The settings in this dialogue box should correspond to your Control Panel setup for the communications port. Select the Pulse option button if you do not have touch tone dialing.

When you are ready to dial, select OK. Cardfile dials the number and displays the message shown in Figure 10-37. Pick up the phone and select OK so you are ready when the person you are calling answers.

Figure 10-37. Cardfile Dialing a Phone Number.

Merging Cardfile Data Bases

You can merge the contents of another Cardfile data base into the current one by selecting the Merge... command on the File menu. When you select this command, you will see the File Merge dialogue box, as shown in Figure 10-38.

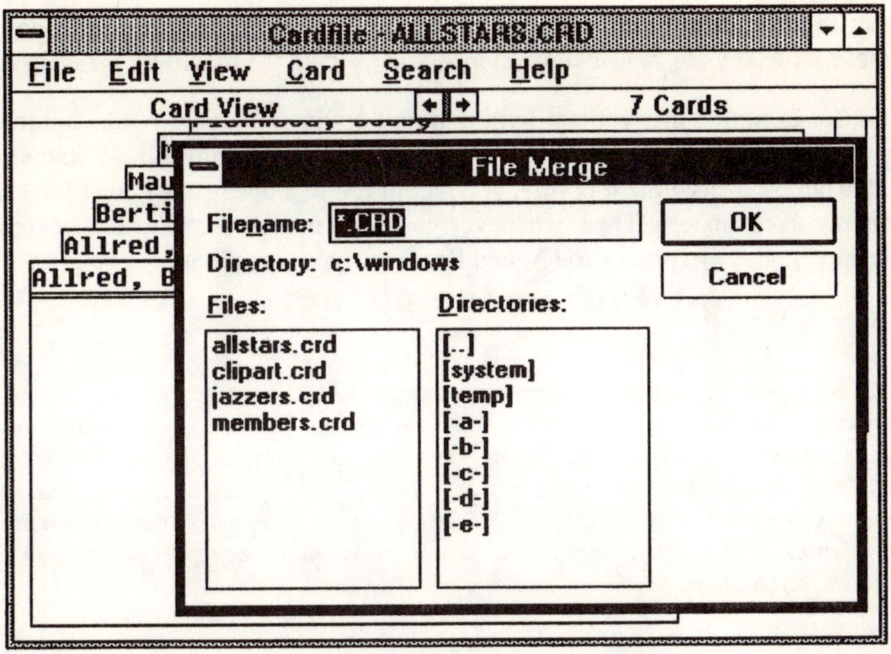

Figure 10-38. The File Merge Dialogue Box.

Select a file to merge from the list of files in the File Merge dialogue box. Observe that the dialogue box lists the current file a long with the others—you are permitted to merge a file into itself.

Printing

Cardfile has the usual Print, Page Setup..., and Printer Setup... commands on the File menu. The Print command prints the card at the top of the stack. To print the entire file of cards, select the Print All command.

THE RECORDER ACCESSORY

Recorder is a program that records user-input macros. If you have ever used a DOS keyboard macro enhancer program such as Superkey, you will already understand what Recorder can do for you. If not, some introduction is necessary.

Recorder records macros—sequences of keystrokes and mouse actions. When you want those same keys or mouse movements, you execute the macro by pressing a key.

Suppose, for example, that you are writing a report with Windows Write, and that the report repeats the phrase "Ackermann Scholarship Fund" many times. Rather than typing the phrase every time it occurs, you record it into a macro, assigning the Ctrl+A shortcut key to the macro. Then, whenever you want to type the phrase, "Ackermann Scholarship Fund," you press Ctrl+A, and Recorder types the phrase for you.

***

YOU COULD MARK THE FIRST INSTANCE OF A FREQUENTLY-USED PHRASE, COPY IT TO THE CLIPBOARD, AND THEN PASTE IT EVERY TIME YOU NEEDED IT, BUT THIS APPROACH HAS THREE LIMITATIONS. FIRST, YOU COULD HAVE ONLY ONE MACRO. SECOND, YOU COULD NOT USE THE CLIPBOARD FOR ANYTHING ELSE. THIRD, THE CLIPBOARD CAN ONLY RECORD TEXT KEYSTROKES. IF YOUR KEYSTROKE MACRO INVOLVED KEYBOARD CURSOR MOVEMENT, ALT+ KEYS, CTRL+ KEYS, MENU SELECTIONS, OR MOUSE MOVEMENTS, THE CLIPBOARD APPROACH WOULD NOT WORK.

***

Recorder can record macros that repeat themselves. You can also build running demonstrations or tutorials by recording macros.

Recorder is not however, an interactive macro language such as you will find in some spreadsheet and data base programs. Recorder macros are simple playbacks of the input actions that you made while Recorder was recording.

Recording a Macro

You will begin by recording a simple keyboard substitution to use in Notepad. You can build similar macros for other Windows word processing applications such as Write and Word for Windows.

First you prepare to record the macro. You must be at the place in an application where you are going to use the macro. If you want Recorder to type the name of your company, for example, you must be where you can type it in order to record it.

In this example, you run the Notepad and have it active and waiting for keystrokes. Set the Word Wrap toggle command on in Notepad's Edit menu. You want a macro to type your company name because that text appears frequently in your correspondence.

Running Recorder

You run Recorder to record a macro, load a macro file, and play back macros. Once your macros are recorded and ready to run, you can run Recorder as a minimized icon to keep it out of the way of your other applications. Initially, however, you must start it up to begin recording. Figure 10-39 shows the Recorder application window running on top of the now inactive Notepad window.

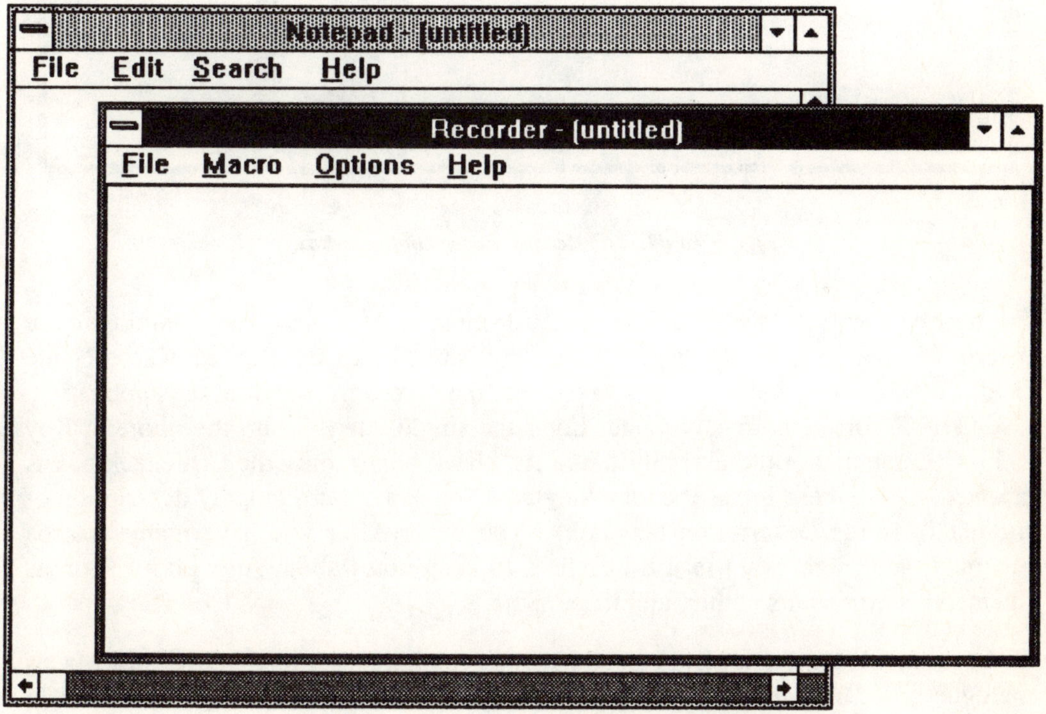

Figure 10-39. The Recorder Application Window.

To set up the macro, select Record on the Macro menu. You will see the Record Macro dialogue box shown in Figure 10-40.

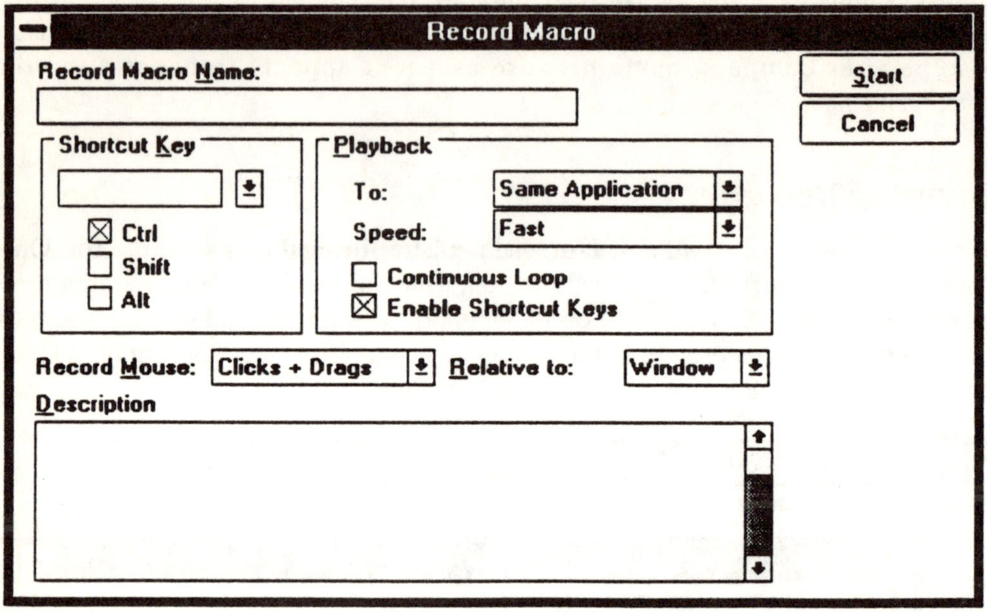

Figure 10-40. The Record Macro Dialogue Box.

For now, you will use the default settings for most of the fields. You should give the macro a name, so enter the value "Company Name" into the Record Macro Name field. You also need a shortcut key to execute the macro from within the application. Use Ctrl+C. for the company name. Enter the single letter C into the Shortcut Key field. Observe that of the Ctrl, Shift, and Alt check boxes, only the Ctrl check box is selected. Leave these boxes the way they are. You can enter a lengthy description of the macro in the Description text box if you wish. After you have many macros recorded, you might want to use this field to keep notes about such information as the macro's origins, its author, and its purpose.

To begin recording the macro, select the Start command button. The Record Macro dialogue box disappears, Recorder minimizes itself to an icon, and you are back in Notepad, ready to type. Observe that the Recorder icon is flashing—this tells you that you are recording a macro. Every keystroke and mouse click that you enter into your application will be recorded for playback.

Enter your company's name. For this example use "Beiderbecke Brassworks." When you are done, press Ctrl+Break or click on the blinking Recorder icon. You see the Recorder dialogue box shown in Figure 10-41.

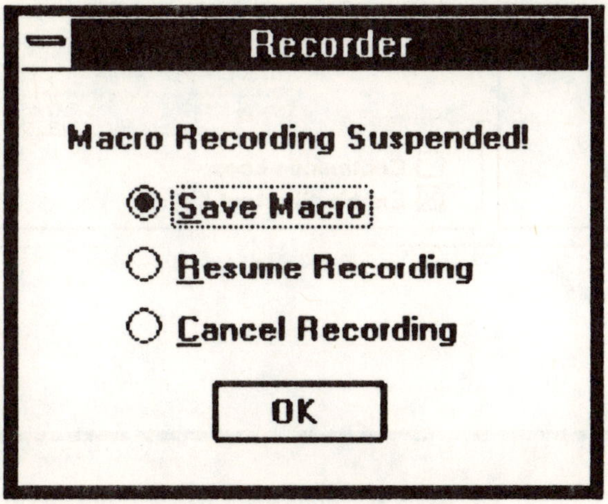

Figure 10-41. The Recorder Dialogue Box.

Select the Save Macro option button and then select OK. The macro is now recorded in Recorder, and you are back in Notepad. To verify that the macro is recorded, activate Recorder. Its work space now contains one macro, as shown in Figure 10-42.

The macro description in the Recorder work space does not describe the keystrokes of the macro, it only lists its shortcut key and name.

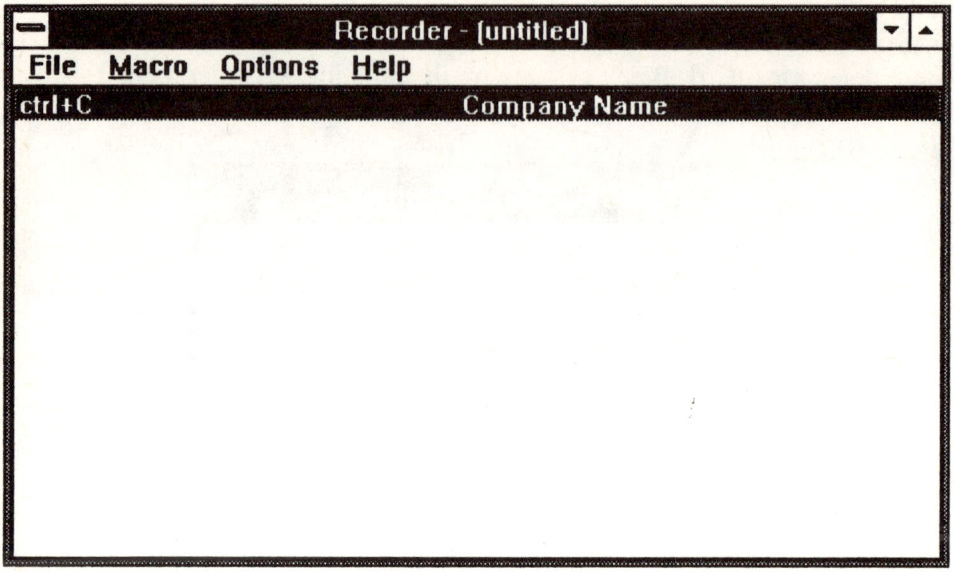

Figure 10-42. The Recorder Application Window with one Macro.

Minimize Recorder to an icon again. To test your new macro, press the Ctrl+C shortcut key—"Beiderbecke Brassworks" should be typed for you. After you are confident that the macro is working correctly, delete the test text from the Notepad work space and type a memo that uses the macro.

Nested Macros

You can call an existing macro while you are recording another. To enable this feature, you must turn on the Enable Shortcut Keys check box in the Playback field of the Record Macro dialogue box. This check box is usually on by default.

Another frequently-used keyboard sequence is the name and address of your company. Using the procedure you just learned, start with an empty Notepad and begin recording a macro named "Company Name and Address," with Ctrl+A as its shortcut key. When Recorder returns to Notepad and begins recording, press Ctrl+C as the first key. Then press the Enter key and type the company address. Figure 10-43 shows the Notepad with the text typed by Recorder when you pressed Ctrl+C (the company name) as well as the text that you added for the new macro (the company address).

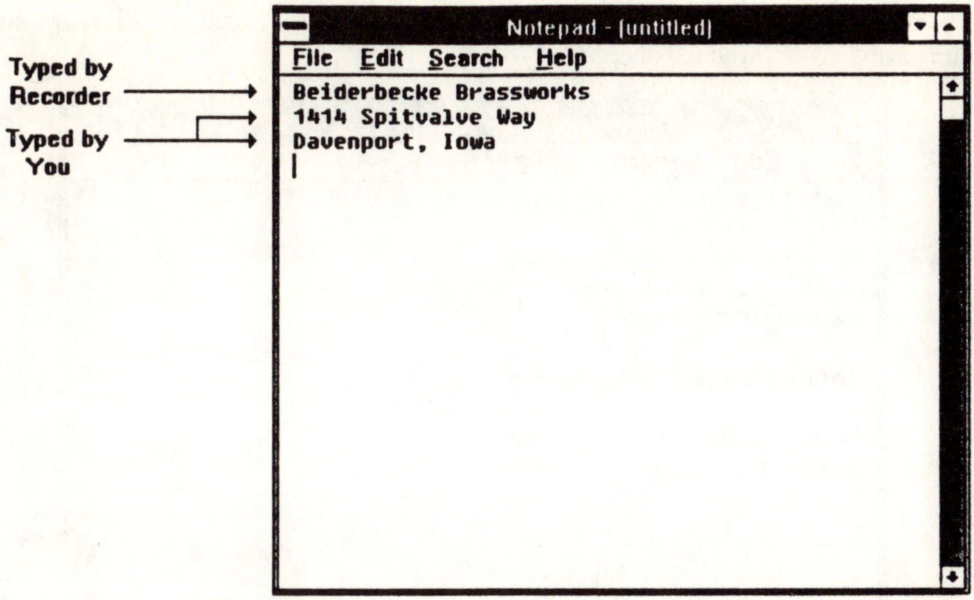

Figure 10-43. The Notepad with Text Typed by the Recorder.

After you have typed in the address, save the macro. If you activate the Recorder window again, you will see that the new macro is added to the list. Return to Notepad, clear the work space, and press Ctrl+A to see your nested macro execute.

Building Document Templates with Recorder

Perhaps you send a lot of memos in your work, and they all have the same format. You would like to automate the preparation of that format. You can use Recorder to build document templates for this purpose.

To build a template for interoffice memoranda, start with an empty Notepad and begin recording a macro named "Memo." Use Ctrl+M for the shortcut key. For the first keystroke in the macro, press the F5 key. The F5 key is Notepad's shortcut for its Time/Date command on the Notepad Edit menu—pressing it inserts the current date into the memo template. Press the Enter key twice to go down two lines and then press Ctrl+A to insert your company's name and address. Type "Interoffice Memorandum," then press the Enter key twice. Then type "From:" and your name. Press Enter and type "To:." Press Enter and type "Re:." Then use the up arrow key to move the cursor up to the To: line, and space over just under your name. Click the Recorder icon or press Ctrl+Break to interrupt recording, and save the macro. Figure 10-44 shows the entire macro as displayed in Notepad.

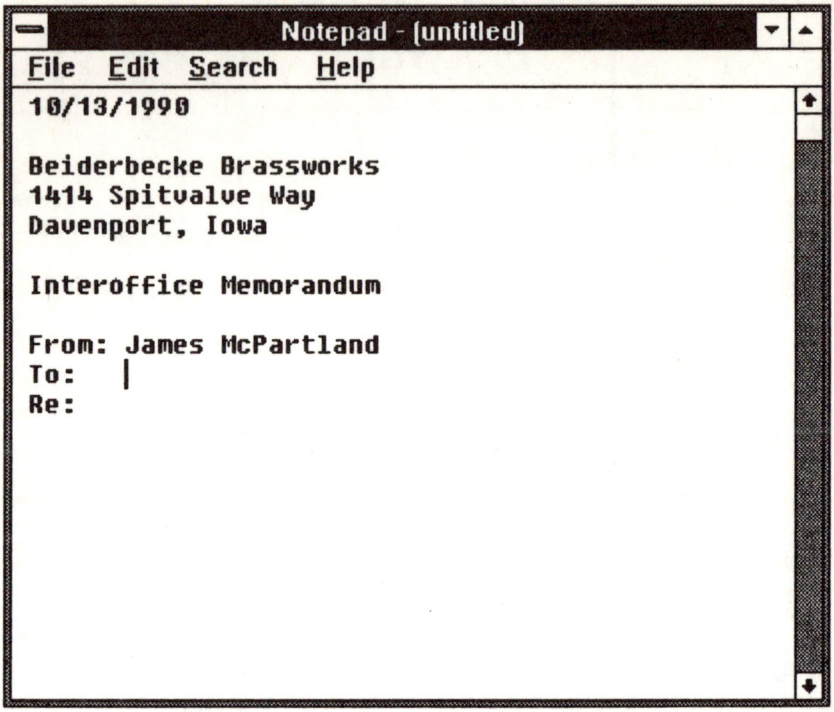

Figure 10-44. Notepad Displaying a Macro.

Whenever you need to send a memo, press Ctrl+M to display the memo template described by this macro. Recorder will write the current date at the top of the page, insert your name, and leave the cursor at the point where you would begin typing the name of the addressee.

You might substitute another macro for your name instead of having the Memo macro type it explicitly. Doing this enables you to share the Memo macro with other Windows users who want to use your Memo template with their own Name macros.

Command Macros

Besides recording text keystrokes, Recorder can record commands. Among the deficiencies of Notepad and Write, in my opinion, are the absence of single keystroke commands to delete a word and a line of text, closing up the remaining text. To delete a word, you must use the keyboard or mouse to mark the word you want to delete and then press the Del key or select the Delete key on the Edit menu. To delete a line, you can use a similar approach or you can press Home, Ctrl+Del to delete from the cursor to the end of the line, and Del to delete the resulting blank line. Both procedures require multiple keystrokes and mouse actions to do a common, routine task.

You can fill this void with two macros: the Alt+Del macro, to delete a word, and the Shift+Del macro, to delete a line. Begin with the nonsense memo shown in Figure 10-45.

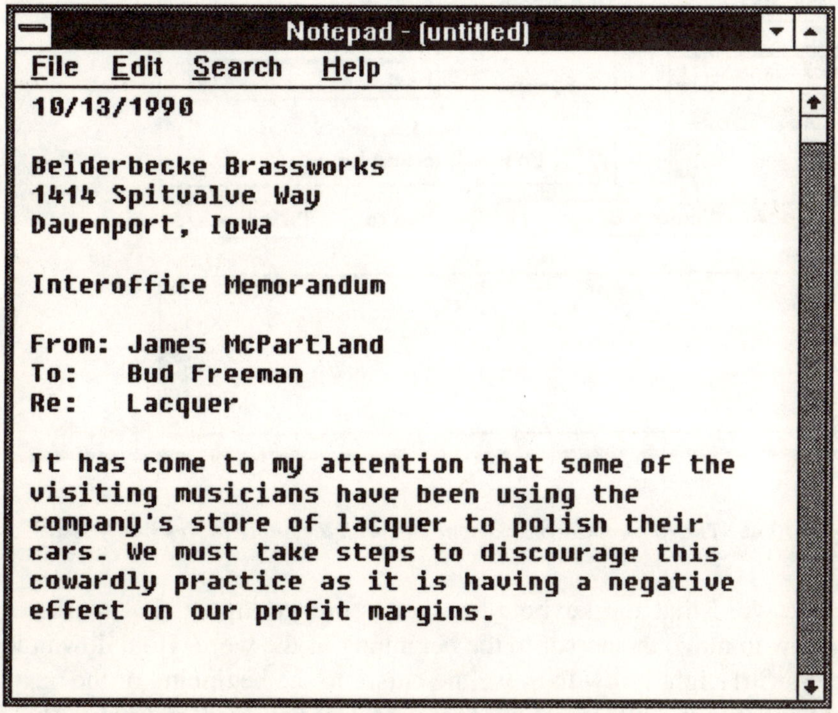

Figure 10-45. A Nonsense Memo.

Recording a Delete Word Macro

Position the keyboard cursor on a word and begin to record a macro called "Delete Word" that uses the Alt+Del shortcut key. The differences here are that you are using Alt instead of Ctrl and the Del key instead of a letter. Figure 10-46 shows the Record

Macro dialogue box with the Shortcut Key drop-down list box selected. This list has all the keys that you can select as shortcut keys. The Alt check box, hidden now by the drop-down list, is selected and the Ctrl and Shift check boxes are not. Select the Start command button. Recorder returns you to the memo in Notepad and begins recording.

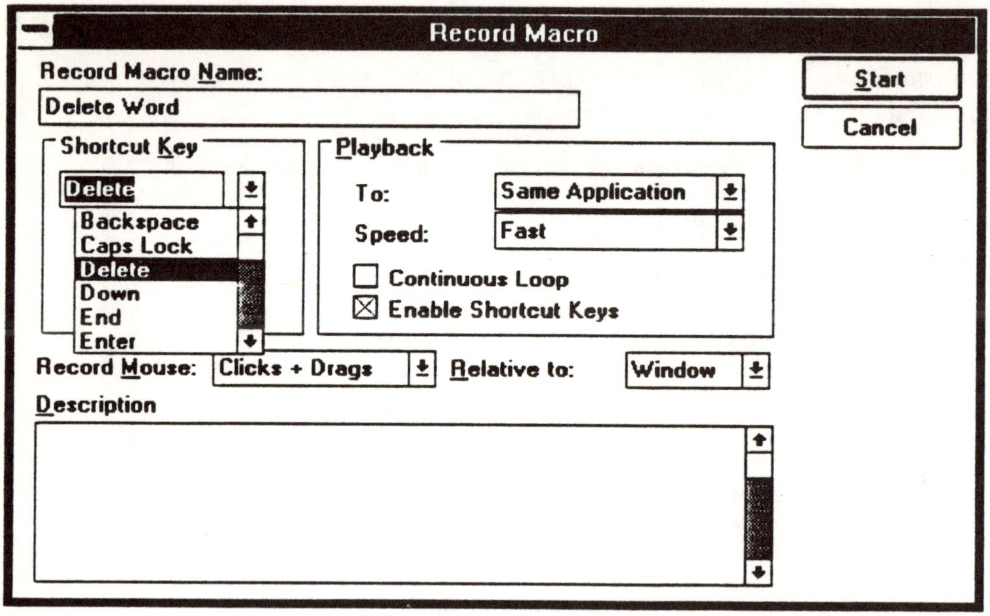

Figure 10-46. The Record Macro Dialogue Box with the Shortcut Key Box Selected.

To delete the word that the keyboard cursor is on, you must first mark it. Press Ctrl+left arrow to move the cursor to the beginning of the word. Hold down the Shift key and press Ctrl+right arrow to move the cursor to the beginning of the next word, marking all the text in between. Now press the Del key to delete the word. All of these keystrokes are being recorded into your Delete Word macro. Select the Recorder icon and save the macro.

Recording a Delete Line Macro

To record the Delete Line macro, repeat the steps you used for recording a Delete Word macro, with these differences. Use Shift+Del as the shortcut key. In Notepad,

Shift+Del normally does the same thing that the backspace key does, so you can reuse it without giving up a feature. After you have begun recording, delete the line by pressing the Home key, then the Ctrl+Del key, then the Del key. Click the Recorder icon or press Ctrl+Break and save the macro.

You now have macros to delete words and lines from within Notepad.

Other Possible Macros

You can use the techniques you have just learned to add new commands to virtually any application, thereby combining many of the application's existing commands into one. For example, to move a marked block from one location to another in Notepad or Write, you cut it to the Clipboard and paste it to where the cursor is positioned. That operation could be a Move Block macro. Copying a block would use the Clipboard's copy operation instead of its cut operation.

Many word processors use document layout templates that describe the formats of different documents or sections within a document. You can write Recorder macros to set up such templates within Write by adjusting margins and indents to defined settings at the touch of a key.

The possibilities for macros that enhance the use of applications is limited only by your imagination.

On-Line Help

With all these macros in place, what about on-line help for the user? How does one remember all the keystrokes? Recorder is itself your on-line help facility for recorded macros. Select the recorder icon, and you get a list of all the macros' shortcut keys and names—in the Recorder application window. What's more, the Recorder application window acts as a menu. Double click an entry, and the macro runs.

Saving Macro Files

With this much work invested, you will want to save the macros in a file for later retrieval. The Recorder's File menu has the usual New, Open..., Save, and Save As... commands. The default file name extension for Recorder macro files is .REC.

Merging Macros

You can merge the macros of one .REC file into the set of macros that are currently in memory. For example, perhaps you want the macros for deleting words and lines to be available for Windows Write as well. You might have several Write .REC files that support the different kinds of documents you use. If you have the Notepad's macros saved in a file named MEMO.REC, for example, you can merge them into your Write macros and then save your Write macro files. By doing this you only have to record a generic set of macros once.

You merge macros by selecting the Merge... command on the File menu. The File Merge dialogue box is similar to the one shown in Figure 10-38—you learned about it in relation to Cardfile. If you merge macros with shortcut keys that conflict with those that are already in memory, Recorder will display the warning message shown in Figure 10-47. You will need to modify the properties of the new macros in order to assign them new shortcut keys.

Figure 10-47. A Recorder Warning Message.

Modifying a Macro's Properties

The Properties... command on the Recorder's Macro menu displays the Macro Properties dialogue box shown in Figure 10-48.

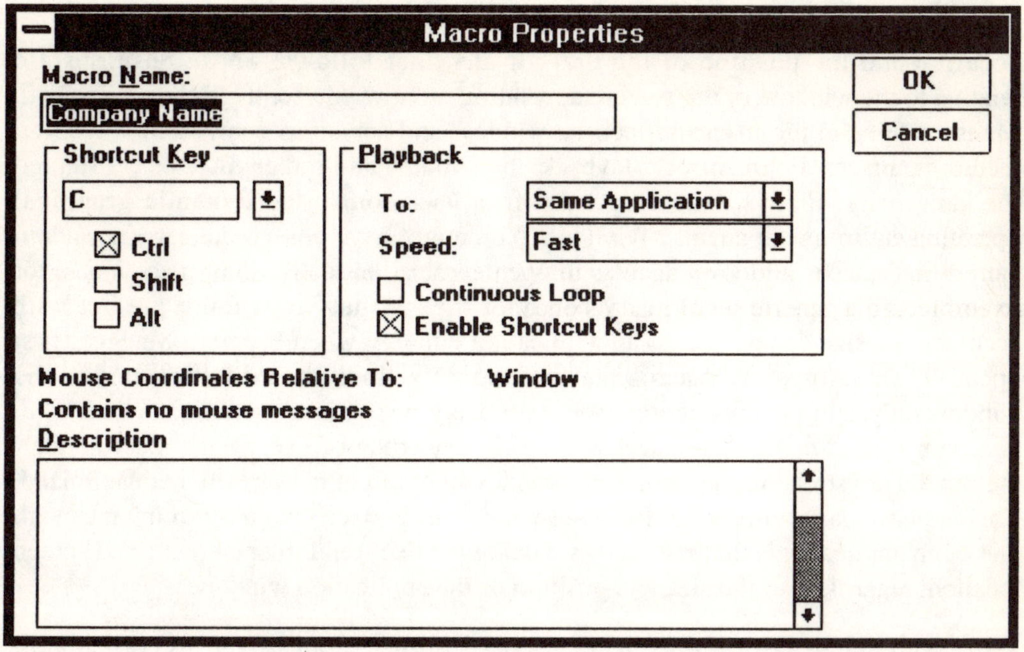

Figure 10-48. The Macro Properties Dialogue Box.

The Macro Properties dialogue box displays the properties of the highlighted macro in the Recorder work space. It has most of the same information as the Record Macro dialogue box. You can modify the properties of a macro, such as its name and shortcut key, but you cannot modify the keystrokes or mouse actions that the macro records. To modify a macro's keystrokes and mouse actions you must delete the macro and record it again from the beginning.

Deleting a Macro

After prompting you to confirm the action, the Delete command on the Recorder's Macro menu deletes the macro that is highlighted in the Recorder work space.

The Macro and the Mouse

Although Recorder will record mouse actions into a macro, mouse actions do not integrate well. The Record Macro dialogue box that you saw in Figure 10-40 allows you to specify in the Record Mouse field that you will record Clicks + Drags, Everything, or Ignore Mouse.

When you record clicks and drags, Recorder records the position where the click occurred and the position of the drag, if any, that follows. Those positions are relative to the window or the screen, depending on how you set the Relative To field. Mouse actions in the macro reflect the window and screen as configured when you record the macro. For a correct playback, the window and screen must be configured the same way; that is expecting a lot in a user-controlled dynamic graphical operating environment such as Windows. You might have observed a certain random pattern in the way Windows decides to open application windows or place icons, for example. This apparent arbitrary behavior means that you cannot predict with accuracy the size or position of an application window when Program Manager first opens it. Therefore, any macros that use mouse actions should be oriented to the window only, and the application should probably be run in a maximized window. In fact, you should make Alt+spacebar the first keystroke of every such macro and X the second keystroke to maximize any window that might not already be maximized. This is particularly important if a mouse action in a macro is going to interact with one of an application's dialogue boxes. Dialogue boxes tend to open in a fixed screen location, regardless of the size and position of the application window.

When you select Everything in the Record Mouse field of the Record Macro dialogue box, every movement of the mouse goes into the macro. If you use this option, do not try to end the recording session by clicking the Recorder icon. The mouse movement and click that you use to end the session will become part of the session. Use the Ctrl-Break key instead.

If a macro has mouse actions, the Macro Properties dialogue box, shown in Figure 10-48, displays the resolution of the video screen where you recorded the macro. Instead of saying, "Contains no mouse messages," the line just above the Description field will say something like, "Recorded on (compatible) 640 by 480 display." A macro that uses the mouse does not work properly if you run it on a system with a screen resolution that is different from the one where you recorded the macro.

In normal practice, using the mouse in a macro is replete with problems, often not worth the bother, and seldom necessary. Anything you can do with the mouse, you can do with the keyboard. Even if you prefer using the mouse in your routine operations, you should use the keyboard equivalent operations when you are recording macros.

One application for using the mouse in macros however, is in the preparation of demonstrations or computer-assisted presentations. In such uses, the video effects are essential to the message and the operating environment is tightly controlled, so it is worth working around the inherent mouse-in-macro problems to gain the advantages of the visual effects.

Global vs Application-Specific Macros

The To: drop-down list box in the Playback field of the Record Macro and Macro Properties dialogue boxes allows you to choose between Same Application and Any Application. If you choose Same Application, the macro will run only when the application in which you recorded it is active. If you choose Any Application, the macro will run at any time.

Real Time vs Fast Macros

The Speed: drop-down list box in the Playback field of the Record Macro and Macro Properties dialogue boxes allows you to choose between Fast and Recorded Speed. The Fast setting plays the macro back as fast as it can. The Recorded Speed setting plays the macro back at the same speed as you recorded it; if you are a slow typist, the macro will be slow. This option is useful when you are developing macros for demonstrations.

Continuous Loop Macros

If you select the Continuous Loop check box in the Record Macro and Macro Properties dialogue boxes, the macro repeats itself indefinitely until you press the Ctrl-Break key. This feature is useful for running non-stop demonstrations.

Ctrl+Break Interruption

You can stop running a macro by pressing the Ctrl+Break key. This feature allows you to stop a continuous-loop macro or to terminate a particularly long-running macro after you realize that you did not mean to execute it.

You can suppress the Ctrl-Break interruption of the macro by turning off the Control+Break Checking toggle command on the Options menu. When you do this, the macro repeats until you reset the computer. This measure prevents someone else from stopping an ongoing demonstration.

Suppressing Shortcut Keys

Turning off the Shortcut Keys toggle command on the Recorder Options menu allows you to prevent the shortcut keys from running the macros. You would turn this option off if you had global macros and were running an application that used some of the same shortcut keys for itself. By default, the command toggle is on.

When shortcut keys are suppressed, you can still run the macros from the Recorder application itself, as described next.

Running a Macro from Recorder

You can activate the Recorder application window and run any macro by double clicking its entry in the work space list or by moving the highlight bar to it and selecting the Run command on the Macro menu. Recorder deactivates itself, returns to the current application, and runs the macro.

Minimize on Use

The Minimize on Use command toggle on the Options menu is normally on. It tells Recorder to minimize itself to an icon when you begin recording a macro and when you run a macro from within Recorder itself. You can turn this toggle off to tell Recorder to become an inactive window rather than an icon. This feature allows you to have easier access to Recorder while you are recording and testing macros.

Setting Defaults

Recorder maintains a number of defaults with respect to how it records macros. You can change the values of these defaults by selecting the Preferences... command on the Options menu. When you select this command, you see the Default Preferences dialogue box shown in Figure 10-49.

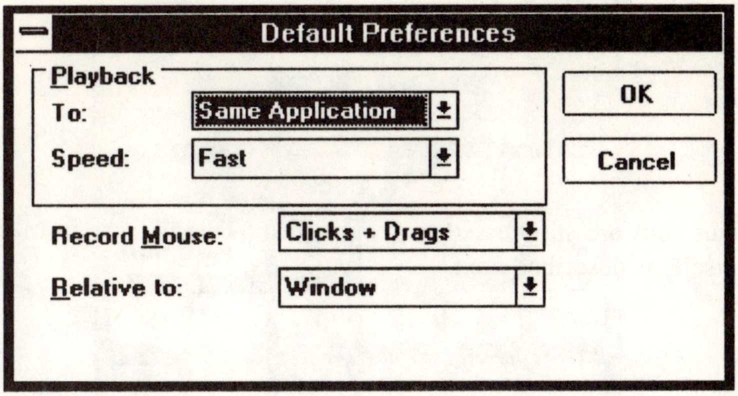

Figure 10-49. The Default Preferences Dialogue Box.

You can change the default values for running macros in the same or all applications; running them fast or at recorded speed; recording mouse actions or not, and, if so, which ones; and running macros relative to the window or the screen.

THE CALCULATOR ACCESSORY

Calculator is a small accessory application. You can run it, minimize it as an icon, and have it nearby on your desktop for whenever you need it. There are two calculators built into the application: the Standard Calculator and the Scientific Calculator.

The Standard Calculator

Figure 10-50 shows the standard calculator. It resembles the typical pocket calculator, with the usual four functions: square root, percent, reciprocal, and memory.

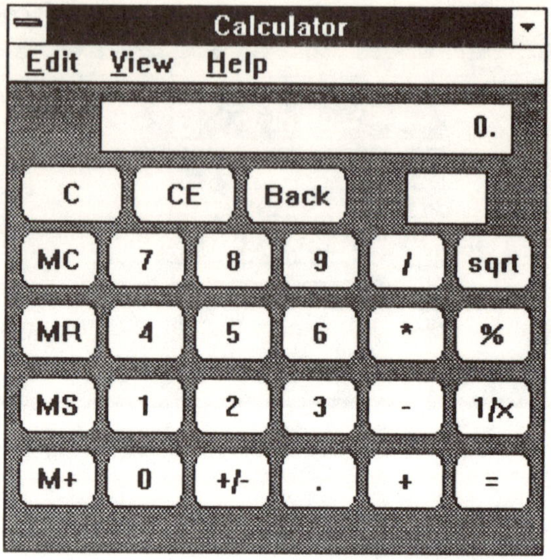

Figure 10-50. The Standard Calculator.

Entering Numbers

You enter numbers into the Calculator by clicking its digit command buttons or by typing the numbers in on your keyboard. Turn on Num Lock on your keyboard and use the numeric keypad for the most familiar way to enter numbers.

Use the . (period) function button or key to begin entering digits to the right of the decimal place. The Back command button and the keyboard's backspace key remove the last digit you entered. The CE (Clear Entry) command button and the keyboard's Del key clear the current entry from the Calculator's display without modifying the current calculation. The C (Clear) command button and the keyboard's Esc key zero out the Calculator completely.

Calculating

The +, -, *, / arithmetic operators and the = operator work just like they do on any standard calculator. The Enter key and the = key on the keyboard will both do what the = command button does. The sqrt command button and the @ key compute the square root of the number in the display. The 1/x command button and the r key compute the reciprocal of the number in the display. The +/- command button and the F9 key change the sign of the number in the display.

Memory

The Calculator has a one-value memory. When the memory is other than zero, the box immediately above the / and sqrt function buttons displays an M.

The MC command button and the Ctrl+C key reset memory to zero. The MR command button and the Ctrl+R key display the value in memory. The MS command button and the Ctrl+M key store the value currently displayed by the Calculator into memory. The M+ command button and the Ctrl+P key add the value currently displayed by the Calculator to the value that is in memory.

The Scientific Calculator

Switch to the Scientific Calculator by selecting Scientific on the View menu. Figure 10-51 shows the Scientific Calculator.

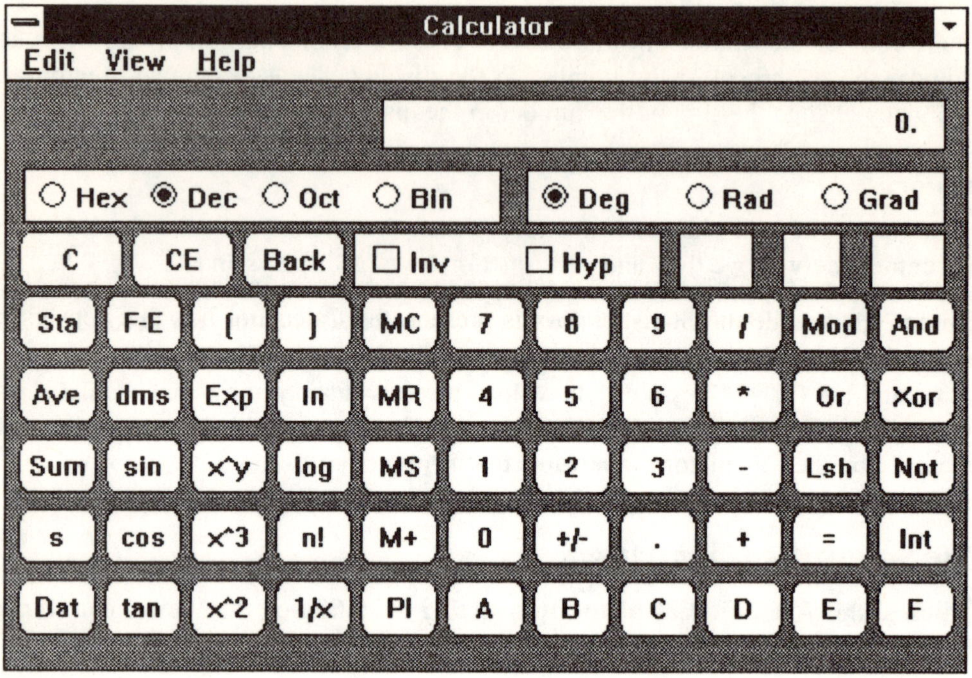

Figure 10-51. The Scientific Calculator.

Number systems

You can set the Calculator to work in the hexadecimal, decimal, octal, and binary number systems by selecting the appropriate Hex, Dec, Oct, or Bin option button. The keyboard keys to select these systems are F5, F6, F7, and F8 respectively. By default, Calculator operates in the decimal number system.

Calculator does not allow you to enter digits that do not work with the number system you select. Binary accepts 1 and 0; octal accepts 0 to 7; decimal accepts 0 to 9; and hexadecimal accepts 0 to 9 and A to F.

When a number is already displayed, changing number systems converts the displayed value to its representation in the new number system.

When you select Hex, Oct, or Bin, the box to the right of the number system option buttons changes to show three option buttons labeled Dword, Word, and Byte.

Selecting Dword causes the display to show the full value of the word. Selecting Word displays the value represented by only the lower 16 bits. Selecting Byte displays the value represented by the lower eight bits. Word and Byte affect the display only; they do not change the value.

Statistical Functions

The Scientific Calculator supports statistical functions. Select the Sta command button or press the Ctrl+S key. You will see the Statistics Box shown in Figure 10-52. Observe that while the Statistics Box is present, the Calculator box that appears just above the 9 and / keys contains the value "stat."

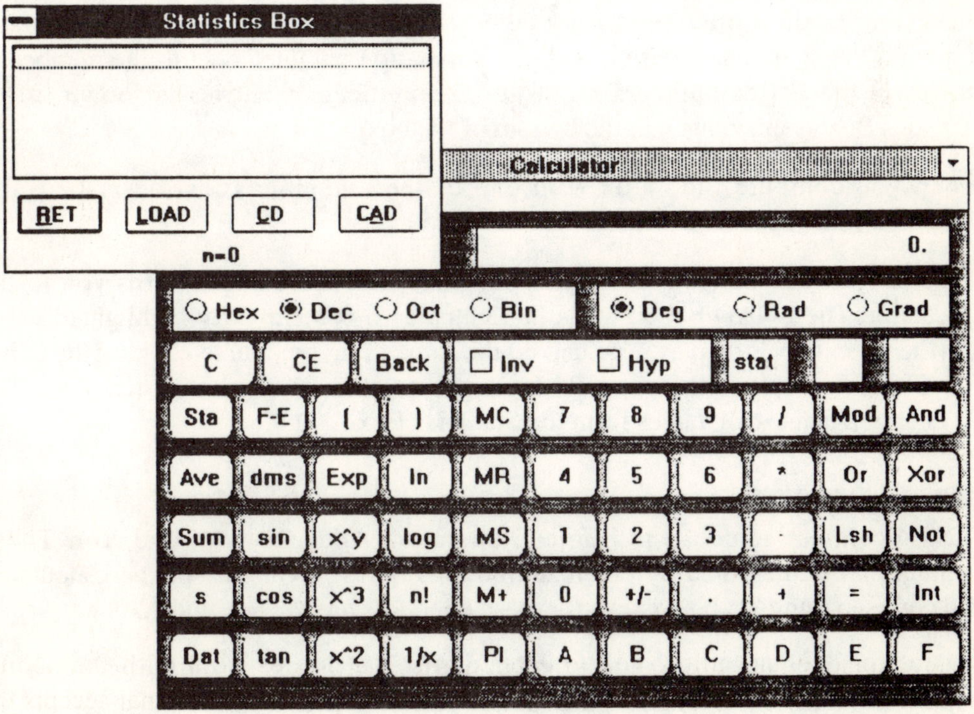

Figure 10-52. The Statistics Box.

You might need to move the Statistics Box around so you can see more of the Calculator. Select the RET button in the Statistics Box to return to the Calculator. Enter a value and select the Dat command button or press the Ins key. The value appears in the Statistics Box. You can enter more values in the same way.

Mean. If you want to take the mean of the numbers, select the Ave command button or press the Ctrl+A key. If you select the Inv check box in the Calculator, the Mean command computes the mean of the squares.

Sum. To take the sum of the numbers, select the Sum command button or press the Ctrl+T key. If you select the Inv check box in the Calculator, the Sum command computes the sum of the squares.

Standard Deviation. To take the standard deviation of the numbers, select the s command button or press the Ctrl+D key. If you select the Inv check box in the Calculator, the Standard Deviation command computes the standard deviation with the population parameter set to the number of entries in the list of numbers. If the Inv check box in the Calculator is not selected, the Standard Deviation command computes the standard deviation with the population parameter set to the number of entries in the list of numbers minus 1. The number of entries is shown in the Statistics Box as the value n at the bottom of the box.

When you compute the value with one of the commands just described, the computed value appears in the Calculator's display.

The Statistics box has four command buttons. The RET button returns you to the Calculator. The LOAD button loads the Statistics Box's currently highlighted value into the Calculator's display. You can do the same thing by double clicking the entry. The CD button deletes the currently highlighted value from the Statistics Box. The CAD button deletes all values from the Statistics Box.

Logical Operations

The Calculator includes the Boolean operators And, Or, Not, and Xor. These operators are represented by command buttons on the right side of the Calculator. The corresponding keyboard keys for these operators are: &, |, ~, and ^.

The Lsh command button and the < key perform a left shift on the value in the display. If the Inv check box is selected, Lsh performs a right shift.

Other Operators

The Mod command button and the % key calculate the modulus of two numbers—the remainder derived when the second number is divided into the first.

The Int command button and the ; key deliver the integer portion of a number. If the Inv check box is selected, Int delivers the fractional portion of the number.

Calculating Expressions

You can use the (and) command buttons to establish precedence as you enter values and operators into a calculation. The box just above the And key displays the current depth of parentheses—for example, (=3 to mean there are currently three unterminated left parentheses.

Trigonometric Input

When you are in the decimal number system, the box just below the display includes the Deg, Rad, and Grad option buttons that allow you to set the trigonometric input to degrees, radians, or gradients. The keyboard keys for these three functions are F2, F3, and F4 respectively.

Notation

When you are in the decimal number system, the F-E command button and the v key switch the display between scientific and normal notation.

Math Functions

Table 10-7 lists the Calculator's math functions, describing their function when the Inv and/or the Hyp check boxes are selected.

Table 10-7. Math Functions.

Command Button	**Keyboard Key**	**Inv**	**Hyp**	**Description**
cos	o			cosine
		x		arc cosine
			x	hyperbolic cosine
		x	x	arc hyberbolic cosine
dms	m			degrees-minutes-seconds
		x		degrees
Exp	x			permits scientific notation input
ln	n			natural (base e) Logarithm
		x		e ^ displayed number
log	1			common (base 10) logarithm
		x		10 ^ displayed number
n!	!			factorial
PI	p			3.14159265359
		x		6.28318530718
sin	s			sine
		x		arc sine
			x	hyperbolic sine
		x	x	arc hyperbolic sine
tan	t			tangent
		x		arc tangent
			x	hyperbolic tangent
		x	x	arc hyperbolic tangent
x^y	y			x ^ y
		x		yth root of x
x^2	@			square
		x		square root
x^3	#			cube
				cube root

The Clipboard

The Calculator's Edit menu includes Copy and Paste commands. You can copy the value currently displayed by the Calculator to the Clipboard to use in another application. You can also paste a value from the Clipboard into the Calculator.

If the Clipboard contains certain text values, they will execute functions on the Calculator. Table 10-8 shows the corresponding values.

Table 10-8. Clipboard to Calculator Function Values.

c	MC
e	Switches to scientific notation
e+	Same as e, indicates positive exponent
e-	Same as e, indicates negative exponent
m	MS
p	M+
r	MR
: letter	Ctrl+letter
: number	Function key (:3 = F3)
\	Dat

SUMMARY

This chapter has described a number of Windows accessories. It marks the last of the chapters that teaches Windows to the new user. Chapter 11—the last chapter in the book—addresses the Windows power user, describing some of the advanced uses that you, a potential power user, can make of the Windows graphical operating environment.

Chapter 11

The Windows Power User

This chapter presents some procedures that you can use to modify the way Windows operates. It requires a deeper understanding of PC/AT architecture than do the preceding chapters. The chapter assumes that you know what conventional, extended, and expanded memory are and that you understand the fundamental differences between the 8088, the 80286, and the 80386 microprocessors from an advanced user's viewpoint. You should also know how DOS memory-resident programs load and execute and how regular DOS programs use memory and video systems. In addition, you should understand the configuration of the network you use—if any. Finally, you should be familiar with multitasking and time slicing so that you can properly adjust these parameters when necessary.

This chapter offers brief introductions to the subjects mentioned above. The techniques discussed in this chapter will enable you to tune the performance of Windows to better match your hardware and your operating requirements.

PC/AT MEMORY

There are three kinds of random-access memory that a PC/AT can have: conventional, extended, and expanded. Windows uses all three types of memory, depending on your computer and what hardware and software you have installed.

Conventional Memory

All PC/AT computers have conventional memory, with a maximum of 640K. These computers can address up to 1 Mbyte, but the space from 640K up is used by other devices, such as video cards, network cards, and the BIOS read-only-memory.

Expanded Memory

Expanded memory is a technique whereby a PC/AT computer accesses extra memory that it cannot normally address. Programs can use this memory, however, by having small segments of it temporarily mapped into holes—address ranges not used by devices—in the conventional address space above 640K. Any PC/AT can have expanded memory. There is a standard method for implementing expanded memory called the LIM 4.0 specification, commonly abbreviated as EMS.

In order for Windows-compatible EMS to exist in a computer, the memory hardware must be installed and a software driver that conforms to the LIM 4.0 specification must be loaded. Drivers that implement LIM versions earlier than 4.0 will not work with Windows. Windows will not attempt to use the EMS, but it will still be available to applications.

Extended Memory

AT class computers with 80286, 80386, and 80486 microprocessors can have extended memory. These processors have an operating mode called the "protected" mode in which they can address memory above the 1Mbyte range. DOS does not run in protected mode. It runs in "real" mode, which can address only the first 1Mbyte of memory. DOS runs this way because the 8086 and 8088 microprocessors do not have the equivalent of protected mode, and DOS must work with all PC/AT machines, regardless of the microprocessor. The standard definition of how extended memory is used by programs is referred to as the XMS specification.

The 8086 and 8088 microprocessors run in real mode only. The 80286, 80386, and 80486 microprocessors can switch between real and protected modes—when they run DOS, they stay in real mode; when they run Windows, they run in protected mode, unless you tell them not to.

The High Memory Area

A characteristic of the 80286, 80386, and 80486 microprocessors is that they can address the first 64K of extended memory without switching into protected mode. This extra memory is called the "high memory area" (HMA). Many memory-resident programs, such as network shell programs, use the HMA—if it is available. They load themselves into the HMA to minimize the amount of conventional memory they occupy.

OPERATING MODES

Windows operates in one of three modes: 386 enhanced, standard, or real. If you do nothing to influence the mode, Windows will examine your hardware and select a mode under which to run.

386 Enhanced Mode

Windows runs in 386 enhanced mode if you have a 80386 or 80486 processor and at least 2 Mbyte of memory. In this mode, Windows uses conventional and extended memory to load and execute multiple tasks. The tasks run concurrently. You can multitask DOS applications along with Windows applications. Windows can run the DOS applications in a Windows applications window or it can run them in full-screen mode. Windows does not use expanded memory in 386 enhanced mode.

Standard Mode

Windows runs in standard mode if you have a 286 processor and at least 1 Mbyte of memory. You can have a mix of Windows and DOS applications loaded at one time. Windows uses conventional and extended memory to load tasks. Windows can multitask Windows applications, but DOS applications suspend while you are inside the Windows graphical operating environment. Likewise, while you are running a DOS application, all Windows tasks suspend, and the DOS application takes over the screen. Windows does not use expanded memory in standard mode.

Real Mode

Windows runs in real mode on 8086 and 8088 processors. Those processors cannot address extended memory, so real mode does not use that type of memory. Applications must confine themselves to the 640K limits of these processors. Windows can multitask to a limited extent in real mode—but only with Windows applications. The multiple tasks must fit together within the 640K space, and the background application will run while the foreground application is waiting for input from the user. DOS applications and Windows applications do not coexist in memory in real mode. When you switch to a DOS application, Windows swaps the Windows applications to disk and loads the DOS application, swapping back when you switch to a Windows application. If you have expanded memory installed—and it complies with the LIM 4.0 specification—Windows will use it for swapping, thus speeding up the task switching operations.

Specifying a Mode

You can use a command-line switch to tell Windows to run in a mode other than the one it would normally select, but your hardware must be compatible with the mode you select.

Specifying 386 Enhanced Mode

If you have a 386 with less than 2 Mbyte, you can use the /3 command-line switch when you run Windows to specify that Windows should run in 386 enhanced mode.

Specifying Standard Mode

The /S command-line switch tells Windows to run in standard mode. You can use this mode if you have a 386 with between 2 and 3 Mbyte and you will not be running any non-Windows DOS applications. Windows runs faster in standard mode under these conditions.

Specifying Real Mode

The /R switch tells Windows to run in real mode regardless of the hardware. You need this mode to run Windows applications that were developed to run under Windows versions earlier than 3.0.

The Control Panel's 386 Enhanced Process

The Control Panel, which you learned about in Chapter 5, has the 386 Enhanced icon if you are running in 386 enhanced mode. When you select this icon, you see the 386 Enhanced dialogue box shown in Figure 11-1.

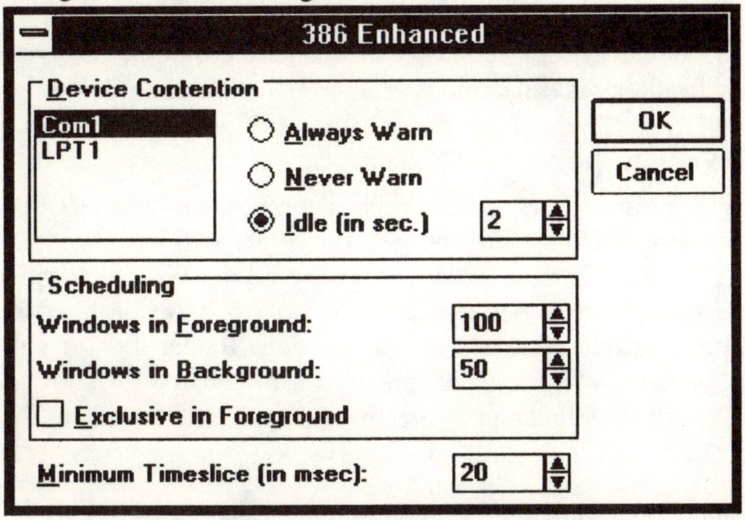

Figure 11-1. The 386 Enhanced Dialogue Box.

You can use this dialogue box to adjust the details of the 386 enhanced mode multitasking process for non-Windows DOS applications and Windows applications that were developed for Windows versions earlier than 3.0.

Device Contention

When a non-Windows DOS application or a pre-version 3.0 Windows application contends for a device while another application is using it, the strategy that you define with the Always Warn, Never Warn, or Idle option button prevails.

When two applications attempt to use the same COM port or LPT device, Windows intercepts their requests and attempts to arbitrate. You can tell Windows what to do by selecting the Always Warn, Never Warn, or Idle option buttons.

The Always Warn option alerts you with a warning dialogue box, informing you that two applications are contending for the same device. You must select one of these two applications to be granted access to the device at the time the contention occurs.

The Never Warn option tells DOS to grant access to any application that tries to use it. This option can result in output from two applications being mixed.

The Idle option includes the warning dialogue box but adds a period of time after a device becomes available that the warning will still appear. This allows you to set up a condition in which two applications can use a device one after the other, but a third application cannot use the device between the time the first one is done with it and the time the second one takes it over.

Task Scheduling

The Minimum Timeslice field specifies the number of milliseconds in a timeslice. Every non-Windows DOS application gets one timeslice. The Windows operating environment gets one timeslice, sharing it among all the Windows applications that are running. This value does not control the priority of tasks or the amount of time allocated to a task in one cycle of the task schedule. Rather it defines the length of one timeslice, which is the length of time a task runs before Windows switches to another task. Priority is a function of the proportion of total timeslices that Windows gives to a particular task in the task-switching cycle.

The Windows in Foreground field specifies the time, in relative terms, that Windows applications share when a Windows application is in the foreground. This number—which ranges from 1 to 10,000—is added to the Background Priority values of all the non-Windows DOS applications. The total represents the total processing time to be shared among all tasks. The ratio of the Windows in Foreground field to the total determines the number of timeslices that Windows gives to the Windows applications when one of them is in the foreground.

The Windows in Background field specifies the time that Windows applications share when a non-Windows DOS application is in the foreground. This number—which ranges from 1 to 10,000—is added to the Foreground Priority value of the foreground application and the Background Priority values of all the non-Windows DOS applications. The total represents the total processing time to be shared among all tasks. The ratio of the Windows in Background field to the total determines the number of timeslices that Windows gives to the Windows applications when a non-Windows DOS application is in the foreground.

The Exclusive in Foreground check box specifies that when a Windows application is in the foreground, non-Windows DOS applications are effectively suspended.

RUNNING SETUP

The Setup application in the Program Manager's Main group allows you to change certain hardware devices in your Windows installation. You use the Setup program to change your display monitor, keyboard, or mouse; to configure Windows to run in a network; and to install applications into the Windows environment. When you run Setup from the Program Manager, or as the program file SETUP.EXE from the File Manager, you see the Setup applications window shown in Figure 11-2.

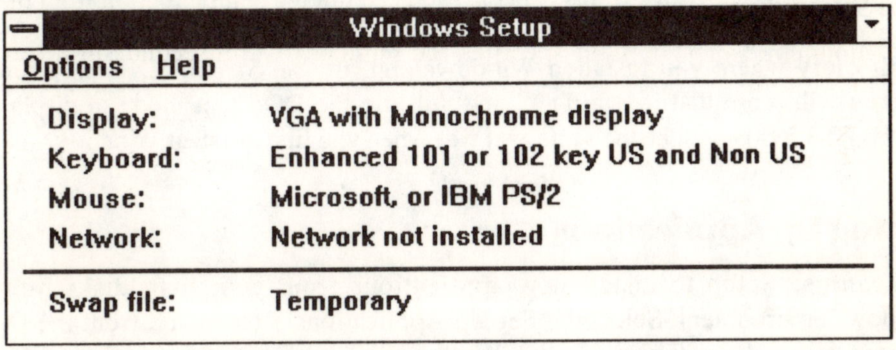

Figure 11-2. The Setup Applications Window.

Changing System Settings

The Setup window lists the current configuration. To change one or more of the settings in this window, choose Change System Settings... on the Options menu. You will see the Change System Settings dialogue box shown in Figure 11-3.

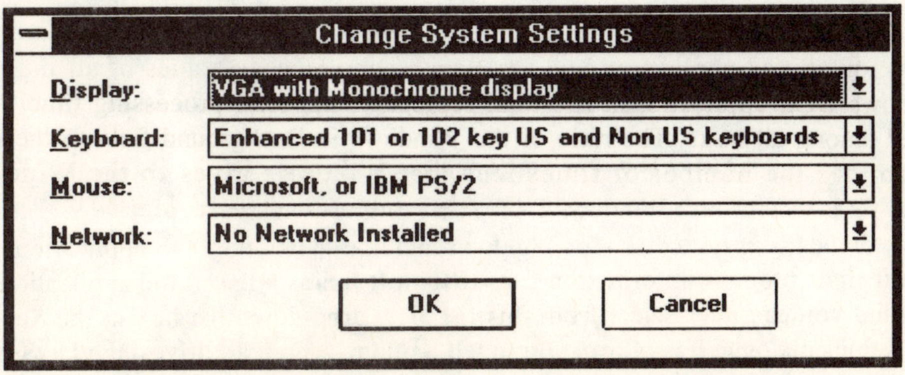

Figure 11-3. The Change System Settings Dialogue Box.

Each of the fields on the Change System Settings dialogue box is a drop-down list that lists the possible devices for the field. Select the devices that match your new configuration and choose OK.

Because you have changed an integral part of the Windows setup, Windows can no longer run without being reloaded. You are given the opportunity to restart Windows or return to DOS. There are no other choices.

If you have made a change in Setup that is not compatible with your hardware, Windows might not operate correctly. If this happens, you can run the Setup program from the DOS command line. Re-boot your computer and stay in DOS. Change to the WINDOWS subdirectory where you installed Windows and run the SETUP.EXE program. The program will sense that it is in DOS and will use the DOS text mode to display your options. The format will be the same as it was when you first installed Windows.

Setting Up Applications

You can use Setup to install new applications from your hard disks into your Windows environment. Select the Set Up Applications... command from the Options window. You will see the Set Up Applications dialogue box shown in Figure 11-4.

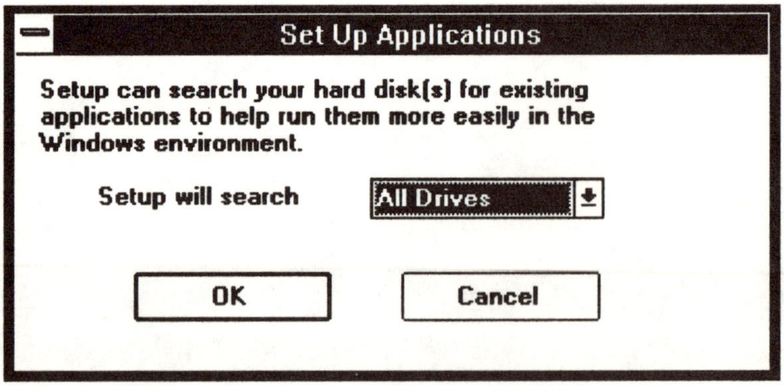

Figure 11-4. The Set Up Applications Dialogue Box.

Setup searches your hard disks for Windows and non-Windows DOS applications for which it finds program information files (PIFs). It builds a list of the applications it finds, and you can later select from this list. The drop-down list box in the Set Up Applications dialogue box allows you to tell Setup to search all drives, the DOS path only, or a specific hard disk drive.

Choose the search you want and select OK. Setup searches the disks and prepares a list. When the search is done, you will see the list in the Set Up Applications dialogue box, as shown in Figure 11-5.

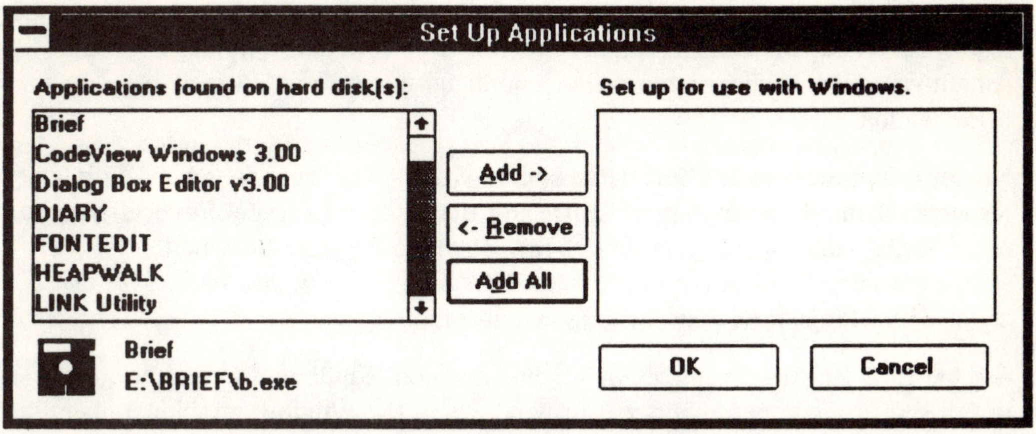

Figure 11-5. The Set Up Applications Dialogue Box.

Press the down arrow key, and a dotted outline surrounds the entry. Move the outline box down and the icon in the lower left corner of the screen becomes either a diskette, as shown in Figure 11-5—to indicate a non-Windows DOS application—or a tiny screen with a window—to indicate a Windows application. Select applications to add by clicking them or pressing the Enter key. Selected applications are highlighted.

Use the Add -> command button to add selected entries to the list of applications that you want to set up for use with Windows. You can use the <- Remove command button to remove an application from the list. When you have the list of applications the way you want it, select OK. Setup adds the Windows applications to the Program Manager group named Windows Applications and the non-Windows DOS applications to the Program Manager Group named Non-Windows Applications.

INTEGRATING NON-WINDOWS DOS APPLICATIONS: THE PIF EDITOR

In Chapter 2 you learned how to use the DOS Prompt icon from the Program Manager to run non-Windows DOS programs. You also learned how to execute programs by using the Run... command and by installing the programs into a group with command-line executions.

The applications that you ran in those ways used default system settings to acquire the system resources needed in order for them to run. They ran in full-screen mode, required a set amount of memory, used the video system in a common way, and used default values for keyboard interaction, command-line parameters, and disk directory manipulation.

Not all DOS programs fit these default settings, however, and some work with fewer resources than the defaults reserve, freeing that excess for other applications. You can describe such a DOS program in a file called the Program Information File (PIF). If an executable DOS program file has a matching PIF, Windows will load that file and use its settings instead of the default values.

In Chapter 2 you saw examples in which some non-Windows DOS applications ran in full-screen mode and others ran in windows in the Windows graphical operating environment. When Windows is in real or standard mode, such applications run in full-screen mode. When Windows is in 386 enhanced mode, such applications optionally run in windows in the Windows graphical operating environment. The option to run a DOS application in a window is one of the PIF settings.

The PIF Editor is an application in the Program Manager's Accessories group. You can use it to create and modify PIFs for non-Windows DOS applications. To run it, you select the executable file PIFEDIT.EXE from the File Manager. You cannot run the PIF editor by selecting one of its .PIF document files, because selecting a .PIF file from within the File Manager is one way to run the non-Windows DOS program that goes along with the file.

PIF Editor in Standard and Real Mode

When you run the PIF editor in standard or real Mode, you will see the PIF Editor application window shown in Figure 11-6.

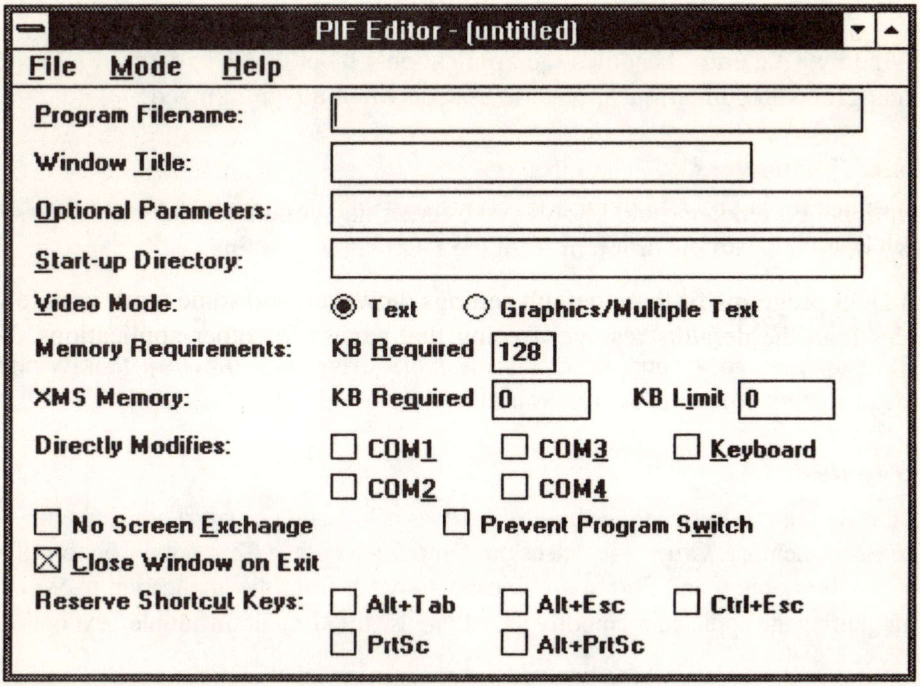

Figure 11-6. The PIF Editor Application Window.

As shown in Figure 11-6, the fields in the application window are empty. The File menu has the usual New, Open..., Save, and Save As... commands for creating, saving, and reloading a PIF. The convention is that a PIF has the same name as the executable program file that it describes; therefore, a PIF for the TWRP.EXE program is named TWRP.PIF. When you save a file, the PIF Editor suggests a filename that matches the program.

The Mode menu allows you to switch to the PIF Editor for 386 enhanced mode, in case you want to edit a PIF for that environment.

The following sections discuss each of the fields on the real and standard mode PIF Editor application window.

Program Filename

The Program Filename field allows you to enter the full path to the executable program file. For example: **d:\twrp\twrp.exe.**

Window Title

The Window Title entry becomes the application's label under its icon in a Program Manager group and under the application's icon when it is minimized.

Optional Parameters

The Optional Parameters field allows you to enter any command-line parameters that you use when you run the program from the DOS command line.

Start-up Directory

The Start-up Directory entry specifies the DOS drive and directory that Windows will make current when the application runs.

Video Mode

Select the Text option button if the application does not use graphics and uses only one page of text video memory. Otherwise select the Graphics/Multiple Text option button. If you choose the Text option and find that you cannot switch from the application to Windows without quitting the application, modify the PIF to use the Graphics/Multiple Text option.

Memory Requirements

Leave the Memory Requirements value at 128K—unless you know that the application needs more memory. This number tells Windows not to run the application unless there is at least this much memory available. Windows gives all of the conventional memory to the application when it runs, regardless of this value.

XMS Memory

The XMS Memory fields tell Windows how much extended memory, under the XMS standard, must be available in order to run the application. These fields also specify the maximum XMS to give to the application. Few DOS applications use XMS.

Directly Modifies

If the application reads and writes the communications ports by making direct hardware accesses, select the corresponding COMn check box. Windows will not allow the application to run if it knows that another application is using the same device.

If the application reads the keyboard directly, select the Keyboard check box. Windows will not attempt to process any keys while the application is running. You must exit from the application to return to Windows.

No Screen Exchange

If you never intend to copy the application's screen to the Clipboard, select the No Screen Exchange check box to save memory.

Prevent Program Switch

The Prevent Program Switch option saves memory by preventing you from switching back to Windows from an application until you exit from the application.

Close Window on Exit

With the Close Window on Exit check box selected, you will return immediately to Windows when the application exits. Otherwise, you will be able to view the screen that follows the application's termination and press any key to return to Windows. This feature is necessary when applications write messages to the screen and exit immediately. If you do not use this option, the screen will be given up to Windows before you have a chance to read such an application's output.

Reserve Shortcut Keys

Windows normally uses certain shortcut keys to manage its multitasking environment. If an application needs some of these keys for its own use, you can reserve them by selecting the appropriate check box.

PIF Editor in 386 Enhanced Mode

When you run the PIF Editor in 386 enhanced mode, you see the PIF application window for 386 enhanced mode, as shown in Figure 11-7.

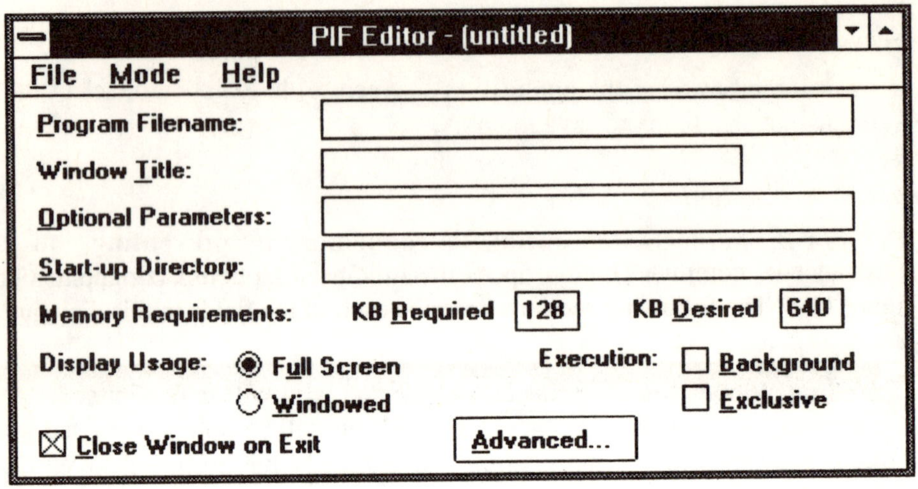

Figure 11-7. The PIF Application Window for 386 Enhanced Mode.

The Mode menu allows you to switch to the PIF Editor in standard mode in case you want to edit a PIF for that environment.

The Program Filename, Window Title, Optional Parameters, Start-up Directory, and Close Window on Exit fields on the Mode menu, and the Reserve Shortcut field in the Advanced Options dialogue box are the same as for the standard mode PIF editor. The following sections discuss the unique fields on the Advanced Options dialogue box.

Memory Requirements

The KB Required field lists the amount of memory that must be available in order for Windows to run the application. The KB Desired field is the amount of memory that Windows will give the application if this memory is available; 640K is the highest amount an application can receive. Set the number lower to leave more memory available for other applications if you know that the program can run properly and efficiently with the lower amount.

Display Usage

You can run the application in Full Screen or Windowed mode by selecting the appropriate option button in the Display Usage field.

Execution

The Background check box allows the application to continue to run while it is in the background. The Exclusive check box prevents other programs from running while the application is in the foreground.

Advanced

The Advanced... command button opens the Advanced Options dialogue box shown in Figure 11-8. The following sections describe each of the fields in this dialogue box.

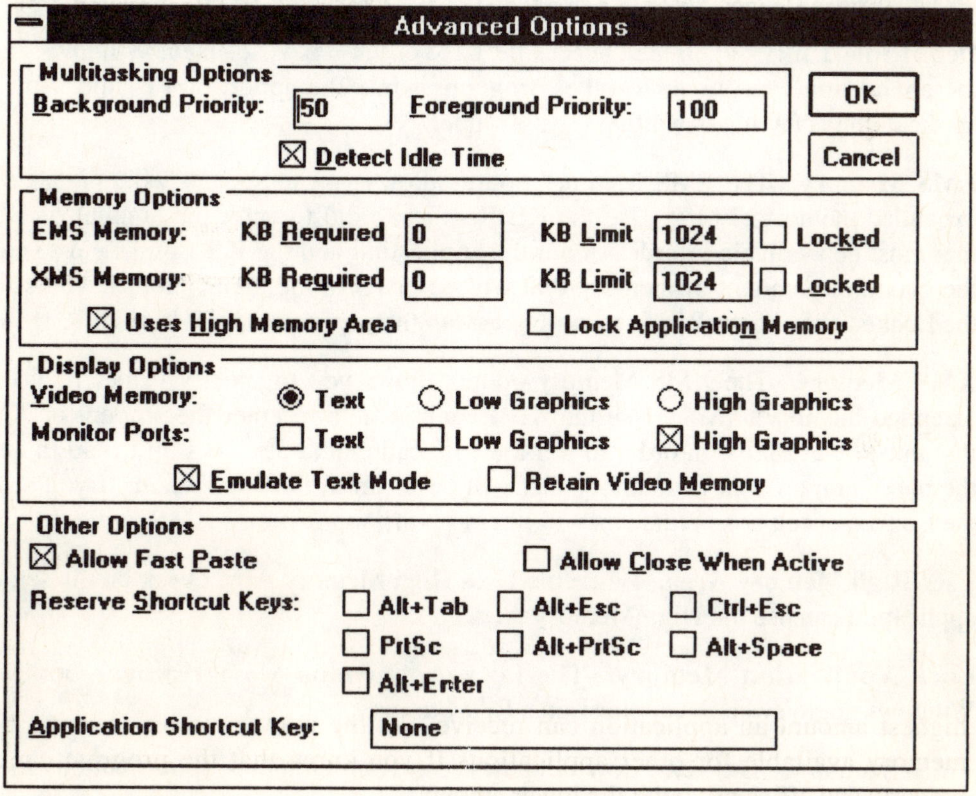

Figure 11-8. The Advanced Options Dialogue Box.

Background Priority. The Background Priority field enables you to enter a value used in calculating the number of time slices that an application receives when it is running in the background. Enter a value from 0 to 10,000. This value is summed with the background and foreground values of other applications that are running, and the ratio of this value to that sum determines the ratio of the total number of time slices that this application receives while it is in the background.

Foreground Priority. The Foreground Priority field is similar to the Background Priority field, except that the number you enter is used in calculating time slices for an application running in the foreground, rather than the background. Enter a value from 0 to 10,000. This value is summed with the background and foreground values of other applications that are running, and the ratio of this value to that sum determines the ratio of the total number of time slices that this application receives while it is in the foreground.

Detect Idle Time. When the Detect Idle Time check box is selected, Windows gives the application's resources to other programs while the application is idle. An idle application is one that is waiting for user input.

EMS Memory. The EMS Memory option allows you to specify values related to expanded memory (EMS). Use the KB Required field to enter the amount of EMS that must be available in order to run the application and the KB Limit field to enter the maximum amount of memory that will be given to the application. If you select the Locked check box, Windows will not swap the application's EMS to disk.

XMS Memory. The XMS Memory option allows you to specify values related to extended memory (XMS). Use the KB Required field to enter the amount of XMS that must be available in order to run the application and the KB Limit field to enter the maximum amount of memory that will be given to the application. If you select the Locked check box, Windows will not swap the application's XMS to disk.

Uses High Memory Area. When the Uses High Memory Area check box is set, the application can use the High Memory Area.

Lock Application Memory. The Lock Application Memory check box tells Windows not to swap the application's RAM to disk.

Video Memory. The Text, Low Graphics, and High Graphics option buttons in the Video Memory field tell Windows how the application will display data and, therefore, how much memory to reserve for saving video memory.

Monitor Ports. The Monitor Ports check boxes tell Windows that the application will write directly to the video ports. Windows monitors the application's use of these ports so that when you leave and return to the application Windows can properly restore its video context.

Emulate Text Mode. The Emulate Text Mode option speeds up the application's video displays. Turn it off only if the application's text displays seem incorrect.

Retain Video Memory. The Retain Video Memory option tells Windows to retain all the application's video memory as long as the application runs. Some applications switch video modes—if Windows gives the video memory to another application, the memory might not be available when you try to return to the application.

Allow Fast Paste. Some applications cannot keep up with the speed at which the Clipboard pastes characters. Turn off the Allow Fast Paste check box if the application loses pasted characters.

Allow Close When Active. If the Allow Close When Active check box is selected, you can close down the application from within Windows without returning to the application to exit from it. Depending on how the application shuts down, you could lose data if you select this option. If the application retains unwritten data in memory pending an orderly exit, those records will be lost if you close the application from Windows. Select the Allow Close When Active option only when you know what the application does to shut down.

Application Shortcut Key. The Application Shortcut Key is a key combination that activates the application while it is minimized and you are in the Windows graphical operating environment. To assign a shortcut key, select the field and press the key combination you want to use. The combination must include the Alt or Ctrl key and must not be one of the key combinations that Windows uses for itself. Windows will tell you if you try to use a shortcut key that is invalid or already in use.

WINDOWS IN A NETWORK

A network is a group of computers connected together. In a typical network configuration, one of the computers is the file server and the others are work stations. The file server is unattended, and the users work at the work stations. The file server allows users to share disk files and printers on the network. Figure 11-9 illustrates a basic network.

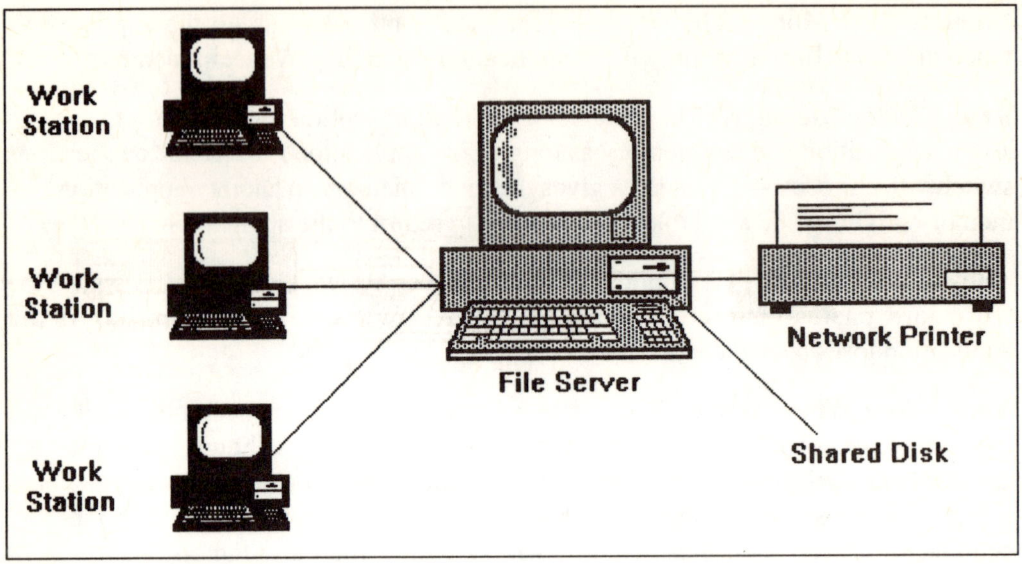

Figure 11-9. A Basic Network.

A work station in a network can have its own disks and printer, and it can share the network disks and printers with the other work stations. A network configuration supports sites where multiple users share common data files, software files, and expensive peripherals such as high-volume disk drives and laser printers.

Many network installations have more than one file server. A two-server network, for example, is usually two independent networks that are bridged together. The users of both networks have access to the shared files and printers of both servers. Figure 11-10 illustrates a two-server network.

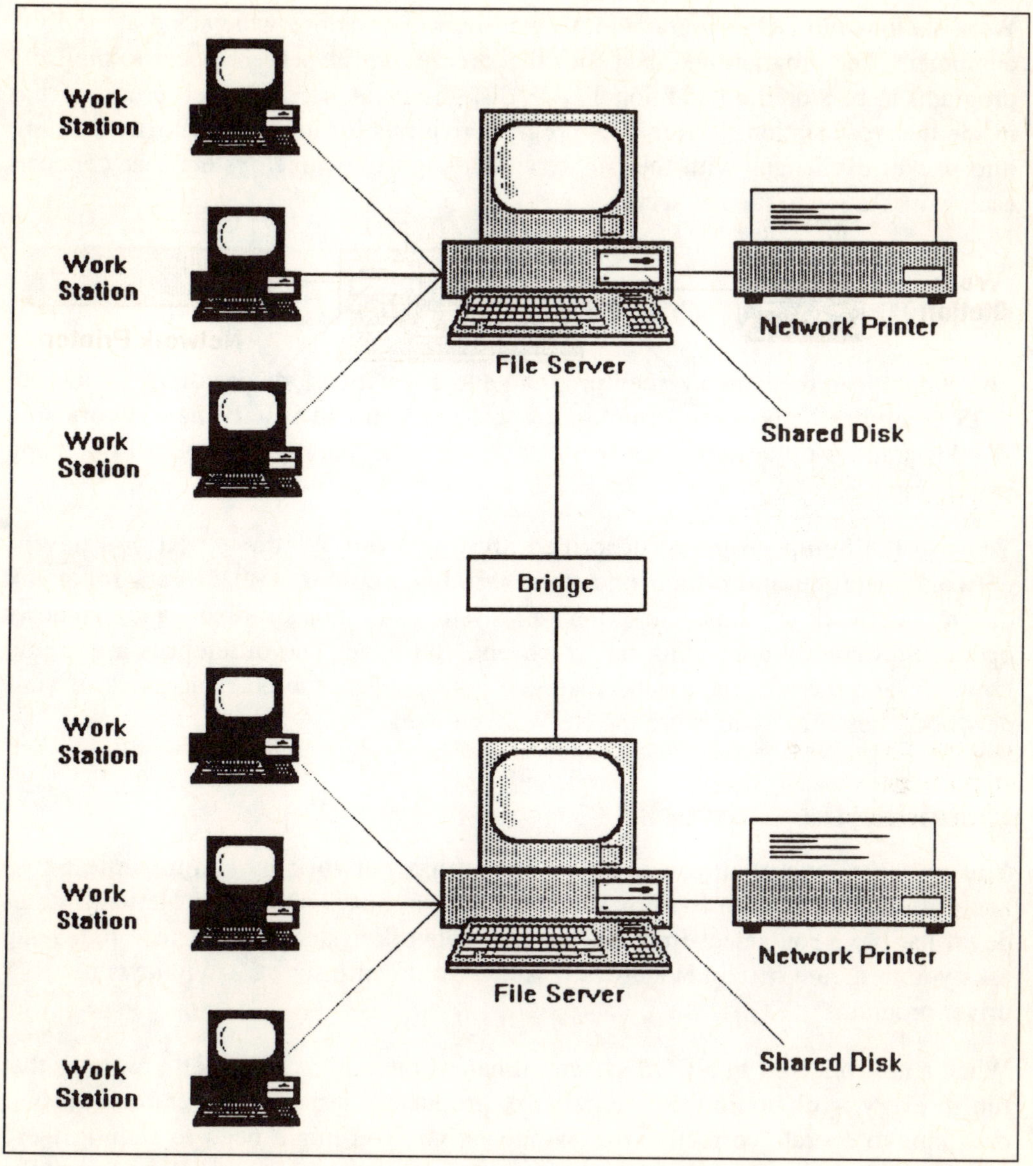

Figure 11-10. A Two-Server Network.

Work stations run DOS programs, just as if the work stations were stand-alone DOS computers. The program and data files that are on the file server appear to the DOS programs to be stored on additional DOS disk drives. A network shell program runs inside the work station. It translates program requests for network disk file accesses into packet exchanges with the file server through the cable system that connects each work station to the file server.

RUNNING WINDOWS IN A NETWORK

You should load the network shell program and any network device drivers into your DOS computer before you run Windows. Then you can install the network into Windows and use the network's features through the Windows graphical operating environment.

You use the Setup program, described above, to tell Windows that you have a network installed and which one it is. Windows comes with drivers for many different network systems. These network systems are not all alike—and Windows operates differently depending on which one you have. The differences are minor, however, and the commands and dialogue boxes reflect the characteristics of your network. These discussions use the NetWare network.

Installing the Network

You tell Windows that you are running with a network by running the Setup application. The Change System Settings dialogue box includes the Network drop-down list box. You select from the various network systems in the list, and Setup asks you to mount certain Windows diskettes so it can install the Windows network driver programs.

When a network runs in a DOS system, it has its own driver and shell programs that run in every work station. Some network products released new versions of their programs to operate correctly with Windows 3.0. You might need to acquire these new network drivers and shells before you can use the network and Windows at the same time. Windows tells you if the resident network driver is the correct version when you load Windows. If it is not, Windows will still operate, but it will not activate any of its network capabilities.

Signing On and Off the Network

Users on a network are known to the network by their user identification or "usernames." When you sign onto the network, you must specify your username and a password—if one has been assigned to you. If you are running in a multi-server network, you must specify the server to which you are signing on. You can be signed onto more than one server at a time, and you can do so under different usernames—if you know the passwords for them.

Signing On

When the network is installed and Windows is running, execute the Control Panel. Figure 11-11 shows the Control Panel application window with a network installed.

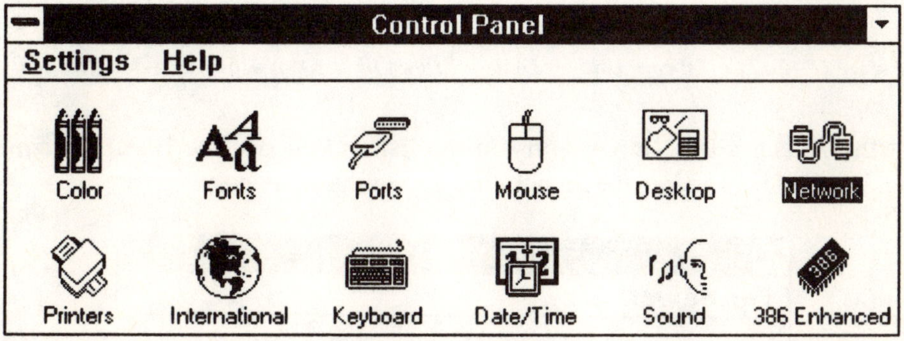

Figure 11-11. The Control Panel Application Window with a Network Installed.

The Network icon tells you that Windows recognizes the network. Choose the icon. Figure 11-12 shows the Network Utilities dialogue box with its drop-down list box selected.

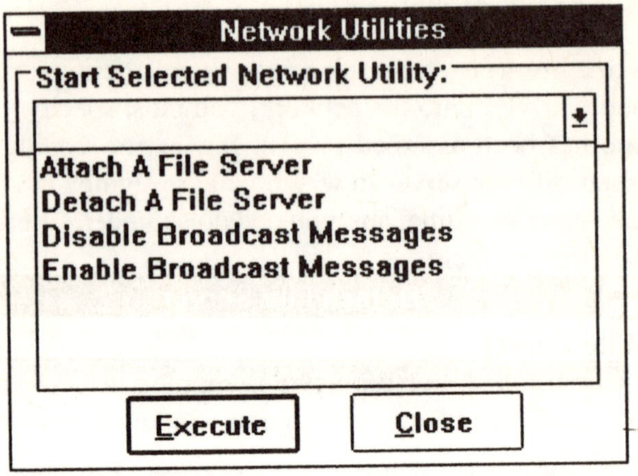

Figure 11-12. The Network Utilities Dialogue Box with its Drop-Down List Box Selected.

Select the Attach a File Server entry in the list and choose the Execute command button. Figure 11-13 shows the Attach File Server dialogue box.

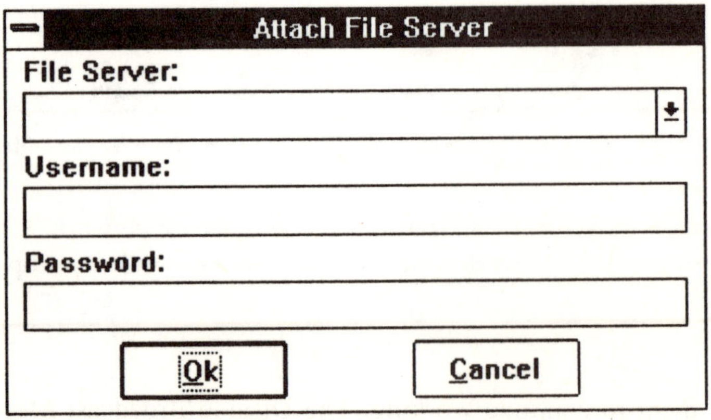

Figure 11-13. The Attach File Server Dialogue Box.

Select the File Server drop-down list box to see a list of the file servers that are in the network and choose one of them. The name of the file server you choose appears in the File Server field. Enter your username and password and choose the OK command button. If you have entered everything correctly, you are now signed onto the network. If you have entered your username or password incorrectly, you will get an error message.

After you are signed onto the network, choose the Close command button on the Network Utilities dialogue box and exit from the Control Panel application.

Signing Off

Select and execute the Detach a File Server entry from the list on the Network Utilities dialogue box. Figure 11-14 shows the Detach File Server dialogue box.

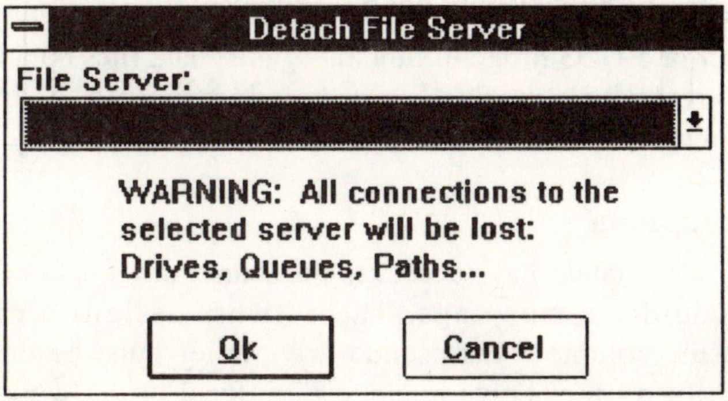

Figure 11-14. The Detach File Server Dialogue Box.

Select the file server name from the drop-down list box on the Detach File Server dialogue box and then select the OK command button. You are now signed off of the file server. When you have signed off of the last server in the network, you are signed off of the network.

Broadcast Messages

Occasionally another user on the network will broadcast messages to you or a group of users. These messages interrupt whatever you are doing, and you must acknowledge them to continue working. The Disable Broadcast Messages entry on the Network Utilities dialogue box disables those messages. The Enable Broadcast Messages enables them again.

Networks and the File Manager

Drives on a network file server are organized into volumes. You must address these drives as volumes rather than by their actual drive letter on the server because there is the possibility that a work station can have a local disk drive with the same drive letter.

Within volumes, data files on the network are organized into a directory structure just like the DOS directory structure, except that the network usually imposes a certain defined set of directories where the network files and programs themselves exist.

DOS applications address disk files through the drive letters on which the files exist. Therefore the user of a DOS program running against data files on a network must be able to translate the network's volume address into a drive that DOS programs—including Windows—understand.

Pseudo-Drive Mapping

Programs in the work station have access to the shared disks on a network through a system of pseudo-drive mappings. The network assigns a drive letter to a subdirectory on the volume. This pseudo-drive letter must be one that the work station does not always use. Drive mappings are local to the work station because different work stations have different drive letters available to be mapped.

The work station can address the pseudo-drive letter in the same context that it would address a real disk drive in its own configuration. The network translates the pseudo-drive into a directory on a volume on a file server—this translation is transparent to the DOS program. You establish the drive mapping and then use the drive as if it were a normal DOS disk drive.

When you run the File Manager with a network installed, the network drives appear at the top of the Directory Tree window, with a NET icon, as shown for the F drive in Figure 11-15.

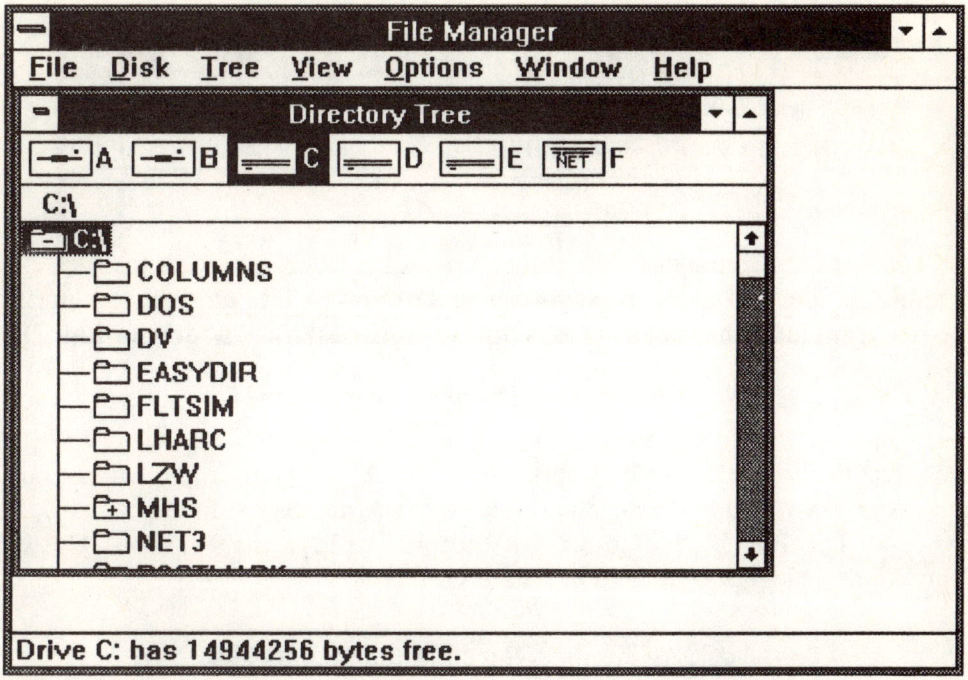

Figure 11-15. Network Drives at the Top of the Directory Tree Window.

Connecting a Network Drive

The Connect Net Drive command on the File Manager's Disk menu enables you to assign pseudo-drive mappings. Figure 11-16 shows the Connect Network Drive dialogue box that appears when you select this command.

Figure 11-16. The Connect Network Drive Dialogue Box.

You select the drive letter to be mapped from the Drive Letter drop-down list box in the dialogue box, and you enter the server, volume, and path into the Network Path text box. The Previous... command button displays the Previous Network Connections dialogue box shown in Figure 11-17.

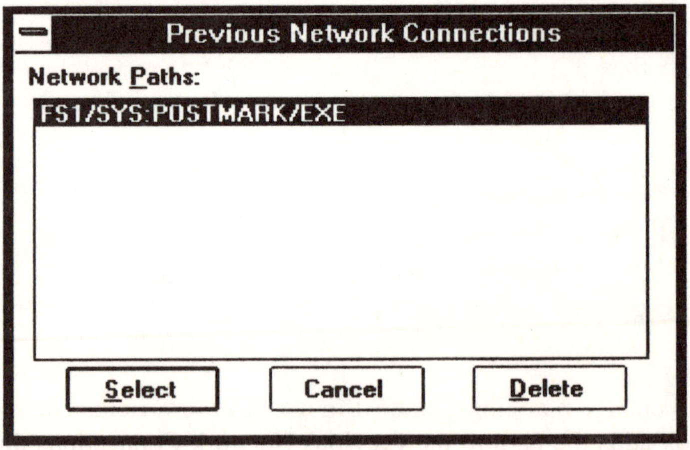

Figure 11-17. The Previous Network Connections Dialogue Box.

You can select a drive mapping from among the list of the previous drive mappings that you used. The Connect Network Drive dialogue box also has a Browse... command button that enables you to browse the network in order to build a path for the mapping. Figure 11-18 shows the Browse Connections dialogue box.

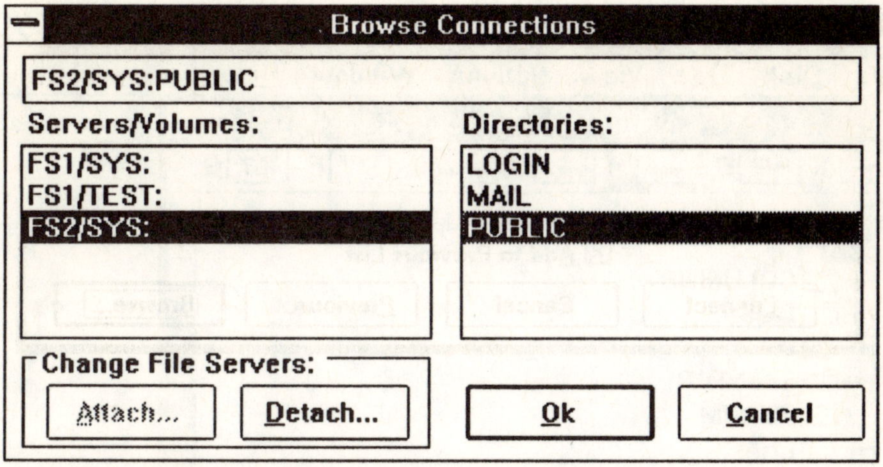

Figure 11-18. The Browse Connections Dialogue Box.

The Browse Connections dialogue box lists the servers to which you are attached and the volumes that are installed in these servers. When you select one of these servers, the Directories list shows the directories at the first level on the volume. You can then select from this list, which replaces itself with a list of directories that are below the one you selected. This process continues until you are at a directory that has no subdirectories. The subdirectory lists have a [..] entry at the top to allow you to return to the parent directory of the current subdirectory.

As you select entries from the lists in the Browse Connections dialogue box, the selections you make append themselves to the text box at the top of the dialogue box. This text box is the path you are building for the drive mapping. When that path is complete, select the OK command button—this returns you to the Connect Network Drive dialogue box, where the selected path is now filled in. If your network requires a password to change mappings, enter it in the Password field. The Add to Previous List check box adds the path to the Previous Network Connections dialogue box for a later selection. Select Connect, and the drive mapping is complete, as shown in the File Manager's Directory Tree in Figure 11-19.

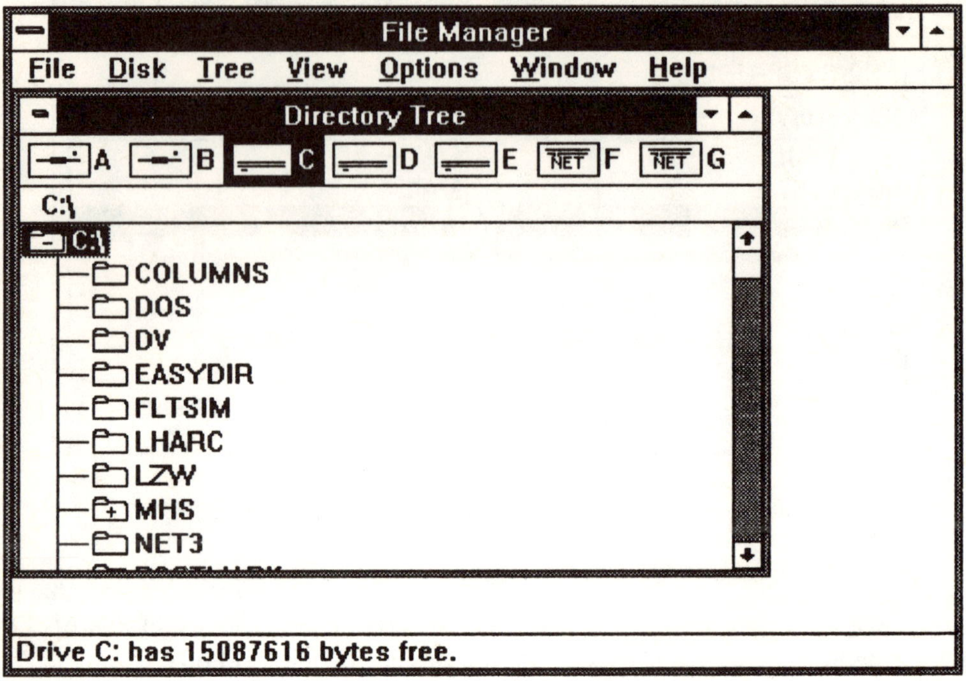

Figure 11-19. The File Manager's Directory Tree.

Disconnecting a Network Drive

The Disconnect Network Drive... command on the File Manager's Disk menu displays the Disconnect Drive dialogue box shown in Figure 11-20.

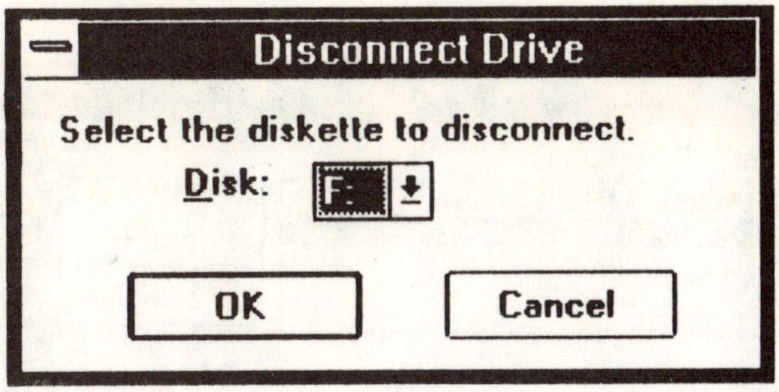

Figure 11-20. The Disconnect Drive Dialogue Box.

Select the network drive you wish to disconnect from the drop-down list box and then select OK. The drive mapping is deleted, and the File Manager removes the network drive's icon from the Directory Tree.

Connecting to Network Print Queues

To print to a file server's shared printer, you send your print output to a print queue on the file server. The server manages the queuing and printing of the job in a manner very much like the Windows Print Manager.

To tell Windows to send print output to the network printer, you must first connect the network print queue to one of your printer ports. When an application prints to that printer port, the network shell intercepts the print output and sends it to the server's print queue.

Usually, you assign the network print queue to a printer port assignment that does not exist in your hardware, and you install a printer driver for the printer on the server, associating it with the printer port. You do all of this with the Control Panel's Printer function.

Figure 11-21 shows the Control Panel's Printers dialogue box.

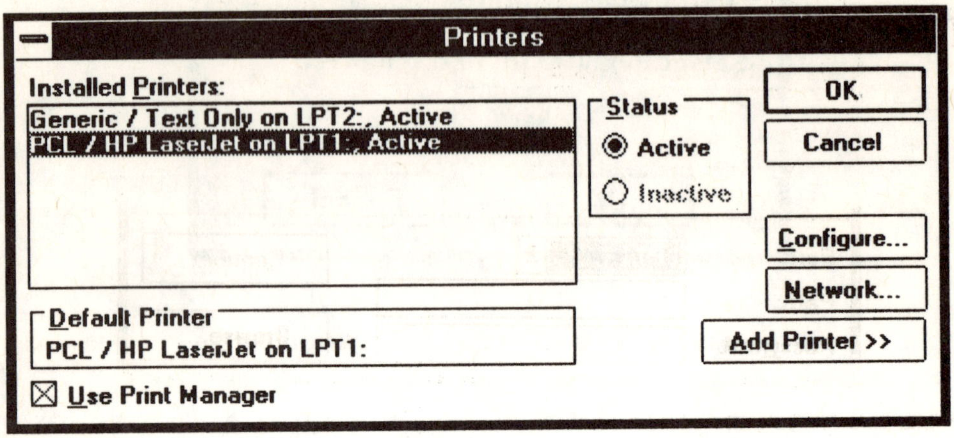

Figure 11-21. The Control Panel's Printers Dialogue Box.

Observe that the Network... command button is enabled on the dialogue box. Assume that your work station has a local printer attached to LPT1. In this example it is installed with the HP Laserjet driver. Your work station has no LPT2 port installed, but you have installed the Generic printer driver and configured it to print to LPT2. You learned how to make these installations in Chapter 5 when you learned about installing printers with the Control Panel.

In this example the Generic printer driver describes the network printer. To associate LPT2 with the network printer, select the Network... command button. You will see the Printers-Network Connections dialogue box shown in Figure 11-22.

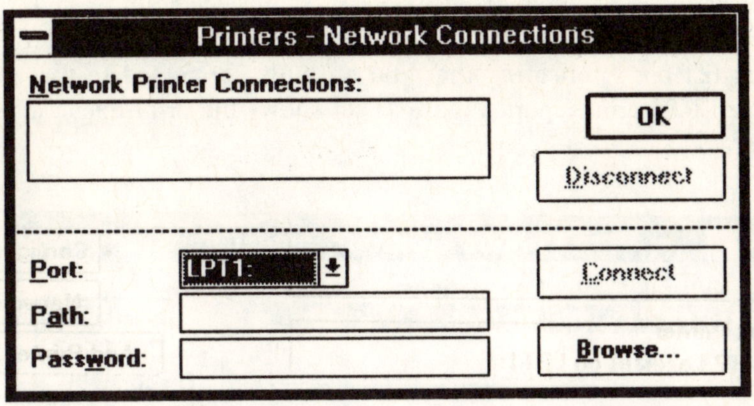

Figure 11-22. The Printers-Network Connections Dialogue Box.

Select LPT2 from the Port drop-down list box and then select the Browse... command button. You will see the Browse Queues dialogue box shown in Figure 11-23.

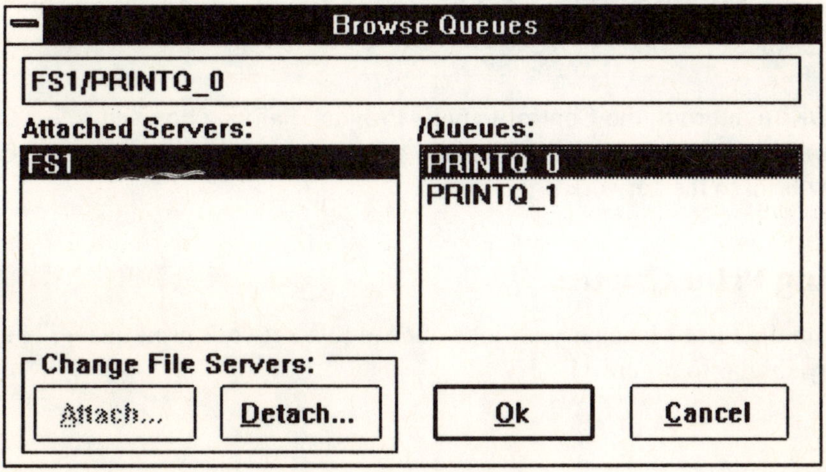

Figure 11-23. The Browse Queues Dialogue Box.

The Browse Queues dialogue box initially lists the attached servers. Select one of these servers, and the /Queues list shows the print queues on that server. Each queue represents a printer to which the server can print. Select one of these printers. The box at the top of the /Queues list builds the path to the queue as you make selections. When the queue name is the one you want, select OK. The Printers - Network

Connections dialogue box now shows the queue you selected in its Path field. Select the Connect command button, and the port and queue appear in the Network Printer Connections list box, indicating that you are now connected to that print queue through your LPT2 printer port. Figure 11-24 shows the print queue added to your connections.

Figure 11-24. The Print Queue Added to Connections.

Select OK to return to the Control Panel's Printers dialogue box and select OK there. Any application that selects the Generic printer from its Printer Setup... command will now print to the network printer.

Viewing Print Queues

If you run the Print Manager with jobs queued to a network print queue, you will see a display similar to Figure 11-25.

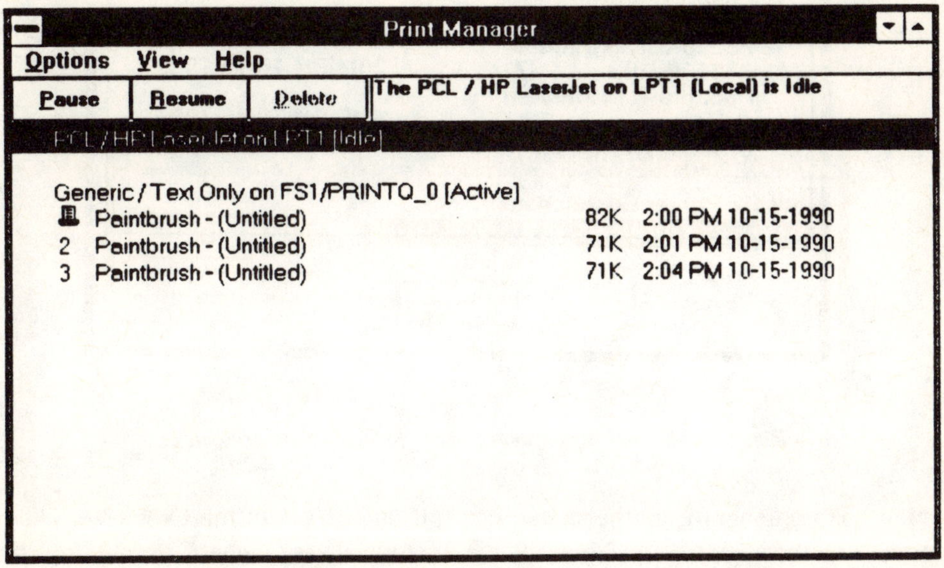

Figure 11-25. The Print Manager Run with Jobs Queued to a Network Print Queue.

The list of jobs that appears in the Print Manager's work space for a network printer consists of jobs that you submitted. The same print queue might have other jobs submitted by other users. To see the entire list of print jobs, highlight the printer entry in the Print Manager work space and select the Selected Net Queue... command on the View menu. You will see a display similar to the one in Figure 11-26, showing all the jobs queued to the selected network queue.

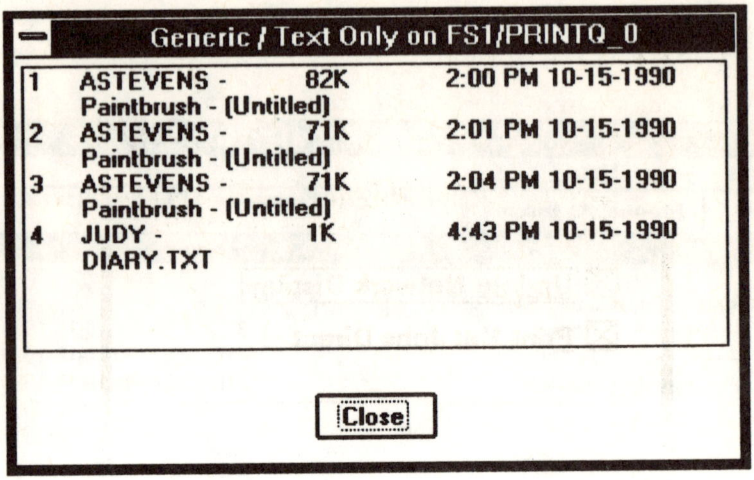

Figure 11-26. All Jobs Queued to the Selected Network Queue.

To view the contents of another network print queue, select the Other Net Queue... command on the View menu. You will see the Other Net Queue dialogue box shown in Figure 11-27.

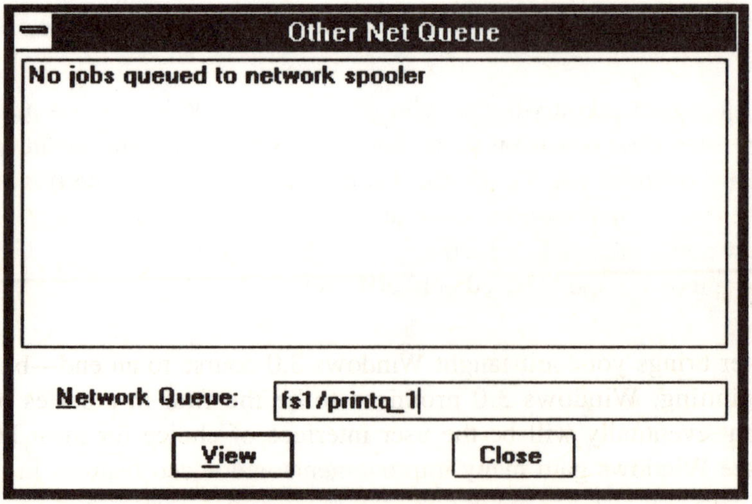

Figure 11-27. The Other Net Queue Dialogue Box.

Setting Network Options

The Network... command on the Print Manager's Options menu displays the Network Options dialogue box shown in Figure 11-28.

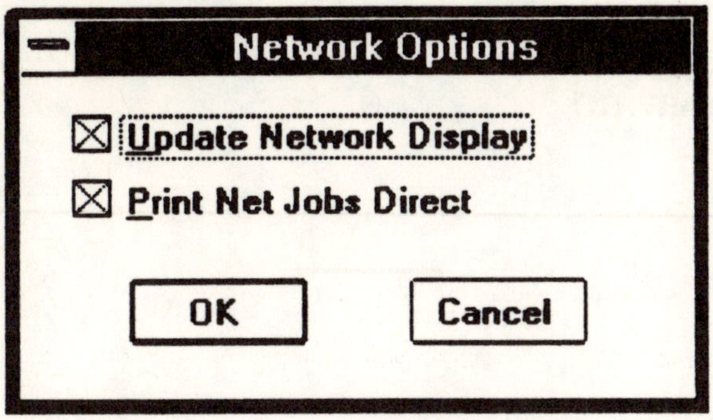

Figure 11-28. The Network Options Dialogue Box.

When the Update Network Display check box is selected, the Print manager updates the list of queued jobs in its work space periodically. Turn off the Update Network Display check box to prevent the Print Manager from periodically reading the queue status and perhaps adversely affecting network traffic loads. To view a current display of the status of the network queues, select the Update Net Queues command on the View menu.

As a default, jobs printed to a network queue bypass the Print Manager and print directly to the network queue. To force network print jobs to go through the Print Manager, turn off the Print Net Jobs Direct check box.

SUMMARY

This chapter brings your self-taught Windows 3.0 course to an end—but this end is also a beginning. Windows 3.0 promises to be the first in a series of Windows releases that eventually will be the user interface of choice for most PC/AT users. You will see Windows gain many improvements and added features in the next few years, and you will also see many powerful applications emerge to take advantage of the full graphical operating environment of Windows 3.0.

Glossary

386 ENHANCED MODE. The mode in which Windows can run if you have a 386 or 486 and at least 2Mbyte of memory. This mode allows multitasking of DOS and Windows applications.

ACTIVE WINDOW. The window into which user inputs go. The active window has its title bar highlighted.

APPLICATION WINDOW. The first window that appears for an application. An application has only one application window. *See also* Document Window.

ARROW KEYS. The up, down, right, and left arrow keys on the keyboard. These keys are typically used to move a text cursor.

BITMAP. The internal representation of a graphics image. Wallpaper is stored in bitmap format. Paintbrush can work with bitmap files with the extension .BMP. *See also* PCX Files.

CASCADED WINDOWS. An arrangement of document windows that displays them in an overlapping cascade. *See also* Tiled Windows.

CHECK BOX. A square box in a dialogue box that you can set to on or off. When a check box is set to on, it contains an X. When a check box is set to off, it is blank.

CLICK. To press and release the left mouse button once, with the mouse cursor pointed at the screen item you wish to select. *See also* Double Click.

CLIPBOARD. The Windows application to which you cut and copy text and graphics from applications and from which you paste text and graphics to applications. This is the method by which most Windows applications can share information.

COM PORT. *See* Communications Port.

COMMAND BUTTON. A rectangular box in a dialogue box. A command button has a command label in it. When you click the command button, you execute the command.

COMMUNICATIONS PORT. A hardware device to which you can connect a modem, terminal, plotter, or serial printer.

CONTROL MENU. The menu that accompanies most windows. It allows you to restore, close, move, size, minimize, and maximize the window. Minimized applications icons have Control menus as well.

COPY. To write text or graphics from an application to the Clipboard.

CURSOR. A pointing icon associated with the keyboard or mouse. The cursor takes different forms depending on its current purpose.

CUT. To write text or graphics from an application to the Clipboard and then delete the text or graphics from the application.

DEFAULT. The initial setting for a parameter—usually established by the system. You can change the default setting for many parameters.

DESKTOP. The portion of the screen that holds application windows and icons.

DIALOGUE BOX. A box with various kinds of fields in which you can enter data.

DIRECTORY. A group of files organized together in a structure consisting of a root directory and subdirectories.

DIRECTORY TREE. The File Manager's display, made up of a disk drive's root directory and the subdirectories under it and each other.

DIRECTORY WINDOW. The window in which the File Manager displays the contents of a directory.

DISK. A mass storage medium. *See also* Diskette and Hard Disk.

DISKETTE. A removable disk medium.

DOCUMENT WINDOW. The window or windows in which an application displays data. An application can have multiple document windows, all of which remain within the borders of the application window. Some applications use the work space of the application window for data display and do not have document windows.

DOS. Disk Operating System. DOS is the operating system under which Windows operates.

DOUBLE CLICK. To click the left mouse button twice rapidly in order to choose an item on the screen. *See also* Click.

DRAG. To press and hold the left mouse button while you move the mouse cursor across the screen. The object under the mouse cursor follows the cursor if the object is subject to being dragged. When the object is at its destination, release the mouse button.

DROP-DOWN LIST BOX. A list box that has only one visible entry which displays the current setting. When you click its down-arrow, the box opens to reveal a list of settings from which you can choose.

EXTENSION. The one- to three-character extension to a file name. The file name and its extension are separated by a period. *See also* File Name .

FILE. A collection of information stored into one logical file on a disk.

FILE NAME. The one- to eight-character name of a file. *See also* Extension.

FIXED DISK. *See* Hard Disk.

FLOPPY DISK. *See* Diskette.

FONT. A character set defined by the shape and design of its characters. *See also* Point Size.

FOOTER. A body of text that is printed at the bottom of every page in a document. *See also* Header.

FORMAT. To prepare a diskette for use.

GROUP. A logical grouping of pointers to executable program files, maintained by and accessible through the Program Manager.

HARD DISK. A high-capacity, non-removable mass storage medium.

HEADER. A body of text that is printed at the top of every page in a document. *See also* Footer.

HIDDEN FILE. A file with the "hidden" attribute set. Such files do not appear in a normal file directory.

HIGHLIGHTED. The state of an item when you have selected it and it is ready to be activated or acted upon by a command.

ICON. A small picture that represents an application. When an application is inactive and minimized, it appears as an icon at the bottom of the desktop.

INACTIVE WINDOW. An application window that is displayed while another window is active. The inactive window's title bar is displayed without highlighting.

LIST BOX. A text box on a dialogue box that contains a list of selections. You can select and choose one of the selections. If the list is longer than the box, the box has a vertical scroll bar.

MACRO. A recorded sequence of keyboard and mouse actions that you can play back by pressing a shortcut key.

MARK. To select a block of text or part of a picture in order to delete it or to cut or copy it to the Clipboard.

MAXIMIZE. To cause a window to occupy the entire screen.

MENU. A vertical list of selectable commands. A menu displays in its own small window that pops down from the menu bar.

MENU BAR. A horizontal display of menu names. The menu bar appears at the top of an application window under the title bar. When you select a menu name, its menu pops down.

MINIMIZE. To reduce an application window to an icon.

MODE. One of the ways in which Windows operates. *See* 386 Enhanced Mode, Real Mode, and Standard Mode.

NETWORK. A configuration of computers organized into a file server and work stations. The work stations support users, while the file server is unattended. The users share the files in the file server and use the printers connected to the file server.

NON-WINDOWS DOS APPLICATION. A DOS program that Windows runs either in a window or by giving it the entire screen.

OPTION BUTTONS. A set of two or more selections in a dialogue box. Only one of the options may be selected at one time. The buttons are represented by small round circles. The selected option button has a dark circle inside the button. The others are empty. Option buttons are also called radio buttons.

PARAMETER. A value that controls or affects the operation of an application and that appears on the applications command line following the application's executable file name.

PASTE. To write a block of text or a picture from the Clipboard into an application.

PATH. The DOS path that leads from the root directory to the file name. The path is expressed as a string such as C:\WINDOWS\SYSTEM\filename.

PCX FILE. A graphics file format that Paintbrush can read and write.

PIF. Program Information File. A file that describes a non-Windows DOS application in a way that allows Windows to run it.

PIXEL. Picture Element. The smallest item of information in a graphics picture. A picture is made up of rows and columns of pixels, each one being a single dot of color.

POINT SIZE. The size assigned to the characters in a font.

PRINT QUEUE. A queue of jobs waiting to be printed by the Print Manager.

PROTOCOL. The method by which the two ends of a communications link coordinate the connection. Protocols exist at several levels—from the hardware protocols that physically connect the two computers to the data protocols that the two computers use to synchronize the transfer of data files and to perform error detection and correction.

RADIO BUTTONS. *See* Option Buttons.

READ-ONLY FILE. A DOS file that has the read-only attribute set. You can read the file but you cannot modify or delete it.

REAL MODE. The mode in which Windows runs if you have an 8086 or 8088 processor. This mode is required in order to run earlier Windows applications.

ROOT DIRECTORY. The top directory in the directory structure of a disk device.

SCROLL BARS. Horizontal and vertical bars that appear on the bottom and right side of a window when its contents do not fit in the visible work space.

SELECT. To point to an item before choosing it for an action.

SERIAL PORT. *See* Communications Port.

SHORTCUT KEY. A keystroke that provides a shortcut to what is otherwise a more complex action. Many menu commands have shortcut keys. Fields in dialogue boxes and recorder macros can also have shortcut keys.

STANDARD MODE. The mode in which Windows runs if you have a 286 processor and at least 1Mbyte of memory. Standard mode multitasks Windows applications and swaps DOS applications.

SYSTEM FILE. A DOS file that has the system attribute set.

TEXT BOX. A box in a dialogue box into which you enter text data.

TILED WINDOWS. Windows arranged so that their borders touch each other and each window is fully visible. The windows are all the same size and shape. *See also* Cascaded Windows.

TITLE BAR. The top bar of a window in which its title appears. When the window is active, the title bar is highlighted.

WALLPAPER. The bitmap pattern that displays on the Desktop. You can select wallpaper patterns to personalize your Windows operating environment.

WILDCARD. A component in a file name that enables you to make the name ambiguous so that a file selection function will find multiple matching files. Wildcards are represented by asterisks and question marks.

WORD WRAP. The ability of a text editor or word processor to automatically move the word and the cursor to the next line when the word you are typing goes past the right margin.

WORK SPACE. The area in a document window in which the application displays the document data and the user makes changes.

Index